The Holy Grail, Cosmos of the Bible

by Lee Perry

> ## CORRECTION
>
> Murphy's Law struck on pages 85 and 114, when an uncorrected, computer backup disk was used in lieu of the corrected original. Thus, the eminent scholar Samuel Noah Kramer is incorrectly referred to as Stanley (sic) Noah Kramer. This typographical error will be corrected in future reprints.

Dec. 3, 1999 Ray & Ria —
Many thanks for the hospitality,
Lee Perry

Philosophical Library

New York

The Holy Grail, Cosmos of the Bible
Copyright© 1991 by Lee Perry.
All rights reserved.

Printed in the United States of America.
No part of this book may be used or
reproduced in any manner whatsoever
without written permission,
except in the case of
brief quotations
embodied in
critical
articles
and reviews.
For information
address Lee Perry, c/o
~~Box 38491, Atlanta, GA. 30334, USA.~~
(see small book for current address.)
Published by Philosophical Library, Inc.,
31 W. 21st Street, Eleventh Floor, New York, NY 10010, USA.

Library of Congress Cataloging-in-Publication Data:

Perry, Lee, 1935-
    The Holy Grail, Cosmos of the Bible / Lee Perry.
            p.   cm.
    Includes bibliographical references and index.
    ISBN 0-8022-2557-8 : $39.95
    1. Grail—Miscellanea. 2. Religion—Miscellanea.
    3. Cosmology—Miscellanea. 4. Mythology—
    Miscellanea. 5. Bible—Miscellanea.
    I. Title.
    BF1999.P525 1990
    291—dc20   90-47086
                    CIP

This book is dedicated to Dr. Benedict Kiely, an almost-Jesuit friend of humankind, who once said that the only sure reality was himself, myself, Frances, and Carole, standing in a circle, beside his garden gate, under the stars, on a balmy night in Dublin, Ireland.

Contents

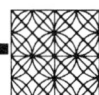

Acknowledgments

Those who graciously allowed me to quote from their works are mentioned in the bibliography. Those who graciously allowed me to copy their photographs or art are mentioned in the list of illustrations.

Without the catalysis of my friend Charles Longstreet Weltner, this book never would have been written.

Without the patient proofreading of my friends Charles N. Hooper, Ron Johnson, Jeanney Kutner, Jon Weintraub, and Sherie Welch, and the careful work of my publisher, Rose Morse Runes, and of my copy editor, George Nammack, typographical errors would have marred the finished product. Blame me alone for the inevitable errors that remain.

Without the encouragement of my former pastor, Rolfe Gerhardt, of Northwest Unitarian Congregation, Atlanta, I would have quit writing soon after starting, and would have kept these things to myself, as did the Welsh knights in *Perlesvaus*.

Without the constructive criticism of Diane Cowgill of Northwest Unitarian Congregation, this book would have recorded my personal quest instead of charting a quest for all persons who are willing to think about religion.

Without the support of my wife, Carole, and of our surviving children, Bruce, Brendan, and Conor, the tasks of working two jobs, helping Carole to maintain the family's vegetable garden, and cutting, splitting, and stacking the firewood that heats our home, while researching and writing this book, would have been impossible. To my children Kevin and Steven, who are with God, I say thanks for happy memories which kept me at the wordprocessor when my arthritic back was screaming for relief. To Tigger, my Pangar Ban, who is tabby not white, go thanks for hours of companionship when everyone else had gone to bed. I'll swear that cat knew what I was at!

Thanks to Chris Duncan and Greg McMahan of LazerAge, Partners in Publishing, in Atlanta, whose composition and computer-aided drawings converted my computerized draft and hand sketches into the finished product. The quality of their work is obvious.

Thanks to the many craft and trade people I never met, who skillfully manufactured this book.

Thanks to the thousands of storytellers, scribes, and translators who faithfully brought the ideas of the ancients to us of this generation, so we may know how far we have come and how far we must go.

And last, but certainly not least, thank you, God, for allowing me to rediscover the toolkit of the prophets.

Lee Perry

Preface

The massive labors that have gone into Lee Perry's book are the result of a curious beginning. Because I had some part in that, I now tell the story. For many years, my father occupied some of his leisure moments pursuing a goal as elusive as the Grail itself: the trisection of the angle. True, there is a well-accepted theory that trisection cannot, in fact, be done by Euclidean methods. But he had supreme confidence in the power of reason, and persisted in his quest. I followed his lead, and more than twenty-five years of that endeavor had passed. There was no trisection, but slowly, painfully, within my mind there began to emerge a comprehension of a movement of geometric figures that accomplished — at any point in that movement — a whole series of trisections, with infinite sub-sets of trisections. Pouring frantic effort into capturing my new-found concept on paper, I committed it all to writing, and with the help of my friend in Congress, now Senator Wyche Fowler, Jr., of Georgia, the idea emerged in print, published in the Congressional Record in 1979.

The trisection movement works. But only one person knew that, and *I* was that person. Why? Because no one else was interested for long enough to understand a fairly complex set of geometric relationships.

Only one person — that is, until Lee Perry chanced to look at one of my drawings, and asked, "What's that?"

The research for this book was launched by that question. Lee understood (praise be!) exactly and precisely what I had labored so hard to discern and to describe! And, while there is *still* no Euclidean trisection, the world now has *The Holy Grail, Cosmos of the Bible*.

Charles Longstreet Weltner

Foreword by the Author

Church. State. Greed. Hate. Aldous Huxley got it right. The cross borne by humanity connects those four words. Not just in Belfast, Beirut, and Bombay. Everywhere. Examples: Descendants of the Patriarch Abraham are keeping their respective covenants with YHWH and Allah by sacrificing each other's children in Israel. Hindus and Moslems again are killing each other in India. Irish Catholics and Protestants periodically exchange insults, paving stones, bullets, or bombs in the North of Ireland. Protestant fundamentalist missionaries are teaching Central American natives to shun their brothers and sisters who remain Roman Catholic. The pattern: First, shun. Then, hate. Finally, kill. In God's name?

John Locke, whose writings inspired our constitutional guarantee of religious freedom, wondered whether persons who would compel his worship according to their faith cared as much about his salvation as they did about their power over his person and purse.

Will humans ever stop hating, killing, and stealing from each other in the name of God?

Many generations ago, a group of gurus founded a new faith for the avowed purpose of ending the bloody conflicts that occur in India between Hindus and Moslems. Adherents of the new faith are called Sikhs. The gurus failed. Now, there are three groups of true believers at each other's throats. The bloodshed did not end. It increased. So much for ecumenical movements.

If ecumenical movements cannot bring an end to collection plate greed, and to religious intolerance, prejudice, and hatred, what will free us sheep from the cross of Church-State-Greed-Hate? Personal enlightenment? An understanding of how our shepherds herd us?

Most people agree that Judaism and Christianity have visionary components. The Bible tells us that Ezekiel and Peter had visions. Many adherents of Judaism and Christianity will not be surprised by the suggestion that biblical narratives about the Tabernacle, Ark of the Covenant, Temple of Solomon, and Paul's experience on the Damascus road similarly are founded on visions.

Many adherents of Judaism and Christianity are aware that theologians, exegetes, historians, and philosophers have used various disciplines in an attempt to draw a bright line between history of fact and history of faith as expressed in biblical narrative. Those efforts have produced libraries full of written materials and endless scholarly disputations but have left the essential fact about Judaism and Christianity untouched. Each of those faiths remains a hermeneusis, that is, an interpretation of data. Each encompasses an astonishingly wide variety of competing religious beliefs and practices, many of whose adherents and practitioners insist that they have an absolute monopoly on religious truth.

The role that the concept of the Holy Grail played in the composition of Hebrew and Christian biblical narrative was suppressed by mainline Christianity during the thirteenth and fourteenth centuries by bloody crusades and inquisitions. As a direct consequence of the torture and slaughter of thousands of "heretics"—persons whose religious views were at variance with those of the religious power structure—most moderns think the Grail was a chalice, if they ascribe to it any real substance.

Grail tales tell us much about the Holy Grail, if we open our eyes and use our intellects. One story tells attentive readers that the Grail is something upon which the image of a chalice, and many other images, appear, then disappear. Still another tells us almost all we need to know about the nature of the Grail. In this second story, the king of the Grail castle has invited to a sumptuous banquet a knight of mixed parentage, Christian and Islamic. The guest wonders how the platters refill themselves while the meal progresses. The guest asks his host the source of this miracle. The king replies that the Grail is the source. The guest asks where the Grail may be found. The king replies that the Grail is lying on the dining table right before the eyes of the guest. The guest responds that he does not see the Grail; that all he sees is an *achmardi*.

The guest saw an *achmardi* without realizing that he had seen the Grail. What is an *achmardi*? It is a piece of green silk upon which a pattern has been sewn using golden threads. Now you know what those of us who were raised on Celtic lore have known all our lives. Now you are equipped to understand how I found the Holy Grail.

Justice Charles Longstreet Weltner of the Supreme Court of Georgia is known to many people as a champion of civil rights, open and ethical government, and a free press. Few people realize that he is a scholar of ancient and modern languages and of ancient mathematics, particularly geometry. In an academic paper, Justice Weltner suggested that a relationship might exist between the visions of the prophet Ezekiel and a certain ancient Babylonian mathematics tablet because the tablet illustrates circles, each of which is surrounded by four eyes.

When Justice Weltner employed me as his law assistant, he knew that I was a graduate of Georgia Institute of Technology, and had earned some of my law school tuition and expenses working as an engineering draftsman.

I asked Justice Weltner's permission to test his speculation by determining whether or not other verbal images of the prophet's visions also might be found within the pattern of lines. One Friday night, I drew the pattern of lines from the tablet on a piece of poster-paper and proceeded to find within the pattern of lines a line-form image corresponding to every verbal image of the prophet's two visions. I drove to Justice Weltner's home the next day, and showed him my findings. Neither Justice Weltner nor I had any idea what I had found. We knew nothing beyond the possibility that I had found something.

Justice Weltner suggested that I read other biblical verses that refer to the "cherubim" of Ezekiel's visions. Having spent the remainder of the weekend reading biblical stories, I reported for work on Monday morning insisting that the verbal images of the stories of the Tabernacle, Ark of the Covenant, and Temple of Solomon probably were written in reference to line-form images visible within the pattern of lines on the tablet.

For months, I did not have any idea what I might have stumbled upon, even after finding the same phenomenon occurring among holy stories of many cultures, ancient and modern. Then an image from an ancient Irish story popped into my mind, leading me to reread that story of my youth and to go where I knew it led me: to the original, unedited versions of the story of King Arthur and the quest for the Holy Grail.

That the Holy Grail might be a pattern of lines was a possibility of which I was aware. That the Holy Grail is the pattern of lines that appears on the Babylonian tablet is a mathematical probability I have been forced to accept.

Years later, I learned that concepts sprung from conversations between persons having expertise in different academic fields are said to be the product of "cross-fertilization of ideas."

A person who suggests that he has found the Holy Grail must expect almost everyone to spring to the conclusion that he is either a crackpot or a huckster. Fortunately, I grew up in a family of engineers who had invented various practical gadgets of modern society and was prepared for total disbelief at worst, and honest skepticism at best, when any discovery, either sensational or mundane, is announced to the public.

What I was not prepared for, however, was the opinion of a few Christians that I should keep my rediscovery of the beliefs of the original Christians to myself because publication of those beliefs might destroy the Christian Religion. How can knowledge of the beliefs of the original Christians—the beliefs upon which Christianity was founded—possibly destroy Christianity? Moreover, Christians who are willing to think about their religion are entitled to know the roots of their faith! Christians who are not willing to think about their religion should cherish their current beliefs and should ignore my findings and conclusions.

The works of the great mythologist Joseph Campbell have convinced me that my rediscovery of the Grail—the toolkit of the prophets—will revive rather than destroy Christianity by leading the clergy away from disputations with scientists that the clergy cannot win; by leading the faithful back into the fertile fields of cosmology where religion germinated and flourished before the clergy tried to seize command of all fields of human endeavor.

So just what is the Holy Grail? Answer: A pattern of lines that can be put to a variety of uses. Rocks or bricks stacked according to this pattern of lines become the classical vaults and domes of houses of worship of many religions, past and present, including Judaism, Christianity, Hinduism, and Buddhism. Surprise! Ancients of all skin colors understood the simple mathematics which caused their religious structures to stand!

Simple but effective mathematics which leads to the construction of large vaults and domes logically leads to the speculation that Heaven is a vault or dome.

The same pattern of lines projected up onto the presumed dome of Heaven and down onto the round earth leads to systems for finding points on the presumed curvature of Heaven and on the known curvature of earth; that is, to astronomy, and to land and ocean navigation. Surprise! The ancients knew about such things!

Finally, because those geometric patterns work so well for the stacking of stones and the finding of points in space and time, might ancients who believed in divination have concluded that they are powerful *mandalas* from which to divine the nature and will of the Creator? Surprise! That apparently is what happened in more than one ancient religion, including Judaism and Christianity!

The foregoing leads inevitably to this question: If the ancients were so technologically adept, why did European science collapse during the Dark Ages? The answer is to be found, at least in part, in the so-far futile efforts of two competing religions, Christianity and Islam, to convert everyone to their respective faiths at the point of a sword! Libraries were burned

deliberately by Christian and Islamic fundamentalists who were trying to destroy all knowledge that was not founded solely on the Bible or the Koran. The American feminist movement recently has rediscovered the great mathematician Hypatia, the daughter of Theon, who was murdered by a mob of raging Christian fundamentalists because she would not give up her "heresy," that is, mathematics.

The answer to the question of how we westerners reacquired the knowledge of the ancients similarly will be unpleasant to many of us at this time when we suddenly find ourselves confronting Iraq. The great Islamic universities of Spain led European Christians to the knowledge that built the Christian cathedrals of Europe; that led Europe toward the Renaissance.

Those of you versed in modern science are attuned to vibrations that the rest of you may not yet have felt. Was Grail theory an early "unified theory" of the cosmos? It was, as you will be thrilled to discover!

Scholars know that Grail tales encode theories of ancient earth-science and sky-science underlying the cosmogony and cosmology of Judaism, Christianity, Hinduism, and Buddhism. Put simply, the green silk on the banquet table in the Grail castle represents the green earth. The golden threads sewn into the Grail *achmardi* represent the rays of the sun, which fructify the earth. Grail tales thus allegorize the cosmic union of the sky father and the earth mother, which gives us the plants and animals that sustain human existence, that is, the banquet from the Creator!

Would you like for me to show you one example of how ancient religionists thought that they had divined the nature of the Divinity from a pattern of lines used by ancient architects to stack stones and used by ancient astronomers and navigators to find points in time-space?

The Romans called him Jupiter-Dolichenus. Ancient Semites called Him El. El is the Lord-God of our Bible; the God of Abraham. The country of Israel is named after Him. Next to the photograph of the bronze statuette, we see an optical illusion created by bold-facing certain lines within the pattern of lines from the Babylonian tablet; the pattern of lines known to the Christian Gnostics as the *Katapetasma*, and known to Celts as the Holy Grail.

Will you consider the possibility that this bronze image of God was divined from this pattern of lines; that you, yourself, right now, are observing the toolkit of the prophets in use? Are you prepared to learn that early Christians believed that the body of Christ was not of flesh and blood; rather, was a "mere optical illusion"? Are you prepared to consider whether or not the last-mentioned optical illusion first was seen among this pattern of lines?

The Holy Grail, Cosmos of the Bible was not written to be read by everyone. It was written only for people who are able to think about religion.

Lee Perry

Jupiter-Dolichenus, a/k/a El, on his cosmic bull. Courtesy of Kunsthistorisches Museum, Vienna.

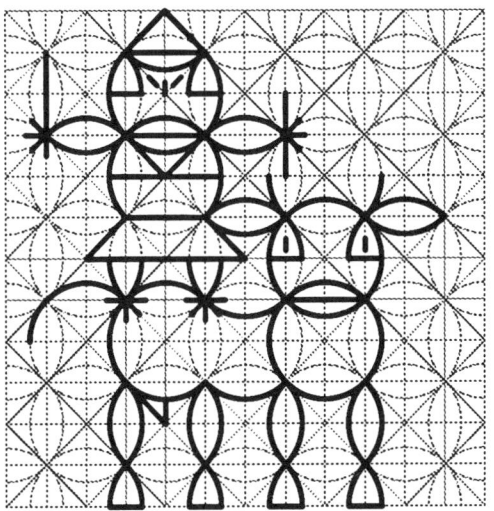

Frontispiece. Symbols of the four Evangelists, from the Book of Kells, fol 129v, Trinity College, Ireland, *circa* 800 A.D. Courtesy of The Board of Trinity College Dublin, and the Green Studio Ltd., Dublin.

Chapter One

Should I Read This Book?

Classify Yourself

Eagles should read this book. Lions, Oxen, and Men should not. You should classify yourself. The four categories of the ancient human enlightenment profile under which you should classify yourself are represented by the four "living creatures" of the Vision of the Prophet Ezekiel: Lion, Ox, Man, and Eagle.[1]

Persons represented by the Lion are those whose minds are untamed; whose actions are governed by animal emotions. Persons represented by the Ox are those whose minds have been broken (in the sense of the breaking of a wild horse) to perform valuable but menial service to mankind. The analogy between persons in this category and the animal which symbolically represents them lies in the fact that the virile bull first is deprived of his "manhood," then is trained to perform the menial but necessary task of pulling a cart or plow. The actions of persons represented by the Ox are governed by emotions and thinking processes which have been put into their minds by other human beings of the Man category to make the Oxen fit to do the menial work of Man. The third category of the profile, Man, represents those persons who have learned to tame the minds of persons of the Lion category, and to break them to the yoke of Oxen, but who have not learned to tame their own emotions or to avoid being misdirected by their own thinking processes. Persons in the Man category often mislead themselves with the same words they use to tame Lions or to break Oxen. The fourth category of the profile, Eagles, represents those persons who have disciplined their minds sufficiently to be able to cast aside, during periods of reasoned analysis, all emotional reactions and preconceived thinking patterns, and to construct for themselves theories which enable them to fly high toward the goal of understanding themselves and the physical universe in which they live. Eagles have sufficient wisdom to realize that never during their lives on Earth will they understand the Creative Force which made all of us, but Eagles, of all humans, are most apt to come closest to that oldest of all human intellectual aspirations.[2]

If you have classified yourself as an Eagle or as a person who would like to become an Eagle, then read on. If not, please put this book aside and read something else. The publisher and I do not want to field complaints from Lions, Oxen, and Men who would growl, bellow, or scream about the contents of this book or the fact that it was written and published. Look at it this way: Folks who do not like to watch football games on television should change the channel. They have no right to watch a game and then fuss at sports fans about the way the game is played.

Why are potential readers being put through this screening process? Because this book presents an unusual hypothesis about the origins of many religions, probably including yours. Moreover, the subjects of inquiry are not platitudes such as "Jesus loves me, this I know, for the Bible tells me so." We shall be encountering disturbing subject matter generally known only to scholars of religion; data generally unknown to most preachers, priests, and rabbis who minister weekly to flocks of believers. Although much of what we shall explore may be found in the libraries of theology schools, you should not be angry with your religious leader for not having let you in on these scholarly secrets. Even if he attended theology school, the information with which this book is concerned was probably not on the academic menu.

A word to the wise is sufficient. The remainder of this book is for Eagles and aspiring Eagles only.

One more cautionary remark: It will prove helpful to readers if they have, and can keep, a sufficiently vigorous sense of humor to enable them to laugh at the childish and just plain silly efforts of human beings to comprehend the incomprehensible.

The Hypothesis

The principal questions raised in this book may be outlined in a few paragraphs, as follows:

1. Does a geometry problem inscribed on a clay tablet almost 4,000 years ago in Mesopotamia (modern Iraq) contain the loose end of a thread of scientific and religious speculation about Mankind and the Cosmos which was woven throughout the fabric of the ancient religions of India, Persia, Mesopotamia, Palestine, Egypt, the Sea Kingdoms, Africa, Greece, Rome, and the Celtic and Germanic territories stretching from Russia across Germany to Ireland?

2. Did this same skein of reasoning later bind the human sacrifice religions of the Sea Kingdoms together with the human sacrifice religions of Meso-America, and provide the warp and woof of the colorful fabric of the "mystery religions" of Mithras, Osiris, Attis, Dionysus, Sol Invictus, and Jesus the Anointed? Were the religions of Judaism, Hinduism, and Buddhism exempted from this thinking?

3. Was one of the "mysteries" of the intellectual elite of certain of the mystery religions that the Earth is round, not flat, and spins clockwise once daily around a polar axis which points always to the same spot on the "vault" of Heaven, while the Earth revolves once a year around the sun? When Galileo announced his telescopic verification of the sun-centered hypothesis of Aristarchus of Samos, did the leaders of the Christian Church threaten him with death unless he publicly renounced his discoveries because they realized that the common man probably would learn from Galileo one of their innermost secrets? Did the Church's leadership believe that Galileo's empirical discoveries about the Earth's rotations should be kept from the common man because that knowledge ultimately might lead to discovery of the origins of the Christian Faith in the pagan faiths it officially supplanted but never obliterated?

4. Did the ancient Sumerians, who ruled Mesopotamia before the oldest of the Babylonians, and the Akkadian-speaking Babylonians who followed them, memorialize this astronomical knowledge of the Earth's rotations by building temples using such "modern" architectural and structural engineering concepts as arches, vaults, and domes springing from penden-

tives? Were those temples earthly versions of the images they saw in the day and nighttime skies? Were those temples based upon the line forms of the time-calculating device they used to plot the apparent courses of the sun, moon, planets, and stars? Were those temples prototypes of the hundreds of "Greek Cross" churches erected by the Christian Church—including Hagia Sophia at Constantinople, and the original structure of St. Peter's at Rome? Do the ground plan (a drawing) and the vault, arch, and dome elevation (the same drawing) of those temples and churches consist of the lines and curves found on our almost four-thousand-year-old Mesopotamian tablet?

5. When prophets of these ancient cultures looked at that drawing, did they think they saw, as signs and revelations from their creator gods, abstract images of the faces of a lion or another cat; of an ox, a bull, or a cow; of a man, a giant, a god, or an angel; of an eagle, a hawk, an owl, or some other bird? Did they see on it abstract images of thrones, chariots, mountains, tents, lambskins, altars, cups, bowls, scepters, swords, trumpets, and a large variety of other symbols or objects—including the image of a Man on a Cross, upon whose chest appeared the letters IC, XC, and XP? Did intersecting circle segments shaped like the body of a fish, appearing at the Man's feet, together with the letters of the Koine word for fish and with the letter combinations on His chest, suggest to the prophets that His name and title should be Jesus Christ (i.e., "anointed") Son of God Savior? Did the Cross upon which He appeared to hang portend to the prophets the manner of His death, as the other indicia had suggested to the prophets the reason for His being born, i.e., to save mankind?

6. Was human sacrifice, followed by the burning of the sacrificial flesh to send its essence up the axis of the Earth to the Heavens to provide food for the gods, and the eating of the flesh and drinking of the blood of the human sacrifice as a means of passing the essential strengths of the sacrificed (hence, godly) human on to the partakers of the cannibal feast, suggested to the minds of ancient religionists by their contemplations

of the image on the drawing of a human body lying across an altar, prepared for blood sacrifice?

7. Is this drawing the Holy Grail of the King Arthur Round Table legends and of related continental Grail quest stories? In *Perlesvaus*, Sir Gawain is warned by a priest, "for behoveth not discover the secrets of the Saviour, and them also to whom they are committed behoveth keep them covertly."[3] Was the secret of the Holy Grail that the Christ story, like many pagan religions before it, was divined from this drawing by prophets?

8. Are present-day major religions of the world (including Christianity, Judaism, Hinduism, and Buddhism) still injuriously infected by legends sprung from marriages between the line forms of the drawing and the fertile imaginations of mystics?

9. Is "science" beliefs which a person is willing to question; "religion" beliefs which a person is not willing to question; and "magic" science and/or religion run wild? Did early man notice that white light (as from the sun or a fire) was separated into its colored components (the multi-colored hues of the rainbow) when it passed through substances such as raindrops, fog, water, oil, ice, and rock crystals? Did early "men of science" attribute this to the characteristics of those substances, and group them together into what we, today, would call "prisms"? Did early men of religion and philosophy decide, instead, that the presence of what we, today, call an "interference pattern" meant that God (or some now-forgotten god or goddess) was present? Did early magicians learn enough of the science of producing the rainbow phenomenon so as to be able to produce a rainbow at their pleasure in order to convince the gullible that they were able to summon God (or some god or goddess) to carry out their commands in acts of magic such as raising the dead to life? Was ancient knowledge of magnetism and static electricity similarly used by men of religion and magic to gain power over the general populace? Was the science which the ancient architects and builders used to erect structures of stone, and which ancient astronomers used to determine units of time, also used by men of religion and magic to capture true believers?

One purpose of this book is to place the drawing, the Holy Grail, and its spawn of science, religion, and magic before modern persons of the Eagle category in the hope that they can help mankind discard certain obsolete and dangerous concepts, as growing children discard their teddy bears, so mankind can get back onto the track of development from which our religions knocked us nearly two thousand years ago. If we could grow up, we might attain by modern means what we never have attained by the primitive means of our cannibal past. We might learn quite a lot about God.

Notes
CHAPTER ONE. Should I Read This Book?

1. Ezekiel 1:5,10; 10:14,15,22. The Christian order is: Matthew —the winged man; Mark — the winged lion; Luke — the winged ox; and John — the eagle.

2. Wilmshurst 155-56.

3. Evans 82.

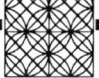

Chapter Two

Principles and Procedures

The story begins here: A friend, who is a scholar of ancient languages, keeps on the window ledge of his office a black and white photographic enlargement of one panel of a Babylonian clay tablet written almost 4,000 years ago. A photograph of this tablet panel appears as **Illustration 2-1**,[1] and a line drawing of that photograph appears as **Figure 1**. We shall refer to this line drawing as "the Holy Grail," realizing that at this time we have only a hypothesis unsupported by proof.

Human beings usually do not see things as they are. More often, we see things as we have been taught to see them. If you grew up in a fundamentalist religious congregation, your knee-jerk reaction to the word "Babylonian" probably was that Babylonians were bad people! How many times we have heard our preachers, priests, and rabbis thunder that "fact"! When my friend first said the tablet was from the Old Babylonian period of approximately 1800 B.C. to 1600 B.C.,[2] my reaction was negative. When he said that the tablet had been recovered by archaeologists from an ancient school library which had been buried by the sands of a desert in Iraq, and was concerned with mathematics rather than religion, my ears perked up because technical training had convinced me

that mathematics is a "good" subject for study. Oxen think as they have been trained to think.

The ancient Babylonian teacher posed for his students a geometry problem based on a line drawing cut by him with a stylus into the soft clay of what was to become, when baked in the sun, a mathematics textbook. The problem has been translated as follows: "A square, the side is 1. Inside it are 4 quadrants and 16 boat-shapes. I have drawn 5 regular concave-sided tetragons. This area, what is it?"[3]

This Babylonian school for scribes was their equivalent of our modern American high schools, although admission was limited to a privileged few.[4] We should ask ourselves how many high-school students are graduated these days without ever having studied a single concave-sided tetragon, much less a covey of five of them! We should be ashamed of the answer!

My friend first became interested in the form of the drawing on the tablet after reading Joan Oates' *Babylon*,[5] which made reference to an appearance of the same tablet panel in H.W.F. Saggs' *The Greatness That Was Babylon*.[6] He told me that he thought this panel of the "ancient copybook" might be related to the "creatures of the Vision" of the Prophet Ezekiel[7] because Ezekiel speaks of four "eyes" around rings or wheels,[8] and there are four eye shapes visible around each of the circles incised in the clay tablet. See **Figure 2**. However, because his interests were focused in another direction, he never explored this possibility. I posited that *if* this four-eyed circle is related to Ezekiel's Vision, then *every* image

Illustration 2-1. A geometry problem from a Babylonian cuneiform tablet of the early second millennium, B.C. Courtesy of The Trustees of the British Museum, London.

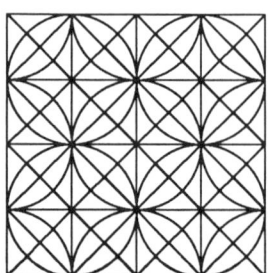 

Figure 1   Figure 2

mentioned in the Vision should appear within this pattern of lines. That single idea gave birth to this book.

The tablet evidently was from the old Babylonian city of Nippur.[9] The river Kebar, or Chebar, where Ezekiel first saw his Vision while in exile, apparently was an irrigation canal which flowed from the Euphrates River through the old city of Nippur.[10] Scholars tell us that Ezekiel saw his vision by the river in 593 B.C.[11] Our Babylonian tablet was over a thousand years old in Ezekiel's time!

You will recall that the words of the ancient mathematics teacher are "boat-shapes" rather than "eye-shapes." We need to depart from the story-line in order to focus our minds on some principles and procedures which will guide us on our quest.

A large part of our potential problem in correct analysis should be gone because only Eagles or fledgling Eagles should be reading this book. Eagles cannot be misled into believing that things which are the same are not the same simply because different people use different words to describe them. Any Eagle can understand that the line forms highlighted in Figure 2 can be described as "boat-shapes" or "eye-shapes." A mere change of descriptive words cannot stop the flight of an Eagle. This point must be kept in mind as we proceed: A pattern of lines referred to as a "mountain" by one ancient writer may be called a "tent" by another, and yet the reference may be to the same form of lines which you Eagles will be able to see for yourself on the Holy Grail.

Please tentatively accept the following, although proof will not be offered until later: We usually will be considering a three-dimensional drawing, rather than a two-dimensional drawing, when we use the Holy Grail. We must be prepared at all times for an ancient writer's perspective of the line forms on the Holy Grail to be presented to us as front-view, side-view, or top-view of the object he is describing.

Are any of you Eagles beginning to get a feeling that you may not be able to understand what is to come? You will be required to learn nothing more difficult than a Babylonian high-school student would have learned almost four-thousand years ago.

Before we return to the storyline, two more matters need mention. Many words can be saved if you keep in mind that Eagles think in terms of hypotheses and proofs. The Noah of our Bibles is a *fact* as far as Lions, Oxen, and Men are concerned. At this stage of this book, Eagles must accept Noah as an *hypothesis subject to proof*. Each of you Eagles must make your personal decision about whether the proofs of our hypotheses are sufficient to convince you.

We shall explore many fantasies of Lions, Oxen, and Men by treating them as hypotheses subject to proof, and shall find in them seeds of understanding of ourselves and our universe. Thomas Jefferson once wrote: "Man is fed with fables through life, leaves it in the belief he knows something of what has been passing, when in truth he has known nothing but what has passed under his own eye."[12] Images from the Holy Grail shall pass under our eyes, perhaps evaporating some of our most precious and most dangerous fantasies.

Notes
CHAPTER TWO. Principles and Procedures

1. Saggs Plate 24. My friend, the scholar of ancient languages, is Justice Charles Longstreet Weltner of the Supreme Court of Georgia, a well-known champion of civil rights, open and ethical government, and a free press. He is less well known as a student of many languages of the ancient Near East.

2. Neugebauer 14-15,29; Oates 184-85; Saggs 450.

3. Oates 185; Saggs 453.

4. Oates 103,125,163-66,170.

5. Oates 185.

6. Saggs 453.

7. Ezekiel 1:5-28; 10:1-22; Weltner 3387.

8. Ezekiel 1:18; 10:12; Weltner 3384.

9. Saggs 451. Our tablet could have come from Tel Harmal, Oates 184, or from another of the ancient libraries. Your author chose not to verify the inference drawn from Saggs that it came from Nippur. This was done to avoid the inevitable questions of, "Why do you ask?", and, "What are you writing?" Scholars, like moonshiners, are intolerant of trespassing in their fields. If the tablet was found in a library in a city other than Nippur, this is of no consequence to our hypotheses because we have no reason to suppose that knowledge about our tablet had not diffused throughout all Babylonian schools for scribes. Greek students later worked a variation of the same problem. Neugebauer 180. It seems highly improbable that our geometry problem would have remained the sole property of only one scribal school for the more than one thousand years which separate our tablet from the life of Ezekiel.

10. 886 *The New English Bible With The Apocrypha* fn. 1.1-3; Ezekiel 1:1-2.

11. Id. 886. Weltner suggests 592 B.C. as the year of Ezekiel's Vision by the river. Weltner 3384. While the scholars debate about one year, we shall move on.

12. Malone 106. From Thomas Jefferson's letter to Thomas Cooper, December 11, 1823.

Chapter Three

Science, Religion, and Magic — The Tachyon Trinity

My friend had not worked the geometry problem on the Babylonian tablet. The repressed engineering draftsman in me could not get home fast enough, and could not go to sleep, before the problem had been drawn on poster paper and solved. Here began my personal fascination with this quest.

You will recall that the ancient tablet reads: "A square, the side is 1. Inside it are 4 quadrants and 16 boat-shapes. I have drawn 5 regular concave-sided tetragons. This area, what is it?"[1]

Our ancient teacher wants us to visualize one large square that has been divided into "4 quadrants," that is, four smaller squares, each of which is equal to one-fourth of the larger square. The four quadrants are illustrated in **Figure 3**. Our teacher says we are to visualize sixteen "boat-shapes." A single boat-shape is bolded in **Figure 4**. All sixteen of these boat-shapes are bolded in **Figure 5**. He next requires us to find five "regular concave-sided tetragons." A single regular concave-sided tetragon is illustrated in **Figure 6**. All five of the concave-sided tetragons are shown in **Figure 7**. He asks us to tell him the area of the five regular

concave-sided tetragons. We know that the area of all five is five times the area of any one of them, so we have reduced the problem to one of how to calculate the area of one regular concave-sided tetragon.

Pick any one of the four regular concave-sided tetragons bounded by any one of the four squares. One practical or graphic method for solving the problem works like this: Calculate the area of one of the four squares. Then calculate the area of the circle that is within and touching that square. See **Figure 8**. Subtract the area of the circle from the area of the square, leaving the area of the regular concave-sided tetragon lying within and touching that circle and square. Multiply that area by five, producing the answer to the problem. Can you see at a glance why this works? If not, turn to **Figure 9**, where your attention has been directed to the fact that each of the concave-sided triangles lying *inside* the square but *outside* the circle is identical to one-fourth of the area of one regular concave-sided tetragon. Now you see it! The area of the square minus the area of the circle equals the area of the regular concave-sided tetragon.

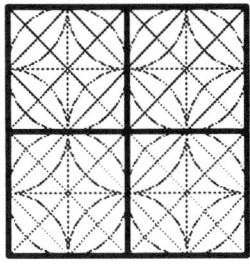

Figure 3

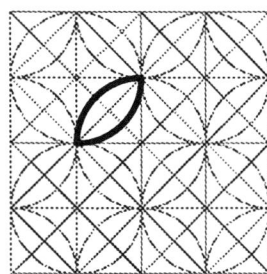

Figure 4

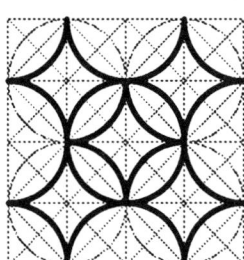

Figure 7

Figure 5

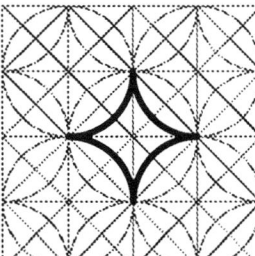

Figure 6

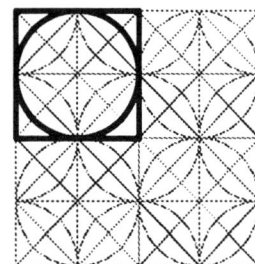

Figure 8

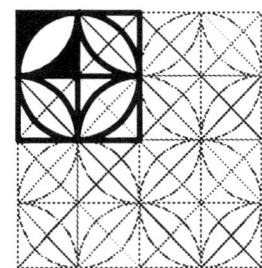

Figure 9

How could a Babylonian high-school student of 1800 B.C. to 1600 B.C. subtract the area of a circle from the area of a square? Were you not taught that Greek mathematicians who lived a thousand years later than our tablet were the first persons to discover the formula for the area of a circle, involving use of the concept of π? The bibliography of Joan Oates' *Babylon* led me to *The Exact Sciences In Antiquity*, in which Neugebauer tells us that the ancient Babylonians *did* have reasonably accurate approximations of our modern value for π and *did* have reasonably accurate formulas for the calculation of the area of a circle.[2] In *Mathematics In The Time Of The Pharaohs*, Gillings tells us that the ancient Egyptians also had a reasonably accurate value for π.[3]

Why are we not taught about the brilliant mathematical and astronomical discoveries of the ancient Babylonians outlined by Neugebauer? These people understood algebraic quadratic equations![4] They methodically plotted the apparent courses of the stars, the sun, the planets, and Earth's moon.[5] The Egyptians also were competent at mathematics, as well as arithmetic, and were accomplished astronomers.[6] Why are we taught in school that the Greeks were the world's first mathematicians and astronomers?[7] Why do our schools slight or ignore the achievements of the Babylonians and Egyptians? The answer is fascinating — but we are getting ahead of our story. First things first.

Here is an interesting tidbit from Gillings for our speculations: He tells us[8] that the ancient Egyptians denoted fractions by placing the hieroglyph ⬯ , representing an open mouth, and being equal to our letter "r," over any integer to indicate its reciprocal. Where did the ancient Egyptians get that hieroglyph? Have any of you Eagles ever seen a symbol like that? Note from Figure 2 that each boat-shape delineates one fourth of the circle, i.e., a fraction or part of the circle.

Mathematicians will say that our solution to the problem on the tablet is not sufficiently "rigorous" to merit their serious interest. True enough, as seen from their perspective. Rigorous mathematical proof would bore many Eagles of "arts-only" academic persuasions. This is a book for *all* Eagles, as well as for fledgling Eagles. The academic "diet" of Eagles is as varied as the food diet of real eagles. It is difficult to write a book about ancient science and religion which always will please the tastes of persons as varied as divinity students and students of quantum mechanics.

Why not avoid the problem of a mixed audience of religion and science students by writing two separate books? You might ask that question because you are thinking of science and religion in the modern way. "Religion" is something that is said and done on the holy days of the religious congregation to which you belong. "Science" is something quite distinct from religion and is practiced in laboratories during the remainder of the week. This dichotomy did not exist in ancient Babylonia, Egypt, and Palestine.[9]

How did ancient science and religion get mixed up together, as in the ancient pseudo-science of astrology, which combines principles of the true science of mathematical astronomy with ancient religious concepts about predestination? Perhaps because the two systems of thinking we call "science" and "religion" are not as mutually exclusive of subject matter as we moderns would prefer to believe. Is our definition of *science* truly a system of beliefs which we are willing to challenge?—Our corollary being *religion*, a system of beliefs which we are not willing to challenge? Is *magic* science or religion run wild? We usually think of the Christ story as a subject of religion. However, significant numbers of students of religion study the Christ story using the methodologies of scientists, although this necessarily involves challenging views traditionally advocated by Christian churches. On the other hand, most of us know a person who will not allow anyone to speak contrary to his or her natural-science theories. Has such a person allowed his science to become a religion? Can one man's science thus be another man's religion, although the subject matters of their studies may be identical? And under our definitions, does it depend upon whether the challenge of theories is tolerated or forbidden, rather than upon the subject matter under discussion? Anyone who has read any version of the Bible realizes that ancient thinking about natural science and religion are interwoven throughout the Scriptures. After further study, we shall attempt to untwine them.

Science and religion can become jumbled together when peoples share cultures with each other. As example, consider the widespread growth of "Cargo Cults" in the New Hebrides and Solomon Islands of the Pacific Ocean. The May, 1974, edition of *National Geographic* contains a story entitled "Tanna Awaits The Coming Of John Frum."[10] Tanna is one of the islands in the New Hebrides group near Australia. The mythical John Frum whose coming the islanders are awaiting is described by

them either as a god come to Earth from Heaven, or as King of the United States. When John Frum comes someday, the islanders will enjoy a work-free existence and an abundance of *cargo*, their word for the material wealth of modern society. They seek to hasten the coming of John Frum by praying and making flower offerings before red-painted wooden crosses, by marching in military formations with red-tipped bamboo sticks held on their shoulders like bayonet-tipped rifles, by painting "U.S.A." on their bare chests and backs, and by faithfully observing the taboos and performing the ceremonies of their former Stone Age society. They treasure memorabilia such as G.I. dog-tags and helmet liners, which remind them of the good days during the 1940's when United States servicemen came to the island, bringing and leaving behind large quantities of *cargo*.

The Tanna Islanders often refuse to cooperate with the governing authorities of the New Hebrides Islands because they fear that such conduct would compromise their fidelity to John Frum and prevent his coming. The beliefs of John Frum Cult members can cause much grief for themselves as well as for the civil authorities. To prove their faith that John Frum will come to save them, they have thrown their money into the ocean, slaughtered their livestock, and eaten up all their food, only to be disappointed when John Frum did not come to save them, obviously because of some unknown transgression on their part.

The Tanna Islanders lived in the Stone Age until Captain James Cook arrived in 1774, after which many of them were converted to Christianity. An airline owned by the islanders brings tourists from Australia to see the island's active volcano, but John Frum remains a real part of their lives.

What does the story of the John Frum Cult prove? The natural reluctance of all human beings to break with the customs and beliefs of their past? That new religions blend with, rather than replace, old religions? Universal human desire for pennies from Heaven? The ever-present human yearning for the coming of a saviour who will press us to his bosom and care for our every need, as the good fathers of all mythology always have cared for their children? These things, perhaps. In the logical analysis of the anthropologists, the John Frum Cult illustrates what can happen when a technologically and materially rich culture encounters a mythologically rich but technologically and materially poor culture. Whether some, or all, of this is proven is debatable, but the evidence of the scholars suggests that a similar cultural collision may have occurred in the Fertile Crescent of the Middle East during the period preceding the birth of the new form of the Hebrew Religion and the beginnings of the concepts we call Christian.

The "tachyon," a hypothetical particle sprung from the brilliant mind of the American physicist Gerald Feinberg,[11] speeds up as it loses energy until at zero energy its velocity is infinite. By analogy, do a religious fanatic's expressions of faith increase in frequency and amplitude as his religion's claims of historicity and holy magic are exposed to the light of scientific reason?

Notes

CHAPTER THREE. Science, Religion, and Magic — The Tachyon Trinity

1. Oates 185; Saggs 453.

2. Neugebauer 46-47,52,78.

3. Gillings 139-146.

4. Neugebauer 150; Oates 185.

5. Neugebauer 97-144; Oates 187-189.

6. Neugebauer 71-96.

7. The Greeks, themselves, made no such claim. Rather, they freely acknowledged their indebtedness to the Babylonians and Egyptians. See, *e.g.*, 1 Heath GM 5, 24-25, 67, 86, 128, 137-138, 141, 174, 177, 202.

8. Gillings 20.

9. Frankfort 31-61; 125-184; 223-254.

10. At 706-715.

11. 2 *World Book Dictionary* 2134 (1979).

Chapter Four

Ezekiel's First Vision

We shall commence proof of the hypothesis that the Prophet Ezekiel was exposed to Babylonian theories of science, religion, and magic while in exile in Babylonia. The supporting evidence will be incomplete in this chapter. The proof cannot be concluded until we have studied other stories in and out of the Bible, have learned something of the historical settings in which those stories were written, and have studied the ancient theories of science which the stories were intended to complement.

The subject matter of this chapter is going to seem strange to most readers. This is because the beliefs of one generation about science and religion often seem like magic ceremonies or sheer nonsense to later generations. As example, some of our most distinguished Puritan founding fathers caused the murder of innocent women they sincerely believed were witches. The Bible said there were witches,[1] so they believed there were witches. The Bible said that people should not suffer a witch to live,[2] so they believed that witches should be discovered and executed.[3]

Contrary to the beliefs of many Protestants, Roman Catholics were not the only Christians who wallowed in the witchcraft mania. John Wesley wrote in his Journal of May 25, 1768, that "The giving up of witchcraft is, in effect, giving up the Bible."[4] John Calvin favored the burning of witches.[5]

One wonders, at times, whether English-speaking Christian fundamentalists believe that the Bible originally was written in the English language of King James! The Hebrew word which the King James version translated as "witch" means "poisoner," and is not a reference to the pointed-hatted, wart-nosed, crackle-voiced hags who stir bubbling cauldrons of bats' wings on Saturday morning television cartoon shows.[6] Neither was the word "witch" as used in the King James Bible considered by Christian witch-burners to be a reference to practitioners of all forms of magic.[7] English Puritan fundamentalists who hacked all Roman Catholic symbols off English churches[8] did not destroy the sexually explicit "Sheela-na-Gig"

fertility goddesses carved on Christian churches,[9] perhaps because they realized it was not nice to fool with Mother Nature! Those baptized Christians who admitted *under torture* that they had made a pact with the Christian Devil were burned as "witches," and this supposedly was done for the good of their souls – to purify them by fire so they could go to Heaven.[10] A witchcraft confession during a Christian inquisition was invalid *unless* made under torture.[11] If all of this somehow makes little sense to you, then so much the better.

Fortunately, we no longer burn women as witches. But you may rest assured that we do other things based upon our present-day theories about science and religion which will amuse and disgust future generations, who will wonder how we could have been so stupid! Here is the point: Let any of us who is without silly beliefs about science and religion throw the first snide remark at the ancient Babylonians or at their captive, the Prophet Ezekiel.

The authors of many Bible stories tried to convince the ancient people for whom the stories were written that the heroes of the stories were magicians. Instead of stating conclusively that a certain story hero was a magician, the storysmiths presented evidence they knew would convince their readers and listeners. Magicians of tribes in the ancient Middle East went about changing something into something else.[12] To prove to their ancient readers that Moses was a magician, the authors of the Moses story wrote that Moses, with the help of God, changed his rod into a serpent and back into a rod.[13] That was credible evidence to the ancient readers for whom the Moses story was written that Moses was, indeed, a holy magician. In a similar vein, the authors of the Christ story sought to convince their readers that Christ was a magician by writing that He changed water into wine.[14] The ancient readers for whom those stories were written would conclude from this evidence, the authors hoped, that the hero of the story was a holy magician. Why? Because the common folk believed in magic and expected their great religious leaders to be great holy magicians?

We shall engage in further thinking like this in the chapters of this book which are yet to come. The point, at present, is to lay a foundation for understanding of other things which ancient holy magicians (magi) did: They divined (discovered) the will of the gods, predicted future events, and found missing or misplaced items.[15] Trying to convince ancient Persians, Babylonians, Egyptians, and Hebrews that their magicians could *not* do such things would be like trying to convince a modern Christian fundamentalist that Christ really did not walk on water.

The activity of ancient magicians upon which we presently must focus our attention was their supposed ability to prophesy the will of the gods and predict the future. By what means was such divination or prophecy carried out? The answer is this: Magicians divined or prophesied by looking at or into objects which were believed to have power.[16] Ancient science postulated that all matter was composed of earth, air, fire, and water.[17] Magicians sought to discover the will of the gods and predict the future by releasing birds into the *air* to observe their flight.[18] A cup was a favorite divining medium of the Biblical hero Joseph.[19] Divining cups were used to divine with *water*.[20] Magicians divined by raising the dead from the *earth* (necromancy) to ask them questions.[21] Divining from dreams was highly popular among the Egyptians, as the Joseph story of our Bible suggests.[22] Other familiar divination devices were marking random lines on the *earth* (geomancy), studying the colors and facets of natural crystals (crystallomancy), studying the viscera of sacrificed animals, and looking at lamps or other *fire*.[23] The point of it all was to use *something* which was believed to have *power*. Hebrews and Christians practiced divination albeit the Bible forbids it.[24]

We shall explore the hypothesis that magicians of many tribes from many lands divined or prophesied using the line forms on our Babylonian tablet; that those line forms, later known as the Holy Grail, comprised the centerpiece concept drawing of ancient science, and represented no less than the following: (1) the four seasonal positions of the Earth as it makes its yearly rotation around the sun, (2) the facet lines of quartz crystals which produce the rainbow-like manifestation we now call an "interference pattern," but which signaled to the ancients the presence of a god, (3) the line forms of the device the ancients used to plot the course of the sun, moon, stars, and planets, thereby telling the time of day, and day of the year, and (4) last – but

far from least – the arch, vault, and dome plan and elevation lines of temples constructed of mud bricks or other dry masonry. In summary, we shall explore the hypothesis that ancient prophets believed that the Holy Grail had more than enough *power* associated with it to make it a good object from which to divine the will of the gods and the future course of events.

What Ezekiel is doing should become clear to you. He has associated the wonders of the Holy Grail – whatever he might have perceived them to be – with Yahweh, his God and ours.

We will be comparing the King James Version of the Bible with the *Oxford Study Edition Of The New English Bible With The Apocrypha*.[25] The King James Version will be used for the main storyline. The Oxford differences, if any, will be set in parentheses.

Ezekiel wrote that he was among the captives (exiles) by the River of Chebar (River Kebar) in Chaldaea when the Heavens were opened and he saw visions (a vision) of God.[26] He said that the word of the Lord came to him and the hand of the Lord was (came) upon him.[27] He described a whirlwind (storm wind) coming out of (from) the north, a great (vast) cloud and a fire infolding itself (flashes of fire and brilliant light about it.).[28] A brightness was about it, as the color of amber, out of the midst of the fire. (Within was a radiance like brass, glowing in the heart of the flames.)[29]

As One and Only God, Yahweh had taken over the roles played by the myriad gods and goddesses of earlier religions, including the storm god El, the "God" of Isaiah.[30] Ezekiel quite naturally associated the coming of God with the coming of a thunder and lightning storm. The direction from which the storm came, the north, reflects the ancient Hebrew regard of the north as a place of mystery, a subject for further study in later chapters.[31] Science historians tell us that the ancients knew that the natural phenomenon we call "electricity" could be produced by rubbing the petrified resin we call "amber" with a woolen cloth or the hair side of an animal hide.[32] Ezekiel apparently realized that the same phenomenon which causes amber to attract particulate matter causes a thundercloud to discharge lightning. Static electric sparks and lightning bolts have the color of amber (yellow) or the color of molten brass. The Hebrew word which the King James translates as "amber" and the Oxford translates as "brass" is *chashmal*, which any fluent speaker of modern Hebrew will translate as "electricity."[33]

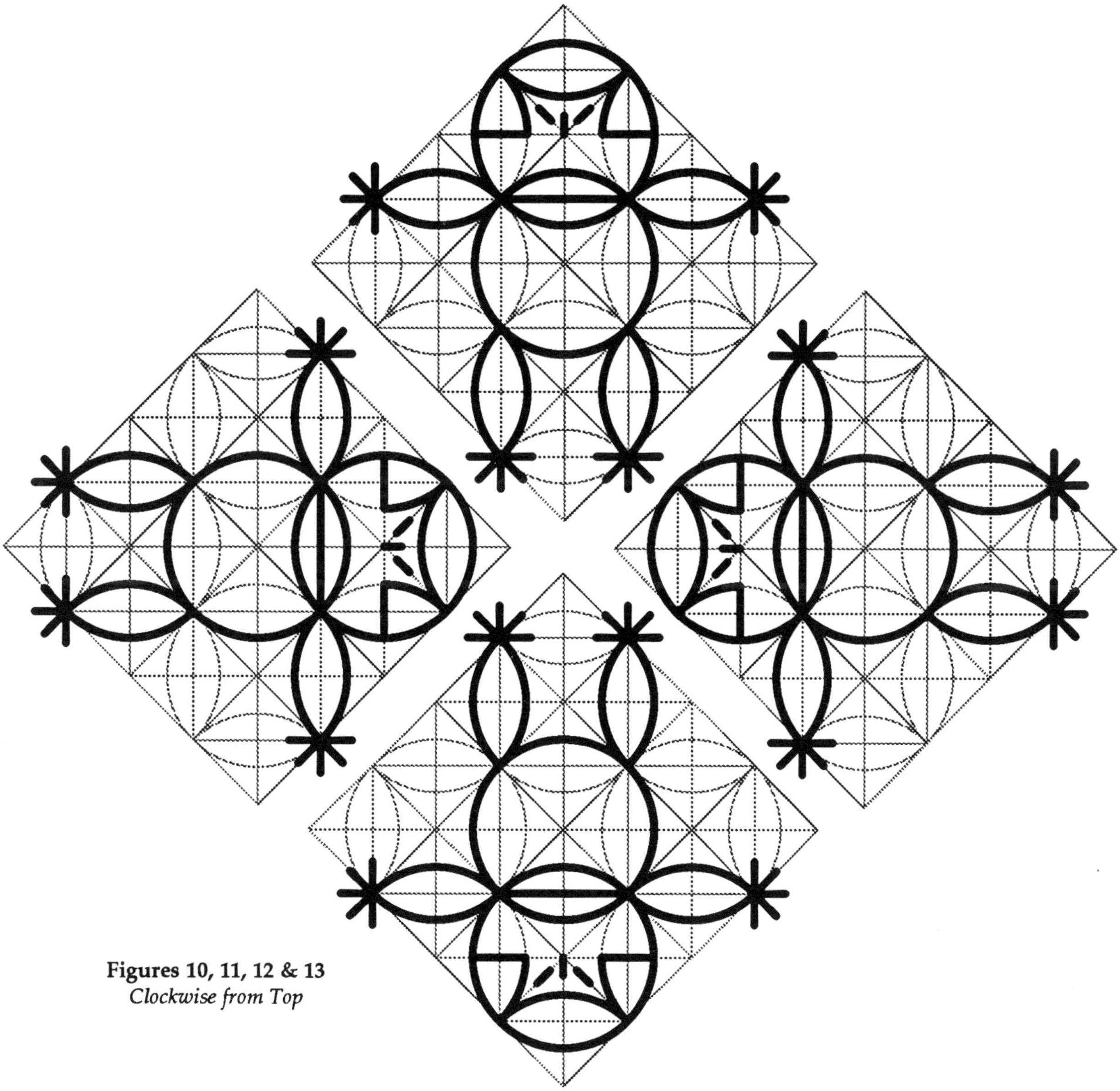

Figures 10, 11, 12 & 13
Clockwise from Top

Ezekiel wrote that out of the midst of the fire came the likeness of four living creatures; that they had the likeness of a man. (In the fire was the semblance of four living creatures in human form.)[34] We have reached "square one" of our analysis. We must find on the Holy Grail the "likeness" or "semblance" of a "man" or "human form." The human form consists of one head, one body, two arms, two hands, two legs, and two feet. Turn to **Figure 10**. Do you see one likeness or semblance of a man or a human form? He is a fat little fellow with a round head, a Dutch-boy hairdo, squint-eyes, a sharp nose, a big belly, fat legs and arms, and long narrow fingers and toes – like a cartoon character. "So what?" you say. "Proving what?" you ask. You

are correct. Proving nothing. One instance proves absolutely nothing about our hypothesis. However, just as a few hundred grains of sand can produce a cup of sand, and a few hundred cups of sand can produce a sack of sand, so also can a few hundred sacks of sand make a pretty decent sandbox in which children can play. Get the point? Stay with us as we collect grains of sand, one at a time.

Where are the other three of our four man-likenesses or human forms? Some of you who have good visual skills already have seen them, haven't you! Look at **Figure 11**, where other Grail lines have been boldfaced to show him on his right side. That makes two. In **Figure 12**, we see him standing on his head. That makes three. In **Figure 13**, we see him

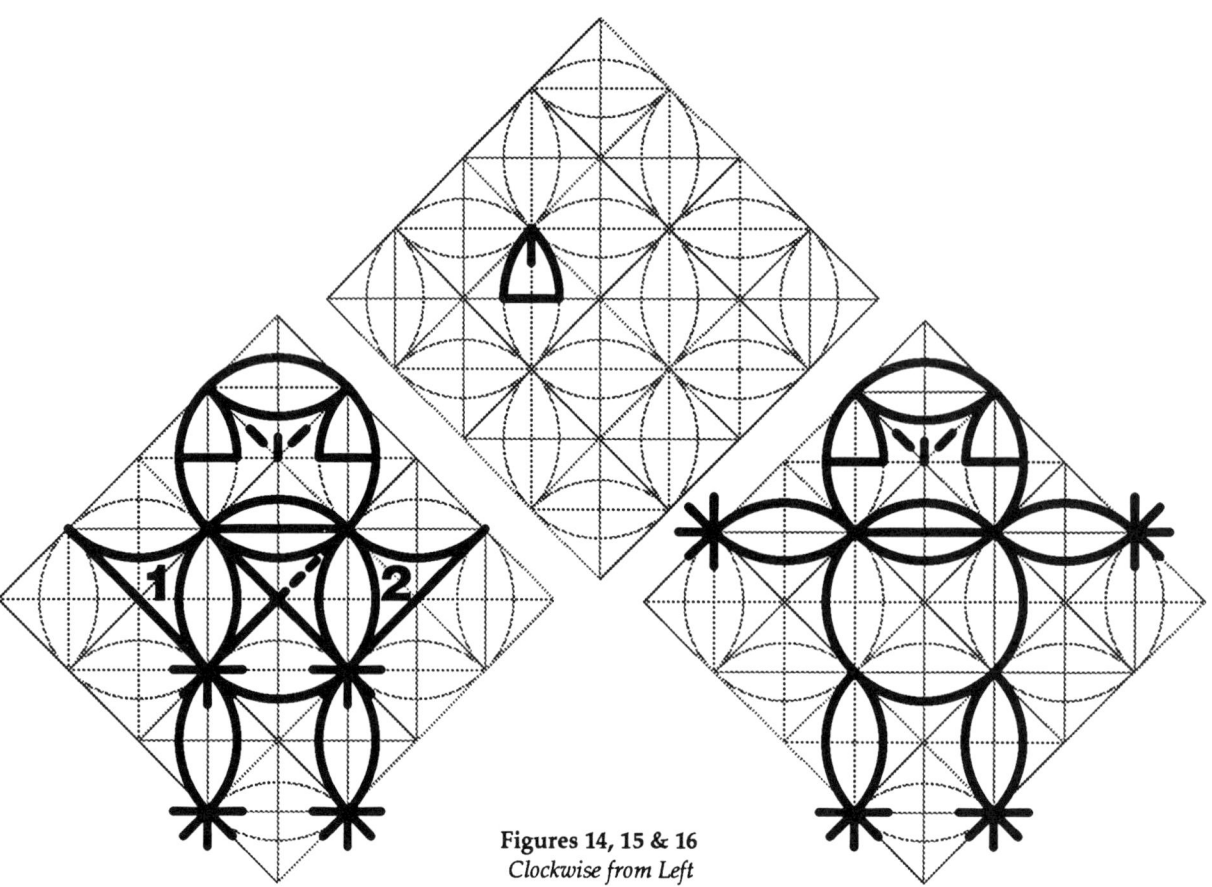

Figures 14, 15 & 16
Clockwise from Left

on his left side. That totals four man-likenesses or human forms. In the Babylonian myth of Utnapishtim, from which the Noah story of our Bibles was copied by later Hebrew storytellers, we find that Utnapishtim lies on his side.[35] Buddhas sometimes lie on their sides. But we are getting ahead of our story. Eagles must learn to flap their wings before they can learn to fly.

Ezekiel told us that every one of the four living creatures had four faces and four wings.[36] The lines of the Holy Grail satisfy that requirement. In **Figure 14**, we see the "wings" of each of the creatures. Wings numbers one and two are outstretched, whereas wings numbers three and four are folded across the body and on top of each other. The dotted lines illustrate the portions of the right wing folded across the body which are covered by portions of the left wing folded across the body. This satisfies the requirements that two of the four wings must be stretched upward or spread and two of the four wings must cover each creature's body.[37] Faces are discussed in a moment when we analyze other verses. More is to be said about wings, also.

At this point, there is a variance between King James and Oxford. King James says that the creatures' *feet* were straight feet and the *soles* of their feet were like the soles of a calf's foot.[38] Oxford says that their *legs* were straight, and their *hooves* were like hooves of a calf.[39] The lines of the Holy Grail will satisfy either of these requirements. Both versions agree that the *bottoms* (soles or hooves) of their feet were like calves' feet. **Figure 15** shows lines which can be understood to be a bottom view of a calf's hoof. You city folks should get out your encyclopedias and see what a calf's sole looks like. Country folks already have understood.

If the proper reference should be to "legs," as in Oxford, then it is quite obvious that the "legs" illustrated in **Figure 16** meet the straightness requirement. If, instead, the King James version is correct, and the reference should be to "feet" instead of "legs," then the "feet" illustrated in *top* view in Figure 16 certainly are "straight" in the sense that they are comprised of straight lines and also in the sense that they point straight forward. In either event, we have found lines on the Holy Grail which abstractly represent the images of Ezekiel's Vision.

Figure 17

The requirement that the feet sparkle like the color of burnished brass (bronze)[40] almost certainly is another reference to the color of static electric sparks and lightning, although the word used is not *chashmal*. Ezekiel seems to be visualizing these creatures' being projected upon the "firmament"; i.e., upon the "vault" of the Heavens.[41] As the editors of the Oxford edition put it: "The ancients considered the sky a *vault* (Gen.1.6); i.e., a solid roof over the world supporting a great *torrent* of *flood* waters above which God was enthroned Lord over the universe and all in it."[42] Hebrew legends outside the Bible say that Adam was so large that when he lay down he stretched from one end of the Earth to the other; that when he stood up, his head was level with the divine throne.[43] If you are able to forget what you know about the sky, and look at the sky from Ezekiel's viewpoint, then you will appreciate how the horizon line of the sky (where the creature's "feet" are) would be sparkling with bolts of lightning from the approaching storm. Picture half a transparent ball sitting on a table top with the cut edge down. When Ezekiel looked up at the sky, he would have thought he was seeing a vault above his head like an ant would see if he looked up from the table top at the transparent dome above his head.[44] Now treat **Figure 17** as if it represents the dome of the sky. See the creature's feet touching the horizon?

Ezekiel next wrote that the creatures had the hands of a man (human) under their wings on their four sides.[45] What we have seen so far has been "spaced out" in the sense that those words are used in American street slang. The discussion about "wings" and "hands" gets spaced out in another sense. Here, we jump into three-dimensional space analysis. You might as well learn, right now, that the ancients were extremely conscious of space and its dimensions. Think about a square box. If we walk around it, we see that it has four sides, a bottom, and a top. Ezekiel appears to be thinking that way. The Bible is loaded with images and objects appearing in groups of seven. *Many* explanations have been offered by the theologians for the "sacred seven."[46] Here is one more explanation for the ancients' fascination with the number seven. This explanation comes from Stone Age mathematics and science.[47] Ancient mathematicians and scientists would have viewed our square box with four sides, a top, and a bottom, as having six planes (that is, flat surfaces) and one center point. Six planes and one center point equals seven. They would have considered that you could move in six directions away from the center point of the box; in the directions of, and perpendicular to, the six sides.[48] We would call movements in these directions "vectors." The corollary principle, of course, would be that you can move to the center point of the box from the six sides in directions perpendicular to those six sides on only six vectors. Thinking this way, they would picture the box expanding out from its center in six directions and contracting in towards its center in six directions.[49] More of this later. You have enough of it now to understand the references to "wings" and "hands."

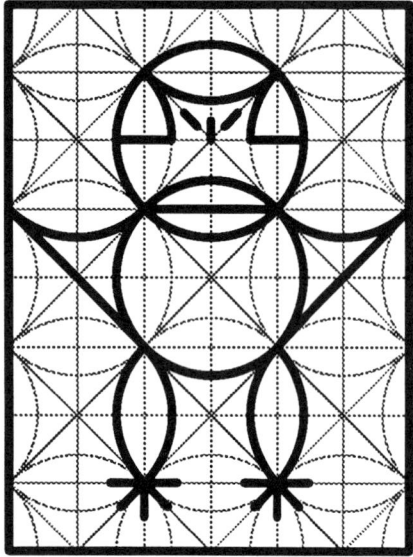

Figure 18

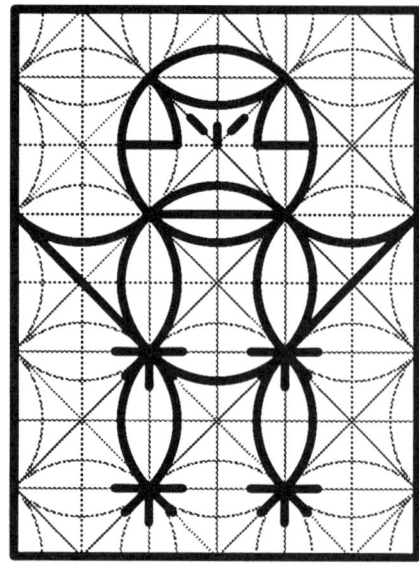

Figure 19

Human hands have five digits – a thumb and four fingers. We already have located the "wings." We know that the "hands" are under the "wings" on their four sides.[50] Until now, we have considered the Holy Grail as if it were two-dimensional. Now we must treat it as if it were a plane (two-dimensional) drawing of a three-dimensional object. As such, it has four sides, excluding its top and bottom, or six sides including its top and bottom. Look at **Figure 18**, and treat it as if it were to represent a view of each of the four sides. Our little fat man – with his wings extended – now is looking at us out of the plane on each of the four sides of the block. Think of this as a child's toy block with the same little man painted on each of its four sides. Just as Ezekiel told us, these four have their faces and their wings.[51] Think of the block as expanding outward along its six vectors and then contracting inward along its six vectors, with the little fat men growing smaller as the block contracts and larger as the block expands – but always with the wings of each of the four little fat men touching at the four corners of the block.[52] Just as Ezekiel told us, the four men would not turn as they go straight forward.[53] But we are evading the question of "hands," you tell me. No, we are not. We are laying a foundation so we can understand that reference. Here we go with hands: Look at **Figure 19**, where the thumb and four fingers of each "hand" that is under each "wing" are illustrated.

Was finding "hands" under "wings" difficult? Let us do something simple for a change. We have jumped back to plane or two-dimensional perspective. Ezekiel said that each of the four living creatures had four faces: the face of a man, the face of a lion on their right sides, the face of an ox on their left sides, and the face of an eagle.[54] The Ox face is easy to see. Look at **Figure 20**. Much less abstract than "hands," you must agree! The eagle face is easy to see also. The drooping eyes and beak are illustrated in **Figure 21**. The cat face is like a Picasso painting. See **Figure 22**. The man's face also is

Figure 20

Figure 21

Figure 22

Figure 23

abstract. We must see him as having his hair across his forehead in "bangs," his side hair down over his ears in a Dutch-boy haircut, and very large lips. You can see him in **Figure 23**. Are you glad you stuck with us in this *strange analysis*? We are beginning to fill our first cup of sand, are we not?

Draw in your mind's eye the "lion face" on the right side of one man-likeness, and the "ox" face on his left side. Remember his right is your left, since he is looking at you out of the page. This is your first examination.

We later shall learn that the twelve divisions of the Zodiac are fixed along the Ecliptic by four "Guardian Stars" which lie on or near the Ecliptic. These stars define a cross in the sky. They are Regulus, lying in the constellation Leo (the *lion*), Aldebaran, lying in the constellation Taurus (the *bull*), Fomalhaut, formerly lying in the constellation Aquarius (the water-bearing *man*), and Antares, lying in the *former* constellation of the *eagle*, which now is in the constellation Scorpio, the scorpion.[55] We also shall learn why lion, ox, man, and eagle were chosen by the early Christian Church as the symbols for the Four Evangelists – Matthew, Mark, Luke, and John.[56]

We already have noted that the creatures' wings are stretched upward (or spread), that two wings of each creature are joined one to another (touching the wings of its neighbor's) and two wings of each creature cover each creature's body.[57] We already have discussed in detail the reasons why they went (moved) straight forward and turned not when they went (or never swerved in their course).[58] The "spirit" that moves the creatures is, of course, the relevant force of nature, depending upon what the Holy Grail is being used to describe at any given time.[59] For instance, if we are loading a dome on a square in erecting a temple, the inward and outward

displacements of the walls of the square are forces of downward compression transferred to lateral thrust. In Ezekiel's time, each force of nature, such as lightning, was represented by a separate god or goddess, or one god or goddess presided over a collection of forces which were grouped with each other, such as lightning, thunder, and rain. In Ezekiel's mind, as in ours, *God* presides over *all* forces of nature, hence is responsible for everything which the Holy Grail can be used to describe.[60]

Ezekiel said the appearance of the creatures was as if burning coals of fire or lamps (torches) were going up and down among them (darting to and fro among them); that the fire was bright (radiant) and out of the fire went forth (came) lightning.[61] He says the creatures ran and returned as the appearance of a flash of lightning.[62]

Ezekiel next wrote about wheels. He said that as he saw the living creatures he saw one wheel upon the earth (ground) by each of them.[63] No one ever has been able to prove that the mathematics of the ancient Babylonians included spherical geometry and spherical trigonometry. Neugebauer has succeeded in demonstrating, however, that the Greeks did not need those branches of mathematics because they reduced spherical surfaces to plane surfaces by a system of stereographic projections.[64] When Ezekiel is speaking of "wheels" on the earth or ground, he evidently is treating the ground as flat, not round, and seems to be projecting the round vault or dome of the sky down onto it using the technique he must have learned from Babylonian astronomers. We study this in detail in later chapters. Ezekiel writes that the wheels have one likeness or appearance (they were all alike) and he tells us that their appearance and their work (their form and working) was as if there were a wheel in the middle of (inside) a wheel.[65] He says when they went, they went upon their four sides and turned not when they went. (When they moved in any of the four directions they never swerved in their course.)[66] In **Figure 24**, we see an expanding and contracting

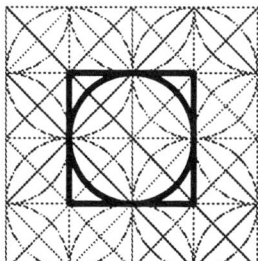

Figure 24

Figure 25

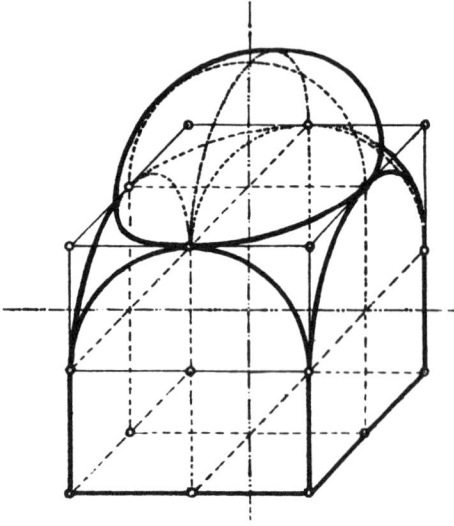

Illustration 4-1. The cuboctahedron as the Byzantine Christian and Moslem solution to the architectural problem of setting a dome on a cubical supporting frame. Courtesy of Dover Publications, Inc., New York.

square with a circle inscribed on it. In **Illustration 4-1,**[67] we see an isometric projection of an architect's line-drawing for the erection of a Byzantine dome upon a square foundation. The square and the circles expand when the dome gets larger, and contract when it gets smaller. We shall study *much* more about the theory of setting domes (the Heavens!) on squares (the Earth!) as we progress.

Figure 25 shows how we satisfy the requirement that there be one wheel upon the earth or ground by each of the four creatures.[68] The reference to the "work" of the wheels is one of the very best clues we have that Ezekiel is relating the colors of the rainbow[69] to what we call an "interference pattern." A black and white interference pattern appears as **Illustration 4-2.**[70] The "work" of the facets of this piece of quartz in separating white light into the colors of the spectrum produces colored wheels inside each other, with spoke-like projections between the "hubs" of the wheels and the "rims" of the "wheels." Thus, their "appearance" and their "work" is as if there were a wheel in the middle of (inside) a wheel.[71] Like so many other topics, the interference pattern will be the subject of detailed study later in this book. In passing, let us notice the resemblance between the interference pattern and **Illustration 4-3,**[72] which is a picture of a Celtic Cross which still stands in Ireland. Is this similarity accidental? We shall see! Right now, back to the task at hand.

Illustration 4-2. A black-and-white copy of a color photograph of the uniaxial interference pattern which can be viewed by naked eye in quartz and other crystals. Note the misalignment of the circle at the fracture. Courtesy of Dover Publications, Inc., New York.

Another difference exists at this point between King James and Oxford. King James says that the appearance and the work of the wheels was "like unto the colour of a beryl."[73] Oxford says that "The wheels sparkled like topaz."[74] Might this possibly be a reference to the gem which is known as a "cat's eye"? Ezekiel said of the "rings" that they were so high that they were dreadful and "were full of eyes round about them four."[75] We already have noted that the four "eyes" around the circles of the Holy Grail look like a cat's eyes. The editors of Oxford indicate that the Hebrew is uncertain of meaning at this point in the Ezekiel story.[76] The bit about the "rings" being so high they were dreadful possibly

Figure 26

Illustration 4-3. Muireachdach's Cross, Monasterboice, County Louth, Ireland. Courtesy of the Office of Public Works, Republic of Ireland.

may prove that Ezekiel realized that his vault of the Heavens was a good distance away. He is anticipating his next verses, of course, because the last time we considered rings or wheels[77] they were on the ground (like a temple ground plan) and he has not yet told us that they also can be lifted up from the ground (as in a temple elevation drawing), as he does in a later verse.[78]

Oxford varies from King James at this point in the analysis, as it affirms that all four creatures had "hubs" and each "hub" in turn "had a projection which had the power of sight."[79] If the circle which is bold in **Figure 26** is treated as a top view of a dome (like our dome on the table) then each "wheel" or "hub" would have a projection (the dome) which would have the "power of sight" because of its four "eyes all round."[80] Thus, we have another instance in which it does not matter whether King James or Oxford is the correct translation because either word formula fits the lines of the Holy Grail.

The next few verses of Ezekiel are concerned with the dynamics or movements of the wheels and the living creatures. Ezekiel said that when the living creatures went (moved), the wheels went by (moved beside) them; when the living creatures were lifted up (rose) from the earth, the wheels were lifted up (rose).[81] Recall our expanding and contracting block and the Byzantine dome-on-square drawing. Continuing with dynamics, where the spirit was to go, they went; there was their spirit to go (they moved in whatever direction the spirit would go); and the wheels were lifted up over against them (the wheels rose together with them)—for the spirit of the living creatures was in the wheels.[82] When those went, these went (when the one moved the other moved); and when those stood, these stood (when the one halted, the other halted); and when those were lifted up from the earth, the wheels were lifted up over against them (the wheels rose together with them)—for the spirit of the living creature (creatures) was in the wheels.[83] We shall study in some considerable detail the use of the Holy Grail as the ground grid, and arch, vault, and dome elevation, for the erection of public places of worship, commencing before the Sumerians and continuing through Christianity.

When we study the book of the Shepherd of Hermas, we shall read about a Christian tower being erected, and the author will tell us that what makes the tower stand is the work of certain "virgins" whose actions he describes.[84] Could those "virgins" be references to the same human forms of

 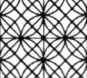

Figure 27

Figure 28

Ezekiel's Vision, simply dressed differently and renamed for purposes of another story made up on the Holy Grail? See **Figure 27**, where we have put a "skirt" on one of our Grail humanforms. The unfortunate thing about this book is that we cannot study everything from ancient religion to ancient structural engineering all at once. Modern architects and engineers, and ancient ones also, knew it was not "living creatures" or "virgins" which caused their buildings to stand. Rather, it was the action of the pendentives bearing the weight of the dome upon the square walls below. Religious writers, divining using the engineers' drawing, seemingly did not understand the principles of engineering, or preferred to ignore them in favor of stories about "living creatures" and "virgins."

The next verse takes us back to Ezekiel's concept of the sky as a dome over the Earth. The time has arrived for us to understand this peculiar bit of ancient cosmology. Ancient religionists thought of the world as a square and the sky as a dome over the square of the Earth.[85] That is why the Bible speaks of the four corners of the Earth.[86] That is why "Greek Cross" Christian churches have a dome erected upon a square at the transcept.[87] It will come as a shock to many Christians that their Greek Cross churches are copies of ancient pagan temples, but that is not the worst shock this book has in store for true believers.

Ezekiel said that the likeness of the firmament upon the heads of the living creature was as the color of the terrible crystal, stretched forth over their heads above. (Stretched over the heads of the living creatures was a vault glittering like a sheet of ice.)[88] The vault which looks like a sheet of ice is, of course, Ezekiel's vault of the sky. If we turn to **Figure 28**, we see one of the four living creatures standing with his straight legs on the ground or

earth and his head touching the vault of the Heavens. As did Adam. In the same figure, we see that under the firmament their wings were straight, the one toward the other. (Under the vault their wings were spread straight out, touching one another.)[89] Here, we should, once again, picture the four little men painted on the four sides of a block. See **Figure 29**. Ezekiel tells us that each of the living creatures had two wings which covered their bodies on "this side" and two more wings which covered its body on "that side."[90] You can picture this without reference to another drawing, can you not? Oxford says, instead, that one pair of wings was spread straight out while one pair of wings covered the body of each.[91] Different, but not materially so. We already have discussed wing positions *ad nauseam*.

The next verse apparently expresses Ezekiel's science or his religion about the noises of the

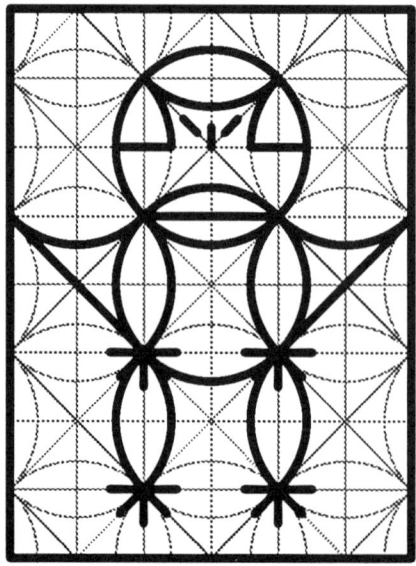

Figure 29

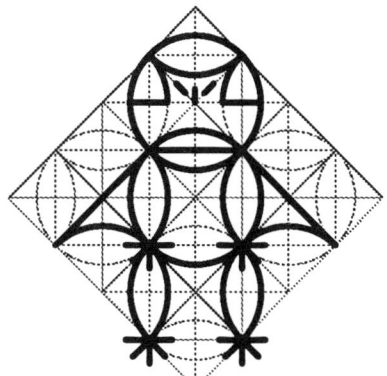

Figure 30

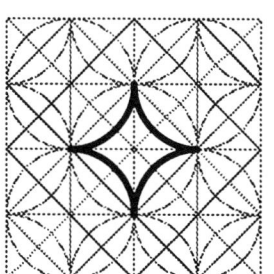

Figure 31

oncoming thunder and lightning storm. The Babylonians had a myth about the Great Bird Imdugud, whose enormous black wings were the black storm clouds.[92] Ezekiel says he heard the noise of the wings of the living creatures, which sounded to him like the noise of great waters, the noise of a host of people or the voice of the Almighty.[93] He says that when the living creatures stood, they let down their wings.[94] Surely the latter is a reference to the calms which come and go in association with violent thunder and lightning storms. Oxford puts it thus: "I heard, too, the noise of their wings; when they moved it was like the noise of a great torrent or of a cloud-burst, like the noise of a crowd or of an armed camp; when they halted their wings dropped."[95] Poetic, and rather descriptive of storm noises, would you not agree?

Ezekiel closes his references to storm noises by saying that there was a voice (sound) from the firmament (from above the vault) that was over their heads when they stood and let down their wings (halted with drooping wings).[96] A last clap of thunder as the storm went away? Can you see the wings let down or drooping? Turn to **Figure 30**.

Ezekiel's next vision is important insofar as the Holy Grail is concerned because it is so graphic. Have you ever seen a campstool made of four legs, joined at their midpoints, upon which a canvas seat is suspended? Stools of this sort are familiar objects in the Middle East these days as they have been for thousands of years. Many have seats made of leather instead of canvas. We see the frame of one of these stools in **Illustration 4-4**.[97] Now look at **Figure 31**, where we have bolded the lines of our now-famous "concave-sided tetragon." That is

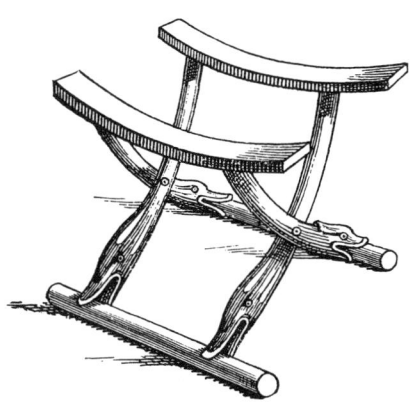

Illustration 4-4. An Egyptian campstool-type portable throne. Courtesy of Dover Publications, Inc., New York.

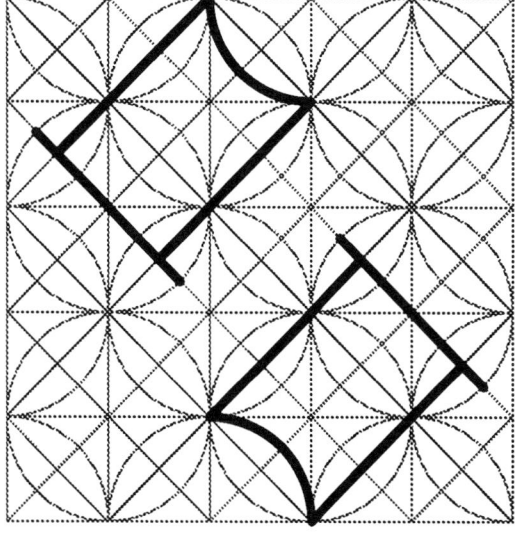

Figure 32

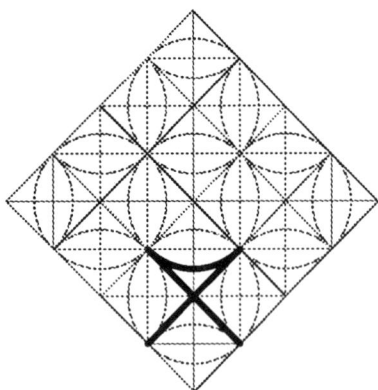

Figure 33

Figure 34

exactly what the seat cover of one of those camp-stools looks like in top view. The legs of such a stool are shown in top view in **Figure 32**, and the legs and seat of such a stool are shown in side view in **Figure 33**. **Illustration 4-5**[98] is of a star sapphire, whose lines center our "concave-sided tetragon." Ezekiel said: Above the firmament (vault) over their heads was (there appeared) the likeness of a throne, as the appearance of a sapphire stone (a sapphire in the shape of a throne).[99] He next said that (high above all) upon the likeness of the throne was the likeness as the appearance of a man above upon it (upon the throne, a form in human likeness.).[100] Turn to **Figure 34**. There sits our little fat man on his camp-stool or mobile throne! Hang on, Eagles! You only have begun to see the images which the fertile minds of storytellers could divine from the Holy Grail! Have we drawn YHWH on the Throne of Heaven?

The color of amber (brass glowing like fire in a furnace) which Ezekiel saw on his human likeness seated upon the throne is the Hebrew word chashmal, which, as we have discussed before, means "electricity" in Modern Hebrew.[101] He saw the appearance of fire, and it had brightness round about (encircling radiance) as the appearance of the bow that is in the cloud in the day of rain (like a rainbow in the clouds on a rainy day); such was the appearance (sight) of the brightness (encircling radiance) round about the fire.[102] Did Ezekiel see the light phenomenon we moderns call a corona around the sun? A corona looks like a rainbow circling the sun. He evidently considered that he had seen the Glory of the Lord. We shall study more about the "Glory of the Lord" in religion and magic, and about solar coronae, later in this book.

One passing thought: If some of the images on the Holy Grail seem to be very abstract, please recall that the persons who wrote these stories are the same persons (or their relatives) who visualized among the stars such forms as a bear, a scorpion, a hunter, and a large variety of other constellations which are much more abstract in form than the images we have found on the Holy Grail.

Illustration 4-5. An asteria; a star sapphire from Sri Lanka. Courtesy of Dover Publications, Inc., New York.

Notes
CHAPTER FOUR. Ezekiel's First Vision

1. Deu. 18.10.

2. Ex. 22.18.

3. Robbins 9, 28-29, 46-47, 341-343, 440-441, 497, 548-549.

4. Robbins 170.

5. Robbins 178, 219.

6. Robbins 46.

7. Robbins 281-282, 471-477.

8. Webber 18-20.

9. Cavendish 173; Sharkey Fig. 6.

10. Robbins 1, 7, 8, 45, 218, 281-282, 471, 546-551.

11. Robbins 11, 101, 104-105, 498-510.

12. Budge EM 5,7; Budge AAS 212.

13. Ex. 4.1-5.

14. John 2.6-11.

15. Oates 178-180.

16. Oates 178-180; Griffith & Thompson 157-169.

17. Schwaller de Lubicz TEM 82-85; Cirlot 6.

18. Oates 178-180.

19. Gen. 44-2, 5, 15.

20. Oates 178.

21. Robbins 138.

22. Gen. 41.1-46; Deut. 13.1-5.

23. Robbins 137-139, 545; Griffith & Thompson 161, 163, 167, 169.

24. Lev. 19.26, 31; Lev. 20.6, 27; Deu. 18.10-12, 20; 1 Sam. 15.23; 2 Kings 9.22; 2 Kings 21.6; 2 Kings 23, 24; Is. 8.19; Morgan 17-86.

25. Oxford University Press, New York, 1972.

26. Ez. 1.1,3.

27. Ez. 1.3.

28. Ez. 1.4.

29. Ez. 1.4.

30. Is. 14.12-15 (Oxford); Graves & Patai 57,59. "Israel" means "El strives." Graves & Patai 229.

31. Is. 14.13 (Oxford); Ps. 48.1-2 (Oxford); Graves & Patai 35,57,59.

32. Graves & Patai 38.

33. Graves & Patai 38.

34. Ez. 1.5.

35. Heidel 80.

36. Ez. 1.6.

37. Ez. 1.11.

38. Ez. 1.7.

39. Ez. 1.7.

40. Ez. 1.7.

41. Ez. 1.22-23.

42. Oxford 887.

43. Graves & Patai 61-62.

44. We assume that Ezekiel entertained thoughts about the supposed vault or dome of the sky similar to those of his contemporaries, which appears to have been the case.

45. Ez. 1.8.

46. Cirlot 283-285.

47. Cirlot xvii.

48. Cirlot 184, 283, 300-303, 343.

49. Cirlot 184, 283, 300-303, 343.

50. Ez. 1.8.

51. Ez. 1.8.

52. Ez. 1.9.

53. Ez. 1.8-9.

54. Ez. 1.10.

55. Allen 256, 345-346, 362-364, 385. Fomalhaut currently is said to lie in the Southern Fishes.

56. Cirlot 337-339; Webber 185-190; Stafford 101; VanTreeck & Croft 48-51. The Christian order is: Man, Lion, Ox, and Eagle.

57. Ez. 1.11.

58. Ez. 1.12.

59. Ez. 1.12.

60. 1 Kings 19.11-12.

61. Ez. 1.13.

62. Ez. 1.14.

63. Ez. 1.15.

64. Neugebauer 161, 185, 218-220.

65. Ez. 1.16.

66. Ez. 1.17.

67. Ghyka, Plate XIV.

68. Ez. 1.15.

69. Ez. 1.28.

70. E.A. Wood, Plate V. The careful observer will see the wheels within wheels despite the fact that this color plate is illustrated in black and white in this book.

71. Ez. 1.16.

72. From the author's collection.

73. Ez. 1.16.

74. Ez. 1.16.

75. Ez. 1.18.

76. Oxford 887.

77. Ez. 1.15.

78. Ez. 1.21.

79. Ez. 1.18.

80. Ez. 1.18.

81. Ez. 1.19.

82. Ez. 1.20.

83. Ez. 1.21.

84. 3 Hermas 10.15.

85. Cirlot 15-16, 308.

86. Is. 11.12.

87. Cirlot 15-16, 308.

88. Ez. 1.22.

89. Ez. 1.23.

90. Ez. 1.23.

91. Ez. 1.23.

92. Frankfort 6.

93. Ez. 1.24.

94. Ez. 1.24.

95. Ez. 1.24.

96. Ez. 1.25.

97. Erman 184.

98. Kunz, Color Plate 1.

99. Ez. 1.26.

100. Ez. 1.26.

101. Ez. 1.27; Graves & Patai 38.

102. Ez. 1.27-28.

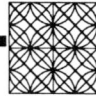

Chapter Five

Ezekiel's Second Vision and Our First

We have discovered that the images of Ezekiel's First Vision can be found on the Holy Grail. The conclusion might be reached that his First Vision was constructed from the Holy Grail. You may be inclined toward that view. You may entertain doubts. More proof follows as we analyze Ezekiel's Second Vision.

It will not be necessary for us to discuss most of the images of Ezekiel's Second Vision because they are identical to those of his First Vision. You should read Chapter Ten of the Book of Ezekiel before you continue with this book. You will note that, skeptic or not, you have gained skill in the finding of images on the Holy Grail.

In his Second Vision, Ezekiel substitutes the word "cherub" for the word "ox" but the cast of characters otherwise remains the same.[1] We know he is writing about the *same* living creatures he saw by the River Chebar (Kebar) because he tells us so

expressly.[2] The plural of "cherub" apparently is "cherubim" or "cherubims."[3] Scholars have attempted to explain the words "cherub," "cherubim," and "cherubims."[4] We shall not engage in such word-play, as we already have good cause to believe that we are working with images created from the lines of the Holy Grail by the fertile minds of ancient storysmiths.

The man clothed with linen[5] is illustrated in **Figure 35**.

It is possible to see the Holy Grail from a top view as the "horned" bowl of an altar, holding "coals of fire."[6] **Illustration 5-1** is a photograph of an ancient Hebrew altar, complete with its "horns."[7] We shall see the form illustrated in **Figure 36** being interpreted as an altar or a hearth. We shall come to understand that the four crossed lines in the middle of this altar or hearth signify "fire" or "sun." Thus, we understand Ezekiel's reference to the man clothed with (dressed in) linen going in among the cherubim to fill his hand with coals of fire to scatter them all over the city.[8] The "city" is a reference to twelve pyramid-shaped tents (one for each of the twelve tribes) around a central square supporting a dome. The central square (Earth) and dome (Heaven) represent the Temple. See **Figure 37**. The

Figures 35, 36 & 37
Clockwise from Top

Illustration 5-1. An Israelite horned altar from Megiddo. Courtesy of Ira Block Photography, Ltd., New York

British Museum, London, contains a remarkably similar painting of the twelve tents of the twelve tribes of Israel surrounding the Temple.[9]

Are we contending that the entire Bible is fantasy constructed from images found on the Holy Grail? No. The *entire* Bible is *not* fantasy. We *are* suggesting that *many* of the *stories* found in the Bible, Old Testament and New Testament, reveal their origins in the minds of ancient storysmiths because their images can be found on the Holy Grail. If you cannot endure being confronted with that hypothesis, you should reclassify yourself and read some other book! When we study one of the stories from the *Shepherd of Hermas*, one of the books of the *Pseudepigrapha*, we shall read an elaborate tale about twelve mountains surrounding a plain, like twelve tents surrounding a square (Earth) upon which has been erected a dome (Heaven). In later chapters, we shall learn about "correspondence theory," that is, the ancient theory that what is on Earth corresponds with what is in Heaven.[10] Might the "coals" which are scattered around the "city" *also* be a reference (in "correspondence theory") to the stars scattered around the City of God, i.e., around the dome of Heaven? If the words "cosmology" and "cosmogony" are not in your vocabulary, you should get a dictionary and look them up. Those are the words which customarily are used to describe the genre of story we are reading.

In the First Chapter of the Book of Ezekiel, we found Ezekiel in the great outdoors, under the dome or vault of the sky, watching and hearing the pyrotechnics of a thunder and lightning storm. In the Tenth Chapter, we find him back in Jerusalem, in spirit if not in body, where he has been transported "in the visions of God."[11] The city has been taken over by worshipers of other faiths.[12] Things are in such a mess that God has picked up and packed out.[13] When worshipers of an ancient god chose to worship a new god, the old god often got miffed and left his temple, according to the pattern of thinking in vogue in Ezekiel's time. Apparently, Ezekiel believes Yahweh acts that way also.[14] The next thing to be anticipated from Yahweh, in usual Old-Testament thinking, is for Him to demolish the city and slaughter its inhabitants because His followers have chosen to believe in some other god or gods.[15] To avert such destruction, Ezekiel must get his people to change their ways.[16] Have you ever heard the story of the sweet little seven-year-old girl who was asked by her Christian Sunday School teacher why God lost His temper so often in the Old Testament and destroyed entire towns and populations? Her answer: He was not yet a Christian! Could it be that God has not changed—only our perceptions of Him?

Chapter Ten of Ezekiel differs from Chapter One because Chapter Ten takes place in and around a "house," according to King James, or a "temple," according to Oxford.[17] It seems clear that the house or temple is The Temple of Jerusalem, from which Yahweh has departed because the residents of Jerusalem are worshiping other gods. Ezekiel wants us to think of the cherubims (cherubim) standing by the right side of the house (temple) and a cloud filling the inner court.[18] Turn to **Figure 38**. Let's pretend that our little fat man (wearing an ox-face and wings, and with his hands under his wings) is lying on his back on the Holy Grail, which is drawn on the ground. In your mind's eye, pivot him at his

Figure 38

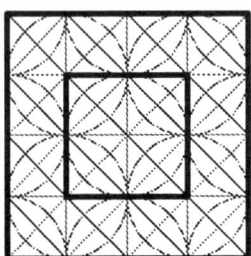

Figure 39

Figure 40

　　　　Ezekiel's Second Vision and Our First

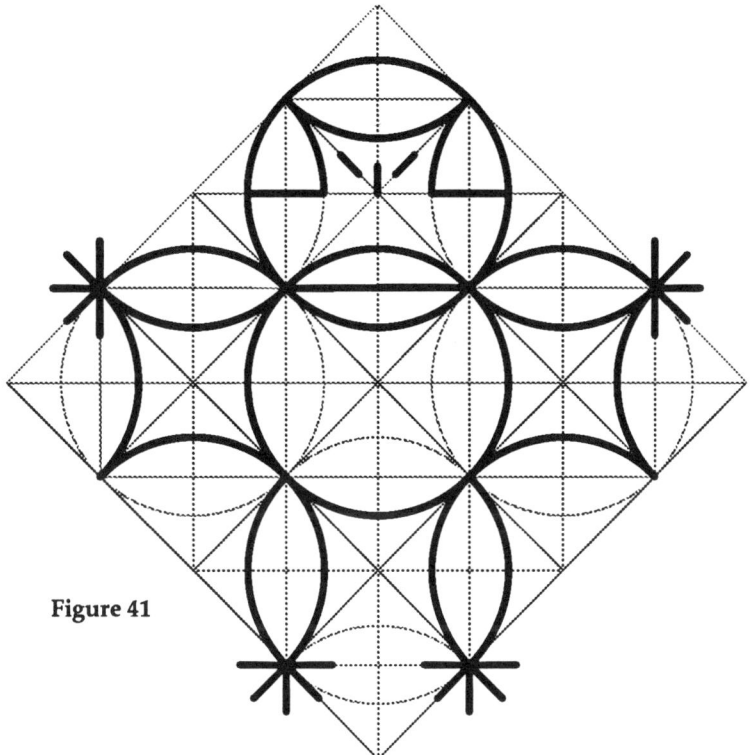

Figure 41

feet and swing him up out of the page, by himself, to a standing position. Now spin Figure 38 clockwise ninety degrees. Now he is standing at the right side of the temple or house. The square on the Holy Grail represents the exterior lines of the ground plan of the temple or house. Treat **Figure 39** as an expanded ground grid or ground plan of the Temple. The "inner court" is illustrated by the inner bold-faced square in Figure 39. The "cloud" which fills the "inner court" in **Figure 40** is our old friend the "concave-sided tetragon."[19]

The Bible tells us that YHWH, or El, rode on clouds, and that the Son of Man came with, or in, the clouds of Heaven.[20] **Figure 41.**

The "glory" around our manform's head[21] is illustrated in **Figure 42.** Note his pointed beard in Figure 42. Early Christian art illustrates such a halo or glory around the head of Jesus Christ.[22] Haloes or glories in early Christian art resemble the interference pattern we saw in Illustration 4-2, and also resemble the shape of the Celtic cross we saw in Illustration 4-3. They also resemble Figure 42. As we previously have mentioned, glories are natural phenomena resulting from white light being divided into its component colors, but signaled to ancient religionists the presence of a god.[23] We shall read about a natural phenomenon known as the "Spectre of the Brocken," a condition in which a glory appears around the head of a just-plain human being.[24]

The "inner court" of the Temple also has a glory around it, as well as a cloud in it.[25] **Figure 43.** We learned in Ezekiel's First Vision that God's presence

Figure 42

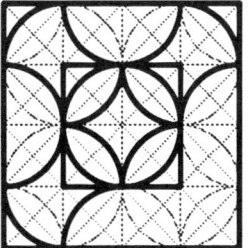

Figure 43

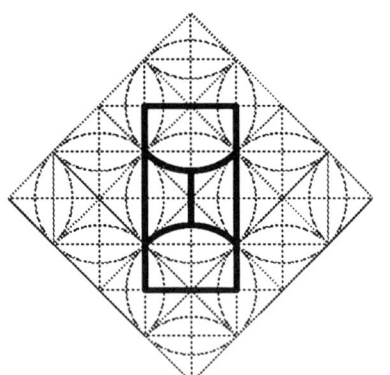

Figure 44

Figure 45

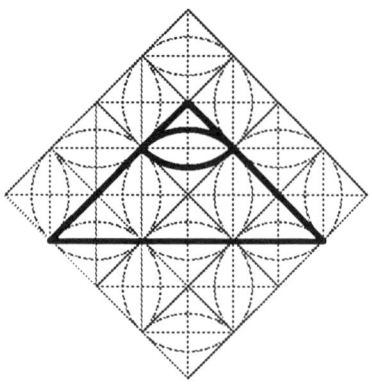

Figure 46

Figure 47

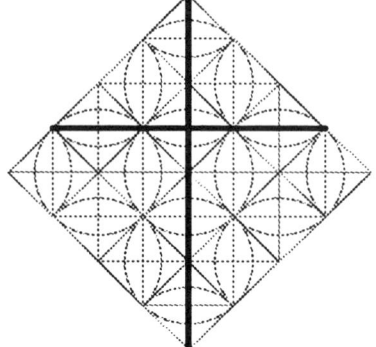

Figure 48

Figure 49

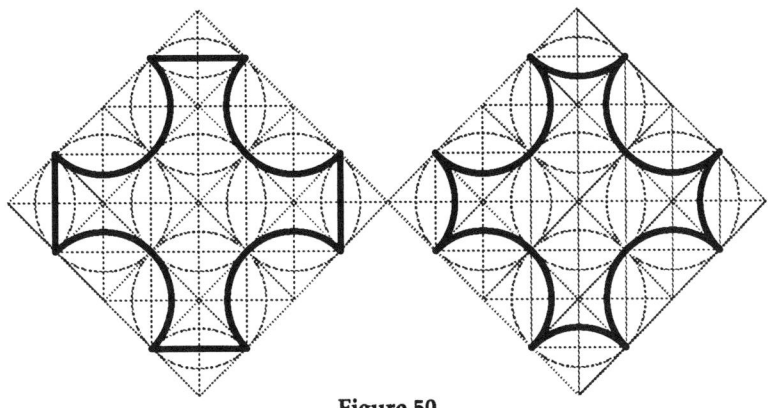

Figure 50

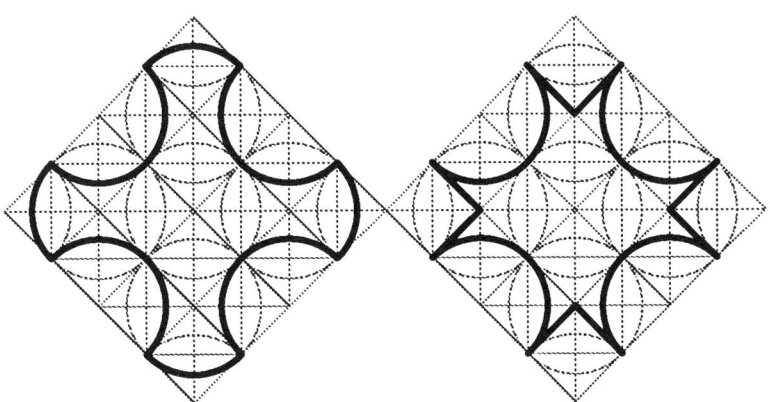

Figure 51   Figure 52

can be announced by the arrival of a cloud.[26] Ezekiel means that God has returned to the Temple of Jerusalem.[27] It was the tradition in many of the Middle Eastern countries that the god of the temple entered the temple from the east, i.e., the sun rises in the east. Not surprising, therefore, that Yahweh returned to the Temple in Jerusalem by way of the east gate.[28] The "threshold" and "gate" (or "gateway") are illustrated in **Figure 44.** The gate, seen in front view in Figure 44, looks like the swinging doors to a saloon in a typical American western movie. Note that the center of the gate is the center of the Holy Grail. We shall study *much* more about this gate in later chapters. Can you picture YHWH back in the Temple sitting on his "throne"? Turn to **Figure 45.**

At this point in the analysis, other images started presenting themselves to me on the Holy Grail. In **Figure 46,** we see the shape of a pyramid with an

eye at its top; the same figure that appears on the back of the United States one-dollar bill. That form is the image of the Babylonian storm god Enlil, known as "the great mountain."[29] The engraver of the dollar bill evidently played a prank upon all citizens of the United States by implying that the one god upon whom the United States was founded was the great god Enlil of the Babylonians! Turn to **Figure 47,** where we see our little, bearded man. Turn to **Figure 48,** where we see a Roman cross. Turn to **Figure 49,** where we see our bearded man crowned and hanging on a Roman cross! The pointed beard he wears in Figure 49 is like the pointed beard which Christ wears in early Christian art.[30] Other forms of crosses are illustrated in **Figure 50,** and **Figure 51.** The Greek letters Chi and Rho appear on the Holy Grail. **Figure 52.** Those letters signify Christ, and are called "the *Christogram.*"[31] Our little man is hanging above the shape of a

Figure 53

Figure 54

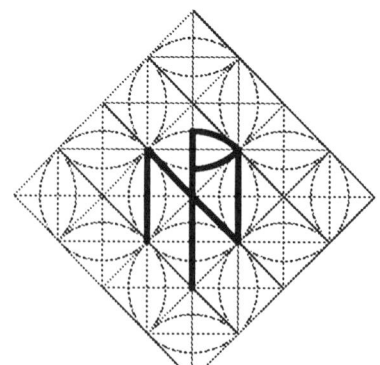

Figure 55

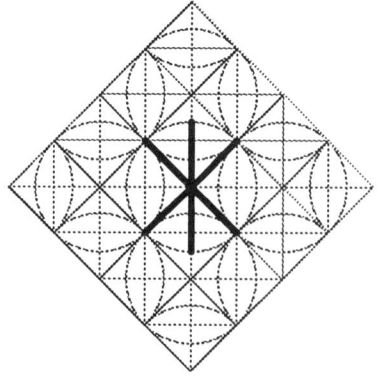

Figure 56

Figure 57

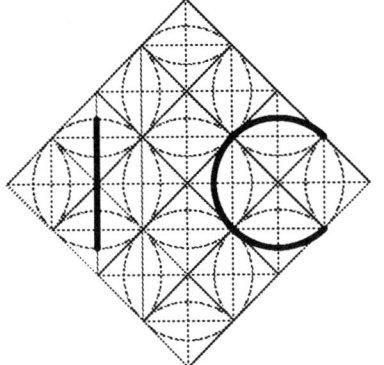

Figure 58

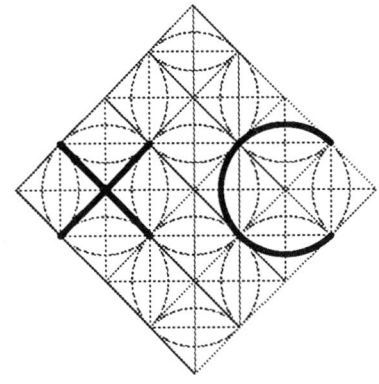

Figure 59

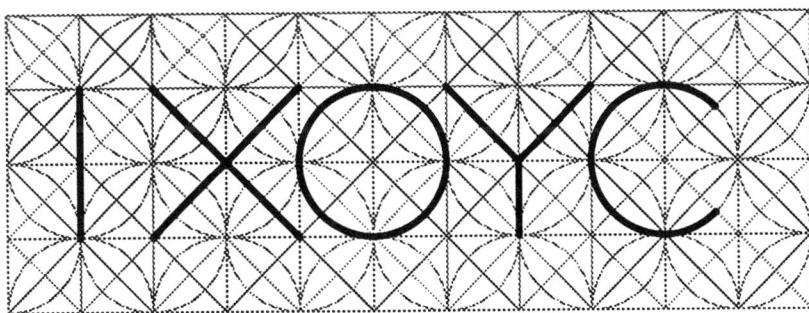

Figure 60

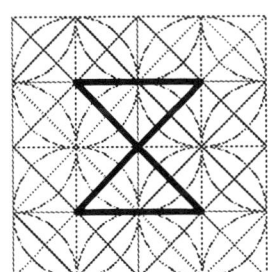

Figure 61

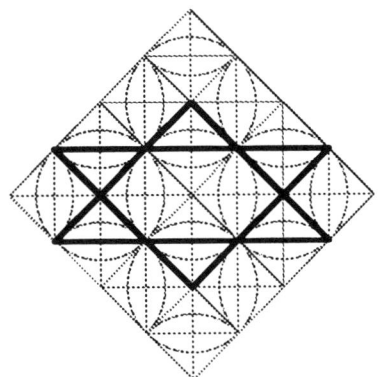

Figure 62

"vesica piscis," a geometry generator which became the Christian fish symbol for Jesus Christ.[32] See **Figure 53**. A crowned and bearded Man on a cross at whose feet appears the Christian fish symbol and above whose head appear the Greek letters of the "Christogram"? What have we stumbled upon?

A trip to the library of a nearby theology school revealed more. Books on Christian symbolism confirmed that the monogram illustrated in **Figure 54** stands for Christ.[33] Another Christian monogram, which is a contraction of the letters XPICTOC NIKA, *Christos Nika*, that is, Christ Conquers,[34] appears in **Figure 55**. Another monogram, appearing in **Figure 56**, was taken from IHCOYC XPICTOC, *Iesous Christos*, Jesus Christ.[35] The exact lines of one of our "Ezekiel Wheels" form another monogram, appearing in **Figure 57**, which stands for Jesus Christ (IX) crucified (on the cross +) as eternal God—the circle signifying eternity.[36] Another Christian monogram, seen in **Figure 58**, was IC, a contraction of IHCOYC, that is, Jesus.[37] Still another, shown in **Figure 59**, was XC, a contraction of XPICTOC, *Christos*, Christ.[38] Also listed in these books was the famous acrostic IXOYC, the word for fish, which stands for Jesus Christ Son of God Savior.[39] **Figure 60**. All of these monograms can be found on the Holy Grail!

What have we found? You may or may not agree, if you complete the quest laid before you in this book.

Christianity is not alone in this respect. We can find on the Holy Grail the "Drum of Siva" of the Hindu Religion.[40] **Figure 61**. The flattened form of the Star of David appears on the Holy Grail. **Figure 62**. The seven-branched Menorah is there, also.

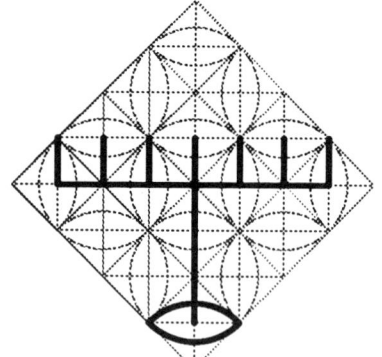

Illustration 5-2. Egyptian scarab necklace. Courtesy of Thames & Hudson, Ltd., London.

Figure 63

Figure 64

Figure 63. The scarab beetle of the Egyptian Religion figuratively hopped from the page at me one night. **Figure 64.** If you are not familiar with typical Egyptian scarabs, look at **Illustration 5-2,**[41] and compare that photograph with Figure 64.

We have completed five chapters. We have seen only a tiny sampling of the images which the fertile minds of ancient storysmiths apparently drew from this wellspring of religious symbols!

The mythological Egyptian scarab beetle supposedly rolled the sun across the sky, an allegory based upon the way that Egyptian dung beetles roll balls of manure.[42] Is this our first clue to the realities of the Holy Grail? Does the Holy Grail somehow relate to the *sun* and to the passage of *time*?

Notes
CHAPTER FIVE. Ezekiel's Second Vision and Our First

1. Ez. 10.14, 20-22.

2. Ez. 10.20, 22.

3. Ez. 10.1.

4. Graves & Patai 70, 74, 77; Frankfort et al. 230.

5. Ez. 10.2.

6. Ez. 10.2.

7. *Splendors Of The Past* 75. This photograph appears by permission of its owner, Ira Block Photography, Ltd., 215 West 20th Street, New York, New York 10011.

8. Ez. 10.2.

9. Rosenau 85.

10. Cirlot xvi, 62.

11. Ez. 8.3.

12. Ez. 8.3-18; 9.1-11.

13. Ez. 9.9.

14. Ez. 9.9.

15. Ez. 11.8-12.

16. Ez. 11.4.

17. Ez. 10.3.

18. Ez. 10.3.

19. Ez. 10.3.

20. Is. 19.1; Dan. 7.13; Mat. 24.30; Mat. 26.64; Mark 13.26; Mark 26.64; Rev. 1.7.

21. Ez. 10.4.

22. Beckwith 260.

23. Baer & Baer 1-6; Krupp 133-134. The Stone Age shaman's drug-induced trip to Heaven across a rainbow bridge created by quartz crystals' being struck by rays of sunlight was brought forward into esoteric Christianity, complete with the Tetramorphs but minus any specific reference to the drugs. Rev. 4.1-8.

24. Minnaert 224-226; Schaaf 43.

25. Ez. 10.3-4.

26. Ez. 1.4; 10.3.

27. Ez. 10.4.

28. Ez. 10.18-19.

29. Frankfort 137, 142, 153, 193.

30. Beckwith 157.

31. Van Treeck & Croft 27-29; Stafford 55; Webber 91.

32. Lawlor 32-35; Van Treeck & Croft 29. Critics will note that the legs of our Grail manform hang straight down. Although the stereotyped, modern depiction of Christ on the Cross illustrates both feet nailed to the upright beam of the Cross with a single spike, the very earliest depictions of the crucifixion show Him, arms extended to a horizontal beam, *legs straight down*, either sitting or standing on a lower horizontal beam. Smith 61-62. Our Grail manform can be visualized either sitting or standing on a lower horizontal beam. Critics who prefer shoulder-length hair in depictions of Christ should visualize the lines of His hair bolded as in Figures 237 and 238.

33. Van Treeck & Croft 27-29; Stafford 55; Webber 91.

34. Van Treeck & Croft 29; Webber 92.

35. Van Treeck & Croft 29; Stafford 54.

36. Van Treeck & Croft 29.

37. Van Treeck & Croft 29; Stafford 54; Webber 92.

38. Van Treeck & Croft 29; Stafford 54; Webber 92.

39. Van Treeck & Croft 29.

40. Sahi 99.

41. Lamy 85. Hebrew and Christian theology students often are exposed these days to archaeological discoveries about the historical and mythological foundations of the Old and New Testaments. Some students leave seminary as a direct result of their studies of archaeological materials. Those who graduate rarely mention such matters to the congregations of true believers to whom they minister. The casual reader quickly may get a good taste of the Semitic mythology that underlies the Old and New Testaments by reading Volume V, Semitic, *The Mythology Of All Races*, by Stephen Herbert Langdon, Cooper Square Publishers, Inc., New York, 1964. Langdon was a giant among Semitic scholars. His last-mentioned work is the one book I recommend if you do not have time to read others. Be prepared to read Sumerian and Babylonian precedents for your favorite Old and New Testament stories, and to be exposed to considerable evidence indicating that those pre-Bible myths were composed to describe events occurring among the constellations of the stars of the sky. If a Sumerian story served as precedent for a Bible story, and the Sumerian story is a myth about the apparent motions of the greater and lesser lights of the sky, then what conclusion might one reach about the latter-day version of the story found in the Bible? Can cosmic allegory become historical reality?

42. Budge EM 35-43; Budge AAS 135-137.

Chapter Six

Introductory Cosmology and Cosmogony

We are exploring stories, hoping to find the seeds of understanding of ourselves and our universe. The tower story of the Book of the Shepherd of Hermas is a parable, i.e., a fantasy. "Hear therefore what I shall say concerning the parable of the tower...."[1]

Are you looking for the Book of the Shepherd of Hermas in your King James Bible? It is not there. It was blackballed by a divided vote of the fathers of the Church when they decided which religious writings would be canonized as the "Word of God."[2] Not that there was anything evil about Hermas. The worst thing ever said about it by the fathers of the Church was Jerome's comment that it was "foolish." Irenaeus quoted it under the name of Scripture. Origen thought it was a most useful writing, and that it was divinely inspired. Eusebius wrote that although it was not deemed canonical, it was read publicly in early Christian churches, and this was corroborated by Jerome. Athanasius cited it, called it a most useful work, and observed that although it was not strictly canonical, the fathers caused it to be read for direction and confirmation in faith and piety. It was attached to some of the most ancient manuscripts of the New Testament.[3]

Why, then, have many modern Christian lay persons never heard of Hermas? You should talk with your religious leader about the Church politics which led to the acceptance of some books and the rejection of others. A detailed discussion of such matters is outside the scope of this writing. One tidbit which escaped from the "smoke-filled rooms" of the "platform committee" of the Church *does* deserve our notice: The need to have only four Gospels apparently was of supreme importance. Irenaeus wrote that because there are four winds, there also must be four Gospels, as the Holy Spirit, the inspiration for all divine writing, is embodied in the wind.[4] Recall that the symbols chosen by the fathers of the Church for Matthew, Mark, Luke, and John were the Tetramorphs, lion, ox, man, and eagle.[5]

We shall consider stories from two collections of Judaeo-Christian writings which have been studied by scholars of religion, but not by most lay persons, down through the years. One is called the *Apocrypha*. Some, but not all, of the Apocryphal writings are attached to Oxford, the second Bible with which we are working. The other collection is called the *Pseudepigrapha*.

The reasons why some of these writings were not canonized are apparent from their contents. Can you imagine a modern Christian fundamentalist preacher telling his flock that when Christ was seven years of age and playing with his childhood companions he commanded clay figures of oxen to walk and clay figures of birds to fly?[6] Modern preachers do not seek to convince true believers that Christ was born a holy magician. Such preaching would be out of touch with "modern realities." Even worse, imagine a modern fundamentalist Christian preacher reading this to his congregation from the pulpit: "Another time, when the Lord Jesus was coming home in the evening with Joseph, he met a boy, who ran so hard against him, that he threw him down; To whom the Lord Jesus said, As thou has thrown me down, so shalt thou fall, nor ever rise. And that moment the boy fell down and died."[7] Convincing words, preacher, if your point is that Christ was born a shaman, but not very convincing if you are talking about the "Sweet Jesus" of the modern Christian Church.

The reasons why others of these writings were not canonized are difficult to imagine. Our preachers, priests, and rabbis have been using many of them as text sources for generations! Why would a writing which is equal to or better than other writings which were canonized fail to become "The Word of God" by vote of the Church's fathers? The answer often was party politics.

As our story goes, Hermas, brother of Pius, Bishop of Rome, was in a private place in a field when he was visited by a lady.[8] She sat him down, held up her bright wand, and showed him a vision of a great tower built upon "the water" using bright square stones.[9] The tower was built upon "a square" by six young men who came with her.[10] Thousands of other men brought stones from "the deep" and

from "the ground" with which the six young men erected the tower.[11] The stones from the deep were polished and square and fitted together without spaces at their joints so the tower appeared to be built of one stone.[12] Some of the stones from the ground were imperfect in enumerated particulars and were not used in the building, whereas other stones from the ground were fitted into the structure.[13] The rejected stones fell in "the way," "the fire," or "the water."[14] Hermas asked the lady what the vision meant; whether it held profit for him.[15] She responded: "You are very cunning, in that you are desirous to know those things which relate to the tower."[16]

How many of you ever watched Groucho Marx's show on television years ago? If a contestant said the magic word, a horn blasted and a rubber duck fell into view on a string with a monetary prize in its bill. The magic word in the last sentence of the last paragraph is "know." "Knowing" Jesus Christ was the pet theory of the Gnostics, whereas "believing" in Jesus Christ was the magic word of the followers of the Apostle Paul. Hermas got blackballed from the Canon of the Bible. So much for the way that the "Word of God" was formulated in the real world of Church politics.[17]

We need to pause for a lesson in Biblical physics. An early Christian listening to a reading of the Book of the Shepherd of Hermas believed that everything on Earth is formulated from the "elements" earth, air, fire, and water.[18] Good science? Not by modern standards. The Irish chemist Lord Boyle long ago proved that earth, air, fire, and water are not elements at all.[19] The congregation also believed that the Earth was a large island, surrounded by sea water, covered by a vault or dome of the sky above which God sat enthroned, opening and closing the sluice gates, allowing fresh water to fall as rain from the sky.[20] According to the pattern of Eastern thinking of which early Christianity was a part, land first rose from the cosmic ocean in the form of a square island.[21] This is why the Bible refers to the four corners of the Earth.[22] Four posts, four gods or goddesses, or four angels held up the vault of the Heavens, according to some cosmologies, whereas a single center post, like a tent post, or a single cosmic man, like Hercules, held up the Heavens according to other cosmologies.[23]

The necessary antecedents of such cosmic terms as "the deep," "the way," "the water," and "the fire" were familiar to the persons for whom the parable of the tower was written. Nowadays, when Mom says to Dad that she and their son are going to

"the ballgame," and their son is wearing his Little League baseball uniform and carrying his bat and glove, Dad need not ask, "Which ballgame?" The necessary antecedent of "the ballgame" quite obviously is the Little League baseball game in which their son is going to play. Similarly, when an early father of the Church told his congregation that Jesus is "the way" and "the light,"[24] he need not have specified *which* way, and *which* light, because the congregation understood the words were a reference to familiar cosmology and cosmogony. We must learn this ancient cosmology and cosmogony if we are to understand the original meaning ascribed to the Christ story by the persons for whom it was written.

The polished and squared stones from "the deep" are the facet lines of a piece of clear quartz crystal, as we shall study later. Not until we consider this system of cosmology in detail in later chapters will we understand its infusion into early Christian doctrines. Note that a "Sea" was used in the Hebrew Temple.[25] It should be rather obvious, even to readers who have not been initiated into the use of allegory in the Bible, that the metal "Sea" in the Temple is not something on which a ship could sail; rather, that it is one of the furnishings of the Temple.

One major distinction between the "science" of early Christians and our present-day science is our scientific methodology. We are inquisitive. We question. We observe. We record. We theorize. Early Christians would not have presumed to do such things. Instead, they awaited revelations or visions. They believed that God would reveal to them what they needed to know, and would keep the rest to Himself. As Hermas puts it: "Whatsoever is fit to be revealed unto thee shall be revealed: only let thy heart be with the Lord, and doubt not whatsoever thou shalt see."[26] Doubting *everything* you see is the heart of the modern scientific method.

The lady next explained to Hermas the allegory of the tower. The tower is the Church.[27] The tower is built on "the water" because the lives of Christians are saved by (baptismal) water; the tower is supported by God's "invisible power and virtue."[28] This is mixed science, cosmology, and religion. Hermas says: "[T]he world itself is upheld by the four elements."[29] The congregation is supposed to believe, literally, that God's "power and virtue" hold up the water which holds up the land which holds up the Church. The allegorical meaning of good stones and bad stones is explained in generous detail. However, you figured it out for yourself — good Christians versus bad Christians. The good

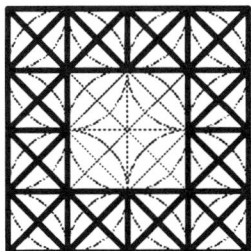

Figure 65

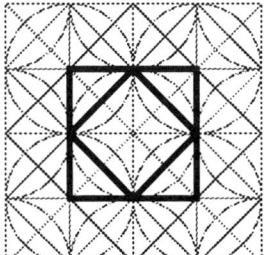

Figure 66

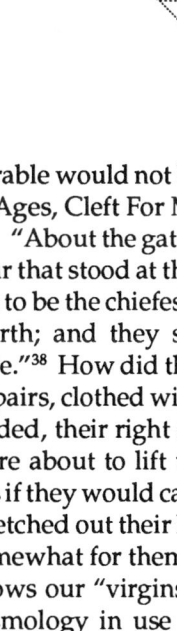

Figure 67

ones are the building materials of the Church.[30] The six young men are said to be the first appointed angels of God.[31] Hermas writes in allegory about framing up and building God's creatures.[32] We are supposed to think of the framing up and building of structures. Is this what Jerome thought was "foolish"?

Get ready to play Grail games! Here we go again! Hermas was transported to the top of a mountain by an angel.[33] He saw from the top of the mountain a great plain with twelve mountains "about it."[34] The mountains are described in considerable detail, indicating that some of them are "nice" mountains and some are "nasty" mountains.[35] We see the plain and its surrounding mountains on the Holy Grail in **Figure 65**. Each mountain looks like a pyramid seen from top view; like the twelve tents of Ezekiel's Second Vision. "In the middle of the plain he showed me a huge white rock, which rose out of the plain, and the rock was higher than those mountains, and was square; so that it seemed capable of supporting the whole world."[36] Visualize on the plain a square rock rising above the tops of the mountains. See **Figure 66**, which is a top view of the plain and the rock. The inner square is the rock; the outer square the plain. "It (the rock) looked to me to be old, yet it had a new gate, which seemed to have been newly hewn out in it. Now that gate was bright beyond the sun itself; insomuch, that I greatly admired at its light."[37] Here we go with the "gate" again. See **Figure 67**. This

parable would not have anything to do with "Rock of Ages, Cleft For Me" would it?

"About the gate stood twelve virgins; of which four that stood at the corners of the gate, seemed to me to be the chiefest, although the rest were also of worth; and they stood at the four parts of the gate."[38] How did the "virgins" look? They "stood in pairs, clothed with linen garments, and decently girded, their right arms being at liberty, as if they were about to lift up some burthen," and looked "as if they would carry the whole heaven."[39] "They stretched out their hands, as if they were to receive somewhat for them to do."[40] **Figure 68**. **Figure 69** shows our "virgins" lifting up "the rock." Pagan cosmology in use in the Christian Church? An allegorical reference to Our Lady's lifting up Her Holy Infant? Beautiful prose? Or lousy science? Later, we shall study about pillars holding up a dome representing the dome of Heaven.[41]

We shall not prolong our agony by going through another version of essentially the same story about the six men building the tower from stones which, in the second version of the same tale, come from the "good" mountains (but not from the "bad" mountains) as well as from "the deep."[42]

The punch line of this fable is that "these commands cannot be kept without these virgins."[43]

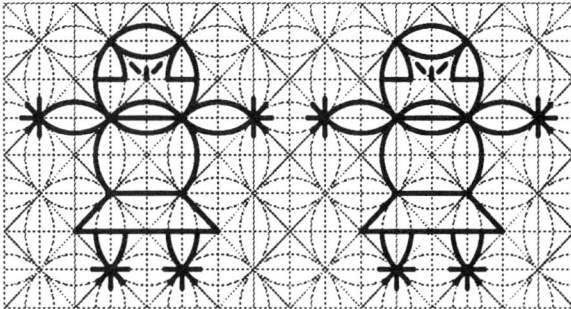

Figure 68

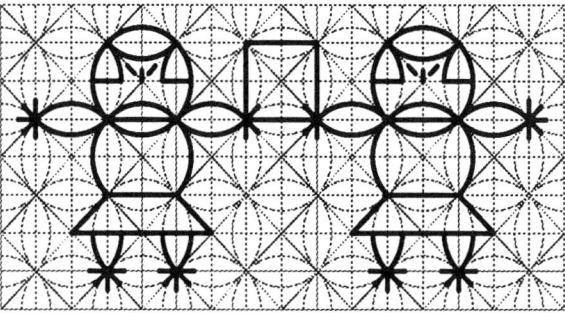

Figure 69

Figure 70

The virgins are for the purpose of "lifting up" the stones of the structure.[44] True enough. If ancient builders set out to erect a tower on a square foundation, the proportionalities (which we shall study when we get to the science part of this book) had to be maintained at all times by accurate measurements. Having dragged you through all this, the key point to be kept in mind is that the Holy Grail should be associated with the process of erecting structures on square foundations. The rest of the parable is a wild mixture of ancient science, cosmology, and religious thinking which is almost incomprehensible to readers who have not yet learned the "mysteries" of the early Christian Church.

There is one bit of theology we need to pick up before we leave Hermas. The allegory of the rock and gate are explained thus: "[T]his rock, and this gate, are the Son of God."[45] When Hermas asked how that could be, inasmuch as the rock was old but the gate new, this answer was given: "The Son of God is indeed more ancient than any creature; insomuch that he was in council with His Father at the creation of all things. But the gate is therefore new, because He appeared in the last days in the fullness of time; that they who shall attain unto salvation, may by it enter into the kingdom of God."[46] The reason the stones were carried through the gate to build the tower was "that no man shall enter into the kingdom of God, but who shall take upon him the name of the Son of God."[47] In the Egyptian *Book of the Dead*, the dead person takes upon himself the name of the god Osiris, and thereby passes into paradise.[48] Osiris was a god who died and was born again.[49] The worship of Osiris predates Christianity by many hundreds of years. We shall find other fathers of the Church expressing the view that Jesus Christ is not new but is ancient, whereas his appearance was recent. The meaning of the statement that Jesus "appeared" may not be comforting to some readers.

What is the point of the allegory about Christ's being "the rock" and "the gate"? Let us use a parable. A new religion has been founded. It is called Christianity. You are one of its teachers. Your congregation believes in the cosmic "rock" and the cosmic "gate." You have done your best to get them to forget the cosmic "rock" and the cosmic "gate," and to believe in Jesus Christ. You have failed. You *cannot* get the "rock" and the "gate" out of their minds. What next? How about an allegory? Christ *is* the "rock," you tell them, and they buy it! Christ *is* the "gate," you tell them, and they buy it! The "rock" and "gate" of their former pagan faith now are assimilated to Christianity. You have been as successful as possible. In this fashion the pagan Samain became Christian All-Saints, and the pagan Saturnalia became Christmas. We Irish say: What cannot be cured must be endured. But, at least the label can be changed!

When the authors of the New Testament wrote that Christ is "the way" and "the light," they were using words of ancient cosmology which were chock-full of meaning to the ancient readers and listeners for whom the Christ story was composed. If we learn the original meaning of those buzz words, we will be able to understand the original message of the Christ story.

Christian preachers still assert that only through Jesus can a person enter Heaven, despite the fact that such theology excludes most of humanity from paradise. We have seen "the rock" in Figure 66. We have seen "the gate" in Figure 67. Turn to **Figure 70**, where we see "the gate" superimposed upon "the rock" superimposed upon our little man. Only through Jesus, "the gate," will we enter Heaven?

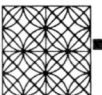

Notes
CHAPTER SIX. Introductory Cosmology and Cosmogony

1. 1 Hermas 3.36. We are working from the Jones-Wake translation of the Book of the Shepherd of Hermas, published in The Lost Books Of The Bible, Bell Publishing Company, New York, 1979.

2. Lost Books 8-16.

3. Lost Books 10, 197.

4. Lost Books 9.

5. Cirlot 337-339; Webber 185-190; Stafford 101; VanTreeck & Croft 48-51. The Christian order is: Man, Lion, Ox, and Eagle.

6. 1 Infancy 15.1-6. (Jones-Wake translation)

7. 1 Infancy 19.22-24. (Jones-Wake translation)

8. 1 Hermas 3.4-5, 38.

9. 1 Hermas 3.23-24.

10. 1 Hermas 3.25.

11. 1 Hermas 3.26.

12. 1 Hermas 3.27. We shall study about a crystal tower in the Grail quest stories we analyze. Quartz crystals are important sacred objects of Old and New World shamans. See, e.g., Krupp 317. Shamans from the Stone Age to present have used the quartz crystal to produce the rainbow-like interference pattern. See, e.g., Krupp 133-134.

13. 1 Hermas 3.28-30.

14. 1 Hermas 3.31-32.

15. 1 Hermas 3.33.

16. 1 Hermas 3.34.

17. Lost Books 8-16.

18. 1 Hermas 3.130.

19. 3 World Book Encyclopedia 319 (1983).

20. Oxford 887; Graves & Patai 21, 40-44; Talbott 116-119.

21. Talbott 134-138. This square island customarily is said to have been a stone. Talbott 135-136.

22. Is. 11.12.

23. Krupp 88-90; Spanuth 210-211; Talbott 172-215; Davidson 26-27.

24. John 8.12; John 14.6.

25. 1 Kings 7.23-26; 2 Chron. 4.1-6,10.

26. 1 Hermas 3.40.

27. 1 Hermas 3.38.

28. 1 Hermas 3.42.

29. 1 Hermas 3.130.

30. 1 Hermas 3.45-81.

31. 1 Hermas 3.43-44.

32. 1 Hermas 3.44.

33. 3 Hermas 9.5.

34. 3 Hermas 9.5.

35. 3 Hermas 9.6-12.

36. 3 Hermas 9.13.

37. 3 Hermas 9.14. In a Germanic myth, we are told that Valgrind is the name of the gate of the gods; that it is old; and that few people know "with what bolt that gate is barred." Hollander 58.

38. 3 Hermas 9.15.

39. 3 Hermas 9.16-17.

40. 3 Hermas 9.24.

41. Cirker 5.

42. 3 Hermas 9.22-280.

43. 3 Hermas 10.15.

44. 3 Hermas 9.27.

45. 3 Hermas 9.109.

46. 3 Hermas 9.110-111.

47. 3 Hermas 9.113.

48. 2 Budge, Osiris 2-3.

49. Lamy 6; Krupp 19; 2 Budge, Osiris 11.

Chapter Seven

The Secret Society of Storysmiths

Why would an author weave a story around images that can be found on the Holy Grail? One possible answer is that the Holy Grail was regarded by ancient writers as a source of power; hence, they really and truly believed that the will of their gods and the future course of events could be prophesied by divining upon it; furthermore, they believed the images they imagined based on the lines of the Holy Grail were revelations from their gods. A cynic might suggest that the Holy Grail may have become a plaything of the Sophists, who delighted in making up stories based on its line forms and in convincing the gullible of the truth and wisdom of their fabrications. The stories from Ezekiel and Hermas inclined me toward the first of those two theories about the motives and intentions of the ancient authors. But how shall we explain the writing from the *Pseudepigrapha* known as "The Letter of Aristeas," which contains a story about "the most exquisite and beautiful table ever produced"?[1] Here is a story which *may* have been written primarily for

the purpose of proving that the author could make up a tale incorporating images which can be seen on the Holy Grail.

During the Middle Ages, the craft of stone masonry was practiced by secret societies of masons. Guilds of masons surrounded themselves with a cloak of secrecy which helped them to keep their architectural, engineering, and building construction techniques to themselves. They initiated their membership using rituals dating back into the dim recesses of prehistory. We shall study some of the "mysteries," initiatory rituals, and practical construction techniques of the operative stone-masons who erected the great cathedrals of Europe. For now, we need to realize only that operative stone-masons had a method by which two strangers claiming to be stone-masons could test each other to discover the truth of their claims to brotherhood. Fraternal handshakes, passwords, signs, and countersigns are familiar to persons who have joined college fraternities or sororities, or other secret societies, including the tree-hut clubs of our childhood.

The identification procedure used by the stone-masons worked like this: A companion mason (second degree of initiation) received at the end of his probationary period a mason's mark or seal which remained for life his sign or password. He had to draw and then "prove" his mark or seal when questioned about his membership in the brotherhood. Two utter strangers were thus able to prove to each other their membership in the guild of masons by drawing and proving their seals or marks. This proof was accomplished by drawing the mark or seal upon the "ground grid" from which the mark or seal was derived.[2] How many of you can recognize a familiar friend among the four mason's marks and their ground grids shown in **Illustration 7-1**?[3] The French *fleur-de-lis* came from the Holy Grail? What next, Santa Claus and the Easter Bunny?

Could it possibly be true that writers of religious literature spanning hundreds of years and dozens of different cultures *also* had some sort of formal or

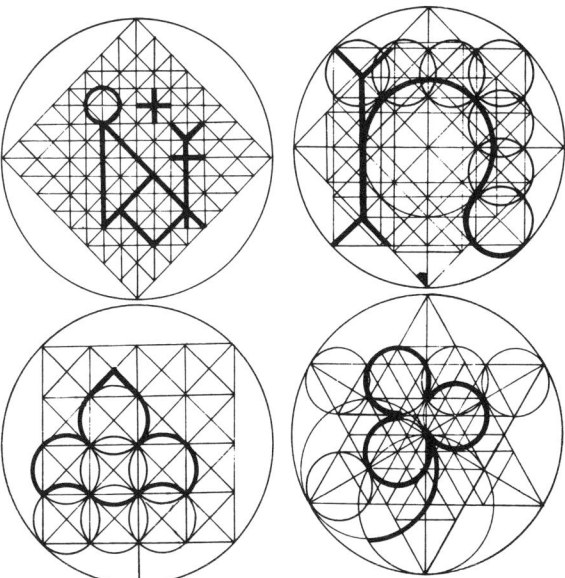

Illustration 7-1. Masons' marks. Courtesy of Dover Publications, Inc., New York.

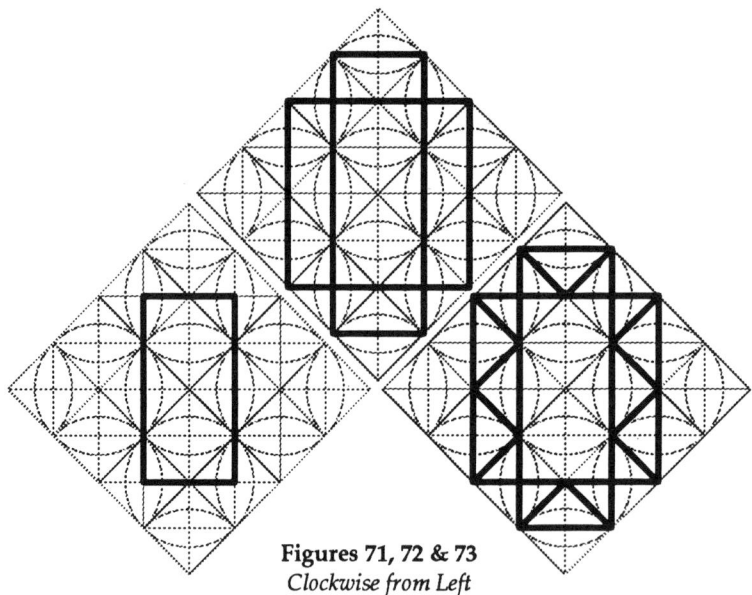

Figures 71, 72 & 73
Clockwise from Left

informal secret society, and that the ability to make up a story using images visible on the Holy Grail proved that an author was a member of that elite group? An affirmative answer is suggested, and proof of that hypothesis is one of the most fascinating aspects of this quest.

Proof of that hypothesis will be presented to you by our plodding through stories written around images visible on the Holy Grail. Our methodology is obvious. You should not be asked to accept or reject my conclusions. Instead, you should reach your own. You must gain proficiency in the finding of images on the Holy Grail if you are to complete this book with maximum comprehension. So here we go, quite literally, back to the drawing board.

The Letter of Aristeas tells the story of one of the world's first book collectors and his desire to bring to his library in Alexandria all of the great books of the world. As the legend goes, Ptolemy Philadelphus finally agreed to pay what must have been one of the highest prices ever paid for a single literary work. He traded some 100,000 captives for the Jewish Laws.[4] Lest the uninitiated fall into the trap of believing that they are reading accurately reported history, let me warn you that the Letter of Aristeas savors as much of legend as beef stew savors of beef. We have not yet learned the purpose of ancient myth or legend. We should reserve judgment on the ancients until we understand the role that mythology played in their lives. We also must realize that myth still plays an important role in our lives. Some of our mythmakers, called "advertising executives," create fictional characters to help manufacturers sell their products. Perhaps we shall learn that the role of the mythmaker has not changed; only his employer.

The story of the table is one of the backwaters of the main storyline of the Letter of Aristeas. It is, however, one of the most important stories analyzed in this book because its images are so many and so vivid.

We read that Ptolemy wanted a table made as a gift to the Jews. He wanted it to be fit for sacrificial use in the Temple in Jerusalem, so he specified that it must conform to Jewish Law. However, to the extent that Jewish Law imposed no limitation on the design and decoration of the table, he wanted it to be as large and as beautiful as possible.[5] The narrator reveals that there must have been some reason why the table already in use in the Temple had been made of small dimensions.[6] "Wherefore we must not transgress or go beyond the proper measure."[7] There *was* a reason for the Temple's sacrificial table to be small. It will make you sick at the stomach. It also will convince you that early Hebrew Humanists led the Hebrew People in great strides away from savagery and toward civilization *long* years before the rest of us made that trip.

The author of the Letter of Aristeas tells us the following about the king who ordered the table built: "[H]e was a man of most lofty conceptions and nature had endowed him with a keen imagination which enabled him to picture the appearance which would be presented *by the finished work*."[8] Is the author giving us a clue to *his* motives and intentions? If we, his readers, have

Figure 74

"lofty conceptions" and "keen imagination," we will be able to "picture the appearance" which will be presented by *the author's* finished work? "Lofty conceptions" may not be of much practical use to you in this analysis, but the keener your imagination the easier it is going to be for you to follow the author through the intricate line-patterns of his story.

"They made the table two cubits long, one cubit broad, one and a half cubits high, fashioning it of pure solid gold."[9] A "short cubit" was approximately eighteen inches,[10] so the table was 36 inches long, 18 inches wide and 27 inches high.[11] It had "a border of a hand's breadth round about it."[12] "And there was a wreath of wave-work, engraved in relief in the form of ropes marvelously wrought on its three sides."[13] "For it was triangular in shape and the style of the work was exactly the same on each of the sides, so that whichever side they were turned, they presented the same appearance."[14] Turn to **Figure 71** for a top view of the center part of the table, minus the border. The proportion is two Grail blocks wide by four Grail blocks long, that is, the same 1 to 2 proportion as 18 is to 36. Now let us add the border. Look at **Figure 72** for the border of a hand's width that is "round about it." Now let us turn to **Figure 73**, where the "wreath of wave-work" has been bolded. Note that this wreath of triangular

"wave-work" *does* present the same appearance on all of its sides. The reference to its being wrought in the form of ropes on its three sides probably means that the triangle work is to be visualized sticking up out of the other surfaces "in relief."[15]

We need to jump ahead in the story for a moment to fix in our minds an image which was familiar to the ancients for whom the story was written. Turn to **Illustration 7-2**, which is a photograph of a bowl removed from an archaeological dig in Iran.[16] Painted inside the bowl is our old friend the concave-sided tetragon, with its four points or horns extending upward toward the rim of the bowl. Further along in the story of the table, we learn of the two silver and two golden bowls on the table.[17] In describing the golden bowls, the author says that "there was a mosaic, worked in the form of rhombus, having a net-like appearance and reaching right up to the brim."[18] Turn to **Figure 74**, where we see a concave-sided tetragon enclosed by a circle. The circle represents the rim of the golden bowl seen from top view, that is, looking down on the bowl as it sits on the table. The concave-sided tetragon is drawn on the bottom of the bowl, and its four horns or sharp points extend upward to the rim of the bowl, just as the author of Aristeas says they should. The concave-sided tetragon is one of the forms of a rhombus, and has a "net-like appearance," that is, it resembles a fishing net, held in position by four cross ropes and four border ropes. **Figure 75**. Take a look at Figure 74 and Illustration 7-2 again. Now visualize the sides of our Grail bowl outside the concave-sided tetragon being cut away and thrown away, leaving nothing but the concave-sided tetragon. See how the four horns or tips of the concave-sided tetragon now stick up out of the surface of the table? What we have is an upside-down version of pendentives supporting a dome erected on a square, as shown in

Illustration 7-2. A pre-Sumerian bowl. J.C. Hinrichs Verlag, Leipzig.

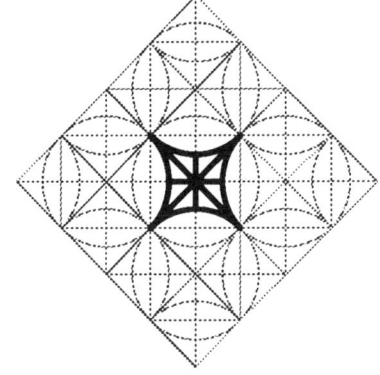

Figure 75

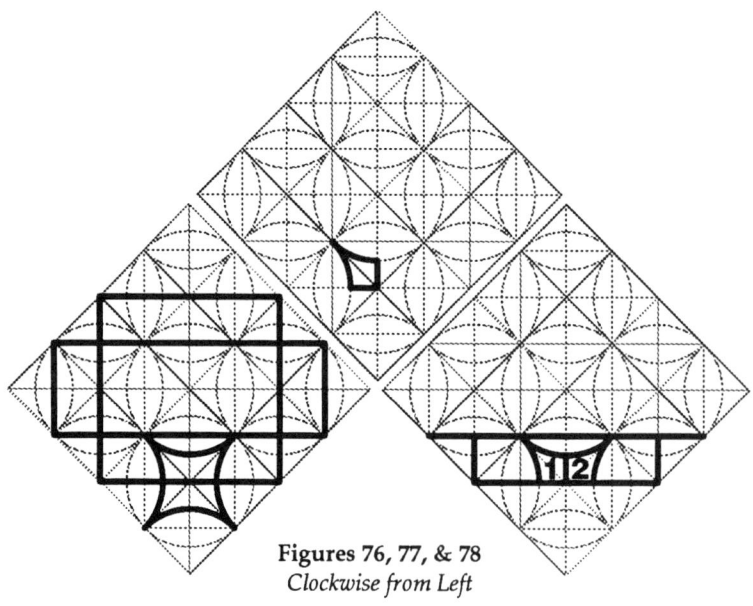

Figures 76, 77, & 78
Clockwise from Left

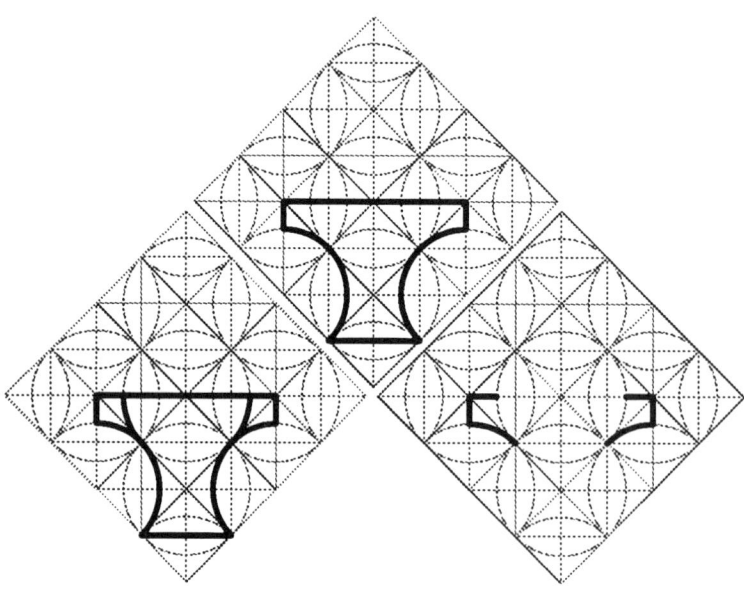

Figures 79, 80, & 81
Clockwise from Left

Illustration 7-3. Do you have this image firmly in mind? Back to the story.

We are told that "of the two sides under the border, the one which sloped down to the table was a very beautiful piece of work, but it was the outer side which attracted the gaze of the spectator."[19] Turn to **Figure 76**, where a top view of the outside edge of the border of the table and the outside edge of the inner portion of the table have been bolded. Also bolded on this drawing is one concave-sided tetragon, part of which should be visualized as being under the border of the table. If we define the lines illustrated in **Figure 77** as a "side," then we do, indeed, have two "sides" under the border. See **Figure 78**. Changing from top view to side view, we should take the lines bolded in **Figure 79** to be the "side" which "sloped down to the table."[20] We see the table in side view in **Figure 80**. Our choice of the lines bolded in Figure 78 to represent a "side" located "under the border"[21] is confirmed as correct by the next verse, which reads: "Now the upper edge of the two sides, being elevated, was sharp since, as we have said, *the rim* was three-sided, from whatever point of view one approached it."[22] See **Figure 81** for two sides under the border, the upper or elevated edges of which are sharp like spear points. The rim of the table has an underneath, a front and a top side which are "three-sided from whatever point of view one approached it."[23] The points of the concave-sided tetragon will be referred to as "spigots" in just a very few minutes.[24] In a few minutes, we also will find these "sides" being referred to as "small shields."[25] Remember your early training as Eagles. Things can be the same although called something different. In the story of the table, such antics of the mythmaker run rampant.

The author of the Letter of Aristeas may be enjoying a Sophistic romp! He tells us he is describing a table. We think he is describing the Holy Grail. Sophists were a group of itinerant teachers of rhetoric — the art of debate. To understand how Sophists thought, consider the two schools of thought about modern-day sporting events. One group of modern sports enthusiasts says it does not matter whether you win or lose; rather, it only matters how fairly and how well you play the game. The other school of thought about modern sporting events believes that winning is everything and losing is nothing; that one must win at sports although, to win, the rules of the game must be bent or broken. Sophists were of the latter view when it came to debate. Truth was irrelevant. Winning the debate was all that mattered. Sophists delighted in convincing their opponents of the

"truth" of an assertion, although Sophists well knew that there was no truth in the assertion.[26] We have Sophists in our society today. We call them "lawyers."

We next are told that "there were layers of precious stones on it in the midst of the embossed cord-work, and they were interwoven with one another by an inimitable artistic device."[27] "For the sake of security they were all fixed by golden needles which were inserted in perforations in the stones."[28] "At the sides they were clamped together by fastenings to hold them firm."[29] Turn to **Figure 82** for the bolding of one "precious stone," which is nothing but a circle with a concave-sided tetragon in it. In Figure 83, all five of the circles with their concave-sided tetragons have been bolded, and you can see that the center of these is layered above the other four, treating the Holy Grail as a top view. Treating **Figure 83** as a side view, we see that "precious stone" number 1 is above "precious stone" number 2, that "precious stone" number 3 is above "precious stone" number 4, and that "precious stone" number 5 sticks out from the side of the block of stones. We do, indeed, have "layers of precious stones."[30] One of the "golden needles" can be seen in **Figure 84** running through a "perforation" of a "stone." You can run the rest of them through the other stones in your mind's eye. The "fastenings"

| Figure 82 | Figure 83 |

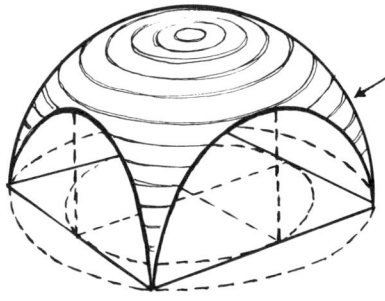

Illustration 7-3. Pendentives supporting a dome on a square. Courtesy of Doreen Yarwood and Bounty Books, London.

Figure 84

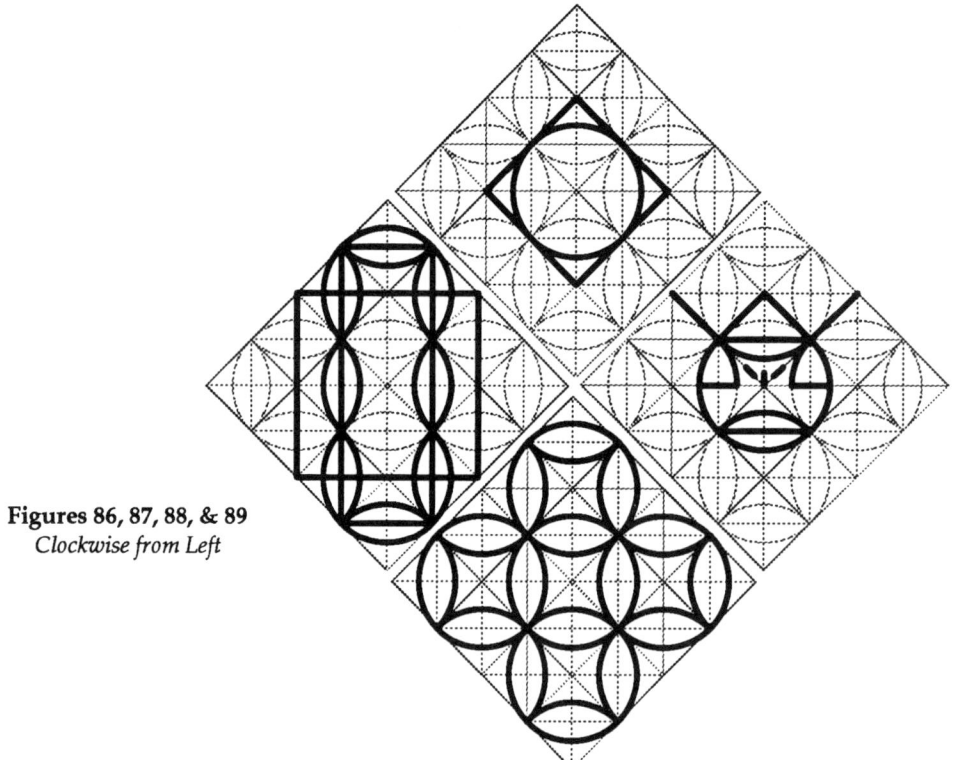

Figures 86, 87, 88, & 89
Clockwise from Left

with which the stones were "clamped together" in order "to hold them firm" are drawn for you in **Figure 85**. Try to see them for yourself before turning to that drawing. Now turn to the drawing. Were you correct? If you pictured the circles as being three-dimensional balls, it is quite obvious that the lattice-work formed by the "fastenings" would hold the "precious stones" firmly in place!

The mythmaker of the Letter of Aristeas next wants us to visualize from the lines of the Holy Grail that "On the part of the border round the table which slanted upwards and met the eyes, there was wrought a pattern of eggs in precious stones, elaborately engraved by a continuous piece of fluted relief-work, closely connected together round the whole table."[31] "And under the stones which had

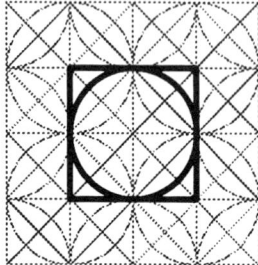

Figure 85

been arranged to represent eggs the artists made a crown containing all kinds of fruits, having at its top clusters of grapes and ears of corn, dates also and apples, and pomegranates and the like, conspicuously arranged."[32] The "pattern of eggs in precious stones" which is "closely connected together round the whole table" as a "continuous piece of fluted relief-work" is seen in **Figure 86**. Remember that the horns of the concave-sided tetragons "slanted upwards." The bit about the "part of the border round the table which slanted upwards and met the eyes" is a pun because the horns of the concave-sided tetragons do join with the eye shapes around each of the circles! Figure 86. The "crown" is illustrated in **Figures 87 and 88**. The four points of the crown should be visualized sticking up from the headband of the crown at 45 degrees. We shall study this crown in great detail in later stories. A "cluster of grapes" is illustrated in **Figure 89**. American readers first must learn that "corn" in Biblical-era stories from the Middle East does not mean Indian maize, but refers to wheat or barley. Look that one up in your dictionary, just to satisfy yourself. Then turn to **Figure 90**, where we illustrate, side-view, an "ear of corn," that is, a stalk of wheat. See the pomegranates? Perhaps you do not know the shape and appearance of a

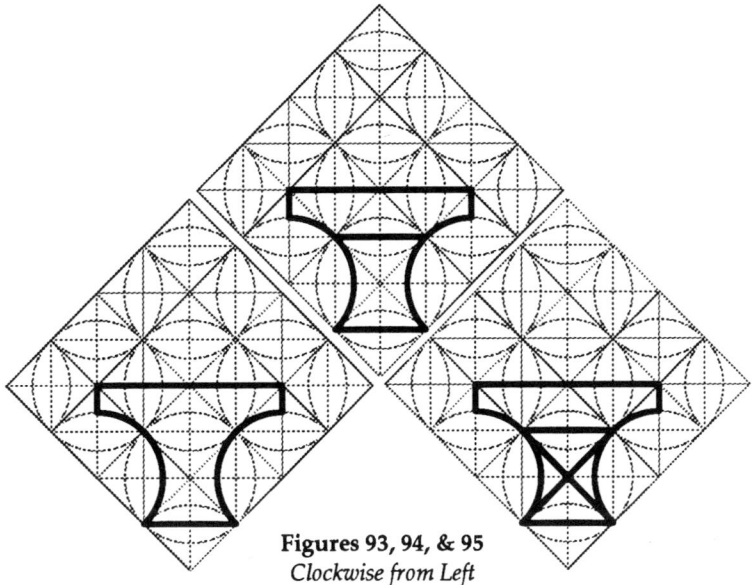

Figures 93, 94, & 95
Clockwise from Left

pomegranate and its blossom end. Look that up in a reference book, then turn to **Figure 91**, where we have illustrated a "pomegranate." You city folks may have to look up the shape of the stalk of wheat, also, if you never have seen one face to face. **Figure 92** illustrates a cluster of dates. Surely, we do not have to bold-in the shape of a nice, round "apple." We are told that the artists building the "table" fastened the fruit-shaped precious stones "edgeways round the sides of the table with a band of gold."[33] Do that yourself, in your mind's eye.

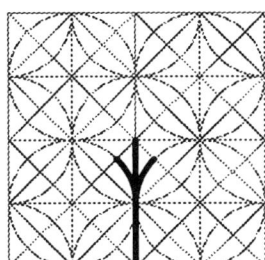

Figure 90

Figure 91   **Figure 92**

You must force yourself to see these forms without line-bolding.

Shift your perspective. We have been looking at the "table" from top view. Here we go into a side-view analysis of the "table." "And after the crown of fruit had been put on, underneath there was inserted another pattern of eggs in precious stones, and other fluting and embossed work, that both sides of the table might be used, according to the wishes of the owners and for this reason the wave-work and the border were extended down to the feet of the table."[34] "They made and fastened under the whole width of the table a massive plate four fingers thick, that the feet might be inserted into it, and clamped fast with linchpins which fitted into sockets under the border, so that which ever side of the table people preferred, might be used."[35] "Thus it became manifestly clear that the work was intended to be used either way."[36]

Figure 93 shows the "table" in side-view perspective. The "pattern of eggs in precious stones," the "fluting and embossed work," and the "wave-work and the border" are shown (but not bolded) extending "down to the feet of the table." **Figure 94** shows the "massive plate four fingers thick" which was "fastened under the whole width of the table" so "the feet might be inserted into it." Figure 94 also shows one of the table's feet inserted into the "massive plate." **Figure 95** shows the "linchpins which fitted into sockets under the border" with which the feet are "clamped fast." The statement that "the work was intended to be used either way" is pregnant with meaning because,

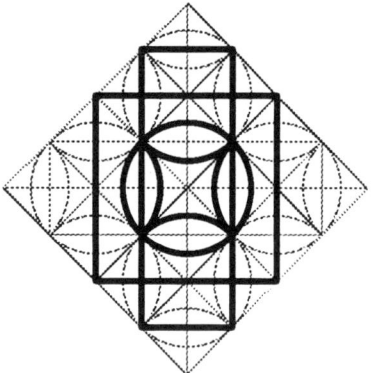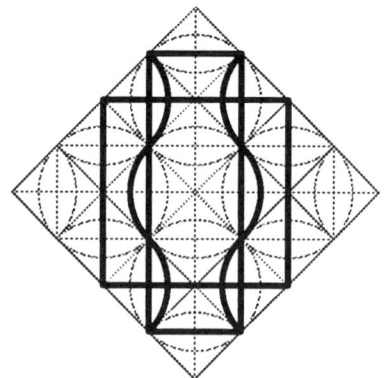

Figures 96 & 97

as we shall learn when we study ancient architectural and structural engineering techniques, the Holy Grail *was* used both as a plan (top view) and as an elevation (side or front view) for the erection of arches, vaults, and domes. When coupled with the statements that the table was constructed so that "both sides of the table might be used according to the wishes of the owners" or "so that which ever side of the table people preferred might be used," the statement that the table "was intended to be used either way" certainly seems calculated to convey to readers the appearance of sameness from each perspective.

Our mythmaker next tells us that on the table "they engraved a 'maeander,' having precious stones standing out in the middle of it, rubies and emeralds and an onyx too and many other kinds of stones which excel in beauty."[37] "And next to the 'maeander' there was placed a wonderful piece of network, which made the centre of the table appear like a rhomboid in shape, and on it a crystal and amber, as it is called, had been wrought, which produced an incomparable impression on the beholders."[38] The "network" is our old friend the concave-sided tetragon, in another of its mythological roles, and is illustrated in **Figure 96**. The "meander" is illustrated in **Figure 97**. The "network" is located next to the "maeander," as the author says it should be. We would not have understood the reference to "crystal and amber" which "produced an incomparable impression on the beholders" unless we already had studied something about the role of those substances in the generation of the interference pattern and static electricity — and, more importantly, in the generation of High Magic. The phrase "as it is called," used in reference to "a crystal and amber," indicates that a conventional word formula for

describing Grail images existed among Grail authors by the time our mythmaker spun this yarn!

Other possible explanations as to why a mythmaker would want to write a story of a "table" using line forms taken from the Holy Grail present themselves to us for consideration. Among the Irish of my generation, storytelling served the same function now served by watching television or going to the movies. The storyteller entertained. We knew we were listening to fantasy. Suppose that future archeologists who dig up the pre-nuclear holocaust remains of our society find films and writings about Donald Duck and Superman. Will they be wise enough to realize that we really did not believe that ducks can talk and men can fly, or will they conclude that our religion taught us that they could? Will they see these mythological characters of our society as we see them: sources of entertainment with a dose of morality thrown in for good measure?

Some of the Bible-era stories that we accept as accurately recorded historical facts about real people *may* have been about fictional characters whose role was to entertain and to instill cultural values. Could it possibly be that the story of the table from the Letter of Aristeas was intended to entertain average imaginations by conjuring up images of gold and jewels, which tribespeople never could possess, while at the same time challenging persons who have a "keen imagination"[39] to bridge the allegorical gap, and to conclude that the wealth of ideas behind the Holy Grail was far more valuable than all the gold and jewels one could possess?

The message of Irish folklore rings clear: Real gold and jewels can be snatched from your possession by a more warlike or cunning person than yourself. But treasures of the mind only can be stolen by destroying the mind itself or the body in

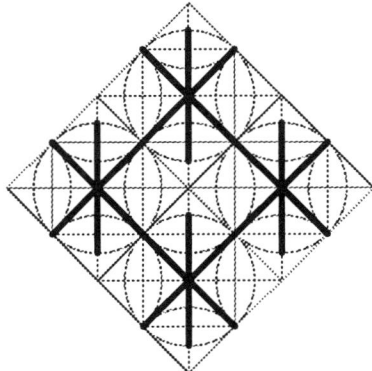

Figure 98

which it resides. An Irish-American captive survived imprisonment in North Vietnam with all of his mental faculties fully operational because the bare concrete walls of his small cell became projection screens upon which his mind played out the images of such dramas as the building of his dream home, the planting of his dream garden, fishing and hunting trips with the son he never had held in his arms, and an endless array of other fantasies which he hoped to convert into realities after the day of his fantasized release from captivity. His tormentors took from him his clothing, food, and water at frequent intervals. They never took the one thing which sustains the Irish against all odds — his fertile imagination!

Imagine yourself an unwashed desert herdsman, sitting cross-legged and barefooted before a small fire of animal dung. The flames illuminate the wrinkled face of the storyteller of your Biblical-era tribe, as he tells the story of this wondrous golden table covered with jewels and ceremonially fit and proper for use in the High Magic of Temple sacrifice. Are the more "lofty conceptions"[40] of physics and cosmology described by the Holy Grail more valuable than any jewel-bedecked golden table?

What comes next are some of the most graphic images of the story of the table. "They made the feet *of the table* with heads like lilies, so that they seemed to be like lilies bending down beneath the table, and the parts which were visible represented leaves which stood upright."[41] If you never have looked down the throat of a lily, then drop by a florist on the way home from work tomorrow, or look the lily up in your encyclopedia or flower reference book. Notice the ⚹, which divides the throat of the lily into six segments. **Figure 98** shows the four "feet" of the "table" from bottom view, from which perspective they have an appearance similar to a

down-the-throat view of a lily. **Figure 99** shows the "leaves which stood upright." The "leaves" of these "flowers" are the very first images which most people see on the Holy Grail.

A valuable clue emerges from the next verse. "The basis of the foot on the ground consisted of a ruby and measured a hand's breadth *high* all round."[42] A ruby that is a hand's breadth high all around is one whopping big ruby! It likely is a storyteller's ruby, not a real stone found or dug by a real person. Has the mythmaker deliberately exaggerated the size of the ruby pedestals of the "feet" of the "table" so that even the most literal-minded or gullible of his readers will know that fantasy rather than fact is intended? Exaggeration is a familiar device of honest, fun-oriented mythmaking. Television soap-opera characters, for instance, invariably are prettier, nastier, richer, etc., than real persons with whom we rub shoulders daily. Notice that the author of Aristeas does not say that the foot looked like a ruby. He says it "consisted of a ruby." A real foot basis (pedestal) of a real table could look like a ruby but it is highly unlikely that any table this size ever existed with one foot — much less four — consisting of a ruby. There is no doubt that the author understood the difference between something having the appearance of a ruby and something consisting of a ruby because in the very next verse he tells us that the basis (pedestal) of the "foot" of the "table" "had the appearance of a shoe and was eight fingers broad."[43]

You might want to conclude that the author of the Letter of Aristeas did not intend to deceive us into believing that he was writing about historical facts, no matter how literal-minded or gullible we might be. You might want to conclude, subject to additional proofs, that our author was not a Sophist; rather, that he was a *very* imaginative maker of myth. Do you understand the expression, "in joke"? An "in joke" is a joke in which the punch line will be understood only if the listener is "in on" some secret known to the joke teller. An "in joke" serves

Figure 99

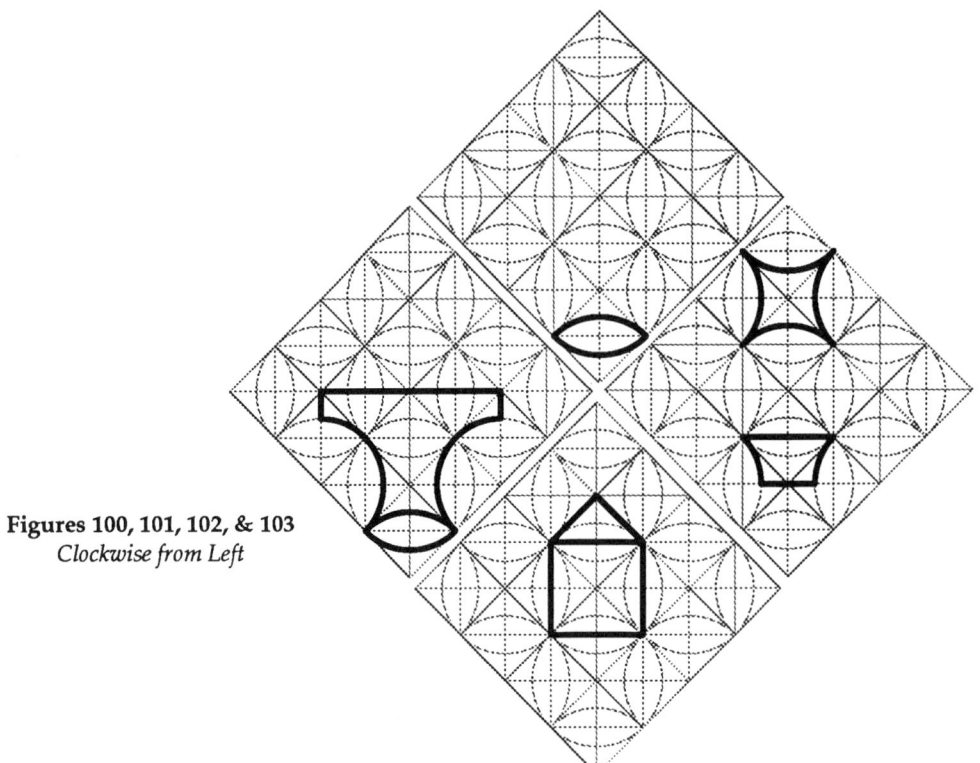

Figures 100, 101, 102, & 103
Clockwise from Left

two useful purposes. It entertains. It reinforces our basic human need to feel that we are part of some "tribal" group. No doubt, the highest pleasure was derived by those "in-group" listeners who realized that the story of the table was not a story of a table!

Our mythmaker next tells us that "It [the basis of the foot of the table] had the appearance of a shoe and was eight fingers broad."[44] "Upon it the whole expanse of the foot rested."[45] **Figure 100** shows one basis (pedestal) of one "foot" of the "table." The "whole expanse of the foot" rests upon it.[46] Also, it has the "appearance of a shoe," if one looks at **Figure 101**.

Continuing the side-view analysis of the feet of the table, the storysmith says that "they made *the foot appear like* ivy growing out of the stone, interwoven with akanthus and surrounded with a vine which encircled it with clusters of grapes, which were worked in stones, up to the top *of the foot*."[47] The herb akanthus (acanthus) was so popular among the ancients that a stereotypical representation of it became the decorative feature of the capital (top) of Corinthian columns. Turn to **Figure 102**, where we see bolded lines which have the appearance, in top and side views, of the capital or top of a Corinthian column. As to the "ivy growing out of the stone," the reference may be to the triangular front end of

an ivy leaf sticking up out of our cosmic "stone." **Figure 103**. The "vine which encircled" the "foot" and the "clusters of grapes" are easy to see. "All the four feet were made in the same style...."[48] And so they are.

We now reach a juncture in the story of the table at which you may wish to make a decision. Our mythmaker writes: "[E]verything was wrought and fitted so skillfully, and such remarkable skill and knowledge were expended upon making it true to nature, that when the air was stirred by a breath of wind, movement was imparted to the leaves, and everything was fashioned to correspond with the actual reality which it represented."[49] Some readers may wish to accuse the storyteller of being a liar, a deceiver, or a cheat. The laws of probability indicate to us that our author is making up a story based upon abstract images which can be visualized on the Holy Grail. How, then, can he honestly and truthfully write that "when the air was stirred by a breath of wind, movement was imparted to the leaves"? You may prefer to give him the benefit of the doubt by concluding that he had no more intent to deceive than the cartoonists who illustrate the comic strips of our daily newspapers, or who draw the animated cartoons we watch at the movies and on television; that he expected his readers to be

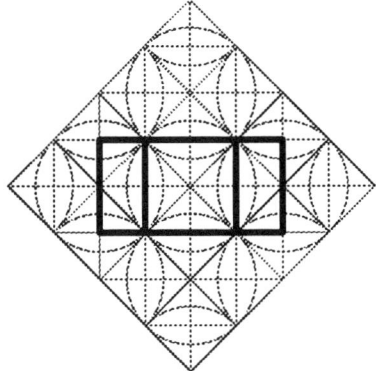

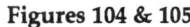

Figures 104 & 105

bright enough to know that he was making up a story, rather than describing an actual table. Under this hypothesis, if we take his writings literally we misread his motives, his intentions, and his work product. We con ourselves into reaching wrong conclusions because of our own lack of knowledge of the mythmaking process and its objectives. We mislead ourselves with gullibility born of ignorance.

If you accept my hypothesis about the motive and intentions of the author, you will conclude that our author created a beautiful *allegory* rather than an artful *deception*. In any event, he has let us know that he was a member of a select brotherhood of creative religious writers who were familiar with the "mysteries" of the Holy Grail.

We are told that "they made the top of the table in three parts like a triptychon, and they were so fitted and dovetailed together with spigots along the whole breadth of the work, that the meeting of the joints could not be seen or even discovered."[50] A "triptychon" or "tryptych" is an altarpiece made in three panels.[51] The "top" of the "table" indeed is "in three parts like a triptychon." **Figure 104.** We can see "spigots along the whole breadth of the work." **Figure 105.**

The story continues: "The thickness of the table was not less than half a cubit, so that the whole work must have cost many talents."[52] Did the storyteller hope or expect that he would be richly rewarded for his work? Is that the meaning of the statement that "the work must have cost many talents"? Was the story commissioned as, in later years, the writing of symphonies and the carving of statuary was sponsored by wealthy patrons of the arts?

We are told that "since the king did not wish to add to its [the table's] size he expended on the details the same sum of money which would have been required if the table could have been of larger

dimensions."[53] This is another reference to the king's desire to build the table five times as large as the sacrificial table then in use in the Temple in Jerusalem, which desire was frustrated by the size requirements imposed by Jewish Law.[54] The same idea is expressed by the final verse of Chapter Three. "The most exceptional artistic skill was employed, so that the cost of the stones and the workmanship was five times as much as that of the gold."[55] We later shall learn that ancient religionists followed ancient scientists into the belief that numerology was an important study. The Pythagoreans believed that everything should be explained in terms of number.[56] They are credited in most modern textbooks with having developed the famous "right angle triangle theorem," which holds that the sum of the squares of the two sides of a right triangle is equal to the square of the hypotenuse. Thus, if side "A" equals 3, and side "B" equals 4, then side "C," the hypotenuse, equals 5, this being the famous 3-4-5 triangle which inspired the speculations of the ancient religionists.[57] One can play all sorts of games with the number series 3-4-5. Three and four add together to produce seven, the favorite number of Old Testament authors. All three numbers add up to twelve, another number often found in Biblical stories.

Ancient scientists, as we shall study, were working with the concept of number as it appeared to relate to observable phenomena — such as the cycle of the seasons and the growth of plants, animals, and rock crystals. There was considerable truth in their theories, as confirmed by modern science — which now is finding that chemical "codes" which can be expressed in numbers determine the birth, growth, and death of plants and animals, and the patterns of crystalline growth. But ancient religionists were not content to limit

Figure 106

Figure 107

themselves to the realm of the observable. They ultimately managed to extend number theory beyond the farthest reaches of religion and magic into the sphere of ultimate nonsense. This book attempts to confront fantasies and distill from them information valuable to modern persons of the Eagle category. However, we shall avoid to the maximum extent feasible the ancient mystique of numerology because it either lacks sense or your author lacks enough sense to comprehend its sense.

We already have considered the golden "mixing bowls" which sat upon the "table." Now, we consider them in detail. "Of the mixing bowls, two were wrought in gold, and from the base to the middle were engraved with relief work in the pattern of scales, and between the scales precious stones were inserted with great artistic skill."[58] **Figure 106** shows a "pattern of scales," that is, lines which closely approximate the side-view appearance of a balance beam scale with pans held by rods on each end of the balance beam. "Precious stones" already have been discussed *ad nauseam*. "Then there was a 'maeander' a cubit in height, with its surface wrought out of precious stones of many colours, displaying great artistic effort and beauty."[59] "Upon this there was a mosaic, worked in the form of a rhombus, having a net-like appearance and reaching right up to the brim."[60] The rhomboid and net-like appearance of a concave-sided tetragon were discussed earlier.

The mythmaker continues: "In the middle [of the golden bowls] small shields which were made of different precious stones, placed alternately, and varying in kind, not less than four fingers broad, enhanced the beauty of their appearance."[61] "Small shields" in a bowl are bolded in **Figure 107**. The "precious stones" are obvious to you by now, are they not? "On the top of the brim there was an ornament of lilies in bloom, and intertwining clusters

of grapes were engraven all round."[62] You should have no trouble finding the "lilies in bloom" and the "intertwining clusters of grapes." "Such then was the construction of the golden bowls, and they held more than two firkins each."[63]

We next consider the "silver bowls." "The silver bowls had a smooth surface, and were wonderfully made as if they were intended for looking-glasses, so that everything which was brought near to them was reflected even more clearly than in mirrors."[64] We shall learn more about these golden and silver bowls when we reach the scientific part of this book. Gold is the color of the sun; silver the color of the moon. The moon reflects the light of the sun.

The remainder of the story of the table is filled with images now comprehensible to you, such as "golden vials."[65] A golden vial is bolded in **Figure 108**.

The best students often do extra-credit assignments. Chapter 4 of the Letter of Aristeas would give you practice using your newly-acquired skills to find images on the Holy Grail. It purports to be a description of the Jewish Temple and the ministrations of its priests. As the tale goes, the Jewish city lies smack in the middle of the whole of Judea on the top of a mountain of considerable altitude.[66] Guess where the Temple is situated in

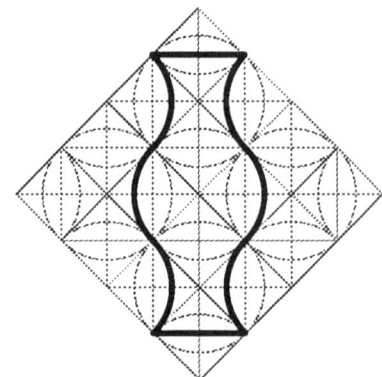

Figure 108

the city? On the summit of the mountain, of course![67] And what was the appearance of the veil of the Temple? Have you noticed how a concave-sided tetragon looks like a wind-filled mainsail of a square-rigged sailing ship?[68]

In a New Testament story, we are told that Peter fell into a trance during which he saw a vision of "heaven opened, and something coming down that looked like a great sheet of sailcloth... slung by the four corners... and in it he saw creatures of every kind...."[69] Algonquian tribes of Canada tell a story about how Fisher (a mammal kin to the weasel) climbed the cosmic mountain of Earth and punched

a hole in the sky, through which creatures descended to Earth. According to the story, Fisher was wounded by an arrow, and remained in the sky as the Algonquian version of Ursa Major, the Great Bear Constellation.[70] We shall learn that Celts called the polar guardian "Arthur," i.e., awful bear, and during our studies of the Grail quest stories, we will learn about the wounded Fisher King. But we are getting ahead of our story! Suffice it here to suggest that our concave-sided tetragon was a popular figment of many imaginations.

Notes
CHAPTER SEVEN. The Secret Society of Storysmiths

1. Platt & Brett 148. We are working from the Platt & Brett edition of the Letter of Aristeas, as published in *The Forgotten Books Of Eden*, Bell Publishing Co., New York, 1981.

2. Ghyka 117-123.

3. Ghyka 122.

4. Platt & Brett 140.

5. Aristeas 3.1-15.

6. Aristeas 3.10.

7. Aristeas 3.12.

8. Aristeas 3.13.

9. Aristeas 3.16.

10. Platt & Brett 148. Our translators have used the "short cubit" of approximately 18 inches. The term "cubit" was applied to a wide variety of lengths. If you are an expert on the lengths of cubits, and prefer to use a longer "cubit," then you may indulge yourself by doing so. Not being an expert in such matters, your author prefers not to raise an issue with our translators about which "cubit" should be employed in the Story of the Table.

11. Aristeas 3.16.

12. Aristeas 3.18.

13. Aristeas 3.19.

14. Aristeas 3.20.

15. Aristeas 3.19.

16. Moortgat Tafel 17.

17. Aristeas 3.44.

18. Aristeas 3.46.

19. Aristeas 3.21.

20. Aristeas 3.21.

21. Aristeas 3.21.

22. Aristeas 3.22.

23. Aristeas 3.22.

24. Aristeas 3.40.

25. Aristeas 3.47.

26. 18 World Book Encyclopedia 485 (1983).

27. Aristeas 3.23.

28. Aristeas 3.24.

29. Aristeas 3.25.

30. Aristeas 3.23.

31. Aristeas 3.26.

32. Aristeas 3.27.

33. Aristeas 3.28.

34. Aristeas 3.29.

35. Aristeas 3.30.

36. Aristeas 3.31.

37. Aristeas 3.32.

38. Aristeas 3.33.

39. Aristeas 3.13.

40. Aristeas 3.13.

41. Aristeas 3.34.

42. Aristeas 3.35.

43. Aristeas 3.36.

44. Aristeas 3.36.

45. Aristeas 3.37.

46. Aristeas 3.37.

47. Aristeas 3.38.

48. Aristeas 3.39.

49. Aristeas 3.39.

50. Aristeas 3.40.

51. 2 World Book Dictionary 2237.

52. Aristeas 3.41.

53. Aristeas 3.42.

54. Aristeas 3.1-14.

55. Aristeas 3.65.

56. Ghyka 5.

57. 1 Heath GM 79,144-149. The Greek Pythagoreans get credit for the so-called "Pythagorean Theorem" although they do not deserve this credit. The more-ancient Egyptians, East Indians, and Babylonians were well aware of the 3-4-5 triangle and its properties. 1 Heath GM 144-149; Neugebauer 35-36; Gillings 1. Why, then, do our textbooks adamantly ignore these realities, and continue to bestow laurels upon the Pythagoreans—who freely acknowledged their indebtedness to those more-ancient peoples? 1 Heath GM 5,67,86,128. Because our discovery of the truth about ancient geometry might lead to our discovery of other, related truths, which, in turn, might lead to our discovery of the very origins of the Christian faith? Christian fundamentalist leaders tell us that we must accept the *entire* Bible as literal truth because they fear that our questioning *anything* eventually might lead to our questioning *everything*? Do they either know or suspect something they are not telling us? Do they either know or suspect that although the physical principles of God's Universe can survive probing questions, Christian fundamentalism cannot?

58. Aristeas 3.44.

59. Aristeas 3.45.

60. Aristeas 3.46.

61. Aristeas 3.47.

62. Aristeas 3.48.

63. Aristeas 3.49.

64. Aristeas 3.50.

65. Aristeas 3.57.

66. Aristeas 4.3.

67. Aristeas 4.4.

68. Aristeas 4.8-9.

69. Acts 10.10-17 (Oxford).

70. Joseph Campbell HAOWM, Vol. 2, Part 2, pp. 177,194-195.

Chapter Eight

The Tabernacle and
Ark of the Covenant

"Ancient Near Eastern temples and their furnishings were believed to be based upon celestial models rather than human design...."[1] We shall be told in later chapters that the Holy Grail was brought to Earth from Heaven by a band of angels. We shall study the Holy Grail's scientific use as a celestial model; as a device for measuring the passage of time. Was the Holy Grail the model for the Tabernacle, the Ark of the Covenant, the altar, and other furniture and furnishings of the Tabernacle?

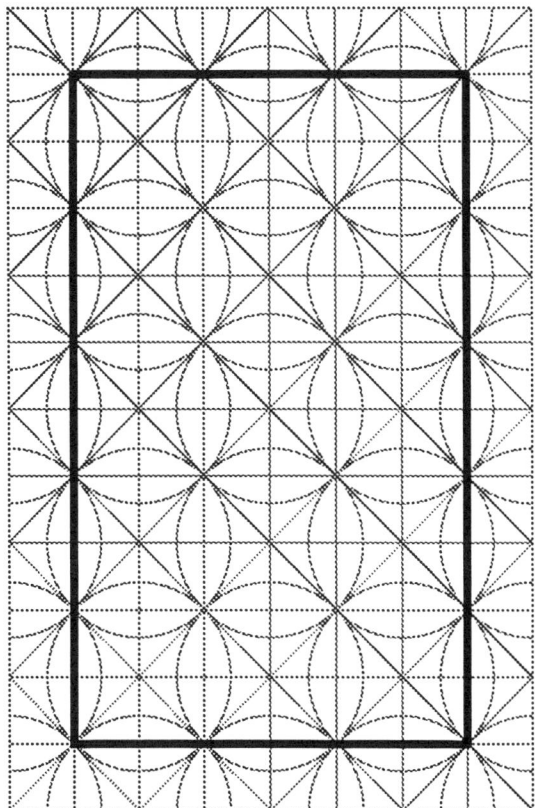

Figure 109

Let us study that question by determining whether the Tabernacle-related verses of Exodus can be interfaced with the Holy Grail. As with Ezekiel's Visions, we shall take the main story line from the King James Bible, setting the Oxford version in parentheses.

"And let them make me a sanctuary; that I may dwell among them." ("Make me a sanctuary, and I will dwell among them.")[2] The concept is specific: If the Hebrews will make God a sanctuary, they believe he will dwell among them, instead of in Heaven, or, perhaps, in addition to dwelling in Heaven. Thus, the concept of God's dwelling among mankind is older than the New Testament.

"According to all that I shew thee, *after* the pattern of the tabernacle, and the pattern of all the instruments thereof, even so shall ye make *it*." ("Make it exactly according to the design I show you, the design for the Tabernacle and for all its furniture. This is how you must make it.")[3] The Hebrews are of the opinion that God wants His sanctuary on Earth and all of its furniture and furnishings — and the garment of the High Priest — to be modeled after something that God has in His mind.

"And they shall make an ark *of* shittim wood: two cubits and a half *shall be* the length thereof, and a cubit and a half the breadth thereof, and a cubit and a half the height thereof." ("Make an Ark, a chest of acacia-wood, two and a half cubits long, one cubit and a half wide, and one cubit and a half high.")[4] The proportions of the Ark are 5 half-cubits long, 3 half-cubits wide and 3 half-cubits high. That gives us the lowest common proportionality in whole numbers. We are concerned only with proportionality, not actual length, width, or height, because you are going to use whatever size cubit pleases you.[5] **Figure 109** shows a top view of outside lines of a rectangle that is 5 units long by 3

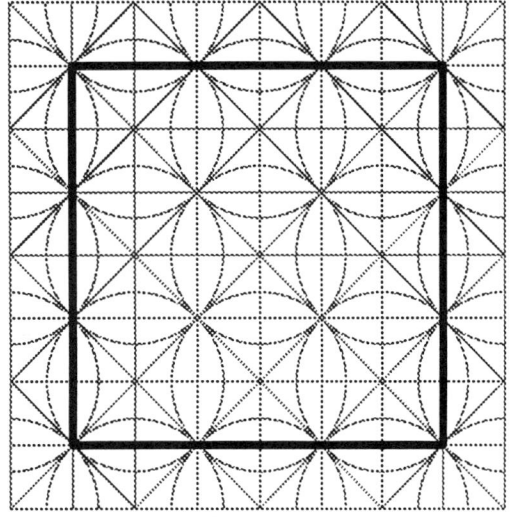

Figure 110

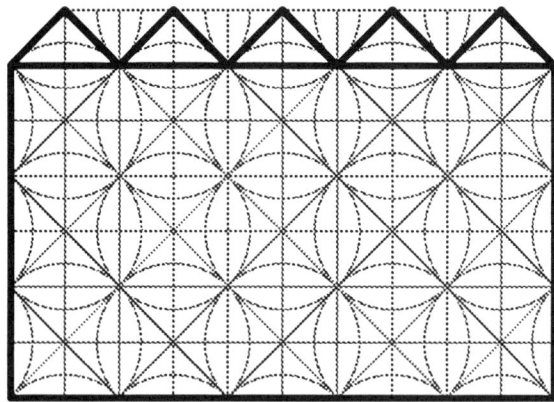

Figure 111

Figure 112

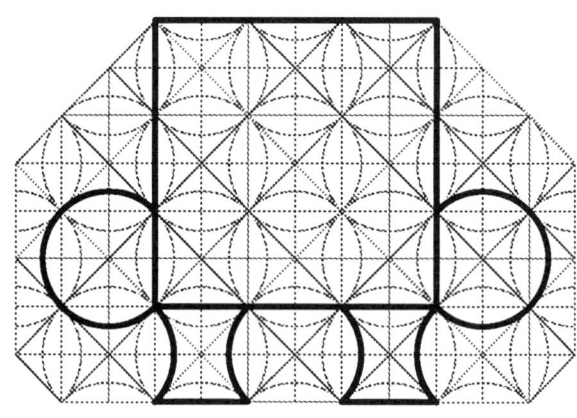

Figure 113

units wide, and **Figure 110** shows an end view of the same rectangle, which is 3 units wide by 3 units high.

"[A]nd shalt make upon it a crown of gold round about." ("[A]nd put a band of gold all round it.")[6] Is this a reference to the series of crown-like points which can be visualized in side view in **Figure 111**, and in end view in **Figure 112**, sticking up from the top of the rectangle? We already have seen these crown points, and shall see them again in later chapters when we study the Crown of Thorns that has become the Crown of Gold.

"And thou shalt cast four rings of gold for it, and put *them* in the four corners thereof; and two

rings *shall be* in the one side of it, and two rings in the other side of it." ("Cast four gold rings for it, and fasten them to its four feet, two rings on each side.")[7] In **Figure 113**, we see one ring at each of the two front corners of the rectangle. Two more rings should be visualized at the two back corners of the Ark, giving us a total of four rings. We see the same "feet" we studied when analyzing the story of the table from the Book of Aristeas.

"And thou shalt make staves *of* shittim wood, and overlay them with gold. The staves shall be in the rings of the ark: they shall not be taken from it." ("Make poles of acacia-wood and plate them with gold, and insert the poles in the rings at the sides of

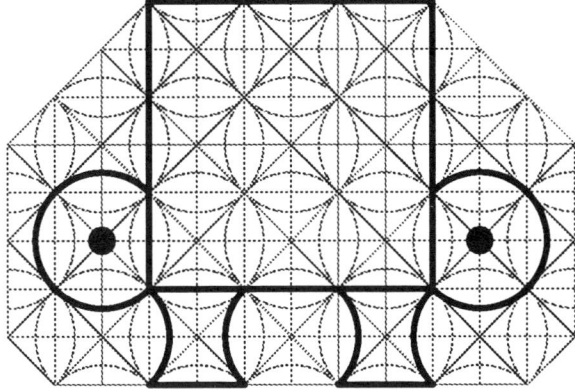

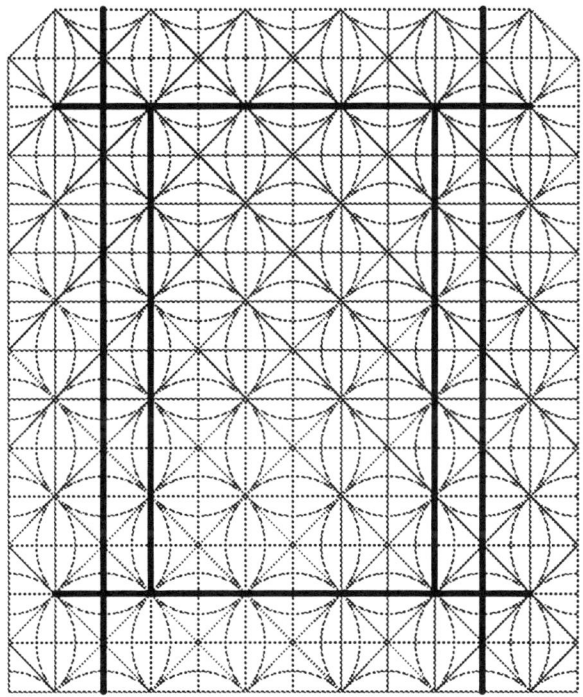

Figure 115

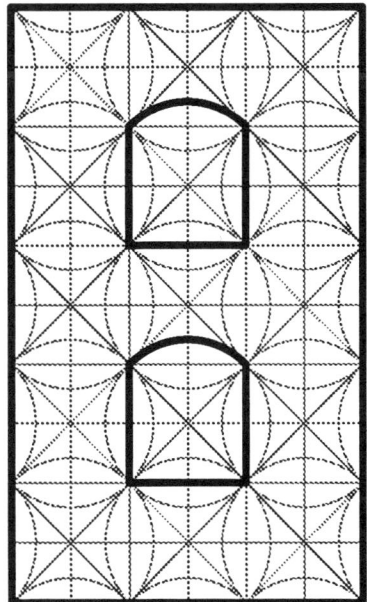

Figure 116

Figure 117

the Ark to lift it. The poles shall remain in the rings of the Ark and never be removed.")[8] We see the poles in an end view in **Figure 114**, and should visualize them running the length of the Ark. We also see them in top view, running the length of the Ark, in **Figure 115**. In the Grail quest stories, we encounter various items which cannot be removed from their places. Are the Grail quest stories parodies of Biblical stories? Why would they be?

"And thou shalt put into the ark the testimony which I shall give thee." (Put into the Ark the Tokens of the Covenant, which I shall give you.")[9] Is this a reference to the Ten Commandments, given to Moses on the Mount on two stone tablets? Hebrew

and Christian fundamentalists should take a deep breath. Exhale. Ready? In **Figure 116**, we see the Ark in top view with its lid off. Inside, in the form traditionally utilized in religious art, lie the two stone tablets. In **Figure 117**, we see our little

Figure 118

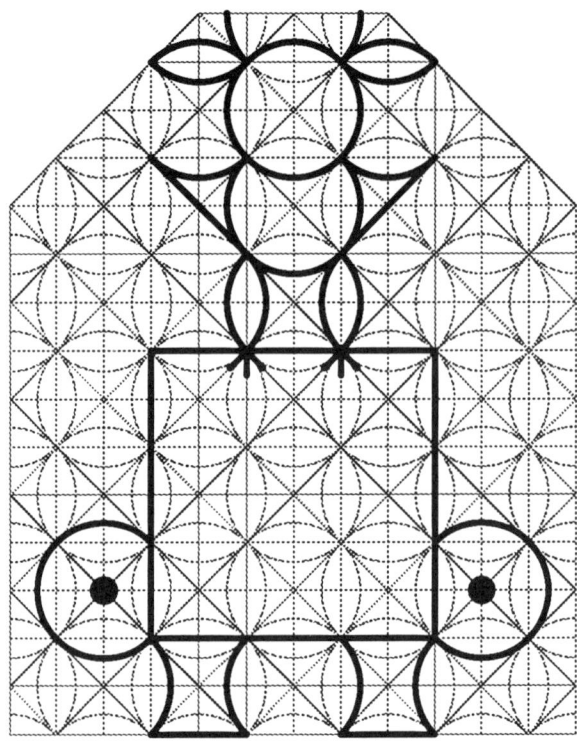

Figure 119

manform holding one of the tablets in his right arm and the other in his left arm. He is standing on three circle segments which we later shall learn were the symbol for "mountain" in the earliest written form of the Sumerian language.

"And thou shalt make a mercy seat *of* pure gold: two cubits and a half *shall be* the length thereof, and a cubit and a half the breadth thereof." ("Make a cover of pure gold, two and a half cubits long and one cubit and a half wide.")[10] "And thou shalt make two cherubims *of* gold, *of* beaten work shalt thou make them, in the two ends of the mercy seat. And make one cherub on the one end, and the other cherub on the other end: *even* of the mercy seat shall ye make the cherubims on the two ends thereof." ("Make two gold cherubim of beaten work at the ends of the cover, one at each end; make each cherub of one piece with the cover.")[11] "And the cherubims shall stretch forth *their* wings on high, covering the mercy seat with their wings, and their faces *shall look* one to another; toward the mercy seat shall the faces of the cherubims be." ("They shall be made with wings outspread and pointing upwards, and shall screen the cover with their wings. They shall be face to face, looking inwards over the cover.")[12] In **Figure 118**, we see one of the

two cherubim with his wings outspread and pointing upwards. He covers with his wings the lid of the Ark. His feet are at one end of the Ark, and he is facing away from us and toward the other end of the Ark, where the other one of the two cherubim would stand. He is of one piece with the cover and faces the cover. Visualize the other cherub at the other end of the Ark for yourself. Seen in top-view perspective, our two manforms should be visualized as cut-out dolls, connected to the cover of the Ark at their feet, otherwise cut free from the cover, and swung up to the perpendicular through a 90-degree arc.

A better way in which to visualize our two cherubim is, of course, from an end-view of the Ark. Turn to **Figure 119**, where we see the Ark from end-view perspective, illustrated *with* feet, and with one of our two cherubim facing toward the other end of the Ark, his back towards us, and his wings outspread and pointing upwards.

"And thou shalt put the mercy seat above upon the ark; and in the ark thou shalt put the testimony that I shall give thee. And there I will meet with thee, and I will commune with thee from above the mercy seat, from between the two cherubims which *are* upon the ark of the testimony, of all *things* which I will give thee in commandment unto the children

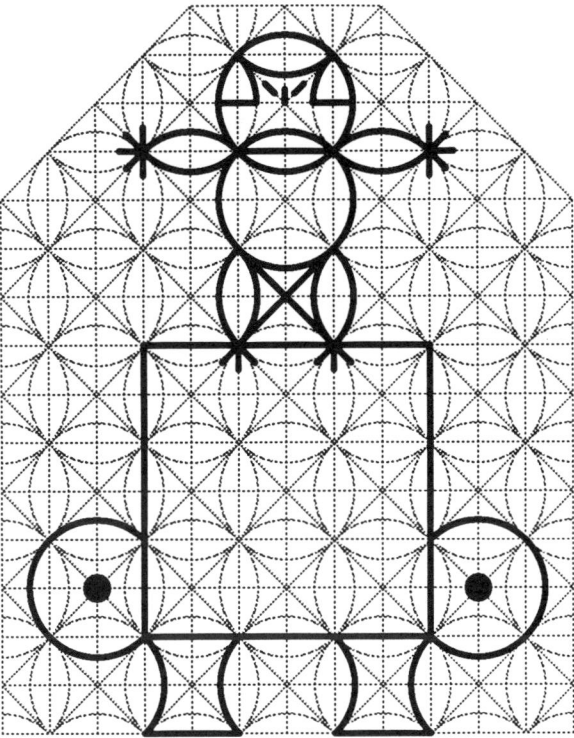

Figure 120

of Israel." ("Put the cover above the Ark, and put into the Ark the Tokens that I shall give you. It is there that I shall meet you, and from above the cover, between the two cherubim over the Ark of the Tokens, I shall deliver to you all my commands for the Israelites.")[13] Hebrew and Christian fundamentalists should take another deep breath. Exhale. Ready? In **Figure 120**, we see the Ark from an end-view perspective, complete with feet, with our little manform sitting on his throne, as we saw him sitting on the same throne above the vault of Heaven in our analysis of the Ezekiel story. Is our little manform playing the role of Yahweh? Picture him located, horizontally, in the middle of the cover of the Ark, and then superimpose on this Figure the two cherubim standing at either end of the cover, as in **Figure 121**. You have satisfied the requirements of this story.

Take your King James Bible and your Oxford Bible and read Exodus 25.23-29 for yourself. By combining our analysis of the story of the table from the Book of Aristeas with the analysis we just have completed of the Ark of the Covenant, you should have no trouble visualizing the Table of the Bread of the Presence for yourself. You may agree or disagree with this analysis, or with the conclusions to which

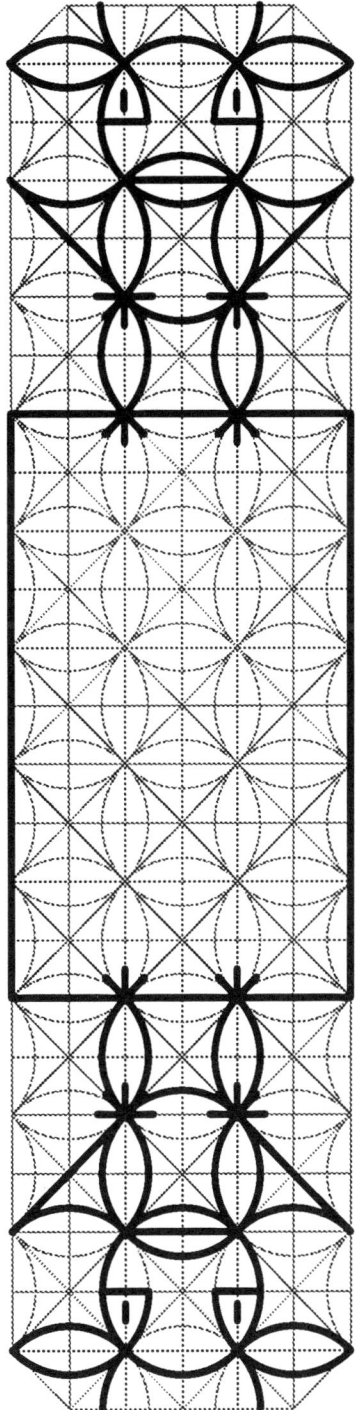

Figure 121

it may lead us, but you nonetheless are able to visualize the Table without any further assistance! That is one of the fascinating things about this book. Lay aside, at least for the moment, beliefs which impede this analysis, and look at the images with coldly analytical eyes. Reach no conclusions yet.

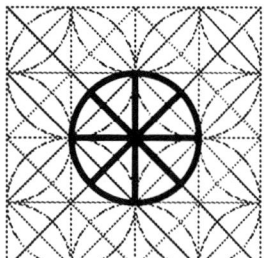

Figure 122

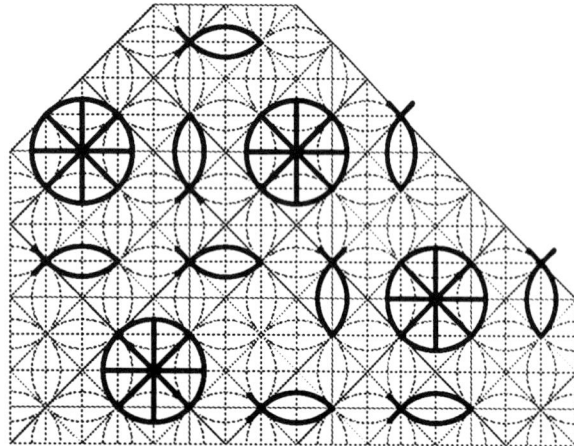

Figure 123

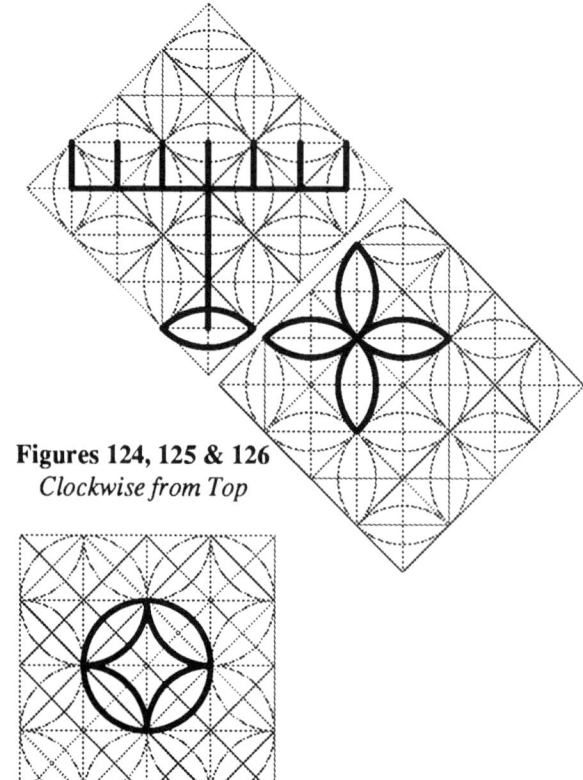

Figures 124, 125 & 126
Clockwise from Top

Illustration 8-1. An ancient loaf of Greek bread preserved in an oven by the volcanic ash covering Pompeii. Courtesy of Museo Nazionale Archeologico.

Read the entire book, then reach conclusions for yourself. Apply the scientific method to religion, and see where this leads you. Perhaps to a better concept of religion than the one with which you started?

"And thou shalt set upon the table shewbread before me always." ("Put the Bread of the Presence on the table, to be always before me.")[14] **Illustration 8-1** shows a loaf of ancient Greek bread removed by archaeologists from an oven in which it was preserved by volcanic ash.[15] Turn to **Figure 122**, and visualize, from top-view perspective, a round loaf of bread, which swells upwards and is crossed with four strokes of the baker's knife, in the form of the ancient Greek loaf illustrated in that photograph. The Holy Grail is covered with these "loaves of bread." The Holy Grail also is covered with Christian-style "fishes." See **Figure 123**. Loaves and fishes? Multiplied?

We already have seen that the ancient seven-branched form of the Menorah can be found on the Holy Grail. **Figure 124.** Read Exodus 25.31-40 for yourself in your King James and Oxford Bibles. Our unknown author wants us to visualize a different Menorah from the one illustrated in Figure

124. He wants us to see, from top-view perspective, each of the six branches complete with "bowls made like unto almonds, *with* a knop and flower" (King James) or with "cups shaped like almond blossoms, with calyx and petals...." (Oxford)[16] A "knop" is a small, rounded protuberance. "Calyxes" are the outer leaves that surround the unopened bud or protuberance of a flower. We see a flower in **Figure 125.** We see calyxes surrounding an unopened bud of a flower in **Figure 126.** We see a bowl having four "almonds" around its rim in Figure 126. The Menorah of Exodus 25 is quite different from modern Menorahs. It is a lampstand, not a candleholder. King James calls it "a

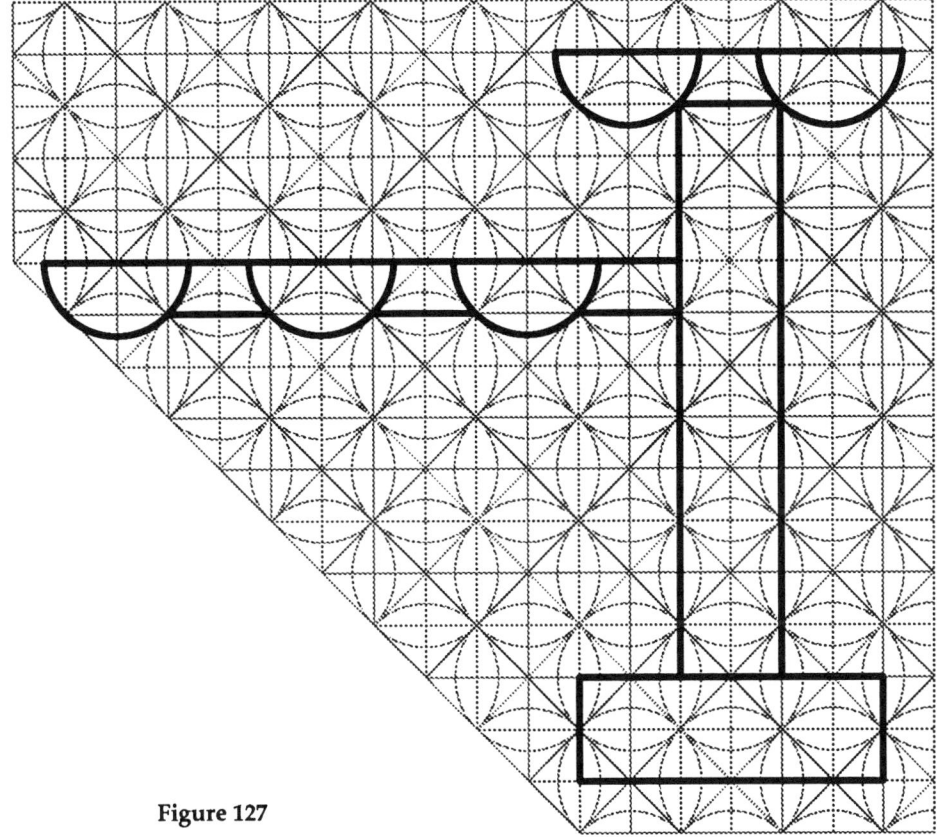

Figure 127

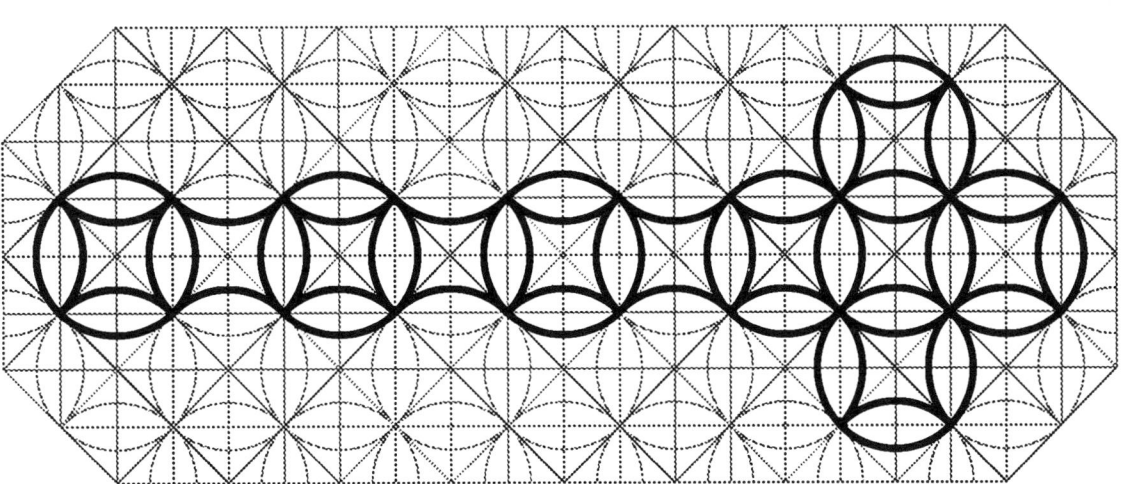

Figure 128

candlestick"[17] but says that "thou shall make the seven lamps thereof."[18] Oxford expressly calls it a "lamp-stand."[19] It has six branches, three on each side, with three cups on each branch, and has four more cups on the main stem.[20]

We see the main stem of the lampstand in side view in **Figure 127**, with two of its four bowls or cups. The other two bowls or cups on the main stem should be visualized behind these two. We also see in Figure 127 one of the six branches, with its three bowls or cups. In **Figure 128**, we see the central

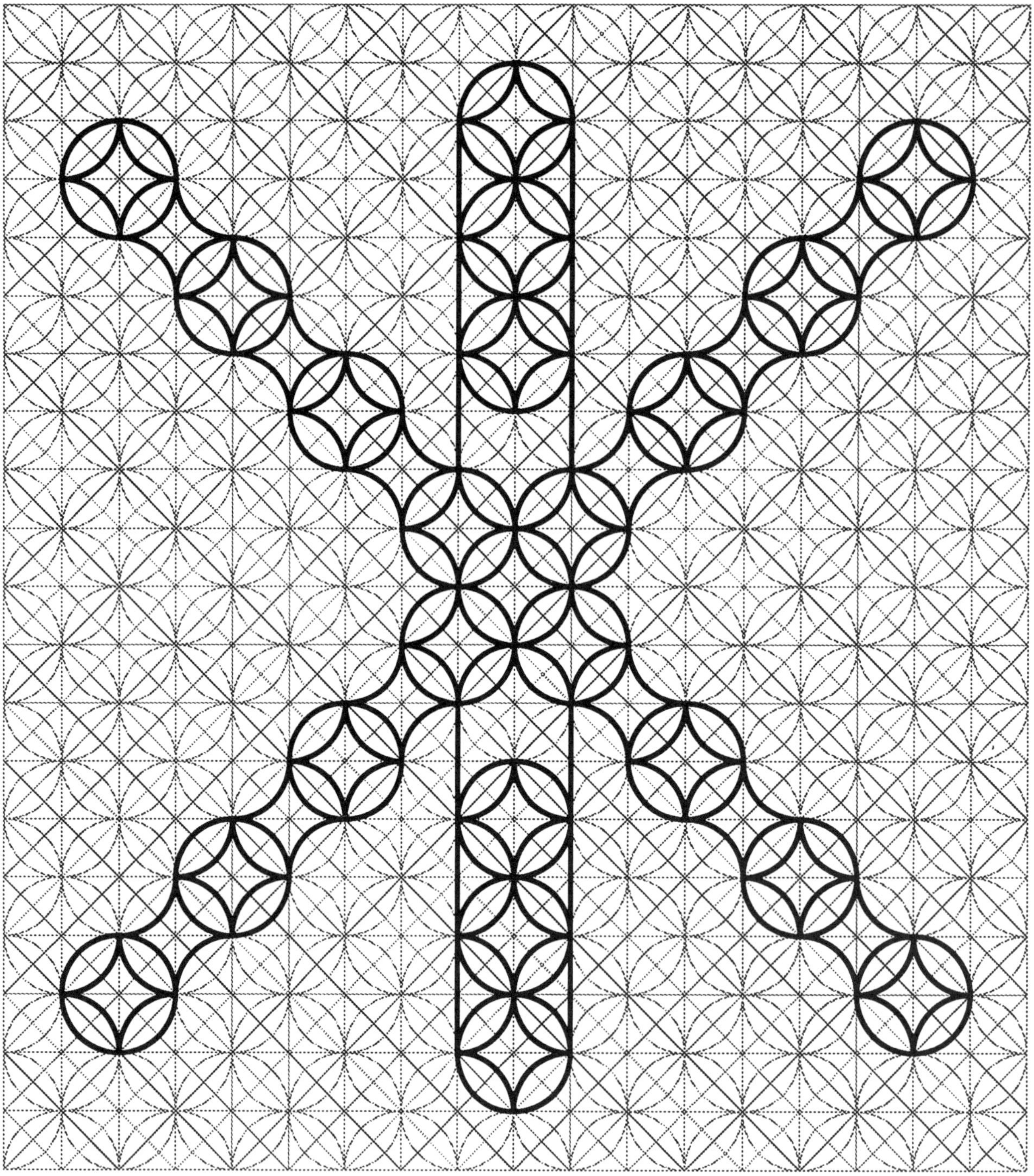

Figure 129

The Tabernacle and Ark of the Covenant

Figure 130

stem in top view, complete with all four of its calyx-shaped cups or bowls, and one of the six branches with its three calyx-shaped bowls or cups. In **Figure 129**, we see the entire lampstand in top view.

In **Figure 130**, we see a set of tongs and a snuff-pan with handle — both as required by Exodus.[21] All these things (the lamp and its fittings) are to be made according to the "pattern" or "design" which was showed to Moses by God on the Mountain.[22] God directed Moses to build for God a lamp and its fittings according to patterns or designs that may be visualized on the Holy Grail? God gave these instructions to Moses when He and Moses were alone together on the Mountain, this being a part of the work Moses must do before God would agree to live on Earth among the Hebrews? Note that our Menorah is in the form of the Christ symbol IX ("Jesus Christ") illustrated in **Figure 131**. Note, also, that it is in the form of a sunburst, as portrayed in **Illustration 8-2**.[23] Store that information in your

reservoir of trivia for future *important* use in later chapters.

Moses is instructed to make seven lamps to be used with the lampstand.[24] Experts in ancient cosmology tell us that the seven "lamps" of Exodus are an allegorical reference to the sun, the moon, and the five visible planets — Mercury, Venus, Mars, Jupiter, and Saturn.[25] The Exodus Menorah has six branches with three "bowls" or "cups" on each branch, and four more "bowls" or "cups" on the central stem. That equals twenty-two bowls or cups in which seven lamps are to sit. How can that be? Are some bowls or cups always left empty while others always contain a lamp? Are the lamps moved around among the bowls or cups? There are six branches. Does each branch have one lamp while the seventh lamp is moved around the four bowls or cups on the central stem? Is this a model planetary system, and, if so, what does the lamp in the middle represent? Did the ancient Hebrews know things about our solar system which we do not give them credit for knowing? Is it a coincidence that 22 divided by 7 equals 3.14, the two-decimal-place equivalent of our modern value for π?

We next encounter the design or pattern for the sanctuary itself, which is made of linen hangings or curtains (the Tabernacle) inside a goat-hair tent (the Tent of the Presence) which is covered with two layers of tanned skins.[26] There are 10 linen hangings or curtains of the Tabernacle, with cherubim worked into them.[27] Each hanging or curtain of the Tabernacle is 28 cubits long by 4 cubits wide.[28] They are joined together into one whole by loops and fasteners.[29] The goat-hair hangings or curtains form a tent, known as the Tent of the Presence, which is over the Tabernacle, that is, over the linen hangings or curtains. Each goat-hair hanging or curtain is 30

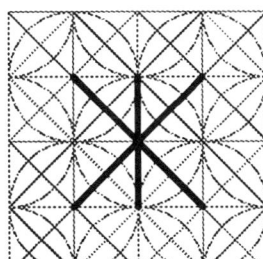

Figure 131

Illustration 8-2. Sunrise over Lake Sidney Lanier. Courtesy of Brendan Perry.

Figure 132

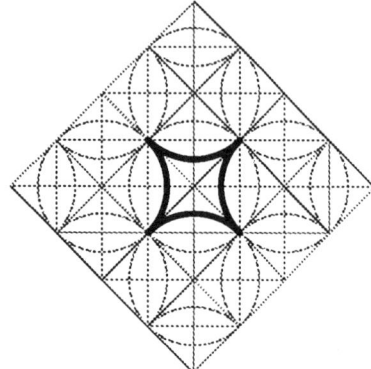

Figure 133

Figure 134

cubits long and 4 cubits wide, and there are 11 goat-hair hangings or curtains fastened together to form the Tent.[30] We are told that the additional length of the tent hanging (Oxford) or the remaining half curtain (King James) is to fall (Oxford) or hang (King James) over the back (Oxford) or backside (King James) of the Tabernacle.[31] We are told that on each side there will be an additional cubit in length of the tent hangings, and that this shall fall over the "two sides of the Tabernacle to cover it."[32] The Tent then is covered with rams' skins, and by an outer layer of badgers' skins (King James) or sea-cow hides (Oxford).[33] Regarding Oxford's reference to "porpoise-hides,"[34] which, strictly speaking, should be translated as "sea-cow hides," see the textnote in Oxford.[35]

Ready to play Grail games? Here we go. Each Tabernacle hanging or curtain is 4 cubits wide by 28 cubits long, producing a proportion of 1 to 7, because 4 times 7 equals 28. Thus, one Tabernacle hanging is 1 Grail square wide and 7 Grail squares long, and 10 Tabernacle hangings, fastened together, along their *lengths*, without overlaps, are 10 Grail squares wide and 7 Grail squares long. If, instead, the Tabernacle hangings are fastened together along their *widths*, the resulting cloth would be 1 Grail square wide by 70 Grail squares long. The numerals are 1 and 7 either way, leading to the speculation that we may be involved in "holy" numerology rather than the erection of a real-world tent!

Note that we are not told the shape of the tent–whether it is circular, square, rectangular, triangular, etc. Note that we are not told whether the hangings or curtains of the Tabernacle and the Tent merely are sidewalls, or somehow are to be folded so as to produce both sidewalls and a roof. Should the shape of the tent be known to us, or does the shape matter?

Note that cherubim can be seen all over the Tabernacle! A single cherubim is illustrated in

Figure 132. Our old friend the concave-sided tetragon appears in this story in the role of a "ram's skin." **Figure 133.** Note that the Tent of the Presence is covered by these "rams' skins." The outer covering over the entire Sanctuary is covered by "sea-cow skins." **Figure 134** illustrates a single "sea-cow skin." Note that the entire Sanctuary is covered by these "sea-cow skins."

Were the Tabernacle and the Tent of the Presence allegories instead of realities? Allegorical of what? We shall learn that early Christian religious leaders insisted that the sky is a tent![36] The Hebrew week had 7 days and the Hebrew lunar month had 28 days, while the solar months of the Egyptian calendar contained 30 days, plus extra days which were "intercaliated" to bring the lunar cycle into close approximation with the solar cycle.[37] Is the Tabernacle circular, like the dome of the sky? Does the Tabernacle represent a Hebrew lunar year of 28-day lunar months? Is the Tent of the Presence circular, like the dome of the sky? Does the Tent of the Presence represent a solar year comprised of 30-day solar months, which has been synchronized with the Hebrew lunar year by the insertion of intercaliated days?

People who have not read Hebrew history cannot understand the depth of the controversy which continued through the years as result of two conflicting desires of the Hebrew religious leaders. First, they wanted to rely upon their ancient lunar calendar. Second, they wanted to celebrate holy days at the proper time of the solar year.[38] The Egyptians had a lunar calendar, a solar calendar, and a solar-lunar calendar.[39] Egyptian astronomers had the skills necessary to keep the year synchronized — to the extent that Egyptian religious leaders would permit it![40] Did the Hebrew religious leaders wrap the two calendrical systems (Hebrew lunar and Egyptian solar) into an elaborate allegory which was understood by educated Hebrews — who would not have been offended by use of the superior Egyptian calendrical system? Did the allegory hide this from the Hebrew masses, who would have been displeased to learn that their priests were using a calendrical system developed by the Egyptian neighbors whom they had been taught to hate?

The next stage of the works is to make planks (Oxford) or boards (King James) of acacia (Oxford) or shittim (King James) wood for the Tabernacle and get them into place as uprights (Oxford) or "standing up" (King James).[41] Each plank or board is 10 cubits long and 1 & 1/2 cubit wide.[42] The planks

are arranged thusly: There are twenty planks on the south side of the Tabernacle, facing south, and twenty planks on the north side of the Tabernacle, facing north, six planks for the west "sides" (King James) or "far end" (Oxford), two planks for the corners "at the far end" (Oxford) or "in the two sides" (King James) and there shall be eight more planks somewhere else that is not specified.[43] It would seem that a circle is not contemplated, as the two rows of twenty planks apparently face each other on the north and south sides of the Tabernacle. We are not told whether the upright planks are inside the Tabernacle, outside the Tabernacle but inside the Tent, outside the Tent but inside the hide coverings, or outside the hide coverings. We are not told what structural role the upright planks play in the total concept of the Sanctuary.

Is the number 4, which we encountered as the number of bowls or cups on the central stem of the lampstand, somehow related to the Four Tetramorphs — the four guardian stars which lie approximately 90 degrees apart along the Ecliptic? There were three bowls or cups on each of six branches on the lampstand. That is 18 bowls or cups. The number of "planks" is 56, a number well known to ancient astronomers as related to the lunar cycle and eclipses of the moon. Nineteen years, plus nineteen years plus eighteen years is *one* of several cycles which can be used to predict some (but not all) eclipses of the moon at Stonehenge. Those three numbers sum to 56. Is this a mere coincidence? We shall discuss these matters thoroughly, and attempt to answer these questions, in the science chapters at the end of this book.

We next are told that bars of acacia (Oxford) or shittim (King James) wood are to be made and erected, five for the planks on "the one side," five for the planks on the "other side," and five for the planks on the west.[44] The middle bar is to go from end to end. Implying that some or all of the others do not?[45] We see four of the upright planks in **Figure 135**, and we see four of the upright planks being held together by the five bars in **Figure 136**.

 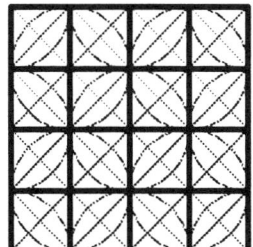

Figures 135 & 136

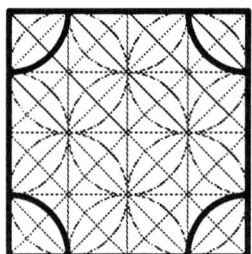

Figure 137

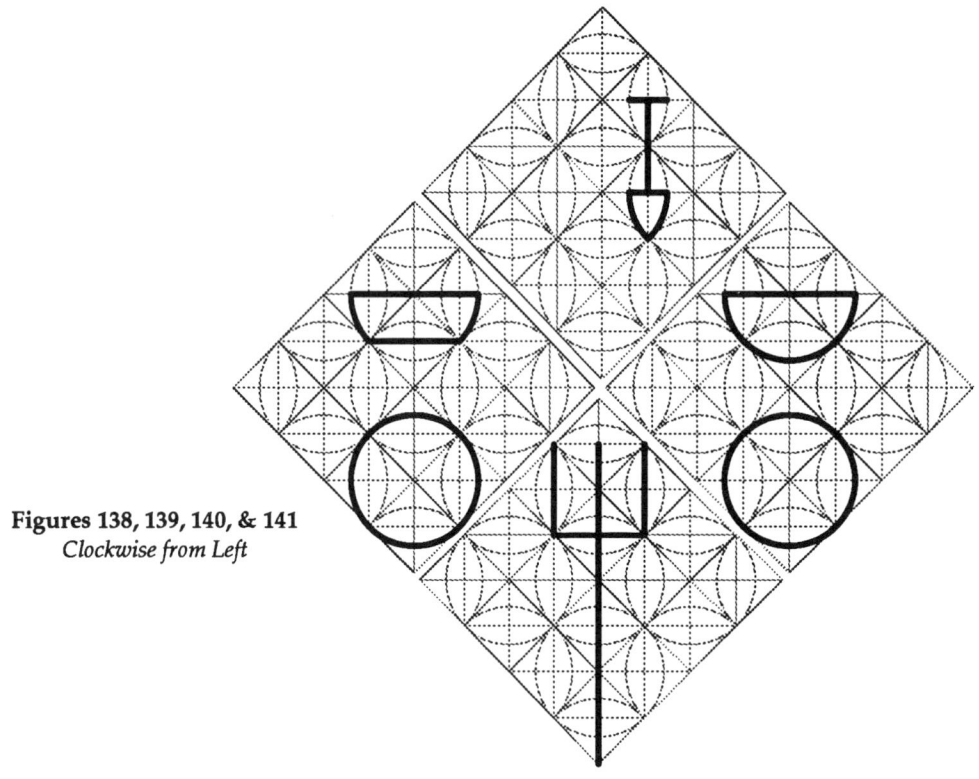

Figures 138, 139, 140, & 141
Clockwise from Left

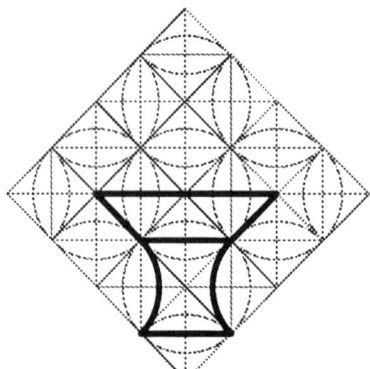

Figure 142

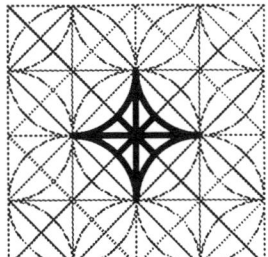

Figure 143

Whatever the form in which the boards and bars were to be erected, we have found them on the Holy Grail, and that may suffice for our purposes.

The Tabernacle is to be set up according to the "design" (Oxford) or "fashion" (King James) showed to Moses by God on the Mountain.[46] We must ask these questions: Did God give Moses the complete plans and specifications for construction and erection of His Sanctuary? Did Moses forget part of what God told him? Did some storyteller to whom the oral tradition was entrusted forget part of the story before the oral tradition was reduced to writing? Did some translator(s) mangle the written text? Did some religious leader require a scribe to rewrite something in the text? Was there ever a Sanctuary? A Tabernacle? A Tent of the Presence? Were they realities, before parts of the plans and specifications were lost? Or were they mere fantasies, seen among the lines of the Holy Grail by religious mythmakers who did not care that the plans and specifications are so incomplete that these items cannot be constructed? The simple answer to these questions is that your author does not know. Do you? Does anyone? We *do* know this much: The shapes and decorations of the fabrics and of the boardwork and its bracing system can be seen on the lines of the Holy Grail. Draw your own conclusions.

We shall skip the making of the Veil of the Holy of Holies and the installation of the Ark of the Covenant, the Lampstand and the Table.[47] You should have no difficulty in following this portion of the story based upon what we already have seen.

We next study the Altar. It is of acacia (Oxford) or shittim (King James) wood, is square, five cubits by five cubits, and is three cubits in height.[48] It has "horns" at (Oxford) or upon (King James) its four corners.[49] It is like our actual Hebrew altar seen as Illustration 5-1 during analysis of Ezekiel's Second Vision. **Figure 137** shows the "altar" in top view. Its equipment includes pots (Oxford) or pans (King James); shovels; tossing bowls (Oxford) or basins

(King James); forks (Oxford) or fleshhooks (King James); firepans; and a grating (Oxford) or grate (King James) of bronze (Oxford) or brass (King James) network.[50] A pot or pan is illustrated in **Figure 138**. A shovel is illustrated in **Figure 139**. A tossing bowl or basin is illustrated in **Figure 140**. A fork or fleshhook is illustrated in **Figure 141**. A firepan is illustrated in **Figure 142**. Our old friend, the concave-sided tetragon, is featured in its newest role as a brass or bronze network grating in **Figure 143**.

"[A]nd upon the net shalt thou make four brazen rings in the four corners thereof." ("[A]nd fit four bronze rings on the network at its four corners.")[51] The four rings at the four corners of the net or network are illustrated in **Figure 144**. The altar is to have two carrying poles (Oxford) or staves (King James) inserted into rings on two of its sides.[52] You can see that image for yourself, based on prior experience with rings and carrying poles. The altar is to be left a hollow shell (Oxford) or made hollow with boards (King James).[53] That is easy to visualize. "[A]s it was shewed thee in the mount, so shall they make *it*." ("As you were shown on the mountain, so shall it be made.")[54] God's instructions for the altar were complete, Moses remembered them exactly, the storytellers to whom the oral tradition was entrusted remembered the story precisely, no scribes wrote it down erroneously, no translators mistranslated it, and we

Figure 144

Figure 145

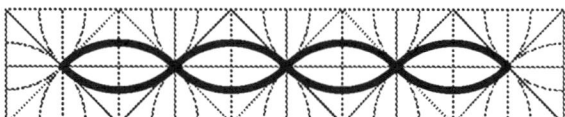

Figure 146

Figure 147

have the story today, in English, sufficiently intact for us to see the exact image of the altar on the Holy Grail and to make such an altar if we wish. Religious fundamentalists will be delighted! Or will they?

What about Aaron's vestments? They are decorated with rosettes (Oxford) or ouches (King James), and chains.[55] A rosette or ouche is seen in **Figure 145**, and a chain is seen in **Figure 146**. Aaron's breastplate shall consist of four rows of three precious stones which are held in place by "gold rosettes" (Oxford) or "their inclosings" (King James).[56] Aaron's breastplate is illustrated in **Figure 147**. We see rows of precious stones like we saw in the story of the table from the Letter of Aristeas. We see one stone for each of the Twelve Tribes of Israel. The story continues, telling us of "bells" and "pomegranates" as decorations on Aaron's vestments.[57] But we have seen enough, have we not? Now we must analyze the story of Solomon's Temple.

Notes
CHAPTER EIGHT. The Tabernacle and Ark of the Covenant

1. Oxford 82-83, fn. 40.

2. Exodus 25.8.

3. Exodus 25.9.

4. Exodus 25.10.

5. There were several "cubits" during Biblical times. For instance, Ezekiel uses a "cubit" which is equal to "a cubit and a hand breadth" to give the measurements of the altar for his idealized Temple. Ezekiel 43.13. Your author does not know, and makes no assumption, as to which "cubit" was intended by the unknown author(s) of the Story of the Tabernacle.

6. Exodus 25.11.

7. Exodus 25.12.

8. Exodus 25.14-15.

9. Exodus 25.16.

10. Exodus 25.17.

11. Exodus 25.18-19.

12. Exodus 25.20.

13. Exodus 25.21-22.

14. Exodus 25.30. Is this the same "bread" as the "bread from heaven"? Exodus 16.4.

15. Splendors of the Past 135.

16. Exodus 25.33.

17. Exodus 25. 31, 32, 34.

18. Exodus 25.37.

19. Exodus 25. 31, 34.

20. Exodus 25.32, 34. Oxford is explicit: "On the main stem of the lampstand there are to be four cups shaped like almond blossoms, with calyx and petals...." Exodus (Oxford) 25.34.

21. Exodus 25.38.

22. Exodus 25.40.

23. By the author's son.

24. Exodus 25.37.

25. Zechariah 4.2,10; Cirlot 257-259, 283-285; Graves & Patai 13, 25, 52-53. Your author is not the first person to suggest that many allegedly historical stories were composed as myths to encode data concerning the apparent movements of the sun, moon, planets, and stars. "By astral-mythology these scholars mean that all myths, legends and even many symbolisms, originated in the personification of the heavenly bodies. They argue, further, that the accounts in the Old Testament, not only of the patriarchs, but of even much more firmly established narratives, are merely the reflections of an astral-theology which originated and was developed in the priestly schools of Babylonia, and which made the phenomena of the heavens as the basis of its teachings." Farbridge 132-133. The Semitic Babylonian Epic of Gilgamesh speaks of Ishtar (Venus) cohabiting promiscuously with whoever her fancy dictated, including the lion and the eagle. Farbridge 171. Modern religious fundamentalists should have no difficulty in accepting the Gilgamesh Epic as astral-mythology. But how should we regard the Story of the Ark of the Covenant? The Prophet Jeremiah tells us that the day will come when "men shall speak no more of the Ark of the Covenant of the Lord; they shall not think of it nor remember it nor resort to it; it will be needed no more." Jer. 3.16 (Oxford). Jeremiah also spoke against worship of the Queen of Heaven. Jer. 7.18; 44.17-19, 25. Would Jeremiah be displeased with modern religious fundamentalists who continue to treat Biblical astral-mythology as if it were the Word of God? Why did the rabbis who wrote the *Mishnah* discourage, if not forbid, the use of the *Merkabah* (the Heavenly Throne of Ezekiel's Visions) for liturgical purposes? Barnstone 705. Because they knew that Ezekiel's Visions are Hebrew rewrites of Semitic Babylonian astral-mythology?

26. Exodus 26.1, 7, 14.

27. Exodus 26.1.

28. Exodus 26.2.

29. Exodus 26.3-6.

30. Exodus 26.7-11.

31. Exodus 26.12.

32. Exodus 26.13. (Oxford)

33. Exodus 26.14.

34. Exodus (Oxford) 25.5, 26.14.

35. Oxford 82, note n.

36. Dreyer 211-212. Rabbi Joel C. Dobin suggests in reference to what Christians call the "Old Testament" that the "richness of its imagery and of its nuance is lost to biblical scholars who do not recognize the mythic origin of the message because they are ignorant of the astrological components of the Bible." Dobin 139. He explains to us in detail that the story of Samson and Delilah is an astrological allegory, with Samson exhibiting the characteristics of a "Leo" while Delilah exhibits the characteristics of Samson's 180-degree opposite along the band of the Zodiac, that is, an "Aquarius." Dobin 113-118. He tells us that the story of Samson and Delilah is not "the only time that a fairytale is included in the Bible to teach a lesson." Dobin 118. He demonstrates that the Tale of Joseph also "is played out in the best of astrological allegories." Dobin 111. His thesis is that we should learn to read the Bible "with an astrologically aware and open mind." Dobin 145. He means, of course, that we should become aware of *ancient Hebrew* astrology in order to understand what the Hebrew authors of the "Old Testament" meant by what they said. Dobin 226. Of the Rabbis of the first century, C.E., he tells (or reminds) us "that these men were mystics, that they believed that all secrets would be revealed by a proper mystical understanding of the Scripture...." Dobin 185. He hopes that he has done more than "just reclaim Astrology for Judaism"; rather, that he has "also indicated a direction, that can be taken by our daughter religion, Christianity, towards reclaiming an integral portion of its lost, or deliberately abandoned, heritage." Dobin 226. Lloyd Graham later will tell us that "there is not an incident in the whole Christ story that is not written in the stars...." Graham 354. The New Testament makes no effort to conceal "Old Testament" use of allegory. In reference to the story of the Sons of Abraham, we are told, most explicitly, that "This is an allegory." Galatians 4.24 (Oxford). *The* Holy Bible of Christian fundamentalists puts it thus: "Which things are an allegory...." Galatians 4.24 (King James). Christian fundamentalists may decline to accept the word of a Rabbi. Will they permit themselves to ignore the "Word of God," i.e., Galatians 4.24?

37. Krupp 169-175; Langdon BMATSC 10-11, 15, 17, 18, 92; Charles xv-xix; Harrelson 20-37, 64-67; H. Brown 2-20. Rabbi Joel C. Dobin *might* be of the opinion, if we were to ask him, that the reference to the number 28 is to the "Great Cycle of 28 years, that is, a Saturn cycle," which is an important component of Hebrew Astrology. Dobin 199.

38. Charles xv-xix.

39. Krupp 173-175.

40. Krupp 174-175.

41. Exodus 26.15.

42. Exodus 26.16.

43. Exodus 26.18-25.

44. Exodus 26.26-27.

45. Exodus 26.28.

46. Exodus 26.30.

47. Exodus 26.31-37. We later shall learn that the four (Exodus 26.32) or the five (Exodus 26.37) pillars are the pillars of cosmology which hold up the Heavens.

48. Exodus 27.1.

49. Exodus 27.2.

50. Exodus 27.3-4.

51. Exodus 27.4.

52. Exodus 27.6-7.

53. Exodus 27.8.

54. Exodus 27.8.

55. Exodus 28.13.

56. Exodus 28.15-20.

57. Exodus 28.33. We have seen the "pomegranates." We shall see the "bells" when we discuss the origin of the Roman Catholic Mass.

Chapter Nine

Solomon's Temple

Solomon built for the Lord a "house" that was 60 cubits long by 20 cubits wide by 30 cubits high.[1] It had a "porch" (King James) or "vestibule" (Oxford) that was 10 cubits deep, front to back, by 20 cubits wide, i.e., the "porch" or "vestibule" was the same width as the "house."[2] The window lights, that is, openings, were narrow (King James) or were embrasures (Oxford).[3] The walls were constructed with "chambers" (King James) or "arcades" (Oxford).[4] He made "rests" (King James) or "rebates" (Oxford) to bear the beams so the beams would not have to be set into the walls.[5] The house was constructed from stones that were not dressed at the construction site using iron tools.[6] The entrance to the middle "chamber" (King James) or "arcade" (Oxford), and to the "third" chamber (King James) or "highest" arcade (Oxford), was by means of "winding stairs" (King James) or "a spiral stairway" (Oxford).[7]

An "embrasure" is a window in a thick wall which has a narrower opening on the outside of the wall than it has on the inside of the wall. If you ever have been inside an old fortress or castle, you have seen embrasures from which the soldiers fired cannon, muskets, or arrows, depending on the age of the structure. **Figure 148** shows an embrasure from an inside-the-building perspective. The two inside vertical lines represent the narrower slot in the outside wall, and the two outside vertical lines represent the wider slot in the inside wall. The top and bottom lines represent, of course, the top and bottom of the embrasure. **Figure 149** represents an arcade in the sense of a view down a passageway

with an arched roof, and **Figure 150** represents an arcade in the sense of a side view of a row of arches supported by columns, i.e., a colonnade. **Figure 151** shows the insides of two vertical walls equipped with two triangular rebates supporting the ends of a horizontal beam that bears on the rebates rather than setting into the walls. A winding or spiral stairway is seen, in top view, in **Figure 152**.

The insides of the walls and the floor were covered with beams and boards (King James) or braced with struts, roofed with beams and coffering and walled and floored with boards (Oxford).[8] Remember the boards of the Tabernacle? He built an "oracle" or "most holy place" (King James) or "Most Holy Place" (Oxford) that was twenty cubits long, twenty cubits wide, and twenty cubits high, in front of which there was "the house" (King James) or "the sanctuary" (Oxford) which was forty cubits long.[9] The wall boards were cedar and the floor boards were fir (King James) or pine (Oxford).[10] The boards inside the walls were carved with knops and open flowers (King James) or open flowers and

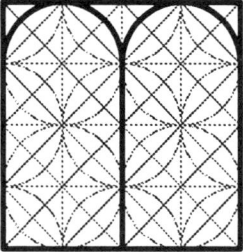

Figure 150

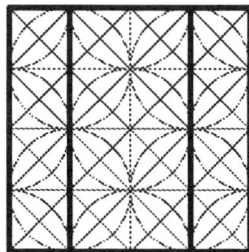

Figure 148

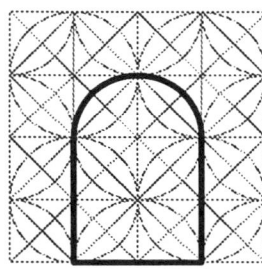

Figure 149

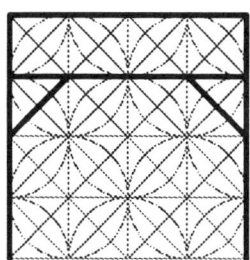

Figure 151

Figure 152

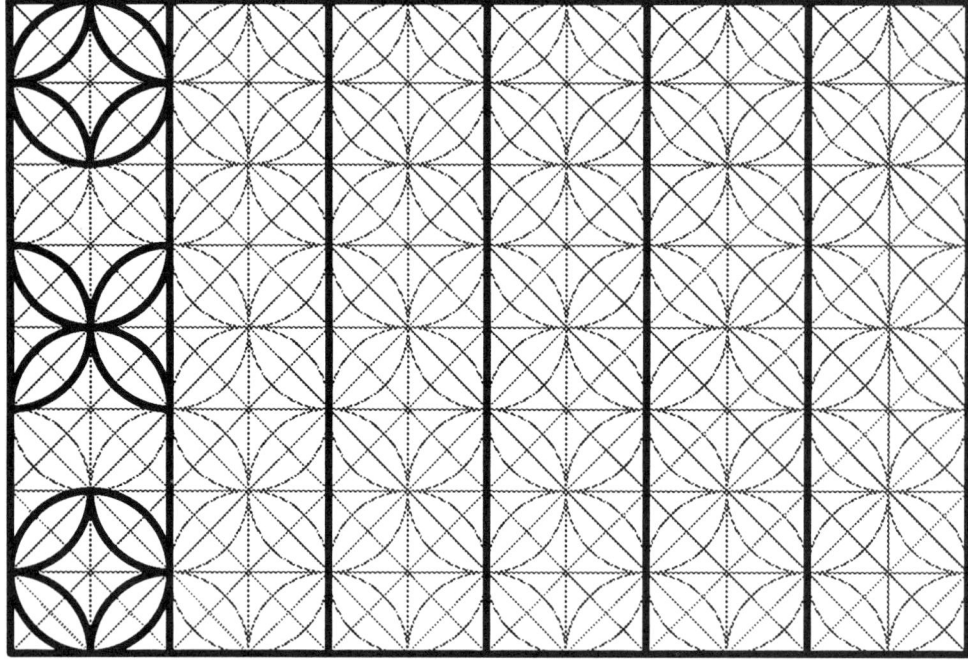

Figure 153

gourds (Oxford).[11] This sounds familiar. See **Figure 153**, where we have bolded six boards. Only one of these boards has two of its knops, and one of its open flowers, or one group of its gourds, bolded. You should be able to visualize all the others!

The "oracle" (King James) or "inner shrine" (Oxford) of the "house" was prepared to receive the Ark of the Covenant.[12] It had two identical cherubim of wild olive wood with wings outspread, the inner wing of each touching the inner wing of the other, the outer wing of each touching the opposite wall.[13] Around all the walls of the house, he carved figures of cherubim, open flowers, and palm trees.[14] **Figure 154** is our familiar open flower. **Figure 155** is our palm tree. Two cherubim touching wings and walls appear in **Figure 156**. You can do the various doors for yourself.[15] He overlaid the walls, floors, cherubim, altar, etc., with gold.[16] The pentagonal doorposts[17] suggest the "Seal of Solomon," the five-pointed star, which corresponds to the "Seal of David," the six-pointed star.[18]

He then built the House of the Forest of Lebanon 100 cubits long, 50 cubits broad, and 30 cubits high.[19] He constructed it with 4 rows of cedar pillars (King James) or columns (Oxford) and a cedar roof, which rested on cedar beams (King James) or lengths (Oxford), which rested on the pillars or columns.[20] We find a wide divergence of meaning between the versions of 1 Kings 7.3 found in King James and in

Oxford. King James refers to "the beams, that *lay* on forty five pillars, fifteen *in* a row," whereas Oxford refers to "the beams, which rested on the columns, fifteen in each row; and the number of beams was forty-five." Thus, the King James version of 1 Kings 7.3 says that the total number of pillars was 45 and that there were 15 pillars in a row. By simple arithmetic, 45 total pillars divided by 15 pillars to a row equals 3 rows of pillars with 15 pillars to a row. But the King James version of 1 Kings 7.2 said that there were 4 rows of pillars supporting beams. Something is amiss. On the other hand, the Oxford version of 1 Kings 7.3 says that the columns were 15 in a row and the number of beams was 45. The Oxford version of 1 Kings 7.3 therefore makes no claim as to the number of rows of columns, leaving us to postulate that the number of rows either was 4, as in *both* the King James and Oxford versions of

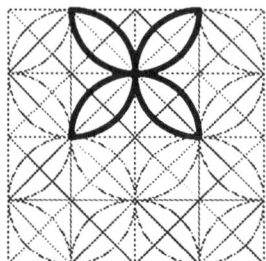

Figure 154

Figure 155

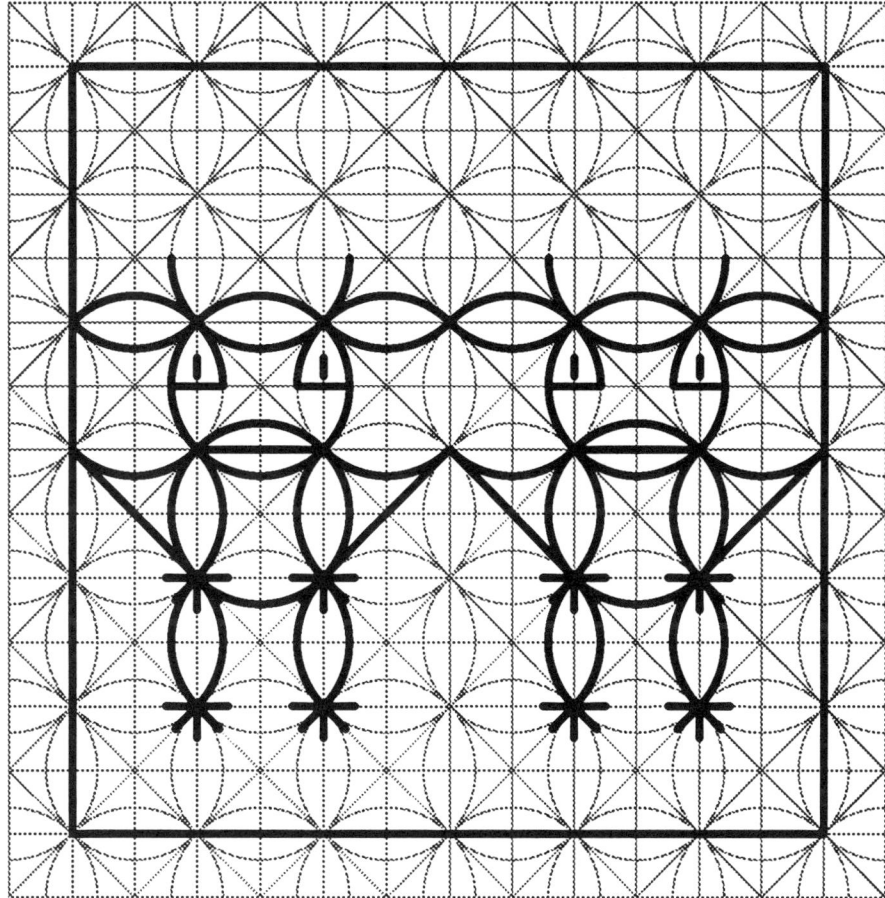

Figure 156

1 Kings 7.2, or was 3, as in the King James version of 1 Kings 7.3. Assuming 4 rows of 15 columns each, that would total 60 columns, which is too many columns for 45 beams. Assuming 3 rows of 15 columns each, we would have 45 columns, or 1 column for each beam, which also seems incorrect. Did Yahweh misinform Solomon as to the proper number of columns and beams? Did Solomon fail to hear Yahweh's instructions to David correctly? Did some person to whom this oral tradition was entrusted, before the story first was written down, fail to remember the correct number of columns or beams? Did some scribe or translator of the written story make an error of some sort? Did the pious author of the story not know, or not care, that some of his readers would be troubled by their inability to determine the proper number of columns and beams?

The House of the Forest of Lebanon had 3 rows of square window frames and its door frames were square.[21] According to King James, twice said, the windows were built so that "light *was* against light *in* three ranks."[22] Oxford translates these verses this way: "[T]he windows corresponded to each other at three levels,"[23] and "window corresponded to window at three levels."[24] **Figure 157**. There also was a "porch of pillars" (King James) or "colonnade" (Oxford) that was 50 cubits long and 30 broad.[25]

This building — which was larger than the Temple of the Lord — was to be used as *Solomon's* hall of judgment and residence.[26] It was made of

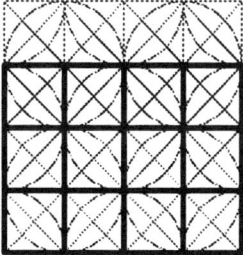

Figure 157

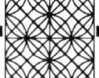

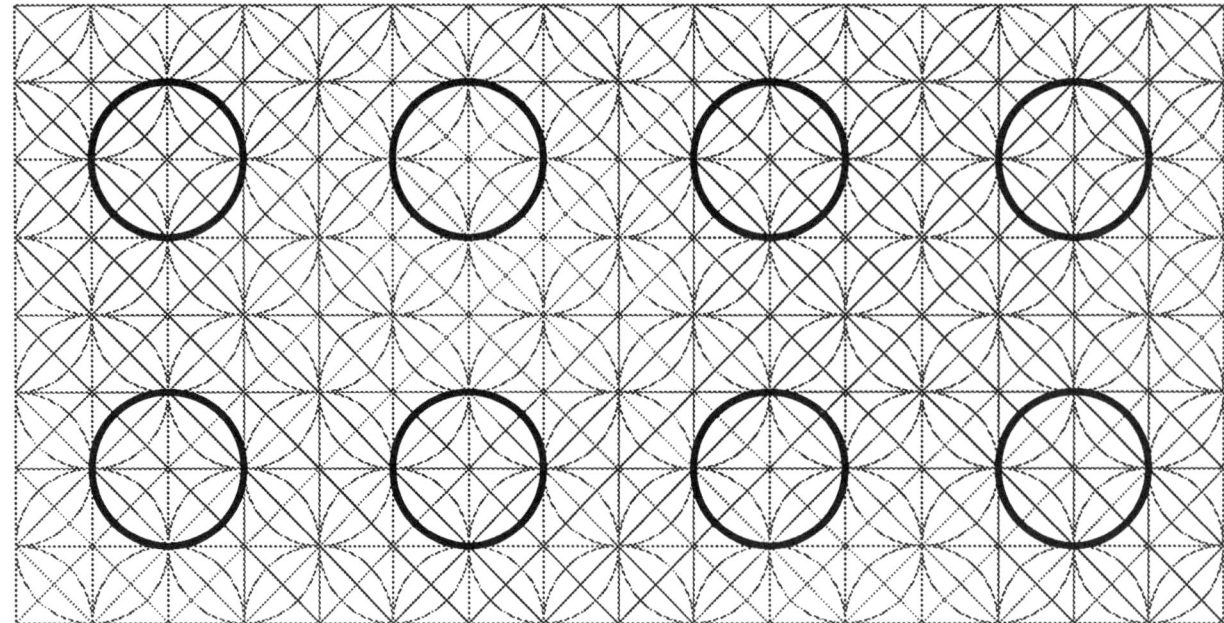

Figure 158

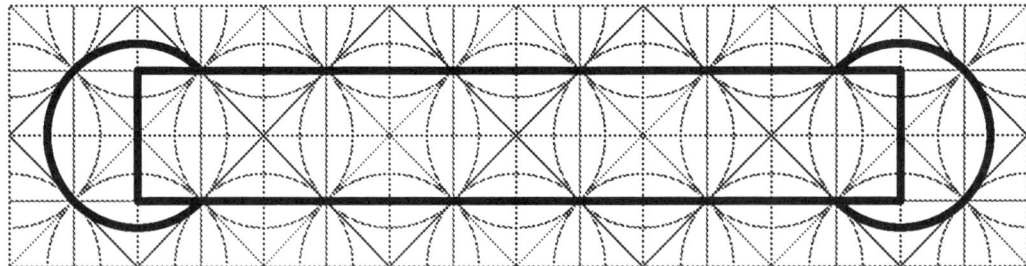

Figure 159

Figure 160

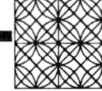

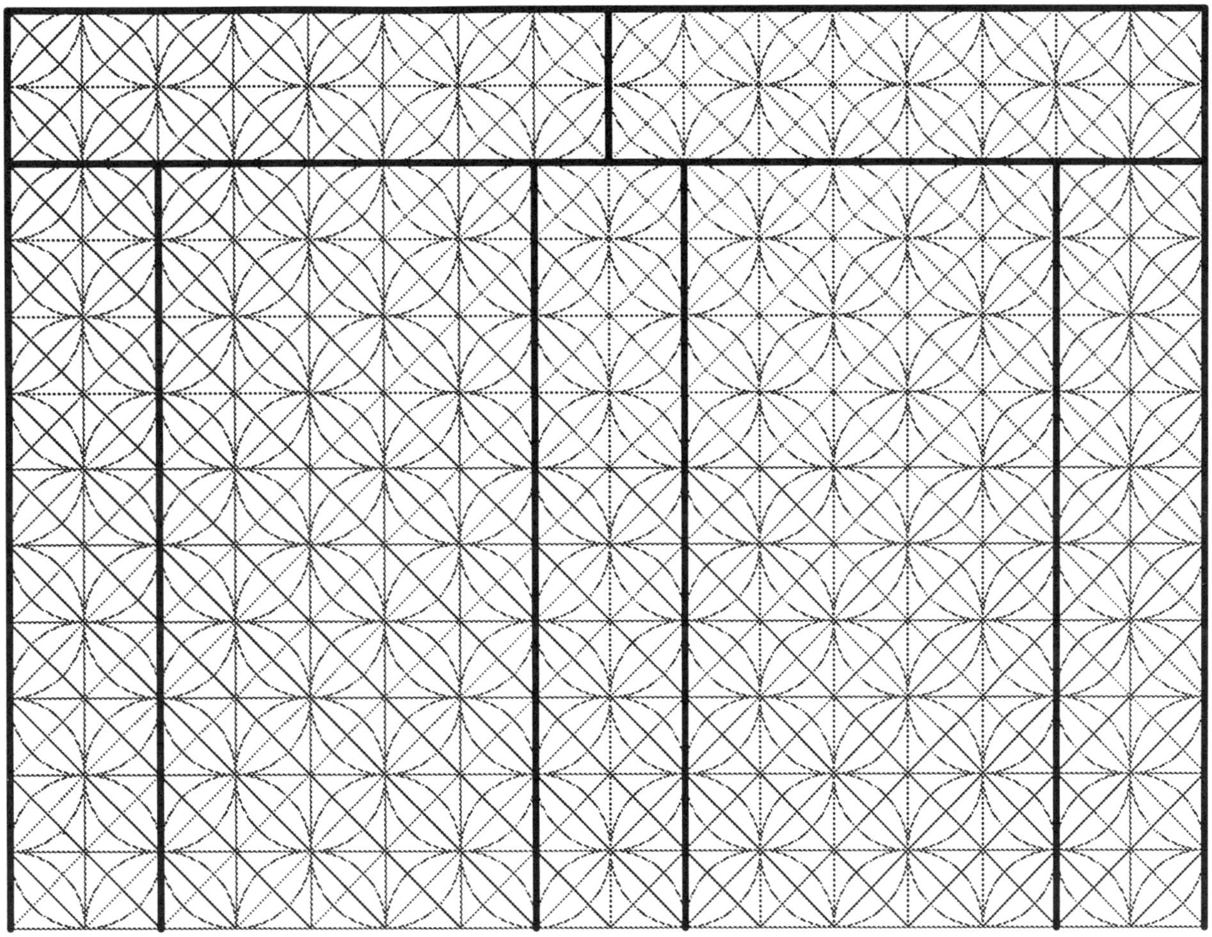

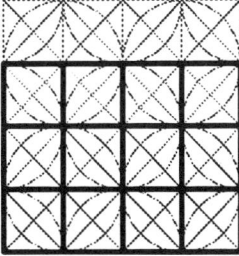

Figure 161

costly, large, sawed stones.[27] **Figure 158** shows parts of two rows of columns from a top view. **Figure 159** shows, in top view, columns supporting a beam. **Figure 160** shows part of a row of columns supporting arcades. **Figure 161** shows part of a row of columns with a beam resting on the columns. **Figure 162** shows parts of three rows of sawed stones. Note that these stones are not staggered for maximum strength. Square window and door frames are visible all over the Holy Grail.

He then cast for the Temple the columns Jachin and Boaz. They were brass (King James) or bronze (Oxford) and were 18 cubits high. Their chapiters (King James) or capitals (Oxford) had nets of checker work and wreaths of chain work (King James) or bands of network in festoons of chain-work (Oxford). On top of the network were two rows of pomegranates. The capitals at the tops of the pillars were shaped like lilies.[28] These are familiar images to a seasoned Grail student like you.

He made a "sea" of metal, round in shape, with a 10 cubit diameter and a 30 cubit circumference.[29] Think about that one for just a moment. The circumference of a circle equals its diameter times π. The modern value of π is 3.1416. We already have learned that the ancient Babylonians and Egyptians had a value for π almost that accurate. We are told that the diameter equalled 10 cubits. Hence, the circumference would have been 31.416 cubits, not 30 cubits, as given. Did Yahweh not know the

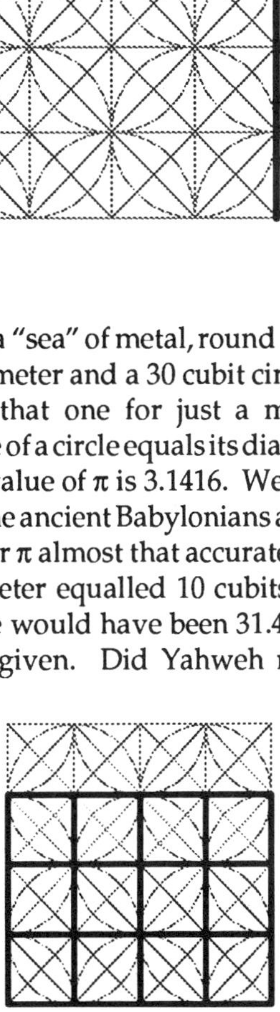

Figure 162

Figure 163

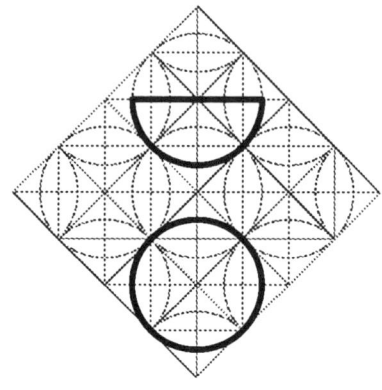

Figures 164 & 165
Left to Right

correct value for π? Or did Solomon forget the value for π that Yahweh had given him or David? Or is the pious author of this story simply revealing his ignorance of, or his lack of concern for, simple Babylonian and Egyptian mathematics? We know that the diameter must "come out uneven," or that the circumference must "come out uneven." Both cannot "come out even" in the real world.[30] We are most explicitly told that "a line of thirty cubits did compass it round about" (King James) or that "it took a line thirty cubits long to go round it" (Oxford).[31] We are safe in the speculation that the author of this story never had stretched a line around this "sea"; or, having stretched one, that he cared more for the holy numerology of a 1 to 3 ratio of diameter to circumference than he did for the accurate measurement, which would have visibly exceeded 30 cubits; or, that his "sea" was a fantasy rather than a reality. In any of these cases, we are lead to the speculation that we are reading the works of a craftsman of fabulous stories rather than

a craftsman of fabulous metalwork. If we were to assume an 18 inch "short" cubit, this "sea" would have been 15 feet in diameter! Anyone having the technical competence to make such a casting surely would not have been so imprecise as to ignore over one cubit out of 30 cubits when measuring its circumference.

We next encounter a very interesting Grail image. We are told that the sea "stood" (King James) or "was mounted" (Oxford) on twelve oxen, with three oxen facing each of the major compass points (north, south, east, and west); that the oxen had their "hinder parts" (King James) or "hindquarters" (Oxford) turned inward.[32] Turn to **Figure 163**, where we see the "sea" supported by three oxen's faces, all of which are facing in the same direction. If you are not able to unravel that complex image, which requires multiple uses of several lines, then look at one ox face in **Figure 164**, and the "sea" illustrated in side and top views in **Figure 165**. Then look back at Figure 163 and

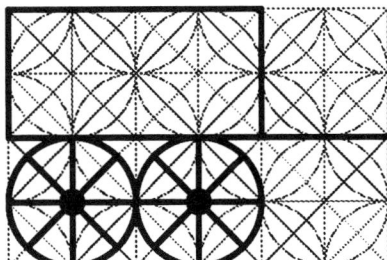

Figure 166

unravel the overlapping lines. Let the direction that this set of three oxen is facing be equal to north, south, east, and west. Three oxen times four directions equals twelve oxen. Note that their hinder parts or hindquarters do, indeed, turn inward.

A paraphrased and combined reading of the Oxford and King James versions produces the following condensed version of the story of the "bases of brass" (King James) or "trolleys of bronze" (Oxford). Ten of them were made, all alike, and they were decorated on their square panels with lions, oxen, cherubim, and palm trees, familiar images which we shall not repeat. Each had four wheels on axles, constructed like chariot wheels, and an opening for a basin set within a crown, which opening had a round, level edge.[33] A trolley with chariot wheels is seen in **Figure 166**. The crown with a round, level edge at its inside circumference is illustrated in side view in **Figure 167**, and in top view in **Figure 168**. A basin for one of the ten trolleys[34] can be visualized in place in Figure 168. We shall see the form of this four-wheeled wagon utilized throughout the stories yet to be encountered in this book, culminating in the cart used by the Maid of the Cart in the Grail quest stories. The imagination of mythsmiths is a wondrous thing!

We need not repeat the images of the pots, shovels, and tossing-bowls[35] or the images from the stories of the outfitting and dedication of the Temple.[36] Read the outfitting and dedication stories for yourself. The image of the cloud filling the Temple, indicating that God had moved into His new house, also is familiar to us.[37]

Without the assistance of lines bolded on the Holy Grail, you should now read in King James and Oxford the *other* story of Solomon's Temple, which commences at 2 Chron. 3. The major discrepancy we find between the King James and Oxford translations occurs in 2 Chron. 3.4, where King James says the height of the porch of the Temple was "an hundred and twenty" whereas Oxford says it was "twenty." Oxford says that the reference to a height of 120 for the porch "is either an error or else an exaggeration characteristic of the Chronicler."[38] The Chronicler evidently was given to exaggeration. He has the Temple adorned with precious stones as well as covered with gold.[39] He "enlarged" the pillars Jachin and Boaz from their 18 cubit height of 1 Kings 7.15 to a height of 35 cubits in the King James translation of 2 Chron. 3.15, which the Oxford translation of 2 Chron. 3.15 reduces back to 18 cubits. Who cares, you say? Hebrew and Christian fundamentalists — that is who! If you believe in the doctrine of Biblical inerrancy, then you cannot permit yourself to admit that a scribe or translator might have made an accidental copybook error, or that a pious religionist might have deliberately enlarged the height of the Temple's porch or columns — because the Bible is the Word of God; hence, is without error!

We perhaps have seen enough Hebrew stories bolded on the Holy Grail. Let us now explore the

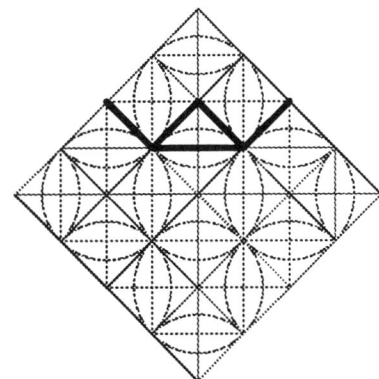
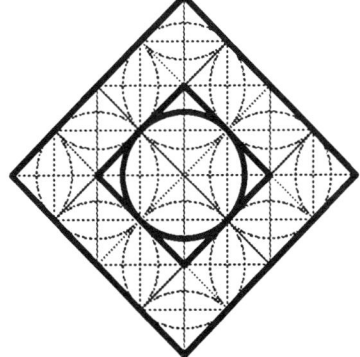

Figures 167 & 168
Left to Right

earliest uses of the Holy Grail for mythmaking that your author has been able to locate. We must take with us one image from the story of the Temple of Solomon. We are told that at the tops of the pillars Jachin and Boaz there were "the *two* bowls of the chapiters" (King James) or "the two bowl-shaped capitals" (Oxford) and "the two networks, to cover the two bowls of the chapiters" (King James) or "the two ornamental networks to cover the two bowl-shaped capitals" (Oxford).[40] **Figure 169** shows the net in the bowl with which we first became familiar during the analysis of the story of the table. This will be the first image of the next chapter.

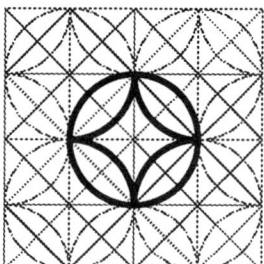

Figure 169

Notes
CHAPTER NINE. Solomon's Temple

1. 1 Kings 6.2.
2. 1 Kings 6.3.
3. 1 Kings 6.4.
4. 1 Kings 6.5-6.
5. 1 Kings 6.6.
6. 1 Kings 6.7.
7. 1 Kings 6.8.
8. 1 Kings 6.9,15.
9. 1 Kings 6.16-17,20.
10. 1 Kings 6.15.
11. 1 Kings 6.18.
12. 1 Kings 6.19.
13. 1 Kings 6.23-28.
14. 1 Kings 6.29.
15. 1 Kings 6.31-35.
16. 1 Kings 6.21,22,28,30.
17. 1 Kings 6.31.
18. Runes 158-159.
19. 1 Kings 7.2.
20. 1 Kings 7.3.
21. 1 Kings 7.4-5.
22. 1 Kings 7.4-5.
23. 1 Kings 7.4.
24. 1 Kings 7.5.
25. 1 Kings 7.6.
26. 1 Kings 7.7-8.
27. 1 Kings 7.9-12.
28. 1 Kings 7.15-22.
29. 1 Kings 7.23.
30. Schwaller de Lubicz EM 67.
31. 1 Kings 7.23.
32. 1 Kings 7.25.
33. 1 Kings 7.27-37.
34. 1 Kings 7.38 (Oxford).
35. 1 Kings 7.40.
36. 1 Kings 8.
37. 1 Kings 8.11.
38. Oxford 453, fn.4.
39. 2 Chron. 3.6-7.
40. 1 Kings 7.41; 2 Chron. 4.12 (Oxford).

Chapter Ten

Sumerians, Persians, Babylonians, and Assyrians

"KISS" is the acronym for "keep it simple, stupid," advice which your author has accepted from a friend. We must search through the writings and archaeological debris of the Sumerians, Babylonians, Assyrians, Persians, East Indians, Egyptians, Africans, Sea People, Greeks, Romans, Teutons, Celts, and American Indians to determine whether their cultures might have been influenced by the Holy Grail. The time span is from 5,000 B.C. to the present. Necessarily, we only can study brief excerpts from their writings, and glance at a few objects of clay, stone, or metal from the cultural treasure houses of these ancient people. We *must* keep it simple.

We shall attempt to satisfy two conflicting demands. Enough data must be presented to convince academicians and lay persons who specialize in these (and other) cultures that they should expend their time and resources using the skills they have acquired from this book to make in-depth studies within their areas of specialization. Most data must be avoided — to convince nonspecialized readers that they should read the next few chapters, although they may have no interest in the cultures to which they relate. We have resolved our conflicts in past chapters, and should not allow our cultural preferences and blind spots to keep us from attaining the Holy Grail.

The Tigris River rises in eastern Turkey and flows southeasterly through Iraq, where it joins with the Euphrates River, which also rises in Turkey but flows through Syria southeasterly before it reaches Iraq. The two rivers of the "Cradle of Civilization" join together in southeastern Iraq to form the Shatt al Arab, which is joined by other waters from Iran before it reaches the Persian Gulf. Along and between the tributaries of this immense watercourse, archaeologists have uncovered clay bowls and other objects which attract our interest because of their shapes and decorations. These items have been dated to the period of approximately 5,000 B.C. to 3,000 B.C. We shall not learn the names assigned to these people by the archaeologists because the names give us no clue as to who these people were, or from whence they came; hence, would be excess baggage to carry with us on our quest.

Turn back to Figure 169, which represents the bowl-shaped capitals and networks on the tops of the columns Jachin and Boaz of the Temple of Solomon. Visualize Figure 169 as representing the network whose points reach up to, and touch, the rim of the bowl which appears in the story of the table. Now look at Illustration 7-2, where we saw a round bowl painted with a concave-sided tetragon whose four points reach up to, and touch, the rim of the bowl.[1] A mere coincidence? Notice the tripartite cross in the center of the bowl in Illustration 7-2, and the single cross in the center of the bowl in **Figure 170**. Notice the cross (white on dark background) surrounded by a trinity of dark rings in the center of the bowl in **Illustration 10-1**.[2] From the outside decorative ring in the center of the bowl in Illustration 10-1 radiate five triple sets of wavy lines. Could this decoration have been intended to

Illustration 10-1. A pre-Sumerian bowl. J.C. Hinrichs Verlag, Leipzig.

Figure 170

represent the sun, surrounded by corona rings, casting its rays out across the dome of the sky? How shall we interpret the comb-shaped decorations on both of these bowls? Were they designs to please the women? Or were they an index by which rotary motion around the rims of the bowls could be measured, much as right ascension along the Ecliptic is measured on a modern German equatorial telescope mount? Is this a system for measuring degrees around a circle? Were these two bowls used as containers for food or drink, or for some other purpose?

For what other purpose could these bowls have been used? We should look at a few lines from a Babylonian hymn to the sun of *later* years. The numbers at the left margin are the lines of the hymn, which will indicate omitted lines and let you find these lines in the original.

1. Illuminator [. . .] the heavens,
2. Who lightens the darkness [. . .] in upper and lower regions;
5. Your beams like a net cover [. . .]
17. Illuminator, dispeller of darkness of the *vault* of the heavens,
18. Who sets aglow the *beard* of light, the corn field, the life of the land.
22. You suspend from the heavens the circle of the lands.
25. Whatever has breath you shepherd without exception,
26. You are their keeper in upper and lower regions.
27. Regularly and without cease you traverse the heavens,
28. Every day you pass over the broad earth.
33. Shepherd of that beneath, keeper of that above,
34. You, Samas, direct, you are the light of everything.
35. You never fail to cross the wide expanse of sea,
42. By night you continue to kindle.
43. To unknown distant regions for uncounted leagues.
44. You press on, Samas, going by day and returning by night.
53. [In] the seer's bowl with the cedar-wood appurtenance,

54. [You] *enlighten* the dream priests and interpret dreams.
87. Your wide net is spread [. . .]
149. You grant revelations, Samas, to the families of men,
150. Your harsh *face* and fierce light you give to them.
151. You manage their omens and preside over their sacrifices,
152. To all four points of the compass you probe their state.
153. So far as human habitations stretch, you grant revelations to them all.
154. The heavens are not enough as the vessel into which you gaze,
155. The sum of the lands is inadequate as a seer's bowl.[3]

Read that hymn again. Slowly. Think about each line. The author seems to believe that the sun is in motion, but his words prove nothing of the sort because we speak of the sun "coming up in the morning" although we know it is the Earth's rotation which causes the sun "to rise" and "to set." Note the inference that the author believes the sun travels continuously in a circular orbit, once daily around a round earth; that it does not "die" on the western horizon at night and is not "born again" the next morning on the eastern horizon, as the ancient Egyptian man-on-the-street is supposed to have believed. Note the seer's bowl and its wooden gnomon post, and its corresponding heavenly bowl into which the sun god gazes. The "Doctrine of Correspondences," under which things on Earth are thought to be copies corresponding to things in Heaven, will become particularly important when we study the Holy Grail as the heavenly model for earthly buildings constructed with vaults, arches, and domes. The references to the "net" of the sun and to the four points of the compass should not go unnoticed. Everyone seems to have discovered that a person should not look the sun in the face.[4] The dots in square brackets denote illegible words, resulting from damage to the clay tablet from which the translator provided us with this wonderful insight into the mind of an ancient Babylonian. The words in brackets are necessary in English grammar. As we noted earlier, the sun was one of their gods. Our religious leaders would call the author of this ancient hymn a pagan.

Before we return to the analysis of pre-Sumerian bowls, let us look at a few more lines of Babylonian "Wisdom Literature."

36. Who knows the will of the gods in heaven?

37. Who understands the plans of the underworld gods?

38. Where have mortals learnt the way of a god?[5]

From the god? From other mortals who profess to know the way of the god?

33. Who but Marduk restores his dead to life?

34. Apart from Sarpanitum which goddess grants life?

35. Marduk can restore life from the grave,

36. Sarpanitum knows how to save from destruction.[6]

Jesus saves?

254. O wise one, O savant, who masters knowledge,

255. In your anguish you blaspheme the god.

256. The divine mind, like the centre of the heavens, is remote;

257. Knowledge of it is difficult; the masses do not know it.

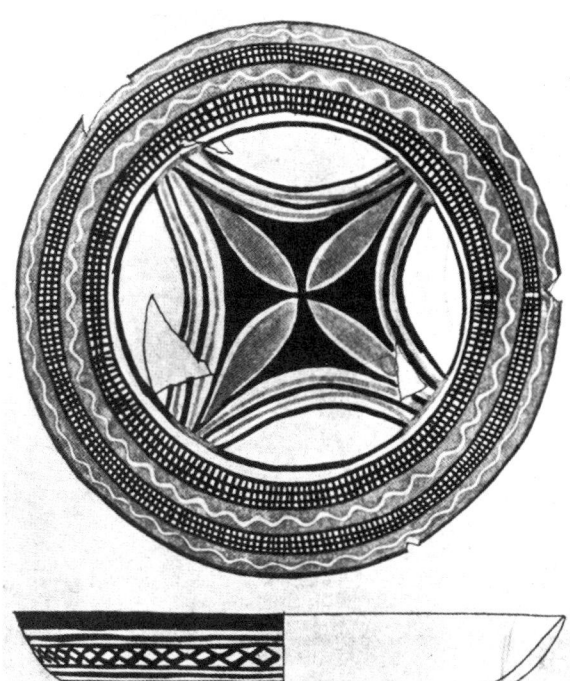

Illustration 10-2. A pre-Sumerian bowl. J.C. Hinrichs Verlag, Leipzig.

264. Though a man may observe what the will of the god is, the masses do not know it.[7]

The masses (Lions, Oxen, and Men) seem always to worship a humanform god who serves as their personal protector-provider; an "all-father" who looks after their material and spiritual needs, as do all father role-models. The Eagles seem always to seek God. In this book, we often "blaspheme" the little humanform on the Holy Grail as we learn about the many roles he has played in mythology. We do *not* blaspheme God. We seek God. We will not find Him, or Her, but we will come closer than do the masses.

Perhaps we are not so distant from the Babylonians as we might presume. One last bit of Babylonian wisdom before we go back to the bowls:

6. I have gone shares in business; loss is unending.[8]

Times change? People do not?

We already have discussed the fact that the four guardian stars which lie along the Ecliptic form a cross that orients the Zodiac in the sky. They were known as the Guardian Stars of Persia, and will be discussed more thoroughly when we consider scientific uses of the Holy Grail. Writers have suggested that Christians got more than the Cross from the astrology of the Zodiac. As example: "Indeed there is not an incident in the whole Christ story that is not written in the stars... by pagan Initiates... [T]he gospels follow minutely the pagan sequence. Within each sign lie the details; to mention only those pertinent to this point in the story, the first decanate of Leo is the Crater or Cup, the solar crucible; the second is Centaurus, the soldier on horseback.... The color symbol of the Centaurus decanate is purple, a sign of royalty.... [T]he second [decanate of Virgo] is Hercules, the Hellenic Christ, who died at this point from wearing the purple robe of the centaur Nessus. The last decanate of Virgo is a crown of thorns, Corona Borealis. 'Then came Jesus forth, wearing the crown of thorns, and the purple robe' (John 19:5)...."[9] Are these the ravings of a religious tract-writer, or could there be some "gum" to what he says? Was the Christ story divined from events which occur among the stars?

What do you see in the bottom of the bowl in **Illustration 10-2**?[10] Four "boat-shapes" around a tripartite concave-sided tetragon centered by one of our familiar Grail flowers? Could the border decorations — which look somewhat like railroad track — be used to measure degrees of rotation of one or more objects around the rim of the bowl? The

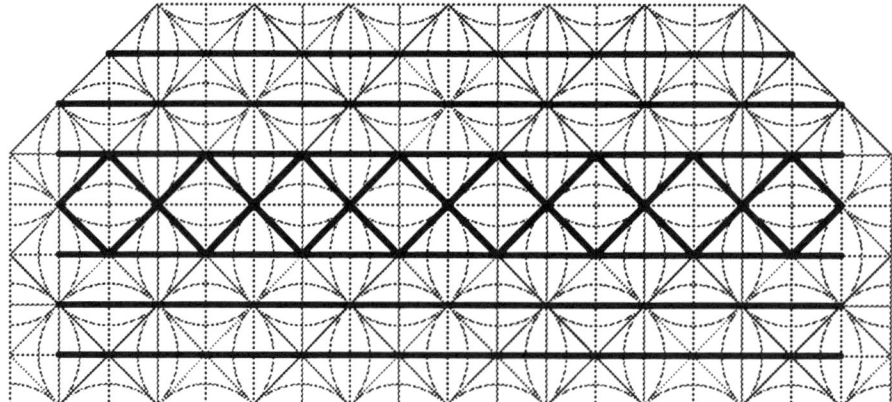

Figure 171

Illustration 10-3. Grail-form object from a pre-Sumerian archaeological dig. J.C. Hinrichs Verlag, Leipzig.

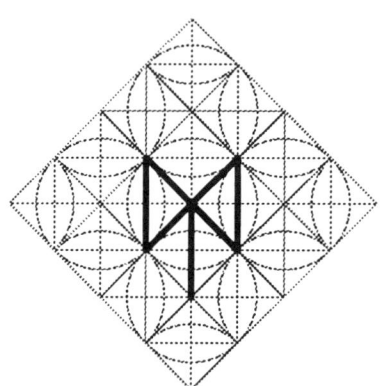

Figure 172

Illustration 10-4. A pre-Sumerian bowl. J.C. Hinrichs Verlag, Leipzig.

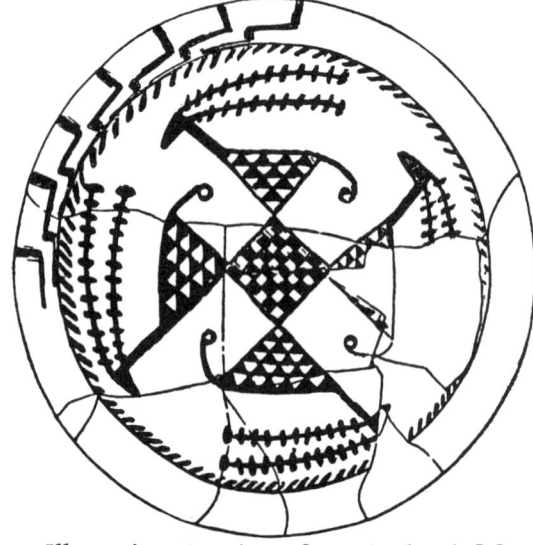

Illustration 10-5. A pre-Sumerian bowl. J.C. Hinrichs Verlag, Leipzig.

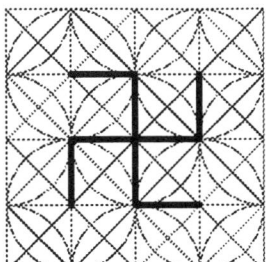

Figure 173

decorations on the side of the bowl in that photograph are seen in **Figure 171**. The "double-headed axe" in **Illustration 10-3**,[11] an ancient symbol for "god,"[12] is illustrated in **Figure 172**.

In **Illustration 10-4**,[13] four abstract birds are catching four abstract fish, while eight more abstract fish swim freely, the motion of all four birds and eight fish being to the left while a swastika, a solar symbol, rotates to the right. (If you are not aware that a swastika is a solar symbol and that a rightward-rotating swastika goes in the correct direction whereas a leftward-rotating swastika goes in the

incorrect direction, then please accept these statements as correct until, during our East Indian studies, we learn about swastikas and their correct direction of rotation.) Do the birds and fish illustrate the counterclockwise rotation of the Heavens? Does the swastika illustrate the clockwise rotation of the Earth? In **Figure 173**, we see a clockwise-rotating swastika centered on the Holy Grail.

In **Illustration 10-5**,[14] four abstract animals with long horns and curly tails rotate to the left along scribed lines which incline toward the animals' leftward rotation. Seven marks are around part of the bowl's rim. The pattern of triangles on the "bodies" of each of the animals is seen on the Holy Grail in **Figure 174**, and the "checkerboard" in the middle of the bowl is seen in **Figure 175**. Horns like these are seen in **Figure 176**. Store these forms in your memory until we study the cosmic mandala and tetractys.

Figure 175

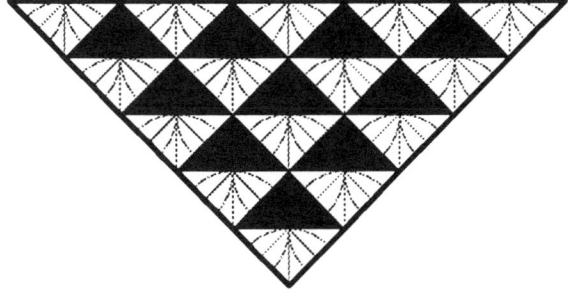

Figure 174

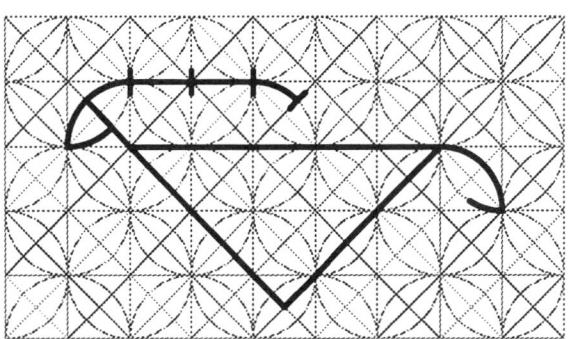

Figure 176

Figures 177, 178, 179, & 180
Clockwise from Left

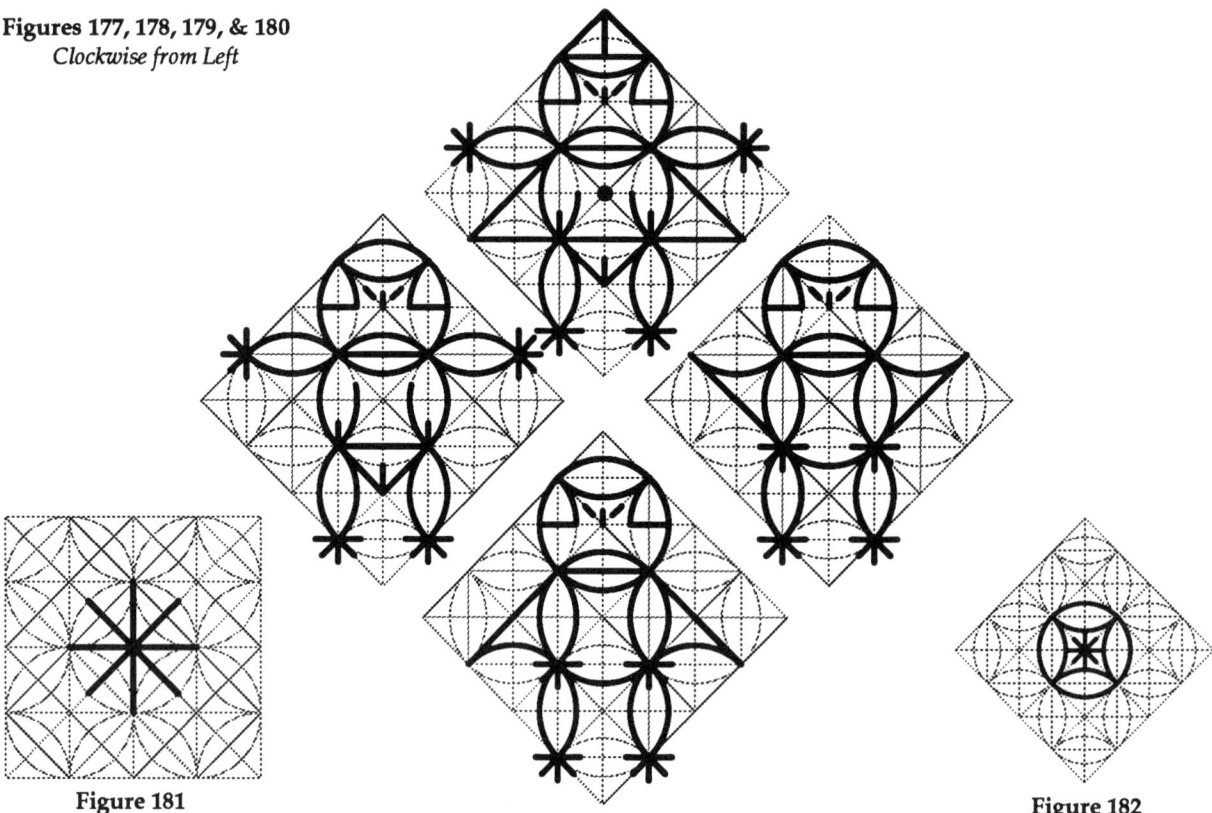

Figure 181

Figure 182

The clay figurine "earth mother," with her enormous football-shaped legs and breasts, shown in **Illustration 10-6**,[15] may be seen in **Figure 177**, where she is standing with her arms held straight out, horizontally, and with her pendulous breasts hanging down because she is not holding them up in her arms as in the photograph! Her breasts and pudendum are grossly exaggerated, but we shall have proof soon and later that the ancients saw her this way.

Illustration 10-6. A pre-Sumerian "mother earth goddess," illustrating her breasts and legs shaped like those of our Holy Grail womanform. J.C. Hinrichs Verlag, Leipzig.

The Sumerians considered the sun, moon, planets, and stars to be gods.[16] They were some of the first people to study mathematical astronomy and to dabble in astrological lore, although only a few specifics are known about their studies of those subjects.[17] May we speculate that they learned some of this from the early people whose discarded pottery we have been observing? Circular motions are illustrated on these bowls. Whether these early people believed the Earth rotated clockwise, or that the Heavens and the sun rotated counterclockwise, we cannot say with certainty based upon the evidence we have examined. We can wonder from the evidence whether Aristarchus of Samos may not have been the first sky-watcher to consider a theory of heliocentricity! Certainly, we should not accept as an article of faith the notion that no person could have entertained such thoughts before the "heretics" Copernicus, Galileo, and Kepler! [18]

The book from which these photographs were taken is written in German, which your author cannot read, but that does not matter, because we can "read" these Grail images. This is the wonderful thing about symbols: we may communicate by

Illustration 10-7. Early Sumerian pictograph for "star," "heaven," or "god."

Illustration 10-8. Early Sumerian pictograph for "Earth," i.e., the planet not the soil.

Illustration 10-9. Early Sumerian pictograph for "woman."

Illustration 10-10. Early Sumerian pictograph for "mountain."

Illustrations 10-7 through 10-10 courtesy of the University of Chicago Press, Chicago.

symbols with persons far separated from us in time, culture, and language.

During archaeological digs at Tel Halif, in modern Turkey, dome-shaped rock buildings were uncovered which connect with rectangular structures only slightly longer, along their long axis, than the diameter of the domes. Their ground plan is that of a Roman or Christian cross.[19] They resemble the internal rock structures of some of the cruciform "passage graves" found in Greece and in Ireland; notably, Newgrange in Ireland.[20] They also resemble the domed monastery buildings which stand on Skellig Michael, an escarpment of rock which lies in the Atlantic Ocean a few miles off the west coast of Ireland.[21] Anchorite monks followed the Egyptian Christian ritual rather than the Roman Catholic ritual while cloistered in those rock domes on the Skelligs.[22] We must withhold discussion of these remarkable buildings until we reach our Irish studies and our scientific studies.

Before considering some Sumerian, Babylonian, and Assyrian stories, let us glance for a moment at the Babylonian-Hebrew demoness Lilith,[23] who, in

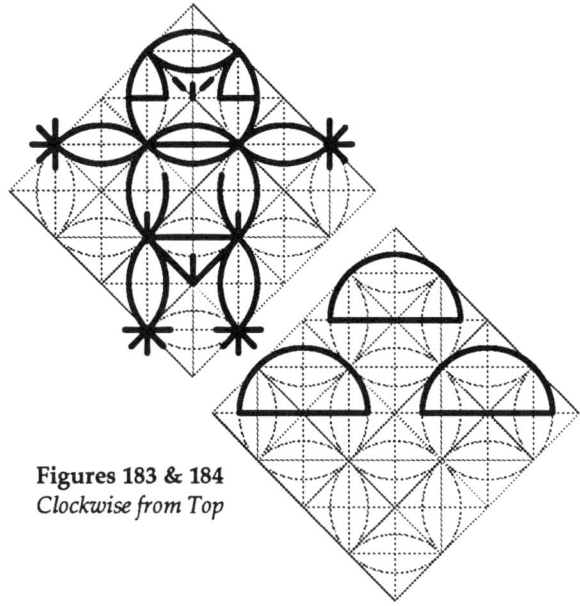

Figures 183 & 184
Clockwise from Top

Hebrew legends outside the Old Testament, was Adam's first wife, until he divorced her because she would not engage in "missionary position" sexual intercourse with him, which would have required her to be beneath him.[24] She has Grail wings in downward position only, and the talons of a raptor. She is a woman-owl. **Figure 178.** In **Figure 179**, we see our Grail humanform in his usual "wings up" position. In **Figure 180**, we see his customary "wings down" stance.

The eight-pointed symbol for the goddess Inanna,[25] later was used in icons of Mary, Our Lady, Mother of Jesus.[26]

Stanley Noah Kramer, an eminent Sumerologist, tells us that the Sumerians first began to write by use of pictographs around 3000 B.C.[27] **Illustration 10-7** is the earliest Sumerian symbol for "heaven" or for "god." Kramer says it represents a star.[28] It appears dead-center on the Holy Grail in **Figure 181.** Shall we henceforth think of "god" in "heaven" when we see that symbol? Our sun is a star, and it lies at the apparent center of our own solar system, just as this star symbol lies in the middle of the Holy Grail. Shall we ignore that as a coincidence? The polestar lies at the Earth's rotational center of the sky. Shall we ignore that as a coincidence? **Illustration 10-8** is the earliest Sumerian symbol for "Earth."[29] Four of these "Earth" symbols around a "god" symbol form one Ezekiel Wheel on the Holy Grail! See **Figure 182.** Shall we ignore that as a coincidence? **Illustration 10-9** is the earliest Sumerian symbol for "woman." Kramer says it represents a female *pudendum*. It is to be found on the Holy Grail on our humanform at the proper location for the female *pudendum*, albeit somewhat exaggerated in size. See **Figure 183.** In an Irish story we study later, we are told that her "lower hair" hangs down to her knees, and so it does! **Illustration 10-10** is the earliest Sumerian symbol for "mountain."[30] It appears on the Holy Grail in **Figure 184.**

Do you recall our Grail figure of Moses on the mountain with the two tablets of the Ten

Commandments in his arms? **Figure 185**. "The earlier Bibles say that Moses, when he came down from the mount, had horns on his head, as Michelangelo portrays him. The authors of the King James Version, believing this to be an error, made it read 'the skin of his face shone'.... Modern scholars believe it should read *rays* rather than *horns*...."[31] The choice is yours. In **Figure 186**, we see short "horns" arising from our little man's head, as in Michelangelo's portrayal of Moses, whereas in **Figure 187**, we see our Grail man's face "rayed" or "shining" because it is centered by the Sumerian pictograph for "star" or "god." Our manform has been "sun-struck" in a pictographical sense! Read the contents of note 4 of this chapter if you want to consider an hypothesis as to which god was the God of Moses.

We have seen a sampling of early Sumerian writing. Now we must move on to a famous Sumerian, Babylonian, and Assyrian tale about the demi-god Gilgamesh and his visit with a man whom the Sumerians called Ziusudra, the later Babylonians and Assyrians called Utnapishtim, and the even later Hebrews called Noah. This is the story of the flood.

Gilgamesh's companion, Enkidu, is dead, and Gilgamesh laments Enkidu's death and fears his own. He seeks Utnapishtim, who has attained immortality, to learn from him how to conquer death. He comes to a barmaid, who evidently is

Figure 185

Figure 186

Figure 187

beside a cosmic "sea," which is the border between the world where Gilgamesh lives and the otherworld of Utnapishtim. Gilgamesh tells the barmaid: "May I not see death, which I dread!"[32] We pick up the epic with her response:

1. "Gilgamesh, whither runnest thou?
2. The life which thou seekest thou wilt not find;
3. (For) when the gods created mankind,
4. They allotted death to mankind,
5. (But) life they retained in their keeping.
6. Thou, O Gilgamesh, let thy belly be full;
7. Day and night be thou merry;
8. Make every day (a day of) rejoicing.
9. Day and night do thou dance and play.
10. Let thy raiment be clean,
11. Thy head be washed, (and) thyself be bathed in water.
12. Cherish the little one holding thy hand,
13. (And) let the wife rejoice in thy bosom.
14. This is the lot of [mankind...]."[33]

The remainder of the Old Babylonian tablet is broken away. We pick up the story on an Assyrian tablet, which tells the same tale. Gilgamesh has found Urshanabi, the boatman of Utnapishtim, and he asks him to ferry him across the "sea" to Utnapishtim, after telling him about the loss of his friend and his personal fear of death.[34] Gilgamesh meets and talks with Utnapishtim, who tells Gilgamesh the story of the flood as follows:

1. Gilgamesh said to him, to Utnapishtim the Distant:
2. "I look upon thee, Utnapishtim,
3. Thine appearance is not different; thou art like unto me.
4. Yea, thou art not different; thou art like unto me.
5. My heart had pictured thee as one perfect for the doing of battle;
6. [But] thou liest (idly) on (thy) side, (or) thy back."[35]

Turn to **Figure 188**, where we see Utnapishtim lying on his back and side!

7. [Tell me], how didst thou enter into the company of the gods and obtain life (everlasting)?"
8. Utnapishtim said to him, to Gilgamesh:

9. "Gilgamesh, I will reveal unto thee a hidden thing,
10. Namely, a secret of the gods will I tell thee.
11. Shurippak — a city which thou knowest,
12. [And which] is situated [on the bank of] the river Euphrates–
13. That city was (already) old, and the gods were in its midst.
14. (Now) their heart prompted the great gods [to] bring a deluge."[36]

The names of the "great gods" then are enumerated.[37] We learn that the gods are tired of listening to the noisy prattle and petty arguments in which residents of the city are engaged — a reaction not unlike that which parents experience when listening to rancor among their children! To regain a little peace and quiet, the gods, led by Enlil, have decided to get rid of the city and its inhabitants. But one of the gods, Ea, decides to tell Utnapishtim of the impending flood.[38] We rejoin the story:

23. "Man of Shurippak, son of Ubara-Tutu!
24. Tear down (thy) house, build a ship!
25. Abandon (thy) possessions, seek (to save) life!
26. Disregard (thy) goods, and save (thy) life!
27. [Cause to] go up into the ship the seed of all living creatures.
28. The ship which thou shalt build,
29. Its measurements shall be (accurately) measured;
30. Its width and its length shall be equal."[39]

Utnapishtim agrees to follow Ea's commands, then asks:

Figure 188

35. "[But what] shall I answer the city, the people and the elders?"[40]

Ea tells Utnapishtim to tell the city dwellers and their leaders that he may no longer dwell in the city; that he must go to dwell with Ea while the rains and the floods come to the city. At morning's first light, Utnapishtim gathers pitch and whatever else is needful to build his craft. He provides food and drink for the craftsmen, and the ship is constructed in the form of a cube.[41]

81. "Whatever I had of silver I loaded aboard her;

82. Whatever I [had] of gold I loaded aboard her;

83. Whatever I had of the seed of all living creatures [I loaded] aboard her.

84. After I had caused all my family and relations to go up into the ship,

85. I caused the game of the field, the beasts of the field, (and) all the craftsmen to go (into it)."[42]

The Babylonians and Assyrians knew from whence came their high civilizations — the craftsmen! They, too, were to be saved!

91. I viewed the appearance of the weather;

92. The weather was frightful to behold.

93. I entered the ship and closed my door.

97. A black cloud came up from out the horizon.

98. Adad [the storm god] thunders within it,

101. Irragal [god of the underworld] pulls out the masts;

102. Ninurta [god of wells and irrigation] causes the dikes to give way;

103. The Annunaki [judges of the underworld] raised their torches,

104. Lighting up the land with their brightness;

127. Six days and [six] nights,

128. The wind blew, the downpour, the tempest, (and) the flo[od] overwhelmed the land.

129. When the seventh day arrived, the tempest, the flood,

130. Which had fought like an army, subsided in (its) onslaught.

131. The sea grew quiet, the storm abated, the flood ceased.

140. On Mount Nisir the ship landed.[43]

For six days, the ship stood fast on Mount Nisir.[44]

145. When the seventh day arrived,

146. I sent forth a dove and let (her) go.

147. The dove went away and came back to me;

148. There was no resting-place, and so she returned.

149. (Then) I sent forth a swallow and let (her) go.

150. The swallow went away and came back to me;

151. There was no resting-place, and so she returned.

152. (Then) I sent forth a raven and let (her) go.

153. The raven went away, and when she saw that the waters had abated,

154. She ate, she flew about, she cawed (and) did not return.

155. (Then) I sent forth (everything) to the four winds and offered a sacrifice."[45]

The gods smelled the sweet savor of the sacrifice and came to accept it, but they denied Enlil any of the offerings because it was he who had brought on the deluge to destroy the people. The god Ea spoke for the gods, saying, toward the end of his declamation,

193. "Hitherto Utnapishtim has been but a man;

194. But now Utnapishtim and his wife shall be like unto us gods.

195. In the distance, at the mouth of the rivers, Utnapishtim shall dwell!"[46]

Gilgamesh falls asleep. When he awakes, Utnapishtim has arranged for his boatman, Urshanabi, to take Gilgamesh back to his world. On the way back to Gilgamesh's world, Urshanabi tells Gilgamesh of the secret of the gods, a plant with which an old man becomes young again. Gilgamesh removes the pelts he wears, dives into the water, brings up the plant from the bottom, then bathes in the clear water. A snake comes up, eats the plant, and that, my friends, is why snakes are able to shed their skin and thereby become renewed![47]

We just have encountered one of the principal purposes of myth — to explain observable phenomena. Snakes shed their skins and become renewed thereby (observable) because their mythological prototype ate the plant of life (mythological explanation).

Would you believe that the Babylonians and Assyrians were fond of puns in their myths? Enlil, who was responsible for the flood, was known as "the Great Mountain." Rainfall in the mountains upstream causes the Euphrates River to rise downstream. Enlil, as personification of this natural

Figure 189

Figure 190

Figure 191

phenomenon, therefore caused the flood! The myth teaches that tidbit of natural science, wrapped in holy mythology.

Compare the Babylonian and Assyrian version of the myth with the later Hebrew story.[48] The Hebrew story discarded the moral of the earlier myth: that mankind should be grateful for, and enjoy, what God has given us — food, beer, wives, and children. The Babylonians believed that becoming like unto a god was for *some* mortals, not *all* mortals, according to the whim of the gods. Christianity and Islam later promised that *everyone* who would give up the beer, the wife, and the child, and die for the Faith would live the good life with God forever. Teaching that doctrine was an excellent way to raise an army for wars against the Moslem "heathens" and the Christian "infidels," that is, to teach man to kill man in the name of God. For the sake of the sheep? Or for the sake of the shepherds?

The doctrine still serves that purpose in modern Lebanon and Iraq for the recruiting of "holy warriors" to kill the "infidel." We should ask ourselves whether this change in religious philosophy was for the better.

Where are the Grail images in the Utnapishtim story? You should be able to find the man and woman images, the bird images, the cat images, and the ox images for yourself by now. In later chapters, we will see **Figure 189** being used as the image of an ass, mule, donkey, or horse; **Figure 190** being used as the image of a cow; and **Figure 191** being used as the image of a bull. We already have found the animal pelts in the story of the Tent of the Presence. Gilgamesh is seen wearing a pelt across his chest in **Figure 192**. Utnapishtim's boat, a perfect cube, is the Holy Grail itself! In later chapters we will find **Figure 193** being used as the image of a river. The outer two lines are the riverbanks, and

Figure 192

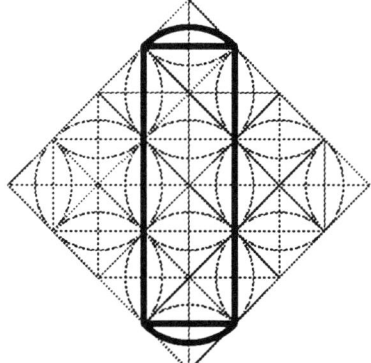

Figure 193

Figure 194

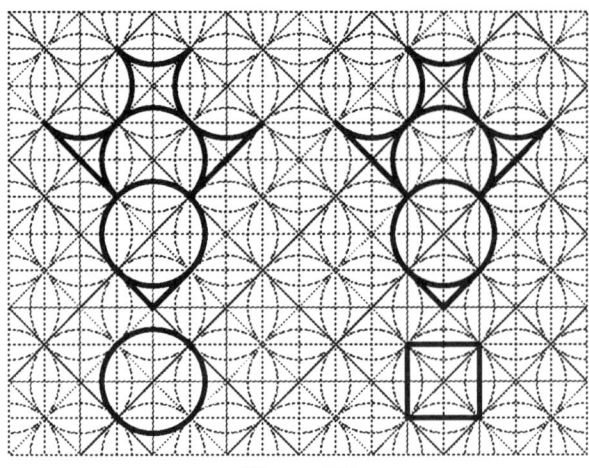

Figure 195

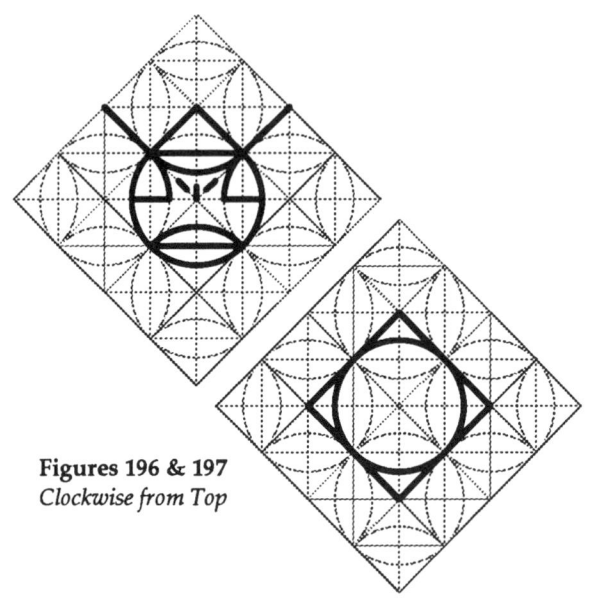

Figures 196 & 197
Clockwise from Top

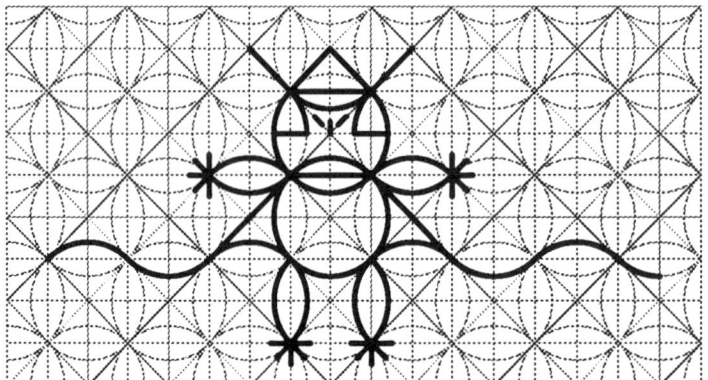

Figure 198

the round circle segments at each end are flat-perspective representations of the rounded bottom of the river. We learned that Utnapishtim stands at the end of the river. He stands at the end of the river in **Figure 194**. The birds flying down to water or earth are illustrated in **Figure 195**. The image of the ascending and descending dove assumes supreme importance when we study Christian symbols derived from the Holy Grail.

Babylonian and Assyrian mythmakers visualized many varieties of gods whose bodies were part lion, ox, man, and eagle.[49] They delighted in the various combination-critters they could dream up by mixing the heads, bodies, legs, and feet of these four Grail creatures. One such myth commands our attention because it invites comparison with the Tabernacle and Temple stories.

Gudea, the head man of a Babylonian city-state, "saw a gigantic man with a divine crown, with wings like a great bird, and with a body which ended below in a floodwave. To the right and left of this man, lions were lying. The man commanded

Gudea to build his temple. Then day broke on the horizon. Next, a woman emerged and proceeded to raze a building plot. In her hand was a stylus of gold and a clay tablet on which constellations of stars were set down; these she studied. Then came a warrior who held a tablet of lapis lazuli upon which he sketched the plan of a house. Before Gudea stood a brick mold and a basket; bird-men unceasingly poured water into a trough; and a male donkey to the right of the god was impatiently pawing the ground."[50] The story goes on to say that the god did more than decree the building of a temple by Gudea. The god also decreed the introduction of laws and customs to regulate the community.[51] Does this sound somewhat familiar?[52]

Here come the Grail images: The divine crown is seen in front view in **Figure 196**, and is seen in top view in **Figure 197**. We shall discuss the divine crown in detail later. The crowned gigantic man with bird wings and a body which ended below a floodwave is seen in **Figure 198**. Day breaking on the horizon is shown in Illustration 8-2, which should be compared with **Figure 199**. The woman with the stylus and tablet appears in **Figure 200**. (Visualize the man with tablet for yourself.) Note that a Sumerian "star" symbol appears on her tablet. We shall wait until the science chapters to appreciate the fact that the Holy Grail is the building plan for many religious structures, including Christian cathedrals, and a grid for dividing the sky. The brick mold appears in **Figure 201**. A basket, seen from top view, appears in **Figure 202**, and the same

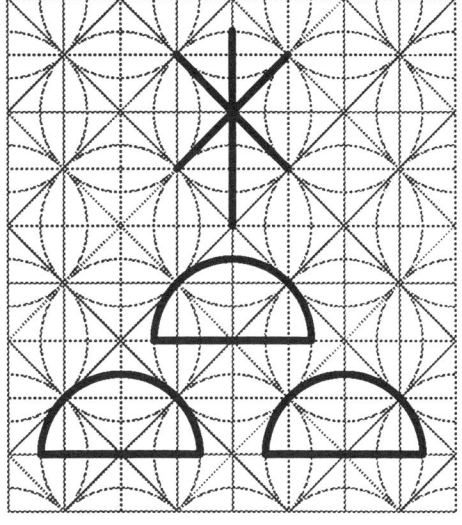

Figure 199

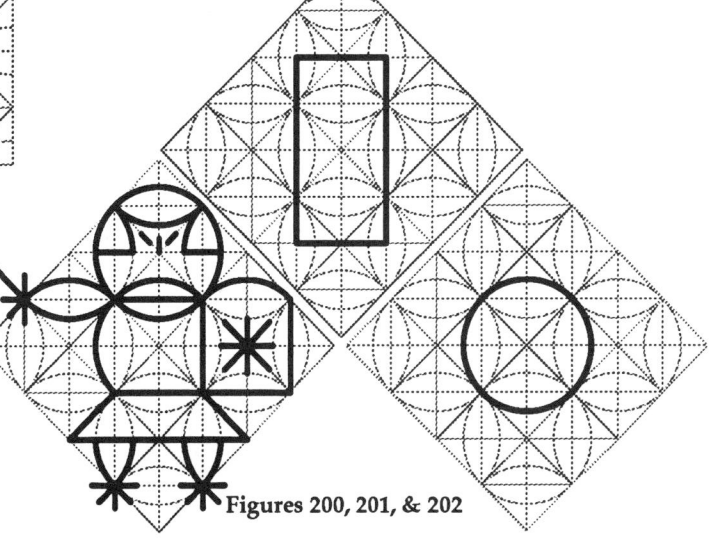

Figures 200, 201, & 202

basket appears in side view in **Figure 203**. A bird-man appears in **Figure 204**. He is pouring water from a pitcher into a trough. Another pitcher is bolded separately, below him, to help you unravel the lines of that complex image. A donkey appears in **Figure 205**.

We could study many more Babylonian myths, but we must move on to the images of other cultures.

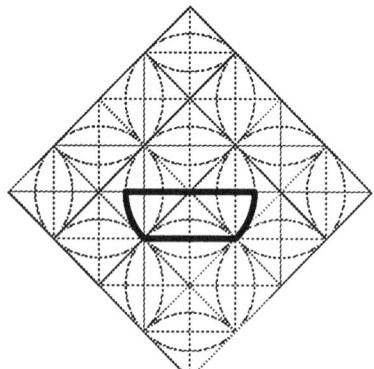

Figure 203

Figure 204

Figure 205

Notes
CHAPTER TEN. Sumerians, Persians, Babylonians, and Assyrians

1. Moortgat Tafel 17.

2. Moortgat Tafel 17.

3. Lambert 127-135.

4. Exodus 33.20-23. The ancients learned that the sun's reverse image safely could be viewed by allowing the sun's rays to pass through a narrow opening in or between rocks, and to fall upon a rock surface. Examples of such sun-viewing stations, which were used by tribal shamans to establish the arrival of the solstices or equinoxes, are to be found in North America. Krupp 126-156. Exodus 33.20-23 describes this technique. The shaman stands at a predetermined location. "[T]hou shalt stand upon a rock." Exodus 33.21. The sun's rays penetrate between the rocks or through the man-made hole. "[W]hile my glory passeth by... I will put thee in a clift of the rock." Exodus 33.22. Oxford uses the word "crevice" instead of "clift." Exodus 33.22. The shaman views the reverse image of the sun projected onto a rock. "[A]nd thou shall see my back parts: but my face shall not be seen." Exodus 33.23. We shall discuss this technique of solar observation in detail in the science chapters of this book. Another way to view the "sun god" is to watch his "back parts" as "they" go over the western horizon, i.e., to view the sunset.

5. Lambert 41.

6. Lambert 59.

7. Lambert 87.

8. Lambert 278.

9. Graham 354-355.

10. Moortgat Tafel 4.

11. Moortgat Tafel 4. Is this "axe-head" not an axe-head at all but a stereotypical representation of a human internal organ? Does it represent the lungs of our Grail humanform? Before male-dominated, Indo-European culture and religion reached Europe, did this "axe-head" symbol represent a butterfly that emerged from a bull's skull, an epiphany of the "great goddess" in her regenerative aspect? Gimbutas 270-275. You should be able to see for yourself among the lines of the Holy Grail such a butterfly emerging from a bull's skull, a symbol of life following death. Gimbutas discusses motion-oriented ceramic designs (including spirals, whirls, and combs) and suggests their possible relationship to apparent astral movements along the Zodiac, and to phases of the moon. Gimbutas 279-303. Is Gimbutas' "fat lady" avatar of the "great goddess" our Holy Grail womanform? See Gimbutas, generally. Does Gimbutas show her readers photographs of the Holy Grail, cast in ceramics? Gimbutas 297. Was Holy Grail astronomy known in Europe before the Indo-Europeans arrived? Many questions need answers!

12. Service & Bradbery 42; Spanuth 109-112.

13. Moortgat 31.

14. Moortgat 32.

15. Moortgat Tafel 5.

16. Kramer 122-123; Wolkstein ix-xix.

17. Kramer 90-91.

18. Dreyer 310-311. Kepler's mother was tried by the Church for witchcraft in 1620. The records of the trial are extant. Robbins 544. Galileo was tried by the Church and threatened with the death penalty if he did not recant his theories of astronomy. Dreyer 416. It was dangerous to speak contrary to Christian dogmas about *science*, as well as about the historicity of the Christ story.

19. Moortgat 26; Lloyd 75.

20. McMann 24.

21. Lavelle 27, 45-51.

22. O'Shea 10.

23. Wolkstein 6, 179. A clay plaque from the Old Babylonian period of 2000-1600 B.C. illustrates Lilith wearing a hat or crown as in Figure 178, and with wings as in that Figure. Wolkstein 6, 179. Scholars have identified Lilith as the "owl" of Isaiah 34.11. Wolkstein 179.

24. Graves & Patai 12, 65-69.

25. Wolkstein 60.

26. Beckwith 327.

27. Kramer 302, 304.

28. Kramer 302, 304.

29. Kramer 302, 304.

30. Kramer 302, 304.

31. Graham 149; Exodus 34.29-30, 35.

32. Heidel 70.

33. Heidel 70.

34. Heidel 71-77.

35. Heidel 80.

36. Heidel 80.

37. Heidel 80.

38. Heidel 80-81.

39. Heidel 81.

40. Heidel 81.

41. Heidel 82-83.

42. Heidel 84.

43. Heidel 84-86.

44. Heidel 86.

45. Heidel 86-87.

46. Heidel 88.

47. Heidel 88-93.

48. Genesis 6.5-8.22.

49. Heidel 133.

50. Frankfort 189-190.

51. Frankfort 191.

52. Exodus 25.8, et seq.; Exodus 35.1, et seq.

Chapter Eleven

Persians, Mandaeans, and Zoroastrians

So much to cover in so few pages. We must be brief, even cursory, in our analysis. Readers would profit from a study of the Saint John Christians, sometimes called the Mandaeans or Nasoraeans, a sect of gnostics who regard Jesus Christ as a false messiah, consider John the Baptist their holy prophet, and cling to ancient fertility rites and sky-worship as aspects of their faith. Saint John Christians still exist in Near Eastern Countries around the Fertile Crescent. Look them up in your encyclopedia. They regard the polestar as a central sun around which all the heavenly bodies sail on the celestial ocean. "Wearing a jewelled crown, ... [the polestar] stands before Abathur's door at the gate of the world of light; the Mandaeans accordingly invariably pray with their faces turned northward."[1] Note the reference to the cosmic "gate." The ancient Hebrews also revered the north. Was there a time when the religions of the Near East could recall their common origins? When they did not regard each other with such disgust and hatred?

Nearly everyone knows that Moslems are obligated to make at least one pilgrimage to Mecca during their lives. There, they walk in vast numbers in a circle around the *Kaaba*, a square building representing the cosmic "rock," which was on that very spot before there was an Islamic faith. The *Kaaba*, by tradition, was first built in Heaven, then on Earth, for Adam, Seth, Abraham, and others of the patriarchs. We are told that the *Kaaba* was an ancient Sabaean temple, the ancestors of the present-day Moslems having been sky-worshiping baptists before Mohammed converted them to Islam; that Arab astronomers knew the polestar as Al Kaukab al Shamaliyy, the word Kaukab being the same word as the Assyrio-Chaldean word Kakkab or the Hebrew word Kohabh, which we know these days as Cochab, as in Bar Cochab, "son of a star," the name of the leader of the famous Jewish revolt against the Roman Emperor Hadrian.[2] We have more in common with each other than our religious leaders are willing for us to know!

There, we did it! We made our point without getting ourselves mired up in a study of ancient celestial religions and their modern-day counterparts!

We already have mentioned the stars Regulus, Aldebaran, Fomalhaut, and Antares. When our Grail stories were being conceived, these stars were located, respectively, in the constellations Lion, Bull, Waterbearer (i.e., Man), and Eagle; whereas, these days, Fomalhaut lies in the Southern Fishes, and Antares in the Scorpion. Lion, Ox, Man, and Eagle were known as the "Four Royal Stars" of Persia or the "Four Guardians of Heaven."[3] The Christian Church later used them as symbols for the Four Evangelists: Matthew, Mark, Luke, and John.[4] Their right ascensions (a term of mathematical astronomy) are about six hours apart, so they evidently were used by all of the ancients from the Fertile Crescent to India "to mark the early equinoctial and solstitial colures, four great circles in the sky, or generally the four quarters of the heavens."[5] Four circles in the sky? There are four circles on the Holy Grail, surmounted by a fifth circle!

A story was told in ancient Persia (modern Iran) about a fabulous structure known as the Takt-i-Taqdis, or Throne of Arches, constructed by King Chosroes II to house the True Cross on which Christ was crucified.[6] A large, circular, walled ruin with a central lake has been identified by some writers as the remains of the Takt.[7] Other writers have compared the Grail Castle of the Grail quest stories with the Takt. The Grail Castle also has been "located" in the British Isles *and* in Southern France.[8] The four circles of the Heavens, discussed in the last paragraph, are one thing; stories like these may be something else.

It has been suggested that the Takt was built on the most sacred spot in the entire realm of King Chosroes II, that is, on the holy mountain of Shiz in Iran.[9] Another sacred building on a sacred mountain! The Persian religion-founder Zoroaster reputedly was born there.[10] The Grail scholar John

Matthews tells us that: "Like the Grail temple, it [the Takt] was domed, roofed with gold and lined with blue stones to represent the sky. There were stars, sun and moon, astrological and astronomical charts outlined in jewels, balustrades covered with gold, golden stair-cases and rich hangings, all resembled the temple of the Grail. The whole structure of the Takt was built above a hidden pit in which teams of horses walked round and round causing the building to revolve with the seasons and to help the calculation of astrological and astronomical observances. This recalls the turning castles of Celtic myth, themselves often repositories for sacred objects, as well as the turning island upon which the Grail King Nasciens found himself, as described in Robert de Borron's *Joseph*, written over six hundred years after the Takt had been razed to the ground."[11] We need not concern ourselves with whether the Takt was fact or fantasy. It is enough for our purposes that legends exist of a fabulous structure, used to survey the skies, turned by teams of horses. The Holy Grail has four "horses," as does the Revelation of Saint John the Divine, a document written by gnostics.[12] We shall see the circle in the middle of the Holy Grail, previously referred to as the "sea," being called the "pit." We learn about the "pit" in this chapter.

Who was Zoroaster and what sort of religion did he found? He was an Iranian prophet who fathered a religion named Zoroastrianism about the year 1500 B.C. The Zoroastrian religion still exists, principally in and around Bombay, India, where the people are known as Parsis. The central theme of the religion is a conflict between good and evil, or light and darkness. Zoroastrianism teaches that there will be a final battle between good and evil during which the latter apparently will prevail. "Then a virgin bathing in a lake will be impregnated by the seed of Zoroaster, preserved there, and the final saviour, Saoshyans, will be born. He will raise all the dead and assemble the court for the final judgment. The wicked will be returned to hell, whence they came, to be purged of their bodily sin. Then all will pass through a stream of molten metal, to prove the righteousness of all. The heavenly and demonic forces will wrestle in combat until the powers of evil are annihilated and Ahriman [the devil] himself is rendered eternally impotent. The world will be perfected as the mountains are laid low and the valleys filled up. Ohrmazd [the creator god] and the saviour will offer in sacrifice the last animal to die in the service of man, and from that

rite all men will receive the elixir of immortality. Heaven will descend to the moon and the earth will ascend to the moon, and all men will dwell in perfection with Ohrmazd forever."[13] Christians will understand why their religious leaders remain silent about Zoroastrianism! Is Christianity as "unique" in its doctrines as Christian leaders adamantly claim?

In Zoroastrianism, it is said that Ohrmazd created Gayomard, an archetypal man, who was immortal, sinless, happy, and without need, like the Hebrew Adam, and the primeval bull, whose sacrifice was the source of all animal and plant life.[14] The ancient Zoroastrian palace at Persepolis is decorated with lions attacking bulls, "perhaps symbolizing the sequence of the seasons."[15] Ahriman, the Zoroastrian devil, is symbolized by a snake.[16] The Garden of Eden had its snake-devil! Zoroastrianism and Mithraism are directly related to each other. When we study the mystery religions, we shall learn that Mithraism and Christianity were running neck to neck in a race for converts, and that Mithraism almost prevailed over Christianity.

How did the ancient Zoroastrians who were the contemporaries of the ancient Hebrews imagine and worship their god? They considered all buildings too small to house their formless god, who was represented by a sacred fire on a sacred mountaintop.[17] Ancient Hebrews and ancient Zoroastrians perhaps could have enjoyed a beer together at an ancient Babylonian tavern if their religious leaders had preached humanism rather than destructive ethnocentrism.

We need to know something about the death beliefs and rituals of Zoroastrians, so we will understand references to them found in the Grail quest story *Perlesvaus*, which we shall study in detail. Zoroastrians believe that if a person's good thoughts, words, and deeds outweigh his evil ones on the scales of justice, his soul is allowed to cross the Bridge of the Separator, whereas if an evil soul tries to cross the bridge, the pathway becomes narrow and the evil soul falls into hell, where the punishment is tailored to fit the crime — but from which *all* souls are freed after they have received sufficient punishment. A Zoroastrian priest comes to claim the body, bringing with him a dog to scare away anything evil. The body is left in a sacred building, preferably on a mountaintop, where the vultures consume the flesh and the bones are bleached white by the sun. The bones then are cast into a central pit.[18] The pit was much feared by Egyptians, Hebrews, and Christians. Other peoples'

religions always have something about them which makes them appear at least strange, if not positively disgusting. That goes for all of us, including Christians, who still practice ceremonial cannibalism.

Our Persian studies do not stop with this short chapter. To the contrary, you should expect to encounter references to Persian religion and culture throughout the remainder of this book. The total impact of Persian religion and culture upon Western society best can be understood incrementally, as we proceed, rather than by attempting to summarize all of it in this one chapter.

Notes
CHAPTER ELEVEN. Persians, Mandaeans, and Zoroastrians

1. Allen 456; 6 Encyclopaedia Britannica Micropaedia 555 (1974). The Koran tolerates "Sabians" like the Saint John Christians. Sura II.62.

2. Allen 457.

3. Allen 256, 345-346, 362-364, 385.

4. Cirlot 337-339. The Christian order runs like this: Matthew — the winged man; Mark — the winged lion; Luke — the winged ox; and John — the eagle.

5. Allen 256.

6. Matthews 57. Many "True Crosses" are held as relics by the Christian Church.

7. Matthews 23, 57.

8. Matthews 35, 56.

9. Matthews 23.

10. Matthews 23.

11. Matthews 23.

12. Revelation 6.

13. Cavendish 40-42.

14. Cavendish 41.

15. Cavendish 41.

16. Cavendish 43.

17. Cavendish 45.

18. Cavendish 43, 46-47.

Chapter Twelve

India and Pakistan:
Deep Wells of Cosmology

The Harappan civilization emerged after 2300 B.C. in the Indus River Valley of what is today modern Pakistan. Like the Sumerians and Egyptians, the Harappans practiced irrigation farming and raised domestic animals along a fertile river valley, upon whose fragile ecology they depended for their wealth if not their survival.[1] The Harappans erected their cities with fired bricks.[2] "[T]he evidence is overwhelming for town planning of a singularly advanced kind,"[3] which included streets laid out on a grid pattern, and spacious homes with bathrooms served by pottery pipes for fresh and waste water.[4] Enough said to show that the Harappans were technologists rivalling the Sumerians and Egyptians.

Harappan pottery showed the influence of southeastern Iran.[5] Left-spinning and right-spinning swastikas as popular pottery designs are indications that the apparent movements of the sun played some role in the thinking of these people.[6] Iranian potters also decorated their wares with the eight-pointed spoked symbol we have seen so often on the Holy Grail. Compare **Illustration 12-1**,[7] with **Figure 206**. The most popular pottery decoration of the Harappans was, however, the intersecting circle, yielding rosettes, or, when combined with chequers, the so-called stretched-hide motif.[8] Does that pattern sound familiar to you? See **Illustration 12-2**[9] and **Illustration 12-3**.[10] The eminent Oriental scholar V. Gordon Childe has stated the opinion that the Indus River civilization

must be regarded either as non-Aryan or pre-Aryan.[11]

The Aryans invaded the Indus River basin in about 1500 B.C. "The story has been repeated for millennia, sung in temples, chanted in halls, told by word and actions of how a warrior people came out of the vastness of inner Asia through the passes of the northwest to fall upon the fortified cities of India and to conquer; riding horse-drawn chariots, driving herds of cattle, sheep, and goats, worshipping cosmic deities like Indra of the thunder and Agni of the fire, sacrificing, quarreling, gambling, drinking, singing, dancing – the Rig-Veda account of the Aryan tribes is one of the oldest epics in the world. It is part of an oral tradition which lies at the heart of Hinduism. The Aryans were a pastoral people moving along routes already ages old, a people already affected by the sedentary world with which they were in contact even before arriving in India. They were organized into a rough class system headed by warrior chiefs whose rank was retained partially by accumulated wealth counted by herds and partially by prowess in battle. They spoke an Indo-European language and both by speech and cosmology were one with that group of pastoral nomads who inhabited the heart of the Eurasian continent in the early second millennium B.C. and whose later migrations so profoundly affected the ancient world."[12] Irish readers who know their history may be amused by that last

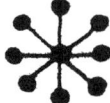

Illustration 12-1. Ancient Iranian-style pottery design. After Fairservis.

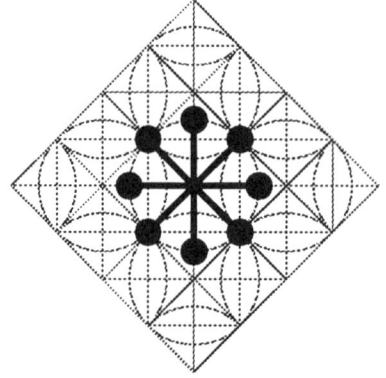

Figure 206

quotation. The neighborhood had gone down fast. Our distant cousins had moved in!

"Hinduism is a cosmic religion and its mythology rests on the cosmic symbolism which underlies all ancient religion."[13] "The basis of this symbolism is found first of all in the five elements, earth, air, fire and water, and the akasa, or space, and their manifestation in sun and moon and stars, earth and sky and sea, rock and tree and animal, and then in the cycle of human birth, marriage and death. Now the characteristic of this symbolism is that it always involves opposition. Nature is composed of light and darkness, life and death, creation and destruction, and the same symbol will signify both of these aspects. Water brings life to the earth, but it also brings destruction by flood or by drought when it is withheld. Fire is the element which cooks the food and gives heat to the body so that it can bring forth life, but it also burns and destroys. In Hindu mythology Siva is the God of destruction, but he is also the renewer of life, who by his grace recreates what he has destroyed. It is this ambivalence of the symbol which makes it [Hinduism] so bewildering, yet once the basic pattern has been discerned it is seen to have its own logic. Nature is a conflict of opposites which is always seeking an equilibrium, always seeking to harmonize the conflicting forces within her and to restore the primal unity from which everything originally came."[14]

Figure 207

"We are told in the sastras that traditionally the temple was built in the image of a human body, the body of the primal man Purusa, who, it is thought, was sacrificed, his body cut into pieces which were then sprinkled over the earth in a fundamental act of creation. These pieces of the body of primal man are the squares of the Mahapurusa mandala on which every Hindu temple is based."[15]

A Hindu legend tells of the entirety of creation emerging as a flowering lotus stem from the navel of Vishnu, as Padma Nabla, while he sleeps.[16] **Figure 207** shows our little manform lying on his back, asleep, with a flowering lotus emerging from his navel.

Illustration 12-2. Ancient Harappan pottery design from Chanhu-daro. After Fairservis.

Illustration 12-3. Ancient pottery design from Mohenjo-daro. After Childe.

Another Hindu legend tells how Agni constantly changes his form by entering different things.[17] Form-changing will become familiar to you as we explore ancient Irish mythology and the Grail quest stories. Vishnu sometimes appears as a dwarf; other times as a man-lion. We already are familiar with man-lions, and we shall encounter the dwarf as a principal actor in many Grail quest stories.

We are told that Hindus equate the concepts of space and consciousness. "Space is conceived of as built up of a network of lines of force running from north to south, east to west, and the points of intersection of these lines are filled with magical energy. The Hindu temple is built on this idea of space, its construction surrounded by magic rites. The mandala pattern on which the temple plan is based is a grid system of squares, created by intersecting lines of force which cut each other at right angles. These opposing directions of parallel lines are oriented to the cardinal points of the compass thus linking the here and now with a cosmic field of consciousness. This point on which I am standing is not just isolated, a point without meaning or relationship with any other point; on the contrary it has meaning in so far as it is the intersection between the All and the All, a point of sunya at the crossroads of infinitely extended directions."[18] Our informant tells us that "[t]his idea of consciousness as space probably goes back to a very primal folk sensibility."[19] The Hebrew Prophet Ezekiel seems to have understood. Spatial relationships are a large part of his Visions; of his consciousness of God.

We have encountered several holy mountains in our studies. Have you ever noticed that the body of a yogi sitting cross-legged, his hands on his knees, while he is lost in meditation, assumes the cone-like form of a mountain?[20] We begin to

Figure 208

comprehend the Hindu concept of the oneness of man and nature.

"The authority of the king is based on his position at the very navel of the world. The kingdom becomes as it were the image on the earthly plane of the cosmos, whose hub is the throne of dominion. The king is thus a 'symbol' of power invested at the centre of life. In Indian thought he... commands the wheel of the cosmos. All emperors aspire to a semi-divine role mirroring, through symbolic identity, Indra who is the legitimate ruler of the universe.... In so far as the temple is a microcosm, reflecting on the earthly plane the whole structure of the cosmos, the designer and builder of the temple takes on the role of 'maker of the universe' – Visvakarma or Pantocrator.... This idea... seems to have been imported into India from Persia...."[21] The idea made its way to the Golden Crescent. Solomon was a temple-builder and a law-giver. Moses was a tent-erector and law-giver.

Our little manform's bellybutton is at the hub of one of our Ezekiel wheels, Figure 207, and his bellybutton is in the middle of a top view of the now-familiar throne upon which our manform sits. See **Figure 208**. Is a Hebrew Ezekiel wheel (Merkaba) somehow related to the Hindu Chakra, the Wheel of the Cosmos? Was our manform once referred to as Indra and Vishnu, as well as YHWH and Arthur? Is there some relationship between the Pantocrator of the Hindus and the Pantocrator of the Christians? Did founders of religions steal ideas from each other just as Tin Pan Alley songwriters stole lyrics? Is our Holy Grail manform *The Hero With A Thousand Faces*?[22]

Those were deep questions. Here is a simple one: What, do you suppose, is the symbolism of the domed roof of the Buddhist temple, i.e., the stupa? The dome of the sky?[23]

We first were initiated into the spatial concept of "the center" when we were studying the First and Second Visions of the Prophet Ezekiel. Now consider this: "The figure of the yogi is very much interrelated with this experience of the centre, for he stands or sits lost in contemplation, at the hub of the spinning universal wheel. As such, again like Jehovah, he is a lawgiver, because he has been initiated into the order (dharma, cosmos) of the universe, and is thus able to impart to man the word or logos on which the universe is founded. The journey to the mountain is thus the path to the source of life. In the mandala, we sometimes see depicted the river of life, flowing from the mountain, like the river Ganges flowing down from Siva's

Illustration 12-5. Jesus Christ surrounded by the Cosmic Mandorla or Vesica Piscis and the Four Tetramorphs: Lion, Ox, Man, and Eagle. Chartres Cathedral, France. Courtesy of Jon Weintraub.

knotted hair."[24] We shall encounter a river flowing from a mountain during our study of the Grail quest stories.

Our informant calls to our attention a stone seal from the Indus River, Culture which the scholars suggest may depict a prototype of Siva sitting cross-legged, in yogi fashion, with four animals, representing the four points of the compass, illustrated around him.[25] A god surrounded by four animals? See **Illustration 12-4** and **Illustration 12-5**.

Have you ever noticed that eastern holy men carry umbrellas? The dome of the umbrella represents the dome of the sky; its handle the axis of the world. "It is carried above an important dignitary, or the image of a deity, to indicate that the person or symbol below the umbrella is in fact the centre of a universe."[26] One gets the impression that rotation around the axis of the Earth is an important aspect of Hindu thinking.

We should pay most careful attention to Sahi's comments about the cosmic pillar. "The symbol of the cosmic pillar is related to a myth concerning a magical lake which is meant to lie in the depths of the Himalayas. It is thought that when the sun rises over this lake, which is known as Udaya or Anavatapta, a pillar arises from the center of the lake and grows upwards until it reaches its greatest height at mid-day, thus becoming a throne on which the sun and the moon rest awhile at their zenith before once again taking their path downward, a movement which is followed by the pillar itself, which gradually sinks back, absorbed once again into the lake at sunset. From this myth we see the

Illustration 12-4. Jesus Christ surrounded by the Cosmic Mandorla or Vesica Piscis and the Four Tetramorphs: Lion, Ox, Man, and Eagle. Canterbury Cathedral, England. From the author's personal collection.

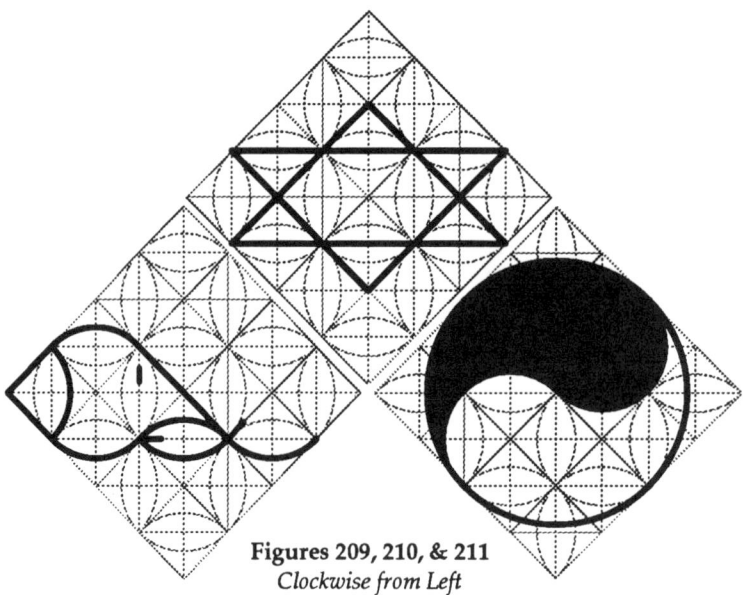

Figures 209, 210, & 211
Clockwise from Left

relation of the pillar to the sun at mid-day and the axis of the universe arising out of the cosmic ocean."[27] Is the Hindu cosmic pillar arising from the lake somehow related to the Celtic sword which arises from the lake in the hand of the Lady of the Lake? Is it related to the manform which plunges into the fountain at Noon in the Grail quest story *Perlesvaus*?

Related directly to the symbol of the pillar are the four points of the compass. The cardinal points of the compass "are symbolized by four creatures who support the throne of the sun. In India, as exemplified in the Sarnath capital, these four beasts are represented as the lion and the elephant, the horse and the bull. In these four beasts, much more than in the four beasts of Western apocalyptic literature (which also owe their form to Persian eschatology), there can be seen a certain balance of elemental forces. The elephant and the bull are related to the forces of water and earth, whereas the lion and the horse are related to the forces of fire and air, heat and speed."[28]

Sahi's comments about the figure of the standing god, complete the trinity of related cosmological concepts: "The figure of the standing Buddha, and later of Vishnu, repeats in the anthropomorphic form the same pillar-like structure. Crowned by the sun, which is here represented by the great orb of a halo, the Lord stands erect, himself the very axis of the universe."[29] Does Christianity have a similar concept?

We have grown accustomed to Lion, Ox, Man, and Eagle representing the Four Winds or the Four Cardinal Points of the compass. Now we must look to the Holy Grail to see if we can see in **Figure 209** an abstract image of an elephant's head, in side view.

Note how many of these symbols are Persian in origin! Could it be that the symbols of Throne and Crown, which appear so many times in a concordance to the Old and New Testaments of Christian Bibles, are related also to eastern thinking? "The figure of the king enthroned with attendants becomes a common feature of Buddhist and Jain art and later Hindu iconography, in which the deity is given the entourage of temporal authorities, very much as we find Christ depicted as enthroned in the manner that was customary in the Byzantine imperial court."[30] "The crown in Indian art is very much like the tall peak of the mythical mount – the sikhara of the northern temple is both the image of the mount Meru, and the crown of the cosmic man Purusa."[31] Is there some relationship between the cosmic man the Hebrews and Christians call Adam, and the cosmic man the Hindus call Purusa? Ezekiel's Visions included the form of God sitting on His throne. We shall encounter thrones and crowns throughout our Grail quest studies.

Jyoti Sahi, in *The Child and the Serpent*, has already given us deep insights into Hindu cosmology. Sahi's writings concerning sacred dance raise our understanding to even higher levels. Drop a stone into a pool of still water. The point where the stone enters the water is "bija" or seed. It is the germ of life of the pattern of waves. It is the center, seen or unseen, of the ritual mandala which contains a square with four gates, like a garden with four entrances, which represents (like the Garden of Eden?) the entire cosmos. This forms the temple stage, or mandapa, on which classical Hindu ritualistic dancing is performed. Thus, the dance is a cosmic play on a cosmic stage.[32] Sahi tells us: "[A]s the mandala is a grid pattern having eight divisions rather like a chessboard, the basic dance steps of classical Indian dancing are built on patterns of eight. The great oil lamp in the centre of the stage has a thick wick, and a thinner wick, representing the sun and the moon."[33] Hebrew and Christian fundamentalists, hang tight to your Old Testament Noah story. "The drumming with which the [dance] performance begins is meant to symbolize the cosmic deluge and the dawn of a new age."[34] Hindus recognize cosmology when they see it! Hebrew and Christian fundamentalists insist that the Noah story is accurately-reported historical fact. Each holds a "truth" to be self-evident. We shall encounter chessmen moving themselves on a chessboard during our Grail quest studies. Cosmic dancers on a cosmic stage?

Siva is the Hindu god of the dance. He is associated with the sacred bull, whose horns represent the moon. He was known in the Vedas as Rudra, the howler, and has been called the dancer in the pine forest.[35] Store those bits of trivia until we study the mystery religions which preceded the advent of Christianity. Can you visualize on the Holy Grail our human form dancing in a pine forest?

We already have seen the "Drum of Siva." Sahi tells us that "As Siva dances he carries in his hand the little drum which is shaped rather like an hourglass, and which conveys the idea of the pulsating rhythm of cosmic time.... The drum is the creative aspect of the dance, its fertility. The shape of the drum is two triangles or cones meeting each other, which in tantric thought symbolizes the act of marriage – the 'hieros gamos', the meaning of heaven and earth."[36] Is the classical hourglass of western societies a copy of the Drum of Siva – a symbol of cosmic time as well as a device to measure the time of day? Overlap the two cosmic triangles, as in **Figure 210**, and you have the Star of David.

Why are we spending so much time reviewing quotations from the writings of Jyoti Sahi about Hinduism? Because fundamental concepts of cosmology, perhaps divined from the Holy Grail by ancient mystics, still play a "front stage" role in Hindu thinking, whereas this same cosmology, which once played a prominent part in the thinking of early Hebrew and Christian writers, is barely discernible in the thoughts of present-day Judaeo-

Christian writers. The hypothesis we are pursuing is that our diverse religions may have more in common, at least in their origins, than modern purveyors of religion may want us to realize.

Ancient Hindu mystics and modern scientists share beliefs about spiral forms and spiral motions. Spirals, they believe, are to be associated with life force; with growth.[37] Modern astronomers observe spiral galaxies and believe they are watching the birth of new stars.[38] Modern biologists observe the spiral form of DNA and believe they have isolated the genetic codes which cause us to be tall or short, fat or skinny, blue-eyed or brown-eyed, etc.[39] Were the ancient mystics taught these beliefs by space travelers, or were they space travelers themselves? Some persons prefer this explanation, which currently cannot be disproved. But another explanation appeals to others of us. We believe that Stone Age people were highly intelligent, not stupid, because their brains were as large as ours.[40] Spirals are visible in sea shells, in plant structure, and on the Holy Grail. Ancient mystics were close observers of nature and did not have to see spiral nebula or DNA, that can only be observed by use of sophisticated modern equipment, in order to conclude, quite correctly, that spirals are fundamental to life force; to growth.

The spiral of Eastern mystical thought with which we need some familiarity is the yin-yang wheel. See **Figure 211**. "By studying attentively the geometry of the yin-yang pattern we begin to discern the rhythms of a spiralling motion. The pattern is created by drawing a circle with, inside, a figure of eight, that is two circles having half the radius of the greater circle, and touching both each other and the larger surrounding circle. This figure of eight, or the two-petalled white lotus, was from ancient time a symbol of eternity. The dividing wall of the yin-yang pattern is made by taking one half of the figure of eight pattern, that is an S-shaped line, whose length is equivalent to exactly half of the total circumference of the greater circle. In turn the inner circles of the yin-yang pattern can be broken down into further yin-yang patterns in an endless progression inwards like the path of an inward spiralling pattern. The moon has been related to the spiralling patterns of shells, and the mathematical progression which seems to govern the volutes of growing organic forms. The spiral has been connected from ancient times with the very force of life - the movement of fluid substances or the growth of cellular structures. The twisting forms of horns which are meant to contain life-force, or the curling patterns of flowing hair, which is also associated with life energy, both follow a spiralling movement. In Islamic art, for example, the spiralling shape of the ram's horn is thought to symbolize the energy of life. In India, hair has also been very much associated with vitality, and thus the hair of the yogi is piled above his head in a spiral topknot, while the dancing Nataraja allows his hair to flow out like streams of cosmic force."[41]

Note that the *analemma* and the ancient and modern mathematical symbol for infinity also take the form of the figure of eight. Note in reference to the supposed magical property of hair that when Delilah wanted to rob Samson of the strength that enabled him to pull down the columns of a temple with his bare hands, she cut off his hair.[42] Mere coincidences? We shall see!

Sahi tells us that "In Eastern thought the vegetation is referred to as the hair of Mother Earth, again connecting spiralling movement with growth and life."[43]

We cannot leave Sahi without trying to understand the sun as a symbol in Hindu and Buddhist thinking. "In mythology, Hindu as elsewhere, the sun is seen either as the father or the son.... The sun as he appears as the divine child is more generally identified with the cycle of the year or seasons. The following is a description of the birth of the Lord Buddha, which is a favourite theme of Buddhist iconography: 'Mahamaya, wife of Suddhodana, of Kapila Vastu, dreamt one night of a white elephant entering her womb. She became pregnant and her womb became transparent like a crystal casket. She felt an urge to withdraw for meditation to the forest and there, while beneath a Sal tree, she gave birth from her side. The child was born in full awareness and looking like a young sun; he leapt on to the ground and where he touched it there sprang up a lotus. He looked on the four cardinal points, to the four half points above and below, and saw deities and men acknowledging his superiority. He made seven steps northwards, a lotus appearing at each footfall. His birth was greeted by Asita, a sage from the Himalayas who likened him to Sakanda or Kumara.'"[44] We shall encounter the yet-unborn god in a crystal casket womb when we reach our Grail quest stories. Note how the birth of the Lord Buddha is associated in Eastern thinking with the sun, the cardinal points of the compass, and the birth of the year (Skanda).[45]

Other legends tell of the birth of Manu, the primal man, from the mind of his father, the sun, or the birth of Kumara, whose name was mentioned in the Buddha legend, quoted above. The child deity Kumara "is described in popular myth as coming out of the mind (man) of his father. This mind is symbolized by the fiery third eye of Siva, from which the child springs as from a womb."[46] According to another tradition, the child-god Ganesa "was born of the mind of the father via the eye (which is another epithet for the sun); but on the other hand he was born of the virgin mother, who is also the queen of the waters of regeneration."[47]

Sahi tells us that in Eastern thinking "the sun is like a door leading up to a reality beyond the cycles of nature.... Arising out of this view of the sun and its significance, from very ancient times the door has been invested with solar symbolism.... This circular movement of the door is symbolized by the swastika, an ancient sun symbol which is often to be found over the door. This symbol clearly goes back as far as the Mohenjodaro civilization, as it is found in terra-cotta seals of that period, but probably it is even older than that."[48] "The symbol of the door is the entry into death and final dissolution, into the source of being, but it is also the exit into life."[49]

"Water is connected with the door in its aspect of initiation. Nearly all initiations involve a ritual dying and entry into water to wash away the past."[50] Christian baptism once meant that the person "died" as a pagan and was "reborn" a Christian? "The frame of the door is slowly converted into the halo, or aura, around a figure of the deity. Sometimes his aura encloses the whole body but sometimes it simply arises out of the shoulder and encircles the head of the divinity. Haloes, as we know them in Western Christian art, are probably of Eastern origin."[51] "This idea of the window already seems to presume an ascent. The halo appears to crown the figure of the Lord - it is the door of the heavens opening up above man."[52]

"As we can see from the whole structure of the Hindu temple, what is being depicted is the mandala of the universe.... In order to set about this journey [to the center of the temple symbolizing the center of the universe] man [as devotee of an initiation ceremony] has to surrender himself. The rituals of initiation into the mandala all entail a testing of the neophite."[53] In Illustration 12-4, we see Christ, the Son of God, framed by an eye-shaped mandorla. We studied Christ as the Gate to Heaven when considering the Book of the Shepherd of Hermas. We considered glories and haloes in religious literature and shall study their observation by modern man and presumed similar observations by ancient man. We studied the cosmic concept of "water" in the Hermas story, and its relationship to Christian baptism.

Our thoughts are spiralling, like ribbons of chocolate in a cookie-mixing machine! All the ingredients are not yet in the mixing bowl, ready to be stirred together into a sweet-tasting conglomeration called "religion." We cannot swallow all of Eastern thinking in one small cookie. We cannot go forward with our studies without looking at the Eastern symbols of the tree and the snake.

"The creation of mandalas... which are organized patterns often based on structures of four or multiples of four, indicate an organized view of reality, which also reflects a new ordering of social relationships, and man's understanding of his place in the universe. This is interesting because many mandalas depict an ideal garden or paradise, at whose center there is often a tree under which is depicted a figure of the deity.... Krsna is popularly depicted as standing with his beloved beneath the kadamba tree. This tree is the centre of the universe, the 'axis mundi.'"[54] "The tree is a symbol in Indian thought of birth. The mother of Buddha, Maya, goes to meditate under a tree when she becomes pregnant, and the child is born from her side. Later the Lord Buddha himself sits under the forest tree in order to be reborn into a higher mode of life."[55] "Each stage in the Buddhist journey to enlightenment is described as a 'hieros gamos', a sacred wedding or kalyanam. Each moment of the yogi's victory over temptation brings yet another shower of petals from the tree which rejoices in his attainments."[56]

"The sacrificial significance of the tree has been realized in many religious traditions. As the tree stands at the intersection of life and death, and is a symbol of the cosmic structure, myths concerning the self-immolation of a cosmic man or woman have come to be connected with the tree. This immolation is, we must remember, basically creative, because to die in this context means to be born again."[57] Might there be some connection between the story of the death of Christ on a wooden cross, by which He and those who believe in Him attained a higher being, and an act of ritual suicide by some village girl in India, who immolates herself, as did the Earth Mother of the legends, in order to pass into a higher state of existence?[58]

Sahi tells us of India what Frazier tells us of Europe: "Human sacrifices were above all appreciated by the deities of the grove, and so, according to Tucci, petty kings made it the excuse for military campaigns against neighbouring kingdoms, for the captures they made during these raids would be sacrificed in their sacred groves."[59] We later shall mention the "Flower Wars" of the Aztecs by which human victims were obtained for sacrifice to the sun.

Sahi already has helped us to understand the concept of the spiral. Snakes spiral. Time can be seen as a spiral.[60] "According to folk belief, the shedding of the serpent's skin is accompanied by a new lease of life.... Wherever snakes are worshipped, a tradition of sacrifices to serpents has been found. These sacrifices in primitive societies even entailed human sacrifices. Many are the tales of dragons who demanded young men and women to be sacrificed to them. In India certain naga tribes (that is, tribes worshipping snakes) were head-hunters. In this cult the serpent is once again the symbol of time itself, which requires the offering of the fruits of youth in order that it might itself remain youthful. The death of the serpent is the death of the aeon, and all that is vital in the cosmos. To renew the world which had grown old and tired, a human sacrifice had to be made. Death and life are the binomials of the serpent cult – the upward and downward tendencies of cyclic nature."[61] What do Christians and Hebrews say of the serpent and the Tree of Life in the Garden of Eden? And of the purpose of the life and death of Jesus Christ? Why do Westerners portray the old year as a tired old man with long whiskers, wearing holy robes, and, like the Roman god Saturn, carrying the sickle of the Grim Reaper, Father Time, with which he soon shall be sacrificed, so that the new year, the babe in diapers, may become the New Year King? Christ carried his cross to his destruction. The Old Year carries the sickle of time with which he will be cut down so the year may be born again. Does any relationship exist between these stories?

We got ourselves out of step in some of the preceding paragraphs by referring to the "mandorla" symbol without saying what it is. Christ, you will recall, is seen surrounded by the mandorla in many of Europe's cathedrals. Illustration 12-4. Sahi tells us, "In the world of pure form, the intersection of two globes or circles produces a structure which is fascinating to the artist and mathematician alike. Euclid devotes his first geometric proposition to the analysis of this form, which was known in the West as the mandorla. This symbol emerges naturally out of the curvilinear, and the opening or splitting of rounded forms. It is thus the form of the opening into the womb, the yoni, and has been worshipped as a symbol of fertility from very ancient times. Through a natural homology which is intrinsic to symbolic thinking, this form has been found in the fish and also in the eye."[62]

We shall study the mandorla or eye-form, found all over the Grail, in its role as *vesica piscis*, a principal Christian symbol for Christ, and as a geometry generator, from which many of the principal forms and proportions of European cathedrals were designed. During the lifetime of Eusebius, one of the founding-fathers of the Christian Church, Psalm 110.3 read, in part, "From the womb before the daystar I begat Thee,"[63] whereas the same verse of King James reads: "from the womb of the morning: thou hast the dew of thy youth." In Indian symbolism, the purna kumbham, or full vessel, a symbol of plenty, is covered by our familiar eight-pointed symbol.[64] Early drawings of Our Lady, Mary, the Mother of Jesus, showed this same symbol on her cowl. Our Lady was the full vessel, or the womb before the "daystar," from which the Son (the sun) was delivered? We shall learn that Our Lady was referred to as the "Queen of Heaven," a title previously reserved for Inanna, the Sumerian goddess whose name was given to the planet we call Venus. We shall learn that Venus in its role as the morning star ("daystar") announces the rising of, or mythologically gives birth to, the sun.

We leave the writings of Jyoti Sahi and go to the book *Mandala Symbolism*, by Carl Gustaf Jung, one of the pioneers of modern psychiatry. Several quotations from this work help us to put the symbol of the mandala into even sharper focus. Jung tells us that as he worked with mandalas, it became increasingly clear to him that "the mandala is the centre. It is the exponent of all paths. It is the path to the centre, to individuation."[65] He tells us that "the goal of psychic development is the self."[66] "The Sanskrit word *mandala* means 'circle' in the ordinary sense of the word.... Very frequently they contain a quaternity or a multiple of four, in the form of a cross, a star, a square, an octagon, etc. In alchemy we encounter this motif in the form of *quadratura circuli*."[67]

Jung tells us that "the 'quaternity of the One' is the schema for all images of God, as depicted in the visions of Ezekiel, Daniel, and Enoch, and as the representation of Horus with his four sons also shows. The latter suggests an interesting differentiation, inasmuch as there are occasionally representations in which three of the sons have animals' heads and only one a human head, in keeping with the Old Testament visions as well as with the emblems of the seraphim which were transferred to the evangelists, and – last but not least – with the nature of the Gospels themselves: three of which are synoptic and one 'Gnostic.'"[68] Jung makes reference to the "copper man" of the alchemists, whom we will encounter in the Grail quest story *Perlesvaus*.[69] Many of the symbols of alchemy can be found on the Holy Grail. The famous Irish chemist Lord Boyle debunked alchemy, showing that it was a philosophy rather than a science, but he did not root out from our thinking every vestige of this pseudo-science. We still refer to a man standing "four-square," a concept drawn directly from the philosophy of alchemy.[70] We already have encountered in the story of the Shepherd of Hermas the alchemists' "stone that is no stone," i.e., Christ.[71]

Jung further enlightens us about the swastika as a religious symbol. "In Tibet, the leftward-moving swastika is a sign of the Bon religion, of black magic. Stupas and chortens must therefore be circumambulated clockwise.... The rightward-moving swastika in Tibet is therefore a Buddhist emblem."[72] We know that the Earth rotates clockwise, to the east, thereby creating the incorrect illusion that the sun moves east to west. We already have learned that the swastika is a sun symbol. Clockwise movement in a circle is "right" and counterclockwise movement in a circle is "wrong" according to Eastern thinking. Did they understand what rotated around what, and in which direction, before Galileo supposedly first discovered such matters?

Jung states that "The mandala, though only a symbol of the self as the psychic totality, is at the same time a God-image, for the central point, circle, and quaternity are well-known symbols for the deity. The impossibility of distinguishing empirically between 'self' and 'God' leads, in Indian theosophy, to the identity of the personal and supra-personal Purusha-Atman. In ecclesiastical as in alchemical literature the saying is often quoted: 'God is an infinite circle (or sphere) whose centre is everywhere and the circumference nowhere.'"[73] Jung reports that the Egyptians rolled wheels around their temples on certain occasions; that a philosopher defined God as "a circle consisting of glowing light." Ezekiel apparently agreed with this symbolism.[74] Jung tells us that "Egyptians customarily represent God, the Lord of the world, as sitting on the lotus, a water-plant." East Indians

apparently would agree with that symbolism.[75]

If the religionists who established our many and varied faiths were in such total agreement with each other as to these fundamentals, why is it that we adherents of these faiths are constantly at each other's throats about which faith should be the one true faith for all of mankind? Is it because those who interpret our articles of faith are more interested in establishing a monopoly over the collection plate than they are in achieving the common goals of all religions?

Jung states in unequivocal words his understanding of the main problem of humankind and its solution. "The political and social *isms* of our day preach every conceivable ideal, but, under this mask, they pursue the goal of lowering the level of our culture by restricting or altogether inhibiting the possibilities of individual development.... This problem cannot be solved collectively, because the masses are not changed unless the individual changes.... The bettering of a general ill begins with the individual, and then only when he makes himself and not others responsible. This is naturally only possible in freedom...."[76]

We entrap ourselves by allowing others to think for us. We are not enslaved. We enslave ourselves. We are at fault, not our leaders. Fish swim. Birds fly. Leaders lead. Only if we let them. The people of the Philippines grew tired of being led by President Marcos. They laid down in the streets, peacefully, daring his army officers to drive their tanks across their bodies. MacSwiney. Ghandi. King. Aquino. It works.

Notes
CHAPTER TWELVE. India and Pakistan: Deep Wells of Cosmology

1. Fairservis 221-222; Childe 176.
2. Fairservis 251.
3. Fairservis 261-262.
4. Fairservis 255,261-262.
5. Fairservis 222,281,287,290.
6. Fairservis 222,275; Childe 182,185.
7. Fairservis Fig 44.
8. Childe 181.
9. Fairservis 289.
10. Childe Plate XXXII.
11. Childe 185.
12. Fairservis 345.
13. Sahi xi.
14. Sahi xi.
15. Sahi 40.
16. Sahi 40-41.
17. Sahi 62.
18. Sahi 65.
19. Sahi 65.
20. Sahi 67-68.
21. Sahi 73.
22. See Joseph Campbell, generally.
23. Sahi 74.
24. Sahi 76.
25. Sahi 76.
26. Sahi 78-79.
27. Sahi 79.
28. Sahi 79-80.
29. Sahi 80.
30. Sahi 81.
31. Sahi 82.
32. Sahi 98.
33. Sahi 98.
34. Sahi 98.
35. Sahi 99.
36. Sahi 99.
37. Sahi 82,105-106.
38. Jastrow 5,28-29; Washburn 23-24.
39. 9 World Book Encyclopedia 192 (1983).
40. Jastrow 123,127.
41. Sahi 105.
42. Judges 16.17-19.
43. Sahi 106.
44. Sahi 125.
45. Sahi 125.
46. Sahi 125.
47. Sahi 126.
48. Sahi 127.
49. Sahi 128.
50. Sahi 129.
51. Sahi 131.
52. Sahi 131.
53. Sahi 132.
54. Sahi 149.
55. Sahi 151.
56. Sahi 152.

57. Sahi 153.

58. Sahi 153.

59. Sahi 154-155.

60. Sahi 161-163.

61. Sahi 167.

62. Sahi 175.

63. Eusebius 44.

64. Sahi 173-175.

65. Jung v.

66. Jung v.

67. Jung 3.

68. Jung 4.

69. Jung 16.

70. Jung 23.

71. Jung 28.

72. Jung 36.

73. Jung 40-41.

74. Ezekiel 1.28.

75. Sahi 73-75.

76. Jung 65.

Chapter Thirteen

Mixing the Ingredients

We should explore *A Dictionary Of Symbols*, by J. E. Cirlot. Cirlot may help us to stir together into a coherent whole, seemingly unrelated information we have picked up during our quest.

We are told that experts on symbolism have a "tendency to espouse the theory that all symbolist traditions, both western and oriental, spring from one common source. Whether this one source once appeared in time and space as a primeval focal point, or whether it stems from the 'collective unconscious', is quite another matter."[1] Eminent scholars of the human mind, such as Jung, would tend, as we have seen, toward the view that our symbolism, western and eastern, is so much alike because all of mankind is so much alike; because we share a collective unconsciousness. Readers of this book may tend toward the other view. Was the Holy Grail the source of western and eastern religious symbolism?

We further are told that "most writers agree in tracing the beginnings of symbolist thought to prehistoric times — to the latter part of the Paleolithic Age."[2] We have collected some evidence from ancient potsherds which would tend to support this theory. Cirlot mentions the ancient *Tabula Smaragdina*: "What is below is like what is above; what is above is like what is below."[3] This seems to be another way of expressing what we have called "correspondence theory," under which the ancients posited that the Earth and Heaven are reflections of each other; that what occurs in the one occurs in the other; that the god acts (or speaks) and the god's actions (or words) are reflected in many ways on Earth, as, for instance, in spirals on sea shells, in whirlpools of water and waterspouts, in smoke, tornadoes, and sandstorms, and in the tendrils of grape vines.

The experts apparently suggest that mankind passed through these stages: animism, totemism, lunar and solar cultures, cosmic ritualism, polytheism, monotheism and, finally, moral philosophy.[4] We are told that, "[d]uring the neolithic era the geometric idea of space was formulated; so also were the significance of the number seven (derived

from the concept of space), and the relation between heaven and earth, the cardinal points, and the relations between the various elements of the septenary (the planetary gods, the days of the week) and between those of the quaternary (the seasons, the colours, the cardinal points, the elements)."[5] A slow spread of these ideas across the entire globe is suggested.[6] We have seen that the geometric idea of space and the color spectrum were associated with the Creator by the Prophet Ezekiel. We have watched the Holy Grail diffuse through various societies, and our voyage is anything but complete!

Cirlot tells us that the early East Indian Zodiac "had only eight constellations and each constellation was supposed to be a 'form of God.' All of these 'forms of God' in the end became deities, each one presiding over one particular constellation; this is what happened in Rome, for example. The eight Indian signs of the Zodiac are: Edu (ram), Yal (harp), Nand (crab), Amma (mother), Tuk (balance), Kani (arrow), Kuda (pitcher), Min (fish)."[7] We see them in **Figures 212 through 219.**

Why would ancient East Indians portray God by such diverse symbols? Because they believed the choice was not theirs? Because they believed that the gods had portrayed themselves to the East Indians in those forms, and that there was nothing they could do about the symbolism except accept it as revealed to them? Remember our studies of the pre-scientific concept that mankind should not go looking for God; rather, that mankind should sit back, relax, and receive messages (revelations) from God as to what God wanted mankind to know? Were the East Indians silly to portray God as diversely as a fish and a mother? What of the early Christian fish and mother symbols? Is this pre-scientific blind acceptance of symbols which the religious leaders of the day said were revelations from the Creator? If we accept the viewpoint of many modern scholars that mankind was about as intelligent back then as now,[8] then it would seem to follow that in ancient times the common man used a fish as symbol for his god because his religious leader said he had received a revelation indicating

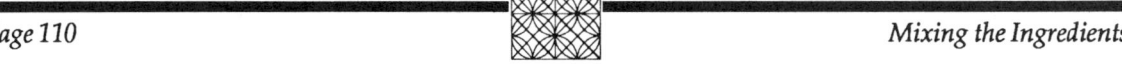

Figure 212

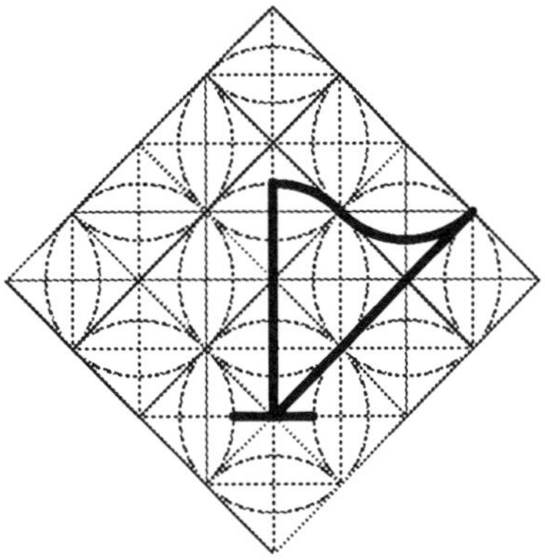

Figure 214

Figure 213

Figure 215

Figure 216

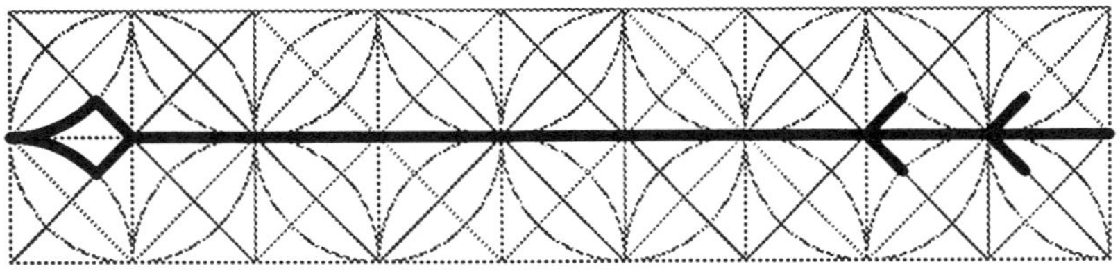

Figure 217

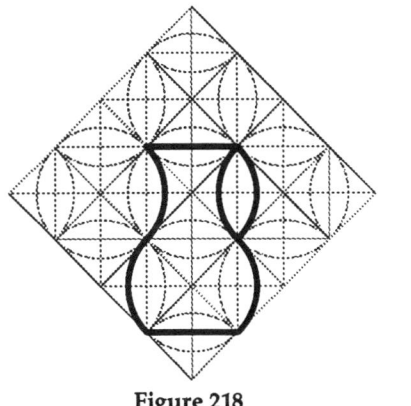

Figure 218

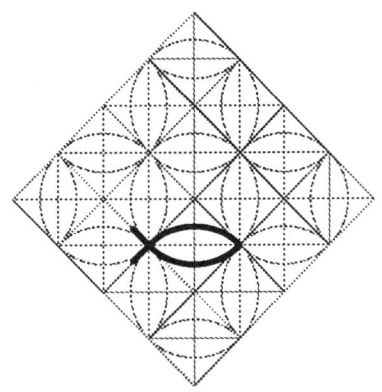

Figure 219

that the god should be symbolized by a fish. Blind faith. But what was the source of that religious leader's "revelation"? Some of us already can speculate, with some degree of accuracy, about the correct answer to that question!

We are told that "The dodecatemorian [that is, twelve-part] system of the Zodiac first appears in the form in which we know it as late as the 6th century B.C. Egyptian and Chaldean science was partly assimilated by the Syrians, Phoenicians and Greeks, reaching the latter largely through secret societies. Herodotus points out, in writing of the Pythagoreans, that they were obliged to wear linen clothes 'in accordance with the Orphic ceremonies, which are the same as the Egyptian....'"[9]

We have posited the existence of secret societies of scholars existing through the ages, who could demonstrate their knowledge of the origins of ancient cosmology by creating stories from line forms divined or "seen" on the Holy Grail. We have suggested that the story of the table from the Letter of Aristeas is such a tale, proving brotherhood in one of those secret societies. We soon shall study some of the many secret societies and "mystery religions" which immediately predated a late-emerging secret society whose members called themselves "Christians."

We later shall discover that the inhabitants of the British Isles apparently divided the year into eight equal parts. Is this because the ancient East Indian Zodiac had eight, rather than twelve, signs?[10]

Cirlot tells us something we later will study: "Frazer points out that 'under the names of Osiris, Tammuz, Adonis, and Attis, the peoples of Egypt and Western Asia represented the yearly decay and revival of life, especially of vegetable life.'"[11] Tammuz remains today a month of the Hebrew Calendar.[12] Ezekiel and the other prophets never were able to obliterate his name from the Hebrew folk consciousness.[13] Shall we add the name of Jesus Christ to that list? If you cannot endure the posing of that question, you should put this book down before we reach our studies of the Grail quest stories.

And what did the founding fathers of the Christian Church think about all this pagan symbolism? Did they seek to purge it from the minds of Christian converts? Or were they masters of human psychology; aware that they could not obliterate symbols of religion deeply imbedded in the minds of the common folk; that the best they could hope to accomplish with the problem of ancient, pagan symbols was to give them Christian meanings? Lion, Ox, Man, and Eagle. The Four Guardian Stars of Persia? The Watchers? The Four Archers? Or Matthew, Mark, Luke, and John? Pagan science books were to be burned, as we later shall learn. Pagan symbols, we shall learn, were to be Christianized — because the folk mind refuses to yield up to the founders of new religions the familiar symbols of faith.

Cirlot tells us: "St. Augustine shows that teaching carried out with the help of symbols feeds and stirs the fires of love, enabling Man to excel himself; he also alludes to the value of all things in nature — organic and inorganic — as bearers of spiritual messages by virtue of their distinctive forms and characteristics. All the medieval lapidaries, herbals and bestiaries owe their origin to this concept. Most of the classical fathers of the Church have something to say about symbolism and since they enjoyed such a high reputation in Roman times, one can see that this was the period when the symbol came to be so deeply experienced, loved and understood."[14]

We do not have time in this book to study these medieval books about rocks, plants, and animals, which were a strange mixture of observed characteristics of the real world with Church-born and Church-preserved fantasy. The purpose of these Church writings was to teach Christian virtues.[15] Neither do we have time to study the lives of those brave European scholars who went about their studies of rocks, plants, and animals unburdened by thoughts of the mythical phoenix bird and the dragons of the storytellers; who began to teach us, through the eyes of modern scientists, not only how things most probably are in the real world but, through their explorations of science, began to give us another viewpoint of the Creator. The Isaac Newton of our physics books was an Isaac Newton of God, a very religious man, who learned much about the Creator from mathematics and physics rather than from Church prayer books and hymnals.[16] But professional religionists do not like such thinking! God is their property; the source of their livelihoods. Scientists should stay in their laboratories and stay off the turf owned by the religionists!

It is the sole prerogative of the religionists to tell us what we shall believe, say, and do in respect to God, and the rest of us, including all scientists, should keep our mouths shut and obey the professional religionists. If we hush not, we shall go to Hell! Really?

Cirlot refers to a writing which is unknown to most of the good men and women who minister daily to flocks of true believers of the major religions of the world. The *Clavis Melitoniae* is "an orthodox version of ancient symbolism" which was of "immense cultural value, particularly during the Middle Ages," and which was known to "most mediaeval authors."[17] Are we saying that the scholar-writers knew something unknown to the common folk; something which could be used to instill in the common folk cultural values thought useful by the scholars? Useful to what end? For the good of the common folk? Or for the good of their masters? Cirlot tells us that "St. Thomas Aquinas himself speaks of the pagan philosophers as sources of external and demonstrable proofs of Christian truths. Concerning the intimate nature of mediaeval symbolism, Jung observes that, in those days 'analogy was not so much a logical figure as a secret identity', that is to say, a continuation of primitive, animistic thought."[18] Knowing a secret unknown to most people is incomparably "sweet."[19]

Why should we not tell the secrets of the scholars of religion right now? Why continue the mystery until later in the book? Because we need to explore other cultures whose values have been affected by the Holy Grail before we let the cat out of the bag. Stick with us. It will be worth the effort.

Cirlot discusses the symbols of rotation and the center, symbols already familiar to us from our brief study of Hinduism: "The idea of rotation is the keystone of most transcendent symbols: of the mediaeval *Rota*; of the Wheel of Buddhist transformations; of the zodiacal cycle; of the myth of the Gemini; and of the *opus* of the alchemists. The idea of the world as a labyrinth or of life as a pilgrimage leads to the idea of the 'centre' as symbol of the absolute goal of Man, Paradise regained, heavenly Jerusalem. Pictorially, this central point is sometimes identified with the geometric centre of the symbolic circle; sometimes it is placed above it; and at other times, as in the oriental *Shri Yantra*, it is not portrayed at all, so that the contemplator has to

imagine it."[20] Again, he discusses the "four symbolic ways of referring to the Centre; the Hindu Wheel of Transformations in the centre of which is a space which is either quite unadorned or else filled with just the symbol or image of a deity; or the Chinese *Pi*, a disc of jade with a hole in the centre; or the idea that the polestar, piercing the sky, points the way along which the merely temporal world must move in order to rid itself of the restrictions of time and space; or, finally, in the West, the Round table with the Holy Grail standing at its centre point."[21] Is the Holy Grail somehow related to Buddhist, Hindu, Chinese, etc., concepts of cosmology? Most westerners think of it as a Christian symbol although, as we shall study later, the Christian Church prefers that we do not think of it at all!

Remember the Hindu temple plan in the form of a man? Cirlot tells us, without hesitation, that "[t]he typical Romanesque church combines the symbolisms of the dome, and of the circle and the square, with two new elements of the greatest importance: the subdivision of the main body of the building into nave and two aisles (symbolic of the Trinity) and the cross-shaped plan, derived from the image of a man lying prostrate with his arms outstretched whereby the centre becomes not man's navel (a merely symmetrical division) but his heart (at the intersection of the nave and transept), while the main apse represents the head."[22] Those of you who have studied the science chapters at the end of the book have seen the Holy Grail in use as the foundation plan of Christian cathedrals. The Church's one foundation *is* Jesus Christ! Take the words of the hymn literally, and see where it leads you!

Turn back to Illustration 12-4. Christ is seen in an aureole or mandorla surrounded by the Four Tetramorphs (Lion, Ox, Man, and Eagle) in this photograph of a stained glass window from Canterbury Cathedral in England. Cirlot defines the word "aureole" for us: "A circular or oblong halo surrounding bodies in glory. According to a 12th century text, attributed to the abbey of St. Victor, the oblong shape derives from the symbolism of the almond, which is identified with Christ. This, however, does not change the general sense of the aureole... as a relic of solar cults, and as a fire-symbol expressive of irradiating, supernatural energy... or as a manifestation of the emanation of

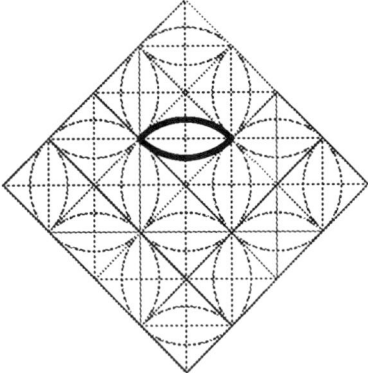

Figure 220

spiritual light (which plays such an important part in Hindu doctrine).... The almond-shaped aureole, which usually surrounds the whole of the body, is usually divided into three zones, as an active expression of the Trinity."[23] The Holy Grail is covered by almond-shapes. One is bolded in **Figure 220**.

Cirlot defines the symbol of the center: "In all symbols expressive of the mystic Centre, the intention is to reveal to Man the meaning of the primordial 'paradisal state' and to teach him to identify himself with the supreme principle of the universe. This centre is in effect Aristotle's 'unmoved mover' and Dante's 'L'Amore che muove il sole a l'altre stelle'.... Similarly, Hindu doctrine declares that God resides in the centre, at that point where the radii of a wheel meet at its axis.... In diagrams of the cosmos, the central space is always reserved for the Creator, so that he appears as if surrounded by a circular or almond shaped halo (formed by the intersection of the circle of heaven with the circle of the earth), surrounded by concentric circles spreading outwards, and by the wheel of the Zodiac, the twelve-monthly cycle of labour upon the land, and a four-part division corresponding both to the seasons and to the tetramorph(s).... In some liturgical crosses, as for example that of Cong in Ireland, the centre is marked by a precious stone."[24] A precious stone centers Ezekiel's vision.[25] Stanley Noah Kramer told us that the eight-pointed "star" symbol is the Sumerian symbol for "god," and is one of the oldest written symbols of mankind.[26] Do you get the impression that the scholars of religion have maintained a continuing dialogue with each other across time and space but out of sight and hearing of the common man?

Cirlot deals with the term "cosmogony": "The basis of most cosmogonies is the 'cosmic sacrifice', expressing the idea that the creation of forms and matter can take place only by modifying primordial energy. Such a modification, so far as most primitive and protohistoric peoples are concerned, was seen to exist in such painful forms as mutilation, struggle or sacrifice. In Babylonian cosmogony it assumed the form of the killing of the original mother Tiamat (the dragon), whose body was used in the creation of heaven and earth.... Hindu tradition links the struggle of the gods with a tribe of devils called Asuras, or with monsters of some other kind. According to the Rig Veda, the gods would sacrifice a primeval being, the giant Purusha. In Persia it was a bull which was sacrificed by Ahriman or Mithras. In Scandinavia it was the giant Ymir who was dismembered by the Aesir gods and then used as the material for the creation of the world. Clearly, then, these cosmogonies have a psychological implication because they express the central idea that there is no creation without sacrifice, no life without death (this being the basis of all inversion-symbolisms and of the Gemini). Here we have the origin of all the bloody sacrifices of the world's religions.... Similarly, it is not possible to transform the human soul in any way, except through sacrifice."[27] Good parents sacrifice their freedom to raise their children. The Christian religion is dominated by the concept of sacrifice.

Look with particular attention at these words of Cirlot: "Here we have the origin of all the bloody sacrifices of the world's religions."[28] Did a priest look at the Holy Grail thousands of years ago and decide that the gods were revealing to him that they wanted human beings to be stretched out on altars to be sacrificed so the seasons would continue their rotation? Did yet another priest look at the Holy Grail and decide, instead, that the gods were revealing to him that they wanted human beings hung from their necks from ropes suspended from pine trees so the seasons would continue their rotation? Did priests later look at the Holy Grail and tell the common people that the gods revealed to them that human beings should be impaled on stakes so the seasons would continue their rotation? Did other priests convince their flocks that men should be hung on crosses with spears stuck through their sides so that the seasons would continue their rotation? Did humanists come into power at later times, and convince their flocks that the earlier priests were wrong about the form on the Holy Grail being a human form; rather, that it was an animal form and, hence, that animal sacrifice, instead of human sacrifice, was demanded by the gods? Did even later humanists who held power over the minds of the common folk teach that no more human sacrifice was necessary because God had given his Son in sacrifice upon the Cross to save forever all of mankind who would believe in the efficacy of this sacrifice?

Putting an end to the practice of human sacrifice *was* a problem faced by humanists at the time that Christians first emerged from their secret societies and began to try, first through persuasion, later by force of the Roman army, to convince all of mankind of the historicity and efficacy of God's sacrifice of his first-born Son. The story of Abraham's aborted sacrifice of his son Isaac, in which the ram became surrogate for the human child, was the ancient Hebrew societal justification for ceasing their sacrifice of their first-born children. But many people other than the Hebrews continued human adult and infant sacrifice to some extent until the Christianized Romans stamped it out with force of arms. More on this later. We now must continue with Cirlot's discussion of symbols.

Here is one you may have anticipated: "Like the Tree of Life, the cross stands for the 'world-axis'. Placed in the mystic Centre of the cosmos, it becomes the bridge or ladder by means of which the soul may reach God."[29]

The mythologies of many ancient peoples refer to the sacrifice of a giant. "This cosmogonic myth was very common among primitive and ancient peoples, and it shows how rites involving the sacrifice of humans are an attempt to revive the initial sacrifice and to resuscitate the cosmic forces or to reawake, at least, their favourable proclivities."[30] Cirlot speaks of the ceremonies of ancient Europeans who put living humans into large wicker-work frames shaped like our Grail manform and set them afire during festivals.[31] Knowledgeable Irish know he is writing about one of the human sacrificial rituals of our Celtic ancestors.[32]

The image of the man hanged on the tree is that of the Germanic god Odin. "Of Odin it was said that he had sacrificed himself by hanging. The relevant verses of *Havamal* read: 'I know that I have been hanging from the stormy tree for nine consecutive nights, wounded by the spear, as an offering to Odin: myself offered to myself.'"[33] A peculiar notion for a god to offer himself in sacrifice to himself? In the Christian faith, it is said that God offered his only begotten Son, Jesus Christ, on the Cross, as a sacrifice to save mankind. It also is said in Christian doctrine that God is the Father, the Son, and the Holy Ghost, i.e., that Jesus Christ is God. What is rarely expressed but always implied by Christian doctrine is that God therefore offered himself, in the avatar of His Son, as sacrifice to mankind. This is a concept not entirely at variance from that of a pagan Germanic god who offered himself as a sacrifice to himself — because in both cases the assertion is that God offered himself in sacrifice. We shall study more about the Celts and Teutons when we reach their respective allotments of space in this book.

We moderns assume that human sacrifices must always have died as portrayed in Hollywood movies — trying to escape or fighting for their lives. We are amazed when we learn that many went to their doom joyfully, convinced by the priests of "the spiritual treasures to be found in the being who performs this self-sacrifice."[34] According to Christian theology, Christ played a role not dissimilar from that of the Hebrew scapegoat, which carried away the sins of the entire tribe.[35] From human sacrifice to animal sacrifice then to God-man sacrifice. Thus go the stories.

"The more terrible the situation, the more urgent the need [in the primitive mind] to transform and invert it (as a public calamity or an unsuccessful war) and the greater must be the sacrifice; this explains the sacrifice of the Carthaginians and the pre-Columbian Mexicans."[36] We shall learn that the Carthaginians were the foremost infant sacrificers known to history. Most everyone knows about the mass human sacrifices performed by Mexican Indians prior to their conversion to Christianity. What most people will not be willing to concede is the role human sacrifice played in the earliest forms of Christianity, and in the pagan lives of our European, African, Middle Eastern, and Oriental ancestors. But we shall learn because we need to know. Otherwise, we miss the point of one of the most important messages of our various religions.

Cirlot tells us that "[t]he rose, the lotus flower, the heart, the irradiating point, these are the most frequent symbols of this hidden centre...."[37] Catholics will think of the familiar icon of Jesus, his robe and his chest opened to reveal a valentine-shaped irradiating heart, to which his finger points. A Christian icon representing the mystic center?

Cirlot tells us that the concept of "the beloved," which has inspired poets and writers through the ages, had its "earliest and purest expression" in Persia.[38] Poetic love originated among the Persians? When we think of Persians, we visualize our television screens filled with mobs of Iranian fundamentalists scowling, shaking their fists, and shouting hatred. What have the world's religious leaders done to mankind through the years?

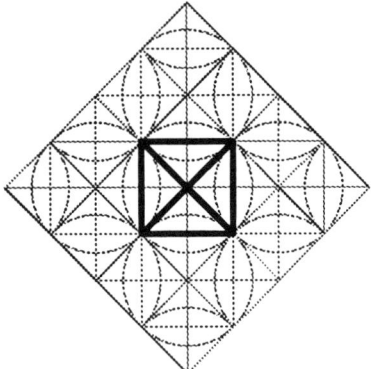

Figure 221

Figure 222

Back to the Cosmic Mountain. Everyone had one! Your Stone Age ancestors really were not part of the "in group" if they had no sacred mountain. Or volcano. Or man-made pile of rocks or dirt, if they lived in a flat place. Cirlot tells us: "As in the case of the cross or the Cosmic Tree, the location of this mountain is at the 'Centre' of the world. This same profound significance is common to almost all traditions: suffice it to recall Mount Meru of the Hindus, the Haraberezaiti of the Iranians, Tabor of the Israelites, Himingbjor of the Germanic peoples, to mention only a few. Furthermore, the temple-mountains such a Borobudur, the Mesopotamian *zigurrats* or the pre-Columbian *teocallis* are all built after the pattern of this symbol. Seen from above, the mountain grows gradually wider, and in this respect it corresponds to the inverted tree whose roots grow up toward heaven while its foliage points downwards, thereby expressing multiplicity, the universe in expansion, involution and materialization. This is why Eliade says that 'the peak of the cosmic mountain is not only the highest point on earth, it is also the earth's navel, the point where creation had its beginning — the root.... The mystic sense of the peak also comes from the fact that it is the point of contact between heaven and earth, or the centre through which the world-axis passes....'"[39] We see the peak of the mystic mountain, and its slope down to the cosmic square representing the Earth, in **Figure 221**. Note that this "navel" of the "Earth" is also the "navel" of our cosmic manform, as seen in **Figure 222**. The cosmic mountain also is found, of course, in the Egyptian pyramid and in the Babylonian "Eye of Enlil" symbol found on the back of every dollar bill issued by the United States of America! The dollar bill is the mystic center of American culture? The prankster-engraver of our currency certainly got that one right!

Cirlot gives us one more useful tidbit about cosmic mountains: "Mount Meru is said to be of gold and located at the North Pole... thus underlining the idea of the Centre and, in particular, linking it to the Pole Star — the 'hole' through which all things temporal and spatial must pass in order to divest themselves of their worldly characteristics. This polar mountain is also to be found in other symbolic traditions, always bearing the same symbolism of the world-axis...; its mythic characteristics were, in all probability, based upon the fixed position of the Pole Star."[40] One thing for certain: Our ancestors certainly were interested in the apparent circular motion of heavenly bodies around the polestar! Another: the Holy Grail, whatever

Figure 223

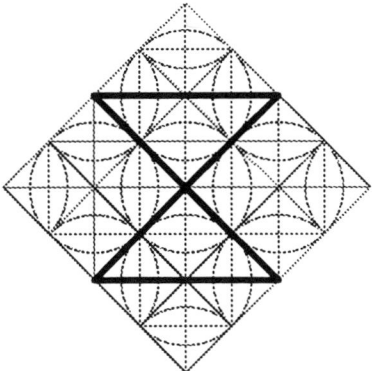

Figure 224

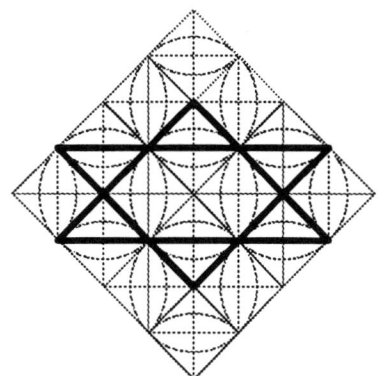

Figure 225

else it might have symbolized, is directly linked to this ancient understanding of polar rotation.

We have alluded to the Egyptian god Osiris, who died and then rose again. Cirlot tells us that his name means that he is the one at the top of the steps.[41] What steps? The steps of the holy pyramid? The steps toward the center? We see Osiris in **Figure 223** standing at the top of the steps of the mystic pyramid.

Take a "fire" triangle with its point toward the heavens, and a "water" triangle with its point toward the earth, conjoin them at their points and you have a drum of Siva.[42] Cross them, instead, to frame a mystic center which is imagined but not drawn, and you have a Star of David.[43] **Figures 224** and **225**.

Cirlot writes of Solomon's Temple: "Solomon's temple, according to Philo and Flavius Josephus, was a figurative representation of the cosmos, and its interior was disposed accordingly: the incense table signified thanksgiving; the seven-branched candelabra stood for the seven planetary heavens; the holy table represented the terrestrial order. In addition to this, the twelve loaves of bread corresponded to the twelve months of the year. The Ark of the Covenant symbolized the intelligibles.... Romanesque, Gothic and Renaissance architects, each in their own way, sought to imitate this superior archetype."[44]

Cirlot discusses at length our four critters: lion, ox, man, and eagle, who were known in certain pagan legends as the "four archers." One archer was posted at each of the four cardinal points to ensure that no one would disrupt the cosmic order, according to pagan storytellers. Christian storytellers used the lion to represent resurrection, the ox to represent passion, the man to represent incarnation and the eagle to represent ascension.[45] Cirlot writes: "In Christian symbolism, the symbolic associations of the four Evangelists (as the archers defending truth and the order of Christ, the 'Centre') are: Matthew, the winged man; Mark, the lion; Luke, the ox; John, the eagle...."[46] In **Figure 226**, we see our manform as an "archer."

Of the concept of "time," Cirlot writes: "[T]he time-pattern usually follows from the division of space, and this applies most particularly to the week.... It was indeed the awareness of the seven Directions of Space (that is, two for each of the three dimensions plus the centre) that gave rise to the projection of the septenary order into time. Sunday, the Day of Rest, corresponds to the centre and, since all centres are linked with the 'Centre' or Divine Source, it is therefore sacred in character. The idea of rest is expressive of the notion of the immobility of the 'Centre', whereas the other six Directions are dynamic in character."[47] We noted

Figure 226

during our study of Ezekiel's Vision the static position of the center, and the movement in and out along the three dimensions, when discussing the expansion and contraction of the box on which our little manform was drawn. It would seem that Ezekiel was well schooled in cosmology.

Hinduism has Brahma, Vishnu, and Shiva. We will allude to the triform goddess Hecate (Diana), of groves and crossroads, who represented birth (the past), life (the present), and death (the future).[48] The Nicene Council of 325 decreed, in effect, a Holy Duality, God the Father and God the Son, and the Council of Constantinople of 381 A.D. created the Christian Trinity, by adding the concept of God the Holy Ghost.[49] Toothpastes do not sell well on the American market unless they have all the ingredients of other toothpastes, plus some mysterious "extra" ingredient. Did Christianity need its Holy Trinity in order to compete with the pagan religions which almost prevailed against it?

Cirlot finally says in point-blank terms what has become increasingly apparent from our readings: "All the great symbols are really images of the world...."[50] He writes that "the world of manifestation, is sometimes represented as a city with four towers and four gates, always with an image of paramount significance in the centre."[51] We already have seen, during our study of the Book of the Shepherd of Hermas, the twelve tents of the twelve tribes of Israel with the Temple, "an image of paramount significance in the centre." We shall find such a "city" during our studies of *Perlesvaus*, one of the Grail quest stories. The author of *Perlesvaus* lets us know that he knows about ancient cosmology. He lets us know he is a "brother" who knows the meaning of the Holy Grail by writing stories using its line forms.

In respect to African societies, Cirlot tells us about "a group of interesting symbols of this kind" appearing on "ritual cups or chalices of Ethiopia" from the period of "the fourth millenary before our era."[52] So much for any notion that Africans are late-comers to this stuff! He describes a cup from Benin, a disk for Morka, and a three-dimensional carving from Yoruba.[53] Let us do some looking for ourselves in the next chapter.

Notes
CHAPTER THIRTEEN. Mixing the Ingredients

1. Cirlot xv.

2. Cirlot xvi.

3. Cirlot xvi.

4. Cirlot xvii.

5. Cirlot xvii.

6. Cirlot xvii.

7. Cirlot xix.

8. Jastrow 123,127.

9. Cirlot xix.

10. Cirlot xix; Burl 34.

11. Cirlot xx.

12. Runes 219.

13. Ezekiel 8.14.

14. Cirlot xx-xxii.

15. 1 World Book Dictionary 191 (1979).

16. Hall 339.

17. Cirlot xxii.

18. Cirlot xxii.

19. Judges 14.18.

20. Cirlot xxvii.

21. Cirlot xl.

22. Cirlot 17.

23. Cirlot 21.

24. Cirlot 40-42.

25. Ezekiel 1.26.

26. Kramer 302,304.

27. Cirlot 64-65.

28. Cirlot 65.

29. Cirlot 69.

30. Cirlot 117.

31. Cirlot 118.

32. Piggott 110-111.

33. Cirlot 138.

34. Cirlot 138.

35. Cirlot 143.

36. Cirlot 158.

37. Cirlot 194.

38. Cirlot 194.

39. Cirlot 219.

40. Cirlot 220.

41. Cirlot 226.

42. Cirlot 238.

43. Cirlot 281,351,361.

44. Cirlot 333.

45. Cirlot 337-339.

46. Cirlot 339.

47. Cirlot 343.

48. Cirlot 351.

49. Booth 13,18.

50. Cirlot 377.

51. Cirlot 378.

52. Cirlot 378.

53. Cirlot 378.

Chapter Fourteen

Black Africa –
Ancient Cultures Dead and Dying

Our discussion of Grail-related symbols from Black Africa must be briefer than most segments of this book because of your author's near total ignorance of ancient Black African cultures, and the apparent dearth of *reliable* informants. By "Black Africa" we mean those regions where the dominant culture is that of black people as distinguished from regions, principally in the North of Africa, where the cultures of Egyptians and other non-blacks have dominated. The apparent absence of reliable informants evidently results from: the absence of ancient written languages;[1] the intentional obliteration by Christian and Islamic missionaries of many aspects of ancient African culture which were deemed incompatible with the dogmas of those faiths, together with the reinterpretation of the remaining culture consistent with the new faith;[2] the ethnocentricity or racism of the published informants;[3] and the general unavailability at bookstores and on publishers' lists of reports of anthropologists and ethnologists who cared enough for blacks to record the truth as best they could perceive it.[4]

Your author is far from the first non-black to encounter these problems. "When Europeans first became acquainted with the religions of the great civilizations of West Africa, such as those of the Yoruba of Nigeria, the Ashanti of Ghana, or the Dahomeans of what is now Benin, they were amazed to discover pantheons, myths and cults as complex and rich as those of ancient Greece."[5] So they set about the process of carefully recording that data for the benefit of mankind? Wrong! "Most Western missionaries had an axe to grind when writing about the indigenous religions."[6] "At the present time the myths of a large number of East African peoples which were current in 1900 survive only in books and articles written earlier in the century, by Europeans.... Furthermore, large numbers of peoples in East Africa are now familiar with the

Illustration 14-1. Serpent plaque from the palace of Obas, Benin, seventeenth century. Courtesy of the Werner Forman Archive, London.

Bible and with Islam, and their new knowledge colours their interpretation of events and their recitation of myths."[7] Thus, it can be quite difficult for those of us, including your author, who are ignorant of ancient African mythology to get an understanding of it which is not *substantially* distorted by our informants.

Not all of this distortion is the fault of white racism. Black racism also plays a part. Those of us who have some understanding of the ancients cannot be other than amused when we read the work-product of *some* "black culture experts" who ask us to believe that a veritable Garden of Eden existed throughout Africa until the white man arrived. If the past cannot be found, or is not pleasing when found, this sort of "expert" cranks out a work-product similar to Adolph Hitler's racist propaganda, except that the "superior race" is black instead of white.

The ultimate frustration occurs when one finally gets his hands on writings of an apparently unbiased scientist who spent years of his or her life carefully recording the day-by-day thoughts and activities of black Africans. Carefully detailed and recorded are customs and practices relating to birth, marriage, death, etc., but little is said of religion and religious art. The informant doubtless was a Christian, and was uncomfortable with non-Christian religious thoughts and artwork. We do not find very much about the Holy Grail. However, the little evidence your author has been able to exhume proves beyond doubt that it *was* known!

Art from the 17th-century palace of Obas, in Benin, **Illustration 14-1**,[8] is covered with solar crosses. Compare those crosses with the one on the Irish Ardagh Chalice, **Illustration 14-2**.[9] Does this solar symbol represent separate thinking in the minds of the ancients of several races? Or exchanges of ideas between their learned persons? The choice is yours. We cannot exclude either possibility. Notice that the serpent illustrated in that art coils counterclockwise around a circle containing a cross centered by a smaller circle.

The Dogon of West Africa excite our interest by telling a tribal myth concerning the Nommo, pairs of twins (the Gemini?), who prefigured human beings, and took form in cosmic placentas in a cosmic egg in the sky. They descended to Earth on a gigantic arch centered by two Nommo of the sky, who were blacksmiths.[10] We shall learn that the Teutonic god Thor and his Saxon counterpart, Weyland Smith, also were blacksmiths. "Four pairs of Nommo, avatars of the first, took up their stance at the four cardinal points and became the first ancestors of man."[11] That is eight Nommo in a circle, the same number as in the ancient East Indian

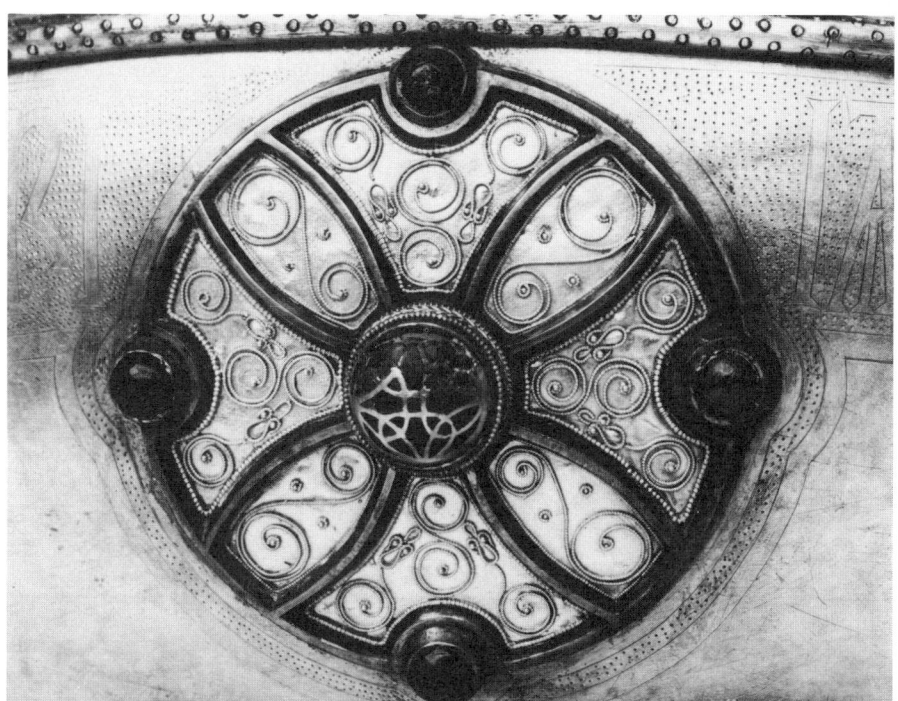

Illustration 14-2. A detail from the Ardagh Chalice, *circa* 700 A.D. Courtesy of the National Museum of Ireland, Dublin.

Illustration 14-3. A Nommo of the Dogon. From Mali. Courtesy of the Werner Forman Archive, London.

Zodiac! **Illustration 14-3**[12] shows one of the Nommo, and we see two Nommo and their blacksmith's anvil, in **Figure 227**.

The Dogon construct "big houses" modeled after that myth. "The building itself, they say, represents a Nommo in his human form. It has four towers, for example, which are his limbs."[13] A cult building having structural members representing members of the human body? We have studied Indian stupas and Christian cathedrals constructed after the form of the human body. Now we learn of African cult buildings designed from the form of the human body. Either the idea was innate among ancients of all races, or it was exchanged between their intellectuals.

Cirlot describes "An African cup from Benin [which] has a sea-serpent in... [a circular] position; here the symbol may be related to the dragon biting his own tail as in the Gnostic *Ouroboros*."[14] Cirlot further relates how a traveler in West Africa in 1910 "found an object like a kind of platform with a cone at each of its four corners and another larger one in the centre, surmounted by a cup or chalice. The central cone is the Mountain of the World (the mystic mandorla); and the four others correspond to the cardinal points."[15] The cup or chalice seen in top-view in **Figure 228** is seen in side-view in **Figure 229**. Take a look at each of the Christian churches in your city or county. Some of those churches will have a tall steeple, with a cross at its top, and the steeple will be surrounded by four smaller cones (or other objects) at the four corners of the bell tower which supports the steeple. Either we all think alike or we have copied each other through the years when devising the symbols of our religions. If forced to make a choice between the theory that this symbolism was born in different minds at different places and times because it is a part of the unconsciousness of all of us, and a choice that it was passed around the world between our intellectuals, the second choice would commend itself to your author over the first.

We now shall cease consideration of the cultures of those regions of Africa lying outside the influence of the ancient Ethiopian and Egyptian societies, hopefully having said enough to make the point that Holy Grail cosmology really is universal. We shall leave to the experts the task of culling from the mass of African folk tales and folk objects additional *genuine* specimens related to the world-wide concept of the Holy Grail.[16] Better a small amount of accurate information than a mass of misinformation.

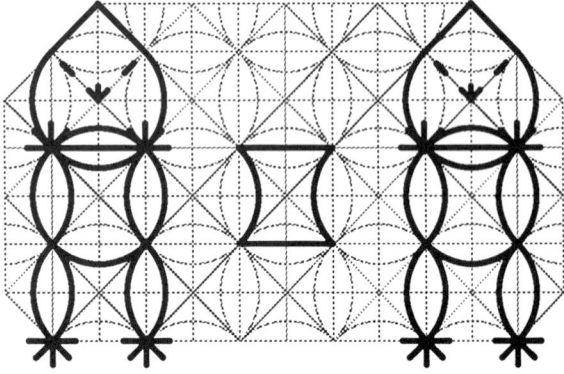

Figure 227

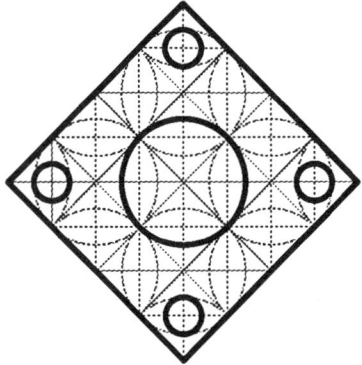

Figure 228

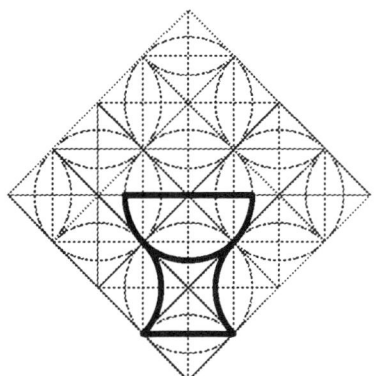

Figure 229

Our discussion of ancient Ethiopia also shall be very brief, but for an entirely different reason. Through the media of translated written language and familiar symbols we are able to establish rapport with them quite easily. The ancient black people of Ethiopia had *their own* written language.[17] Ethiopia was one of the earliest Christian countries, hundreds of years before the first Christian missionary reached Northern Europe.[18] Ethiopian Christianity is an offshoot of the Coptic Church; it is their own blend of the earliest versions of the Gospels with their ancient cult practices and beliefs.[19] Grail-related symbols, already familiar to us, abound in Ethiopian religious art. The Virgin's Prayer at Bartos refers to the four angels who hold up the four corners of the world.[20] Do you need further proof that Africans were brothers with the rest of us in the cosmology of the Holy Grail?

Notes
CHAPTER FOURTEEN.
Black Africa — Ancient Cultures Dead and Dying

1. There were notable exceptions to this general statement. Ethiopians had their own written language for hundreds of years before European languages, other than Greek and Latin, had written forms. Other black Africans read and wrote ancient Egyptian, Arabic, Greek, and Latin. In their zeal to destroy pagan religion, Christian and Islamic missionaries doubtless destroyed other notational systems utilized to preserve data in written form. But the general statement holds true. Most black Africans did not read or write before the introduction of modern European languages.

2. Neither Christianity nor Islam was tolerant of "pagan" religion. Missionaries first sought to destroy African religion. Only to the extent that they failed did they resort to allegory to reinterpret the old religion in light of the new religion.

3. Thousands of Europeans and Americans have written about their missionary conquests, or their rifle or camera safaris, on the "Dark Continent." Many of these writings drip with honey-sweet paternalism or stench from white racism expressed by those travelers toward their black African hosts. Few express even the slightest understanding of the cultural and ecological values expressed through the "quaint" or "barbaric" ceremonies which the haughty traveler had witnessed. Who, today, is prepared to say that people who never polluted a river or lake, and who had better sense than to destroy the game upon which they fed, had nothing of cultural or ecological value for white people? Most "modern" black Africans pollute and destroy their environment as if they were whites. The few who cherish and conserve nature have values we all should emulate.

4. High-quality studies by anthropologists, ethnologists, and persons of other social-science disciplines exist in the libraries of the large universities, but are not available to the general reader, who is precluded by the exigencies of everyday life from taking advantage of those treasure houses.

5. Cavendish 222.

6. Cavendish 207.

7. Cavendish 214.

8. Cavendish 225.

9. From the author's collection.

10. Cavendish 227.

11. Cavendish 226.

12. Cavendish 226.

13. Cavendish 226.

14. Cirlot 378.

15. Cirlot 378.

16. This is a formidable task for a dedicated few, who, in the opinion of your author, need to obtain portable recording equipment and start interviewing tribal elders whose minds are not clouded by the white man's mythology. Knowledge of the millennia dies with each of those "Auld Wans."

17. 6 Encyclopaedia Britannica Macropaedia 1006-1007.

18. 6 World Book Encyclopedia 296 (1983); 6 Encyclopaedia Britannica Macropaedia 1001; Mercier 7.

19. 6 World Book Encyclopedia 295 (1983); Budge AAS 1889-189;

20. Mercier 118.

Chapter Fifteen

Egyptian Religion Explained?

How could so brilliant a people as the ancient Egyptians be so stupid as to worship animals? From ancient to modern times, possible answers to that question have been debated between supporters and detractors of the Egyptians. Stylized animals *do* play as prominent a role in ancient Egyptian art as stylized humans. Equally prominent and stylized in ancient Egyptian art are human bodies with heads of animals, birds, reptiles, and insects. "'Egyptian animal worship'… provoked the merriment of the cultured Greek, and drew down upon the Egyptians the ridicule and abuse of the early Christian writers. But if the matter be examined closely its apparent stupidity disappears." Thus wrote the eminent Egyptologist E. A. Wallis Budge.[1] Budge contended that "[t]he educated Egyptian never worshipped an animal as an animal, but only as an incarnation of a god…. The ignorant people, no doubt, often mistook the symbol for what it symbolized, but it is wrong to say that the Egyptians worshipped animals in the ordinary sense of the word, and this fact cannot be too strongly insisted on."[2] Budge thus shows himself to be pro-Egyptian.

Why were early Christian writers so abusive towards the Egyptians? Early Christians used a fish as a symbol for Jesus Christ, but the Egyptians evidently did not contend that Christians therefore worshiped fish! Did early Christian writers disparage the Egyptians not because Egyptian religion was so different from Christianity but because it was so similar in many fundamental aspects and was in such active competition with Christianity for converts?

The unknown author of *The Letter Of Aristeas*, the book from which came our story of the table,

Figure 230

apparently was anti-Egyptian. He wrote: "Why need we speak of other infatuated people, Egyptians and the like, who place their reliance upon wild beasts and most kinds of creeping things and cattle, and worship them, and offer sacrifices to them both while living and when dead?"[3] Scholars believe it is "highly probable" that the unknown author of *Aristeas* was Hebrew.[4] He has demonstrated to us that he knew how to make up a story about a "table" using line forms visible on the Holy Grail. He apparently also knew secret allegorical reasons for the Hebrew dietary laws. While addressing the subject of meat to eat and not to eat, he wrote: "For the division of the hoof and the separation of the claws are intended to teach us that we must discriminate between our individual actions with a view to the practice of virtue."[5] He also wrote: "For all animals 'which are cloven-footed and chew the cud' represent to the initiated the *symbol* of memory."[6] *Symbol*? *Initiated*? We have suspected that he was a member of some secret society. He seems to have proven us correct by his own words!

Because the author of *Aristeas* knew enough about the Holy Grail to be able to write a complex story about a table using the line forms of the Holy Grail, he may be presumed to have known the origin of the Egyptian goddess Sekhmet, who had the head of a lioness on the body of a human female; and the Egyptian goddess Isis-Hathor, who had the stylized horns of a cow on the head and body of a human female; and the Egyptian god Osiris, who had the head and body of a human male; and, last but not least, the Egyptian god Horus, the son of Osiris and Isis, who had the head of a falcon on the body of a human male.[7] Eagles and falcons look much alike, both being raptors. The heads of horned bulls, horned cows, and horned oxen look much alike. Lion, Ox, Man, and Eagle! Our four critters of Ezekiel's Vision made their appearance in the Egyptian pantheon? Ezekiel told us that the cherubim had "straight" feet?[8] The Egyptian canon of art called for the feet of humans, gods, and combination human-animals to face "straight" sideways in the manner illustrated in **Figure 230**. Here we find another possible meaning of Ezekiel's vague reference to "straight" feet.

Are we being unfair if we conclude that our probably-Jewish author of *Aristeas* was anti-Egyptian? Because of his having written the story of the table based on line forms visible on the Holy Grail, he must be presumed to have known that Moses as well as Hathor was "found" on the Holy Grail. Anti-Semitism is disgusting. What about anti-Hamitism? Ethnocentrism and consequent racism should be deplored by all Eagles at all times. All of humankind is "God's chosen people," not just the people who traditionally have referred to themselves by those words. Israelites did not like to be considered equals with Hamites? Too bad! We shall allow for no favorites in this book.

Why did the author of *Aristeas*, a religionist who knew about the Holy Grail, seek to elevate his religious beliefs by deprecating someone else's religious beliefs? Was it because he was more interested in maintaining or increasing his flock of followers than he was interested in achieving the common goal of all religions — betterment of the human condition? Or was it just another case of the feudin', fussin', and fightin' that goes on to this day between Semites and Hamites; them-uns versus us-uns, with them-uns always being the bad guys?

Let us assume that the well-informed classes in ancient Egypt grasped a line of reasoning that ran something like this: (1) The gods have revealed to us through the Holy Grail an abstract image of a cow with horns. (2) Horned cows are good mothers to their calves. (3) Accordingly, the gods are telling us that human females should be good mothers to their children. Let us assume that the worst-informed classes in ancient Egypt failed to grasp the allegory and merely worshiped the cow, because, according to their best understanding, that is what they were supposed to do to comply with the dictates of the priests. Let us next recall that the ancient Egyptians worshiped a god-man named Osiris who, according to their priests, died a sacrificial death to save mankind, and then was born again; that they believed that if they complied with the dictates of the priests of the Osiris cult, they would be saved from the human affliction of death and would have eternal life, like gods, with Osiris in the sky.[9] Egyptians tried to become like Osiris, just as Christians aspire to become Christ-like. The original thought pattern was identical in both religions: Humans die. The God (Osiris) (Christ) did not. Therefore, we shall aspire to become like the God and, as result, we shall have eternal life like the God instead of death like a human.

How is the typical Christian construction worker of today different from his Egyptian counterpart of yesterday? Relying upon his engineering experts, the ancient Egyptian fellah constructed marvelous structures. Likewise, the modern construction laborer. The religious beliefs of both about the way to salvation are distinctly similar. How could a people as brilliant

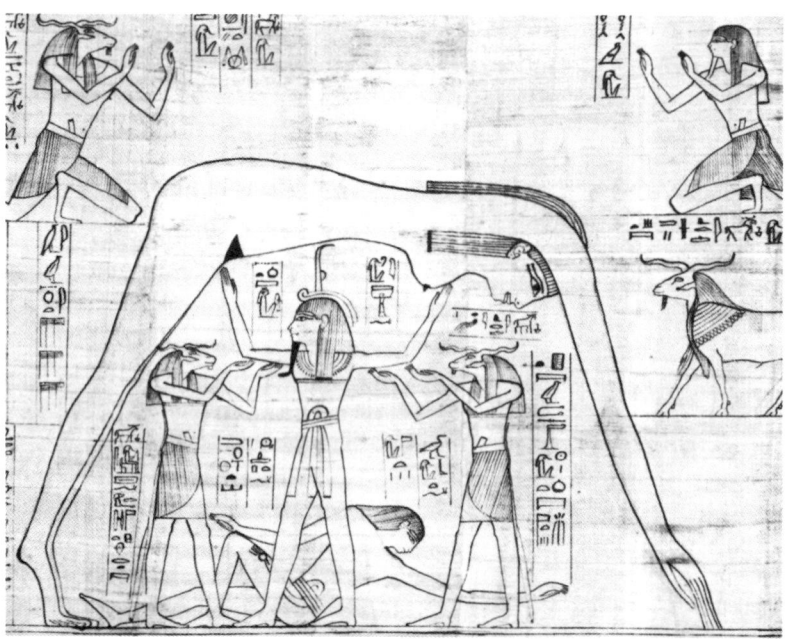

Illustration 15-1. Shu, god of space, holding Nut, goddess of the sky, apart from Geb, god of the Earth. Courtesy of Thames & Hudson Ltd., London.

as the Americans of the twentieth century worship as they do? Is the answer the same as for the ancient Egyptians? In default of reason; as an exercise of unquestioning faith in their religious leaders? If the answer to the last question is in the affirmative, then the next question must be whether our religious leaders deserve our absolute faith. Should we reason with them about the form and content of our religion? Your author does *not* suggest that we be rid of them. When espousing humanism, instead of theology, they do much good in this world.

*   *   *

At no point in our travels will your author be more tempted than now to violate our guiding principle that we shall visit only *briefly* with cultures apparently influenced by the Holy Grail. Several volumes could be written on the impact of the Holy Grail upon Egyptian religion. We shall resist the temptation and be brief.

When lay persons such as you and I look at ancient Egyptian art, we often fail to get the point the artist intended to convey. When we read translations of the texts which accompany the art, we still fail to understand the message. In resignation, we lay the book aside. We admit our ignorance. Egyptologists admit that they have not discovered the logic behind all details of the ancient Egyptian religion, which was

a hodgepodge of beliefs rather than a unified faith.[10] The Rosetta Stone provided the key to the ancient Egyptian language. Is the Holy Grail a key to better understanding of ancient Egyptian religion?

With the last question firmly lodged in our minds, let us look at the legend of the goddess Nut and the god Geb. She was the goddess of the sky; he the god of the Earth. In the beginning, they were separated from each other by the god of space, Shu, much as in the beginning Yahweh separated the waters of the Heavens (the posited heavenly reservoir of rainwater) from the waters of the Earth.[11]

The usual portrayal of this trinity of Nut, Geb, and Shu is in **Illustration 15-1**, where Nut forms the vault of the sky with her arched body, supporting herself on her tiptoes and fingertips, while Shu extends his arms upwards, in the form of an Egyptian Ka-symbol, to hold Nut apart from Geb, who lies below Nut.[12] According to ancient Egyptian texts, Nut gave birth to the sun each morning and swallowed it each evening.[13] Less frequently seen in books on Egypt, probably because it shocked Egyptologists of the Victorian era, is the portrayal in **Illustration 15-2** of Geb lying beneath Nut with his phallus (representing the world axis?) erect.[14] Notice in Illustration 15-2 the positions of Geb's legs, arms, and head. Is he turning towards the right of the picture? Towards the east? The Earth rotates to the east on its axis. Did the ancient Egyptians know that? The least frequently seen portrayal of this couple, who were said to be the parents of Osiris, Isis,

Illustration 15-2. Nut, goddess of the sky, over Geb, god of the Earth, both facing easterly. Courtesy of Michael Holford Photographs, Loughton, Essex, England.

Seth, and Nephthys, is shown in **Illustration 15-3**, in which her head faces in one direction and his head faces in the opposite direction.[15] In this last portrayal, she again is at rest on her fingertips and tiptoes, while he again is in motion.

We are told by our history books that the ancients believed the sky turned and the Earth stood still. This was the theory espoused by the early Christian Church.[16] This certainly is not the symbolism of Illustrations 15-2 and 15-3, in which Nut (the sky) is at rest and Geb (the Earth) is in motion! Of that much we can be certain!

Nut's head is towards the left of the page in Illustration 15-3; Geb's toward the right. We shall assume that the Egyptologists correctly have concluded that the Egyptians employed the same north (up), south (down), east (right), and west (left) schema we still use.[17] If Nut gives birth in this position, the sun will be born in the morning from her vulva in the east and be swallowed in the evening by her mouth in the west. Thus, this artwork may portray a belief that the sun rises in the east in the morning, traverses the sky during the day, and sets in the west in the evening. But another interpretation is possible. Geb may be visualized doing either a forwards somersault or a backwards somersault. If he is doing a forwards somersault, then he is turning, to the west, in the same direction that the sun is "traveling" from Nut's vulva to her mouth. This movement would contradict the apparent motion of the sun across the sky, unless the sun moves faster than Geb's rotation. If, instead, Geb is doing a backwards somersault, he is

turning toward the east — the direction that the Earth really turns on its axis!

Did educated Egyptians know that the apparent movement of the sun, east to west across the daytime sky, results from the easterly rotation of the Earth on its axis? Did educated Egyptians tell the uneducated masses that the sun does the moving because they knew the masses would not believe the converse? Notice that Nut eats her offspring (the sun) in the legend, conduct familiar to peasants who would have observed such behavior among animals, fish, and birds. Was the Nut legend more believable to the common folk than the scientific explanation? Why do we still speak of the sun "rising" each morning and "setting" each evening? In mindless devotion to our religious leaders, do we recite an ancient litany (such as "the sun rises") long after we are, or should be, aware of reality?

The direction of Geb's motion in Illustrations 15-2 and 15-3 is ambiguous. His somersault can be either backwards or forwards. We must not select the direction we would prefer to attribute to the ancient Egyptians. We must be content with the clear expression through this symbolism that the Earth turns while the sky is at rest.

Why do our history books omit this information about the ancient Egyptians? Because of pressure from the Christian Church? The early Christian Church taught that the Earth stands still, in the very middle of the universe, while the heavenly bodies (including the sun and moon) rotate on their respective spheres.[18] Our Egyptian artists apparently knew better. When

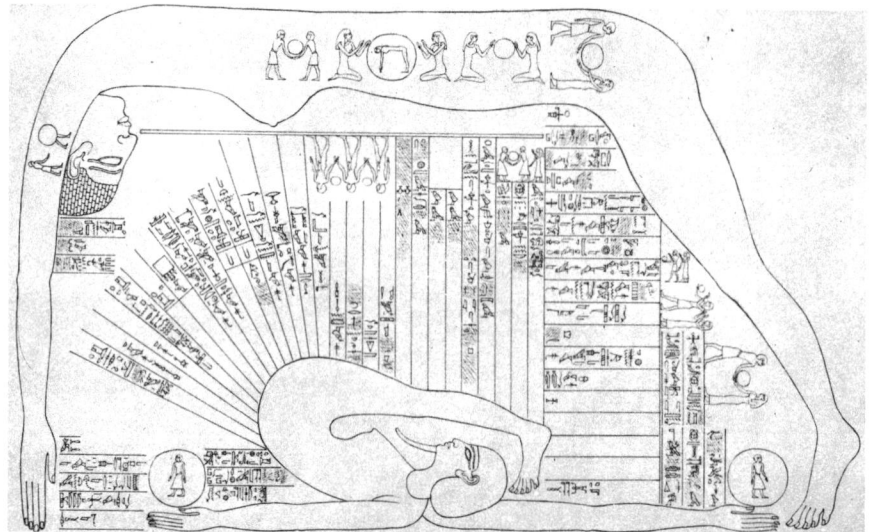

Illustration 15-3. Nut, goddess of the sky, over Geb, god of the Earth, she facing westerly and he facing easterly. Courtesy of Thames & Hudson Ltd., London.

Galileo arrived at the conclusion evidently reached by our ancient Egyptian artists, the Church reacted first with condemnation then with violence, threatening Galileo variously with death, or life in prison, if he did not publicly renounce his theory.[19] Did the leaders of the Church know that the Earth rotates on its axis as it rotates around the sun? If so, why did they teach the opposite to the masses? Because the masses never would have given up sun worship, together with its human sacrificial rituals, if they had known that *in fact* the sun sits "enthroned in the center" with the Earth obediently revolving around it? Why do many textbook publishers still refrain from telling the whole truth about the trial of Galileo? Because Christian fundamentalists would seek to have such books banned in their school districts? Because the corporate purpose of the textbook publishers is to make money, a goal forwarded by the simple strategy of avoiding the whole truth?

Do Nut and Geb appear on the Holy Grail? If so, that is some evidence that the Egyptians may have related the Holy Grail to rotations visible in the sky. Turn back to our humanform in Figures 10 through 13, where we see him (or her) facing north, south, east, and west. Imagine one naked Grail humanform on top of, and facing in the same direction as, a second naked Grail humanform. Now visualize one naked Grail humanform on top of another naked Grail humanform, with their heads facing in opposite directions. Nonsense? You bet it is! But it is not *my* nonsense!

Could the Grail images of Nut and Geb facing in the same direction have been the priestly inspiration for the ancient Semitic "sacred marriage" ceremonies which were celebrated, as acts of religious devotion, among the Semitic Babylonians long after the Hebrews gave this custom up? (The king and the high priestess consummated sexual intercourse each New Year's Day to fructify, symbolically, not only all members of the tribe but their animals and crops as well.) Could this have been the origin of ancient Semitic sacred prostitution, against which the Hebrew prophets of later years vented their holy wrath? Could Grail humanforms facing in opposite directions have been the inspiration for ancient Semitic sacred sexual perversion which, like sacred prostitution, was practiced within the confines of the temple as an act of religious devotion, and later was decried by Bible-era Hebrew reformers? Ask yourself these questions: Why would the ancient Egyptians portray the sky as a woman and the Earth as a man? Where did they get the idea? From their priests? And where did the

priests get it? From the same place they got "animal worship"? From the Holy Grail?

Another parallel question: the New Testament refers to Christ as "the bridegroom," a term which harkens back to the ancient Semitic sacred marriage ceremonies.[20] Notice the missing antecedent of the definite article "the." Not "a" bridegroom but "the" bridegroom, in the same fashion as Christ was referred to not as "a" rock but as "the" rock. More ancient cosmology? Good salesmanship by those spreading the new Christian faith? We already have learned that successful salesmen of new religions often associate with the new god the symbols of the old god because the masses are so satisfied with their ancient symbols that they do not readily give them up. Was the antecedent of the definite article "the" sufficiently understood by the masses to whom the Gospels first were addressed so that nothing more needed to be said? Was the "bridegroom" to which these Biblical passages referred the cosmic bridegroom in the sky; our manform on the Holy Grail? Were the Gospel-writers merely telling their audiences that the correct name of the familiar cosmic manform is Jesus Christ, Son of God, Savior, instead of Indra, Vishnu, Siva, Arthur, Adam, Attis, Mithras, etc.? We already have learned the importance to the ancient mind of knowing the correct name of the god — to make prayers effective.[21]

*　　　*　　　*

Continuing with the "family history" of some of the principal gods and goddesses of ancient Egypt, we are told that Osiris and his sister Isis, children of Nut and Geb, got married and had a son named Horus. Pharaoh married his sister for thousands of years to mimic the mythical marriage of Osiris and Isis. You get the desired effect from an aspirin tablet by swallowing it with some water. The ancients thought you got the desired effect from a myth by mimicking the words and actions of the hero or heroine of the myth. The idea is that you act out what you want to happen and it will happen; a version of the sympathetic magic of the ancient shaman. Isis holds baby Horus in her arms.[22] Our Lady holds Her Son in Her arms.[23] All mothers become like the Good Mother by doing likewise. As we have said, the masses cling to their symbols, and the successful reformer of religion knows this and takes advantage of it.

The myths said that Horus had four sons. When an Egyptian was mummified, parts of his viscera were removed and placed in four canoptic jars, which

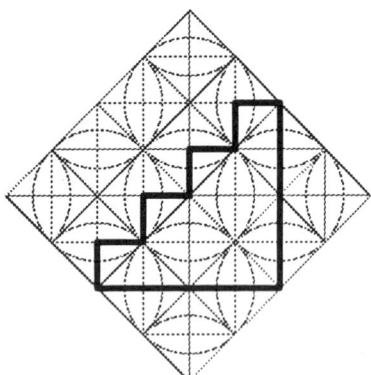

Figure 231

represented the four sons of Horus and were arranged in a north, south, east, and west configuration and placed in a square canoptic jar case.[24] The deceased thereby got for himself the value of the Horus myth.

The four sons (like many Egyptian gods) sometimes were represented in human form and at other times with human bodies and animal heads.[25] Lion, ox, man, and eagle? Not this time. We have, instead, baboon, dog or jackal, man, and falcon.[26] Find them for yourself on the Holy Grail. Budge tells us that the four sons of Horus "originally represented the four supports of heaven, but very soon each was regarded as the god of the four quarters of the earth, and also of that quarter of the heavens which was above it."[27]

Had enough Egyptian cosmology? Ready to move on to another civilization? Before we do, let us rapidly look at a few familiar Egyptian symbols.

In Illustration 5-2, and in Figure 64, we see Khepera or Khepri, the scarab-beetle, who represented the power which "rolls the sun across the sky" like his real-world counterpart, the Egyptian dung beetle, rolls balls of manure.[28] The amulet of the steps to Heaven is seen in **Figure 231**.[29] We are told that the Egyptian sun-god Re or Ra (also known as Atum)[30] "was supposed to travel in one boat (called 'Atet') until noon, and another (called 'Setet') until sunset."[31] The Atet boat and the Setet boat sailed around a

circular sea.[32] We see these "boats" in **Figures 232 and 233**.

Is the "sea" on which the Atet boat and the Setet boat sailed the same "sea" found in Solomon's temple? Is this the same "sea" on which Christ boated and walked?

The Egyptians thought the floor of Heaven was an iron plate. Why? Because lightning appeared to come from Heaven, and iron was associated by them with electricity, as it was by the ancient Hebrews?[33]

Another Egyptian symbol before we move on: **Figure 234** shows the "Ka-arms" which enclose the cosmic sun.[34] **Figure 235** shows the symbol of the Phoenician goddess Tanit, who was believed to demand human infant sacrifice, with her "Ka-arms" raised.[35] We have allowed our religious leaders to talk us into doing positively disgusting things in the name of religion. We still do. When Ian Paisley preaches tribal mythology, children die in Belfast.

Let us leave Egypt with these bits of mythology trivia: The Israelites were not the first people reputed to have a leader who could divide a large body of water.[36] Neither was the story of the sun's standing still in the midday sky originally of Hebrew origin.[37] In a myth far older than the Creation story of the Book of Genesis, the Egyptian creator god created the universe by saying the correct word.[38] Is the Bible nothing but accurately reported history? Or might it contain at least a few retellings of ancient myths which have been modified to prove that "our" magicians are equal to or better than "theirs"? Are such "us-uns is better than them-uns" stories expressions of beautiful religious belief or of disgusting ethnocentricity?

We are no more through with Egypt when we leave this chapter than we were through with Persia when we left Chapter Eleven.

Here is a brain-teaser for professional and amateur Egyptologists: What do we see in **Figure 236**? The bull of Heaven with the sun in its horns, rising or setting over an akhet hieroglyph? This question is answered in the science chapters, where the proof is

Figure 232

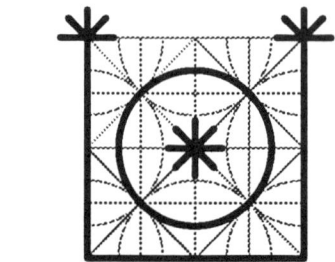

Figure 233

Figure   234

Egyptian Religion Explained?

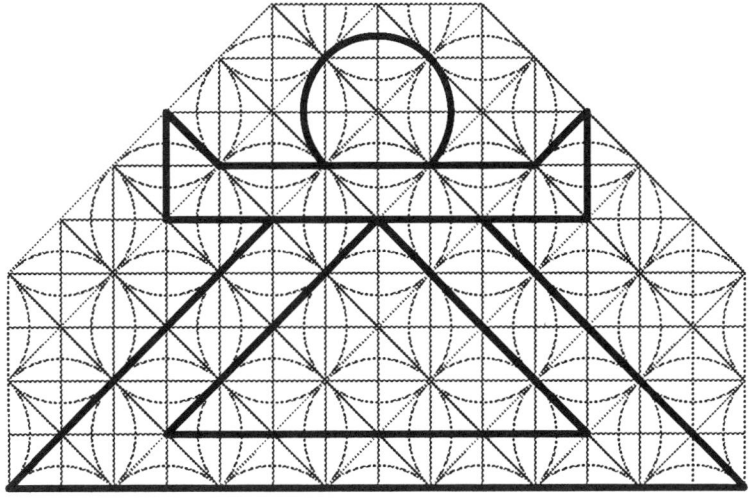

Figure   235

Figure 236

found set in the stones of the Sphinx and the great pyramids of Khufu and Khafre!

We will encounter dwarfs in the Grail quest stories we analyze. The Egyptians had a "domestic god" named Bes, who was "a bandy-legged dwarf with a broad face, wide mouth with protruding tongue, a beard resembling a lion's mane and animal ears and tail."[39] Does that sound like someone you may have met?

Notes
CHAPTER FIFTEEN. Egyptian Religion Explained?

1. Budge EM 232.

2. Budge EM 233; see also Cerny 40.

3. Letter of Aristeas 6.15.

4. 2 Charlesworth, Letter of Aristeas 9.

5. Letter of Aristeas 6.33.

6. Letter of Aristeas 6.40.

7. Erman 268, 271; Lamy 46-47, 82; Cavendish 106.

8. Ezekiel 1.7.

9. Budge EM xiii,1-2, 184; Cerny 147-150.

10. Cerny 39.

11. Lamy 42; Oxford 887, fn.22.

12. Lamy 42. Even the Hebrews had their trinity. Cerny tells us that the Hebrew colony at Elephantine, on the River Nile, in Egypt, built "a temple to Yahve and his two female companions, Ashima and Anat, whose worship was not forbidden among Jews before the introduction of the unified religious law on the occasion of the rebuilding of Yahve's temple at Jerusalem in 515 B.C." Cerny 135.

13. Lamy 42.

14. Cavendish 98.

15. Lamy 21.

16. Dreyer 192, 206-239, 416-417.

17. Lamy 21, 95; Branston 179.

18. Dreyer 207-239, 416-417.

19. Dreyer 416-420; Hall 18-22; 8 World Book Encyclopedia 12 (1983); 4 World Book Encyclopedia 821 (1983).

20. Matthew 9.15; Mark 2.19-20; Luke 5.34-35.

21. Griffith & Thompson 37, 59-63.

22. Branston 199.

23. Branston 198. "The worship of the Virgin Mary and the picture of her with the child Jesus in her arms almost certainly owe a great deal to the influence of the goddess Isis with the young Horus on her lap." Cerny 148.

24. Budge EM 89-91; Lamy 93-95.

25. Lamy 94.

26. Erman 306; Lamy 93.

27. Budge EM 91.

28. Budge EM 35-43.

29. Budge EM 62.

30. Cavendish 109.

31. Budge EM 111.

32. Talbott 269-282.

33. *Hashmal* is the modern Hebrew for "electricity." Graves & Patai 38. The King James Bible translates *hashmal* or *chashmal* as "amber." Ezekiel 1.4, 27.

34. Talbott 286-298.

35. Talbott 285-286; Fox 146-153. Christian priests and preachers traditionally raise "ka-arms" while they say the benediction. With their arms thus raised, their heads take the position of the enclosed cosmic sun. Our brains enlighten our lives? Yes, if we strive to become Eagles.

36. Budge EM 7-10.

37. Budge EM 135.

38. Budge EM 161.

39. Cerny 71.

Chapter Sixteen

The Mystery Religions: Mithraism

The appearances of most objects change as the magnification through which we observe them increases and decreases. The same may be said of religions. Their appearances change with the depth and breadth of our vision.

Christian Sunday school literature and American high-school history books tend to agree on these perspectives of history:

1. The official gods of the Roman state, Jupiter, etc., were mirror images of the Greek Olympian Gods, Zeus, etc. Only their names were changed.
2. The Roman state persecuted Christians because Christians refused to worship the official gods of the Roman state.
3. The competition for converts thus was between only two religions.
4. The Roman state under Emperor Constantine adopted Christianity as its official religion, thereby ending religious intolerance and persecution.
5. Freed from fears of persecution by the Roman state, everyone except the Hebrews voluntarily flocked to the Christian Church, was baptized, and lived happily ever after.

Students of comparative religion learn another reality. The following summary is *far* too general to be entirely accurate but is much more accurate than the foregoing summary:

1. Many years before Christianity became a serious contender against the mystery religions for converts, Jupiter, etc., had been replaced in the minds of many Roman citizens by the savior gods of the mystery religions.[1]
2. The savior gods of the mystery religions had become the official (or some of the official) gods of the Roman state during the reign of some of the emperors, i.e., they sometimes had replaced Jupiter, etc., or had become their official equals.[2]
3. During the three-plus hundreds of years before Christianity became the official religion of the Roman state, religious toleration was the rule; religious intolerance the exception.[3]

Some Roman emperors persecuted some of the mystery religions, because of their national origins, while supporting and even joining others. Most tolerated them all.[4] Several mystery religions built their temples on the very spot in Rome where the Vatican now stands.[5] Their congregations were open to anyone who would accept initiation, and their pageants paraded through the streets of Rome for all to observe.[6]

4. Roman religious tolerance rose to such a high level that persons often were initiated into more than one of the mystery religions, and religious leaders became official clergy of more than one mystery religion.[7] Only Christians and Jews insisted upon religious exclusiveness for both their membership and clergy.[8]
5. Christianity was as tolerated as other savior-god religions until the Roman authorities came to believe that Christians practiced actual, as distinguished from symbolic, human sacrifice and cannibalism, at which time the Roman laws proscribing such practices were applied to Christians in the same manner and to the same extent as these laws were applied to other persons who engaged in those ancient forms of magic.[9] Whether early Christians should have been convicted under Roman laws against human sacrifice and cannibalism is a question we shall discuss later. You must be prepared to hear evidence which goes beyond Christian magic ceremonies through which bread and wine supposedly were converted into the actual flesh and blood of Jesus Christ. You shall have to decide for yourself whether the Roman government had no cause, some cause, or considerable cause for these allegations against early Christian sects.
6. We will discover that systematic religious intolerance and persecution began, rather than ended, with Christianity's ascendancy to the status of official religion of the Roman

state.[10] Persons who would not become Christians were slaughtered, their houses of worship were burned or pulled to the ground, the symbols of their worship were smashed, their treasuries were looted, and their libraries were burned by Roman soldiers and by howling Christian mobs lead by Christian bishops.[11] Those who refused to recite the word formulae of the Church in the exact form prescribed were called "heretics," were hunted down as groups and individually, and were put to the sword or burned to death. We shall study the Arian and Cathar Heresies and the armed crusades mounted by the Church to slaughter these "heretics," whose beliefs were starkly similar to those of many persons today.[12] We shall learn that Constantine chose Christianity as his state religion in lieu of Mithraism for reasons of empire.[13]

What is a "mystery religion?" A "mystery religion" is a religion which imparts to the initiated a secret which ensures salvation.[14] "There was something, whether doctrine, symbol, or divine drama, which could not be imparted except by initiation to those duly qualified to receive, a supernatural revelation which gave the recipient a new outlook on life, the world, and the deity, and security denied to the uninitiated. The 'mystery' consisted in an objective presentation of the history of the cult-deity in his or her struggles, sorrows, and triumphs, repeated subjectively by the initiate in sacramental acts together with prayers and liturgic formulae, or it was a profound intuition of the 'Spirit in Love,' or foretaste of that mystic experience in which 'we know as we are known,' in progressive satisfaction of the two eternal passions of selfhood, the desire for love and also for knowledge. The 'secret,' when imparted, rendered men superior to all trials of life and ensured salvation."[15] "No means of exciting the emotions was neglected in the passion-play, either by way of inducing careful predispositions or of supplying external stimulus. Tense mental anticipation, heightened by a period of abstinence, hushed silences, imposing processions and elaborated pageantry, music loud and violent or soft and enthralling, delirious dances, the drinking of spirituous liquors, physical macerations, alternations of dense darkness and dazzling light, the sight of gorgeous ceremonial vestments, the handling of holy emblems, auto-suggestion and the promptings of the hierophant — these and many other secrets of emotional exaltation were in vogue."[16]

Why do Christian preachers who graduated seminary leave the mystery religions unmentioned to their congregations? It cannot be because they never have heard of them. (We must excuse lay preachers, called to the pulpit from the congregation, who lack formal religious education and, hence, know little about the history of religion.) Are these the reasons: Because persons who know about the mystery religions are apt to realize that Christian doctrine is *evolutionary* rather than *revolutionary*?[17] Because persons who know about the mystery religions may conclude that Christianity was a new and improved brand of mystery religion?[18]

Each of the manufacturers of the various cola drinks on the market today seeks to lure away the competition's faithful consumers by representations that their product is absolutely unique. The blunt truth, however, is that all these drinks taste somewhat alike, and that all will satisfy a burning thirst. Was this true of the mystery religions? Each and every one of them had a god (1) who died and was born again;[19] (2) whose doctrines, if recited and believed, and whose ceremonies, if faithfully performed, would assure the true believer of life everlasting; and (3) who could save the faithful from the otherwise inevitable consequences — death of the human body and dissolution of the human soul.[20] Did Christianity prevail by "market competition," i.e., by providing a "better product," or because it had powerful political allies who could organize a howling mob or command the Roman army to march? Although Christianity's "sugar" was more refined, was it the "product" itself or the tactics of the "salesmen" that made the real difference?

Erudite consumers realize how toothpaste advertising works. If you believe toothpaste advertising, you are forced to conclude that each toothpaste has everything and does everything that all other toothpastes have and do, and also has some secret ingredient which does something none of the others can do. The impossibility of such a proposition is to be ignored. The blunt truth is that baking soda does a remarkably good, yet inexpensive, job of cleaning teeth when used with a proper toothbrush which is agitated in a proper manner. Baking soda, however, merely cleans your teeth. It does not promise you a wonderful night on the town with a beautiful or handsome sexual partner. People want more than clean teeth. They want mystique. If you understand toothpaste advertising, you may understand the mystery religions.

An example from *Encyclopaedia Britannica* may suffice to illustrate the tactics employed by the mystery religions to gain converts. Most people who have graduated high school know that Di-

onysus was a god of vegetation: hence, a god of grapes and wine. As successful businessmen, the priests of Dionysus knew how to compete: cheat. "The Dionysus temple at Corinth had an underground system of tubes and barrels that could be operated by buttons from the outside. The priest showed the worshippers of the god a barrel filled with water. They left the temple together, and the door was sealed from without. By pressing the buttons, the water was let out of the barrel, and wine was poured in. The following day, when the seal was removed, the spectator witnessed the Dionysiac miracle of water turned into wine."[21] Is this why the Bible tells us the story of how Christ changed water into wine before the eyes of a group of partygoers?[22] Christian fundamentalist teetotalers would prefer that the storyteller had written that Christ changed wine into water, but are forced by the doctrine of Biblical inerrancy to concede that the founder of the Christian religion made wine for a party. The Roman engineer Hero invented a vase with a hidden siphon system which was used by magicians to create the illusion of changing water into wine or wine into water.[23] This illusion was a part of the repertoire of magicians in Roman times.[24]

Priestly showmanship to attract "customers" was not, however, confined to the worshipers of Dionysus. Another priesthood employed an engineer to erect a temple dome of lodestone in an attempt to cause an iron image of their goddess to float in the air.[25] That little bit of pious fraud did not work, but a very famous invention did. Highschool students often learn that a Roman engineer named Hero invented the first steam engine, but the authors of those books forget to tell the students the use to which it was put. It was used to open the doors of a miniature temple as if by command of the god.[26] The engineers of Nazi Germany who designed the death-camp cremation ovens and our engineers who designed the atomic bombs dropped on Japan apparently were not the first to prostitute their trade to the power structure.[27]

Before we get down to some particulars of several of the mystery religions, and look for their symbols on the Holy Grail, let us chew on a few more quotations from *Encyclopaedia Britannica* as general background information.

"Before initiation, a confession of sins was expected.... It was believed that the rite of baptism would wash away all the candidate's sins, and, from that point on, his life would be changed for the better, because he had enrolled himself in the service of the savior god.... The initiation ceremonies usually mimed death and resurrection.... In imitation of the Orphic myth of Dionysus Zagreus, a rite

was held in which the heart of a victim, supposedly a human child, was roasted and distributed among the participants to be eaten.... The baptism could be either by water or by fire.... In the religion of Sol, the festivals were determined by astronomy. The greatest festival was held on December 24-25, at the time of the winter solstice. Because from this date the length of the day began to increase, it was regarded as the day of the rebirth of the god and of the renovation of life.... The creeds of the mystery religions were never worked out to the same extent that the Christian creeds were. Nevertheless, the doctrines of the mysteries may be called a theology. One of the central subjects in mystery writings was cosmogony — the theory of the origin or creation of the world.... The theological doctrine of the soul and the myth about its celestial home, its fall, and its redemption were inseparable.... The simultaneousness of the propagation of the mystery religions and of Christianity and the striking similarities between them, however, demand some explanation of their relationship. The hypothesis of a mutual dependence has been proposed by scholars — especially a dependence of Christianity upon the mysteries — but such theories have been discarded. The similarities must rather be explained by parallel developments from similar origins. In both cases, national religions of a ritualistic type were transformed, and the transformation followed similar lines: from national to ecumenical religion, from ritualistic ceremonies and taboos to spiritual doctrines set down in books, from the idea of inherited tradition to the idea of revelation.... The ideas of Greek philosophy penetrated everywhere in this [the cosmopolitan Roman] society.... The mystery religions and Christianity had many similar features — *e.g.*, a time of preparation before initiation and periods of fasting; baptism and banquets; vigils and early-morning ceremonies; pilgrimages and new names for the initiates. The purity demanded in the worship of Sol and in the Chaldean fire rites was similar to Christian standards. The first Christian communities resembled the mystery communities in big cities and seaports by providing social security and the feeling of brotherhood. In the Christian congregations of the first two centuries, the variety of rites and creeds was almost as great as in the mystery communities; few of the early Christian congregations could have been called orthodox according to later standards. The date of Christmas was purposefully fixed on December 25 to push into the background the great festival of the sun god, and Epiphany on January 6 to supplant an Egyptian festival of the same day. The Easter ceremonies rivalled the pagan spring festivals. The religious art of the Christians continued the pagan art of the preceding generations. The Christian representations of the Madonna and child are clearly the continuation of the representations of Isis and her son suckling her breast. The statue of the Good Shepherd carrying his lost sheep and the pastoral themes on Christian sarcophagi were also taken over from pagan craftsmanship.... In theology the difference between early Christians, Gnostics (members — often Christian — of dualistic sects of the 2nd century AD), and pagan Hermetists were slight. In the large Gnostic library discovered at Naj'Hammadi, in upper Egypt, in 1945, Hermetic writings were found side-by-side with Christian Gnostic texts. The doctrine of the soul, as it was taught in Gnostic communities, was almost identical to that of the mysteries.... Thus, the religions had a common conceptual framework. The doctrinal similarity is exemplified in the case of the pagan writer and philosopher Synesius. When the people of Cyrene wanted the most able man of the city to be their bishop, they chose him, and he was able to accept the election without sacrificing his intellectual honesty. In his pagan period he wrote hymns that closely follow the fire theology of the *Chaldean Oracles*; later he wrote hymns to Christ. The doctrine is almost identical.... The similarity of the religious vocabulary is also great.... The Christians took over the entire terminology; but many pagan words were strangely twisted in order to fit into the Christian world.... There are also great differences between Christianity and the mysteries. Mystery religions, as a rule, can be traced back to tribal origins, Christianity to a historical person. The holy stories of the mysteries were myths; the Gospels of the New Testament, however, related historical events.... The mysteries declined quickly when the Emperor Constantine raised Christianity to the status of the state religion. After a short period of toleration, the pagan religions were prohibited. The property of the pagan gods was confiscated, and the temples were destroyed.... The Roman aristocrats multiplied their efforts to maintain the piety of the mysteries, and the pagan philosophers tried to refine their theology.... In 391, however, the Sarapeum at Alexandria was demolished, and in 394 the opposition of the Roman aristocracy was crushed in the battle at Frigidus River (modern stream of Vipacco, Italy; stream of Vipava, Yugoslavia)."[28]

Did you notice the bit about the ceremonial eating of a substance said to be the heart of a human child? We shall continue to learn about actual and symbolic cannibalism. The idea behind the real thing and its ceremonial substitute was the same.

The ancients evidently realized that you are what you eat.[29] They believed that the life-force of an animal was in its blood.[30] This is why Hebrew law required the flesh of animals to be bled-out completely before being cooked and eaten. Variations on this theme of blood-flesh sympathetic magic were: Drink the blood of a goat and you will become goat-like. Eat the heart (either actually or symbolically) of a child and you will become young again like that child. Drink the blood of a god and eat the flesh of a god (symbolically) and you will become like that god, i.e, you will acquire life everlasting.[31] Eat animal flesh of any sort and become animalistic; hence, eat only vegetables.[32] Why this theory of sympathetic magic did not hold constant as to vegetables we are not told. No one seems to have suggested that if you eat a cabbage you become a cabbage!

The Christian Eucharist originated as symbolic cannibalism? The early Church affirmed through the Doctrine of Real Presence that the Holy Magic of the Mass converted the bread and wine into the *real* flesh and blood of Christ.[33] If the Mass of the early Church was not symbolic cannibalism, then what was it?

Did you notice the great difference between the mystery religions and Christianity? Whereas the former unquestionably were based on myths, the latter insists upon its historicity. We are subjecting that claim to examination, rather than accepting it as an exercise in faith.

Let us look at some specifics about several of the mystery religions.

Mithraism. Mithraism was a men-only religion brought to Rome from Persia by way of Chaldea during the first century B.C. by Persian soldiers enlisted in the Roman army, by Persian slaves in the service of wealthy Romans, and by Persian merchants who had settled in Rome because it was the commercial hub of the Roman Empire.[34] Mithraism emphasized servile loyalty and obedience to duty, the "Oxen" virtues which a military commander or homeowner prizes in his footsoldiers, servants, or purveyors of foodstuffs.[35] It is not difficult to understand, therefore, why Emperor Constantine's choice of Christianity over Mithraism as the perfect religion with which to forge an empire was not easily reached. Indeed, Mithraism came closer than any of the other mystery religions to defeating Christianity in the contest for official Roman government approval,[36] and proved harder to stamp out than any of the other mystery religions after the final Christian triumph in arms.[37] Remains of temples of Mithras are to be found wherever the

Roman army marched, including parts of the British Isles.[38]

Mithraism was an offshoot of the ancient Aryan religion of Ahura Mazda from which sprung Zoroastrianism and Parseeism,[39] and from whence came such theological concepts as the angels of the Hebrew and Christian religions and Satan the Prince of Darkness of the Christian religion.[40] "Who is the Mithras of the Mysteries? He is one of the gods, lower than Ahura Mazda (the Supreme Deity of Light of the Persians) but higher than the visible Sun. He is creator and orderer of the universe, hence a manifestation of the creative Logos or Word. Seeing mankind afflicted by Ahriman, the cosmic power of darkness, he incarnated on earth. His birth on 25 December was witnessed by shepherds. After many deeds... he held a last supper with his disciples and returned to heaven. At the end of the world he will come again to judge resurrected mankind and after the last battle, victorious over evil, he will lead the chosen ones through a river of fire to blessed immortality.... No wonder the early Christians were disturbed by a deity who bore so close a resemblance to their own...."[41]

And disturbed they were! Early Christians considered Mithras to be "a mockery of Christ invented by Satan."[42] Adherents of Mithraism similarly were shocked and repulsed by what they supposed to be efforts of Christianity to mimic their faith.[43] If the one religion copied the other, recall that Mithraism preceded Christianity by many years. Cumont, one of the foremost authorities on

Illustration 16-2. Mithras being born from the cosmic rock. Courtesy of Dover Publications, Inc., New York.

Mithraism, suggests that neither copied the other; that both had their origins in a blending of the Persian cult of Ahura Mazda with the Semitic Babylonian astrophysics from whence came modern astronomy and its illegitimate offspring, astrology.[44] Persian magi were found in Babylon and other major cities in profusion.[45] Even the Semitic wanderers who became known as the Hebrews were not immune from their influence.[46] The faith of the Jewish Essenes, most particularly their concept of the final battle between the powers of light and darkness, compares closely with the ancient Persian faith.[47]

In **Illustration 16-1**, we see Mithras encircled by the Zodiac.[48] He is being born, full-grown, from the cosmic egg. Compare that photograph with the lines bolded in **Figure 237**. In **Illustration 16-2**, we see Mithras, wearing his Phrygian cap, being born

Illustration 16-1. Mithras being born from the cosmic egg. Courtesy of the Museum of Antiquities of the University, and the Society of Antiquaries, Newcastle Upon Tyne.

Figure 237

Figure 238

from the cosmic rock.[49] Note the resemblance of that peaked cap to the cap "worn" by our Grail humanform in **Figure 238**, which illustrates his being born from the cosmic rock of our Hermas story. Santa and his elves wear caps like that! In **Illustration 16-3**, we see Mithras slaughtering the cosmic bull,[50] which should be compared with the line forms in **Figure 239**.

Wealthy Romans were baptized into the Mithraic faith with the blood from a bull slaughtered on an overhead grill, through which the blood splashed down on them.[51] We see that grill in **Figure 240**. Poor Romans were thus baptized (washed) in the blood of a lamb.[52] In Christian theology, Christ is referred to as that lamb. St. Peter's at the Vatican is situated at the place where those blood baptisms occurred.[53] Mithras was re-

ferred to as *Sol Invictus* (the unconquered sun) in the Roman mysteries, in which he was represented standing on a steer while holding in his hand a two-edged ax symbolizing his mastery over lightning — which splits trees like an axe.[54] We see him in this form in **Illustration 16-4**,[55] and in **Figure 241**.

Persian religion was "dualistic," by which students of religion mean it taught that the bad as well as the good could be worshiped.[56] Devil worship among European peasants was a remnant of this Persian dualism.[57] The Christian Church's campaign against witchcraft may be explained in part as a final attempt to root out and destroy the folk-culture remains of its Persian competitor.[58] Cumont tells us that Germany is the place where the greatest number of places of Mithraic worship have been discovered,[59] and that Mithraism survived longest in Germany,[60] the very place where the Church's inquisition reached its maximum frenzy.[61]

Cumont suggests that one of the many reasons why Christianity conquered Mithraism is that whereas both had their origins in Persian-Chaldean concepts of our physical universe, Christianity almost completely dissociated itself from its beginnings in ancient astro-physics whereas Mithraism continued to make direct reference to, and insisted upon the verity of, its science until its end.[62] There are, however, visible remnants of this "science" in Christianity. For instance, Christ is said to be "the light."[63] Mithras was said to be the genius or source of light.[64]

We shall learn that as Roman Christianity spread, the common folk did not regard it as being radically different from their existing faiths, except insofar as it claimed historicity.[65] Do we have more

Illustration 16-3. Mithras slaughtering the cosmic bull. Courtesy of Dover Publications, Inc., New York.

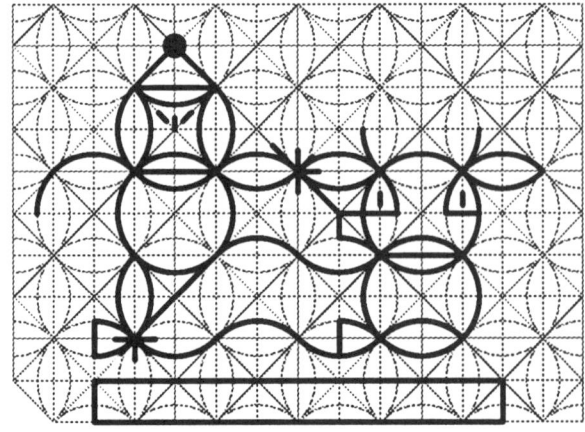

Figure 239

Figure 240

in common with each other than our religious leaders want us to realize? Why do modern faiths insist that they are unique; the one and only way to live? For the sake of their sheep? Or for the sake of their shepherds? We shall learn that the knights of the Grail quest stories always are so fascinated by the Holy Grail ceremony that they fail to ask the question which would save the life of the Fisher King, that is, "Who is served by the Holy Grail?"

Illustration 16-4. Jupiter Dolichenus on his cosmic bull. Courtesy of Kunsthistorisches Museum, Vienna.

Purification by self-flagellations was a liturgical practice of the ancient Persian faith.[66] Iranians now are Moslem, but who among us has not seen mobs of them on our television screens beating themselves with chains while they shriek hatred toward the infidels? In contrast, the concept of courtly love had its origins in ancient Persia.[67] The march of mankind is ever upward toward truth and right?

The concept of "haloes" or "glories" around the heads of gods and goddesses, and around the heads of earthly kings and queens who ruled by the "grace" of those gods and goddesses, also was a Persian concept, which unquestionably was based upon their "scientific" observations of such phenomena around the sun and moon, around earthly light sources such as fire and lamps, and around the heads of real people under certain atmospheric conditions.[68] The Persian concept of the "divine right of kings" was adopted by the Christian Church and continued in Europe by the monarchy until modern times when the great popular revolutions put it in where it belonged — in history's rubbish heap for outdated institutions.[69]

Mithras was not the Persian equivalent of the Hebrew Tetragrammaton; the Christian Jehovah. He was the intermediary between the creator god and mankind,[70] as is Jesus, although he was a trinity,[71] as is Jehovah in Christian doctrine. At the pinnacle of Mithraic theology was Aion, personify-

Figure 241

ing boundless time, whom the Greeks named Kronos and the Romans called Saturnus.[72] Time was pictured as a lion-headed humanform with four extended wings, around whose body coiled a snake.[73] His golden key around his neck unlocked the Capricorn solstitial or golden gate, i.e., "the way" through which the gods descend to Earth (the birth dates of Mithras and Jesus being at the winter solstice) and "the way" through which souls ascend to Heaven when they have been released from the wheel of life and death, that is, from reincarnation.[74] Christians are taught that Jesus is "the way" and "the gate" to Heaven; that only through Him shall the Father be reached. In Christianity, St. Peter, rather than Aion, holds the key to Heaven's gate. Aion's great festival was on December 25th.[75]

Mithraism had its story of the great flood and the surviving boatman,[76] which should come as no surprise to anyone who has been with us throughout this book, because that cosmology apparently had its origins in Sumeria and Assyro-Babylonia.

The supreme god "drives a chariot drawn by four steeds which turn ceaselessly round in a fixed circle."[77] The Romans ran such circumpolar four-horse chariot races in the Circus Maximus,[78] and John the Divine wrote of the four horses in his Revelation.[79] "The first horse is the incarnation of fire or ether, the second of air, the third of water, and the fourth of the earth."[80] Ancient "science" at its very best! The purpose of religion is to "explain" that for which science offers no satisfying answer? Or to convince us to be on our best behavior? Or to con us into accepting the authority of our would-be masters?

Historians give the Semitic Babylonians, their Semitic predecessors, the Akkadians, and their non-Semitic predecessors, the Sumerians, credit for being the first people to conclude from empirical observations and rational analysis that the universe operates according to immutable laws by which future events may be predicted within certain ranges of mathematical accuracy. They tell us that until this "scientific" theory evolved, the ancients had thought that events occurred according to the whims of the gods.[81] But the limits of science rarely satisfy human desire for certainty. Some ancient king wanted to know whether he would win some battle. His mathematician-astronomers could not say, although they could predict with certainty the occurrence of the next eclipse of the moon. The king could not understand why they could do the one and not the other. So he summoned a magus (plural: magi) who "predicted" the king's victory.

Good salesmanship consists of telling the customer what he wants to hear. The magi, from whose title we get our word "magician," accordingly prospered and gained power.[82]

Astrology, the bastard offspring of Babylonian mathematical astronomy,[83] and Mithraism were intertwined with each other for many generations, giving us insight into the hatred which the Christian Church has held for the astrologer.[84] One must understand that magic, per se, was not condemned by the Christian Church. The Church's own magic, such as the Mass and exorcism, was Holy Magic; hence, good stuff.[85] But astrology was the handmaiden of the hated Mithraic cult; hence, its practitioners were in league with the devil.[86] Not until the Protestant leader John Calvin took the pulpit did the astrological doctrine of predestination become a legitimate mind-set for Christian true believers.

Magic, as well as astrology, was a bastard offspring of Persian science, and was intertwined with Persian religion, including Mithraism.[87] "The attraction of the magnet for iron was utilized by the thaumaturgi ("miracle workers") before it was interpreted by the natural philosophers."[88] Cumont concludes that "if astrology was a perverted astronomy, magic was physics gone astray."[89]

Could not Mithraism and Christianity, so obviously brother faiths, reconcile with each other rather than fight until the one lay prostrate before the other? In modern times, Moslems and Hindus slaughter each other periodically in India, in the name of God. Certain gurus thought they could end this age-old religious strife by distilling from each of those two faiths the very best of its essence and creating from the distillate a brand-new religion in which all Hindus and Moslems could be united in love. Their new faith now is a very old faith whose adherents are called Sikhs.[90] Reconciliation did not occur. Instead, there now are three warring factions instead of two, with each of the three sects laying slaughter upon the other two, all in the name of God. For the sake of the sheep? Or for the sake of the shepherds? The wise ones tried the same thing with Christianity and Mithraism. The combined faith was called Manichaeism.[91] The Catholic Church destroyed Manichaeism with spear and sword.[92] For the sake of the sheep? Or for the sake of the shepherds? Does your author have a dream that this book will reveal to us our commonality? Hence, will bring all of us together in human love? A dream? Yes. A realistic expectation? No. Religious leaders will not permit it. For the sake of the sheep? Or for the sake of the shepherds?

Cumont defines the practical reason why this book will have zero impact on the day-by-day lives of Lions, Oxen, and Men. "[O]nly intelligent minds could delight in doubt or surrender to it; the masses wanted certainties."[93] Our religious leaders are excellent salesmen. The masses *still* want certainties, so the clergy will provide certainties! The clergy will preach cosmic allegory as historical fact until the masses learn to read the Bible for themselves.[94]

Notes
CHAPTER SIXTEEN. The Mystery Religions: Mithraism

1. Angus 31-38; Cumont OR 196-211.

2. Angus 31-38, 159-164. "The last battle of the ancient faiths was fought not by Mars but by the hosts of the Unconquered Sun under Licinus, against the Church Militant under Constantine." Godwin 39.

3. Godwin 7; Angus 19-20.

4. Angus 38, 44, 161-162.

5. Cumont OR 55, 71.

6. Angus 39-40; Cumont OR 53, 57.

7. Angus 192; Cumont OR 65.

8. Angus 277-282.

9. Cumont OR 191-195; Smith 50-56, 66, 75, 122-123, 146-147.

10. Angus 41. The Christian Church offered entire populations either the cross or the sword, i.e., conversion or death. Martin 97, 186. Christians were taught to believe that their religion was about historical events, which really and truly had happened, whereas other mystery religions made no pretense or claim of historical truth. Martin 89. The new Christian truth or reality was unwilling to tolerate the ecumenicalism of the pre-Christian mystery religions; hence, religious wars and religious persecutions increased where Christianity extended itself. Martin 90. What was the source of this attitude among Christians? Did Christians really believe that they had an absolute monopoly upon God's truth; hence, that everyone was obligated to become a Christian? Martin 107. Did the Church attempt to conquer the world with cross and sword to save souls, or to fill its treasuries, or, perhaps, with mixed motives?

11. Angus 66, 282-283; Ronan 7-9.

12. Angus 282-283; Baigent 49-57; 383-387.

13. Godwin 58.

14. Angus 39.

15. Angus 52-53.

16. Angus 61.

17. Cumont OR x, xii.

18. Angus 271-277, 284-287; Cumont OR xi.

19. Godwin 26.

20. Godwin 26-29.

21. "Mystery Religions," 12 Encyclopaedia Britannica Macropaedia 784 (15th edition 1974).

22. John 2.1-11.

23. Landels 202.

24. Landels 202.

25. 28 Great Books of the Western World 3.

26. Ronan 114-115.

27. Landels 202.

28. "Mystery Religions," 12 Encyclopaedia Britannica Macropaedia 781-785 (15th edition 1974).

29. Cumont OR 67.

30. Graham 47; Cumont OR 66-71; Cumont MM 180; Godwin 24.

31. Angus 129-133; Smith 122-123, 146-147, 152; Cumont OR 40, 66-71; Godwin 25.

32. Angus 223.

33. Matthews 54. "In the mediaeval mind, Christ's blood contained both the 'soul,' and possibly even the Divinity of the Saviour." Matthews 11.

34. Cumont MM 40-43, 57-64, 70, 74-81, 173-174; Godwin 98.

35. Cumont MM 141-142; Cumont OR 155-156, 158.

36. Cumont MM 199.

37. Cumont MM 200-207.

38. Cumont MM 43, 53, 57-58.

39. Cumont MM iv,1-6, 31.

40. Cumont OR 138, 145.

41. Godwin 99; see also, Cumont MM iv-v, 131, 140-146, 158-160, 188-191, 194-200.

42. Godwin 99.

43. Cumont MM iv-v.

44. Cumont MM 29-31; Cumont OR xviii, 146, 151.

45. Cumont MM 9-11; Cumont OR 139.

46. Cumont MM iv.

47. Dupont-Sommer 51.

48. Godwin 101.

49. Cumont MM 130.

50. Cumont MM 22.

51. Cumont MM 86, 180; Angus 94.

52. Angus 95.

53. Angus 235; Godwin 24.

54. Cumont OR 127, 147.

55. Godwin 154. Mithras is to be associated with the bull because he was one of many Aryan cattle-stealing gods like Hermes and Krishna. Godwin 102. We Irish would add Cu Culainn to that list. Cross & Slover 281-327. In Illustration 16-4, Mithras, or *Sol Invictus*, is shown in his syncretic form of Jupiter Dolichenus. Godwin 154. The head of his axe, held in his right hand, is not visible in this photograph. Notice the "feet" of the "bull" on which he stands in Figure 241. They are like a "calf's foot." Is this the meaning of Ezekiel 1.7? Langdon tells us that the Semitic storm god Adad was represented standing upon a bull, hurling a thunderbolt with his right hand while holding more lightning in his left. Langdon 39. Langdon equates the names Adad, Hadad, El, and Yaw with each other. Langdon 37-45. Langdon tells us that during Hebrew polytheism, El was the Hebrew sun-god, and Yaw was the Hebrew storm-god; that the monotheistic Hebrews of later years used both names (and others) in reference to their One-God. Langdon 37-45. El was the God of Abraham. Langdon 45. Yaw (a/k/a Yaweh or Jehovah) and El are the God of our Bible! The biblical prohibition against the making of images of God did not apply to all Semitic people; only to Hebrews. And, as we have seen, the biblical prohibition of image-making did not prevent Hebrews from visualizing God among the lines of the Holy Grail, sitting on the lid of the Ark of the Covenant!

56. Cumont MM 112-114; Cumont OR 152.

57. Cumont OR 188-195.

58. This is your author's suggestion. There certainly were many other causes of the witchcraft mania sponsored by the Church.

59. Cumont MM 52.

60. Cumont MM 206.

61. Robbins 218-222.

62. Cumont MM 10, 119-123, 187-190, 194-198; Cumont OR 31-33, 146, 160.

63. John 8.12.

64. Cumont MM 1-3, 127, 129.

65. Angus 309-314.

66. Cumont MM 6.

67. Cirlot 194.

68. Cumont MM 93-95; Minnaert 224, 231, 333; Schaaf 38-43.

69. Cumont MM 93-103.

70. Cumont MM 128, 145, 191.

71. Cumont MM 129, 191.

72. Cumont MM 104-110. Thus, our best time-keeping devices are called "chronometers."

73. Godwin 109; Cumont MM 105, 106, 108.

74. Cumont MM 107; Godwin 108.

75. Godwin 108. Christ and Mithras shared a lifestyle as well as a birthday. They, alone, among all the saviors of the mystery religions, lacked female companions. Cumont OR 157.

76. Cumont MM 138.

77. Cumont MM 116.

78. Godwin 57.

79. Revelation 6.2-8. A friend was disappointed that this book fails to analyze the Revelation of St. John the Divine. I deliberately refrained from an analysis of the Book of Revelation because I did not want to deprive you of the electrical tingles that will run through your body as you read it by yourself. You easily can tune in to that revelation by using the skills learned in this book. What is the allegorical line of the story? I speculate that the author is expressing his hopes that his brand of Christianity will prevail over the political, social, economic, and religious malaise of his day; that the then-existing Romanized world order will die, and from its ashes will arise a new world order pleasing to Christian mystics of his mind-set. Would he be pleased with what actually happened? I doubt it. Rome and the Christian Church became allies. Together, they swept away his brand of Christianity, or drove it underground. The Christian Church of Rome taught cosmic allegory as historic truth. The mind-set of Christian true believers was changed utterly. St. John's Christianity taught its adherents to kill off and bury their "Lion," "Ox," and "Man" materiality; to soar like an "Eagle," spiritually at one with the Cosmos. Few moderns, other than Buddhists and Native Americans, can comprehend the essentials of the Christianity that the Roman Army destroyed at the behest of the Church of Rome. The Roman Church shot down free-flying and free-feeding Christian "Eagles," and converted "Lions" and "Men" into "Oxen" to plow its fields; to feed only at its troughs. Materialism prevailed over spirituality. The Roman Church, and Protestant successors to portions of its power, imposed on humankind the it's-here-for-our-taking mind-set which has led to the rape of Mother Earth; to modern destruction of the Cosmos. A pro-environment commercial on American television shows a feathered Native American crying as he rides his barebacked horse past untreated sewage flowing into a river; past rotting garbage strewn across a field of tree stumps; past industrial smokestacks spewing pollutants into the air. Would the author of the Book of Revelation cry over what was done to his Christ Story, and the resulting damage to his Cosmos?

80. Cumont MM 118.

81. Cumont OR 179.

82. Cumont MM 126; Cumont OR 162-163.

83. Cumont OR 164.

84. Angus 164-169, 249-256.

85. Angus 256; Robbins 180-189.

86. Cumont MM 124-126, 206-207; Robbins 46-47.

87. Cumont OR 182-195.

88. Cumont OR 184.

89. Cumont OR 184.

90. 17 World Book Encyclopedia 375 (1983).

91. Cumont MM v, 207-208; Cumont OR 142. Saint Augustine was an adherent of Manichaeism until he became a Christian. 11 Encyclopaedia Britannica Macropaedia 443-444 (1974).

92. 11 Encyclopaedia Britannica Macropaedia 444 (1974).

93. Cumont OR 34.

94. See 4.24, in the King James Bible. See, also, Galatians 4.24 in the Living Bible, which substitutes the words "true story" for the word "allegory," thereby reinforcing the Christian myth of Old Testament historicity and further isolating Christians from the reality of Old Testament allegory.

Chapter Seventeen

More Mystery Religions

Adonis or *Tammuz.* "Under the names of Osiris, Adonis, Tammuz, Attis, and Dionysus, the Egyptians, Syrians, Babylonians, Phrygians, and Greeks represented the decay and revival of vegetation with rites which, as the ancients themselves recognized, were substantially the same, and which find their parallels in the spring and midsummer customs of our European ancestors."[1] We already have noted that the Hebrews worshiped Tammuz although their prophets, like Ezekiel, did their best to end the practice,[2] and that Tammuz remains to this day the name of a month of the Hebrew calendar.[3]

Recall what we have learned about sympathetic magic and your comprehension will be enhanced: Light a fire to cause the sun to shine. Shed tears to start the rains. Throw an object into a fire to bring out the sun or into water to bring on the rains.[4] Nonsense? Of course, but not to our ancestors!

The Greeks evidently borrowed the worship of Adonis from the Semitic Syrians as early as the Fifth Century B.C.[5] The death of Adonis or Tammuz was lamented annually by the bitter wailing of women, and his effigy was thrown into a body of water. The next day "he was believed to come to life again and ascend up to heaven in the presence of his worshippers."[6] Seed grain sprouts when exposed to water. In this sense, seed grain arises from the dead. As it grows, it ascends towards Heaven. "The women wailed because he had been cruelly slain, his bones ground in a mill, and then scattered to the winds."[7] In the Christ story, the Savior of mankind (the grain?) was captured (harvested?), was whipped (threshed?), then was lifted up and exposed to the winds (winnowed?), after which he was placed on a slab (a kern?) in a tomb (a granary?) after having passed by a large, heavy, rolling stone (a millstone?). He then arose from the dead (rose as bread?) to save (feed?) mankind. Did the Christian Lion, Ox, Man, and Eagle intend the Christ story to be understood in that way? Were they creating a universal religion which had within its Holy Writ something they hoped would strike a familiar chord with everyone who believed in any of the dogmas of any then-existing religion?

"In a Babylonian legend, the goddess Istar (Astarte, Aphrodite) descends to Hades to fetch the water of life with which to restore to life the dead Tammuz, and it appears that the water was thrown over him at a great mourning ceremony, at which men and women stood round the funeral pyre of Tammuz lamenting."[8] "Tammuz is described [in a Babylonian hymn] as dwelling in the midst of a great tree at the centre of the earth."[9] We see Tammuz in the great coniferous tree in **Figure 242.** In the comparable northern European legends, Tammuz is called "Balder," and the queen of the underworld is named "Hel."[10] The Greeks called the goddess of death "Hecate."[11] We say, "Oh, Hell"! We can be more polite by saying, "Oh, Heck"! When we swear by the name of the goddess of darkness, are we continuing the Mithraic devil-worship of our European ancestors which the Church tried so hard to stamp out?

"At the approach of Easter, Sicilian women sow wheat, lentils, and canary-seed in plates, which are kept in the dark and watered every two days. The

Figure 242

---

plants soon shoot up; the stalks are tied together with red ribbons, and the plates containing them are placed on sepulchers which, with effigies of the dead Christ, are made up in Roman Catholic and Greek churches on Good Friday, just as the gardens of Adonis were placed on the grave of the dead Adonis. The whole custom — sepulchers as well as plates of sprouting grain — is probably nothing but a continuation, under a different name, of the Adonis worship."[12] Home gardeners often sprout their seeds in cool, damp, dark places before they bring them forth into the sun so their spring gardens may be born again.

Attis and *Cybele.* Attis was to Phrygia what Adonis was to Syria. According to the Pessinus version, Attis sacrificed himself by self-castration.[13] Cybele was Mother Nature.[14] They were supposed to ride about in a chariot pulled by four lions.[15] See **Figure 243**.

Frazer gives this version of the legend: "After his death, Attis is said to have been changed into a pine-tree.... At the spring equinox (22nd March) a pine-tree was cut in the woods and brought into the sanctuary of Cybele, where it was treated as a divinity. It was adorned with woollen bands and wreaths of violets, for violets were said to have sprung from the blood of Attis.... [T]he effigy of a young man was attached to the middle of the tree...."[16] We see the man in the pine tree in Figure

Figure 244

242. We see the pine tree covered by wreaths of violets in **Figure 244**. The second day of the ceremony was celebrated principally by the blowing of trumpets, the third day by the priests' drawing blood from their arms and legs and offering it to cult initiates to be drunk as a sacrament, and the fourth day was the Festival of Joy, the *Hilaria*, the origin of our word "hilarious," which was the celebration of

Figure 243

Figure 245   Figure 246

the resurrection of Attis.[17] The myth recited that "he was born of a virgin, who conceived by putting in her bosom a ripe almond or pomegranate."[18] We see the virgin with an almond in her bosom in **Figure 245**, and the virgin with a pomegranate in her bosom in **Figure 246**.

"[T]he story of his [Attis's] sufferings, death, and resurrection was interpreted as the ripe grain wounded by the reaper, buried in the granary, and coming to life again when sown in the ground."[19] Did the Christian Lion, Ox, Man, and Eagle intend for the worshipers of Attis to see in their stories of the death and resurrection of Christ Jesus enough similarity to the Attis myth to convince them to become adherents of the new faith?

Dionysus. This Greek god of vegetation, hence of grapes and wine, had his origins in Thrace.[20] The Romans called him Bacchus.[21] We tend to analogize his worship to a college beer-bash. Wine, women, song, and dance. Yes and no. His devotees used heavy drugs such as opium as well as alcohol, but the wild dancing and savage behavior of the cult members must be explained in large measure by the ecstasy they sought to achieve and the goal they sought to reach.[22] Ascetics seek to repress or destroy their animal urges so they can spend their time in worthy thought or action. Adherents of the cult of Dionysus sought first to satiate their animal desires, then to concentrate their efforts towards high-level thoughts and actions.[23] College students traditionally have tried both routes toward academic success, with varying degrees of success. The problem with party first and study later is that it can lead to party first then party later, and we must suppose that numbers of the followers of Dionysus may have fallen into this trap!

Alcoholic binges and drug trips are one thing; actual cannibalism another. The myth of Dionysus

recited, in part, that he was sired by Zeus and born of Persephone; that while a child he was captured, dismembered, and eaten by the Titans.[24] While under the influence of alcohol and drugs, his worshipers *actually*, rather than merely *symbolically*, attacked with their bare hands and teeth, killed and ate the flesh and drank the blood of *living* sacrificial victims of this primitive communion.[25] More often than not, in later years of this practice, the surrogate victim was a four-legged animal.[26] Omophagy, the eating of raw flesh, is one thing; cannibalism another. Visitors to Fort George in upper New York State are shocked to learn that Indian allies of the French soldiers who captured the English garrison attacked in similar fashion defenseless captives in order to drink the warm blood spurting from their still-living bodies. Thus were they initiated into the cult of warriors. Now we learn that our "civilized" European ancestors still engaged in such practices in historic times! But, then, how many of us have eaten the consecrated bread and drunk the consecrated wine (or grape juice) at Mass or Communion this month? It is remarkable what intelligent people will do on command of their religious leaders!

The idea behind the savage omophagy of the Dionysus cult, we are told, was that you got such desires out of your system, then you could devote your time to high-level thoughts and actions.[27] Why do "civilized" moderns pay high admission fees to watch men pound each other's bodies with their fists or feet, or twist each other's legs and arms, in boxing and wrestling rings? At least the meat they eat during those events consists of hotdogs, hamburgers, sausages, and pork rinds! We evidently have made *some* small progress toward civilization.

Dionysus and his wife, Ariadne, the original sleeping beauty, travelled around in a chariot drawn by four tigers.[28] A principal symbol of the cult was

Figure 247

Figure 248

a pine-cone on the end of a staff.[29] A dancing *maenad*, i.e., a woman dancing in intoxicated ecstasy, her arms ninety degrees from her whirling body, is seen in **Figure 247**, holding such a staff. The pine tree was particularly sacred to Dionysus.[30] Death and resurrection were central features of his worship. He descended to Hades to bring up his mother.[31] When Christ harrowed Hell, He brought up a crowd.[32] He always outdid his competitors.

Orpheus and *Hercules*. Orphism predated Christianity by several hundreds of years, and has been termed "the harbinger of the Mystery-Religions and Christianity in the West...."[33] "It confronted the situation (Greek social upheaval) by shifting the centre of interest from mere earthly existence, making life here but a preparation for a life beyond. Orphism introduced a theology of redemption. It taught a doctrine of original sin.... Asceticism, 'the Orphic life,' was the primary condition of the attainment of salvation, the means by which the true Orphic delivered his soul from the pollution of the body and escaped the long series of purificatory punishments in Hades. This stern religion, with its anthropology uncongenial to the Greek world-affirming ethic, its emphasis on sin and the need of a cathartic ritual, its relative indifference to civic as compared with personal righteousness, must have appeared to Greek theologians somewhat in the light in which Puritanism appeared to Elizabethan politicians."[34] Orphism was "concerned primarily with the salvation of the individual soul — a startlingly new religious concep-

tion.... Orphism was steeped in sacramentarianism which flooded the later Mysteries and flowed into Christianity. Salvation was by sacrament, by initiatory rites, and by an esoteric doctrine."[35]

The Orphics were skilled craftsmen of religion. They drew, to the maximum extent possible, upon the "commonplace and familiar" rites and myths of the cult of Dionysus, discarding the savageries and crudities of that faith and substituting rites of purification for drunken orgies.[36] Wild dancing to loud music was discarded in favor of quiet music and contemplation.[37] Why did they not make a clean break with the past? Why did they "desire to retain the maximum of primitive ritual" and thereby face the task "of reconciling the archaic with the modern, and of mysticizing the commonplace" through skillful use of allegory?[38] We have said it before and must recognize it again: skillful religion-smiths realize that the common folk will not accept a clean break between their myths and rituals and the myths and rituals of a new religion, although they will accept a new allegorical interpretation of the old myths and rituals. Protestant fundamentalists do not eat the actual body and drink the real blood of Jesus Christ to acquire life everlasting; rather, they eat soda crackers and drink Concord grape juice to "remember" Him. The ancient ceremony of becoming like the god (acquiring life everlasting) by eating the god goes on, but the meaning has changed. The Orphics and the fathers of the Church knew how to lead mankind up from its savagery. We owe them much. Orphism has been referred to as "the most potent solvent ever introduced into Greek religious life."[39] It started the dissolution of the cults of the Olympian gods which Christianity finished.[40]

In later years, Orphism flowed together with Christianity. "Orphics, so very foreign to the Greek

Figure 249

Figure 250

mentality, were perfectly at one with early Christian ethics, and the figure of Orpheus was borrowed in Christian iconography for representations of David and even of Christ himself."[41] "Orpheus, Hercules, and Jesus: all three were born as demi-gods, performed miracles, and descended to the underworld before or after suffering cruel deaths. They were afterwards raised to Heaven by their divine fathers, whence they still radiate beneficent influence to their worshippers."[42] Orpheus was visualized wearing his Phyrigian cap and playing his seven-stringed lyre, surrounded by such Dionysian critters as fauns, centaurs, lions, and goats.[43] We see Orpheus playing his lyre in **Figure 248**. A faun and a centaur are seen, respectively, in **Figure 249** and **Figure 250**. Hercules, club in hand, ready for battle, was seen as in **Figure 251**.[44] Remember the twelve trials Hercules faced? He had to slaughter a lion, a hydra, a boar, and some birds; capture a hind, a bull, some mares, a girdle, some cattle, some golden apples, and the guard-dog of Hell; and clean some stables.[45] Find all twelve "trials" for yourself on the Holy Grail, including the stables. We shall see a rather special stable later during our quest.

Orphics and Buddhists agreed that upon death the soul either would remain on the "Circle of Necessity" or "Wheel of Existence," to be reincarnated in another body, or would leave the system altogether and attain perpetual freedom from rebirth.[46] Orphism described death as a journey through the dark to a point at which "a strange and wonderful light meets the wanderer; he is admitted

into pure and verdant pastures." [47] Modern medicine records the same phenomenon among persons of all faiths, or of no faith, who have been revived after being in clinical medical conditions near death.[48] Christianity and Judaism speak of the valley of the shadow of death, and of a God who maketh us to lie down in green pastures.[49] Does one religion hold the entire truth, sharing it with none else, or can the only religious reality we ever shall see in this life be discovered by following a variety of "ways"?

Figure 251

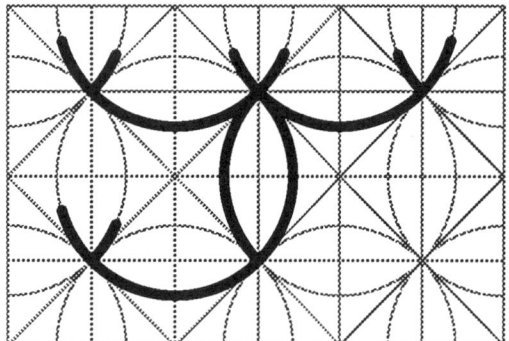

Figure 252

The Pythagoreans, whom we know for their science and mathematics, identified themselves with Orpheus and Hercules.[50] "With the Neopythagorean revival of the last centuries B C came the establishment of a literary canon (the Orphic Hymns), and an elaborate theogony and cosmogony, and Mysteries among whose initiates were Plutarch and, some say, the young Saul of Tarsus."[51] Is this why the writings of St. Paul about Jesus Christ so often coincide with the doctrines of Orphism?

Isis. The goddess Isis "became the chief deity of all Egypt, and, in late times, her worship wholly eclipsed that of her male counterpart Osiris."[52] Isis, her sister Nephthys, her brother Set (whom the Greeks called Typhon), and her brother Osiris were the children of the Earth god, Geb, and the sky goddess, Nut, whom we already have met. Isis married her brother Osiris. Set killed Osiris and cut his body into pieces. Isis found the parts of the body of Osiris, except for his phallus, put them back together again, made a phallus, and thereby conceived by Osiris their son, Horus, whose four children we already have discussed. Set, in the form of a scorpion, found the infant Horus in the swamps, where Isis had hidden him, and killed Horus. We see Set as a Grail scorpion in **Figure 252**. Isis called out to Heaven for help. Thoth, the god of wisdom, stopped the sun boat, the sun stood still, and Thoth descended to Earth to instruct Isis in the magic which she used to bring Horus back to life. Horus grew up, and captured his uncle Set, but his mother felt sorry for her brother and turned him loose, which enraged Horus so much that he cut off his mother's head. Thoth, the god of wisdom, changed the head of Isis into that of a cow, and reattached it to her.[53] We see Isis in her Hathor or cow-goddess form in **Figure 253**. The legend makes no sense?

Figure 253

But you can play it out on the Holy Grail! Maybe it made no sense to the Egyptians, either, and they simply accepted, as an act of faith, that which their mystics "saw" on the Holy Grail.

Isis was known by many names, including the Lady of Heaven or Queen of Heaven, in which role she directed the courses of the heavenly bodies.[54] Her cult made its way into the Mediterranean islands during the Fifth Century B.C., into Athens during the Fourth Century B.C., and into Rome in the First Century B.C. From Rome, her cult spread

Figure 254

Figure 255

throughout Europe. "When her cult finally broke down through the development and mighty spreading of Christianity in Egypt, Isis was to her votaries the type and symbol of all that is greatest and best in woman in her character of the unselfish, true, tender, loving, and eternal World Mother."[55] When, during the fourth and fifth centuries, the Christian Roman emperors sent expeditions deep into Egypt and Nubia to bring an end to the worship of Isis, "[t]he ideas and beliefs which were the foundations of the cult were not even then destroyed, for they survived in Christianity. And the bulk of the masses in Egypt and Nubia who professed Christianity transferred to Mary the Virgin, the new Lady of Heaven, the attributes of Isis the Everlasting Mother, and to the Babe Jesus those of Horus."[56] She was referred to as "nature's mother," and was, indeed, Mother Nature.[57]

Isis is seen wearing her vulture's headdress in **Figure 254**.[58] The throne symbol, one of the meanings of her name,[59] appears in **Figure 255**. Isis, wearing her cow's horns, supporting the disk of the moon, is illustrated in **Figure 256**.[60]

One inscription to Isis reads: "I, by aid of Osiris my brother, put an end to anthropophagy."[61] Budge says: "There seems to be no doubt that the primitive Egyptians were cannibals, and that men only ceased to be so after they learned to grow wheat, barley, and dhura."[62] Isis ended cannibalism "by aid of Osiris" because Osiris was the Egyptian god of vegetation.[63] The "body" of a vegetation god would be bread, and his "blood" would be beer or wine. "Jesus saith... mine hour is not yet come."[64]

Budge quotes from an ancient account of one of the two principal festivals of Isis. "Another priest bore an ark full of objects of mysterious significa-

tions which symbolized the mysteries of the glorious faith. Another carried the awful image of the mighty deity, the emblem of whose meaning no man may speak, it was the symbol of the loftiest of faiths, whose mysteries must be shrouded in deep silence. It was neither like cattle, nor wild beast, nor bird, nor man. This object was a small gold urn hollowed out with wondrous skill; its bottom was perfectly round, and its exterior was adorned with strange Egyptian figures. Its mouth projected into a long low spout with outstretched tube. On the other side, with ample arch, extended a long retreating handle, on which was set an asp with twisted coils, holding erect the streaked scales of its swelling neck."[65] An ark containing objects which symbolized the mysteries of the faith?[66] An "emblem of whose meaning no man may speak" which is "the awful image of the mighty deity"? This cult object "was the symbol of the loftiest of faiths, whose mysteries must be shrouded in deep silence"? And what is it? We are told that it was "a small gold urn hollowed out," that "its bottom was perfectly round," and that "Its mouth projected into a long low spout with outstretched tube." We are told that, "On the other side, with ample arch, extended a long retreating handle." We may make an educated guess at what it was. The "long retreat-

Figure 256

Figures 257, 258, 259, & 260
Clockwise from Left

ing handle" of **Figure 257** is shaped like the "swelling neck" of an asp or cobra which is "erect" and ready to strike. The cup that caught the blood of Christ which issued from His side when He was struck with the lance was said to have appeared on the Holy Grail, as we shall learn in subsequent chapters. Could this ancient Egyptian cult object have been no object at all? Could it merely have been line forms on the Holy Grail? We are told that "It was neither like cattle [Ox?], nor wild beast [Lion?], nor bird [Eagle?], nor man." Lion, Ox, Man, and Eagle? Are we dealing with another fantasy created from line forms visible on the Holy Grail?

Budge answers the last question for us by quoting extensively from the account by the same informant of an apparition of Isis which he "saw."[67] "About its lofty brow was bound a crown of many shapes and varied flowers, and in the midst thereof above the forehead there shone white and glowing a round disc like a mirror or after the semblance of the moon...."[68] The "crown of many shapes and varied flowers" is illustrated in **Figure 258**. The "round disc like a mirror or after the semblance of the moon" above the forehead of the apparition is illustrated in **Figure 259**. Budge continues: "...to right and left it was bound about with the furrowed coils of climbing vipers; above, it stretched forth

ears of corn."[69] A cobra, his hood extended, is seen in **Figure 260**, and "ears of corn," that is, stalks of wheat, are seen in **Figure 261**. Budge's quotation from Lucius goes on: "The tunic was of many colours, woven of fine linen, now gleaming with a snowy brightness, now yellow with the hue of saffron, now blushing with roseate flame. But the cloak it was that dazzled my gaze far beyond all else, for it was of deep black glistening with sable sheen; it was cast round and about the body, and passing under the right side was brought back to the left shoulder. Part of it hung shieldwise down and drooped in many a fold, and the whole streamed seemly to its utmost edge with tasselled fringe. Along its broidered border, and on its surface also, where scattered sparkling stars, and in their midst

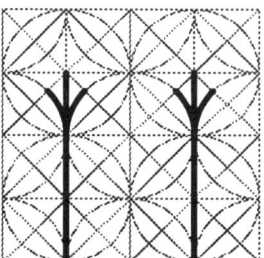

Figure 261

Figure 262

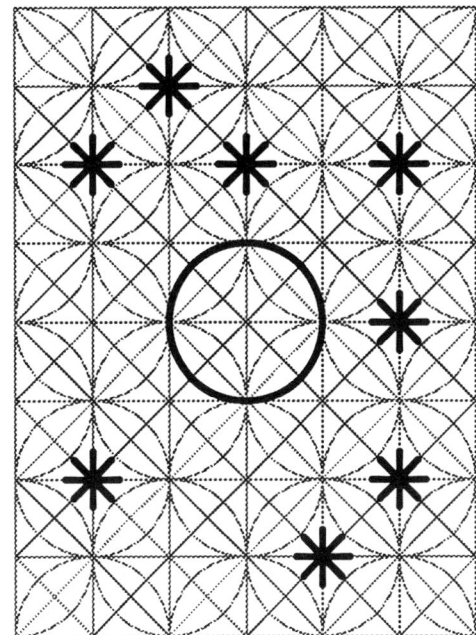

Figure 263

the full moon breathed forth her flaming fire. But wheresoever streamed the embracing folds of that wondrous cloak, there clung a garland's endless wreath, wrought of all manner of flowers, and all manner of fruit."[70]

A multi-colored tunic. A black cloak on which appears the moon and stars. The allegory is not very deep, if you are aware of the astronomical fact that the electro-magnetic phenomenon known as the "northern lights," that is, the *aurora borealis*, has been visible against the dark black skies of Egyptian and other middle eastern deserts under certain atmospheric conditions.[71] The multi-colored "tunic" described by the foregoing words compares almost exactly with the description of the northern lights which you will find in modern encyclopedias![72] Joseph had a coat of many colors.[73] The "cloak" of night, complete with moon and stars, is even less a deep allegory. But notice something more. The passage is simply brimming over with Grail images! The cloak passed under the right side of the apparition's body and was brought back to the left shoulder, as in **Figure 262**. Part of the cloak hung "shieldwise down." Remember our "small shields" of the story of the table? We see in Figure 262 two "small shields" which are "hung shieldwise down" under the apparition's left arm. We see the "full moon" and several "sparkling stars" in **Figure 263**. Remember the Sumerian symbol for "star?" "Flowers" and "fruit" of "all manner" appear on the "cloak." See **Figure 264**. Remember the flowers and fruit of the story of the table?

We have found something quite valuable to us in that description of the Egyptian goddess Isis. We know she was called "Queen of Heaven" and "Our Lady of Heaven," and that she was credited with

causing the "spheres of the heavens" to turn and the heavenly bodies to "travel" their appointed rounds.[74] Ezekiel spoke of something he saw in the skies of Babylonia like unto the rainbow which appears in the sky after a storm. He apparently had no word in his vocabulary with which to describe what he had seen, and only could compare it with another sky phenomenon (a rainbow) for which he did have a word.[75] The northern lights can be visible in the Mesopotamian desert.[76] Is that what Ezekiel saw? If so, a shudder should run through your body and the hairs on the back of your neck should stand up, as happened with me, because Ezekiel twice used the word *chashmal*, which even

Figure 264

Figure 265

to this day is the Hebrew word for "electricity!"[77] One level of science, a rather high one at that, would be represented by early Semitic knowledge that lightning, such as Ezekiel describes in his vision, was caused by *chashmal*, but quite another, and even higher level, would be represented by Semitic knowledge that the northern lights *also* are an electrical phenomenon!

Note what else that description of Isis suggests: that the human form on the Holy Grail was known as "Isis."

We have not mentioned all of the mystery religions. The Greeks, for instance, celebrated at Eleusis the so-called Eleusian mysteries, involving the Demeter myth, whose symbols were wheat, pomegranates, and the opium poppy.[78] The ceremony, which is largely unknown even to this day, apparently climaxed in a way "disappointing to non-initiates: the displaying of an ear of wheat."[79] Have you ever stayed completely sober during a cocktail party, and been bored by what the drunks said which they thought was so erudite? We may speculate that enough juice of the opium poppy would lead a person to find great significance in an ear of wheat! Is it of any significance that an abstract image of the unopened flower bud of an opium poppy can be visualized in side view on the Holy Grail? See **Figure 265**. Note, also, the resemblance between the unopened flower bud of the opium poppy, as seen in Figure 265, and the "small gold urn" illustrated in Figure 257. Is the bud of the opium poppy the "small gold urn"? Is the "loftiest of faiths" nothing but a drug trip?

The Hebrew Faith. "Philo forbade his people to take part in pagan initiations, suggesting that there were Mysteries in their own faith to which they might aspire."[80] Godwin suggests that the work of the Kabbalists proves that whoever wrote the Pentateuch "was already adept at understanding, and concealing, the most profound knowledge."[81] We already have seen for ourselves some of what the authors of the first five books of the Old Testament knew and concealed! We can see the sun in his chariot, being pulled by four horses, surrounded by twelve signs of the Zodiac and four angels, in a mosaic in the Synagogue Beth Alpha, in Israel, painted some time after A.D. 569. That mosaic portrays the same theme we have seen so many times in the mystery religions.[82] Godwin suggests that the seven-branched Menorah symbolized the central sun and six of the seven visible planets.[83] The sun at the center? We are told that the ancients believed the *Earth* was at the center![84] "In the Lesser Mysteries of other gods, it is suggested that the fact of heliocentricity was revealed."[85] In the science chapters of this book, we shall not rely upon *suggestions* but shall see what we can see for ourselves!

Notes
CHAPTER SEVENTEEN. More Mystery Religions

1. 1 Frazer 278.

2. Ezekiel 8.14; Godwin 52.

3. Runes 219.

4. 1 Frazer 285.

5. 1 Frazer 279.

6. 1 Frazer 280.

7. 1 Frazer 283-284.

8. 1 Frazer 287.

9. 1 Frazer 288.

10. Branston 134, 139.

11. Godwin 69, 110.

12. 1 Frazer 295.

13. 1 Frazer 296.

14. Godwin 112, 114; Cumont MM 86-87; Cumont OR 48.

15. Godwin 118-119.

16. 1 Frazer 297.

17. 1 Frazer 297.

18. 1 Frazer 298.

19. 1 Frazer 299.

20. Godwin 132.

21. Godwin 132; 1 Frazer 320.

22. Godwin 132-143; 1 Frazer 320-329.

23. Godwin 133,142; 1 Frazer 324.

24. Godwin 132-133; 1 Frazer 322-324.

25. Godwin 133-134; 1 Frazer 325-329.

26. 1 Frazer 329.

27. 1 Frazer 324.

28. Godwin 133, 139.

29. Godwin 143.

30. 1 Frazer 321.

31. 1 Frazer 324.

32. 1 Peter 4.6. During the Middle Ages, the Church taught that Christ descended into Hades, preached the Gospel to the saints of the Old Testament, and raised them to life in Heaven. This was called the "Harrowing of Hell." Staniforth 92.

33. Angus 150.

34. Angus 151.

35. Angus 154.

36. Angus 153-154.

37. Angus 154; Godwin 146.

38. Angus 155.

39. Angus 202.

40. Angus 202.

41. Godwin 145.

42. Godwin 145.

43. Godwin 146.

44. Godwin 148.

45. Godwin 148.

46. Godwin 37.

47. Godwin 36.

48. Wheeler 1-182.

49. Psalm 23.2, 4.

50. Godwin 144.

51. Godwin 144.

52. Budge 2 Osiris 270.

53. Budge 2 Osiris 272-276; Godwin 121.

54. Budge 2 Osiris 277-278.

55. Budge 2 Osiris 281.

56. Budge 2 Osiris 306.

57. Budge 2 Osiris 288.

58. Budge 2 Osiris 281.

59. Budge 2 Osiris 281.

60. Budge 2 Osiris 281.

61. Budge 2 Osiris 292.

62. Budge 2 Osiris 292.

63. 1 Frazer 301.

64. John 2.4.

65. Budge 2 Osiris 298.

66. Exodus 25.16.

67. Budge 2 Osiris 299.

68. Budge 2 Osiris 299.

69. Budge 2 Osiris 299.

70. Budge 2 Osiris 299-300.

71. Schaaf 77,80.

72. 1 World Book Encyclopedia 863-864 (1983).

73. Genesis 37.3.

74. Budge 2 Osiris 302-303.

75. Ezekiel 1.27-28.

76. Schaaf 77, 80.

77. Graves & Patai 38. In the King James version of Ezekiel 1.4, 27, *chashmal* is translated as "amber."

78. Godwin 33.

79. Godwin 33-34; 147.

80. Godwin 79.

81. Godwin 79.

82. Godwin 83.

83. Godwin 80.

84. Dreyer 416-417.

85. Godwin 34.

 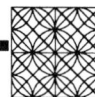

Chapter Eighteen

The Early Christian Church

Question: What do we know about the early Christian Church? Answer: Not enough to please the scholars. Far too much to please the priests and preachers. We already have noted the resemblances between early Christianity and the mystery religions, and have come to appreciate the main problem faced by Christianity's doctrine-smiths and salesmen: how to present to the common people a refined theology and moral code which they would accept voluntarily, so it would not be necessary to force them to accept the new religion at the point of a sword. We shall see that fatherly persuasion did not work, and that holy mayhem almost achieved success. Almost. But not quite.

Paternalism does have its problems! Question: How do we get our children's teeth brushed without doing it for them or without using verbal threats or physical violence? Answer: By associating the brushing of their teeth with their beloved Saturday morning television cartoon characters; by giving them candy-tasting toothpaste instead of harsh-tasting baking soda as dentifrice; by convincing them that toothbrushing is play-time instead of chore-time. Not surprising, therefore, that the scholars and salesmen who birthed and reared to maturity the new faith sought to maximize the humanization of the common people by minimizing the contrasts between the ceremonies and doctrines of the old and new faiths. Modern Christian "Oxen" celebrate their holy day on Sunday by drinking grape juice and eating wafers or crackers, without the slightest understanding of the origins of that liturgy.[1] We have given the churchmen their "lumps" in this book, but we also should give them our thanks. Thanks, Daddy, for teaching me to brush my teeth. Thanks, Father Tomas, for repressing the animal instincts which lie beneath the thin veneer of civilization.

We Irish have a saying about the Kerry Blue terrier: The Kerry Blue is smart enough to herd mice at the crossroads. A similar accolade is due from all modern Christians to Eusebius, A.D. 263-339, who was the Bishop of Caesarea, in Palestine.[2] He wrote one of the very first histories of the Church,

in which he candidly aired the Church's dirty linen, thereby proving the need to define the term "Christian" and to exclude from the Church all who failed to meet the definition.[3] He was a better politician than scholar, but his role as founding father of the Church is not open to the slightest doubt. Eusebius was friend and confidant of the Roman Emperor Constantine. Eusebius sat with Constantine at the Council of Nicaea in 325, which gave Christianity the Nicene Creed recited in many Christian Churches even until this day.[4]

By majority vote of the churchmen assembled at the Council of Nicaea, it was determined that Jesus Christ was *one* of the *two* "Persons" of God, the significance being that the council rejected the doctrine of the Presbyter Arius, later known as the "Arian Heresy," which held that Jesus was created by God rather than being one of the "Persons" of God.[5] The "official" Holy Trinity did not come along until later when, at the Council of Constantinople, in the year 381, the Holy Ghost was added, by majority vote of the bishops, to the Holy Duality of God the Father and God the Son, to give the Church its "God in Three Persons, Blessed Trinity."[6]

In the common parlance of that day, a holy magician was referred to as a "Son of God."[7] Magi reputedly acted through a "medium," often a child; or through a ghost or spirit, often an evil spirit or devil.[8] This is why the Bible says that some persons who reputedly witnessed Christ's miracles thought that He had a devil or evil spirit as His paraclete.[9] Because the common folk expected the Church to accomplish its Holy Magic, such as the Mass, through a ghost or spirit, and were accustomed, also, to worshiping "trinitarian" gods and goddesses, the Christian Church quite obviously needed its "Holy Ghost" or "Holy Spirit," which it gave itself, officially, by vote of the fathers of the Church at Constantinople in the year 381.[10]

Why this introduction to the man Eusebius and to his enduring accomplishments? Because we are going to read some of his writings about the early Church, and it is necessary that we dispel any notion that Eusebius was some sort of right-wing or left-wing radical. He voted with the center.[11] In an effort to maximize accuracy, modern scholars collect "pro" and "con" writings about the early Christian Church and demonstrate that views of Christianity found in the writings of the supporters and opponents of the early Church coincide remarkably with the views expressed in Matthew, Mark, Luke, and John.[12] We do not have the time or space to engage in such a process in this book. We must be brief. We primarily shall limit ourselves to the views of early Christian history expressed by Eusebius, a man to whom modern Christians probably owe more than any other founding father of the Church, with the exception of the Apostle Paul.

A modern Christian fundamentalist will find that stepping into the pages of *The History Of The Church* will cause as many shivers to run through his body as stepping into a mountain stream to receive Holy Baptism. Familiar doctrines of modern Christian faith are absent; unfamiliar aspects of early Christianity are present.[13] The gap between the silent contemplation of a modern Trappist monk and the noisy frenzy of a modern Holy Roller is wide enough. Both call themselves "Christian," but other than their common faith in Christ they have very little in common. Eusebius confronted an even wider spectrum of "Christian worship," and he did something about it. Beliefs and practices which he favored became "Catholic." Beliefs and practices which he disfavored became "heresy." Catholics were blessed. Heretics were slaughtered.[14] Some of these Christian heretics engaged in practices which we moderns would consider despicable.[15] Others thought as we moderns think; their only "sin" was being ahead of their time.[16] The early Church made no distinction. To give an inch one day was to give a mile the next. *No* deviation from official dogma was to be permitted.[17] For the good of the sheep? Or for the good of the shepherds?

Familiar aspects of modern Roman Catholicism missing from the works of Eusebius include the Doctrine of Papal Infallibility, the Immaculate Conception, and the Bodily Assumption of Our Lady.[18] There could be no Papal Infallibility because there was no Pope. "If the Bishop of Rome tried to put others in their place, his brother-bishops 'sternly rebuked' him."[19] Saint Peter was not regarded as founder of the Church at Rome. "[T]he language used of him is used of Paul as well...."[20] Our Lady "is mentioned less than half a dozen times, and though the doctrine of the Virgin Birth is stoutly

maintained, no title of honour is applied to her, nor is it ever suggested that she or any other saint can be the recipient or channel of prayer. Finally, we note that so far from celibacy being imposed on bishops or clergy, such imposition is regarded as rank heresy."[21]

Eusebius quotes Clement approvingly "to rebut those who deprecated marriage, by listing the apostles known to have been married men."[22] Eusebius tells us that Clement wrote: "'Or will they condemn even the apostles? For Peter and Phillip had families, and Phillip gave his daughters in marriage, while Paul himself does not hesitate in one of his epistles to address his yoke-fellow, whom he did not take round with him for fear of hindering his ministry.'"[23] Compare Clement's statement about Paul's "yoke-fellow" with 1 Cor. 9.5, which says either that all twelve of the Apostles and the brothers of Jesus had wives or, at least, that they had the right to have wives. *If* Paul had a *male* "yoke-fellow" and left him at home, then Paul evidently left him at home so as not to be subject to the gossip spoken of the later Cathar priests, who always traveled in groups of two, thereby incurring the odium that they preferred male to female companionship.[24]

The New Testament tells us that Christ is "a priest forever" in the order of Melchizedek. Who was "Melchizedek?" Read the Biblical passages in note 25 of this chapter, and you will know all that your author knows on the subject.[25] Was "Melchizedek" a name once given to our humanform on the Holy Grail? Eusebius tells us that in Psalm 110, David wrote the following words concerning David's "Lord," whom God had created as a priest forever in the order of Melchizedek: "From the womb before the daystar I begat Thee."[26] That line of the Psalm is either missing from, or is badly mangled in, every modern Bible your author has found. The words last-quoted were present in the Bible from which Eusebius was writing his *History*, and Eusebius wanted his readers to understand that, in his opinion, the reference of the Psalmist was to Jesus Christ.[27] Eusebius glosses the quoted phrase by writing that it means "before the creation of the world."[28] Our modern Bibles avoid the necessity of interpreting the quoted words either by deleting them entirely or by substantially recasting them. The lesson: It had not yet become accepted as official Christian dogma that the Bible was the immutable "Word of God." Hence, after Eusebius wrote his *History*, expositors of Christian Truth felt free either to eliminate Biblical passages

Figure 266

Figure 267

which were not in accord with their latest pronouncement of Christian Truth, or to substantially rewrite them so as to mask their original meaning.[29]

Why do the deleted words deserve such extended discussion? Because they have an *explicit* meaning. The daystar is the planet we call Venus, which appears at certain seasons in its role as the morning star and at other seasons in its role as the evening star.[30] Sumerian and Babylonian astronomers knew that the morning star and the evening star were one and the same heavenly body, which was a "wanderer" (planet) rather than a star.[31] Modern astronomers will understand that this single fact proves that the Sumerians were competent astronomers. The "womb" before the daystar is a zodiacal light phenomenon which announces the rising of the sun.[32] How could Jesus Christ be born from the womb before the daystar and *also* be born of the Virgin Mary? Because Our Lady became "Queen of Heaven," in succession to all of the ancient goddesses by whose names the daystar previously had been known? Is this why Our Lady wears on her headdress[33] the ✳ symbol of Inanna, a former Queen of Heaven?[34] And just what is the meaning of that symbol? We already have learned that it was the Sumerian symbol for "star." In the science chapters, we shall learn its astronomical significance, and shall suggest why it is to be found in Bronze Age passage graves in Ireland.[35]

Eusebius says that the Night Visions of the Prophet Daniel were of the coming of Jesus.[36] We have not mentioned Daniel's Night Visions so far in this book. Please get your Bible and read them.[37] Who is the "Ancient of days?" Our Grail manform who sits on the throne? See **Figure 266**. Who is the "one like the Son of man" who came with the clouds of heaven? Our Grail manform with his arms

extended among "clouds" of concave-sided tetragons? See **Figure 267**. Note that Daniel's beasts arose from the sea (of the heavens?) and that a fiery stream (the Milky Way?) came forth before the Ancient of days. Note also that one of Daniel's animals is like a bear. The Little Bear (Ursa Minor) and Great Bear (Ursa Major) are circumpolar constellations which share stars with the two asterisms which Americans call the Big Dipper and the Little Dipper, the locators of Polaris, the current polestar.[38] The astronomical phenomenon called "precession" causes the celestial pole to wobble across several of the stars of the circumpolar constellations over a very long period of years.[39] Most recently, Polaris assumed dominion as polestar.[40] Daniel's bear lost its dominion! Could it be that Biblical authors were writing in allegory about celestial periodic phenomena, including precession, which the Chaldean astronomers had discovered?

Would it not be a mistake if the archaeologists who dig up the remains of American culture were to reach the conclusion that our religions taught us that ducks could talk, and that men could fly by extending their capes? We really do not believe that Donald Duck can talk, or that Superman can fly simply by extending his cape. But if, by chance, some comic-book collector put his treasures safely away in a fireproof vault, found by future archaeologists, the learned scholars of the future might reach wrong conclusions about our beliefs. The archaeologists might conclude from that cache of comic-books, their only tangible evidence of our civilization, that we believed such fables were facts, and find in this primitivism a possible explanation of why we perished. You get the point. Suppose we are treating as historical fact that which Biblical writers intended as allegorical references to what was happening in the skies? Suppose they never intended to mislead us into reaching our conclusions? Who would be at fault? Our religious leaders who insist upon the absolute historicity of the Biblical stories? Do they know one reality yet tell us another? Or are they as ignorant as we?

Did the early Christians wrap their realities in allegory?[41] Eusebius thought they did. He quotes and writes extensively in his *History* about Claudius Philo, who wrote about a group of ascetics whose male members Philo called *Therapeutae*, and whose female members Philo called *Therapeutrides*.[42] Eusebius tells us that these appellations were conferred upon them "either because like doctors they rid the souls of those who come to them from moral sickness and so cure and heal them, or in view of their pure and sincere service and worship of God. Whether he [Philo] invented this designation and applied it to them, fitting a suitable name to their mode of life, or whether they were actually called this from the very start, because the title Christian was not yet in general use, need not be discussed now."[43] Eusebius, how we wish you *had* discussed this further!

Eusebius continues: "This much is certain. He [Philo] lays special emphasis on their renunciation of property, saying that when they embark on the philosophic life they hand over their possessions to their relations, then, having renounced all worldly interests, they go outside the walls and make their homes on lonely farms and plantations well aware that association with men of different ideas is unprofitable and harmful. That, apparently, was the practice of the Christians of that time, who with eager and ardent faith disciplined themselves to emulate the prophetic way of life. Similarly, in the canonical Acts of the Apostles it is stated that all the disciples of the apostles sold their possessions and belongings and shared them out among the others in accordance with individual needs, so that no one was in want among them; all who were owners of land or houses, Scripture tells us, sold them and brought the price they fetched and laid it at the apostles' feet, so that it was distributed to everyone in accordance with individual needs."[44] Have you ever noticed the similarity between early Christian and Marxist doctrines? Both found Utopia in a communistic egalitarianism which the greedy majority of mankind, even in Russia and China, refuses to accept. The parallels between the early Christian cult and modern-day cults are too obvious to require extended discussion.

Eusebius continues: "Having testified to practices very similar to these, Philo goes on: 'The community is to be found in many parts of the world, for it was right that what is perfectly good should be shared by both Greek and foreign lands. It is very strong in Egypt in each of the *nomes*, and especially in the Alexandrian area. The best men in each region set out as colonists for a highly suitable spot, regarding it as the homeland of the *Therapeutae*. It is situated above Lake Mareotis on a low hill, very convenient in view of its security and the mildness of the climate.'"[45]

Are the desert ascetics of America the *real* Christians of today? Are they more faithful to the original ideals of Christianity than those of us who pray on our knees on Sunday then prey on our neighbors for the remainder of the week?

Eusebius is about to answer the question we posed regarding allegory. He writes: "Next, after describing the character of their dwellings, he [Philo] has this to say about the churches in the area: 'In every house there is a holy chamber called a sanctuary or "monastery", where they celebrate in seclusion the mysteries of the sanctified life, bringing in nothing — drink, food, or anything else required for bodily needs — but laws and inspired oracles spoken by prophets, hymns, and everything else by which knowledge and true religion are increased and perfected.... The whole period from dawn to dusk is given up to spiritual discipline. They read the sacred scriptures, and study their ancestral wisdom philosophically, allegorizing it, since they regard the literal sense as symbolic of a hidden reality revealed in figures. They possess also short works by early writers, the founders of their sect, who left many specimens of the allegorical method, which they take as their models, following the system on which their predecessors worked.'"[46]

Hang on tightly to your beliefs about the historicity of the Gospel stories, because here comes the punchline. Eusebius writes: "It seems likely that Philo wrote this after listening to their exposition of the Holy Scriptures, and it is very probable that what he calls short works by their early writers were the gospels, the apostolic writings, and in all probability passages interpreting the old prophets, such as are contained in the Epistle to the Hebrews and several others of Paul's epistles."[47] You remain cynical? Eusebius is ready for you! He thought you might resist

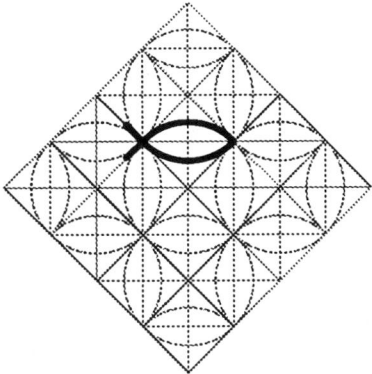

Figure 268

Figure 269

agreeing with him, so, like a practiced advocate, he assaults you with further proofs.

Eusebius writes: "If anyone does not agree that what has been described is peculiar to the gospel way of life but thinks it applicable to other people too, he will surely be convinced by Philo's next paragraph, in which, if he is reasonable, he will find the evidence on this point beyond dispute: 'Having first laid down self-control as foundation for the soul, they build the other virtues on it. None of them would take food or drink before sundown, as they hold that philosophy deserves daylight but darkness is good enough for bodily needs. So to the one they assign the day, to the others a small part of the night. Some think of food only once in three days - those in whom a greater passion for knowledge is rooted; others so delight and luxuriate as they feast on the wisdom that richly and ungrudgingly supplies their doctrines that they hold out even for twice that time, and scarcely taste necessary food once in six days, having accustomed themselves to this.'"[48]

Eusebius' last quotation from Philo apparently proved the point to Eusebius, but certainly proves little to us because it does not describe the vast majority of the present-day Christian community around the world.

Eusebius writes: "These statements of Philo [which we last quoted above] seem to me to refer plainly and unquestionably to members of our Church. But, if after this someone insists on denying it, he will surely abandon his skepticism and be convinced by still clearer evidence which cannot be found anywhere but in the religious practices of Christians who follow the gospel. For Philo states that among the people in question there are women, most of them elderly spinsters, 'who have remained single, not of necessity, like some priestesses of pagan cults, but of their own free will, through their passionate craving for wisdom, with which they were so eager to live that they scorned bodily pleasures, and set their hearts not on mortal children but on immortal, which only the soul that loves God can bring into the world.'"[49]

Immortal children brought into the world by mortal women? A concept like unto that of Our Lady bearing Jesus?

Eusebius tells us that Philo wrote of these people that, "'[t]heir explanations of the sacred scriptures are expressed figuratively in allegories. For the whole Law seems to them to resemble a living being, which for body has the literal precepts, for soul the meaning that is hidden in the words out of sight.'"[50]

Eusebius concludes by stating that "[a]nyone can see that when he [Philo] wrote it he had in mind the first preachers of the gospel teaching and the customs handed down by the apostles from the beginning."[51]

If we are willing to accept the conclusion of Eusebius that these writings of Philo describe early Christians, it would seem to follow that we should be very cautious about accepting *all* verses of Gospel stories as historical, because at least *some* verses of Gospel stories may have been intended as allegory by their authors, and understood as allegory by the ancient readers for whom they were written. We have found on the Holy Grail the structural components of "Solomon's Temple" and its furniture and furnishings. We see a single "fish" in **Figure 268**. We see in Illustration 8-1 an actual loaf of bread taken from a Greek oven buried by a volcanic eruption. We see the lines of an identical "loaf of bread" bolded in **Figure 269**. If we look at

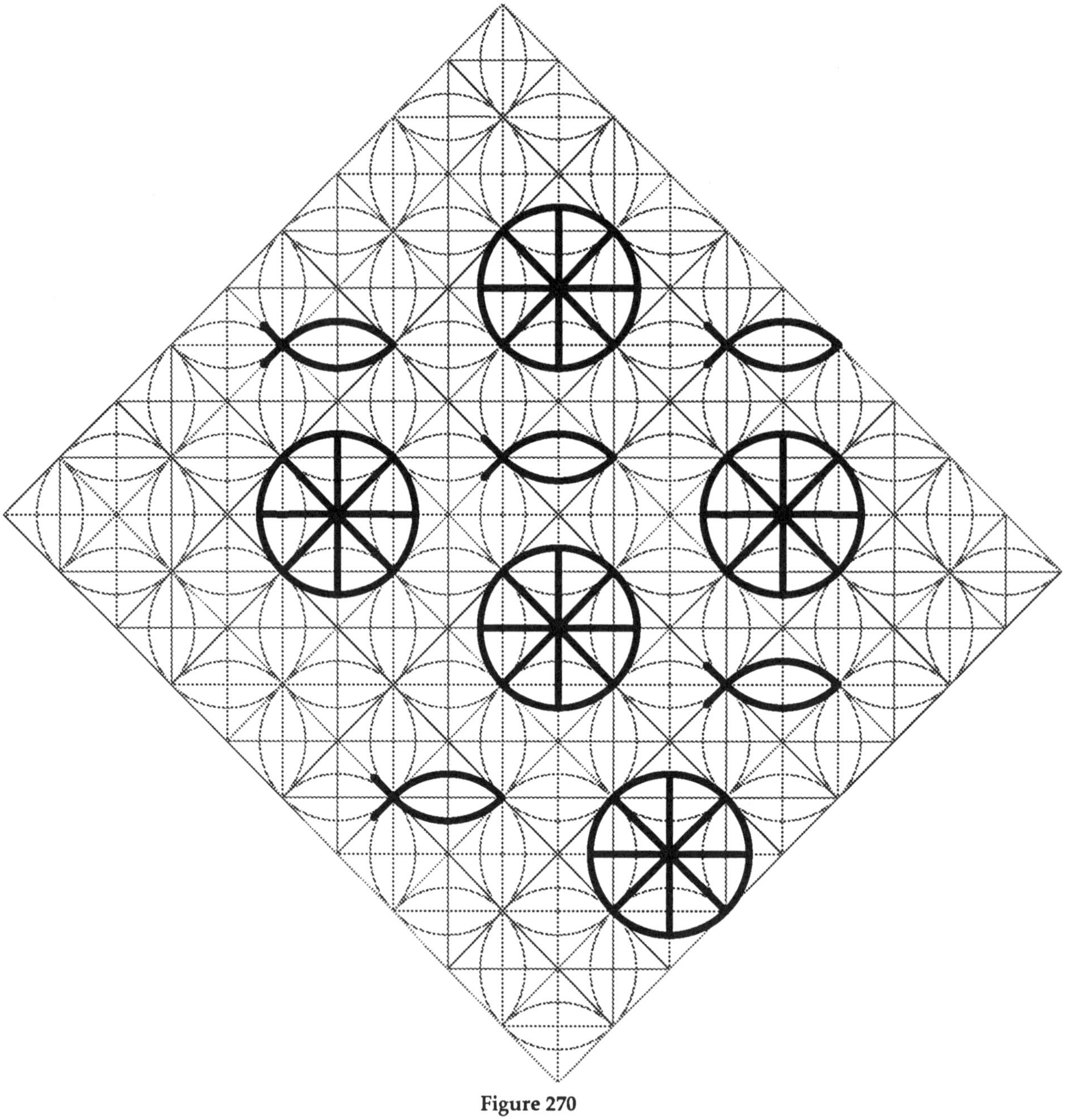

Figure 270

Figure 270, and search for as many of these "loaf" and "fish" forms as we can find, we find quite a few. Expanding Figure 270 by several more Holy Grail squares would multiply the number of these "loaf" and "fish" forms. Loaves and fishes? Multiplied?

One reality is that the Gospels "belong" to the modern-day Christian Church; hence, each Christian, depending on denomination, either has the right to decide what the Gospels mean in his life or has the duty to obey the interpretation of his spiritual advisor. Another reality is that the Gospels are the allegorical writings of ancient cultists who sought to live an ascetic life on Earth in order to enjoy a better life in Heaven. We are using *their* writings for *our* purposes. We had best keep that in mind! Eusebius criticizes a Christian whose teachings he regarded as heretical: "I suppose he got these notions by misinterpreting the apostolic accounts and failing to grasp what they had said in mystic and symbolic language. For he seems to have been a man of very small intelligence, to judge from his looks."[52] Do those words of Eusebius apply to some of us?

We previously alluded to the reason behind Roman persecution of the Christians: Not because most Roman governments were opposed to a wide variety of religions competing for converts among the Roman people but because they believed (rightly or wrongly) that Christians participated in human sacrifice and cannibalism. Does Eusebius tell us anything about this? He answers our questions completely!

Remember that Eusebius's purpose for writing his *History* was not to sweep under the rug the practices and beliefs of persons who called themselves "Christians" but whom he regarded as "heretics" because their beliefs or practices were at variance with his Greek concepts of humanism or with the Nicene Creed. Quite to the contrary, he sought to justify the harsh treatment Christian heretics were accorded by middle-of-the-road Christians who accepted Greek notions of humanism and the Nicene Creed.[53] We are not far into his writings before we learn that he has no sympathy with cannibals.[54] He also expresses his disgust about Christian heretics "who make sport of wretched women."[55] The Roman authorities believed that Christian "worship" included sexual orgies during which male members of the congregation engaged in intercourse with all female members, including their own sisters and mothers.[56] Sexual orgies, incestuous or otherwise, were not the reason for Roman persecutions of the Christians, however, because the Roman laws under which Christians were prosecuted and executed were directed against magic ceremonies involving human sacrifice and cannibalism:

"Any who perform, or procure the performance of, impious or nocturnal sacrifices, to enchant, curse, bind anyone with a spell, are either crucified or thrown to the beasts (in the arena). Any who sacrifice a man, or make offerings of his blood, or pollute a shrine or temple are thrown to the beasts or, if people of position, are beheaded. It is the prevailing legal opinion that participants in the magical art should be subject to the extreme punishment, that is, either thrown to the beasts or crucified...."[57]

Early Christians worshiped at night and practiced holy magic which they believed converted bread and wine into the real body and blood of Jesus Christ.[58] Accordingly, the Roman laws quoted above *could* have been written as a pretense for the persecution of Christians who were, at worst, *symbolic* human sacrificers and cannibals, and who never had engaged in what we might call "the real

thing." Eusebius believed that some Christians who were thrown to the lions were entirely truthful when they protested that they never had participated in ceremonies involving "the real thing."[59] Modern Christians would be comforted if we could reach the conclusion that the Roman authorities (1) wrote such laws as a way of getting rid of Christianity, or (2) believed that no distinction should be drawn between "the real thing" and Christian symbolic substitutes for "the real thing," or (3) erroneously believed that persons who admitted their participation in the Holy Magic of the Mass perjured themselves to conceal their participation in "the real thing."

Eusebius will not allow us that comfort. He tells us that the Cerinthian Christian sect taught "that Christ's kingdom would be here on earth" and that they engaged in drunken orgies "and the immolation of victims."[60] He lists several "schools of detestable heresies," names the men who founded them, and concludes: "Thus it came about that with the help of these ministers the demon that delights in evil enslaved their pitiable dupes and brought them to ruin, furnishing the unbelieving heathen with ample grounds for speaking ill of the divine message, since the talk to which they gave rise circulated widely and involved the whole Christian people in calumny. This was the main reason why that wicked and outrageous suspicion regarding us was current among the unbelievers of that time — the suspicion that we practised unlawful intercourse with mothers and sisters and took part in unhallowed feasts."[61] Lest we miss the meaning of Eusebius's words "unhallowed feasts," our translator tells us: "The reference is to cannibalism."[62]

The words of Eusebius cannot be rationalized away. He tells us that the Romans erroneously thought *all* Christians were human sacrificers and cannibals because *some* persons who called themselves Christians were in fact human sacrificers and cannibals. Can we debate about why Christians were thrown to the lions? Can we deny the origins of the Mass in our cannibal past?

Most modern Christians have no idea how the date of Easter presently is determined, or that the Christian Church permanently was torn asunder by a debate which raged between churchmen as to which method should be used to determine the date of Easter. The problem cannot be understood without a considerable understanding of both astronomy and astrology, as well as an appreciation of the relationship between Christian Easter and

Hebrew Passover. Gale R. Owen aptly has referred to the calculation of Easter as "a mathematical as well as a theological conundrum."[63] We cannot devote very much time to this fascinating topic, and must content ourselves with this: Jesus is reputed to have died either at or near (depending on which method of calculation of Easter you adopt) the Hebrew Passover, when the Pascal lamb was sacrificed, which is either at or near (again, depending on your methodology) the time when the sun reaches the first sign of the Zodiac or what Eusebius calls "the start of the planetary course."[64] Jesus was not the first sacrificial "king" to die at this time of the year. The Babylonians had followed the Persian custom of elevating a common man, often a criminal, to the status of "king," so they could make a "big" sacrifice of their "king" to make sure the wheel of the seasons, the Zodiac, would commence another annual 360 degree rotation; to give the sun an extra magical boost of energy, which their priests said it needed, at the Spring Equinox, when day and night were equal to each other, in order that day once more would commence its annual conquest of night, rather than vice versa.[65]

Those of you who enjoyed our analysis of the stories of the Tower and the Temple of Solomon should read Eusebius's verbal description of his design for the ideal Christian Church building.[66] We simply do not have time to put his words on the Holy Grail. Yes, Eusebius apparently was aware of the Holy Grail and its use by storysmiths as well as architects! By making up his own story on the Holy Grail, he proves himself a brother of those intellectuals of every generation who have known the secret of the Holy Grail!

We will pause just long enough to collect one brief, allegorical reference by Eusebius to that ideal church building. We need this excerpt for use in the science chapters at the end of this book. Eusebius says of his ideal church building that "With one huge gateway, consisting of the praise of our Sovereign Lord, the one only God, he adorns the whole cathedral; and on both sides of the Father's supreme power he supplies the secondary beams of the light of Christ, and the Holy Ghost."[67] Our translator pounces on Eusebius's reference to "secondary beams" like a robin on a worm! He offers us this apology: "Eusebius intends no heresy: As Christ is begotten of, and the Holy Ghost proceeds from, the Father, the Father may not unnaturally be deemed primary."[68] You are entitled to say, "So what?" So this: Under Nicaean dogma, the Father is God, the Son is God and, under the same mainline Roman Catholic doctrine, the Holy Ghost became God by vote of the bishops at the Council of Constantinople in the year 381.[69] All three "Persons" of the Holy Trinity (Father, Son, and Holy Ghost) thus are *primary* under mainline Christian dogma.[70] Eusebius *is* guilty of heresy, the specific heresy being that of the Presbyter Arius, whose views were not adopted in Nicaea because Eusebius and others joined with the mainliners to vote them down![71] Arius held the view that Jesus was secondary to God.[72] Eusebius is revealing his "true colors," which are contrary to the vote he cast at Nicaea. More importantly: We see for the first time in the explicit language of a leading Christian father an allegory based on primary and secondary rays of light, a physical phenomenon known to the ancients long before Sir Isaac Newton split "white" light into the colors of the rainbow by passing it through a prism.[73] The passage of primary and secondary beams of light into quartz crystals gives us the rainbow spectrum "interference pattern" visible inside quartz crystals, which is in the form of a "wheel within a wheel," in the words of Ezekiel, or in the form of the Celtic Cross appearing on the Holy Grail and in Irish churchyards! See Illustrations 4-2 and 4-3, and Figure 42. Salt that bit of trivia away for the moment. We will stir it together with an Anglo-Saxon Holy Grail story, then wrap the entire matter up in the science chapters.

Readers must prepare themselves for another speculation, which goes beyond the possibility that some of the *stories* of the Old and New Testaments are allegories.[74] Could Jesus have been an allegory? The word "Docetism" is defined as follows in a popular dictionary: "An early Christian doctrine that Jesus Christ appeared to men in a spiritual body and since he had no actual human body he only seemed to suffer and die on the cross."[75] Our best information about Docetism comes from the writings of the founding fathers of the Christian Church, who spewed heated words at Docetics, before the Roman army put the Docetics to the sword. Evidently, Docetism was "observed to be rife" in the City of Smyrna.[76] Ignatius wrote that Christ's Passion "was no unreal illusion, as some skeptics aver who are all unreality themselves" and that Christ, Himself, declared that He was "no bodiless phantom."[77] Ignatius denies that "everything our Lord did was only an illusion," and contends that "a man... blasphemes my Lord by denying that He ever bore a real human body...."[78] He tells us that the Docetics "even absent themselves from the Eucharist and the public prayers, because they will not admit that the Eucharist is the self-same body of our Saviour Jesus Christ...."[79] The translator notes that the Docetics claimed "that since the Passion itself is unreal, all suffering for Christ's sake must be vain and pointless."[80]

Polycarp joined the chorus against the Docetics by denouncing "the Docetic heretics who denied the reality of Christ's incarnation."[81] He summed things up like this: "To deny that Jesus Christ has come in the flesh is to be Antichrist. To contradict the evidence of the Cross is to be of the devil. And to pervert the Lord's words to suit our own wishes, by asserting that there are no such things as resurrection or judgement, is to be a first begotten son of Satan. So let us have no more of the nonsense from the gutter, and these lying doctrines, and turn back again to the Word originally delivered to us."[82] The idea that one elite group of religionists, and that group alone, has a monopoly on the "Word of God" is nothing new among Christian fundamentalists!

The interesting thing about these denouncements of Docetism is that Docetism apparently was a popular movement; a movement of and by the people. We have been surprised to find that scholars in many times and places knew about the Holy Grail as a source of religions. Did the average Docetic-in-the-street also know? Will the people ever be the masters of their own destinies? Not until they learn to think for themselves! Not until they accept as fact that many Ways lead toward God.

If the problem with Christian Docetics, who thought Christ was a optical illusion rather than a reality, was not bad enough, the founding fathers of the Church were faced with what to do about Christ look-alikes such as Apollonius of Tyana.[83] They could, of course, send in the Roman army, as they did with the Arian and Cathar Heretics, or, as in the case of Apollonius, they could bury the problem with invective. "[I]t soon became as necessary for every Catholic saint or doctor of the fourth and fifth centuries to have an opinion about Apollonius of Tyana as it was for the French bishops of fifty years ago to have an opinion about Our Lady of La Salette. Eusebius handsomely recognised Apollonius as the first of philosophers. Lactantius

and Arnobius did not deny his miracles, but referred them to magic. St. Jerome also regarded him as a magician; but he found things in his life to praise. St. Augustine, in arguing with the heathen, paid Apollonius a rather mild compliment by allowing that he was purer than Jove.... On the other hand, St. John Chrysostom branded the *Life* as false and Apollonius as a deceiver; and St. John Chrysostom's gradually became the common view.... Nevertheless the cult of Apollonius lingered on almost to the end of the Middle Ages...."[84]

Invective. Followed by swords, spears, and burnings at the stake. John Locke saw the truth about the history of the Christian Church when he wrote: "[T]he Gospel frequently declares that the true disciples of Christ must suffer persecution; but that the Church of Christ should persecute others, and force others by fire and sword to embrace her faith and doctrine, I could never yet find in any of the books of the New Testament."[85] Locke spelled out the consequences to humankind: "Nobody, therefore, in fine, neither single persons nor churches, nay, nor even commonwealths, have any just title to invade the civil rights and worldly goods of each other upon pretense of religion. Those that are of another opinion would do well to consider with themselves how pernicious a seed of discord and war, how powerful a provocation to endless hatreds, rapines, and slaughters they thereby furnish unto mankind. No peace and security, no, not so much as common friendship, can ever be established or preserved amongst men so long as this opinion prevails, that dominion is founded in grace and that religion is to be propagated by force of arms."[86]

Page one of tonight's newspaper tells me that a Christian fundamentalist preacher wants an excellent public servant voted out of office because the officeholder will not sign a written statement that he is a born-again Christian. The officeholder is a devout Hebrew. Page one also tells me that the Islamic "Party of God" has kidnapped another American in Beirut. Page one further says that families are burying their dead killed by the Islamic "Soldiers of God" during last week's commercial airplane highjacking. I think I shall not read page two. What will Ian Paisley preach from his pulpit in Belfast tomorrow morning? For the sake of the sheep? Or for the sake of the shepherds?

Notes
CHAPTER EIGHTEEN. The Early Christian Church

1. "This ignorant Christian custom of eating and drinking commonplace bread and wine in the hope of gaining some Christlike virtue is but a relic of the savage rite of omophagia — the eating and drinking of another person's or animal's flesh and blood to acquire his or its qualities, strength, courage, and so on. But the civilized, so-called, have gone the savage one better; they eat a god instead of a man, and so the savage's anthropophagy is now theanthropophagy." Graham 335. "The officiating priests of Rome would, *sub rosa*, change the words '*Hoc est meum corpus*' (This is my body) to '*Panis es, et panis manebis*' (Bread it is, and bread it shall remain), and the poor, benighted people would bow their heads before the elevated Host and profess their unworthiness just as today." Graham 336.

2. Eusebius 1.

3. Eusebius 1, 7-29.

4. Eusebius 12-13.

5. Henry Chadwick 130.

6. Booth 18.

7. Griffith & Thompson 133. "[C]laiming to be the son of a god was not an actionable offense in Roman law, but, as already mentioned, magicians often claimed to be gods or sons of gods...." Smith 41. The Gospels do *not* indicate that the criminal charge brought against Jesus under Roman law was that He claimed He was the Son of God; rather, the charge was that He was a "doer of evil" or "malefactor," John 18.30, common parlance in Roman law for "magician." Smith 41. "This [John 18.30] would seem too vague to be a legal accusation did not the Roman law codes tell us that it was the vulgar term for a magician." Smith 33. "Thus, in popular thought, 'son of god' and 'magician' are alternative titles...." Smith 81.

8. Griffith & Thompson 165-169; Smith 32-36, 136-139.

9. John 7.20; John 8.48-49, 52; see also, Matthew 9.34; Matthew 10.25; Mark 3.22-30.

10. Booth 18; Graham 87, 452-453.

11. Eusebius 12-13. We must not confuse our Eusebius, who inspired Emperor Constantine to become a sort-of Christian, thereby giving the Church an army with which to slaughter its religious competitors, with another Eusebius, who later baptized the aged Constantine. Eusebius 13; Henry Chadwick 136.

12. Smith 1-7.

13. Eusebius 7-29.

14. Eusebius 82-83, 239. Eusebius quotes the words of a "Catholic" or "blessed" Christian who was thrown to the lions: "'I am God's wheat, ground by the teeth of beasts, that I may be found pure bread.'" Eusebius 147. After our studies of the mystery religions, we better can understand that Christian *allegory*.

15. Hopefully, most of us will agree with Eusebius that rape, human sacrifice, the eating of actual human flesh and the drinking of actual human blood, and other such barbaric practices should be outside the pale of all religions. Eusebius 86-87, 136-139, 158-160, 163-165, 182, 190.

16. Most moderns do not equate the study of geometry and mathematics with Christian heresy. Eusebius 237.

17. A Roman Emperor wrote to a Bishop of Rome: "[S]uch is the regard I pay to the lawful Catholic Church that I desire you to have no schism or division of any kind anywhere." Eusebius 405.

18. Eusebius 10-11.

19. Eusebius 10.

20. Eusebius 10.

21. Eusebius 11.

22. Eusebius 140.

23. Eusebius 140. Paul addresses his "true yokefellow" in Philippians 4.3.

24. Baigent 55. Paul's "yoke-fellow" may have been a *female* who performed wife-like services *other than* sexual intercourse. Walker 115. However, the word "yoke-fellow" means *more than* "servant." "Yoke-fellow" means "associate" or "partner." 2 World Book Dictionary 2422 (1979). Paul's yokefellow most likely was an assistant pastor or assistant to the pastor. The common folk have not changed. Imagine a present-day, unmarried, circuit-riding preacher who takes with him on his travels either a male or a female assistant pastor or assistant to the pastor. If this modern preacher's traveling companion is an unmarried male, wagging tongues will suggest that the preacher is gay. If the preacher's traveling companion is an unmarried female, wagging tongues will suggest that she and the preacher are engaged in hanky-panky outside the vows of marriage. No wonder that Paul, an unmarried man, left his partner in Christ at home when he was riding circuit!

25. Gen. 14.18; Ps. 110.4; Heb. 5.6, 5.10, 6.20, 7.1, 7.11, 7.15 and 7.17.

26. Eusebius 44.

27. Eusebius 44-45.

28. Eusebius 45.

29. Weingreen 28-29 tells us that Jeremiah 44.17-19 was altered in the Hebrew Canon to delete all reference to the "queen of heaven." Those words appear in King James, and in most other Christian Bibles. The words "queen of heaven" were considered to be "too blasphemous even to be allowed to be mentioned [in the Hebrew Canon] for it implied that in their turning to the nature religion of the nations around, the [Hebrew] people had accepted the notion that Yahweh had a consort. The objectionable expression was ingeniously given a different meaning by the simple device of reading the first word differently...." Similar practices continue to this day. The word "allegory," which appears in the King James version of Galatians 4.24, was deleted

and replaced by the words "true story" in the version of Galatians 4.24 found in The Living Bible.

30. Krupp 12; Schaaf 147-148.

31. Krupp 306; Wolkstein 93, 103, 105; Heath *Aristarchus* 66. The Romans did not realize that Venus is *both* the morning star *and* the evening star. They thought it was two different objects. They named the morning star "Phosphorus" and the evening star "Hesperus." The Heavens 104.

32. Minnaert 290-295.

33. Beckwith 327. In medieval thinking, Our Lady *was* the Queen of Heaven. Brooke 32.

34. Wolkstein 60.

35. McMann Fig. 43.

36. Eusebius 40.

37. Daniel 7.1-28.

38. Rey 30-31, 34-35.

39. Rey 127-129.

40. Rey 128.

41. "For it is written, that Abraham had two sons, the one by a bondmaid, the other by a freewoman. But he *who was* of the bondwoman was born after the flesh; but he of the freewoman *was* by promise. Which things are an allegory...." Galatians 4.22-24. Saint Paul *evidently* believed that something (what?) about that Old Testament story was an allegory!

42. Eusebius 89-90.

43. Eusebius 90.

44. Eusebius 90.

45. Eusebius 90-91.

46. Eusebius 91.

47. Eusebius 91.

48. Eusebius 92.

49. Eusebius 92.

50. Eusebius 93.

51. Eusebius 93.

52. Eusebius 152.

53. Eusebius 158-160.

54. Eusebius 38.

55. Eusebius 87.

56. Eusebius 159-160, 195.

57. Smith 75.

58. Smith 50-51; Matthews 54-55.

59. Eusebius 195, 197, 202.

60. Eusebius 138.

61. Eusebius 159-160.

62. Eusebius 160.

63. Owen 140. Hanbury Brown puts it this way: "[T]he date of Easter is… given for all time by a formula which reads like a magic spell. To cast this spell you must invoke the golden number, the dominical letter, and finally the day of the paschal full moon." H. Brown 1.

64. Eusebius 323. "The first day of *nisan* [March-April] was the beginning of the year for the computation of passover. For other purposes, the year began in autumn, on the first of *tishri* [September-October], which was solemnized as New Year's Day...." 1 The Interpreter's Bible 152.

65. Langdon TBEOC 16, 20-33, 58-59; 1 Frazer 109-120, 178-179, 213-253. We shall learn that Grail stories contain many references to this ancient custom.

66. Eusebius 383-401.

67. Eusebius 399.

68. Eusebius 399.

69. Booth 18.

70. 19 World Book Encyclopedia 363 (1983).

71. Eusebius 12-13.

72. 1 World Book Encyclopedia 625 (1983).

73. Krupp 133, 317.

74. Galatians 4.24.

75. Webster's Third New International Dictionary 665. The Compact Edition of the Oxford English Dictionary, 1971, Vol. 1, at page 779, says, *inter alia*, that the *Docetae* believed the body of Jesus to have been either "a mere optical illusion" or "something ethereal and impalpable." An "optical illusion" created by lines boldfaced on the Holy Grail?

76. Staniforth 118.

77. Staniforth 119.

78. Staniforth 120.

79. Staniforth 121.

80. Staniforth 124.

81. Staniforth 142.

82. Staniforth 147. Docetism in Hinduism and Buddhism is not the problem it has been to orthodox Christians. Parrinder 50, 105, 177, 212-213, 214, 245, 263-264. That God appeared to humankind in a human body seems less fabulous than the assertion that He appeared to mankind in such avatars as a swan, a fish, a tortoise, a boar, a man-lion, a horse-headed man, or a firefly. Parrinder 22-23, 75. That God appeared as Rama with an axe, or as a dwarf, is more in the order of Christian believability. Parrinder 22. Note how the incarnation and the avatars *all* appear on the Holy Grail. Why did early Christian theologians write invective against Docetism? Was Christian Docetism actively competing with the Christian historicity movement for true believers? Was the "spiritual flesh" of Gnostic Docetism a precursor, or merely a contemporary, of the "human flesh" of the Gospels? Rudolph 10, 16-17, 25, 131, 148-151, 162-171, 193-194, 205, 275-294.

83. F.W. Groves Campbell 7-120.

84. F.W. Groves Campbell 12-13.

85. 35 Great Books Of The Western World 5.

86. 35 Great Books Of The Western World 7.

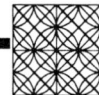

Chapter Nineteen

Teutons and Anglo-Saxons

"It will prove helpful to readers if they have, and can keep, a sufficiently vigorous sense of humor to enable them to laugh at the childish and just plain silly efforts of human beings to comprehend the incomprehensible." That advice first was given in Chapter One.[1] It seems worth repeating at this stage of our Grail quest.

Christianity arrived late in the Germanic territories of northern Europe. Iceland was Christianized in about 1000 A.D. Adam of Bremen wrote about human sacrifice to Odin (Odinn or Woden), Thor (Thunor) and Frey (Fricco) in Uppsala, Sweden, just before 1200 A.D.[2] In contrast, the Germanic Saxons, Angles, and Jutes who arrived to colonize the British Isles in about 450 A.D. were more or less converted to Christianity before the Synod of Whitby in 664 A.D.[3] Christianity first had arrived in Britain during the second century.[4] The Saxon invasion gave Christianity such a heavy blow that it had to be reintroduced in 597 A.D.[5] Viking raiders who settled in England during the ninth and tenth centuries caused some "backsliding" among their Anglo-Saxon cousins, but the Church never again lost its toe-hold in England.[6] For these reasons, the written records pertaining to Anglo-Saxon pre-Christian religious worship are older and fewer than those of northern Europe.

We learn from the *Verse Edda* and *Prose Edda*, written in Iceland, respectively, in about 900 A.D. and 1200 A.D.,[7] that northern European Germanic people told myths about the creation and end of the world which strikingly resemble the Creation story of the Old Testament and the Battle of Armageddon of the New Testament; which contain elements of the Christ story. The customary explanation for these ofttimes startling resemblances is that the Germanic pagans must have modeled their myths after Christian doctrines.[8] We shall explore another possibility: Were these stories born in the minds of ancient storysmiths from line forms visualized on the Holy Grail?

The *Eddas* tell us that in the beginning, there was an All-father; one god named Tiwaz,[9] like the Hebrew Tetragrammaton. Then there was Ginnungagap, a yawning chasm, the place of creation, like the void of Genesis.[10] The northern end of Ginnungagap was Niflheim, a place of fog and ice, to the south of which lay Muspellheim, a place of fire and flame.[11] Water and fire, two of the four ancient "elements," found in a creation myth once more![12] Up from the center of Niflheim bubbled the source of all rivers, known as the Roaring Cauldron of Hvergelmir.[13] Cauldron? Like the Hebrew "sea" in the Temple?[14] It seems that cosmic waters always mystically well up from "the center" or near the holy altar.[15] At the point where the heat and the frost met, there formed a giant in the likeness of a man, whose name was Ymir or Aurgelmir, which means "Mud Seether,"[16] as "Adam," the name of the Hebrew cosmic man, means the soil of the earth.[17] From him sprung the Frost Giants, the opposites of the Fire Giant of the more southern regions.[18] Adam, we learned from Hebrew legends outside the Canon of the Bible, was a giant whose body spread from horizon to horizon.[19] The fire giant, Surt, grasped a flaming sword,[20] like the flaming sword of the Garden of Eden story.[21]

We are told that Ymir fed himself with the milk from a cosmic cow, like the Egyptian cosmic cow, Hathor, who licked away the ice covering a man, who married a giantess, and that they had three sons, including Odin, who killed the giant Ymir and made the world from his bodily remains,[22] much as in the Babylonian creation story the world was made from the remains of Tiamat, a monster.[23] The giant's blood became the oceans, and drowned all the frost giants, except one who escaped in his boat with his wife, in a Germanic version of the flood story.[24] The giant's flesh became the earth and his skull was used by the three sons to form the dome of heaven, held aloft by four dwarfs which had emerged like maggots from the divine cow's body.[25] The four dwarfs supporting the sky stand

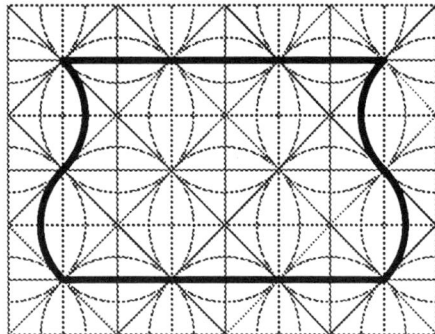

Figure 271

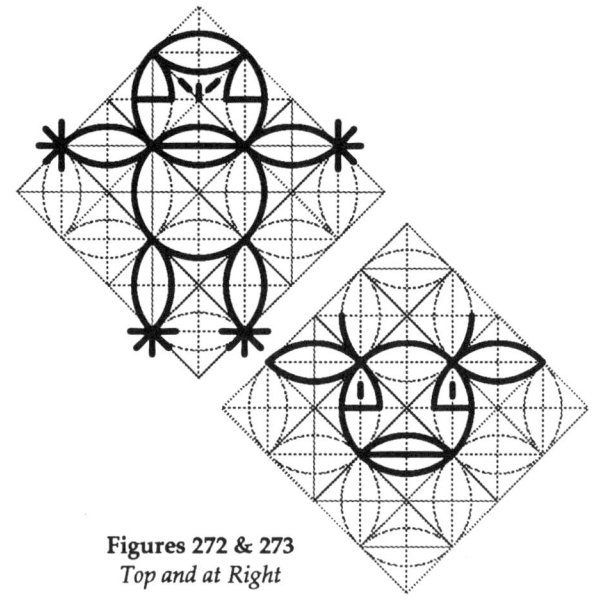

Figures 272 & 273
Top and at Right

at the four cardinal points.[26] Cauldron? **Figure 271?** Giant? **Figure 272?** Cow? **Figure 273?** Two dwarfs standing behind two more dwarfs at the four corners of a square while holding up the dome of the heavens? **Figure 274?** Here we go again!

Odin took his place as father of the gods and of men "aloft in his high seat called Gateshelf."[27] We see him enthroned in **Figure 275.** Odin maintained contact with the world through two ravens, Huginn and Muninn, much as Jehovah sends down to the

world the Holy Spirit in the form of the dove of the Christian Mass.[28] We see the bird-form employed

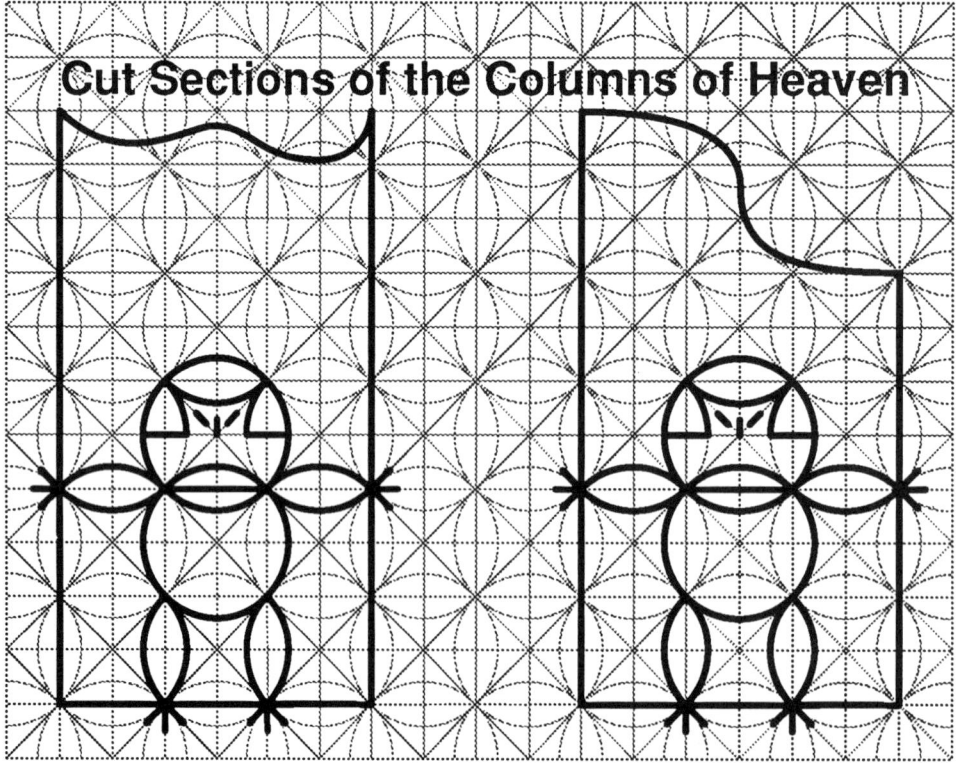

Figure 274

Teutons and Anglo-Saxons

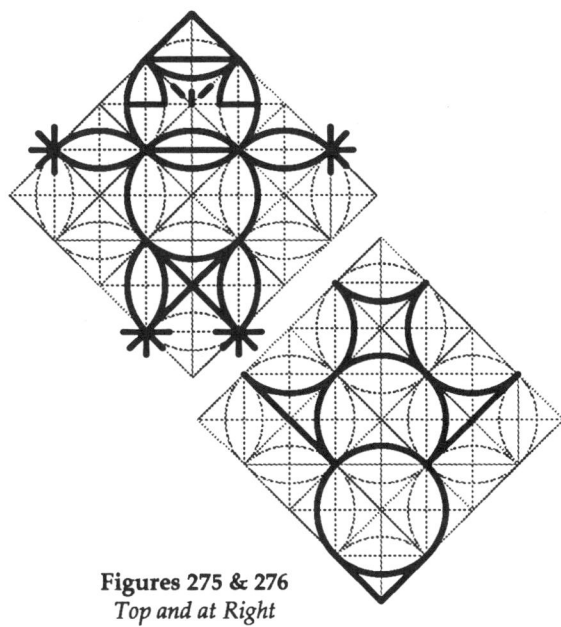

Figures 275 & 276
Top and at Right

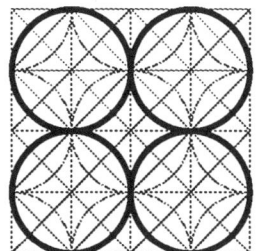

Figure 278

by God and Odin, and also by Noah-Utnapishtim in **Figure 276**.

The regions of the Germanic cosmic world are supported by the mighty ash Yggdrasill.[29] The Mayan Indians of Mexico tell a nearly identical story about the cosmic tree.[30] One of the roots of Yggdrasill is in Heaven, one runs up to Giantland, and a third goes down to Hel.[31] Hel is the Germanic underworld, which is more like the Mayan and Semitic underworlds (it merely is dismal) than the Christian hot spot.[32] By the heavenly root is the well of Urdr, where dwell the three Norns or Fates.[33] By the root which reaches towards the giants lies Mimir's Well, so called for its guardian, a giant named Mimir.[34] A branch of the cosmic tree, with its ash leaves, is seen in **Figure 277**. The cosmic tree represents the world-axis, as does the Christian Cross.[35] We shall find a giant guarding a spring[36] in our Grail quest stories to follow. Odin gains wisdom by consulting with the severed head of Mimir,[37] much as the Aramaeans consulted with mummified heads of first-born children, called Teraphim.[38] We shall learn that the Knights Templar may have sought wisdom from severed human heads,[39] as did our Irish ancestors.[40]

Odin sires the Aesir, that is, the "pillars,"[41] a race of gods,[42] including Balder, the Germanic Christ, by his wife Frig,[43] the Germanic goddess of love,[44] whose name remains to this day a colloquial expression for the act of copulation.[45] One of their sons is the god Thor.[46] There is, of course, a Germanic devil, Loki, who is more in the role of the American Indian "Trickster" than the Christian Satan.[47] Loki is a thief who steals the gods' treasures, including the cosmic apples of youth, seen in **Figure 278**.[48] Loki fathers a cosmic wolf, which will destroy Odin; a cosmic serpent, which will destroy Thor; and the goddess Hel, who is sent down to the underworld to become queen of the ingloriously dead.[49] Men and women who die violently in battle or sacrifice go to the Germanic Heaven, Valhalla, of which we soon shall learn.[50] Everyone else, including those who die of sickness and old age, go to live in the underworld with Hel.[51] It is easy to understand how myths can govern the conduct of the masses![52] As in other mythologies, the cosmic serpent lives in the sea.[53]

In accordance with the Chaldean concept of predestination, even the gods are in the hands of the Fates, and the stories move toward Wagner's "Twilight of the Gods," the Germanic Battle of

Figure 277

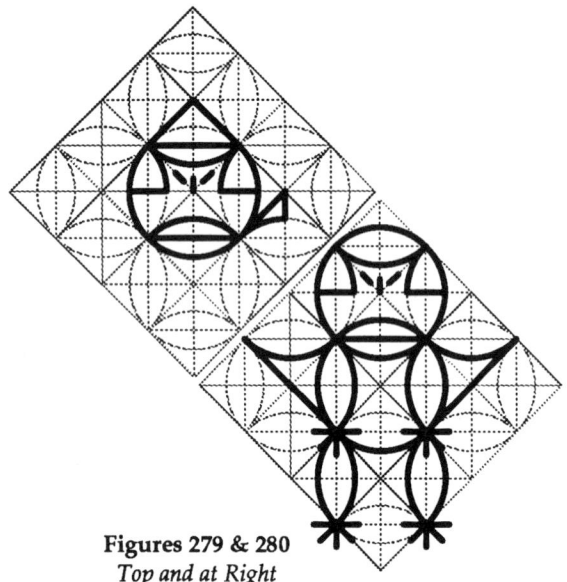

Figures 279 & 280
Top and at Right

Armageddon, called Ragnarok.[54] Heimdall, the watchman of Asgard, blows on his horn, and the gods ride to battle. All the gods fight bravely, but in vain.[55] We see Heimdall, blowing Gjallarhorn[56] in **Figure 279**. Christians say that the Archangel Gabriel will be the horn-blower. We see the Archangel Gabriel, wings spread, in **Figure 280**, and we see him in **Figure 281**, blowing his trumpet. At the Ragnarok, the demons destroy the gods and the world. A new Heaven and Earth arise after the fires of Surt have done their damage. Two human beings survive the cataclysm and repeople the Earth. Balder, the Germanic Christ, and other gods return to Heaven.[57] Davidson concludes her discussion of the Ragnarok, as follows: "It has already been noticed that several points in the account of the ending of the world can be paralleled from Iranian sources."[58] Through Zoroastrianism and Mithraism, the Persians seem to have influenced everyone's religion!

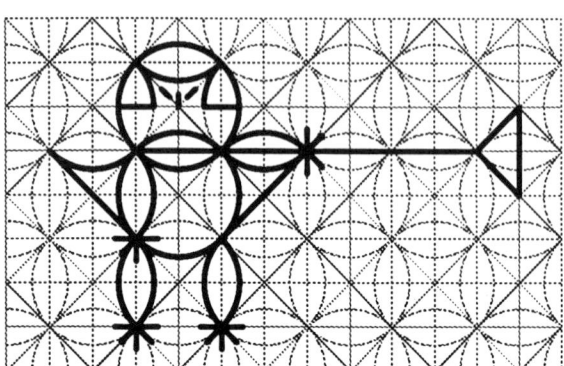

Figure 281

Balder's cremation pyre, laid Viking-style on his ship, Hringhorni, is described in another story, which includes the tale about Odin placing Draupnir, his golden ring, on Balder's pyre.[59] We see the golden ring in **Figure 282**, lying on top of the sticks of wood of Balder's classical Indo-European funeral pyre. We see Balder lying on his pyre in **Figure 283**. Are we observing the origin of the ancient Aryan and present Hindu custom of cremation? People apparently got many customs and beliefs from the Holy Grail!

We have not the time to read an Arab traveler's description of a real, tenth-century, Viking-style, shipboard, cremation ceremony, complete with angel-of-death-assisted *suttee* of a female slave. Those who would like to see how seriously we humans have taken our Holy Grail myths down through the years may want to read the savage horror of that account.[60] Balder's wife, Nanna, whose name comes close to the Babylonian goddess of love, Inanna, dies of a broken heart and is cremated with him, as is a dwarf whom Thor kicks into the flames.[61] Dwarfs are malevolent characters in our Grail quest stories which are to follow. Did our Holy Grail humanform remind many storysmiths of real human dwarfs? See Figure 272.

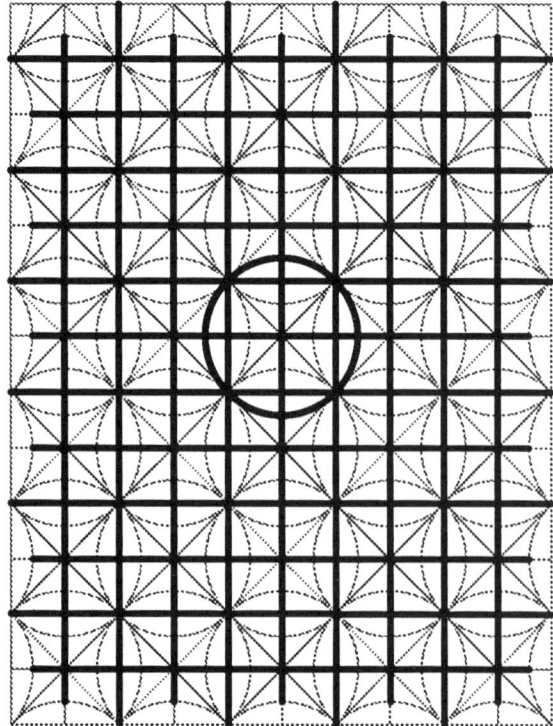

Figure 282

These Skaldic tales are too long to be discussed in detail. We must move on. It only should be necessary to point out that they include a rainbow bridge, a judgment seat, an eagle roosting in the cosmic tree,[62] a snake coiled below the cosmic tree,[63] a hawk, and a squirrel.[64] We never have seen a squirrel on the Holy Grail, but there he is in **Figure 284**. The dew which drips from the cosmic tree "is called honeydew, and men and bees are nourished on it."[65] Samson found the cosmic honey, bees, etc.[66] Knowing a secret *is* incomparably sweet! We are spilling the "honey" of the ages!

The Fates, known as the weavers or the spinners, controlled the destiny of the gods as well as of men until Christianity convinced the common man that God is not subject to the fates.[67] Calvinism took up the concept of predestination as to the lives of men, and carried it forward into our times.[68] Wyrd, one of the three fatal sisters, gave us Shakespeare's "Weird Sisters" of Macbeth.[69]

Branston renders the story of Odin's sacrifice to himself in these words: "...I hung on the windy tree, swung there nights all of nine; gashed with a blade bloodied for Odinn, myself an offering to myself.... Wellbeing I won and wisdom too, I grew and joyed in my growth."[70] In this story, Odin does not die; rather, he lives and gains wisdom,[71] as did

Figure 284

the American Indian warriors who drove hooks through the skin of their chests to which they attached leather thongs with which they roped themselves to the cosmic sacrificial stake representing the world axis.[72] Like modern Freemasons, through an initiatory act of self-sacrifice, their old selves "died" and they were "born again" as better men. "The World Tree is indeed the centre of the shaman's cosmology, as it is in the world of the northern myths. The essential feature of the initiation ceremony, whether among the Eskimos, the American Indians, or the Siberian peoples, is the death and rebirth of the young shaman, and the torments and terrors which he has to undergo if he is to gain possession of the esoteric knowledge necessary to him in his new calling. Before he can attain ability to heal and to pass to the realms of the gods and spirits, he has to undergo a ritual death."[73]

Few Christians realize that the Koran says Jesus did not die on the Cross. "[T]hey said (in boast), 'We killed Christ Jesus the son of Mary, the Apostle of Allah'; but they killed him not, nor crucified him, but so it was made to appear...."[74] We have not mentioned the Koran because it does not contain word-images visible on the Holy Grail. Islam apparently was not affected by Holy Grail mystique.

Was the story of the death of Christ once regarded as an initiation into wisdom instead of a scapegoat sacrifice to remove the burden of sin from mankind? Is this the reason for the longstanding enmity of the Catholic Church against Freemasonry, an initiatory ritual by which men ritually die and are born again?[75] Why did the Holy Father who officially permitted Catholics to become Masons take the name "John" and why did he die?

Valhalla, the Germanic heaven-in-the-sky to which all men *and women* went who died violently in battle *or sacrifice*,[76] was a Viking's paradise: you

Figure 283

Figure 285

fought all day, and if you got killed, the only penalty was that you missed that night's feast of magical boar and the drinking bout of magical mead, but you were up again in the morning, refreshed and ready for another day's "fun."[77] Would a new religion promising endless rounds of hot dogs and beer, and with never-ending Super Bowl and World Series games, attract a following of Americans seeking "conversion"? The magical boar of Valhalla was killed, cooked, and eaten each day, then born again to feed the hungry warriors the next day.[78] The English Christmas custom of bringing before the dinner guests a roasted boar with an apple in its mouth harkens back to the magical boar and magical apples of Valhalla.[79] We see the head of the magical boar in **Figure 285**.

So much for Odin. How about Thor? His name means thunder, and he was, among other things, the Germanic weather god.[80] He was worshiped in holy oak groves deep in the forest, probably because oaks are so often struck by "his" lightning bolts.[81] Branston tells us that "the description and exploits of the Hindu god Indra fit the Norse Thor exactly: both have red hair and a red beard; both are great trenchermen and smiters of tremendous blows; both are equipped with thunderbolts; both are serpent-slayers; and both are protectors of mankind against their enemies."[82] Branston speaks of the "rollicking, irascible strong god Thunor, the divine epitome of all hot-tempered red-haired people."[83]

We Irish know Thor well. Our distant cousins brought him to India as Indra of the Vedas. Our not-so-distant cousins later sold him to their Germanic neighbors as a replacement for the Germanic All-father, Tiwaz.[84] We see him sitting, "Celtic-sullen," in **Illustration 19-1**,[85] wearing his Phrygian cap and resting his sharp-pointed beard on Mjollnir, his "hammer." **Figure 286** illustrates Thor and his

Illustration 19-1. Thor with his hammer, Mjollnir. Courtesy of the Werner Forman Archive, London.

Teutons and Anglo-Saxons

Figure 286

Figure 287

famous "hammer." Other versions of Thor's hammer resemble Christian crosses.[86] "Violent and unpredictable, he was given to fits of uncontrollable rage, but his anger was usually directed against the giants. To his own people, he was a good and utterly reliable friend, who fought on their side in the struggle of life.... [He was] huge, red-bearded, a titanic eater and drinker, massively strong and courageous, but sometimes over hasty in his judgment."[87] He was "your man," blackthorn "hammer" in hand, swaggering happily through Donnybrook Fair!

Hitler's mythmakers stole one of Thor's principal symbols, the fylft, known in modern history as the swastika, for which we Celts *never* will forgive them.[88] The Nazis *may* have adopted the runic letter "sigel," half a fylft, meaning "sun,"[89] as the double "lightning bolt" symbol of their murderous SS troops. It is equally possible that the

SS double "lightning bolt" symbol was derived from the rune for "yew-wood."[90] Yew was used to make bows and wooden fire-starters in olden times, and probably was used as a warrior's protective talisman.[91] "Fire" and "sun" equate with each other, and things equal to the same thing are equal to each other.[92] It is a shame for these ancient symbols to have come to such an ignoble end! The double-axe head symbol of Thor[93] and other ancient weather gods[94] is seen in **Figure 287**. The symbol for Tiwaz, and later for Odinn, was the spearhead.[95] Fylft and spearhead symbols appear on Anglo-Saxon clay pottery,[96] and on a variety of Anglo-Saxon urns.[97] The runic symbol for Ing, another name for the fertility god, is two circle segments intersecting with each other in this form: ◊ .[98] We see all three of these god-symbols in **Figure 288**.

While we are on the subject of "runes," which were letters of the alphabet in which Germanic

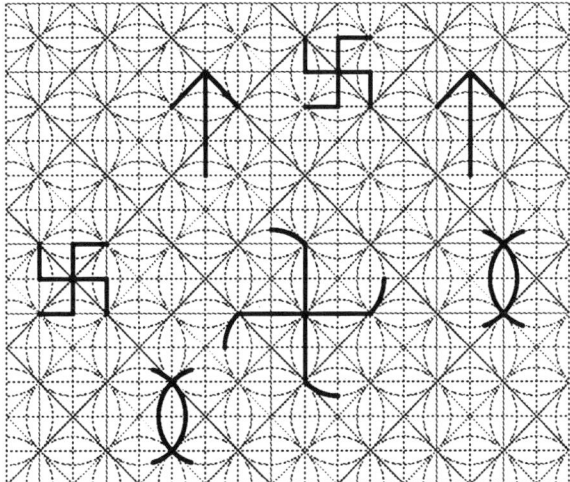

Figure 288

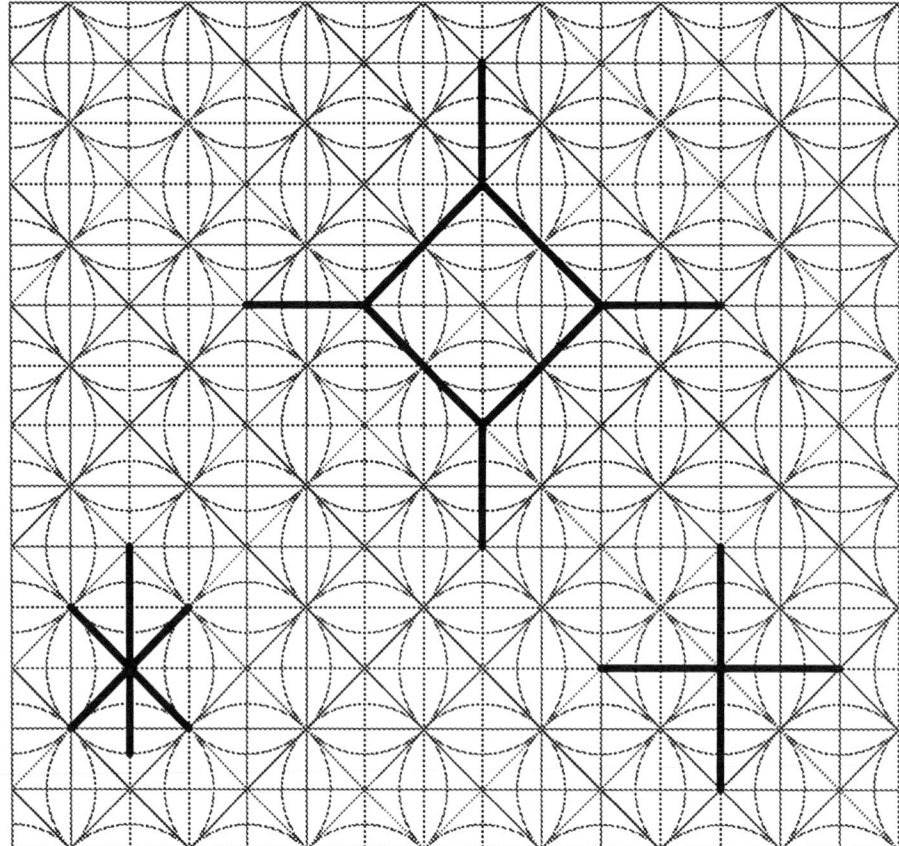

Figure 289

Illustration 19-2. Fricco or Frey, the god of prosperity, peace, and the fruitful earth. Courtesy of the Werner Forman Archive, London.

languages were written, although they became magical objects in the minds of their illiterate northern European cousins, we may as well face up to the rune ✧, usually written + or ✳, which means "year."[99] Those symbols appear on the Holy Grail in **Figure 289**. Each centers a circle that is not bolded on the Holy Grail. They become important to us in our science chapters.

Adam of Bremen wrote about human bodies hanging on trees at the great pagan temple at Uppsala, Sweden, just before 1200 A.D.[100] He tells us: "…the people worship the images of three gods. Thor, the mightiest of the three, stands in the centre of the church, with Wodan and Fricco on his right and left."[101] We see the three of them standing together in **Figure 290**. Thor is identified by his symbols of the hammer, the axe, and the fylft. Odin is identified by his symbols of the hangman's noose and the spear.[102] Fricco, or Frey, the god of sexual love, is identified by his erect phallus, the cosmic lingum, and by his rune. We see Frey in **Illustration 19-2**, wearing his Phrygian cap and sporting his pointed beard, his phallus erect.[103] In **Figure 291**, we

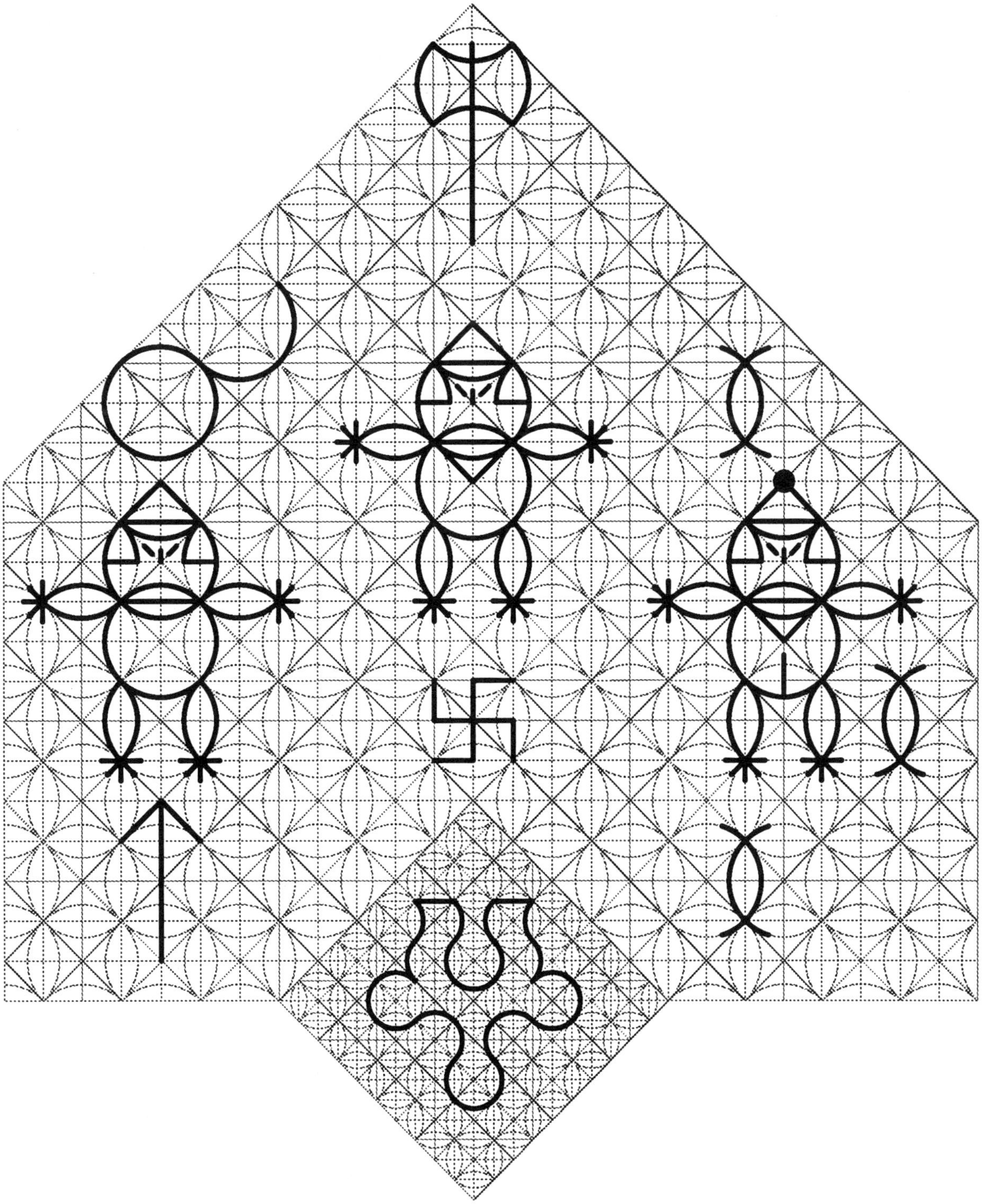

Figure 290

Figure 291

Figure 292

Figure 293

show three Grail humanforms, but the new religion has arrived. Jesus stands, as the Gospels tell us He does, at the right hand of the enthroned Jehovah, and is denoted by the sign of the fish and the Chi Rho (XP) *Christogram*. The Holy Ghost or Holy Spirit stands to the left of the enthroned Jehovah, and is identified by the Holy Dove, in which form He acts as messenger for Jehovah, as the ravens did for Odin. Religions change. The Holy Grail remains constant.

Our week begins with Sun day. Then we celebrate Moon day, followed by Tiwaz day. Next comes Woden's day, Thor's day, Frig's day, and Saturn's day.[104] We are Christian, not pagan. So we say.

Our Celtic ancestors in northern Europe were no less bloodthirsty. The Roman geographer Strabo wrote that we hung our prisoners' heads down; that an old woman climbed a ladder and cut their throats so their blood filled a cauldron below.[105] We shall read about this custom during our studies of the Grail quest stories. The blood was used for holy magic,[106] as in the Mass.

Vikings usually fought wearing mailcoats, but they had an elite band of warriors, the Beserks, whose lives were dedicated to Odin, who fought wearing no mailcoats, protected only by their swords, their bear-skin cloaks, and their wild frenzy.[107] Some Celts customarily fought naked, armed only with a spear.[108]

Students of the classics probably are wondering why we have not mentioned much about the state gods of Greece and Rome. Answer: You scholars of the classics are perfectly capable of putting those stories on the Holy Grail for yourself. You do not need the help of an amateur like your author. Just two Holy Grail images to get you rolling: A gladiator who was armed with net and trident, representing the water element, traditionally fought a gladiator who was armed with sword and shield, representing the sun or fire element.[109] We see the two standing side-by-side in **Figure 292**. We find Ulysses, tied to the mast of his ship, in **Figure 293**. From that point on, it's duck soup.

What about the Valkyries; the "choosers of the slain"?[110] Women who died violently, usually as an act of *suttee* on the funeral pyre of their husbands, went to Valhalla also.[111] Some became Valkyries, who went about cleaning up the cosmic battlefields.[112] The rest kept the ale-cups of their men brimming during the drinking bouts.[113] Women were second-class citizens in Valhalla.

We have this description of the cosmic "web of victory": "... the warp itself is made of men's guts weighted at the bottom with human heads; the shuttles are arrows...."[114] Can you visualize that on the Holy Grail for yourself?

Figure 294

How about the cosmic means of transportation? The sun rode about in a chariot pulled by horses.[115] Thor drove a chariot pulled by a yoke of bulls,[116] or by a yoke of goats.[117] Thor's goats were multi-purpose. He also ate them, then raised his hammer as a magic wand over their bones, whereupon they were born again.[118] Early Christian art portrayed Christ's touching his magician's wand to the mummy of Lazarus, who thereby was born again.[119] Nerthus, that is, Mother Nature, went about in a wagon pulled by oxen.[120] **Figure 294**. Frig or Freya sat on a float pulled by a pair of cats.[121] Ezekiel's

Figure 295

Figure 296

Figure 297

Figure 298

"throne wagon" certainly got around! By the way, Frig or Freya means "Lady."[122] Our Lady learned to behave when she became a Christian. The Germanic cosmic man Ing or Frey, whose name means "Lord," was seen by the Danes walking over the waves.[123] The water was cosmic water of a cosmic sea, until the Church said otherwise. Here is a challenge to Anglophiles familiar with the legend of Weylund Smith's "flying machine":[124] Find "Weylund" and his "flying machine" on the Holy Grail!

The Norse cried for Balder like the Hebrews and their Semitic Babylonian cousins cried for Tammuz.[125] The name Balder, like Frey, means "Lord."[126] Things equal to the same thing are equal to each other. Balder was killed by the blind god Hoder using a spear made of mistletoe fashioned by the Trickster, Loki,[127] much as Christ reputedly expired by the lance thrust of Longeus, a Roman centurion, whose blindness reputedly was cured by the effusion of blood and water from Christ's

side,[128] provided, of course, you can imagine a blind Roman centurion's being on military duty at all, much less officiating at such an important event as the crucifixion of Jesus. A cock-crow announced the advent of Ragnarok, as the crow of a cock announced the sacrifice of Christ, thereby signaling the end of an era.[129] We see the cosmic cock in **Figure 295**. We see Longeus-Hoder spearing the crowned and bearded Christ-Balder in **Figure 296**.

According to Skaldic myth, Loki got his punishment for the death of Balder by being bound by the gods with a serpent above his head dripping venom on him.[130] Loki's wife tried her best to protect him from this punishment by catching as much of the poison as possible in a bowl.[131] Joseph of Arimathaea caught the blood of Christ in the Grail Cup.[132] We see Loki bound in **Figure 297**, the snake over his head, and his wife catching poison in the bowl over his head. In **Figure 298**, we see Joseph catching Christ's blood in the Grail Cup.

When Thor and Heimir (or Hymir) went fishing for the world-serpent, Thor baited his hook with the head of one of Heimir's oxen.[133] We see Thor, identified by his signs, holding his fishing pole and

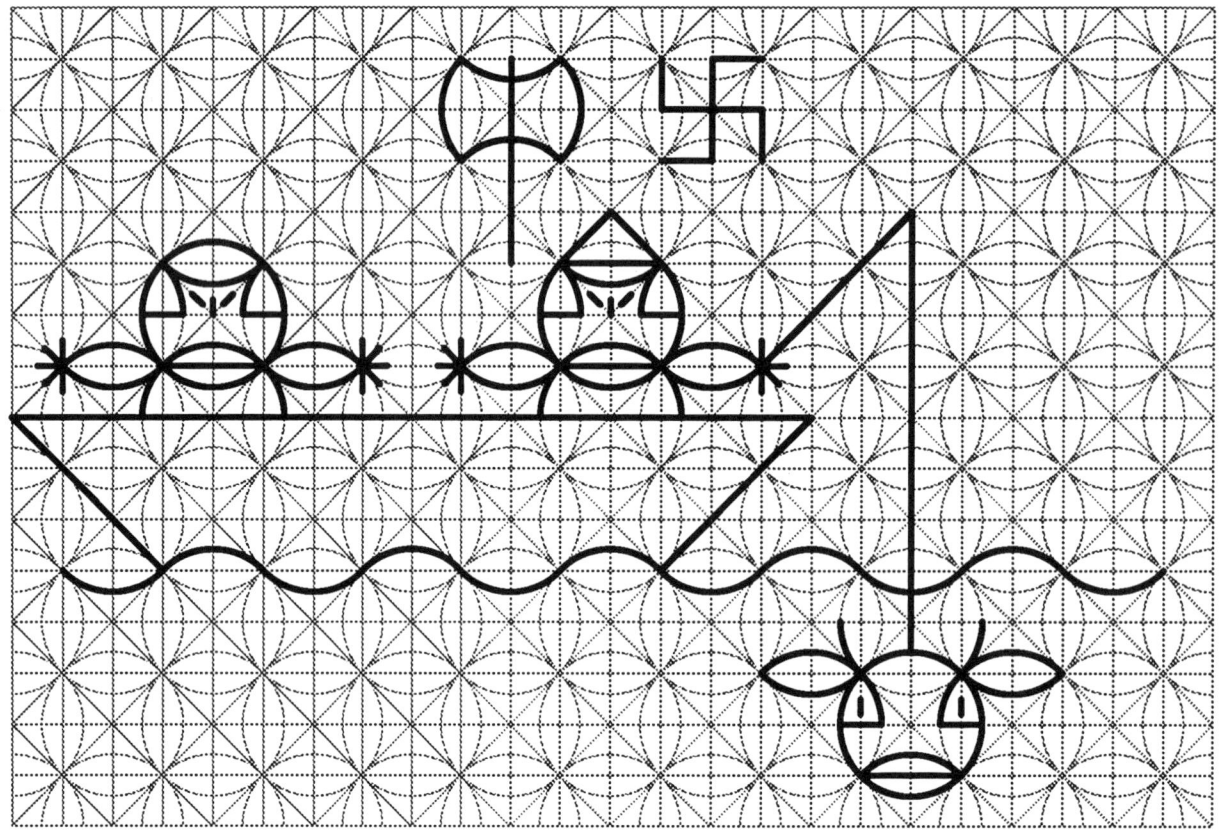

Figure 299

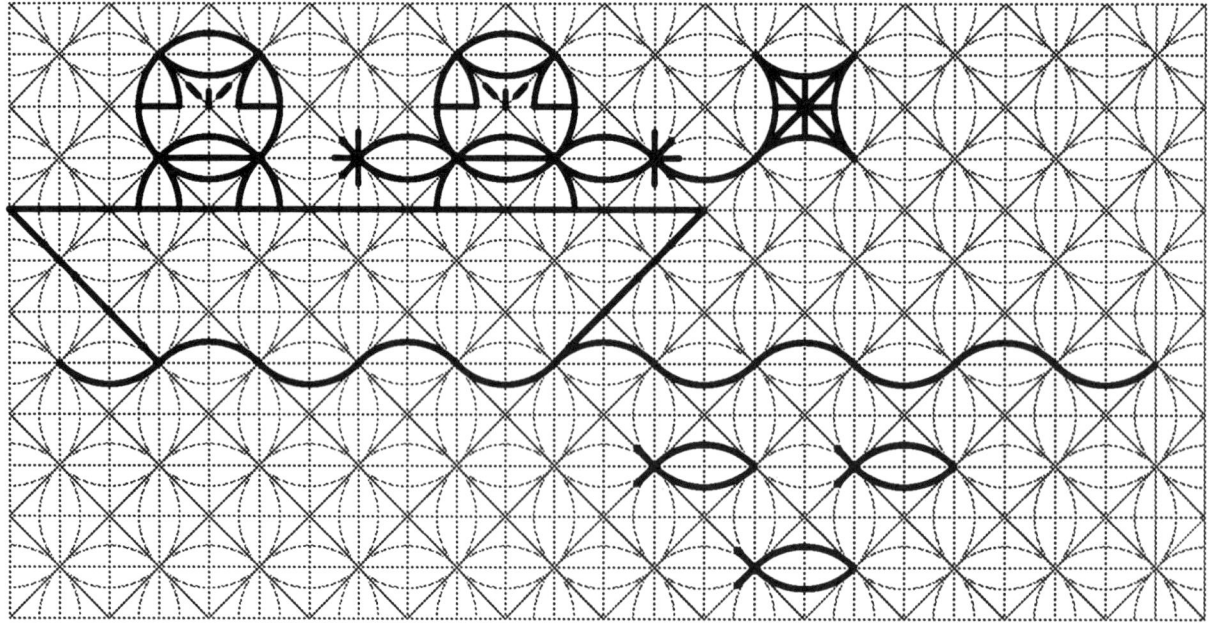

Figure 300

Figure 301

line baited with an ox head, in **Figure 299**. We also see their boat on the water in that Figure. In **Figure 300**, we see our Grail manform fishing with a Biblical-era throw net. We also see in Figure 300 the fish for which he is fishing. In **Figure 301**, we see Christ, identified by his symbols, standing on this "sea." In **Figure 302**, we see Christ, identified by his symbols, having cast his cosmic "net" over a Grail manform. Fishers of men?

Do we have any idea how the Germanic thinking people and the unthinking Germanic masses reacted to the advent of Christianity? Davidson tells us that Bede wrote in his *Ecclesiastical History* that, in 625 A.D., when the King of Northumbria asked for the reaction of his nobles, one responded: "'Of what went before [birth] and of what is to follow [death], we are utterly ignorant. If therefore this new faith can give us some greater certainty, it justly deserves that we should follow it.'"[134] Christianity comforts its adherents for that very reason: It gives them certainty of life after death. "As for the unthinking, of whom there were many, it was largely a matter of new ceremonies replacing the old. 'They have taken away the ancient rites and customs, and how the new ones are to be attended to, nobody knows,' was

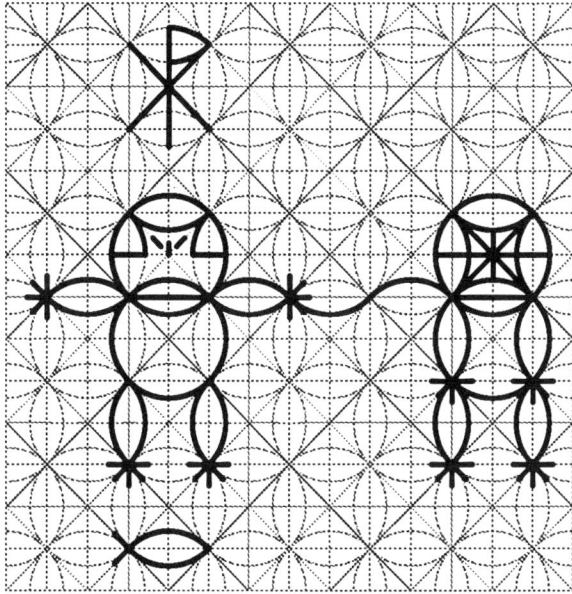

Figure 302

the lament of the country people against the monks, recorded in Bede's *Life of St. Cuthbert*."[135] Cavendish concludes: "In the process the peasant changed his gods, but he did not necessarily change his religion."[136] Let those last words sink in before you proceed.

Remember the story of the table? The table was a valuable gift, you will recall.[137] Gale R. Owen gives us William of Malmesbury's account of the treasures which Hugh, Duke of the Franks, sent to the "devout Christian" King Athelstan, when requesting the hand in marriage of one of Athelstan's sisters:

"[Gifts]... such as never before had been seen in England; *jewellery*, especially of *emeralds*, in whose greenness the reflected *sun* lit up the eyes of the bystanders with a pleasing light; many fleet *horses*, with trappings, 'champing', as Maro says, 'on bits of ruddy gold'; a *vase* of onyx, carved with such subtle engravers' art that the *cornfields* seemed really to wave, the *vines* really to bud, the *forms of men* really to move, and so clear and polished that it reflected like a *mirror* the faces of the onlookers; the *sword* of Constantine the Great, on which could be read the *name of the ancient owner* in letters of gold; on the pommel also above thick plates of gold you could see an *iron nail* fixed, one of the *four* which the Jewish faction prepared for the *crucifixion of our Lord's body*; the *spear* of Charles the Great, which, whenever the most invincible emperor, leading an army against the Saracens, hurled it against the enemy, never let him depart without the victory; it was said to be the same which, driven by the hand of the *centurion into our Lord's side, opened by the gash of that precious wound Paradise for wretched mortals*; the *standard* of Maurice, the most blessed martyr and prince of the Theban legion, by which the same king was wont in the Spanish war to break asunder the battalions of the enemies, however fierce and dense, and to force them to flight; a *diadem*, precious certainly for its quantity of gold, but more for its *gems*, whose splendor so *threw flashes of light* on the onlookers that the more anyone strove to fix his gaze on it, the more was he driven back and *forced to give in; a piece of the holy and adorable Cross enclosed in crystal*, where the eye, penetrating the substance of the stone, could discern what was the *colour of the wood* and what the quantity; a portion also of the *crown of thorns, similarly enclosed*, which the madness of the soldiers placed on Christ's sacred head in mockery of his kingship."[138]

It would seem that William of Malmesbury was a member of that unnamed brotherhood of Holy Grail storysmiths who have lived in all generations

of all European cultures! Artwork in which cornfields *seemed really* to wave, vines to bud, and forms of men to move! Remember the comparable language in the story of the table![139] "Flashes of light" which forced "the onlookers... to give in"? Give in to what? The Holy Magic of the Mass? And, we are told that a piece of the Cross, its color visible, and a portion of the Crown of Thorns, are enclosed in a stone crystal! Is this a reference to the cross and circle of the "interference pattern" which is "thrown" when primary and secondary rays of light enter quartz crystals? We have seen the "interference pattern" in Illustration 4-2. Have the rich and powerful, and their intellectual comrades, always known something they have not told the masses? Suppose we later learn that King Athelstan was a Freemason?

As we discussed above, the shocking similarities between the Skaldic tales and the stories of the Old and New Testaments traditionally have been explained by suggesting that those nasty old pagan Vikings copied into their barbaric myths certain elements of the Word of God, either before or after they "accepted" Christianity, because they considered those elements of Biblical stories significant or, worse, because they sought to parody the Bible.[140] Could there be another explanation? Suppose there was evidence of travel and commerce between the Germanic people of northern Europe and the Semitic inhabitants of Palestine during or before the period when the stories of the Bible were written?

Every child who ever attended Christian Sunday school has heard the tale of how a Hebrew youth named David, armed with a rock in his leather sling, bravely offered himself in single combat against a fully-armed and armored Philistine giant named Goliath, and slew the giant with a single sling-stone to the giant's forehead.[141] Not another "giant story" after what we have been through! Has your author no sympathy with the culture shock you are suffering? None! If you cannot stand the heat, then get out of the kitchen. This is a book for *Eagles alone*.

Few modern children or their parents ever ask the question, "Who were the Philistines?" The "Philistines" have gotten a lot of "bad press" down through the years, as you can tell if you look up the name in your dictionary, which will use words and phrases such as "warlike," "lacking in culture," "commonplace in ideas and tastes," "indifferent to or contemptuous of poetry, music, the fine arts, and the like," or even worse.

The answer to the question really is not all that difficult to discover, like much of what we have discussed in this book. It is just that we have been taught to believe, never to question.

World Book Encyclopedia tells us this about the Philistines: They were driven from Crete and other islands in the Aegean Sea by invaders from the north. They raided along the eastern shores of the Mediterranean, invading Canaan (Palestine) from the west while the Israelites were invading from the east. Pharaoh Ramses III defeated them when they attempted to invade Egypt. They settled in Palestine.[142]

World Book makes it sound as if the Semitic Canaanites, whom the Bible pictures as being fond of wine, women, and song, were caught between what modern military experts would call a "pincers movement" of two warlike tribes, the Philistines and the Israelites, who were bent on occupying as much Canaanite turf as their war machines could take and hold! Nations who do such things these days are called "colonial imperialists." So we have learned that Philistines were a group of Aegean people.

Back to *World Book*, which tells us that Aegean civilization flourished from approximately 3000 B.C. to 1100 B.C. on Crete, mainland Greece, around the City of Troy, and on certain other islands; that these people were highly skilled in the arts and architecture.[143] Hold it! Stop! Did we not learn that *Philistine* today means a person who is hostile to the arts?[144] If Philistines were Aegean people and Aegean civilization was so skilled in arts, crafts, and architecture, how can it be that Philistines were such dunderheads about art and the arts? Were Philistines mentally defective or culturally deprived outcasts from Aegean civilization? Or were they victims of Israelite, hence, Biblical, "bad press," much as George Washington would have been a "British traitor" rather than an "American founding father" had the American Kentucky rifle not sent the British Brown Bess musket to history's trashcan for obsolete military hardware? If *truth*, rather than *belief*, is our goal, we must read on.

Although the reasons are not given, *World Book* tells us that Aegean civilization fell into decay and decline about 1100 B.C.[145] Does this explain why we think Philistines were uncultured dolts?

We are told that the poet Homer incorporated stories told by the Aegean people into his *Iliad* and *Odyssey*.[146] Has reality hit you between the eyes? These people *may* have been *some* of the ancestors of the Greeks of classical history! And they were

opposed to the arts? We must read on. We are assured that archaeologists do not know where the northern invaders came from who established Mycenae on the Peloponnesus of Greece.[147]

And so we reach a dead end and can trace the Philistines no further? So we must accept the view that they were uncultured dolts whose ancestors were cultured Aegean people and whose descendents were the cultured Greeks of the Classical Age? Here is the safest conclusion reached in this book: All quitters have quit us by now! The rest of us are ready to push on! We have an advantage in this analysis: We know Grail-born cosmology and cosmogony when we see it! Most writers who have ventured into this fog bank have been unable to separate cosmic men from real men, and for that reason have failed.

The controversial Christian minister Jurgan Spanuth tried to prove that the Philistines of the Bible were Germanic invaders from northern Europe.[148] He showed his readers pictures of horned helmets of bronze unearthed in Denmark and a bronze statue of a man wearing such a helmet, which was unearthed in Cyprus.[149] He showed his readers Egyptian art in which the Pharaoh Ramses III bragged about the Egyptian defeat of invaders from the north.[150] Ramses' artists portrayed the invaders wearing horned helmets, or wearing horsehair bristle helmets of the type worn by Germanic troops who served in a unit of the Roman Army.[151] A Germanic helmet made of knotted horsehair topped by tightly packed erect horsehair bristles would do a good job of absorbing a downward blow from a club or hacking sword.[152] Germans always have been excellent technologists, albeit they often have been too quick to follow their beserkers.

Spanuth's proof which attracts our attention relies upon the myth of the "world-pillar" or "Heaven-pillar," the cosmic equivalent of the rotational axis of the real world, which supposedly stood at the northernmost reaches of the world according to the cosmology and cosmogony of the ancient cultures we have studied. Spanuth summarizes the Heaven-pillar stories and shows that they describe in cosmic terms the regions of Europe which lie in the direction of the North Star; regions where the petrified tree resin we call "amber," the stuff of Ezekiel's Vision, is found.[153] He attempts to reconstruct the ancient trade routes of North Sea amber across Greece and into Palestine.[154]

Spanuth relies upon the one book that every Christian fundamentalist always must believe, the Holy Bible. He says that the Biblical people of Caphtor, the Caphtorim, were the Philistines.[155] My King James Bible says: "... for the LORD will spoil the Philistines, the remnant of the country of Caphtor."[156] It also says: "Have not I brought up Israel out of the land of Egypt? and the Philistines from Caphtor, and the Syrians from Kir?"[157] The King James Bible also refers to "... the Caphtorims, which came forth out of Caphtor...."[158]

Spanuth contends that the Hebrew word which our Bibles translate as "Caphtorims" or "Kaphthorites" is a reference to the "pillar people,"[159] that is, the people whose pillars Yahweh directed the Israelites to break, and whose sacred groves of trees Yahweh directed the Israelites to cut down and burn.[160] "And ye shall overthrow their altars, and break their pillars, and burn their groves with fire...."[161] Evidently, some Israelites not only disobeyed Yahweh's command to destroy the sacred objects and precincts of the Philistines but "backslid" by worshiping the Philistine Heaven pillar in sacred groves. Accordingly, our Bibles tell us that Yahweh commanded right-minded Israelites to destroy the Philistine-style sacred groves of wrong-minded Israelites, as well as the sacred groves of the Philistines.[162] That this Philistine-style religion somehow involved worship of the sun, the moon, the planets, and the other "hosts of Heaven" is not subject to serious question.[163] The Israelites believed that Yahweh did not want a grove of trees near His altar,[164] but they believed in the pillars of Heaven and Earth,[165] although the pillars obviously belonged to Yahweh.[166]

If we accept those proofs or, for that matter, any of Spanuth's proofs not here discussed, then there is no reason to suppose that Germanic people who brought their Heaven pillar and their sacred groves of trees to Palestine would not also have brought Odin, who hung on the world axis.

"The World Tree, Yggdrasill, formed the centre of the universe."[167] The World Tree "was symbolized in shamanistic ritual by a post with steps cut in it, a ladder, or a small birch tree, up which the shaman climbed to indicate his ascent to the heavens. When he entered into his state of ecstasy, he was believed to pass through a series of heavens, one above the other, until at last he penetrated in his flight into the highest realm of the gods. So in Norse mythology the beliefs about the nature of the world of the gods are inextricably linked with the powerful symbol of the World Tree."[168] "The image of the tree that occupied the centre of the world did not wholly die out. It was replaced by the conception of the Christian cross, believed to stand at the midpoint of the earth when it was raised at Calvary, at the spot once occupied by the fatal tree of Eden."[169]

Morton Smith quotes an ancient magical text written on papyrus: "A spell to get (a revelation in) a dream, (to be said) to (the god of the) pole star... Jesus, Anou(bis?)...."[170] Those lines are someone's reconstruction and interpretation of a torn and tattered tidbit of someone else's reality. This book may be nothing more. Or it may be the closest brush that Christianity has had with its origins in many centuries.

Notes
CHAPTER NINETEEN. Teutons and Anglo-Saxons

1. Page 1.

2. Branston 114; Owen 8, 170.

3. Branston 35.

4. Owen 5.

5. Branston 57; Owen 5.

6. Owen 5-8, 166-169.

7. Davidson 24; Branston 171.

8. Branston 98; Davidson 204.

9. Davidson 56-61.

10. Branston 171.

11. Branston 171.

12. Davidson 200.

13. Branston 171.

14. 1 Kings 7.23-26.

15. Genesis 2.10; Aristeas 4.17; Talbott 222-225.

16. Branston 172.

17. Graves & Patai 60.

18. Branston 172.

19. Graves & Patai 61.

20. Branston 171.

21. Genesis 3.24.

22. Branston 172.

23. Graves & Patai 30-33.

24. Branston 47,172.

25. Branston 172; Davidson 27, 199; Cavendish 180.

26. Branston 176.

27. Branston 172.

28. Branston 172.

29. Branston 172. In a Germanic myth, we are told regarding the ash tree Yggdrasill that it spreads its limbs over all the land; that neither fire nor iron will fell it; that no man knows "from what roots it doth arise"; and that few persons guess "by what it falleth." Hollander 146. Myths arise from fertile ignorance? Knowledge fells myths?

30. Hadingham EMATC 197.

31. Davidson 26; Branston 172.

32. Hadingham EMATC 196; Graves & Patai 278-279.

33. Davidson 26; Branston 172.

34. Davidson 166; Branston 172.

35. Davidson 196.

36. Davidson 166,167.

37. Davidson 45.

38. Graves & Patai 210-211.

39. Baigent 82-85.

40. Nora Chadwick 49-50; Sharkey Fig. 28.

41. Spanuth 92.

42. Davidson 28, 29, 183; Branston 172.

43. Davidson 111.

44. Davidson 111, 123; Branston 127; Owen 23.

45. Owen 23.

46. Branston 172.

47. Davidson 28-29, 177-182.

48. Davidson 179.

49. Davidson 29, 32; Branston 173.

50. Davidson 48, 149, 150.

51. Davidson 32.

52. Davidson 9.

53. Davidson 32; Branston 172-173.

54. Branston 173; Davidson 37-38, 202.

55. Cavendish 186.

56. Davidson 173.

57. Branston 173.

58. Davidson 206.

59. Davidson 36; Owen 98.

60. Owen 98-101; Davidson 52, 62, 150.

61. Owen 98.

62. Davidson 39. In a Germanic myth, we are told that a giant in eagle's shape sits at Heaven's end, creating wind by flapping his wings. Hollander 48.

63. Davidson 193.

64. Branston 175.

65. Branston 175.

66. 1 Judges 15.8-18.

67. Branston 64-65.

68. Davidson 217.

69. Branston 64-71.

70. Branston 98.

71. Davidson 143-145.

72. Cavendish 234.

73. Davidson 144.

74. Sura IV.157.

75. Wilmshurst 210-211.

76. Davidson 149-152.

77. Davidson 28, 70, 152; Branston 99.

78. Branston 99, 117.

79. Branston 151; Davidson 166; Owen 48, 101.

80. Branston 109. Thor was said to be the son of a sky father and an earth mother, and he was called the savior of men. Hollander 75, 87, 101.

81. Davidson 86-88.

82. Branston 109.

83. Branston 109.

84. Davidson 77.

85. Cavendish 181. Thor's hammer, Mjollnir, "has only one small flaw.... Its handle is rather short." Crossley-Holland 52. And so it is, as you can see!

86. Owen 18.

87. Cavendish 181.

88. Davidson 83, 158; Owen 25, 92; Cavendish 188-191.

89. Owen 57.

90. Owen 56.

91. Owen 56.

92. Owen 56.

93. Davidson 82.

94. Branston 125.

95. Owen 57, 59.

96. Owen 29.

97. Owen 35, 109.

98. Owen 30.

99. Owen 56.

100. Davidson 51, 52.

101. Branston 114.

102. Davidson 51.

103. Cavendish 184.

104. The planet Saturn was known to the ancients

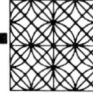

as the "night sun." Talbott 40.

105. Davidson 54.

106. Davidson 40.

107. Davidson 66-67, 70; Owen 14.

108. Nora Chadwick 134.

109. 8 World Book Encyclopedia 194 (1983).

110. Davidson 61, 65-66; Branston 100.

111. Davidson 28, 150-151.

112. Davidson 65.

113. Davidson 28.

114. Branston 101.

115. Branston 79.

116. Branston 110.

117. Owen 47.

118. Davidson 32.

119. Smith Frontispiece. While Professor Morton Smith was visiting the Greek Orthodox Monastery of Mar Saba, in Palestine, in 1958, he discovered a part of a letter from Clement of Alexander, an early Christian theologian of note, containing references to what has come to be known as "The Secret Gospel of Mark," verses which no longer appear in the Gospel attributed to Mark, which tell of Jesus' having freed a young man from a tomb after rolling away the stone blocking the door of the tomb. Meyer 232-234. The verses of the secret gospel indicate that some sort of mystery religion spiritual resurrection (instead of the infusing of life into a human corpse) was involved. The secret gospel has sparked a firestorm of controversy about whether the love between Jesus and the young man was spiritual, or something else, but, in either event, Clement's opinion that "Not all true things are to be said to all men," and similar remarks, found in the letter-fragment, make clear his views that everything about the Christ story should not be told to all persons; that some things should be concealed from Christians of lesser intelligence, even if this requires the telling of an untruth. Meyer 233-

234. Your author does not suggest that Clement thereby speaks for all of the fathers of the Church. Only that Clement's personal views about selective teaching of matters "useful for increasing the faith" could not be clearer. Meyer 233.

120. Branston 129, 131; Owen 30, 41.

121. Branston 149.

122. Branston 132,138.

123. Branston 138-139.

124. Owen 173.

125. Davidson 21, 36, 110, 184; Branston 145-147, 157, 161.

126. Branston 157.

127. Davidson 35, 36, 187; Branston 158-159.

128. Branston 169.

129. Branston 173.

130. Cavendish 185.

131. Owen 26, 170; Cavendish 185.

132. Matthews 5-6.

133. Davidson 35; Branston 120-121; Owen 171.

134. Davidson 221.

135. Davidson 222.

136. Cavendish 187.

137. Aristeas 3.63-65.

138. Owen 201-202.

139. Aristeas 3.39.

140. Davidson 201.

141. 1 Samuel 17.4-51.

142. 15 World Book Encyclopedia 344 (1983).

143. 1 World Book Encyclopedia 73 (1983).

144. 15 World Book Encyclopedia 344 (1983).

145. 1 World Book Encyclopedia 73 (1983).

146. 1 World Book Encyclopedia 73 (1983).

147. 1 World Book Encyclopedia 73 (1983).

148. Spanuth 96, 211.

149. Spanuth 31, 32.

150. Spanuth 22-25, 193.

151. Spanuth 35.

152. Spanuth 34-35.

153. Spanuth 28, 30, 47-55, 91-101.

154. Spanuth 52.

155. Spanuth 96, 211.

156. Jeremiah 47.4.

157. Amos 9.7.

158. Deut. 2.23; see also, Genesis 10.14 and 1 Chron. 1.12.

159. Spanuth 96, 211.

160. Hebrews worshiped the goddess Asherah in groves. They honored the Philistine goddess Astarte, as well as Anat, the Queen of Heaven. Graves & Patai 26-27.

161. Deut. 12.3.

162. Exodus 34.13; Deut. 7.5, 12.3; Judg. 3.7, 6.25, 6.26, 6.28, 6.30; 1 Kings 14.15, 14.23, 15.13, 16.33, 18.19; 2 Kings 13.6, 17.10, 17.16, 18.4, 21.3, 21.7, 23.4, 23.6, 23.7, 23.14, 23.15; 2 Chron. 14.3, 15.16, 17.6, 19.3, 24.18, 31.1, 33.3, 34.3, 34.7; Isa. 17.8, 27.9; Jer. 17.2; Mic. 5.14.

163. Deut. 17.3; 2 Kings 17.16, 21.3, 23.4-5; 2 Chron. 33.3.

164. Deut. 16.21.

165. Psa. 75.3; Job 26.11.

166. 1 Samuel 2.8.

167. Davidson 190.

168. Davidson 192.

169. Davidson 196.

170. Smith 63.

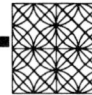

Chapter Twenty

Grail Quest Stories: Parodies and Satires on the Holy Writ?

Legions of scholars have attempted to explain the Grail quest stories. Some have insisted that these fables were written only to entertain.[1] This appears to be the opinion most often held by the general public. Who has not read for entertainment some account of King Arthur and his Knights of the Round Table? Most people think of the Holy Grail as a cup, a dish, a stone, or a jewel, if they ascribe to it any substance at all.[2] Most twentieth-century scholars contend that the Grail quest stories are founded on a pagan ritual connected with the cycle of the seasons; that they describe a vegetation cult like those of Tammuz, Attis, Adonis, and Osiris; that they also involve unorthodox or heretical forms of Christianity; and that the link they fuse between pagan and Christian traditions is important for reasons that have "eluded the scholars."[3]

We Irish who were raised on Celtic legends know that the tales of King Arthur and his knights were composed to record ancient Celtic customs and beliefs, as well as to entertain. We make no attempt to hide the fact that our ancestors were headhunters and human sacrificers.[4] Victorious Knights of the Round Table who bring home the heads of vanquished knights, or who pour human blood over sick or wounded persons to cure injury or illness, are understood by us to be ghostly images of our ancestors. But hold your ire against the Irish. No matter what your skin color or nationality, your ancestors *also* did such things back in those days, albeit your history books may not be as honest as ours.

Ancient people from India to Ireland believed that the welfare of the tribe depended directly upon the well-being of their kings. A virile king who could impregnate his queen assured a lush harvest and the birth of many domestic animals. A languishing king meant a barren land; bad times for the tribe. If such thinking is new to you, then read some of the materials listed under the note following this sentence.[5]

When those of us who were spoon-fed on Celtic history read the Grail quest stories, we think of Balder, the god of vegetation, who died annually after the harvest and rose from the grave during the next planting season. Vegetation gods, who died and were born again, were common among ancient peoples, as those of you who have read the previous chapters know.

Scholars have commented upon the many direct and indirect references to the Christ story which can be found in Grail quest stories.[6] Although to the casual reader these parallels between the lives of Grail questers and the life of Christ seem to be the work of pious Christians, scholars have concluded that during the Albigensian Crusade, the Church declared Grail stories to be pernicious if not heretical.[7] It was comforting to discover that someone else had reached that conclusion. Another view of the scholars seems to be that the Church kept silent about the Holy Grail. "It may have been because they [the Church's fathers] knew that the Grail was associated by some with heresy.... Or they may have recognized the borrowings to be from other, non-Christian sources.... Perhaps they believed that, with the stamping out of the Cathar heresy in Southern France (with which, as we shall see, the Grail had strong links), the matter would die out on its own."[8]

Let us explore the possibility that Grail quest stories are satires or parodies upon the Christ story. If this speculation can be proven, then it would be no wonder that thirteenth-century clerics fulminated against them!

Why would anyone satirize or parody the Christ story? What sort of person would do that? We do not have time and space to study the details of the many early heresies of the Roman Catholic Church. It will be sufficient, at this time, if we understand that early Christians were not of one mind regarding the nature of Jesus Christ.[9] The followers of Manichaeism, named for the Babylonian prophet Mani, and of Arianism, named for the Christian presbyter Arius, as well as the Cathar or Albigensian Christians, and some of the Knights Templar, shared a belief that Jesus Christ was not God; that he was less than God or was a creation of God.[10] Greatly oversimplified, the general idea was that

God was wholly spirit and was "good" whereas the flesh of mankind was "bad." Accordingly, as the theory went, the "good" would not have caused itself to be incarnated in the "bad," i.e., God would not have walked the Earth in the flesh. "The dualist belief that spirit is good and matter evil logically necessitated the denial of the humanity of Christ. If He came from God he was a spirit and could not become flesh and blood. The facts of his earthly life then were not real, but an appearance only, an illusion. He was not born of Mary, was never actually hungry or thirsty or tired, and could have felt no pain on the Cross. There could be no resurrection of a non-existent body. The Church, by accepting lands and wealth, had compromised with the world and therefore with the devil, and so had forfeited all claim to apostolic authority. The true Church, the true successors of St. Peter, were the Cathars."[11] The Roman Catholic Church insisted, of course, that Christ was a divinity incarnate — God in human flesh.[12]

The Grail quest stories were popular during the twelfth and thirteenth centuries, when the Cathar heresy had captured the minds (and purses) of much of Western Europe.[13] Hundreds of years earlier, Arian Christianity effectively had replaced Roman Catholicism in western Europe.[14] In both instances, what the Roman church could not recapture with the intellect, it destroyed with the sword. The Roman Catholic church mounted crusades against the Cathar or Albigensian Christians and the Knights Templar; wholesale genocide was committed against men, women, and children.[15] Moslems believe that Mohammed was a prophet, rather than a divinity.[16] Modern Christians might regard Christ as a prophet, rather than a divinity, had the armies of Rome been less numerous or less ruthless in this genocide.

The Church of Rome despised the Cathar "heretics" for another practical (as distinguished from theological) reason. The Cathars believed in a direct one-to-one relationship between the Christian laity and God, thereby dispensing with the need for a large body of clergy to intercede for lay persons with God.[17] This very real threat of unemployment for Roman Catholic clergymen was reason enough to annihilate the Cathars! The Cathars ordained as their religious instructors women as well as men, practiced contraception and abortion, were strict vegetarians, and their highest orders renounced all pleasures of the body.[18] They believed in reincarnation and meditation.[19] Enough to give the Holy Father an upset stomach!

History records that Saint Augustine spent his early years as an adherent of Manichaeism.[20] We must not allow our religious leaders to make us think of these "heretics" as evil people. We must open our minds to the possibility that their thinking simply was ahead of their time. Martin Luther was next to challenge Roman orthodoxy.

You will recall our earlier discussion of Gnostic Christianity. By way of oversimplification, Gnostics emphasized *knowledge* about Jesus Christ whereas Roman Catholicism emphasized *belief* or *faith* in Jesus Christ. The Cathar or Albigensian Christians and some of the Templars properly should be described as Gnostic in their views.[21] The Poor Knights of Christ and of the Temple of Solomon, known to history as the Knights Templar, were a secret order of Christian Crusaders whose rites of initiation are claimed by modern speculative freemasonry to have been the underpinnings of their rituals of initiation.[22] Many young men nowadays join the Order of Demolay, sponsored by the Masons, without ever appreciating the impact on western society of the death of Jacques de Molay, the last grand master of the Knights Templar, who was slow-roasted to death over a fire by Roman Catholics who were intent on destroying, once and for all, the secret Christian order which had provided some of the very best Crusaders ever to serve Rome, but who had given in to "heresy."[23]

Scholars have suggested that the Knights Templar may have believed as they did because they knew some secret about the origins of Christianity.[24] Those of you who complete this book may reach that conclusion. We are about to study in detail the probable substance of that secret.

What proof is there that *any* secret ever existed about the origins of Christianity? Authors of Grail quest stories alluded to the existence of a secret known to the clergy which should not be revealed by the clergy to the laity. An example: "[F]or behoveth not discover the secrets of the Saviour, and them also to whom they are committed behoveth keep them covertly."[25] Sir Thomas Malory, in *Le Morte d'Arthur*, made passing reference to the existence of mysteries relating to the Holy Trinity.[26] Malory also tells us that only those cleansed of their sins will see the mysteries of the Saviour.[27] Malory's father-confessor of Sir Lancelot tells the knight that he did not see those mysteries when the Grail appeared because he is as barren as the Biblical fig tree.[28] Another of Malory's characters is ruled by the desire to participate in the mysteries of the Holy Grail.[29] Malory tells us that the nature of the quest for the Holy Grail is for each knight to challenge and overcome evil, thereby becoming eligible to participate in the holy mysteries reserved by God for the righteous.[30]

Malory then alludes to the substance of these mysteries by telling a tale about a ship constructed by Solomon. Upon that ship was placed a bed that had spindles made of wood cut from a tree that was grown from a branch planted by Eve. Eve had cut that branch from the tree from which she got the apple she fed to Adam.[31] Malory's story tells us that no man on Earth knows the secret or meaning of this ship or bed.[32] Solomon's wife remarks that the meaning *soon* might be discovered.[33] *Soon* thereafter, we are told that as Solomon slept, an angel wrote these words on the ship: "Thou man that wilt enter within me, beware that thou be full within the faith, for I ne am but faith and belief."[34] A ship that is nothing but faith and belief? With a bed on board the ship with spindles made of a tree that is nothing but faith and belief? No real substance? Just pious fantasy? Or ancient allegory? Is that what Malory is saying?

Malory says that when Sir Lancelot got a fleeting glance at the Holy Grail during a dream, he saw a silver candlestick with six candles move toward a cross, at which time a silver table appeared, upon which sat the Holy Grail.[35] Familiar symbols!

Malory's story continues with the three knights and "Percivale's sister" finding a white hart being led by four lions. They follow the hart and lions to a chapel, where a priest is saying Mass. "And at the secrets of the mass, they three saw the hart become a man, which marvelled them, and set him upon the altar in a rich siege [seat], and saw the four lions were changed, the one to the form of a man, the other to the form of a lion, the third to an eagle, and the fourth was changed unto an ox. Then took they their siege where the hart sat, and went out through a glass window, and there was nothing perished nor broken, and they heard a voice say, In such a manner entered the son of God in the womb of a maid, Mary. And when they heard these words, they fell down to the earth, and were astonied [astonished], and therewith was a great clearness."[36] Is Malory saying that a phantasm of pure light, but not a human being, can pass through a glass window without breaking it?

Christ's appearance from the Holy Grail is described by Malory as follows: "Then looked they, and saw a man come out of the holy vessel, that had all the signs of the passion of Jesu Christ, bleeding all openly, and said, My knights and my servants

and my true children, which be come out of deadly life into spiritual life, I will now no longer hide me from you, but ye shall see now a part of my secrets and of my hid things: now hold and receive the high meat which ye have so much desired."[37]

Le Morte d'Arthur was published during the late 1400's, after the Roman church had destroyed the Cathars and the Knights Templar.[38] Some scholars suggest that the word "Grail" was derived from the Latin word *"gradalis,"* meaning a dish in which costly meats were served in layers or according to degrees of worth.[39] Is this an allegorical reference to a story containing many layers of allegory?

Did any of you turn back to Figure 1 and put the story of the lions that changed into an eagle, an ox, and a man, and the hart (deer) which changed into a man, onto the Holy Grail? The fourth lion evidently remained a lion. Lion. Ox. Man. Eagle. Christ often was portrayed as a white hart during those days.[40] The hart on the Holy Grail is seen in **Figure 303**. Are you beginning to feel that same "great clearness"?

What is the meaning of the "glass window" through which Christ passed as pure light? The Gnostics spoke of a boundary (*horos*) between Heaven and Earth, over which was stretched a veil or curtain (*katapetasma*), onto which were projected, from Heaven, the secret patterns (*paradeigmata*) of creatures and objects.[41] Gnostic Christians said that Christ was the guardian of this veil; was the door

Figure 303

between Heaven and Earth; and that only through Him could humankind enter Heaven.[42] The crossing point between Heaven and Earth (*stauros et axis mundi*) was conceptualized as a cruciform human turning or spiralling![43] In Chapter 29, we will learn that the Holy Grail can be visualized as a stereographical projection of certain crystals, including quartz. Note in Illustration 29-1 the plane between the upper and lower regions, onto which points on the upper half-hemisphere are projected. Is the Holy Grail the veil (*katapetasma*) of the Gnostics? Are the images we have seen on the Holy Grail the secret patterns (*paradeigmata*) of the creatures and objects projected from Heaven? Did the ancients regard the quartz crystal as a microcosm of the Universe, or, conversely, did they regard the Universe as a macrocosm of a quartz crystal? Ancient science and religion woven into ancient cosmology? Ancient Biblical truths?

Notes
CHAPTER TWENTY.
Grail Quest Stories: Parodies and Satires on the Holy Writ?

1.   Bryant 3.

2.   Matthews 5.

3.   Baigent 285.

4.   Darrah 14-15; Nora Chadwick 49-50, 150-151; Powell 180-182; Piggott 109-112.

5.   Darrah 20, 37-70, 104-114; Gantz EIMAS 9; Kramer 140-141.

6.   Baigent 285-303; Matthews 5, 32.

7.   Baigent 62.

8.   Matthews 8.

9.   Eusebius, generally.

10.   Baigent 53-55, 74, 82-85, 383-387. Some of the Knights Templar evidently agreed with the Saint John Christians that John the Baptist was the true Messiah, and that Jesus Christ was a false prophet. Baigent 83-85. Some *may* have been instructed during initiation into the order that they should believe alone in God in Heaven, not in Jesus Christ. Baigent 85; Partner 77-78. The initiation ceremonies for *some* of the *French* Templars *may* have involved the use of the Holy Grail itself! Partner 77-78. Under torture, some French Templars and their retainers described something (what?) shown to them during their initiations; described, variously, as one or more cats, a man with a long beard, or a man's head. Partner 77-78. Do we know what they saw?

11.   Brooke 101; see also Baigent 53.

12.   Henry Chadwick 130.

13.   Baigent 49-57, 285-286.

14.   Baigent 385-386.

15.   Baigent 49-52, 56-57, 74-77; Matthews 20-21.

16.   Baigent 386.

17.   Baigent 52-53; Brooke 101.

18.   Baigent 52-55; Brooke 100-101.

19.   Baigent 52-55.

20.   11 Encyclopaedia Britannica Macropaedia 443-444 (1974).

21.   Baigent 52-53.

22. Baigent 64,66.

23. Baigent 76-80.

24. Baigent 81. Scholars believe, but have been unable to prove, that some Templars were Cathars who had proof that the Christ story is allegorical or docetic, rather than historical; that the Roman church annihilated them by crusade and inquisition to prevent the spread of that innermost secret of the Vatican. Partner 65, 90, 167-168.

25. Evans 82.

26. Malory (Baines) 368.

27. Malory (Baines) 366.

28. Malory (Baines) 379.

29. Malory (Baines) 381.

30. Malory (Baines) 392.

31. Malory (Baines) 412-413.

32. Malory (Baines) 413.

33. Malory (Baines) 414.

34. Malory (Strachey) 397. In a Germanic myth, we are told that the ship Skithblathnir is the best of boats; that it is large enough for all of the gods and their equipment; and that "It may be laid together like a cloth and put in one's pocket." Hollander 62. Why not if, as we should suspect, the ship Skithblathnir appears on the *Katapetasma* or Heavenly Veil of the Gnostics, which became known as the Holy Grail!

35. Malory (Baines) 376.

36. Malory (Strachey) 399.

37. Malory (Strachey) 408.

38. Baigent 286.

39. Evans x.

40. Matthews 88.

41. Walker 34.

42. Walker 35.

43. Walker 35. Meister Eckhart, 1260-1329 A.D., a German Dominican whose roots were in the nature-oriented, Celtic tradition of spirituality, rather than in the redemption-oriented Christianity of Rome, served as vicar-general of the Irish monastic foundation at Ratisbon (Regensburg) in Germany. Fox, *Breakthrough* 1, 30-34. Meister Eckhart expressed these views about Heaven: "Heaven runs constantly in a circle.... [I]t bestows on all creatures their beings and their lives.... Heaven does not have this power of itself but rather from an angel who causes it to revolve. As I have also often said, all the 'images' and preliminary images or 'ideas' of all of the creatures were already created in the angels before they were created corporeally in creatures.... [B]y causing heaven to revolve, the angel pours out all of the first images of creation which he has received from God...." Fox, *Breakthrough* 367-68. Eckhart also stated, "As a result of heaven's revolution, everything in the world flourishes and bursts into leaf." Fox, *Breakthrough* 120. About humans' questing for God, Eckhart said, "[T]he soul can find no rest until it understands God, insofar as it is possible for a creature to understand God." Fox, *Breakthrough* 366. Eckhart says that in its quest for God, the human spirit "storms the firmament and scales the heavens until it reaches the Spirit that drives the heavens.... [I]t presses on ever further into the vortex" of the "circle of being of which the Creator is the center point." Fox, *Breakthrough* 95-96; 354-55. Eckhart compares the human heart, which he says is at the center of the human body, to the center point around which he says the heavens rotate. Fox, *Breakthrough* 367. Can Eckhart's understanding of the gnostic concept of the *Katapetasma* have failed to include the gnostic concept of Jesus Christ as the docetic man-form image on the heavenly veil? Eckhart told his congregation that they ought not to understand God's sending Christ into the world "in connection with the external world, as, for example, that he ate and drank with us. You must understand it with respect to the spiritual world." Fox, *Breakthrough* 200-01. Have some Christians always known Christianity's visionary origins in Babylonian astrophysics?

Chapter Twenty-One

Grail Quest Stories: Their Origins and Purposes

Another Grail quest story is *Parzival*, written by Wolfram von Eschenbach toward the end of the twelfth or beginning of the thirteenth century.[1] Wolfram claimed his story of the Holy Grail is authentic because he got it from a man named Kyot.[2] The consensus of scholars through the years has been that "Kyot" was not a real person; rather, that Wolfram invented him to lend credibility to his tale.[3] The story of Kyot's source of the tale, the pagan sage Flegentanis, "is so completely incredible that few scholars have even taken this 'information' seriously."[4] Here we go bashing away at the scholars once again! The hypothesis is that we take "Kyot" and "Flegentanis" seriously just long enough to see where an assumption of their reality might lead us. First, we must learn what Wolfram had to say about these two "persons."

Wolfram tells us that "Kyot was called *laschantiure*." The word in italics is old German, and has been translated either *"l'enchanteur,"* that is, "magician," or *"le chanteur,"* that is, "singer."[5] Our translators prefer to render the word as "singer," because Wolfram next tells us that Kyot's skill "would not allow him to do other than sing and recite so that many are still made glad thereby. Kyot is a Provencal who saw this tale of Parzival written in heathen language."[6] By "heathen language" Wolfram meant Arabic.[7] Wolfram continues: "Anyone who asked me before about the Grail and took me to task for not telling him was very much in the wrong. Kyot asked me not to reveal this, for Adventure commanded him to give it no thought until she herself, Adventure, should invite the telling, and then one *must* speak of it, of course."[8] Wolfram writes: "Kyot, the well-known master, found in Toledo, discarded, set down in heathen writing, the first source of this adventure. He had first to learn the *abc's*, but without the art of black magic. It helped him that he was baptized, else this story would still be unknown. No heathen art could be of use in revealing the nature of the Grail and how its mysteries were discovered."[9]

Wolfram then tells us of "Flegentanis." He writes: "A heathen, Flegentanis, had achieved high renown for his learning. This scholar of nature was descended from Solomon and born of a family which had long been Israelite until baptism became our shield against the fire of Hell. He wrote the adventure of the Grail. On his father's side Flegentanis was a heathen, who worshipped a calf as if it were his god...."[10]

Wolfram then writes words whose substance we should weigh most carefully: "The heathen Flegentanis could tell us how all the stars set and rise again and how long each one revolves before it reaches its starting point once more. To the circling course of the stars man's affairs and destiny are linked. Flegentanis the heathen saw with his own eyes in the constellations things he was shy to talk about, hidden mysteries. He said there was a thing called the Grail whose name he had read clearly in the constellations. 'A host of angels left it on the earth and then flew away up over the stars. Was it their innocence that drew them away? Since then baptized men have had the task of guarding it, and with such chaste discipline that those who are called to the service of the Grail are always noble men.' Thus wrote Flegentanis of these things."[11]

Those of you who already have read the science chapters of this book know something the remainder of our fellow Grail-questers will find out later! You were promised that we would penetrate myths and find realities. You now know, or will later learn, that the promise has been kept!

Wolfram finishes about "Kyot" by telling us that "Kyot, the wise master, set about to trace this tale in Latin books, to see where there ever had been a people, dedicated to purity and worthy of caring for the Grail. He read the chronicles of the lands, in Britain and elsewhere, in France and in Ireland, and in Anjou he found the tale."[12]

Note that our translators prefer for good reasons to translate *"laschantiure"* as "singer" but do not reject its possible translation as "magician."[13] Note that the "pagan" language was Arabic. In the science chapters which follow, we shall learn that by Wolfram's time the Church had blotted from the minds of all persons except a few scholars almost all knowledge of Greek science, engineering, and mathematics. During these European scientific Dark Ages, these studies had continued unabated among the non-Christian Arabs, and had matured into the beginnings of modern geometry, algebra, calculus, astronomy, physical sciences, and engineering. We shall learn that when the Moors invaded Spain, they brought with them an age of mathematical and scientific enlightenment which enabled, among other things, the "Cathedral Crusade" to commence, that is, design and construction was begun on Europe's wondrous cathedrals. We will get some impression of the depth of our European ancestors' ignorance about matters of simple mathematics and building construction by studying a few basic geometry propositions which were used to erect the great cathedrals. So important did the European stone masons and architects regard some of these childishly-simple concepts that they would impose the death penalty upon any member of their secret societies who revealed this "top-secret" information to an outsider.

During the time when our Christianized European ancestors were being introduced to "pagan" mathematics, science, and engineering, they also were coming into contact with "pagan" philosophy, cosmology, medicine, and religion.[14] One of the major learning centers was Toledo in Spain.[15] Christians learned many subjects from the sublime — algebra — to the ridiculous — magic. Against that historical backdrop, ask yourself whether it is "completely incredible" that a person learned in "pagan" religion and cosmology communicated to pious European Christians his thoughts about the origins of the Christian faith. Whether his name was "Kyot" or "Flegentanis" really is beside the point.

Note that Wolfram says that the Grail quest story still would be unknown to us if "Kyot" had not been baptized as a Christian. Why? Because "Kyot" otherwise would not have realized that there is a definite relationship between the Grail quest story and the Christ story?

Two more questions before we proceed: Why have the baptized (that is, Christian) guardians of the Holy Grail always been "noble men"? Why have the common folk not shared this guardianship with the nobility? You will understand the answers to those questions later, if you do not already.

Scholars have concluded from their studies that Wolfram wrote *Parzival* to conceal something of immense consequence; that Wolfram encourages his audience to read between the lines; and that Wolfram constantly reiterates the urgency of the secrecy.[16] As example to prove those comments correct, consider these words of Wolfram: "I tell my story like the bowstring and not like the bow. The string is here a figure of speech. Now *you* think the bow is fast, but faster is the arrow sped by the string. If what I have just said is right, the string is like the simple, straightforward tales that people like. Whoever tells you a story like the curve of the bow wants to lead you a roundabout way. If you see the bow and it is strung, you must admit the string is straight — unless it be bent to an arch to speed the shot. Of course if I shot my tale at a listener who is sure to be bored, it finds no resting place, but travels a roomy path, namely, in one ear and out the other. It would be labor lost if I annoyed such a one with my tale. A goat would understand it better, or a rotten tree trunk."[17] Worry not, Wolfram, only "Eagles" are reading your tale about the Story of Stories! "Eagles" will snatch up your allegories and parodies as readily as real eagles catch mice running in the grass.

Scholars seem certain that Wolfram's writings are depositories of secrets about the Christian Church.[18]

Wolfram links the Holy Grail with the Crucifixion and the Mass. "Today is Good Friday, and they await there a dove, winging down from Heaven. It brings a small wafer, and leaves it on the stone. Then, shining white, the dove soars up to Heaven again. Always on Good Friday it brings to the stone what I have just told you, and from that the stone derives whatever good fragrances of drink and food there are on earth, like to the perfection of Paradise. I mean all things the earth may bear. And further the stone provides whatever game lives beneath the heavens, whether it flies or runs or swims. Thus, to the knightly brotherhood, does the power of the Grail give sustenance."[19] You will recall from previous chapters that Christ was called "the Stone." You also will recall Eusebius's quotations from Philo concerning the religionists Eusebius says were the original Christians. Eusebius told us that the original Christians were more interested in sustaining their souls by their studies and worship

Figure 304

Figure 305

than in sustaining their bodies by regular consumption of food and drink.

Roman Catholic readers should take a deep breath before continuing. Now exhale. Ready? The dove winging down from Heaven and the wafer on the stone are illustrated in **Figure 304**. The dove, the wafer, and the cup are illustrated in **Figure 305**. These are the images of the Roman Catholic Mass. The dove represents the Holy Ghost, whose coming, on summons from the priest officiating at the Mass, changes the wafer into the body of Jesus Christ through the *holy magic* of the Mass. The wafer, called the Host, represents the body of Christ and becomes the *actual* body of Christ "in real presence," according to Roman Catholic doctrine in vogue at the time of *Parzival*.[20] The cup holds the wine, which becomes, through the magic of the Mass, the *actual* blood of Christ.[21] In **Figure 306**, we see the celebrant of the Mass, bell in his right hand, crozier in his left hand, summoning one of the three "Persons" of God, i.e., the Holy Ghost in the form of the dove, to perform the holy magic of converting

common bread and wine into the flesh and blood of another of the three "Persons" of God, Jesus Christ, so the celebrant may assist the penitents to consume these magical substances and thus acquire life everlasting. Did thirteenth-century clerics fulminate against Grail stories because these stories documented the fact that the Holy Grail was the origin of the Mass? If so, it is no wonder that the Church never acknowledged that the Holy Grail was a sacred relic of the Christian Faith![22] Is the Holy Grail the secret wellspring from whence these Christian

![Figure 306 geometric construction]

Figure 306

symbols were drawn? Is it more? Is it the origin of the Christ story?

The Grail quest story we shall study in detail is *Perlesvaus*. The author is unknown, but is supposed by some scholars to have been a Templar.[23] He knew the Knights Templar well. His references to them are unmistakable.[24] *Perlesvaus* was written at the end of the twelfth or beginning of the thirteenth century.[25] The Grail scholar John Matthews says

that *Perlesvaus* "demands a more thorough study than it has yet received."[26] We shall do our best.

Perlesvaus ends with a colophon by the author which reads, in part: "The lord of Cambrein had this book written for the lord of Neele. It has only once before been written down in the vernacular, and that copy is so ancient that the letters can be read only with great difficulty. And let my lord Johan de Neele know that this tale should be cherished, and should not be told to men of little under-

Figure 307

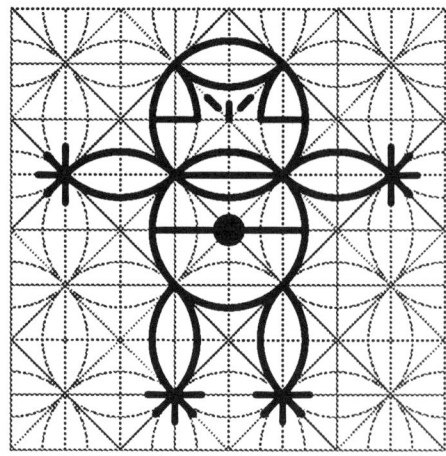

Figure 308

standing, for a good word spread amongst bad people is never properly remembered and passed on by them."[27] Familiar thoughts by an author of a Grail quest story! Words to the same effect as those of Wolfram quoted just a few paragraphs ago! Grail quest authors did not intend their stories for "Men," "Oxen," and "Lions." These are stories for "Eagles" alone!

There is only one problem with selecting *Perlesvaus* rather than one of the more familiar Grail quest stories for intensive study. *Perlesvaus* does not contain the most famous of all Arthurian images — the sword in the stone. You know Malory's story. He would be King of the Brits who drew the Sword Excalibur from the anvil sitting on the stone.[28] Turn to **Figure 307**, where we see (in side view) an anvil sitting on a square block of stone with a crusader's sword stuck through the anvil into the stone. This stuff can be fun!

Sometimes this stuff gets ominous. In a less-modern English translation of *Perlesvaus* than the one from which we shall be working, Sir Gawain arrived at the Castle of the Inquest. The master of the priests of the castle assured him that in the Castle of the Inquest "nought you shall ask whereof it shall not tell you the meaning..." Sir Gawain had seen many things in the forest during his travels. He took the master of the priests at his word, and started asking him the meanings of what he had seen. The master of the priests responded in detail to Sir Gawain's many questions, until the following colloquy occurred: (By Sir Gawain) "Sir, I found a fountain in a forest, the fairest that was ever seen,

and an image had it within that hid itself when it saw me, and a clerk brought a golden vessel and took another golden vessel that hung at the column that was there, and set his own in place thereof. Afterwards, came three damsels and filled the vessel with that they had brought thither, and straightway meseemed that but one was there." The master of the priests then broke his promise to Sir Gawain to answer fully all of Sir Gawain's questions. "'Sir,' saith the priest, 'I will tell you no more thereof than you have heard, and therewithal ought you to hold yourself well apaid, for behoveth not discover the secrets of the Saviour, and them also to whom they are committed behoveth keep them covertly.'"[29] Anyone who is afraid of ancient threats should put this book down right now, because we are about to embark upon a short voyage through *Parzival*, followed by a long voyage through *Perlesvaus*, with the intent and purpose of discovering "the secrets of the Saviour."

Several small, but extremely important, points are made by our translators of *Parzival* in their introduction. We shall study several "pro" stories about King Arthur of Round Table fame. Here is an "anti-Arthur" story. The clergy apparently got peeved about the fact that Christian doctrine had failed to drive King Arthur from the popular imagination. In Wolfram's time, tales about King Arthur were multiplying rather than diminishing in number. The clergy perhaps "sought to offset popular reverence for him."[30] King Arthur was said to be a king of the dwarfs and "a dweller at the Antipodes."[31] Note that many Grail quest stories involve a dwarf, and that our little manform on the Holy Grail can as readily be visualized as a dwarf as a giant. The "antipodes" of the Earth are any two

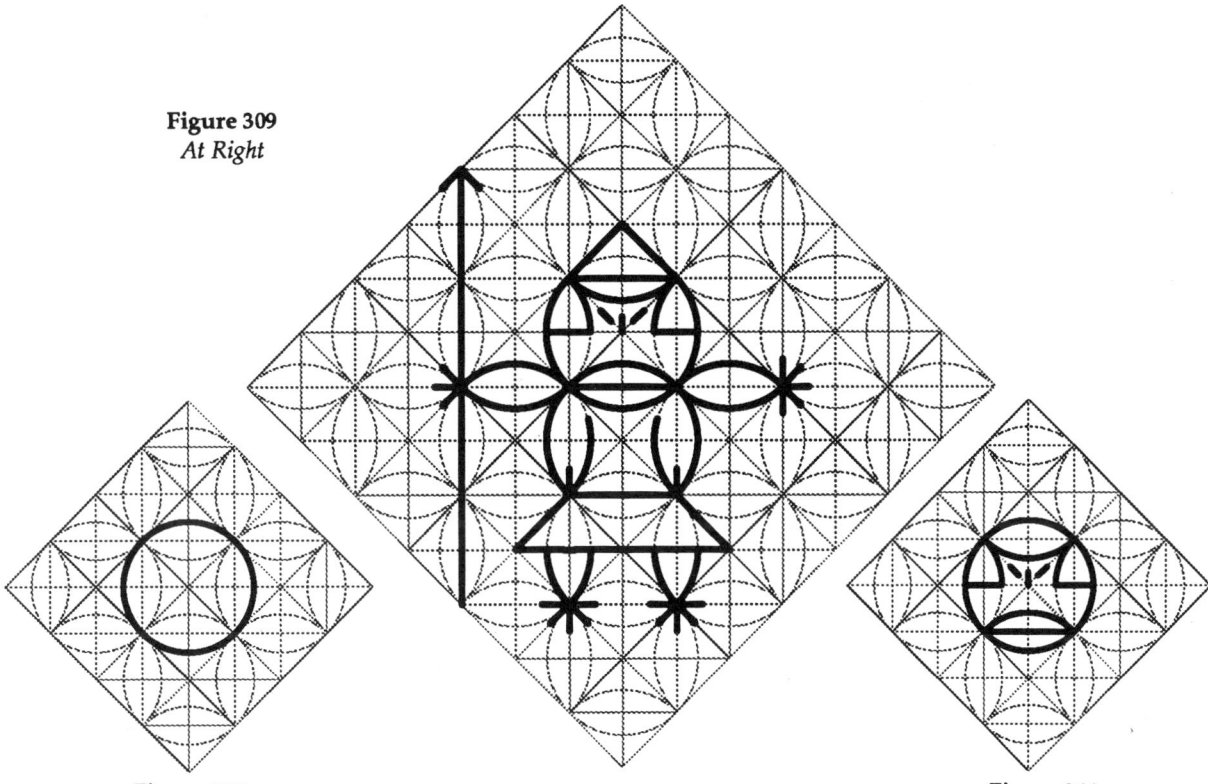

Figure 309
At Right

Figure 310

Figure 311

points on opposite sides of the Earth from each other. For instance, the North Pole and South Pole are antipodes. So is one point on the Equator and another point on the Equator 180 degrees distant from the first point.[32] Add to that bit of trivia Wolfram's etymology for *Parzival*, in English "Perceval," which is *perce a val*, that is, "pierce through the middle."[33] In Wolfram's own words, "In truth, your name is Parzival, which signifies *'right through the middle.'*"[34] Look at our little manform in **Figure 308**. His bellybutton is located at the intersection of the vertical line dividing his right half from his left half, which vertical line is perpendicular to the horizontal line or "belt" around his belly. If his bellybutton is the North Pole of our Earth, and we posit another carbon copy of him pierced through the middle by the South Pole, we do, indeed, have a dweller at the antipodes! Readers may be less amused by this suggestion when they become aware that our little manform, in his role as the locator of the star "Kochab," was used by ancient sailors in the Northern Hemisphere to calculate longitude, and still is used by modern sailors who seek verification that their electronic navigational equipment is functioning properly![35] So many people think of Arthur as a real King of the Brits. A shame it is to cloud their illusions of reality.

Our translators mention in passing the Welsh version of the story of Parzival, and the associations of the Welsh version of the tale with *Yr Wyddfa*, Mount Snowdon, in Wales.[36] Holy mountains are not strange concepts to those who have survived the previous chapters of this book. In a Welsh version of the Grail story, the hero, known as *Peredur*, is sitting with his host "when a great spear streaming blood is carried through the hall."[37] Peredur fails to ask about the spear.[38] We shall encounter "the question unasked" many times in Grail literature. The maidens who carried in the spear next carry before the host and his guest "a great salver between them, and a man's head on the salver, and blood in profusion around the head."[39] Our translators inform us, correctly, that "The Welsh word here translated as 'salver' is *dyscyl*, which... was the semantic equivalent of Old French *graal*, i.e., 'grail.'"[40] We should have learned, before now, that different people see different things when they look at the Holy Grail. Were the Welsh intrigued by the story of Saint John the Baptist? A maiden carrying a spear is illustrated in **Figure 309**. A salver is illustrated in **Figure 310**. A salver is illustrated in **Figure 311** with a man's head on it.

A reader easily could conclude that Wolfram was obsessed with the image of a large jewel. Dur-

Figure 312

ing our analysis of Ezekiel's Visions, and many times since, we have seen that the Grail image illustrated in **Figure 312** may be taken to be a representation of a jewel, i.e., a ruby, an emerald, or some other precious stone. Wolfram writes: "Her crown was a lucent ruby through which her head could be seen."[41] "[T]he helmet was thick and strong and made of a diamond, a good companion in battle."[42] "They had with them the diamond helmet...."[43] "His mouth shone in its redness like a ruby or as if it were on fire, and a full mouth it was, not thin at all."[44] We already have noticed that our Grail manform has large, thick lips!

Wolfram continues on the subject of jewels: "He looked at the diamond headgear, and what a helmet it was!"[45] "They fastened his diamond helmet on: thick and hard it was."[46] "Costly goblets they were, broad, not small in the least, and made of precious stones entirely without gold.... Drink was proffered now in many a jewel of bright color, emerald and carnelian, and some consisted of a single ruby."[47] Remember the "feet" of the "table" which consisted of a single ruby? "Over his grave was set a precious ruby through which he clearly shines. We were permitted to place a Cross on his grave for his comfort for the defense of his soul, after the manner of the Passion by which Christ's death redeemed us.... An epitaph was engraved upon his diamond helmet, which was made fast to the cross above his grave. *Through this helmet a joust slew a man who was brave.*"[48] "[T]he other four were not displeased to be the bearers of a precious stone so clear that in the day the sun shone through. It was a garnet hyacinth, long and wide, and he who measured it for a table top had cut it thin that it might be light to carry. At this sumptuous table the host ate."[49] We are familiar with a "table" that had a "precious stone" in its middle! Wolfram continues: "[A] squire approached bearing a sword. Its

sheath was worth a thousand marks, a ruby formed the hilt...."[50]

Wolfram continues on the same subject: "I will tell you how they [the Knights Templar who guard the Holy Grail] are sustained. They live from a stone of purest kind. If you do not know it, it shall here be named to you. It is called *lapsit exillis*."[51] Our translators tell us that "Many different explanations have been given for these two words [that is, *lapsit exillis*].... The words are apparently a corruption of some Latin phrase, but no one knows for certain what that phrase was. Such interpretations have been made as: *lapis ex caelis*, 'stone from the heavens'; *lapsit ex caelis*, 'it fell from the heavens'; *lapis elixir*, which would correspond to the philosopher's stone,... *lapis lapsus ex caelis*, 'a stone fallen from heaven.'"[52] In any event, Wolfram tells us that "By the power of that stone the phoenix burns to ashes, but the ashes give him life again."[53] Further, Wolfram assures us that "Such power does the stone give a man that flesh and bones are at once made young again. The stone is also called the Grail."[54] Wolfram also tells us that "On the stone, around the edge, appear letters inscribed, giving the name and lineage of each one, maid or boy, who is to take this blessed journey. No one needs to rub out the inscription, for once he has read the name, it fades away before his eyes."[55] We already are familiar, from personal experience, with images fading into and out of our sight on the Holy Grail.

Wolfram has not yet exhausted the subject of precious stones: "He entered the chamber — its pavement shone bright and smooth as glass — and there was the *Lit marveile*, the Wonder Bed. Four wheels, round and made of bright rubies, rolled underneath it...."[56] We have studied in detail a "table" with feet which consisted of large rubies. We have seen four-wheeled carts, and shall see many more.

Wolfram next weaves precious stones into one of the most complex and most important images of his tale. He tells us about a "sumptuous castle hall" and a "winding staircase" leading up to "a narrow tower high above the castle roof."[57] "Up there stood a shining pillar, not made of rotten wood, but bright and firm.... It was circular like a tent.... Of diamond and amethyst — the adventure tells us so — of topaz and garnet, of chrysolite, ruby, emerald, and sard were the costly window columns, so was the roof above. But among these columns was none that could compare with the great pillar which stood in the center. The adventure tells us what wondrous properties it had. Wanting to look at the

Figure 313

Figure 314

many precious stones, Gawan climbed alone to the watchtower. There he found a marvel so great that he could not take his eyes from it. It seemed to him he could see in the great pillar all the lands round about, and it seemed the lands were circling the column and the mighty mountains collided with a clash. In the pillar he saw people riding and walking, others running or standing still. He seated himself at a window to observe the marvel better."[58] Wolfram leaves us hanging about the meaning of the pillar, but not without giving us enough clues to understand the allegory. "To his mistress he spoke and asked her to tell him about the pillar he saw there, of what nature it was. She answered, 'Sir, this stone has cast its glow, by day and all the nights since it was first known to me, for six miles round the countryside. Whatever happens with this space, in water or on meadow, may be seen in this pillar. Of everything it gives a true report. Bird or beast, guest or exile, stranger or friend, one finds them here. Its light gleams for six miles around and it is so strong and solid that neither hammer nor smith could harm it even with the greatest skill....' At this moment Gawan perceived riders in the pillar.... Gawan turned away, yet this only increased his sorrow. He thought the pillar had deceived him...."[59] Later, Wolfram tells us that "[a]t the Castle of Wonders whatever takes place within six miles' distance can be seen in the pillar on my lookout tower."[60]

During our studies of the Shepherd of Hermas, we learned about a crystal tower which is the "one true church." We are yet to learn about the shaman's

quartz crystal; how it splits white light into the component colors of the rainbow; and how it signified the crystallized light of the sun, fallen to Earth. We are told that the lands revolve around an axis; and that the world's axis is a crystal tower rather than a cross of *rotten* wood. Is Wolfram suggesting that the Cathar Christian Church, not the corrupted Roman Catholic Church, is that one true church? Is he saying that the polestar, not the Cross of Calvary, is at the rotational center of the world? Are the many jewels the many different-colored stars in the vault of the sky? Did Wolfram know that the Earth rotates around its pole, and the planets around the sun? Did he know the heretical doctrine of heliocentricity? Did he accept the theory of Aristarchus of Samos rather than the theory of the Holy Father at Rome? Were the heretics Copernicus, Kepler, and Galileo late to learn what the Knights Templar long before had known? Who is the smith who cannot harm the tower with his hammer? Is he the Holy Father at Rome?

The list of stones adorning the bed of Anfortas (the Fisher King of other Grail stories) is too long to quote.[61] Is the wheeled "bed" of the Fisher King Ezekiel's throne wagon in the sky? Wolfram tells us of the Grail Castle's baptismal font: "The baptismal font was a single ruby, and it sat on a circular step of jasper."[62] As was stated, categorically, at the beginning of this long analysis of precious stones, Wolfram was obsessed with precious stones and jewels!

But what shall we make of all this? Look at our humanform's "head" in **Figures 313** and **314**. It does

Figure 315

Figure 316

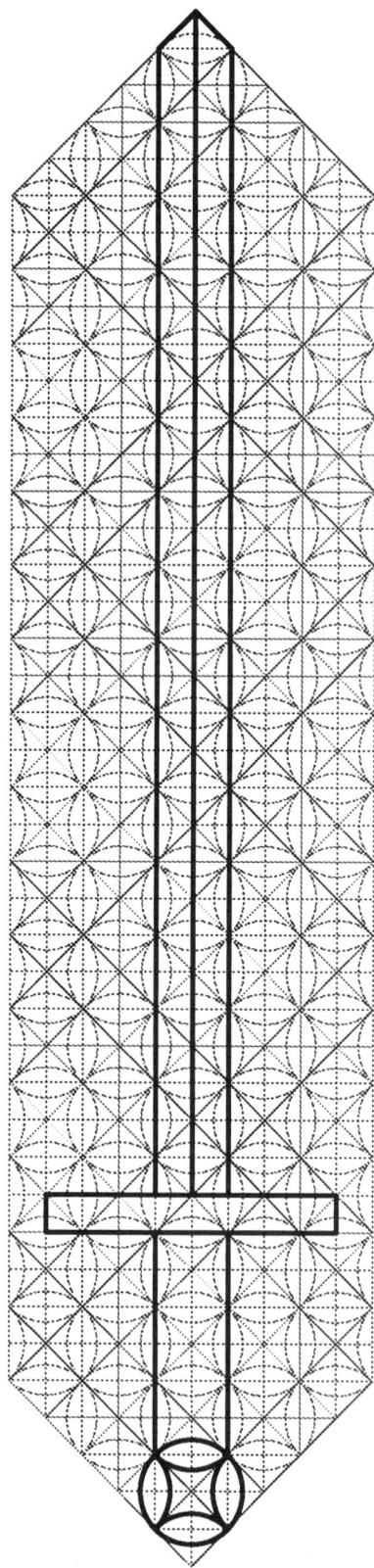

Figure 317

look like "she" is wearing a precious stone on her head as a "crown," or "he" is wearing a precious stone over his head as a knight's battle helmet! Note that the face visor of his helmet is up. The cup in **Figure 315** does look like its body (as distinguished from its stem) is made of half a precious jewel. The baptismal font in **Figure 316** also looks (in top view) as though it is centered by a precious jewel. To construct a proper Christian or Crusader's sword with a properly-sized pommel consisting of a precious stone, we need to extend our lines as in **Figure 317.**

And what about the complex images of the pillar, the tower, and its related items? Could this have any relationship to the Hebrew Tabernacle and Temple stories we already have studied in

Figure 318

great detail? This castle has a circular stairway, like the Temple, and is round, like we presumed the Tabernacle to be. Remember that "it seemed the lands were circling the column...."[63] Those of you who have "fudged" by reading the science chapters at the end of this book again have an advantage. We apparently have been misinformed by our history professors. An intellectual elite of religious leaders, spanning many thousands of years and many areas of geography, evidently was well aware that the Earth was round, spun daily upon its axis, and revolved annually around the sun, the center of our little universe. They seem to have kept this information for themselves and from the herd of humanity for reasons which we shall discuss in detail. Only now, possessed of this information, do we begin to understand why the Church threatened Galileo with death or imprisonment if he did not renounce his theories of heliocentricity, which had been based upon his telescopic observations. We shall encounter the Grail image of the Earth spinning on its axis in *Perlesvaus* in the story of the turning castle.

Wolfram expended many words in an effort to convince us that the Holy Grail is on a precious stone or jewel. But he also says it is borne on *achmardi*.[64] Our translators of *Parzival* give us a translation of the word "*achmardi*." They say it means a color; specifically, emerald-green.[65] Matthews gives us a clue to the probable significance of the color green. "Interestingly, the colour green attributed by Wolfram to the Grail stone is associated with Venus, whose day, Friday, is the Islamic Sabbath...."[66] The translators of Wolfram's other book, *Willehalm*, give us a more complete translation of the word "*achmardi*." It seems that "*achmardi*" is "precious green silk interwoven with gold thread."[67] We have found the lines of the Holy Grail inscribed on a rock, and now find those same lines borne on *achmardi*, that is, sewn in gold thread on precious green silk. The Holy Grail usually is preserved these days on cloth. Minus its construction lines, as illustrated in **Figure 318**, the Holy Grail is popular even to this day in its role as the "wedding ring pattern" of American Colonial-style quilting! Of the Holy Grail sewn with gold thread on precious green silk, Wolfram tells us: "Upon a deep green achmardi she bore the perfection of Paradise, both root and branch. That was a thing called the Grail, which surpasses all earthly perfection."[68] Our translators want to tell us something about their phrase "perfection of Paradise," and, therefore, give us this comment in a footnote: "Wolfram frequently uses this phrase to describe the Grail. There is no one English word which reproduces adequately the meaning of the word *wunsch* in the original. It connotes an absolute ideal, the supreme good."[69]

Wolfram tells us that the Holy Grail provided the assembly with food and drink.[70] "The heathen wanted to know what it was that kept filling the empty gold dishes in front of the table. The marvel intrigued him. Then the beautiful Anfortas, who had been seated next to him, said, 'Sir, do you see the Grail lying there before you?' The speckled heathen said, 'I don't see anything but an achmardi.'"[71] Is Wolfram telling us by these words that the lines of the Holy Grail were sewn in gold thread on precious green silk? The sun's golden threads cause the green Earth to provide humankind with food and drink? Wolfram says that the Holy Grail permitted no one but the lovely maiden, Repanse de Schoye, to carry it.[72] We can speculate that Repanse de Schoye, and the maidens who bear the Holy Grail in front of the host and guests in the tale of *Perlesvaus*, might have carried it in the form of an *achmardi*. We know from those sequences in *Parzival* and *Perlesvaus* that the Holy Grail was portable in that it could be carried by a maiden or maidens. In contradiction of its portability, we also know from

Wolfram that "Repanse de Schoye tends the Grail, which is so heavy that all of sinful humanity cannot move it from its place."[73] Humankind cannot destroy the solar system? We surely can destroy ourselves, and make the Earth unfit for our kind!

Wolfram is concerned with the ancient cosmological concept of everything proceeding outward from the "center" then proceeding inward back to the "center." "Squarely in the middle of Book IX (467-468) — which itself has a mathematically exact centrality in the total work — the question of the Grail is broached between the hero and the hermit uncle."[74] Wolfram is concerned with measurement of the passage of time. The story proceeds from the first Pentecost when Parzival first is knighted by Arthur to the seventh Pentecost when he "becomes truly a knight in spirit."[75] Wolfram is concerned with astronomical and astrological phenomena. "Perhaps the Scorpion's orbit in the sky would help us too in the time before the planets turn backward in their course and the change in the moon begins...."[76] "[H]e ate none of them before the Nones."[77] Our translators tell us that the "Nones" are 3:00 o'clock p.m., "the traditional hour of Christ's death on the Cross."[78] "When the star Saturn had returned to the zenith...."[79] "On days when certain stars appear, the people of Munsalvaesch have reason to lament their woe. These are the stars [planets] whose courses run parallel [along the Ecliptic] one high above the other, and which move irregularly, in contrast to the others. And the change of the moon also hurts the wound sorely."[80] "Saturn climbs so high aloft that the wound knew of its coming before the other frost arrived."[81] "Our father Adam [the Biblical Adam]... knew... the revolutions of the stars as well, and what forces the seven planets had...."[82] "How high above all the stars swift Saturn runs its course!"[83] "As the antarctic pole faces the north star, and neither moves from its place, so my love and yours shall stand true and never leave each other."[84] Remember King Arthur in his role as a dweller at the antipodes? "Seven stars then she named in the heathen language... [naming them].... These are the bridle of the firmament and they check its speed; their opposition has ever contended against its sweep.... Whatever the planets' orbits bound, upon whatever their light is shed, that is destined as your goal to reach and to achieve."[85] "Now the time had waited until Mars or Jupiter had once again come back all angry in their orbits to the point from which they had proceeded."[86] These astronomical and astrological passages are consistent either with Earth-centered, sky-moving astronomy, or with Earth-moving and planet-moving astronomy in a heliocentric system. We know the Earth does the moving around the sun, but we still speak, in the vernacular, of the sun coming up in the morning! It would be the height of folly to attempt to prove Wolfram's knowledge, or lack of knowledge, about the concept of heliocentricity based upon the words he used in these astronomically and astrologically related passages, which were poetry, instead of prose, in the original German.

We cannot leave *Parzival* without commenting on Wolfram's statements about the blood on the snow, the question unasked, the Round Table in the flowery field, the person and appearance of Cundrie *la sorciere*, and without quick reference to some of the familiar images and phrases that appear in *Parzival* but which will not be studied until we analyze *Perlesvaus*.

Wolfram writes that a falcon wounded a goose in flight. "From its wounds there fell upon the snow three red drops of blood.... From the way the drops lay on the snow, the hero's eyes fancied two as her [his love's] cheeks and the third as her chin.... When he saw the drops no longer, Lady Reason gave him his senses back again."[87] An analogous fascination over the Passion of Christ occurs in *Perlesvaus*, causing the hero to fail to ask the question which would heal the ailing Fisher King. We often forget to use our reason when contemplating persons we love. In *Parzival*, if the question is asked by the visiting hero, without his being prompted, "Anfortas shall be healed, but he shall no longer be king."[88] In *Parzival*, the hero asks the question: "Uncle, what is it that troubles you?" In *Perlesvaus*, the heroes always are so fascinated by images of the Passion of Christ that they fail to ask the question. Our translators tell us that in Chretien, "the question is a double one: Why does the lance bleed? and Whom does one serve with this Grail?"[89] We speculate as to the proper answers to the question (or questions) unasked when we analyze *Perlesvaus*.

Wolfram's statements about the Round Table in the flowery field are important to Celts. He says that "[t]hough the Table had been left behind at Nantes, they transferred its rights and privileges to a flowery field with no tents or shrubs in the way."[90] Wolfram apparently understood that tidbit of Celtic cosmology. The ancients believed in a correspondence between Heaven and Earth. Life here was a reflection of life there; life there was a reflection of life here. Remember the dove [Holy Ghost] coming down from Heaven bearing the Host and returning

Figure 319

to Heaven with the essence of all good food and drink found here on Earth? When our ancestors stuck standing stones in a circle in a field, no matter the size, they had, as it were, staked out a little bit of Heaven here on Earth, and had established a sort of Celtic Jacob's ladder by which the denizens of Heaven and Earth could communicate, if not commute. The idea is preserved, more or less intact, in the *original* concept of the Mass.

Wolfram makes an allusion to the Celtic "cauldron of rebirth," into which the dead were put, headfirst, by the gods, to be "born again."[91] "[H]e would stew him some nice big pieces of bread and whirl them around for him in his stewing kettle."[92] Human flesh was regarded as the "bread of the gods" by many ancient peoples.[93] Turn back to Illustration 8-1 for the shape of a typical loaf of ancient Greek bread, then turn to **Figure 319**, where you can see a loaf of that bread in a stew-pot, seen from top view.

Cundrie *la sorciere* could not have won a beauty pageant. When we first are introduced to her, she is riding her mule. "No lady was she in appearance.... [S]he spoke all languages well, Latin, French and heathen [Arabic]. She was versed in dialectic and geometry and even in the science of astronomy.... Her tongue was far from lame, for it had quite enough to say.... She had a nose like a dog's, and two boar's teeth stuck out from her mouth, each a span in length.... Cundrie had ears like a bear's and... a face... hairy and rough. In her hand she carried a whip with thongs of silk and a ruby handle, and the hands of this charming dear looked like a monkey's skin."[94] Wolfram's luck on blind dates must have been similar to mine. The old fellow did have a sense of humor! Do you understand the parody? If not, do not worry. We shall study a story of three girls, a horse, a whip, etc., in *Perlesvaus*, and the correspondence between the

Figure 320

images of that story and those of another famous story will be less elusive, if not inescapable. Want to see Cundrie? Turn to **Figure 320**, where we see Cundrie, complete with bear's ears, a dog's nose, and enormous boar's tusks. She is sitting on her mule, her whip in hand. Why does she speak all of those languages, and why is she skilled in many studies, from dialectic to astronomy? Because Grail stories have been written in all those languages, and more? Because the Grail was used to formulate dialectic, as well as to survey the skies? Remember when we suggested that it would help if you had, and could keep, a sense of humor? It is such a shame that folks must frown so much about religion.

Wolfram is a sly guy. He uses many different techniques to get his message across. For instance, he uses phrases such as "a merchant who is trying to cheat us," and sentences such as "I am to protect us from fraud?" and "*He* was never bent on deception."[95] Is Wolfram trying to tell us, by the shape of the bow rather than the shape of the bowstring, that we are not being told the truth?

Wolfram is not as graphic with his miscellaneous images as is the unknown (presumably Templar) author of *Perlesvaus*. However, a partial list of Wolfram's images which can be found on the Holy

Grail will serve as a substantial clue to many Eagles. We shall wait until we study *Perlesvaus* to illustrate these, and many more, on the Holy Grail by using bolded lines. Many of you may want to try to find some of them for yourself before turning to the next chapter. Wolfram's Grail images include, but are not limited to: anchors with golden ropes looped through them; a field full of tents; a lady leaning out of a castle window; tents on all sides of a city; a trumpet; a drum; a flute; a shield; a knife; a sword; a lance; a whip; a man with a bandage around his head; a horse; a mule; a donkey; a bed with a man badly wounded; a raven; a man riding a horse into a city in stately fashion; soft pillows and cushions; jewels; a man's four comrades; gates; a flag with the image of a transfixed knight thereon; a shield painted inside and out with the image of a transfixed man; a crown that consists of a precious jewel; a helmet that consists of a precious jewel; a tomb covered by a precious jewel in the form of a cross; a great hall; tents, with their stakes and guy-ropes; candles; rushes lightly strewn; goblets, a table; a cloth; a tower; a sparrow hawk; a bell; axes; a drawbridge; steps; a bed on wheels; fishermen; boats; a loaf of bread; couches; a carpet; a bleeding lance; stools; a lady with a wreath of flowers in her hair; basins; towels; blood from wounds; glowing coals; a cloak; books; a casket with holy relics; a turtledove; the Host (bread) of the Mass; a wounded or dead knight lying across the lap of a lady; and a man pierced through with a lance.

We must give Wolfram an *A* for effort. He tried, by many devices, to lead us, the long way around, to reach a definite conclusion he had in mind, to which he did not want to allude directly.

Notes
CHAPTER TWENTY-ONE
Grail Quest Stories: Their Origins and Purposes

1. Eschenbach *Parzival* xvii.

2. Eschenbach *Parzival* xx-xxv.

3. Eschenbach *Parzival* xxiv-xxv.

4. Eschenbach *Parzival* xxv.

5. Eschenbach *Parzival* 224.

6. Eschenbach *Parzival* 224.

7. Eschenbach *Parzival* 224, fn.13.

8. Eschenbach *Parzival* 243.

9. Eschenbach *Parzival* 244.

10. Eschenbach *Parzival* 244.

11. Eschenbach *Parzival* 244. The relationship between *Parzival* and Hermetism, between the Grail and the Hermetic Krater, is far beyond the reach of this book. Kahane 15-17,21,59-61,118-121. This book must leave much work undone. The gist of what Flegentanis wrote is that a "thing called the Grail" was brought to Earth from the sky. The inference is that the Holy Grail first appeared among the apparently-circling course of the constellations of stars. This book assumes, *arguendo*, that sequence of events. Sky, first. Earth, later. However, the sequence of events may be proven by someone to have been like this: (1) Earth-bound human beings, our ancestors, discovered, during the Stone Ages, how to stack rocks to form domes and vaults.

(In fact, examples of their handiwork still stand from modern Turkey, across Europe, to the west coast of Ireland, and elsewhere.) (2) They understood the basic geometry which held up their structures, and were able to replicate on the ground, using ropes and stakes as drawing instruments, the pattern of lines which came to be known as the Holy Grail. (3) They posited that the sky was a domed and/or vaulted object, held up by the same geometry they had discovered on Earth, perhaps from their study of rock crystals. (4) They mentally projected the Holy Grail onto the posited dome or vault of the sky using stars as locators. (5) They located the stars which came to be known as Lion-Ox-Man-Eagle in relationship to the then-existing solstices and equinoxes, thereby giving us an opportunity, by cranking the Precession of the Equinoxes in reverse, to establish the time-window during which the foregoing events may have transpired! (6) They drew the Holy Grail on the ground (on the grassy field known as the "Round Table") in their stone circles, and the correspondences between the Grail in the sky and the Grail on the ground helped to determine the time of year. (Hoyle says that the Aubrey Circle at Stonehenge *is* the Ecliptic!) (7) At some time before, during, or after the foregoing, a shaman or prophet looked over the shoulder of the architect, astronomer, or mathematician who was working with the pattern of lines we call the Holy Grail, and exclaimed, "I see a lion, an ox, a man, and an eagle. The god(s) is (are) sending messages to me." He began to see what we have seen, and spread the "good news" among others of his trade or profession! Other sequences of events can be posited. There is much work to be done by the archaeoastronomers!

12. Eschenbach *Parzival* 244.

13. Eschenbach *Parzival* xxiv.

14. Eschenbach *Parzival* xxiv; Gimpel 82-84.

15. Eschenbach *Parzival* xxiv; Gimpel 82-84.

16. Baigent 295-296.

17. Eschenbach *Parzival* 131-132.

18. Baigent 303.

19. Eschenbach *Parzival* 252.

20. Matthews 54-55.

21. Matthews 54-55.

22. Matthews 8.

23. Baigent 289.

24. Baigent 290.

25. Bryant 1.

26. Matthews 13.

27. Bryant 265.

28. Malory 24-25.

29. Evans 82.

30. Eschenbach *Parzival* xxxii.

31. Eschenbach *Parzival* xxxii. Like other polar guardians, King Arthur limped. Guest 271. Eastern Christian tradition says Christ was lame. Tribbe 221. Is this a coincidence? "Arth-uthr," are the Cymraeg (Welsh) words for "bear-awful." Evans, *Dictionary* 43, 253. The association between King Arthur and the constellation Ursa Major, the Great Bear, has been noted by commentators. Baigent 238-239. Matthews, *Reader* 342-348. The so-called "Mithras Liturgy" refers to "the Bear which moves and turns heaven around, moving upward and downward in accordance with the hour." Meyer 218. The Phrygians spoke of the cosmic goatherd Aipolos, he who "rotates the whole universe in a circle." Meyer 151. Meister Eckhart said that an angel causes heaven to revolve. Fox, *Breakthrough* 367-368. In previous chapters, we have seen our human-form image referred to as YHWH, Moses, and Jesus Christ. Our little human form on the Holy Grail justly has been called "the being with many names." Meyer 153. Have humans slaughtered each other in wars about the proper name to be given to a human-form image among a pattern of lines? Yes, and they still do!

32. 1 World Book Dictionary 92 (1979).

33. Eschenbach *Parzival* xxxv.

34. Eschenbach *Parzival* 78.

35. Morison 154.

36. Eschenbach *Parzival* xxxvi.

37. Eschenbach *Parzival* xxxvii.

38. Eschenbach *Parzival* xxxviii.

39. Eschenbach *Parzival* xxxviii.

40. Eschenbach *Parzival* xxxviii.

41. Eschenbach *Parzival* 14.

42. Eschenbach *Parzival* 30.

43. Eschenbach *Parzival* 33.

44. Eschenbach *Parzival* 36.

45. Eschenbach *Parzival* 40.

46. Eschenbach *Parzival* 44.

47. Eschenbach *Parzival* 48. In the story of Hymir, we are told that, with considerable effort, Thor was able to shatter a crystal wine cup or goblet, a test which won him the right to carry away an ale-kettle or cauldron. Hollander 88.

48. Eschenbach *Parzival* 60-61.

49. Eschenbach *Parzival* 128.

50. Eschenbach *Parzival* 130-131.

51. Eschenbach *Parzival* 251.

52. Eschenbach *Parzival* 251. Is this "stone" a loadstone (lodestone) or magnet stone? Kahane 22, 109-110.

53. Eschenbach *Parzival* 251.

54. Eschenbach *Parzival* 252.

55. Eschenbach *Parzival* 252.

56. Eschenbach *Parzival* 300.

57. Eschenbach *Parzival* 312.

58. Eschenbach *Parzival* 313.

59. Eschenbach *Parzival* 314.

60. Eschenbach *Parzival* 395.

61. Eschenbach *Parzival* 412-413.

62. Eschenbach *Parzival* 425.

63. Eschenbach *Parzival* 313.

64. Eschenbach *Parzival* 129.

65. Eschenbach *Parzival* 10, fn.8.

66. Matthews 19-20.

67. Eschenbach *Willehalm* 208, 292.

68. Eschenbach *Parzival* 129.

69. Eschenbach *Parzival* 129.

70. Eschenbach *Parzival* 421-422.

71. Eschenbach *Parzival* 422. The suggestion that the Holy Grail appears on a piece of cloth also is found in the Norse sagas, where we are told that the vessel Skidbladnir is large enough to hold all of the gods fully armed, but that when that boat is not needed it can be folded up no larger than a piece of cloth and put into your purse. Crossley-Holland 51. We also are told that Thor's mighty hammer, Mjollnir, can be made small enough to be tucked inside your shirt. Crossley-Holland 52. It is difficult to avoid the humor implicit in those representations.

72. Eschenbach *Parzival* 421.

73. Eschenbach *Parzival* 255.

74. Eschenbach *Parzival* xliv.

75. Eschenbach *Parzival* 1.

76. Eschenbach *Parzival* 258.

77. Eschenbach *Parzival* 260.

78. Eschenbach *Parzival* 260.

79. Eschenbach *Parzival* 261.

80. Eschenbach *Parzival* 262.

81. Eschenbach *Parzival* 263.

82. Eschenbach *Parzival* 276.

83. Eschenbach *Parzival* 324.

84. Eschenbach *Parzival* 373.

85. Eschenbach *Parzival* 407.

86. Eschenbach *Parzival* 411.

87. Eschenbach *Parzival* 153-154.

88. Eschenbach *Parzival* 259.

89. Eschenbach *Parzival* 415.

90. Eschenbach *Parzival* 167.

91. Darrah 72-73; Gantz *The Mabinogion* 71-72.

92. Eschenbach *Parzival* 226-227.

93. An analogous concept may be found in Christianity. Ignatius, a founding father of the Christian Church, referred to Christ's human flesh as "a Fruit imparting life to us." Staniforth 119.

94. Eschenbach *Parzival* 169-170.

95. Eschenbach *Parzival* 194-195.

Chapter Twenty-Two

Perlesvaus: Riddling the Coals of the Original Christian Faith

The High Book of the Holy Grail, known to Grail scholars as *Perlesvaus,* was written, according to its unknown author, so "the truth might be known of how knights and worthy men were willing to suffer toil and hardship to exalt the Law of Jesus Christ...."[1] The author suggests that those who hear his story "must be attentive and forget all their baseness...."[2] He tells us the story of the good knight, *Perlesvaus,* descended from Joseph of Arimathaea. Joseph, he says, took Christ down from the Cross, laid His body in the tomb, and kept the lance by which His blood was drawn and the "holy vessel" in which His blood was collected.[3] We are told that Britain and the isles have fallen into great sorrow "through just a few words which he [the good knight] neglected to say."[4] Christ is referred to as "the Holy Prophet," a term consistent with Cathar theology.[5]

We are introduced to King Arthur and Queen Guinevere, and are given the bad news that "a weakness suddenly beset his [Arthur's] resolve and he began to lose his former passion for great deeds."[6] Should we think of King Arthur as a sacred king languishing instead of "standing tall in the saddle"? Arthur and Guinevere lament that knights do not come to their court anymore; nor do any adventures befall them, as in the good old days.[7] Guinevere tells Arthur that she believes he will regain his will to do great deeds if he will go to the Chapel of St. Augustine.[8] Arthur agrees to go and, at Guinevere's insistence, to take along a squire.[9] The squire has a dream that Arthur has gone on without him.[10] The contents of the squire's dream provide our first Grail adventure.

As the squire rode out, in his dream, after Arthur, "he saw the hoofmarks of the king's horse, or so it seemed."[11] Remember that we "must be attentive." The author is going to give us some subtle clues which easily could be overlooked. Do the words "or so it seemed" tell us something? Was what the squire saw something which seemed like the hoofprints of a horse but was not the hoofprints of a horse? Were they, instead, lines on the Holy Grail? See the horse's hoofprints in **Figure 321**. The squire came to "a chapel in the middle of the clear-

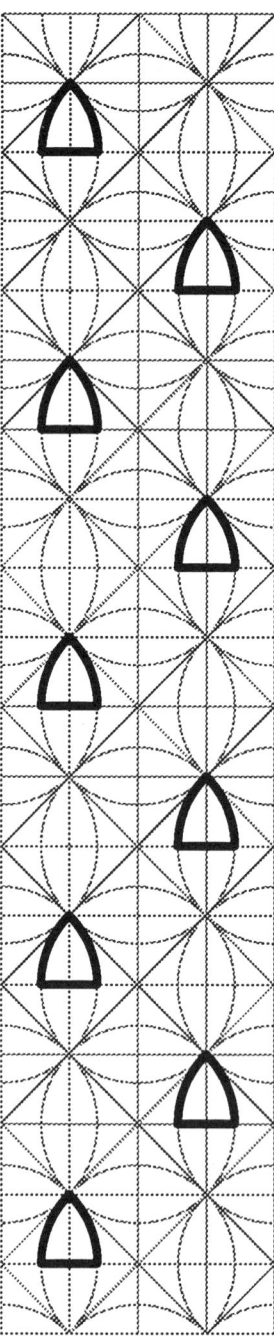

Figure 321

Figure 322

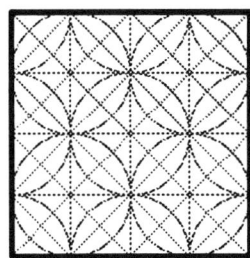

Figure 323

ing, around which he thought he saw a great cemetery with many tombs."[12] The words "he thought he saw" once more tell us, if we are attentive, that we are dealing with appearances rather than realities? **Figure 322** shows the simple chapel. **Figure 323** shows the clearing, in top view. **Figure 324** shows a single tomb, in isometric view. You can imagine the remainder of the tombs for yourself. Recall that the young man who became St. Augustine spent his early years as an adherent of Manichaeism, a syncretized faith which regarded

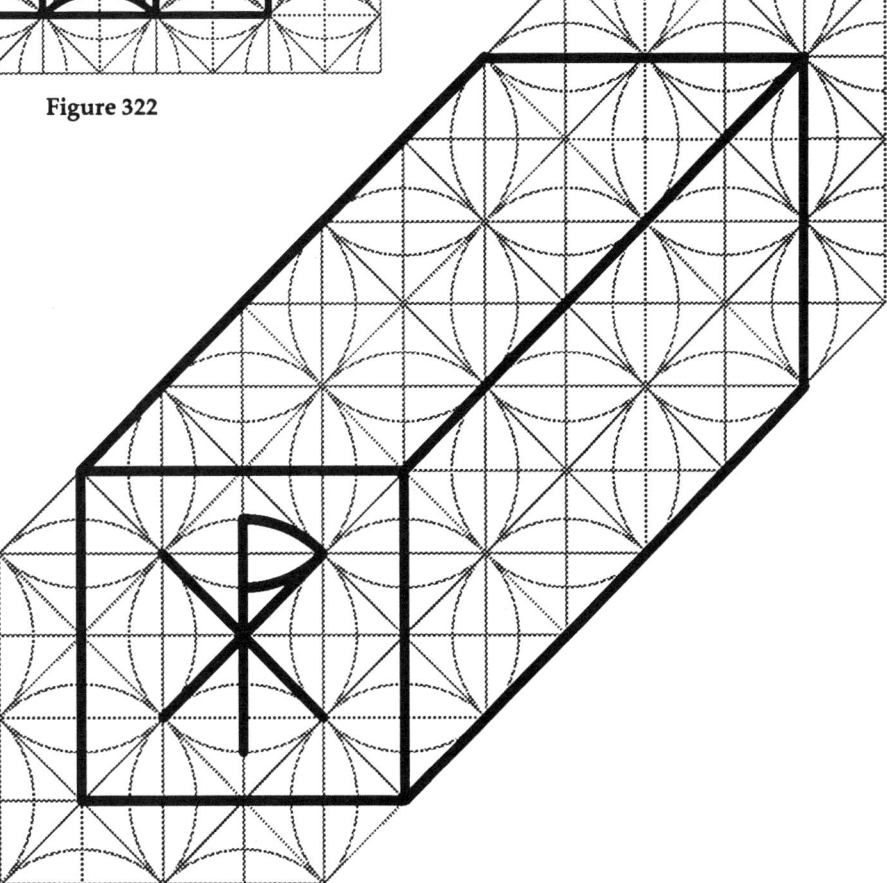

Figure 324

Figure 325
At Right

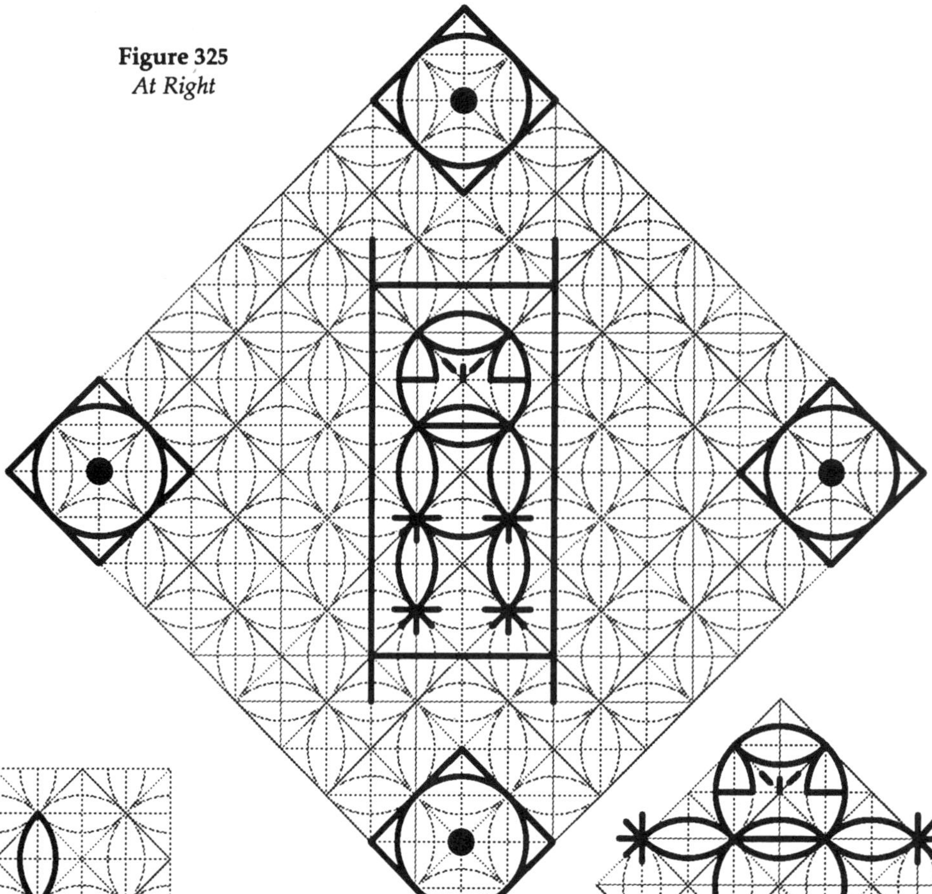

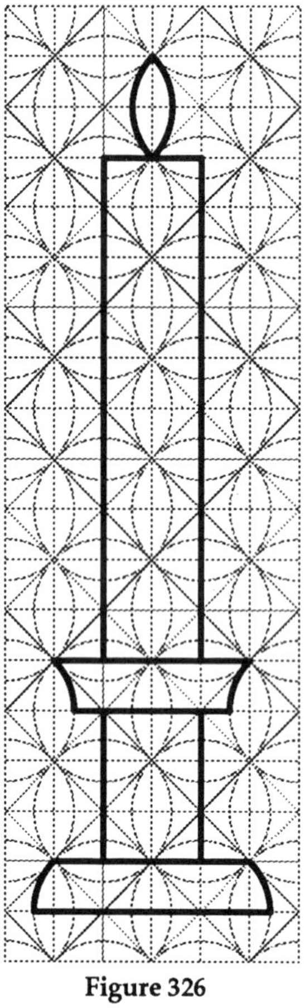

Figure 327

Figure 326

Christ as a prophet rather than as God incarnate.[13] Cathars evidently adopted the practice of earlier heretical Christians of burying their dead in above-ground stone tombs rather than in underground caskets.[14]

Inside the chapel, the squire found "a knight lying on a litter in the middle of the chapel, draped in rich silk, with four candles burning around him in four golden candlesticks."[15] The four guardian stars (Lion, Ox, Man, and Eagle) along the Ecliptic? **Figure 325** shows the knight lying on the litter surrounded by four candles in four candlesticks. A single candlestick with candle is illustrated in side view in **Figure 326**. The knight's body had been left alone, "for statues were its only company."[16] **Figure 327** shows one of our Grailforms in his latest role as a "statue." You can visualize for yourself the

Figure 328

Figure 329

other three. The squire stole one of the golden candlesticks, minus the candle, but was caught by a dark and ugly man on horseback.[17] "[I]t seemed to the boy that the man was clutching a huge, sharp, two-edged knife in his hand."[18] "It seemed" means it had the appearance of a knife while not being a knife at all? When the squire refused to return the stolen candlestick, and tried to escape from the man, "the man came to the attack and struck him in the right side with his knife and thrust it in right up to the haft."[19] The man on horseback is illustrated in **Figure 328**. The squire on his pony is illustrated in **Figure 329**.

The squire awakened from his dream, screaming that he was dying.[20] He had the knife in his side, and the stolen candlestick in his possession.[21] The knife in his side (almost up to the haft) is illustrated in **Figure 330**. The squire died.[22] King Arthur gave the golden candlestick to St. Paul's Church in London because "he wanted this wondrous adventure to be known to everyone, so that people would pray in the church for the soul of the boy who had been killed because of the candlestick."[23]

What did we learn from this Grail quest story? We saw a weapon piercing a human's side, a boy riding a pony, and a man riding a horse, and statues standing in the presence of a dead human body lying on a slab or litter in a chapel. These are images of the Christ story, except that in the Christ story the weapon was a lance, the animal an ass, the statues

were angels, and the chapel was the tomb. We saw golden candlesticks, images of the Revelation of Saint John the Divine. We should recall that the story of *Perlesvaus* is about knights' suffering toil and hardship "to exalt the Law of Jesus Christ." How does the death of a squire who steals a candle-

Figure 330

Figure 331

stick for his king, who presents it to the Church, "exalt the Law of Jesus Christ"? Which "Law of Jesus Christ"? Thou shalt not steal? No, the immoral moral of this cameo is that thy soul shalt be prayed for because thou didst die whilst stealing on behalf of King and Church! You were warned that we would be studying a parody or satire on Roman Catholicism!

The author of *Perlesvaus* has opened verbal combat by accusing the Roman Catholic church of turning the commandment not to steal upside down in order to enrich itself with the booty of the world! This is one of the criticisms hurled by Cathar Christians against the Roman Catholic church.[24] The Cathars insisted that the original Christians gave to the poor whatever wealth they may have accumulated, and lived in physical poverty but not in spiritual poverty.[25] With considerable historical

justification, the Cathars accused the Roman Catholic clergy of the thirteenth century of living in physical wealth and in spiritual poverty.[26] The Cathars considered themselves the true Christian faith because, like the original Christians, they aspired to the existence of a poor church which ministered to the physical and spiritual needs of the poor — rather than a rich church run by men who lived in splendor like feudal lords while they subjected the common folk to physical and spiritual poverty.[27]

By learning to find images of this story on the Holy Grail, we necessarily have learned to find the analogous images of the Christ story. **Figure 331** shows our Grail manform on the Cross, bearded and crowned, with a crusader's lance stuck through His side. Remove the handguard from that lance and you have a Roman lance. **Figure 332** shows the

Figure 332

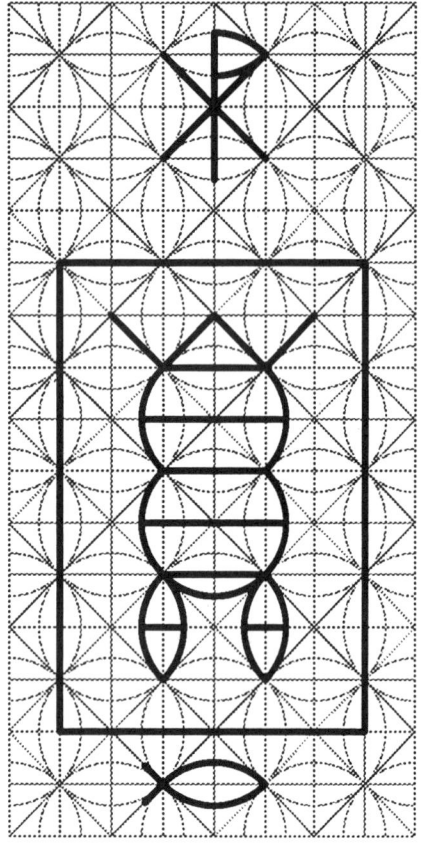

Figure 333

Grail cup catching the blood flowing from His side. **Figure 333** shows Him wrapped in fine cloth and lying on a slab in a tomb. **Figure 334** shows the stone in place in front of the tomb, which is being guarded by two angels. The symbols tell us whose tomb it is.

We have analyzed only four and a half pages of *Perlesvaus*, but look what we have encountered already!

His squire dead, Arthur prepared to set out for the Chapel of St. Augustine by himself.[28] He was given his shield and lance and, "[h]e set himself so firmly in the stirrups that he made the saddle stretch and the horse bow under him...."[29] We see King Arthur, crowned, his lance in his right hand, his shield in his left, astride his stretched saddle on his sway-backed horse in **Figures 335A, 335B,** and **335C**. The pun about the saddle stretching and the horse bowing under Arthur proves our unknown author had a sense of humor. Moreover, it is a rather substantial piece of circumstantial evidence indicating that our author of *Perlesvaus* is drawing his images from the wellspring of the Holy Grail! Queen Guinevere goes to her castle window, and Arthur's knights come to the steps of the castle to see Arthur

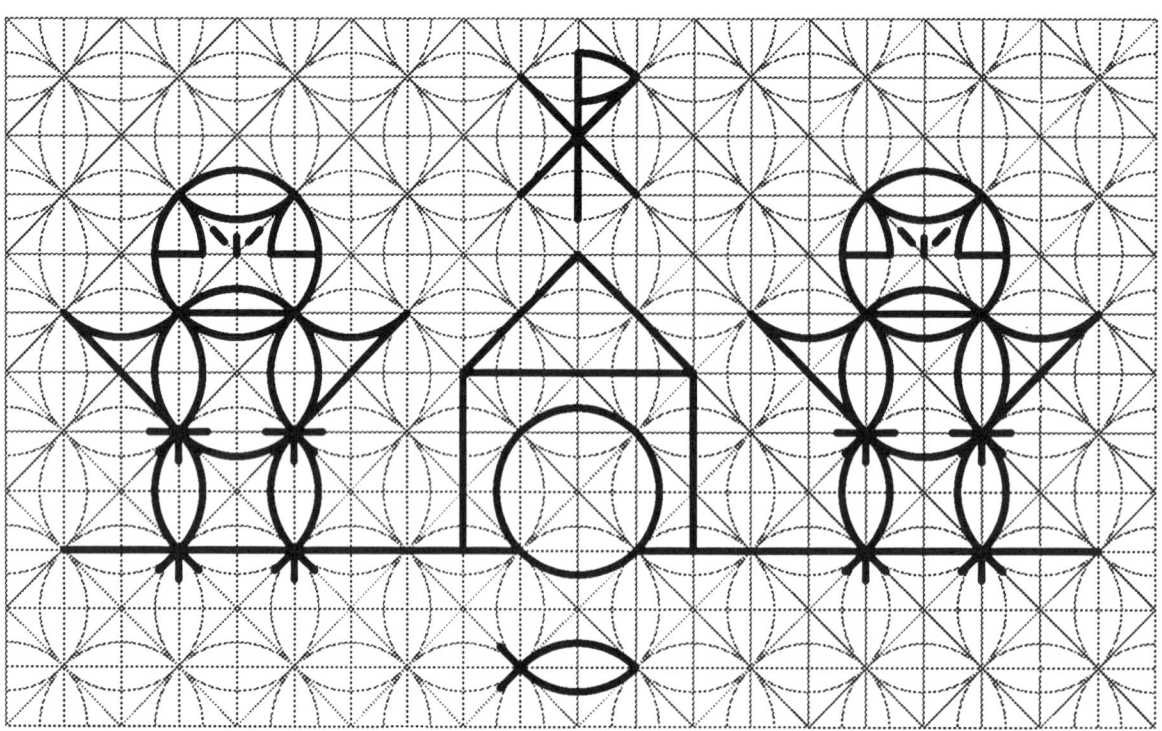

Figure 334

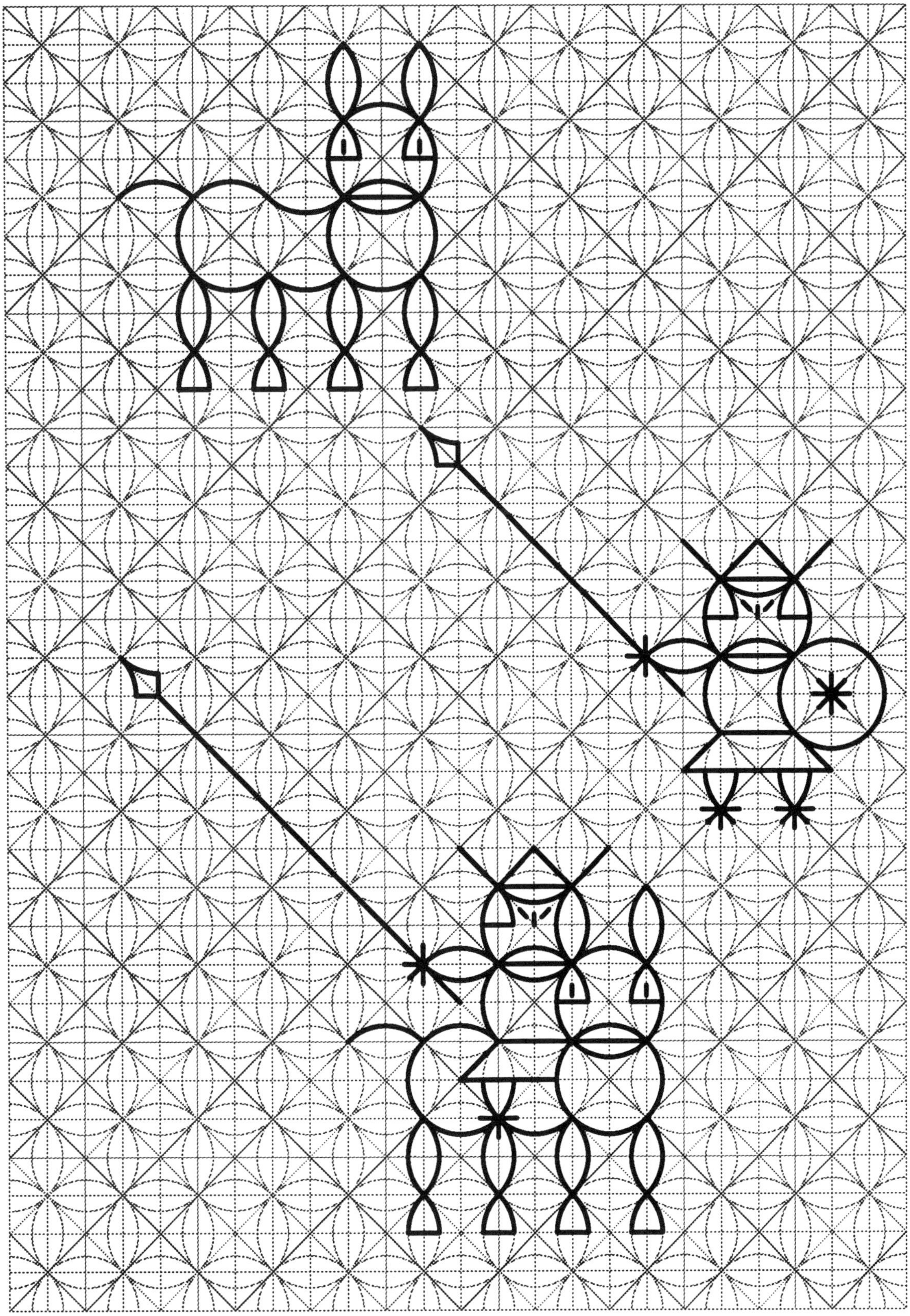

Figures 335A, 335B, and 335C
Top to Bottom

Figure 336

Figure 338

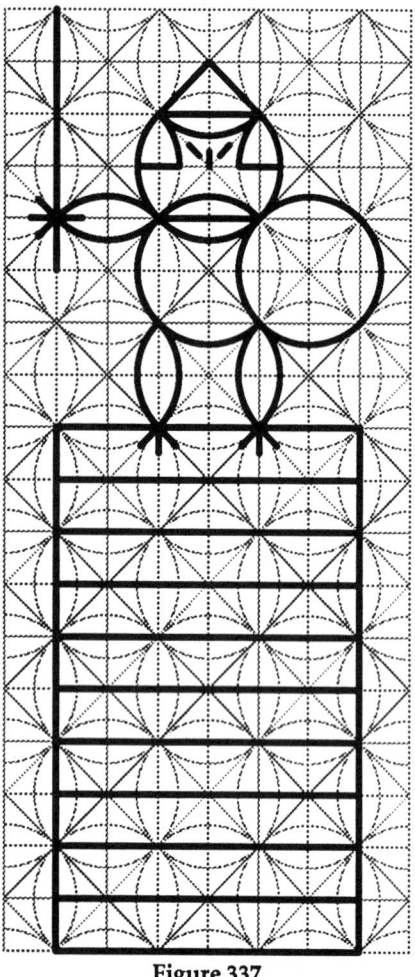

Figure 337

Figure 339

Figure 340

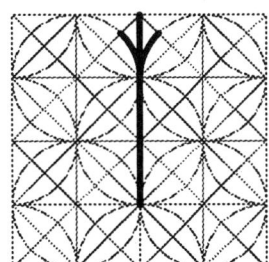

Figure 341

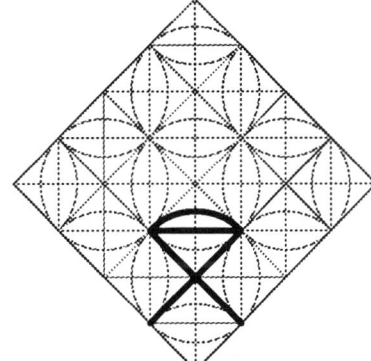

Figure 342

off.[30] In **Figure 336**, we see Queen Guinevere at her window. She wears the pointed head-dress worn by ladies of the thirteenth century. In **Figure 337**, we see a knight standing at the top of the steps of the castle. The visor of his helmet is up.

Arthur rode through the forest to a hut by a chapel, where "He laid his lance on the ground and leaned his shield against the wall, and then ungirded his sword and unlaced the top of his mailcoat."[31] We see his lance, his shield, and his sword in **Figure 338**. The lines of **Figure 339** show the top of his mailcoat unlaced. Recall your preliminary training as Eagles. Lines which are called a "beard" in one story can be referred to as an "unlaced mailcoat" in another story!

Arthur went into the hut, "pulling his horse behind him, though it could hardly get through the door."[32] The crowd in town at tax time kept Joseph and Mary from getting into the inn; they were lucky to get their donkey and themselves into the stable.[33] Satire? Parody? Inside the hut, Arthur found barley and meal, so he led his horse up, took off its bridle and closed the door.[34] Is the door to the hut the "gate" we previously considered? In **Figure 340**, you will see that the door (gate) to the hut is narrower than the horse, so the horse must squeeze through, cartoon-style. The barley is shown in **Figure 341**, and the meal is mounded up in the manger illustrated in **Figure 342**. In

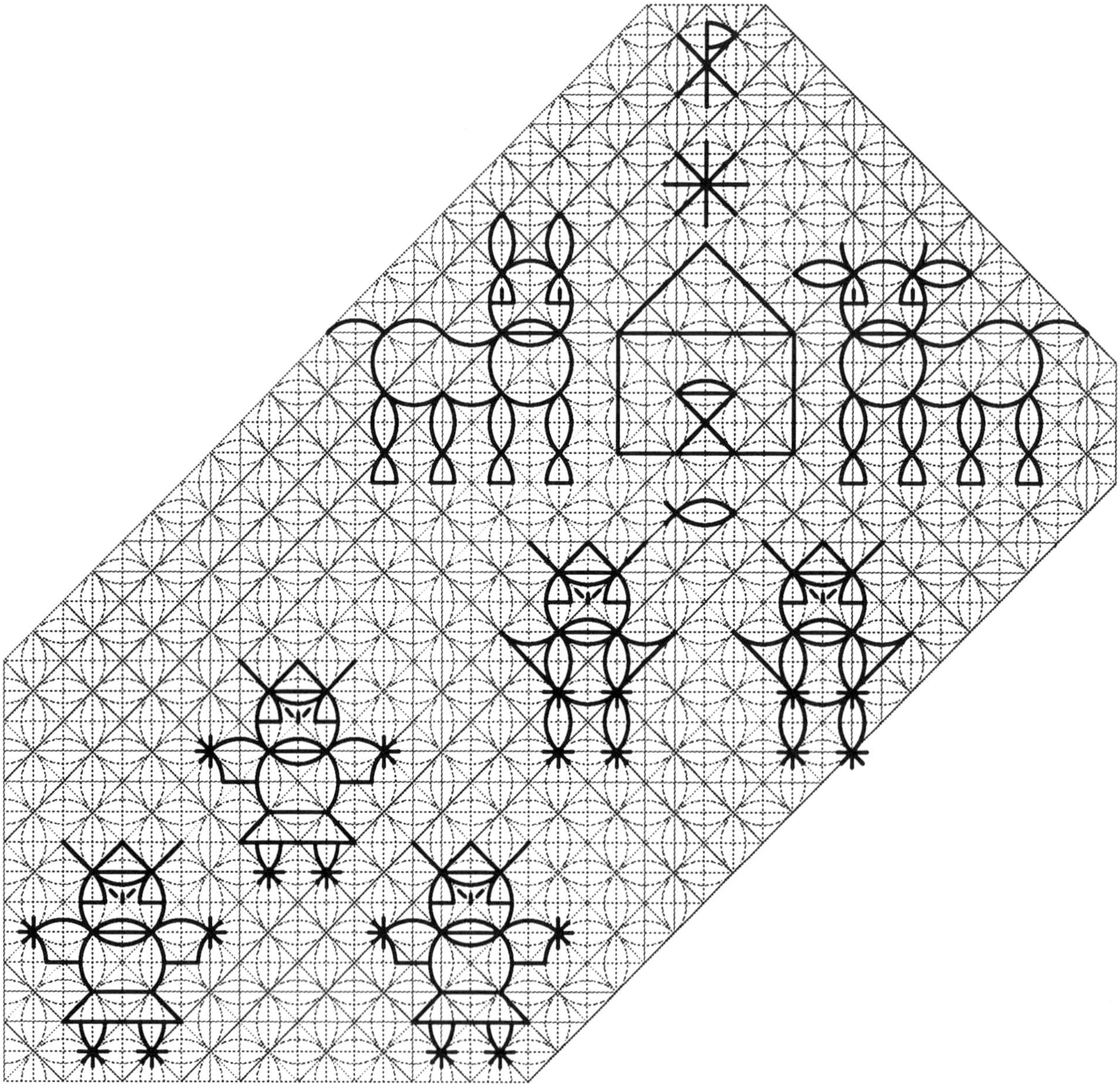

Figure 343

Figure 344

Figure 345

in reference to a cross which is shaped like the cross seen in the interference pattern and behind the heads of our Grail humanforms, as in Illustration 4-2, and in Figures 344 and 345.[35] We should note most carefully that piece of circumstantial evidence, which tends to indicate some relationship between the Christ story, the Holy Grail, the interference pattern, and the sun.

Arthur found the hermit nearly dead and lying in the little church in an open coffin, fully clothed.[36] **Figure 346.** "His beard flowed down as far as his belt and his hands were folded on his chest. He was

Figure 346

Figure 343, we see the manger in the stable. A donkey and a cow, and two angels wearing heavenly crowns stand outside the stable. The *vesica piscis* (Christian fish symbol) and *Chi Rho* Christogram tell us who lies in the manger in this stable. The Star of Bethlehem, in the form of the ancient Sumerian "star," "sun," or "god" symbol, stands over this stable. Three crowned Grail manforms approach the stable, over which stands the star symbol. In **Figure 344**, we see Baby Jesus lying in the manger. A stylized Christian halo in the form of the interference-pattern cross of light frames His head. In **Figure 345**, we see His mother and her earthly husband, as distinguished from the father of the Child, standing beside the manger, halo sun-crosses also framing their heads. And we hardly have begun analysis of *Perlesvaus*!

The Society For The Study Of Catharism, based primarily in France, still uses the term "sun-cross"

Figure 347   Figure 348   Figure 349   Figure 350

holding a cross to him and the figure of Christ was touching his lips."[37] The last passage illustrates just how graphically certain symbols can be seen on the Holy Grail. **Figure 347** shows the hermit's beard flowing down to his belt. **Figure 348** shows Grail manform "hands" (minus arms) folded on his chest. **Figure 349** shows the cross he was holding to him. **Figure 350** shows the figure of Christ (*Chi Rho*) held to his lips. Having seen these images separately, you should look at Figure 1 and picture them all together.

King Arthur "sat down on a seat which had been the hermit's" and listened while angels and demons disputed for the soul of the hermit.[38] **Figure 351** shows Arthur on the hermit's seat. The angels won, with the assistance of Our Lady, despite the fact that the hermit had been a robber and murderer in the forest for sixty-two years but a Christian hermit for only five.[39] Remember that

Perlesvaus was written so "the truth might be known of how knights and worthy men were willing to suffer toil and hardship to exalt the Law of Jesus Christ...." Two laws of Jesus Christ are that a man shall not kill his fellow man and shall not steal from him. The hermit did both, most of his life, but was protected from the demons, because he finally donned the cloth. So the immoral moral of this cameo is that thou mayest kill and steal until thy heart is content yet get into Heaven nonetheless if thou wilst but give all thy (stolen) possessions to the Church and wear the cloth for a few years before thy death? Was the purpose of the doctrine to talk people into being as good as possible for as long as possible? Or was the purpose of the doctrine for the

Figure 351

Figure 352

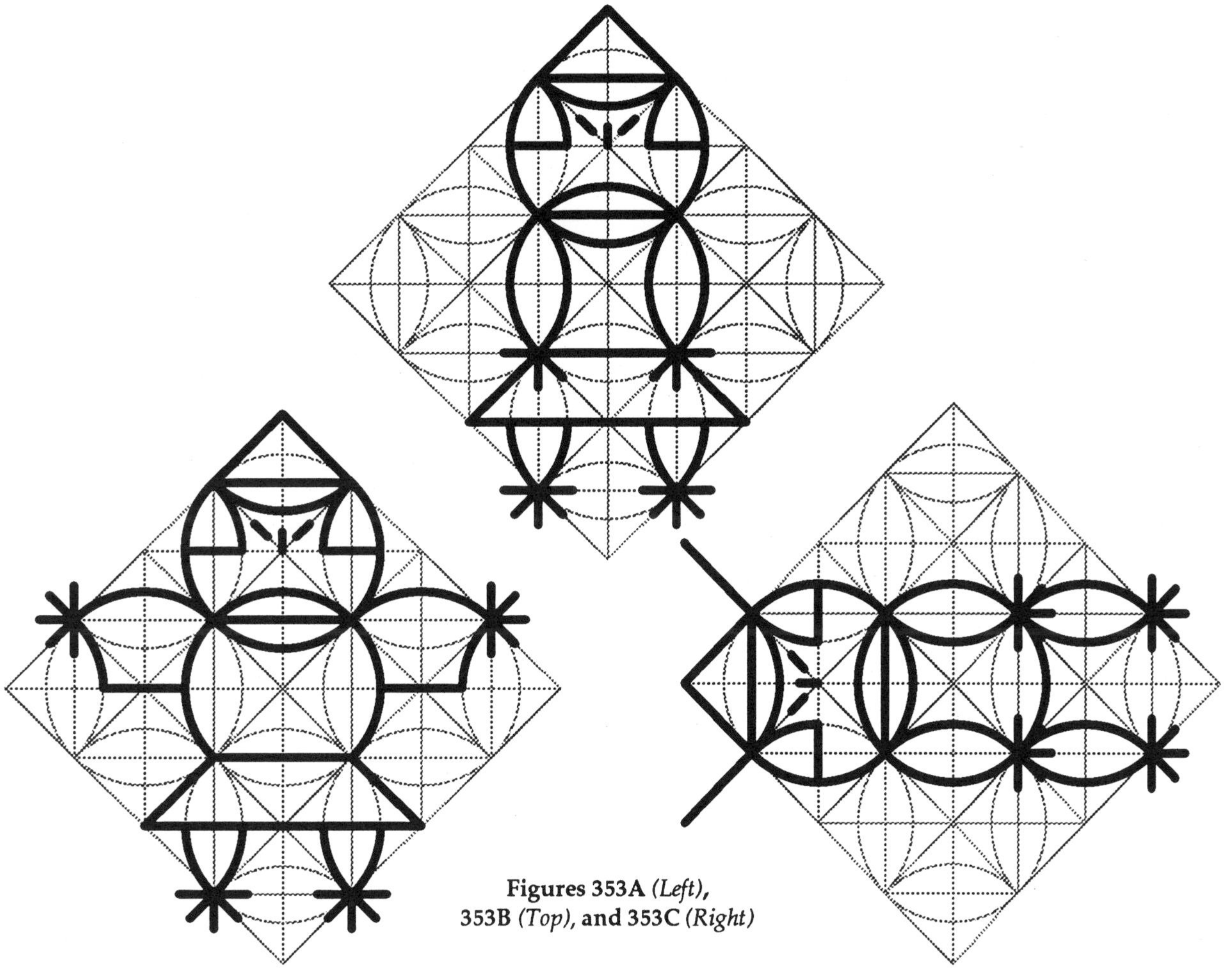

Figures 353A *(Left)*,
353B *(Top)*, and **353C** *(Right)*

Church to take the stolen goods of the thief in return for a promise of his salvation?

King Arthur rode on, coming "to one of the most beautiful glades ever seen, with a swing gate at the entrance."[40] Heaven, itself? Visualize the "swing gate" for yourself. He rode on to the Chapel of St. Augustine, "and it seemed to him that the hermit was dressed for mass."[41] **Figure 352.** Arthur watched from outside as the Mass was celebrated. Our Lady offered her Son to the officiating priest, who "placed him on the altar."[42] But, then, it seemed to Arthur "that the hermit was holding in his arms a man, bleeding from his side... hands and feet and crowned with thorns...." Then as Arthur looked again, he "thought he saw the man's body changed into the shape of the child that he had seen before."[43] Lines on the Holy Grail *do* appear so clearly as one thing, then so clearly as another, as the story unfolds. **Figures 353A, 353B,** and **353C** show the hermit holding a man in his arms. Treat those three drawings as successive frames of a home movie and

you see a priest lowering his arms to receive a man into his arms.

Arthur was excluded from the chapel while Mass was celebrated for the hermit who had been a robber and murderer for sixty-two years and a Christian hermit for five years because Arthur had sinned for three of his forty years.[44] But, then, Arthur had not taken the cloth!

The priest then told Arthur the tale of the questions unasked: "[A] great misfortune has recently befallen us because of a knight who was lodged at the house of the rich Fisher King. The Holy Grail appeared to him, with the lance whose iron head bleeds, but he did not ask what was done with it or who was served from it. And because he failed to ask these questions, all lands are now rent by war; no knight meets another in a forest but he attacks him and kills him if he can...."[45]

The questions unasked are one of the major enigmas of Grail quest stories. Here are some hypothetical answers to the question of what was done with the Holy Grail: Cathedrals were erected

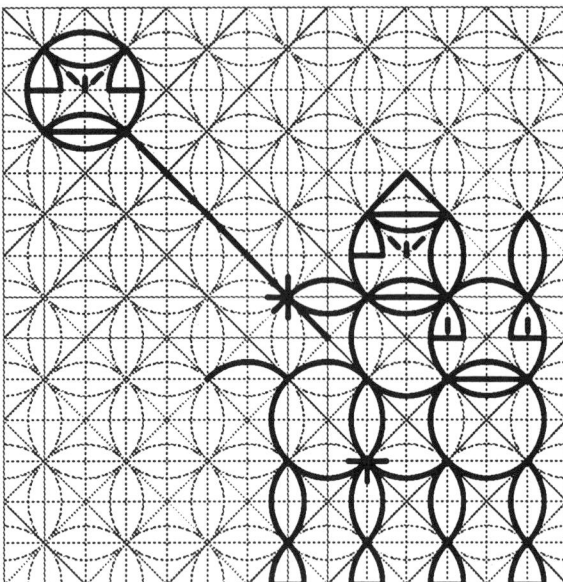

Figure 354

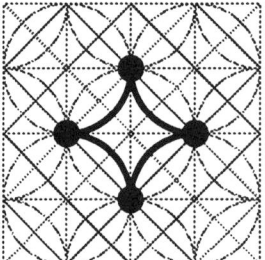

Figure 355

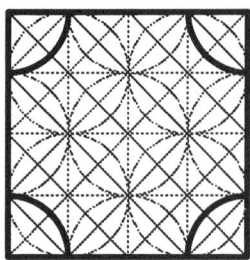

Figure 356

with it. Time was calculated with it in terms of hours, days, months, and years. Symbols and stories of many religions were derived from its lines, as were the initiation ceremonies of the Knights Templar, operative freemasons, and speculative freemasons. Here are some hypothetical answers to the questions of who was, and who was not, served by or from it: The actual body of God "in real presence" was not served from it. Stories derived from the Grail served the interests of the hierarchy of the Catholic Church, who used these stories to seize power over the minds and purses of the common folk. Why would warfare between knights have ceased if the questions had been asked? Hypothetical answer: Because Roman Catholic knights would not have gone about killing Cathar Christian knights to protect Roman Catholicism from the Cathar Christian heresy if they had known what the Cathar Christian knights knew about the origins of the Christian religion. No knight would kill another over lines scratched or painted on a rock, sewn into a piece of cloth, or drawn on a piece of paper.

Our first head-hunting scene next appears. Arthur rode into the forest, and was attacked by a knight with a flaming lance.[46] Pagan storm gods carried flaming lances, that is, lightning bolts. Arthur had ridden through a gate into the Otherworld. He had jousted with, and killed, the knight of the flaming lance.[47] The dead knight's companion knights arrived, and Arthur was beating a strategic retreat back toward the gate out of the perilous

glade when a damsel appeared, demanding that Arthur fetch her the dead knight's head. One of the companion knights had stuck the dead knight's head on his lance.[48] **Figure 354.** Arthur went back, and was asked, by the knight with the head, who had killed his companion.[49] Arthur answered that King Arthur had done so, but evaded the question of where King Arthur could be found.[50] He galloped through the gate into the safety of this world as another companion recognized him.[51]

The damsel bound Arthur's wounds with "blood from the knight's head which still flowed hot."[52] Tourists at Fort William Henry in upstate New York are horrified when told by the tour guides that Indian initiates to the cult of warriors drank the warm blood of their helpless captives when the fort fell to the French and Indians., How horrified would they be if they realized that their own European ancestors similarly were initiated into warrior cults in the not-so-distant past! How horrified would they be if they realized the origins of the Christian Eucharist! The use of the warm blood of victims as a magic potent was bad enough among pre-Christian warriors. How will you regard the blood of the Eucharist the next time you drink it?

The ancients, you remember, thought the blood of an animal contained the essential qualities of the animal.[53] Accordingly, if one ate or drank the blood of a sheep, he was in danger of becoming like a sheep. On the other hand, if one drank the blood of a god, then he would become like that god.[54] We can well imagine some ancient mother telling her young child to drink the blood of gods but not the blood of sheep because you are what you eat! You will recall our earlier discussion of the practices of the mystery religions in which the hearts of sacrificed children were eaten by celebrants either actually or symbolically in an effort to reacquire their youth.[55] Evidently, our author is familiar with human flesh and blood as magic potents. Arthur entered the Otherworld, and killed a pagan storm god, the

Illustration 22-1. The dome of Heaven, supported by four pendentives, with Lion and Ox on the dome, and Man and Eagle above. Courtesy of The Board of Trinity College, Dublin, and the Green Studio Ltd., Dublin.

knight of the flaming lance. The blood of the knight [god] when poured onto Arthur's wounds effects a miraculous cure. The damsel assured Arthur that he "would never have been cured without the blood of the knight."[56] Biting satire, sprung from the pen of a man presumed to have been a Templar!

Figure 357

Christians still profess to believe that they could not have been cured of their sins without the blood of Christ.

The damsel then proceeded to tell Arthur about the knight *Perlesvaus*, known, in English, as Perceval. It seems that near Perceval's childhood home "was a little chapel standing on four marble columns with a wooden roof. Inside was a little altar, and before the altar was a beautiful tomb on which was carved the figure of a man."[57] The four marble columns and domed roof are illustrated in **Figure 355**. Compare this image with **Illustration 22-1**, the dome of Heaven supported by the four columns of Heaven located at the four cardinal directions. Notice Lion and Ox on the dome, and Man and Eagle over it. The little altar is illustrated in **Figure 356**. The little altar represents the Earth under the dome of Heaven. The tomb on which was carved the figure of a man is illustrated in **Figure 357**. The damsel told Arthur that Perceval asked his father who lay in the tomb, and was told, "I have never heard of anyone who knew what lay within, save by what the letters on the tomb say: when the finest knight in the world comes here, the tomb will open and he will see what lies within."[58] The tomb-opening episode occurs later in *Perlesvaus*. We shall see the secret of the tomb.

Branch One of the story of *Perlesvaus* ends with Arthur's returning to his home, renewed by his travels, and promising to hold court as soon as possible.[59] Branch Two begins with his having

Figure 358

Figure 359

Figure 360

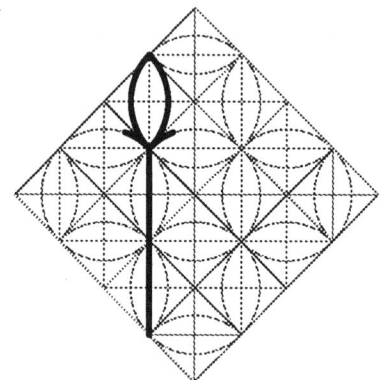

Figure 361

Figure 362

summoned his knights to court on St. John's day. He sat at the head of his table, upon which a cloth had been laid, and his butler served him with his "cup of gold."[60] Arthur appears at the head of his table in **Figure 358**. The cloth on the table appears, in top view, in **Figure 359**. His cup of gold appears in **Figure 360**. The floor "was strewn with rushes and flowers and wild mint...."[61] **Figure 361** portrays a rush. **Figure 362** portrays wild mint leaves or flowers.

While the assembly was awaiting the second course, three maidens entered the hall.[62] The first was riding a white mule with a "head-piece of gold and an ivory saddle...."[63] The head-piece of gold is bolded in **Figure 363**. The saddle appears in top view in **Figure 364**. "The maiden had a most comely body, though her face was not so fair, and she was clad in a rich silken gown, with a fine head-dress flowing all round her head.... And it was well that

her head was thus covered, for she was quite bald."[64] The typical cone-shaped ladies' headdress of that era appears in **Figure 365**. It is easy to picture her bald! You can clothe her. Her face *is* a mess! Your author has thought all along that some author should have commented on the facial features of our Grail humanform. Now, that has been done! A bald maiden? Mother Earth without her hair, i.e., the Earth barren of vegetation, wasted by the illness of the Fisher King?

We are told that "[h]er right arm was hung in a sling embroidered with gold, and her arms rested on the richest cushion ever seen, set about with little golden bells. And in her hands she held the head of a king, sealed with silver and crowned with gold."[65] **Figure 366** shows her arm in the sling. **Figure 367** shows the cushion and the little bells. **Figure 368** shows her arms on the cushion with the little bells. **Figure 369** shows the head of the crowned king in

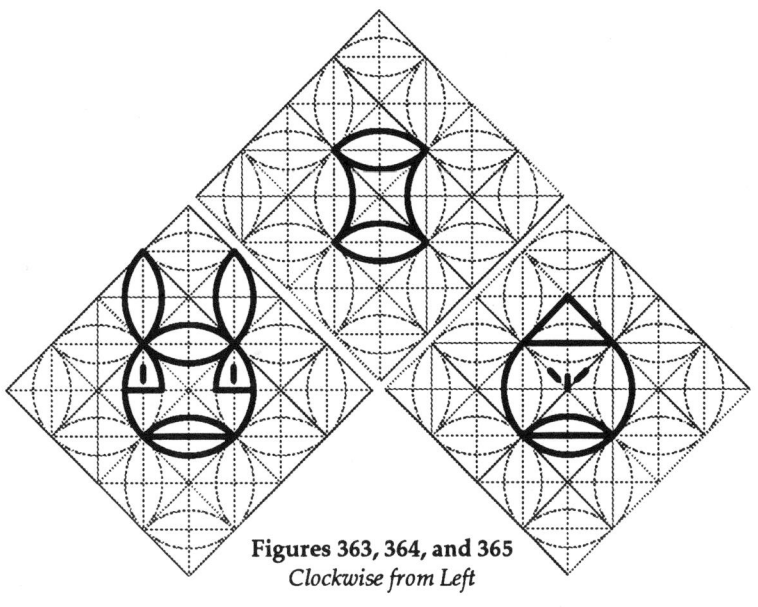

Figures 363, 364, and 365
Clockwise from Left

Figures 366, 367, 368, and 369
Clockwise from Left

Figure 370

Figure 371

her hands. The silver represents the moon; the gold the sun? Remember the gold and silver bowls in the story of the table?

The second maiden "rode like a squire, with a small wooden box tied behind her on which there sat a hunting-dog; and from her neck a shield hung... with a red cross...."[66] The box and hunting dog appear in **Figure 370**. The third maiden "wore a short skirt" and "carried a whip" with which she drove the mounts.[67] She, her short skirt, and her whip appear in **Figure 371**. The Dominicans and Franciscans often served as inquisitors to discover heretics and burn them at the stake.[68] Those two mendicant Roman Catholic orders often were portrayed as "hunting dogs," searching for and killing "wolves," i.e., heretics.[69] Is the hunting dog on the box an allegory for the inquisitor on his throne?[70] If so, then is the second woman the Church Militant? Who, then, is the third woman?

The first maiden told the assembly that the shield belonged to Joseph, the good soldier who took Jesus from the cross, and that she was giving it to Arthur "on these conditions: that you keep the shield for a knight who will come to collect it, and that you hang it on that pillar in the middle of the hall and keep it there; for none but he must take it down or hang it from his neck. With this shield he

will conquer the Grail, and he will leave another shield here, a red shield emblazoned with a white stag. And the hunting-dog that this maiden is carrying will stay here but will greet no-one until the arrival of the knight."[71] The key phrase is "With this shield he will conquer the Grail...." The shield is illustrated in **Figure 372**. Because we realize that the shield is covered with the *Chi Rho Christogram,* we will "conquer the Grail," that is, we will comprehend the relationship between the Holy Grail and the Christ story? Notice how many images of the Christ story appear in the Grail story presently under analysis. The author has changed from substitute images (knife instead of lance) to the actual images of the Christ story: Table. Cup. Mule. Whip. Cross. If we are correct about the stag (Christ) and hunting dog (inquisitor) allegories,

Figure 372

Figure 373

then are we being told that the Dominican or Franciscan hunting dog will recognize the Cathar knight as a true knight of Jesus Christ because he leaves behind the old shield of Christ (the stag) and takes with him the new shield of Christ (the *Chi Rho Christogram*)? Will the Roman Catholic inquisitor recognize the Cathar heretic as a knight in the true image of Christ? And will he let him walk away, carrying the new shield of Christ, instead of burning him at the stake (the pillar in the hall) as a heretic? Was our unknown author dreaming of the day when the Roman Catholic inquisitors would see the light and stop burning Cathars?

We again find the unasked questions: "This weakness has beset him [the Fisher King] because of the knight whom he lodged at his castle, and to whom the Grail appeared. Because the knight failed to ask who was served from it, all lands were engulfed by war; whenever a knight met another in a forest or glade they would do battle without any real cause."[72] The key words are "without any real cause." Think of all the human beings, men, women, and children, who were slaughtered through the years by wars and inquisitions conducted to protect the "purity" of the Roman Catholic faith. If our

hypothesis is correct that the Christian religion was born of the line forms on the Holy Grail, then those persons certainly died "without any real cause."

The maiden showed her bald head to the assembly, explaining that once she "had a beautiful head of hair" but "because he [the knight] failed to ask the question I am now bald, and my hair will not return until a knight goes and asks the question more properly, or goes and conquers the Grail."[73] If we have asked the question properly, and have conquered the Holy Grail, will this symbolic Earth maiden be able to regrow her tresses? Christianity taught us to rape the Earth by convincing us that God put plants and animals here for our use. Modern environmentalists understand the timeless wisdom of Native American and Native African sages who insist that we must preserve all aspects of the plant and animal ecological chains of which humans are only one part. We have raped this maiden too long, but it is not too late for her to regrow her tresses!

The maiden is called the "the maiden of the cart" because she next exposed before the assembly her cart full of the heads of knights who had died as result of the question's not having been asked. The cart had "a gold cross on top as long as the cart itself...."[74] Her cart and its contents symbolize all the human lives destroyed by the Church?

The maidens left the assembly with the cart of heads drawn by three stags (God the Father, Son, and Holy Ghost?) and proceeded into the forest, where they met Sir Gawain. The first maiden told him their story, and expressed hopes he would conquer the Holy Grail.[75] She asked Sir Gawain to escort her past a castle, and he agreed.[76] "They rode on until they came to a great valley. Sir Gawain looked down a wide defile, and there before him was a black castle enclosed by a great circular wall which was ugly indeed and ghastly.... He could see great halls loom up, and... a river flowing down from the peak of an ugly mountain and tumbling through the castle.... Sir Gawain saw the gateway, as ugly as the mouth of Hell, and from within came a great shouting and weeping with many people crying."[77] In **Figure 373**, we see the river flowing down from the mountain and through the castle. The City of Shurippak being flooded by Enlil? Roman Catholicism flooding the world? Knights on black horses rode forth from the castle and

Figure 374

speared heads from the maiden's cart onto the ends of their lances.[78] Sir Gawain defeated the knight with the shield of the golden eagle, then escorted the maidens away from the castle to a "big cross at the edge of the forest," where the maiden showed him the path he should take and they parted.[79] The maiden's cart of human heads is illustrated in **Figure 374.**

Sir Gawain rode on to Kamaalot, where he "came across a chapel standing on four marble columns, and inside was a beautiful tomb, which was wide open to view since the chapel had no walls."[80] Turn back to Figure 355, and to Illustration 22-1, which show a structure like the one the author wants us to visualize. The dome of Heaven over the hearth of Earth! Sir Gawain is told by the widow lady of the castle that the King of Castle Mortal "has designs on the lands of my brother the Fisher King, and the Holy Grail and the lance with the head that bleeds each day…."[81] We are told for the first time that the lance bleeds *each day.* We are not yet told *what time of day.* In Cathar thinking, the Holy Father in Rome was "Rex Mundi," king of the evil world, that is, Satan himself.[82] Is the Holy Father the "King of Castle Mortal"? Is the "widow lady," Our Lady? Some of the allegories in *Perlesvaus* are explained by our unknown author, but the question remains whether additional levels of allegory lie beneath the allegories that are explained; whether the "explanations" are

red herrings dragged across the plot to lead inquisitor "hunting dogs" off the track!

The news arrived that there was to be a great tournament in the vales of Kamaalot, and that the pavilions already were set up.[83] We are familiar with the image of pyramid-shaped tents or pavilions set up around a field. Of course, Sir Gawain acquitted himself well at jousting.[84] He then continued his quest.[85]

Sir Gawain rode on to several adventures, which we must omit to save space. He met the coward knight, who informed Sir Gawain that "nothing but ill comes of war,"[86] a lesson mankind should have learned by now! The coward knight told Sir Gawain why the maiden of the cart wears her arm in a sling: "With that hand she served from the Holy Grail the knight who came to the castle of the Fisher King but failed to ask what was done with the Grail. And because she held in that hand the precious vessel into which the hallowed blood drips from the point of the lance, she does not want to hold anything else in it until she returns to the holy house of the Grail."[87] Here we are informed, once more, that the blood did not drip from the head of the lance just once, when Jesus Christ died, but that it *continues to drip.* We were told previously that it *drips once daily.* The continuing aspect of the phenomenon will be explained soon.

Sir Gawain next arrived at the castle of the haughty maiden, where he was shown three tombs, one each for him, Sir Lancelot and Sir Perceval, and a fourth for the maiden, who told him that she "can have no joy of them while they are alive, but joy I shall have of them dead."[88] Surely, she represents the Church Militant, craving the death of her martyrs! Has she been in her own tomb for many years? The martyr craze has ended in the Catholic church, but she is not dead and buried. She has converted to Islam, and is alive and well!

After other adventures, which we must omit for lack of space, Sir Gawain arrived at the castle of the Fisher King, where he was denied admission unless he brought "the sword with which Saint John was beheaded."[89] The entrance to the castle was guarded by an assortment of critters and objects, which would make a nice extra-credit assignment for *A* students.[90] Sir Gawain saw priests and knights "look up at the sky, rejoicing, and it seemed as though they could see God and His mother on high."[91] On the Holy Grail? Among the constellations? As Wolfram von Eschenbach told us?

Sir Gawain then commenced his quest for the sword.[92] As he traveled, he came upon "a great tent with ropes of silk and pegs of ivory to fix them in the

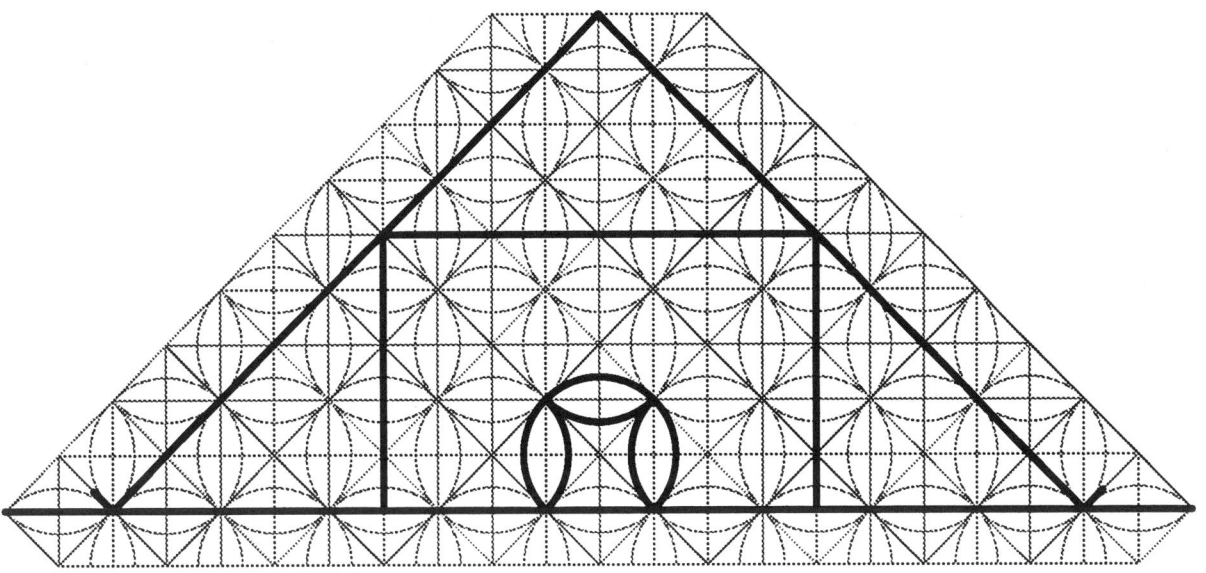

Figure 375

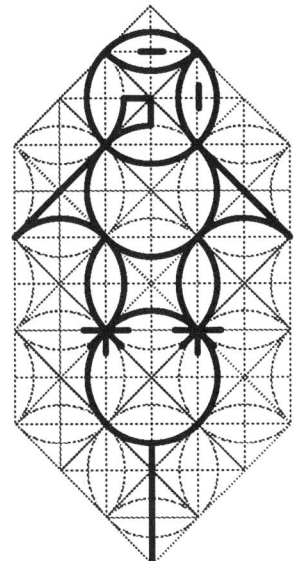

Figure 376

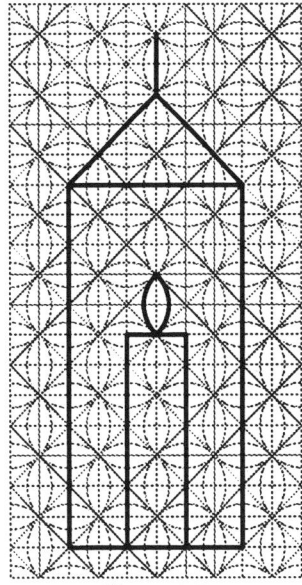

Figure 378

Figure 377

ground, and golden pommels on the tent-poles with an eagle of gold on top of each."[93] The Tabernacle and Tent of the Presence? The tent, its ropes, and pegs appear in **Figure 375**. An eagle on a pommel is illustrated in **Figure 376**. He looked into the tent and saw a rich couch at the head of which lay two pillows.[94] He saw "on either side of the head of the couch... an ivory chair with cushions of gold cloth... and at the foot of the couch hung a golden candlestick which held a great candle."[95] One chair and its cushion is shown in **Figure 377**, in side view. The hanging golden candlestick and its great candle is shown in **Figure 378**. "A table had been set in the

Figure 379

middle of the tent; of ivory it was, and edged with gold and precious stones, and a cloth had been laid upon it with a silver trencher and knives of ivory handles and rich golden plate."[96] You set the table. Use a top view of the table top. Place the cloth, then the silver trencher (plate), then the knife. "Then the dwarf brought two silver basins and a white towel...."[97] "Just then two boys came in bearing

Figure 380

wine and food for the table.... They lit two great candles in golden candlesticks and then left straightway."[98] Finding these suppertime images should be easy for you by now.

The maidens of the tent wanted Sir Gawain to have more than a meal and conversation with them, but he refused, to retain his virginity, in an effort to see the Holy Grail.[99] Because he refused, he had to fight his way out of the situation.[100] Christian knights, Roman Catholic or Cathar, were supposed to make war, not love!

Sir Gawain next entered a "rich and pleasant land bounded by a huge wall" which had "but one gate."[101] Recall our "gate" analysis of the Book of the Shepherd of Hermas. "The land was no more than three leagues wide, but in the middle stood a great tower upon a rock, and at the top of the tower a crane had built its nest."[102] Recall that the true Christian church is the "tower," and Jesus Christ is both the "gate" and the "rock." The rock, the tower built on it, and the crane's nest at the top of the tower are illustrated in top view in **Figure 379**. We see the crane in **Figure 380**. Cranes are fish-eating birds. The original Christians were fishers of men. The Fisher King is Jesus Christ? Who is the crane? The crane has captured the true Christian Church from the Fisher King? Cathar Catholics, rather than Roman Catholics, are the rightful successors to the original Christian fishers of men because Cathar Christians, like original Christians, believe in a poor church serving the temporal and spiritual needs of poor people? If the "fish" are mankind, then is our presumably-Templar author saying that the crane is the Holy Father in Rome, who has nested on the true Christian Church and is feeding on mankind? Is this the intended allegory? It is an allegory that is consistent with Cathar beliefs!

Sir Gawain "left his shield and lance outside and then climbed up the stairs to the hall" to meet the King of the Watch.[103] You should find those images for yourself. The king knew Sir Gawain was on a quest for the sword with which Saint John was beheaded, and told Sir Gawain he could not leave his land "until a year had passed."[104] However, Sir Gawain promised he would return through the king's land with the sword, and the king, wishing to see the sword, let Sir Gawain go.[105]

"[J]ust on the hour of midday he [Sir Gawain] came across a fountain set about with marble; shaded by the forest it was, as if by a bower, and rich pillars of marble stood all around inlaid with bands of gold and precious stones, and from the central pillar hung a vessel of gold on a silver chain. And in the

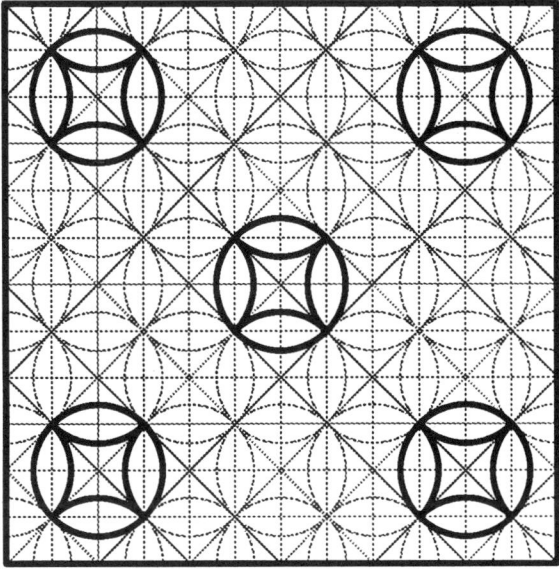

Figure 381

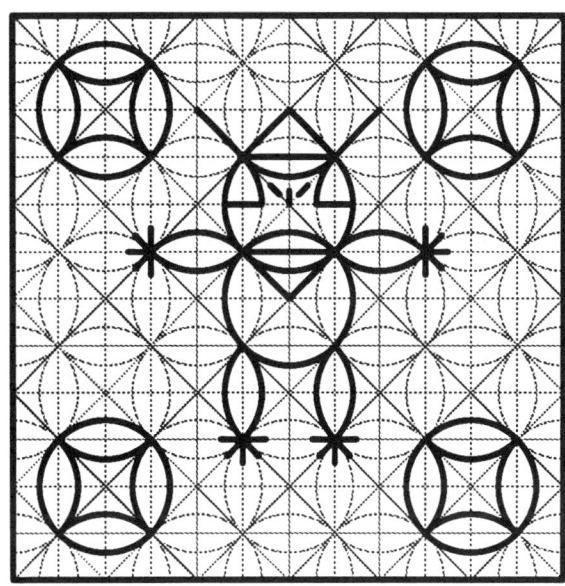

Figure 383

Figure 382

plunged into the water and vanished. Gawain dismounted, but just as he went to take hold of the golden vessel a voice cried out: 'You are not the good knight who is served from the vessel and cured by it.' Sir Gawain drew back and saw a priest come up to the spring: a young man he was, dressed in white robes, and with his arm in a sling, and he was holding a square golden vessel. He walked up to the vessel which hung from the marble pillar and looked inside; then he rinsed the vessel he was holding and poured what he found in the other into his own. Just then three maidens of the most fabulous beauty appeared, all draped in white robes with white drapes to cover their heads; one of them carried bread in a vessel of gold, another brought wine in a vessel of silver. They came up to the golden vessel which hung from the pillar and in it they placed their offerings. And after sitting awhile at the foot of the pillar they began to walk back, but as they went, it seemed to Sir Gawain that there was but one of them, and he wondered much at this miracle. He went after the priest who bore the other vessel, and said... [w]here are you taking that golden vessel and whatever it holds? 'To the hermits,' he replied, 'who live in this forest, and to the good knight who lies sick at the house of his uncle, the Hermit King.'"[106] In **Figure 381**, we see the fountain in top view. In **Figure 382**, we see, in side view, the jewelled central marble pillar of the fountain, representing the world axis, and the golden vessel hanging on the silver chain. In **Figure 383**, we see the statue in the middle of the fountain. The statue

middle of the fountain stood a statue so finely sculpted that it seemed alive. The moment that Sir Gawain appeared before the fountain, the statue plunged into the water of the fountain and vanished just at the moment Sir Gawain appeared before the fountain, which was "just on the hour of midday." Those readers who are not Roman Catholic, or who have never seen a priest bless the holy water, need to be told that the priest holds a candle over the water, says the proper words, then plunges the candle into the water. The act is symbolically sexual. The candle is male; the water female. Thus, the water is activated for holy use (blessed) by the ceremony. Is our author's fountain performing holy magic? Christ is plunged into the water to make it holy water? Is the fountain changing plain bread and wine into a holy substance to be used in magic ceremonies to cure ills, as does the Holy Magic of the Mass? Religious art often has portrayed Christ as a fountain; as the fountain of life.[107]

But we have not as yet answered the question of why the statue (the Christ form?) plunged into the fountain precisely at noon. Is the reason the same reason why the sword with which Saint John was beheaded "bleeds each day at noon"?[108] Yes, the sword bleeds at noon and the statue plunges into the water at noon. Both are the noon mark? Is it just that simple? If you drive a staff into the ground pointing absolutely vertically, it will "impale" the light of the sun just at the moment of noon, that is, the light of the sun will spread out on the ground evenly around your sun lance. Your sun lance will "bleed" at noon, i.e., sunlight will flow down all sides of it rather than some of its sides being in shadow. If, instead, you watch the sun's image on water, the image of the sun will "plunge" into the water just as the sun reaches noon. Has our unknown author told us something important? Has he told us that, in his opinion, Jesus Christ and Saint John the Baptist are in some respect related to the ancient concept of sacrificial kings who died so that the sun might live? Could this possibly be correct?

We moderns cannot even begin to comprehend the fear of the ancients that the sun would not "rise" in the morning. We still speak, in the vernacular, about the sun's "rising" each morning, although we are perfectly aware that what really has happened is that the Earth has rotated on its axis once in approximately twenty-four hours and our side of the Earth again is facing the central sun. Translations of ancient texts leave us no doubt that the common man of ancient times was told that the sun traveled across the Heavens while the Earth stood still. For instance, the Egyptian man-in-the-street evidently believed the sun was "born" each morn-

Figure 384

ing and "died" each night, so that on the next morning, it should arise from the dead and be born again.[109] Under such a system of thought, it is obvious that the sun starts to "die" after reaching its highest point in the sky at noon. Thus, noon is a point at which a sacrifice must be offered to assure that the sun will be born again? The sword with which Saint John was beheaded "bleeds each day at noon, because that was the hour when they cut off that good man's head."[110] In Saint John's case, however, do not worry about the death of a human being to assure another day of sunshine. We are, once more, concerned with a story on the Holy Grail. **Figure 384** shows our Grail manform with his head being cut off by a sword. A legend suffices to keep the sun's chariot rolling? No need, any more, for a human being actually to die? It's called progress. And what of the death of Jesus Christ? He reputedly died at Hebrew Passover, a Spring festival, honoring the Spring Equinox, that is, at the time of the year at which the *day* again becomes equal to the *night* in length of hours. For many years, people in the Middle East had celebrated during the Spring Equinox a New Year's festival during which a false king, usually a convicted criminal, was crowned king for the day, then sacrificed to assure a good planting season.[111] But we must not wander too far from our story about Sir Gawain's quest for the sword with which Saint John was beheaded.

King Gurgaran had the sword.[112] His son had been carried off by a giant.[113] Sir Gawain found out that the king had offered the sword to anyone who would rescue his son and kill the giant.[114] Sir Gawain went to the king's castle and saw the sword. "[T]he king drew the sword from its sheath, and out it came, bleeding, for it was then noon, and he bade that it be held before Gawain until that hour had

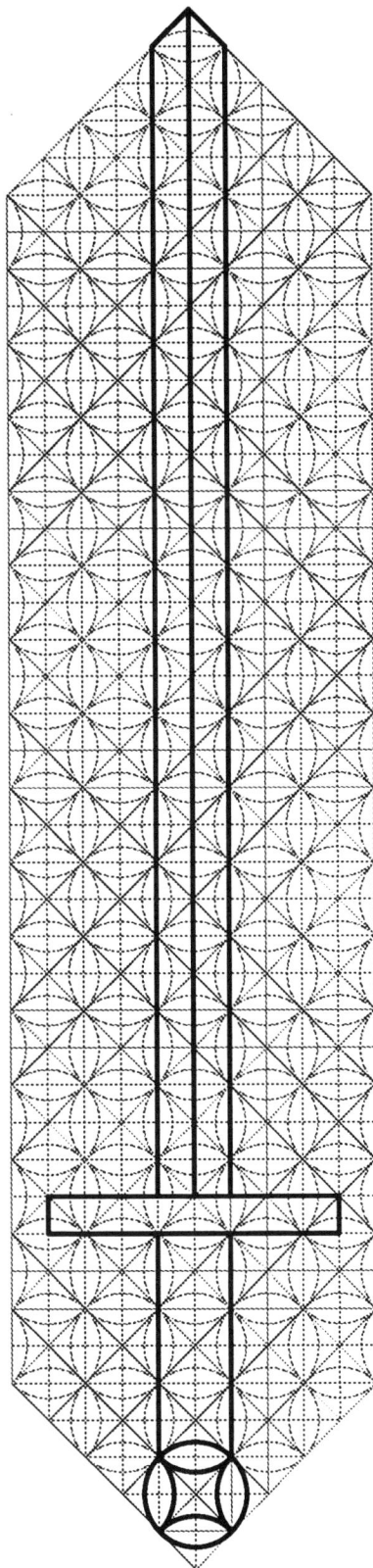

Figure 385

passed. Thereupon the sword became as bright and green as emerald."[115] Of course it glows like an emerald. It has an emerald on its hilt! **Figure 385.**

Sir Gawain rode to "a great high mountain" where the giant lived, "and the entrance to his mountain home was so narrow that a horse could not pass through."[116] Those are familiar words! Sir Gawain had to leave his horse and continue on foot. The giant saw Sir Gawain, "seized a great ax lying beside him, and strode towards Gawain ready to strike, aiming to deal him a two-handed blow full on the head."[117] The giant strangled the king's son to death before Sir Gawain was able to thrust his sword through the giant's heart and cut off his head.[118] Sir Gawain carried the king's dead son to the king.[119]

The king and his men lamented the death of the king's son, then the king "bade that a great fire be kindled in the middle of the city, and had his son placed in a brass vessel full of water to be cooked and boiled over the fire, while the giant's head was hung above the gate. And when his son's flesh was cooked, he had it cut up into the smallest pieces possible, and summoned all the people of his land and gave each one a piece until all the flesh was gone."[120] How could any father do that with his dead son, you are asking yourself? Is that precisely the question our presumably-Templar author wanted us to ask? Would God the Father really have offered the flesh of His Son to the people of the world to eat? Recall that heretical Christians, such as Cathars, did not believe that God appeared on Earth in human flesh. They considered Jesus Christ a holy prophet, at most; an optical illusion, at least. They did not believe in the Eucharist. The line between Roman Catholic heretics like the Cathars and the early founding fathers of the Protestant Reformation is not as distinct as many Christians might prefer it to be.[121] Protestants continue the ritual of eating God, but say that they do this to remember Him rather than to absorb into their bodies the magical essence of His flesh and blood. Progress toward civilization. But, then, so was the Roman Catholic Mass progress toward civilization because bread and wine were used in lieu of the actual human flesh and blood employed by some of the mystery religions and by some of the early sects of Christianity. Have faith in humanity. We shall yet prevail against our masters and ourselves!

Sir Gawain kept his word to the king of the watch by going to the king's castle on his way to the Fisher King with the sword.[122] The king of the watch demanded the sword, saying that he was "descended from the king (Jesus Christ?) who beheaded (replaced as leader of the Christian faith?) Saint John," and that he had more right to the sword than Sir Gawain, but agreed to let Sir Gawain carry it away provided he would "grant to the first maiden who has a request of him whatever she asks, no matter what it might be."[123] Poor Sir Gawain! Did he have to make love not war?

Sir Gawain rode with the sword to the castle of enquiry, where he asked, *inter alia*, about the fountain in the forest, and was told, by the priest, "I will tell you no more than you have heard — and you should be thankful for that much — for no-one should reveal the secrets of the Saviour; they should be kept secret by him to whom they are entrusted."[124]

Is your intelligence being insulted by my continuing to bold lines of the Holy Grail to illustrate images? Have you long-since developed the skill to do it for yourself? O.K., then lead yourself through the story of the appearance of the Holy Grail to Sir Gawain, without my bolding for you a single line.

Sir Gawain rode past the magnificent tomb whose contents remain unknown — because a voice cried out to him, "Do not touch the tomb, for you are not the knight by whom it shall be known who lies within."[125] He crossed the Bridge of the Needle, which appeared to be too narrow for him to cross, but which widened itself to allow him to pass.[126] Is this a reference to the Bridge of the Separator — a tenet of the Zoroastrian faith? "Then he looked at the gate ahead of him, and there he saw depicted Our Lord on the cross, with His mother on one side and Saint John on the other.... And on the right he saw a beautiful angel, his finger pointing to the chapel of the Holy Grail. He had a precious stone in the middle of his chest, and letters written above his head saying that the lord of the castle was as pure and clean of all sins as the jewel. Just then Gawain saw at the gateway a huge and terrible lion, standing there on all fours, but as soon as it saw Sir Gawain it lay down on the ground, and he passed by quite freely. He arrived at the castle and dismounted, and leaving his lance and shield propped against the wall he climbed up the marble steps and entered a most magnificent and beautiful hall, set all around with images of gold. And in the middle he found a rich, high couch, at the foot of which there was a beautiful chess-board, finely wrought, and a golden cushion full of precious stones,... but the chessmen were not set up.... [W]ater was brought in two basins to wash his face and hands.... He saw that the night was very dark, but that there in the hall, without candles, it was as bright as if the sun had been shining, and he wondered to himself where the light could be coming from.... [T]hey led him to the chamber where the Fisher King lay, which seemed to be strewn with grass and flowers. The king was lying in a bed hung on cords... and on his head he wore a sable hat covered with red samite and blazoned with a cross of gold. His head rested on a pillow... with... a jewel... set at each corner...."[127] That passage was a comprehensive test of your Grail skills, and you passed the test easily, did you not?

The Fisher King's hat is a pointed cap, as worn by elves in many European children's stories, including the tales about Saint Nick. Our Grail manform certainly has a big belly, like a bowl full of jelly! Could it be that both Christmas stories, the Christ story and the story of Santa Claus, were born of the Holy Grail?

The next sentence contains a substantial clue. "And there in the room stood a pillar of copper, and on it an angel sat, holding a golden cross on which there was a piece of the real cross where God was crucified, as big as the cross of gold itself...."[128] If we assume that the "cross of gold" is without substance, because it consists of lines on the Holy Grail, then would it not follow that "the real cross where God was crucified" also would have been without substance? Is this what we are being told? Such a view certainly would be consistent with Cathar beliefs that Calvary was an illusion rather than a reality.[129]

Gawain gave the sword with which Saint John was beheaded to the Fisher King, who "took the sword and held it to his lips and face, kissing it very gently...."[130] The Fisher King implores Sir Gawain to remember to ask the questions when the Grail appears.[131]

The Grail then appeared to Sir Gawain. "Just then two maidens appeared from a chapel: in her hands one was carrying the Holy Grail, and the other held the lance with the bleeding head.... Sir Gawain gazed at the Grail and thought he saw therein a chalice... and he saw the point of the lance from which the red blood flowed, and he thought he could see two angels bearing two golden candlesticks with candles burning."[132] Notice that the Holy Grail is not here described as a chalice; rather, as an object in which Sir Gawain thought he saw a chalice. The maidens left the room, went into a chapel, then returned from the chapel and passed in front of Sir Gawain again.[133] "And he thought he saw three angels where before he had seen but two, and there in the centre of the Grail he thought he could

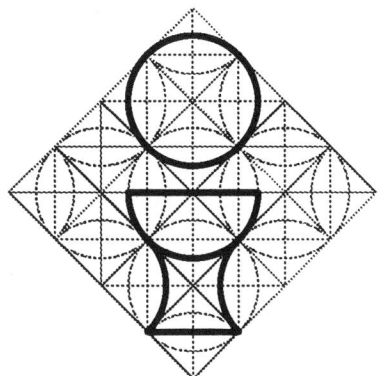

Figure 386

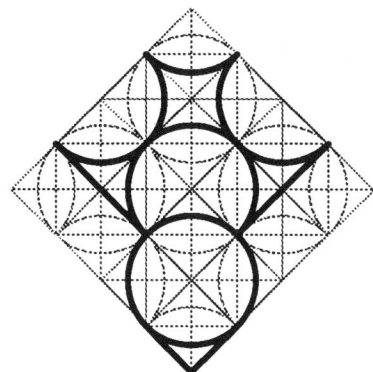

Figure 387

see the shape of a child."[134] Our Grail humanform does look like a fat little baby! The foremost knight in attendance cried out, attempting to get Sir Gawain to remember to ask the questions, but Sir Gawain's eyes and thought were on what he perceived to be three drops of blood, which moved away from him when he tried to kiss them.[135] The two maidens then made their final pass before the table, "and to Sir Gawain it seemed that there were three; and looking up it appeared to him that the Grail was high up in the air. And above it he saw, he thought, a crowned king nailed to a cross with a spear thrust in his side...."[136] Again, the foremost knight cried out for Sir Gawain to speak, but Sir Gawain remained silent, "hearing nothing of what the king had said."[137] Thus, Gawain failed to ask the questions, and left the castle by the road taken by those who similarly had failed to speak.[138]

The allegory of the questions unasked now should be clear to us. The solemn ceremonies of the Roman Catholic church are some of the best drama ever performed. A person need not have been raised as a Roman Catholic to be speechless at the end of the Mass. The pageantry and drama of the Mass fill up our senses and shift our reasoning powers into neutral; much as we become bereft of reason, yet supercharged with emotion, when we are in the presence of a person with whom we anticipate the pleasures of sexual intercourse. However, after we have seen the cup of the Mass with the wafer (Host) of the Mass suspended above it, as in **Figure 386**; after we have seen the dove, representing the Holy Ghost, descending to effect the holy magic of the Mass, as in **Figure 387**; after we have seen the celebrant with bell in one hand and crozier in the other, as in **Figure 388**, might we not want to ask a few questions? If our minds are not ossified by dogma or paralyzed by emotions, might we not wonder whether we have seen on the

Holy Grail the very origins of this high and holy magic? Had the questions been asked, Roman Catholic and Cathar Catholic knights might have found something else to fight about, but it is unlikely they would have continued fighting about lines of a drawing!

The unknown author of *Perlesvaus* believed that if Roman Catholics had known the origin of the Christ story on the Holy Grail, they would have renounced Roman Catholicism and would have accepted the Cathar-Templar view that the man called Jesus was, at most, a prophet, rather than God incarnate? Saint John Christians still believe that Jesus Christ was a *false* prophet, and that John the Baptist was the *true* Holy Prophet of God.[139] The Templars evidently were affected to some extent by the beliefs of the Saint John Christians.[140] Recall the opinion of Eusebius, a principal founding father of the Christian church, that the very first Christians

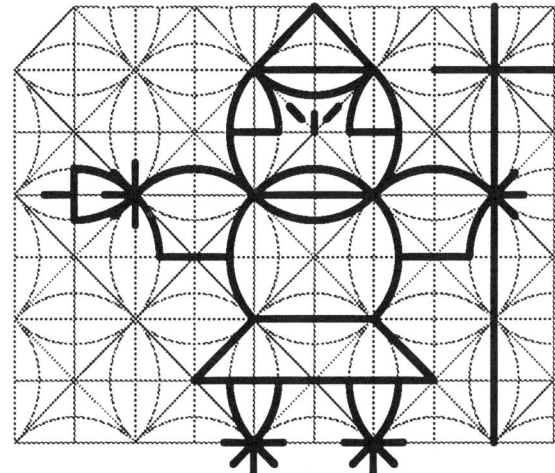

Figure 388

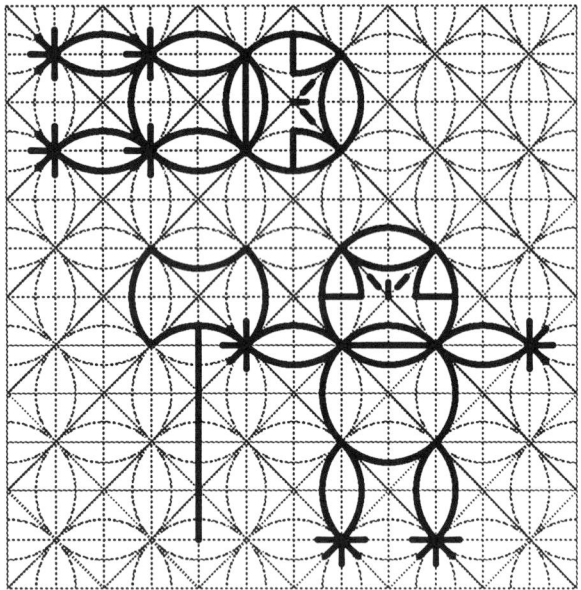

Figure 389

Figure 390

wrote the Gospels as allegory rather than as history.[141] Who has misled whom as to what, and why? So priests can tell their flocks that Roman Catholicism is founded in fact whereas all the other religions are founded in mythology?

What is the significance of Sir Gawain's chess games, which he played alone after he failed to ask the questions? The gold pieces countered his moves of the ivory pieces and checkmated him twice.[142] No man can win against his fate as decreed by God? Predestination? Is this chessboard related to the Hindu concepts of space and sacred dance which we studied previously?

Sir Lancelot's adventures in the Waste City will be understood by students of comparative religion. Many cultures, including some which survived into the last century, had "kings" who reigned but did not rule; who were pampered and adored for a period of time, then sacrificed, supposedly for the good of the tribe.[143] The sins of the tribespeople often were transferred to these persons immediately before they were sacrificed.[144] The idea behind this practice apparently was that individual and collective guilt could be borne away in this manner.[145] Christian true believers seem shocked when they discover that the concept of a king who dies to save mankind from its sins was not unique to Christianity. Long before anyone ever used the term "Christian," the ancient Hebrews distinguished themselves by substituting a goat for a

human being; thus, the term "scapegoat."[146] The later Hebrews further distinguished themselves by driving the scapegoat bearing the sins of the tribe into the desert, rather than sacrificing it.[147] One more signal victory of humanism over religion.

When Sir Lancelot rides into the Waste City, he finds a richly-clad knight holding a huge axe, who says that Lancelot must cut off his head with the axe or he must cut off Lancelot's head.[148] Lancelot suggests that the best alternative would be neither of those choices, but the knight says that the one alternative or the other must occur.[149] Lancelot pledges that he will return to the Waste City a year from that day, at or before the hour he chops off the knight's head, to offer his head as sacrifice, freely, and without contest, just as the knight offered his.[150] The knight refers to himself as "he who must go before the Saviour of the world."[151] Saint John the Baptist? Lancelot accepts the pledge, cuts off the knight's head, then rides out of town.[152] When he looks back, "he could see neither the body of the knight nor his head, and he could not think what had become of them."[153] What had become of them was that they had faded from view, as do all images on the Holy Grail?

We tend to use the word "victim" when thinking of humans who were sacrificed because we, of this generation, cannot imagine anyone's volunteering for the job. We must accept the fact that many persons *did* volunteer to be human sacrifices, to gain or protect honor or to enjoy the wonderful afterlife they believed they would enjoy as result of the gift of their lives.[154] Is our author making sure that we have not overlooked the parallel between these sacrificial "kings" and Jesus Christ, King of the Jews?

The knight awaiting sacrifice is seen lying on his back in **Figure 389**, as Sir Lancelot stands over him carrying the large axe. Is our author expressing the opinion that the human sacrifice scenario in the Story of Stories is as much a fantasy as that of Lancelot in the Waste City? Such a view certainly would be in accord with Cathar theology.

A short sequence of words pertaining to the Hermit King offers us another valuable clue. We are told that the Hermit King rode forth on his white mule whose forehead was marked with a red cross.[155] The hermit astride the mule is illustrated in **Figure 390**. The translation then reads: "The good scribe Josephus tells us that this mule had belonged to Joseph of Arimathea when he was a soldier of Pilate, and that he had passed it on to King Pelles."[156] That is one *very* old mule, if you think about those words for just a moment! We already have learned that storytellers often use exaggeration to make sure that even the most gullible reader realizes that mythology, rather than history, is being written. Does our unknown author mean to suggest that the Grail humanform on the Grail muleform might have been known in a story as Joseph of Arimathea, and later known, in another story, as King Pelles? Does it not follow, then, that the Grail humanform on the Grail muleform also might have been known, in even earlier stories, as Mary, the mother of Jesus, or as Jesus Christ?

Our author does not want to run any risk that we will overlook the parallel between the life of Christ and the lives of other sacrificial kings. Lancelot rides into a burning city, and is offered the kingship of the city if he will agree to extinguish the flames after the passage of a year by throwing himself into the fire.[157] He declines the honor, and a dwarf accepts the crown and the fate.[158] Lancelot's procession into the city, while the city dwellers still think he would accept the crown, might remind you of the entry of another sacrificial king into another town in another story.[159]

Nearly everyone who knows anything about Grail stories realizes that Sir Lancelot never saw the Holy Grail because he refused to renounce his love for King Arthur's wife, Queen Guinevere.[160] Lancelot represents Man? If so, does Gawain represent

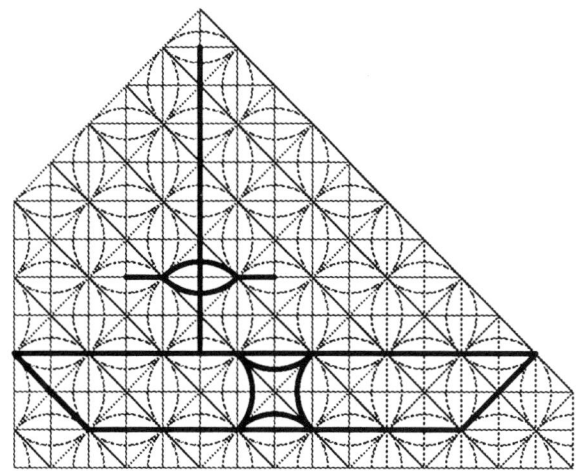

Figure 391

Ox and Perceval represent Eagle? The images Lancelot encounters during his entry into the Grail Castle are familiar to us, and nothing of value would be gained by repeating them here.[161] Lancelot tells the Fisher King that Perceval "goes under many disguises, and conceals his name in many parts."[162] We surely have learned by now that our Grail manform goes under many disguises, and conceals his name among the lines of the Holy Grail. Perceval is referred to as "the knight who has caused you such pain and hardship, but who has now set you free."[163] Free to fly like an Eagle above the trials and tribulations of Lions, Oxen, and Men? What pain? Pain like Odin suffered while hanging on the tree as a sacrifice to himself? We were told that Odin improved himself by his self-sacrifice. We improve ourselves through self-sacrifice? As did Jesus? The Jesus allegory teaches the value of self-sacrifice in reaching the goal of self-improvement? Does this sound more like an initiation into speculative freemasonry than a baptism into the Christian church?

In a cameo referred to as "The Mysterious Ship," we are told of Perceval's arrival by ship to claim the shield hanging on the pillar at Camelot. "The craft was draped in the middle with the finest silken cloth, and the sail was lowered because the sea was so calm and still."[164] **Figure 391**. Perceval takes down from the pillar the shield bearing the cross and leaves his red shield emblazoned with the white stag.[165] The dog that the maiden left with the shield gave Perceval a joyous welcome, and left with him on the ship.[166] Remember that the white stag was at one time as much a symbol of Jesus Christ as was the Cross. Perceval, the self-made knight,[167] left by ship accompanied by the mendi-

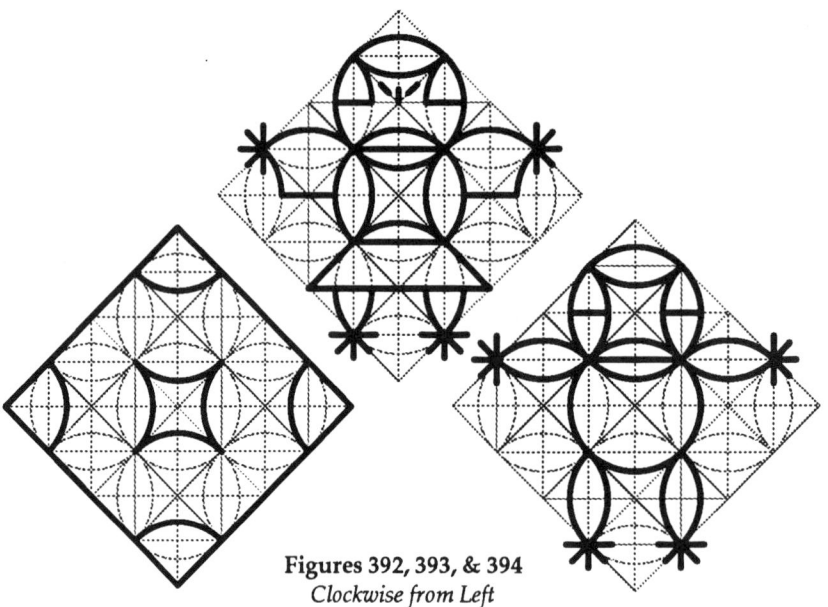

Figures 392, 393, & 394
Clockwise from Left

cant hunting dog[168] and they went away together to found the poor church of which all European self-made "heretics" had dreamed for generations?[169]

Clues dropped among the story lines might lead us to conclude that Perceval does as the author of *Perlesvaus* believed that Christ Jesus did, even if we reject the suggestion that Perceval is playing the role of Jesus, arisen and come again. Perceval stayed three nights at one place — as the moon stays gone from view for three days, then seemingly arises from the dead and ascends into Heaven, there to sit at the right hand of the sun.[170] He is encountered by persons who fail to recognize him.[171] He commits no carnal sin, but is pure, chaste and innocent of excess.[172] Persons grieve that they cannot find him and be his companion.[173] Elsewhere, throughout the stories, Perceval's resemblances to the hero of the Christ story are listed to aid our comprehension of the allegory. When Sir Gawain finds Sir Perceval at the Tournament on the Crimson Heath, Sir Perceval has changed his arms to all-white, and Sir Gawain again fails to recognize him.[174] Sir Perceval is a knight in white who is "the finest knight in the world"; who will be found by Sir Gawain "only with the greatest toil."[175]

Another clue is dropped in the story of the Circle of Gold. It would appear that the queen of the Castle of the Circle of Gold has the crown of thorns which was worn by Christ on the Cross, and that she has had it set in gold and precious stones.[176] Once a year, knights and their ladies come to worship it.[177] According to the story, it will be won by the knight who first beheld the Holy Grail — that knight being Perceval.[178] If Perceval is not playing the role of the arisen Christ, he certainly seems to be an adequate Christ substitute! Gawain finally finds and recognizes Perceval, only to lose him again.[179] Did our author regard the Christ story as an allegory for the pilgrim's progress towards God? Do Eagles perfect themselves through the pain and suffering associated with earthly existence? Does the crown of thorns (self-sacrifice) become a crown of gold (self-perfection)? Are these knights seekers of human perfection, what we would call "Eagles"? The highest orders of the Cathars were called *perfecti*.[180]

Anyone who is following the story in full in Nigel Bryant's translation of *Perlesvaus* realizes that we are avoiding most repetitions of Grail images already bolded during our studies. Those of you following the story in full should be experiencing a thrill which everyone else is missing: You should be finding familiar images for yourself, without any help.

The story of the perilous cemetery is worth telling. The maiden of the story is seeking in the Perilous Cemetery a Christian relic which is to be found there: the sheet that shrouded Jesus Christ in the Tomb when he returned to life on the third day.[181] We are told that the cloth covers the altar in the chapel of the Perilous Cemetery.[182] The maiden must go there alone.[183] As each of us must trod the path toward God by ourselves? The maiden is Perceval's sister.[184] She finds comfort because "looking ahead, she could see a cross, high and tall and wide, and on this cross was carved the figure of Our Lord...."[185] The initiate is comforted by the thought that the master already has trod the lonely road toward perfection? She rides up to the altar, "and was just about to take hold of the cloth when it rose into the air as though a wind had seized it, and hung so high above an ancient crucifix there in the chapel that she could not reach it."[186] Human perfection is an elusive goal? She laments that the cloth has flown from her, alluding to her purity in body and mind and her love for Christ and for her family — as her family needs the cloth to help them out of certain enumerated troubles.[187] Is that which we seek snatched away just as we apparently are about to attain it? Perfection is hard to attain? In answer to her prayers, the cloth descends to the altar once more.[188] Seek, ask, knock, etc.? She takes from the altar "what God wished her to have, placing it [the cloth] religiously at her breast."[189] **Figure 392** illustrates the cloth lying on the altar, in top view. **Figure 393** illustrates the maiden's breast covered by the cloth.

The next cameo has been dangled before us several times, then snatched away before we could take a careful look at it. Our author definitely has been trying to pique our curiosity about the contents of the tomb in the chapel outside Camelot. Other knights have been told to ride on by because the contents were not for their eyes.[190] Now, finally, Perceval rides up to the "chapel sitting on its four marble columns," and dismounts.[191] "Then he laid his hand on the lid, and as soon as he touched it the tomb began to break its seal and open, and the lid leaned to one side to reveal what lay within."[192] Perceval's mother, the "Widowed Lady," saw the lid open and her daughter (Perceval's sister) fall at the knight's feet in joy.[193] She thereby knew the knight was her son, Perceval.[194] She exclaimed that it now was proven that Perceval was the finest knight in the world "for otherwise the tomb would not have opened; and never before has any man known who it was whom you now can see before you."[195] Has anyone failed to understand the "level one" allegory of the man who could open the tomb? What did they find inside? Our author tells us: "She bade the chaplain take the letters sealed in gold which lay in the tomb: he looked at them and read them, and said that the letters declared that he who lay in the tomb was one of those who had helped to take Our Lord from the cross. Then they peered into the tomb, and beside the body they found the pincers, all stained with blood, with

which the nails had been pulled out, but they could not be taken from the body's side or from the tomb. And Josephus tells us that as soon as Perceval left the chapel the tomb closed once more, and was sealed as it had been before."[196] Why could the pincers not be taken from the body's side or from the tomb? Because they were nothing but lines on the Holy Grail? As were the other objects, and characters, in the Story of Stories? Recall that Cathars did not believe that Calvary was history; that Templars were told to worship God rather than Jesus Christ.[197] Cathars believed that the human soul, which was good, was entombed in the human body, which was evil.[198] Is this the meaning of the allegory of the man who could open his tomb? A Cathar *perfectus* or a Templar knight does not allow his soul to be imprisoned in his body; rather, he permits it to fly high as an Eagle? We know that the ancients believed that the soul flew forth from the body, and could be captured by another person.[199] He restoreth my soul?[200]

Our unknown author uses Grail images even better than did Wolfram. As example, consider this tender scene, which occurs when Perceval is about to ride out from Camelot. His sister said to him, "Fair brother, here is the piece of the holy cloth that I took from the chapel in the Perilous Cemetery. Kiss it, and hold it to your face, for a holy hermit told me that our land would never be recovered unless we had this. Perceval kissed it and held it to his eyes and face."[201] **Figure 394** shows Perceval, with the cloth covering his face. Contrast this scenario with what comes next.

After a few more battle scenes, Perceval captures the Lord of the Fens, his mother's tormentor, and brings him to her court, where Perceval recites: "'God commanded in the Old Law and in the New that we should exercise justice on murderers and traitors, and so shall I on you; never shall His commandment be broken.'"[202] Is what follows Biblical "justice"? "He bade that a great vat be made ready and brought into the middle of the court; then he called for the eleven knights to be led forward, and had them beheaded in the vat and left to bleed as much blood as they could. Then he had their heads and bodies thrown out so that only the pure blood remained in the vat. Then he called for the Lord of the Fens to be disarmed and led before the vat with its great fill of blood. He had him bound tightly, hand and foot, and then, mockingly, cried: 'Lord of the Fens! Lord of the Fens! You could never have enough of the blood of my lady my mother's knights, but I will give you enough of the

Illustration 22-2. Human sacrifice? Pagan baptism? Cosmic allegory for the return to the source? From the Gundestrup Cauldron, second century B.C., Denmark. Courtesy of the Werner Forman Archive, London.

Figure 395

blood of your own.' He bade him be hung in the vat by his feet so that his head was plunged in the blood up to the shoulders; and he had him held there until he drowned to death."[203] A fiendish fantasy? Not at all! That is exactly the way our Bronze Age and Iron Age Celtic and Germanic ancestors might have handled this situation. See **Illustration 22-2.**[204] Where did they get the idea for such a bloodthirsty method of execution? From **Figure 395**? Are we more civilized? You might not think so if you ever had watched the reaction of a condemned prisoner when the high voltage surge of electricity strikes his brain or the poison gas enters his lungs!

Do Christians believe that Jesus Christ wants them to kill people who question the authority of their Christian pastors? If so, which Christian pastors? Baptist preachers and Roman Catholic priests are not of one mind although both are Christians. Shall all Christians mimic the Irish of Belfast by killing each other in the name of God? Shall Christians bomb abortion clinics as Christmas presents to Jesus Christ? The very next cameo after the execution of the Lord of the Fens commences with a visit by the Maiden of the Cart. Does she personify the death and destruction caused by the Church? She comes with news that the King of Castle Mortal

has seized the lands of the now-deceased Fisher King and has declared that those who will support the Old Law and abandon the New Law will have his protection.[205] "'My lady,' said Perceval, 'he is neither your brother nor my uncle since he denies God; he is our mortal enemy, and we should rightly hate him more than a stranger.'"[206] Do the Gospels sanction such thinking?[207] What is the "Old Law" and what is the "New Law"? On the first layer of allegory, is Judaism the Old Law and Christianity the New Law? On the second layer of allegory, is Roman Catholicism the Old Law and Cathar Christianity the New Law? The "sin" of the King of Castle Mortal is that "he denies God," which could be a reference to Judaism because Hebrews deny that Jesus Christ was God. However, if, as we have suggested, our unknown author was a Templar, those words can have another meaning: that the King of Castle Mortal (the Holy Father in Rome) "denies God," i.e., worships Jesus Christ as God instead of worshiping Yahweh as God! Accordingly, the meaning of "Old Law" and "New Law" depends upon the religious perspective of the speaker! The New Testament, with Jesus Christ as God, is the "New Law" in relation to the Old Testament, with Yahweh as God. But the doctrines of Cathar and Templar Christianity are "New Law" in relationship to both Judaism and Roman Catholicism! And the Christian doctrines of the Protestant

Reformation are "New Law" in relation to the Christian heresies of the Middle Ages! Can this conundrum be solved? Who justly is entitled to kill whom in the name of God? Your author once saw a cartoon in a magazine which may point us toward an answer. To the left, around their green priest, congregated the green knights, while to the right, around their red priest, congregated the red knights. The green priest and the red priest were saying the same words: "God is on our side." Down from a cloud over the battlefield came these words: "If anyone down there is the least bit interested in the truth, I am sick and tired of watching you guys killing each other in My Name." The Koran says that God is merciful and forgiving.[208] Apparently so.

We shall analyze in some detail the tale of the yelping beast.[209] "Perceval... came upon a beautiful glade in the middle of the woods; and looking before him, he saw a cross: all red it was; and as he looked towards the far end of the glade he saw a most handsome knight sitting in the shadow of the forest, clad all in white, holding a golden vessel in his hand. And when he turned towards the other end of the glade he saw a maiden sitting there likewise, young and fair and of the greatest beauty, draped in white samite with drops of gold, holding a most beautiful golden vessel in her hand."[210]

"Josephus tells us in his divine writing that out of the forest came a beast as white as new-fallen snow, bigger than a hare but smaller than fox: out into the glade she came in alarm, for she bore a litter of twelve in her belly which were yelping like a pack of dogs; and the beast fled through the glade, terrified by the barking of the dogs inside her. Perceval leaned on the butt of his lance, gazing at the beast in wonder; and he felt great pity for her, for she looked gentle and very beautiful, and her eyes were like two emeralds. Towards the knight she ran in terror, but after she had rested there awhile the dogs began to torture her anew and she ran to the maiden; but she could not rest there for long, for the dogs would not cease their yelping and she was very frightened. She did not dare dive into the forest, so she turned to Perceval for protection, and as she was about to jump onto the neck of his horse he held out his hands to catch her so that she would not hurt herself; and still the dogs kept barking. The knight cried out to Perceval, saying: 'Sir knight, let the beast go. Do not try to hold her, for she is not your business or anyone else's: leave her to her own destiny.'"[211]

"The beast saw that she was to have no protector and headed for the cross. The young could no longer stay inside her, and out they came, alive, as dogs; and they were not as gentle or as beautiful as the beast. She humbled herself before them and lay flat on the ground as though begging for mercy, keeping as close to the cross as she could. The dogs surrounded her and attacked her from all sides and tore her to pieces with their teeth; but they could not eat the flesh or pull her away from the cross.[212]

"When the dogs had killed the beast they raced off into the woods as though they had turned wild; then the knight and the maiden came up to where the beast lay in pieces by the cross, and each took a share and placed it in their golden vessels. They collected the blood which lay on the ground along with the flesh, and kissed that spot and worshipped the cross, and then made their way back into the forest. Perceval dismounted, and kneeling before the cross he kissed it and worshipped it, and likewise the place where the beast was killed, just as he had seen the knight and the maiden do. Thereupon a fragrance rose from that place and from the cross, so sweet that none could ever equal it. Then he looked up and saw two priests coming from the forest on foot; and the first cried out to him:

"'Sir knight, draw back from the cross; let us approach.'

"Perceval drew back, and one of the priests knelt before the cross and worshipped it and bowed to it and kissed it more than twenty times with the greatest joy in the world; but the other priest came up behind bearing a great rod, and forcing the first priest aside he began to beat the cross all over with the rod, weeping most bitterly.[213] Perceval gazed at him in wonder.

"'Sire,' he said, 'you seem to be a priest; why do you act so wickedly?'

"'Sire, nothing we do is of any consequence to you, and you will not be told by us.'

"If he had not been a priest Perceval would have lost his temper with him, but he did not wish to do him harm and he turned away and mounted, and rode back into the forest, fully armed."[214]

We are given an explanation of the first level of allegory of the story of the yelping beast.[215] Is there a second level of allegory? Is the innocent white beast the original Christian church? Are the twelve yelping dogs she spawns the twelve Apostles? She is innocent and beautiful. They run wild through the land establishing *their* order of things rather than *hers*, i.e., the many and varied warring Christian churches: Roman Catholic, Cathar Catholic, etc.?

She dies, and a fragrance arises. When the story was written, a fragrance arising meant that a martyr had died. Her litter chews her up into pieces, but is unable to swallow the pieces. Her remains are scooped up into golden vessels and tenderly cared for by a white-clad Templar knight and his lady who were sitting in the presence of the red Templar cross where the beast ran for protection. The Templar knight knows that the original church can not survive; that she must be left to her own destiny? But he scoops up her remains and takes them away with him for proper veneration and preservation? The priest who kisses and loves the cross is Roman Catholic. The priest who beats the cross with the rod is a Templar.[216] Does our unknown author, who presumably was a Templar, mean to tell us that his version of Christianity was most like original Christianity; that everyone else had strayed from the Way? Most Christians still think that way. We are right. They are wrong. We are going to Heaven. They are going to Hell. We are saved. They need to repent. The yelping-dogs allegory fits well, does it not?

We are introduced to the Knight of the Burning Dragon, who is huge, carries an enormous sword and lance, and a shield on which "there is the head of a dragon which throws out fire and flame whenever he wishes...."[217] The prize for killing the Knight of the Burning Dragon is the Circle of Gold.[218] Lancelot and Gawain ride with Perceval looking for that "demon knight."[219] They arrive at the Forbidden Castle, which is "a castle standing in the middle of the open meadows, surrounded by rushing rivers and rings of walls, and there within loomed great, windowed halls. And as they approached the castle they saw that it was turning round faster than any wind; and above the battlements were archers of copper which fired with such power that no armour in the world could withstand their shots. With them were live men sounding horns, horns so loud that it seemed as though the earth were quaking. And down below at the gateway were lions and bears in chains, roaring with such fury that all the forest and the valley rang."[220] The dome of Heaven, with its four archers at their posts, and the constellations of stars in the forms of men and animals? Only Perceval could enter. "[T]he only one who may proceed is he who is to conquer the demon knight and the Circle of Gold and the Grail and the false law of the castle."[221] The Circle of Gold is the Zodiac? The false law of the castle is astrology, and the demon knight is the astrologer? We have been told that the Holy Grail was brought down from the sky by a band of angels. Perceval lays down his lance and shield, takes sword in hand, spurs his horse forward, and strikes the Turning Castle with his sword, which ceases turning, the archers stop shooting, and the animals run to their lairs.[222] It was prophesied that the occupants of the castle "would worship the Old Law until the coming of the Good knight...."[223] Perceval converted the castle residents to "the New Law," that is, Christianity.[224] Note the name of the castle: The Forbidden Castle. Christianity forbade the common man to know the shape and motions of the Earth. Perceval stopped the round Earth from turning? If our perceptions of reality are the only realities in our lives, the Christian church *did* stop Castle Earth from turning!

And what of the encounter between Perceval and the Knight of the Burning Dragon? Grail knights, like Hollywood cowboys, always get the bad guy.[225] "She led Perceval to where the Circle of Gold was kept, and with her own hand she placed it upon his head."[226] Hollywood cowboys ride off and leave the heroine. Perceval rode off and left the Crown of Gold.[227] He needed to continue living to complete his adventures.

"The story tells us that he [Perceval] rode on until he came one day to the Castle of the Copper Tower, where there dwelt many people who worshipped the Tower of Copper and believed in no other god. The Copper Tower was in the middle of the castle, standing on four columns of copper."[228] That is an easy image for seasoned Grail-questers like us! **Figure 396.** "At the gateway there were two men made by the art of sorcery, holding two great iron hammers which they drove and dashed together with such fury that nothing in all the world could pass between them without being completely destroyed."[229] The guards had no power over Perceval, and he rode into the castle.[230] The "demon" in

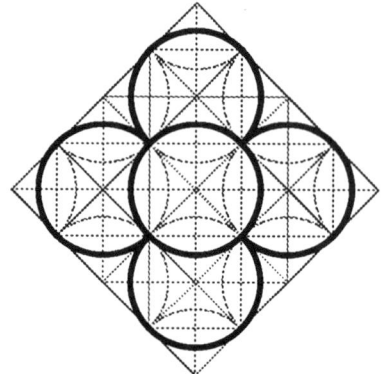

Figure 396

which the residents of the castle believed "provided them with such plenty that they wanted for nothing."[231] "They were not used to fighting, for the entrance to the castle was so strong that no-one could enter...."[232] A group of peaceful "heathens" who wanted for nothing! But Perceval was about to change all that! He drove them between the guards at the gate, and all but 13 of the 1500 residents had their brains dashed out by the guards' hammers.[233] He destroyed the tower.[234] The surviving 13 were baptized, and became good Christians, "and led good lives indeed."[235] Now that they were converted to Christianity, "no-one could go inside to join them without being killed or cut to pieces, unless he believed staunchly in God."[236] Thou shalt not kill, provided, however, that thou shalt convert the heathen or shalt kill them! The survivors became good Christians! They killed all who would not accept their new faith.

The story of Joseus, a man of the cloth who fights rather than prays as the assault upon the Grail Castle proceeds, surely was one pleasing to our presumed-Templar author.[237] The Roman Catholics recaptured the castle.[238] And what did Perceval do with those who did not want to convert to Roman Catholic Christianity? "He killed all those who would not believe in it and the country was ruled and protected by him and the Law of Our Lord exalted by his strength and valour."[239] Which law? Thou shalt not kill? Or thou shalt capture paying parishioners?

As Arthur, Lancelot, and Gawain travelled, they came upon a ruined house (the house of science?) with "a great fire in the middle where a man could warm himself from far away."[240] The sun? They found a room filled with heads and feet of dead men.[241] The Holy Grail is covered with heads and feet of our Grail humanforms. The maiden of the Castle of Beards was doing penance by collecting unburied bodies of knights she found in the forest.[242] Formerly, she had required knights to remove their beards at her castle, or to suffer death or maiming.[243] Templars wore beards at the time of *Perlesvaus*, although most men were clean-shaven.[244] We have seen Grail beards previously.

We are told that "King Arthur, who is now the finest King in the world, was conceived in sin" because his father was not married to his mother, who was married to another man.[245] Yahweh sired Jesus on Mary who was married to Joseph? Remember that Templars and Cathars did not believe in the historicity of the Immaculate Conception.[246] We also are told that the body of Merlin the magi-

cian did not remain in his tomb, but was borne away by God or the devil.[247] As the body of Jesus the Magician was borne away in the Story of Stories? Our author never seems to tire of poking fun at Roman Catholic beliefs which he does not share.

Lancelot returns to the Waste City, to offer his head in sacrifice. "He lay down on the ground with his arms outstretched, and prayed to God for mercy."[248] Lancelot was saved by a maiden, who declared: "All of them [the other knights] broke their promise, for none dared return; and if *you* had failed to return on the day like the others had done, we would have lost this city forever...."[249] Christ and Lancelot both willingly returned to a city to face death. Lancelot did not die. Is our author suggesting that Jesus did not die? Had the Templars accepted some of the beliefs of Islam?[250]

We are told about "a beautiful river... that... came from the Earthly Paradise and ran all around the... [Grail Castle] and flowed on into the forest to the house of a worthy hermit. There its course ended and it vanished into the earth, but wherever it flowed there was a great abundance of all good things."[251] "Eden" was the first name of the Grail Castle.[252] Is our unknown author expressing the opinion that the story of the Garden of Eden was among the many legends created from images that can be seen on the Holy Grail?

The Holy Grail appeared to King Arthur. "The Grail appeared at the consecration in five forms, but they should not be revealed, for the secrets of the sacrament none should tell save he whom God has granted grace. But King Arthur saw all of the transubstantiations, and last appeared the chalice; and the hermit who was conducting the mass found a memorandum upon the consecration cloth, and the letters declared that God wanted His body to be sacrificed in such vessel in remembrance of Him. The story does not say that it was the only chalice anywhere, but in all of Britain and the neighbouring cities and kingdoms, there was none."[253] We are told that "Solomon had cast three bells with which to honour the Saviour of the world and His sweet mother and His saints, and by his command they had brought this one to this island [Britain] because there was none here."[254] Jesus supposedly lived *after* Solomon, but all things are possible on the Holy Grail! Arthur takes the model of the Grail Castle chalice and bell home with him, and requires copies to be made for the churches, "So that the Saviour of the world might be served with greater honour."[255] If the hypothesis of this book is correct, many of our ceremonies and ceremonial objects

Figure 397

Figure 398

may have had their origins in models seen by the ancients on the Holy Grail.

We next are told of Sir Gawain's foster-father, who also was named Gawain.[256] We are told that his mother did not want anyone to know of his birth so she placed him in a "beautiful vessel" in which he was transported to his foster parents, who raised him, then took him to Rome, where he was chosen to become emperor.[257] He did not want to be emperor, however, because people were reproaching him for his birth, which earlier had been hidden from him, so he returned to Britain to live, and, when he died, he left his castle to Sir Gawain.[258] The Biblical parallel is obvious. There lies the baby in the "beautiful vessel"! **Figure 397**. What next?

The story again leaves Sir Gawain, and returns to Sir Lancelot, who has ridden to the Castle of Griffins, where any knight can win the hand of the daughter of the lord of the castle if he succeeds in pulling out a spear fixed in one of the pillars of the castle hall.[259] The resemblance to Malory's sword in the stone is quite obvious. If, however, a knight fails to extract the spear, he loses his head, which is hung on the castle gate.[260] Lancelot puts his life to risk, of course. "He came straight to the pillar and seized

the spear with both hands; and as soon as he took hold of it he pulled it out with such force that the whole pillar came crumbling down."[261] The Samson story also? There Samson stands, his arms extended around two pillars, about to pull them down! **Figure 398**. What next?

Lancelot wins the maiden's hand, but his thoughts are with Queen Guinevere, who has died, so he flees the castle.[262] The way out, through an underground cistern passage, is blocked by a lion and "two serpents called griffins. They have the faces of men, the beaks of birds, the eyes of screech-owls, the teeth of dogs, the ears of mules, the feet of lions, and the tails of serpents...."[263] Ezekiel's critters were rather domestic in comparison!

Lancelot's visit to the tomb of Queen Guinevere would be a good extra-credit assignment for *A* students.[264]

Lancelot again is required to pull a spear-like object out of a pillar. This time it is a crossbow bolt.[265] He extracts it.[266] He is told that his accomplishment of that feat means that he must go to the Perilous Chapel, get a part of the cloth which shrouds the knight in the tomb, and get the sword which lies beside the knight in the tomb.[267] Next, he must go back to the Perilous Castle and get the head of one of the griffins which live in the cistern. Finally, he must bring all three objects back to cure a knight who cannot otherwise be cured.[268] Does this sound like an initiation ceremony? Is our unknown author trying to tell us that the Holy Grail had something to do with an initiation ceremony?

Lancelot responds to the maiden's demand that he face these perils: "I see that you care little for my life, only that your wish be fulfilled."[269] We will understand the maiden's plans for Sir Lancelot in a few more paragraphs.

When Lancelot arrives at the Perilous Chapel, "[h]e could see a shed outside with fodder for horses, and so he went to stable his [horse] there...."[270] Lancelot opens the tomb, sees the bloody shroud covering the dead knight, takes the sword and half of the shroud, and the tomb closes.[271] He is challenged by a maiden, who is glad for him to have the sword and cloth when she learns who he is. She attempts to lure him to her castle, where she has prepared three rich tombs for him, Sir Perceval and Sir Gawain.[272] When he refuses her hospitality, she demands the sword, but he escapes from her by the magic of the sword. He then gains entrance to the Perilous Castle, by the magic of the sword, where, tired from his adventures, he takes a nap in the orchard, and is discovered by the maiden he earlier had jilted, who awakens him with three kisses.[273] He tells her he must get the head of one of the serpents, to cure the sick knight, whereupon she tells him that she told the maiden "that story because I wanted you to come back here to me."[274] Lancelot tells her that he will be on his way, since he now knows he does not need the serpent's head, and, realizing that she is about to be jilted a second time, she tells Lancelot, "I would love you better dead than alive! Truly, I wish your head were hanging with the others at the gateway!"[275] He leaves the Perilous Castle, and returns with the sword and cloth, giving them to the maiden whose demands set him upon the mission in the first place.[276] He tells her that he knows she was "jesting about the serpent's head." She admits that she was, and tells him that "I told you the tale to please the maiden of the castle...."[277] What are we to learn from this story? We have a story about a woman who not only does not care for Lancelot's life but really would prefer to see him dead and buried in a tomb she has built for him in her castle. In order to get him to come back to her, she has had another woman tell him a lie. We already have read about a woman who might represent the Church Militant,

Figure 399

craving its martyred Christian soldiers. Now, do we have a servant or agent of the Church Militant telling a lie in order to get a Christian soldier back into the arms of the Church Militant? Is that what our unknown author is suggesting? The Roman Catholic church lies to its knights in order to induce them to risk their lives for the material gain of the Roman Catholic Church? That allegory would be consistent with Cathar beliefs about the Christian Church of Rome.[278] The tale ends happily, with the sick knight being cured by having the sword and shroud laid upon his wounds.[279] How many of us *still* believe that holy relics can cure bodily afflictions?

Lancelot gets thrown into prison.[280] Lancelot in prison is seen in **Figure 399**. The Bible hero Joseph also got thrown into prison.[281] What next?

Our unknown author assures us that "In the text which records this story, which was set down in the vernacular from the Latin, Josephus tells us that no-one should doubt that these adventures took place at that time in Britain and in all the other kingdoms; and many more occurred than I recall, but these are the best known."[282] These allegorical references are to the best known Biblical tales! No one should doubt that these Grail tales took place, just as no one should doubt that the corresponding Biblical tales took place? Grail tales and Biblical tales report historical facts? Neither is mythology or legend? Or is our author's pen dripping with sarcasm?

We find Perceval sailing the oceans with a mariner or steersman at the helm.[283] They have sailed so far that the mariner knows "neither the sea nor the stars."[284] Remember that *Perlesvaus* was written during the last years of the twelfth century or early years of the thirteenth century. Europeans were supposed to believe what the Church told them: that the flat Earth lay at the center of the universe and the Heavens rotated around it.[285] Belief to the contrary was heresy, a form of treason against the Church.[286] However, every deepwater sailor who had sailed south along the coast of Africa knew the truth.[287] As you sailed south *around* the world, stars were encountered which the curvature of the Earth prevented you from seeing in Europe.[288] Only devout Christian landlubbers believed in a flat world! Their leaders knew better, if the thesis of this book is correct. The term "mariner" or "steersman" is a reference to the Templar leader whose office corresponds to the chairman of the board of directors of a modern corporation.[289]

Perceval and the mariner arrived at a castle on an island in the sea.[290] They came upon "the most beautiful fountain that any man could describe; surrounded it was by rich golden columns...."[291] They met at the fountain "two men... with hair and beards whiter than new-fallen snow, yet their faces seemed young indeed...."[292] Remember that Templars wore beards while most men went clean-shaven.[293] The island-dwellers were well acquainted with the knight (Joseph of Arimathea) who previously had borne Perceval's shield.[294] "Perceval looked beyond the fountain, and in a most fair place he saw a cask which seemed to be made all of glass, and it was so big that inside was a knight in full armour. And as Perceval looked inside he saw that the knight was very much alive. He addressed him again and again, but the knight would not reply, and Perceval gazed at him in wonder. He came back to the worthy men and asked them who the knight was, but they said he could not know just yet."[295] The Lord Buddha?[296] Or was Perceval looking at the next story hero to be born of the Holy Grail?

When one of the masters sounded a gong three times, "into the hall came thirty-three men, all in one company; they were dressed all in white, and each bore a red cross on his chest; and they all seemed to be thirty-two years old."[297] Templars![298]

Perceval returned to the Grail Castle, where he lived until, as he had expected, a ship bearing a white sail with a red cross manned by fair people dressed as for Mass, came to take him away to Paradise.[299]

Our analysis of *Perlesvaus* ends with these words: "Josephus tells us that Perceval thus departed, and from that time forth no earthly man ever knew what became of him, and the story tells nothing more. But Josephus says that Joseus stayed at the castle which had belonged to the Fisher King and locked himself inside so that no-one could enter, and sustained himself with what God sent him. He remained there for a long while after Perceval's departure, and died there; but after his death the house began to crumble and its halls turned to ruins. But the chapel never showed any signs of decay: it remained in fine condition, and so it is still. But the castle had been far from any people and it seemed a rather strange place, and when it had turned to ruins, many people in the neighbouring lands and isles wondered what could be there, and some were tempted to go and look. But those who went never returned, and no-one ever knew what became of them. The news travelled to every land, but no-one thereafter dared to go there, save two Welsh knights who had heard about it; they were fair knights indeed, very young and high-spirited, and they swore to each other that they would go, and full of excitement they entered the castle. They stayed there for a long while. And when they left they lived as hermits, wearing hair-shirts and wandering through the forests, eating only roots; it was a hard life, but it pleased them greatly, and when people asked them why they were living thus, they would reply: 'Go where we went, and you will know why.'"[300] We have been where they went. We know why.

Notes
CHAPTER TWENTY-TWO
Perlesvaus: Riddling the Coals of the Original Christian Faith

1. Bryant 19.

2. Bryant 19.

3. Bryant 19.

4. Bryant 19.

5. Bryant 20; Erbstosser 89; Baigent 54.

6. Bryant 20.

7. Bryant 20-21.

8. Bryant 21.

9. Bryant 21.

10. Bryant 22.

11. Bryant 22.

12. Bryant 22.

13. 11 Encyclopaedia Britannica Macropaedia 443-444 (1974).

14. Erbstosser Figs. 19-26, and accompanying text.

15. Bryant 22.

16. Bryant 22.

17. Bryant 22.

18. Bryant 22.

19. Bryant 22.

20. Bryant 22-23.

21. Bryant 23.

22. Bryant 23.

23. Bryant 23.

24. Erbstosser 89.

25. Erbstosser 86-89.

26. Erbstosser 86-89.

27. Erbstosser 86-96; Brooke 99-103.

28. Bryant 23.

29. Bryant 23.

30. Bryant 23.

31. Bryant 24.

32. Bryant 24.

33. Luke 2.7.

34. Bryant 24.

35. Erbstosser 40.

36. Bryant 24.

37. Bryant 24.

38. Bryant 24.

39. Bryant 24-25.

40. Bryant 25.

41. Bryant 26.

42. Bryant 26. King Arthur "marvelled that she called the child her father and her son." Bryant 26. The Cathars believed that God was good and human flesh was bad; hence, that God would not have become incarnate; hence, that God remains entirely spiritual and Jesus Christ could not have been God incarnate. Brooke 101. Is our unknown author poking fun at the illogic of a human child's being his own father; of the child's mother also being the child's spouse? Recall that in Roman Catholic theology, God the Father, Son, and Holy Ghost "are of one substance, and that substance is God." Bryant 19.

43. Bryant 26.

44. Bryant 27.

45. Bryant 27.

46. Bryant 27-28.

47. Bryant 28.

48. Bryant 29.

49. Bryant 29.

50. Bryant 29.

51. Bryant 29.

52. Bryant 30.

53. 1 Frazer 178-185; Cumont OR 40,67; Cumont MM 180.

54. Graham 335; Godwin 25; Matthews 11.

55. 12 Encyclopaedia Britannica Macropaedia 782 (1974).

56. Bryant 30.

57. Bryant 30.

58. Bryant 30.

59. Bryant 32-33.

60. Bryant 33.

61. Bryant 33.

62. Bryant 33-34.

63. Bryant 34.

64. Bryant 34.

65. Bryant 34. Was Saint John the Baptist the king whose head she held? See Bryant 35.

66. Bryant 34.

67. Bryant 34.

68. Erbstosser 106-110.

69. Erbstosser Fig. 48, and accompanying text.

70. Erbstosser Fig. 47, and accompanying text.

71. Bryant 34.

72. Bryant 34-35.

73. Bryant 35.

74. Bryant 35. She is called the maiden of the cart. Bryant 39,42.

75. Bryant 36-37.

76. Bryant 36.

77. Bryant 37. This castle has been identified as Hell itself. Bryant 73. Are such explanations of the allegories of *Perlesvaus* nothing but "red herrings," dragged across the story to lead Roman Catholic inquisitors off the track? Are there *unexplained* allegories lying beneath the surface of the *explained* allegories? Is this castle *really* the Roman Catholic church? "[T]his is a wicked castle if they rob people thus." Bryant 152. Knowing what we do in regard to Cathar and Templar opinions about the Roman Catholic church, what shall we conclude? Baigent 78-85, 48-55; Brooke 99-103; Erbstosser 86-142.

78. Bryant 37-38.

79. Bryant 40.

80. Bryant 44.

81. Bryant 46.

82. Baigent 53; Brooke 101; Erbstosser 90.

83. Bryant 46.

84. Bryant 47-49.

85. Bryant 49.

86. Bryant 54.

87. Bryant 54.

88. Bryant 55.

89. Bryant 61.

90. Bryant 61. The gatekeepers included "two ghastly figures of copper, which by an ingenious device could fling forth crossbow-bolts... with such fury that no armour could withstand them." Bryant 61. The Templars were alchemists of considerable abilities. Baigent 79. Were they familiar with static electricity?

91. Bryant 61.

92. Bryant 62.

93. Bryant 62.

94. Bryant 63.

95. Bryant 63.

96. Bryant 63.

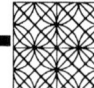

97. Bryant 63.

98. Bryant 63.

99. Bryant 64.

100. Bryant 64-66. One of the knights with whom Sir Gawain fought could be killed only by striking him with a sword on the sole of his foot "for he was of the line of Achilles, whose descendants could die in no other way." Bryant 66. Is our author suggesting that Homer's tale about the Trojan War was born on the Holy Grail?

101. Bryant 67.

102. Bryant 67.

103. Bryant 67.

104. Bryant 67.

105. Bryant 67.

106. Bryant 67-68.

107. Matthews 39.

108. Bryant 69,72.

109. Lamy 21.

110. Bryant 69.

111. Frazer 226-227.

112. Bryant 68.

113. Bryant 68.

114. Bryant 69.

115. Bryant 69.

116. Bryant 69.

117. Bryant 70.

118. Bryant 70.

119. Bryant 70.

120. Bryant 70.

121. Erbstosser 198,203,210-211.

122. Bryant 71.

123. Bryant 71.

124. Bryant 75. The explanations offered to Sir Gawain by the priest of the Castle of Inquiry for the various allegories in *Perlesvaus* are quite different from those suggested by your author. Bryant 73-75. Is your author simply wrong? Or was our presumably-Templar author of *Perlesvaus* attempting to protect himself from the Roman Catholic Inquisition by offering his readers a series of explanations which were "O.K." under mainline Roman Catholic doctrine? For instance, how could an inquisitor suggest that the Black Hermit was intended as an allegorical reference to the Holy Father in Rome, since the author of *Perlesvaus* has his priest of the Castle of Inquiry state that the Black Hermit is Lucifer, lord of Hell? Bryant 73. Note that the priest's explanations of the various allegories pleased Sir Gawain greatly. Bryant 74. Because Sir Gawain was so pleased with the priest's explanations, he did not look behind what the priest said to determine whether there might be a second layer of allegory? Note that when Sir Gawain first came to the Castle of Inquiry, he was assured by the priest that he would be told the significance of *anything* he asked. Bryant 73. However, when Sir Gawain inquired about the fountain, the priest broke that promise by refusing to talk about the fountain - because the fountain had something to do with "the secrets of the Saviour." Bryant 75. Are we being told that the priest of the Castle of Inquiry was less than candid with Sir Gawain? The priest assured Sir Gawain that the maid of the cart "spoke true." Bryant 73. Did the priest?

125. Bryant 76.

126. Bryant 76. Is the author of *Perlesvaus* suggesting that images of the Zoroastrian faith also were drawn from the wellspring of the Holy Grail?

127. Bryant 77-78.

128. Bryant 78.

129. Brooke 101.

130. Bryant 78.

131. Bryant 78-79.

132. Bryant 79.

133. Bryant 79.

134. Bryant 79.

135. Bryant 79.

136. Bryant 79.

137. Bryant 80.

138. Bryant 80-81.

139. Baigent 83; 6 Encyclopaedia Britannica Macropaedia 555 (1974).

140. Baigent 83.

141. Eusebius 91.

142. Bryant 80.

143. 1 Frazer 213-239.

144. 2 Frazer 182-217.

145. 2 Frazer 182-217.

146. Graves & Patai 101; 2 Frazer 195.

147. Frankfort 16; 2 Frazer 195.

148. Bryant 90. Is Lancelot somehow related to the Hindu Avatar of Rama with the axe? Parrinder 22,26,63.

149. Bryant 90.

150. Bryant 90.

151. Bryant 91.

152. Bryant 91.

153. Bryant 91. Hindu true believers are more aware than most Christians that avatars are mere illusions, sprung from the minds of human beings. Parrinder 50,105.

154. Owen 99.

155. Bryant 93.

156. Bryant 93.

157. Bryant 106.

158. Bryant 106-107.

159. John 12.13.

160. Bryant 110-112.

161. Bryant 110-112.

162. Bryant 112. The Germanic god Odin was known by many names, including "The Concealer." Hollander 63.

163. Bryant 116.

164. Bryant 120.

165. Bryant 121.

166. Bryant 121.

167. Bryant 60, 91-92.

168. Bryant 121.

169. Erbstosser, generally.

170. Bryant 127.

171. Bryant 128.

172. Bryant 128.

173. Bryant 128.

174. Bryant 129.

175. Bryant 130.

176. Bryant 131.

177. Bryant 131.

178. Bryant 131.

179. Bryant 136-137.

180. Brooke 100.

181. Bryant 143. The Shroud of Turin evidently was in the possession of the Templars from 1204 to 1307. Baigent 82. The Templars were alchemists. Baigent 79. We cannot fail to discuss the Shroud of Turin. Modern scientific studies indicate that the "photographic negative" image on the shroud probably was produced by light passing through space, which differentiates the shroud from the many dyed versions produced by the Cult of Relics. Tribbe 63,124,141-142,167-169,174-175,208,253; Gimpel 34,48-49,82-91; James 51-52. Does the manner of its production indicate that the Shroud of Turin is the genuine article? Two Roman Catholic Bishops of

Troyes thought it was a fake, which led Pope Clement VII to require it to be labeled as a reproduction rather than as the actual burial garment of Jesus Christ. Tribbe 71-72,171-172. The bishops and the pope did not have at their disposal the modern, scientific tests which have been applied to the shroud, but they may have had information not possessed by most present-day Christians. The French town of Troyes, the seat of the two bishops, became acquainted with Cathar or Albigensian Gnostic Christianity. Partner 60,84,132,139-142; Rudolph 375-376; Walker 172. The Roman Catholic Albigensian Crusade and Inquisition had used genocide and torture to destroy Cathar Christianity; however, Cathar Christianity continued to be practiced in secret by the French Knights Templar. Partner 77-80,139-142,166-168; Rudolph 375-376; Walker 172-173. Roman Catholic spies discovered the secret Christian faith of the Knights Templar, after which the Knights Templar, originally founded at Troyes, were annihilated by Roman Catholic Inquisition. Partner 1-10,59-85. The Shroud of Turin apparently had been in the possession of the Knights Templar. Tribbe 53-67. Gnostic Christians believed that Jesus Christ was a being of light; that He appeared to humankind in spiritual flesh rather than in human flesh. Rudolph 63,157-171. Thus, their relic tends to support their Christology. On the other hand, some modern Christians believe the image on the shroud proves that Christ appeared in human flesh. Tribbe 254. One point surely is proven: Cognitive dissonance pervades Christology. Christian true believers notice evidence that supports their views, and ignore evidence to the contrary, a harmless bit of mental gymnastics unless, once again, it leads the one group to practice genocide upon the other. After the first draft of this note, the international news media reported that carbon 14 dating tests performed on the Shroud of Turin indicate that the Shroud must be dated to the Middle Ages. What will true believers now say?

182. Bryant 143.

183. Bryant 143.

184. Bryant 144.

185. Bryant 144.

186. Bryant 145.

187. Bryant 145.

188. Bryant 145.

189. Bryant 146.

190. Bryant 76.

191. Bryant 147.

192. Bryant 148.

193. Bryant 148.

194. Bryant 148.

195. Bryant 148.

196. Bryant 148.

197. Baigent 53-54,85; Brooke 101.

198. Baigent 53.

199. 1 Frazer 215,239.

200. Psalm 23.3.

201. Bryant 150.

202. Bryant 151.

203. Bryant 151-152.

204. Cavendish 177.

205. Bryant 152.

206. Bryant 152.

207. Matthew 10.34-37.

208. Sura XLII.5.

209. Bryant 154.

210. Bryant 154. Templars wore white mantles emblazoned with the splayed red Templar cross pattee. Baigent 64,69. The cross pattee appears all over the Holy Grail.

211. Bryant 154.

212. Bryant 154.

213. Bryant 155.

214. Bryant 155.

215. Bryant 165-167.

216. Baigent 64,76,85.

217. Bryant 153.

218. Bryant 159.

219. Bryant 159.

220. Bryant 159.

221. Bryant 160.

222. Bryant 160.

223. Bryant 161.

224. Bryant 161.

225. Bryant 163.

226. Bryant 164.

227. Bryant 164.

228. Bryant 164.

229. Bryant 164.

230. Bryant 164.

231. Bryant 165.

232. Bryant 165.

233. Bryant 165.

234. Bryant 165.

235. Bryant 165.

236. Bryant 165.

237. Bryant 170-171.

238. Bryant 172.

239. Bryant 172.

240. Bryant 176.

241. Bryant 176.

242. Bryant 177.

243. Bryant 177.

244. Baigent 68.

245. Bryant 181.

246. Baigent 54,76,85.

247. Bryant 181.

248. Bryant 183.

249. Bryant 183-184.

250. Sura IV.157.

251. Bryant 195.

252. Bryant 195.

253. Bryant 195-196.

254. Bryant 196.

255. Bryant 210.

256. Bryant 197-198.

257. Bryant 197-198.

258. Bryant 198.

259. Bryant 199.

260. Bryant 199-200.

261. Bryant 201.

262. Bryant 203.

263. Bryant 202.

264. Bryant 204.

265. Bryant 217.

266. Bryant 218.

267. Bryant 219.

268. Bryant 219.

269. Bryant 219.

270. Bryant 221.

271. Bryant 221.

272. Bryant 221-222.

273. Bryant 223.

274. Bryant 223.

275. Bryant 223.

276. Bryant 224.

277. Bryant 224.

278. Baigent 51-55,64-85.

279. Bryant 225.

280. Bryant 229.

281. Genesis 39.20.

282. Bryant 234.

283. Bryant 250.

284. Bryant 250.

285. Dreyer 207-223.

286. Dreyer 224-225.

287. Dreyer 39,118,172,249.

288. Dreyer 39,118,172,249.

289. Baigent 131.

290. Bryant 250.

291. Bryant 250.

292. Bryant 250.

293. Baigent 68.

294. Bryant 250.

295. Bryant 250.

296. Sahi 125.

297. Bryant 251.

298. Baigent 64,68-69.

299. Bryant 264.

300. Bryant 264-265. While our presumably-Cathar Grail quest authors were using the Holy Grail to write satires and parodies on the Christ story, a Benedictine visionary, St. Hildegard of Bingen, A.D. 1098-1179, was using the Holy Grail as inspiration for her visions. 1 Fox 6-7,92; 2 Fox ix; Hozeski ix-xi. St. Hildegard despised the Cathars, so we cannot suspect her of being a "closet Cathar." 2 Fox 322-333,344-346. She tells us how her visions did, and did not, come to her: "I spoke and wrote these things [her visions] not according to the invention of my or any other person's heart, but as I saw, heard and perceived them in the heavens through the hidden mysteries of God." Hozeski 4. What did St. Hildegard see in the Heavens? Many images familiar to students of ancient cosmology and cosmogony, and to Grail-questers. The effect of her visions upon St. Hildegard was that she "was able to understand books suddenly, the psaltery clearly, the evangelists and the volumes of the Old and New Testament...." Hozeski 2. We have had similar experiences in the pages of this book! In a "celestial illustration" she saw: a great mountain upon which sat a winged person of great brightness. Before that person was an image filled with eyes. Before that image was a young girl clothed in a tunic, with a cloth covering her feet. She saw heads of people among stars on that mountain. Hozeski 7-8. In another vision, she spoke of a tent of gems with a foundation of topaz and stairs of crystal. Hozeski 41. In another, she saw Abraham, Isaac, and Jacob, and John the Baptist, as stars. Hozeski 83. In yet another, she wrote of an image, in the shape of a human, on an ivory plaque, on the breast of a young woman named "Lady," who brought forth the image from her womb before the daystar. 1 Fox 52; 2 Fox 308. The moist greenness of stone was, to St. Hildegard, a symbol for God. Hozeski 90. She saw such familiar Grail objects as a net, a tower, and a building aligned to the seven stars of the Great Bear constellation to the north. I Fox 71; Hozeski 69-70,97,189. In one vision "a wheel of marvelous appearance became visible right in the center of the breast of the above-mentioned figure which I had seen in the midst of the southern air." 2 Fox 22. She saw God the Father as a living light; His Son as a flash of light; and the Holy Spirit as fire. 1 Fox 23. The cosmic tree, the cosmic egg, the cosmic wheel, the cosmic pillars, and the cosmic web of the universe appear in her visions. 1 Fox 23,35,39,40,47. One of her present-day commentators, a Dominican scholar, believes that there are connections between Hildegard's visions and Celtic-Hindu-Buddhist cosmology, the ancient mother earth goddess religions, the alchemical tradition, and world-axis symbolism which "goes back to pre-Neolithic times." 1 Fox 7,16,48,81. Grail-questers who have reached this point in our analysis should put their skills to the test by reading, with comprehension, the visions of St. Hildegard of Bingen.

Chapter Twenty-Three

French and Welsh Grail Stories

French Tales

Perlesvaus is the centerpiece of our Arthurian studies, but it was not the continental or insular origin of these tales. "Chretien de Troyes was the creator of the Arthurian romance as a literary genre; he was the first known writer in Western Europe to put the Celtic legends of King Arthur and his knights into the long romance form in order to illustrate themes from the twelfth-century codes of love and chivalry. His five romances... were written between 1160 and 1190, a period in France of great interest in British legends and folklore."[1] We shall discuss two of his works, *Yvain* and *Perceval*.

Chretien's word-picture of our Grail giant is exquisite:

> "A creature who looked like a Moor,
> and was so ugly, and so black,
> and hideous, I find I lack
> words to describe him fully, sat
> upon a stump. I notice that
> he held a huge club in his hand.
> I drew close to the creature, and
> I saw his head's size was enormous,
> a huger head than any horse's
> or other beast's, with tufts of hair.
> His forehead was completely bare
> and measured more than two spans wide.
> The creature's head had on each side
> a huge ear filled with mossy plants,
> just like the ears of elephants.
> His brows were full, his face was flat,
> with owlish eyes, the nose of a cat.
> His wolfish mouth was split apart
> by wild boar's teeth, bloodred and sharp.
> His beard was red; his whiskers in
> great knots; his chest merged with his chin.
> His long spine twisted in a hump.
> The creature sat upon the stump
> and leaned upon his club. He wore
> no wool or linen clothing, for
> instead, the fellow was arrayed
> in two wild bulls' hides, newly flayed
> and hung around his neck...."[2]

We see our Grail giant sitting on a stump in **Figure 400**, which illustrates his club in his hand, his tufts of hair, his elephant-like ears, his boar's tusks, his mouth split apart, and his beard. In **Figure 401**, parts of the "boat-shapes" which played the role of elephant-like ears now appear in the role of owlish eyes, and we see, also, his cat-like nose and the bull-hide he is wearing over his chest. In

Figure 400

Figure 401

Figure 402

Figure 402, we see that his chest is, indeed, merged with his chin. Imagine his back being rounded and, ergo, his spine would be rounded also. Three cheers for Chretien for his Grailsmanship! Congratulations, also, to his translator, Ruth Harwood Cline, for her job well done! No easy task to translate Old French verse into modern English verse and not lose the meanings which now are so familiar to us!

Yvain tells the giant he is a knight-errant in search of adventure. The giant assures Yvain he may find adventure at a nearby spring, which Cline's translation describes as follows:

> "An iron basin hangs suspended
> on a long chain that, when extended,
> will reach the fountain, where you'll find
> a great stone. I don't know what kind
> of stone it is: I must admit
> I've never seen a stone like it.
> There is a chapel by the spring;
> it is a very pretty thing.
> Just pick the basin up and spill
> some water on the stone; you will
> start such an awful storm that way,
> no animal would dare to stay...."[3]

Yvain finds the spring beneath a pine tree on which hangs a basin.

> "The spring did seem
> to boil. An emerald, bright green,

Figure 403

> shaped like a sieve, was the great stone,
> with small holes on a ruby throne.
> Beneath the emerald were four
> bright rubies, blazing red and more
> aflame with color than the sun
> at morning in the east...."[4]

Yvain picks up the basin, fills it with water from the spring, and spills the water on the stone.[5] These acts of sympathetic magic start a raging thunderstorm, complete with lightning which splits trees and wind which blows them down.[6] The storm acts as a summons to the knight who guards the spring. If the tale were to proceed as in Frazer's *The Golden Bough*, the knight of the spring would fight Yvain to the death.[7] In Chretien's comic version of this familiar Celtic theme, the knight merely unhorses Yvain and disdainfully rides away, leaving nothing wounded but Yvain's pride.[8] Chretien later tells us, specifically, that the giant is a herdsman tending wild bulls in the glen; that he is as black as any smith.[9] We recall red-headed and lame Thor, who was a blacksmith! Is it without significance that Christian traditions outside the Bible tell us that Jesus Christ was both red-headed and lame?[10] We are told that when the storm subsides, birds sit in the pine tree and sing.[11]

The pine tree and chained basin are seen in **Figure 403**. We see the emerald centered on the four

Figure 404

Figure 405

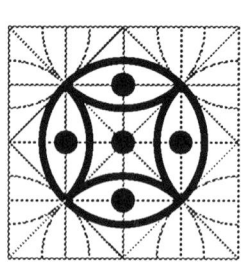

Figure 406

Figure 407

rubies in **Figure 404**, and the sieve in **Figure 405**. The ruby throne, with holes, is seen in top view, and, again, in side view, in **Figures 406** and **407**. The birds in the pine tree are seen in **Figure 408**. We see one of the herdsman's *bulls* in **Figure 409**. The *knight* of the spring rode up to give battle "swifter than an *eagle*, as fierce as any *lion*...."[12]

> All four,
> once more!
> Lion, ox,
> man, and eagle!
> We sniff them out,
> just like a beagle!

King Arthur came with Yvain to experience the phenomena of the spring "...within two weeks at least. Before Saint John the Baptist's feast...."[13] So far, Chretien is writing entertaining stories based on line-forms visible on the Holy Grail, although the reference to John the Baptist is a clue as to what we shall read before the end of Chretien's story. The parody on the Christ story begins with King Arthur's triumphant entrance into town, complete with such Grail-forms as bells, trumpets, horns, drums, cymbals, flutes, and pipes.[14] The priest-bashing begins with this salvo:

> "I give good
> advice to others that I would
> not take myself, just like a priest:
> disloyal lechers, but at least
> they tell us what is right, and teach,
> but do not practice what they preach!"[15]

Yvain is an entertaining tale of knighthood which is filled with Grail-images, such as dwarfs and giants,[16] and passing references to Church dogmas, such as Our Lady in her role as Queen of Heaven.[17] Yvain must keep an appointment to rescue a maiden who is to be burned at the stake at noontime.[18] Yvain, a man of iron, and his side-kick, a lion, save the maiden tied to the pyre, just as the villains light her fire.[19] Hollywood never did better!

The story continues, but we must commend the rest of it to your reading because we must briefly explore Chretien's *Perceval*, which is subtitled *The Story of the Grail*.

Chretien's *Perceval* abounds with familiar Grail-images, and tells the story of the Grail, itself, in these words:

> "Out of a room a squire came, clasping
> a lance of purest white: while grasping
> the center of the lance, the squire
> walked through the hall between the fire
> and two men sitting on the bed.
> All saw him bear, with measured tread,
> the pure white lance. From its white tip
> a drop of crimson blood would drip
> and run along the white shaft and
> drip down upon the squire's hand,
> and then another drop would flow.

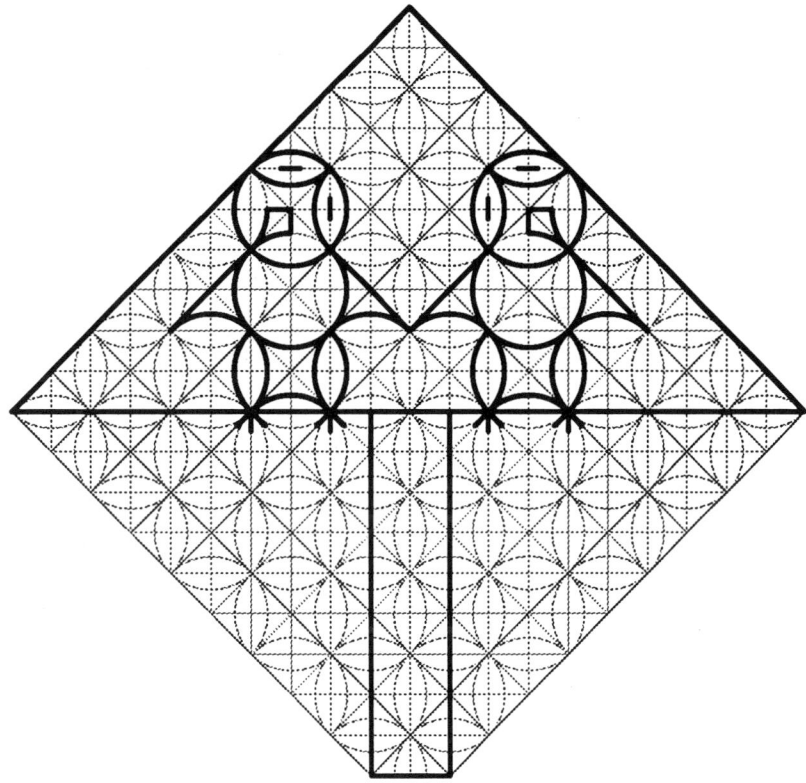

Figure 408

* * * * *

Two more squires entered, and each squire held candelabra....

* * * * *

The squires were followed by a maiden
who bore a grail, with both hands laden.
The bearer was of noble mien,
well dressed, and lovely, and serene,
and when she entered with the grail,
the candles suddenly grew pale,
the grail cast such a brilliant light,
as stars grow dimmer in the night
when sun or moonrise makes them fade.
A maiden after her conveyed
a silver platter past the bed.
The grail, which had been borne ahead,
was made of purest, finest gold
and set with gems; a manifold
display of jewels of every kind,
the costliest that one could find
in any place on land or sea,
the rarest jewels there could be,
let not the slightest doubt be cast.
The jewels in the grail surpassed
all other gems in radiance."[20]

The golden sun, silver moon, and stars of Heaven shine in many jewel-like colors and surpass all gemstones. Is this the meaning?

The hero, of course, fails to ask the relevant questions about the Grail and whom the servers served from it;[21] "about the lance, why it was bleeding, about the grail, whom they were feeding...."[22] As in other Grail quest stories, Perceval

Figure 409

fails to ask the question "… what nobleman was being served… ?"[23]

> "… a dreadful pity you did not
> ask all these questions on the spot!
> To ask one question would procure
> the king's recovery and his cure."[24]

What is the King's illness? Having to share the Godhead with His Son and the Holy Ghost? What would be the King's cure? Common knowledge of the origin of the Christ story? What would be the King's recovery? His former position as One-and-Only God?

Chretien's description of Cundrie riding her mule[25] is good for a few laughs, as well as being an excellent opportunity to exercise your Grail skills, as is his story of the "Maid with Little Sleeves."[26] His story of the mob of peasants attempting to undermine a tower[27] may not be amusing to those of you who already have read the science chapters at the end of this book. His description of the wondrous bed-on-wheels[28] and of the tower with its spiral staircase[29] are worth reading – if you want to practice your Grail skills without help. We must leave Chretien's *Perceval* after reading *his* answer to the question of who is served by the Holy Grail:

> "You were a foolish man to fail
> to learn whom they serve from the grail.
> The man they serve is my own brother;
> my sister, and his, was your mother;
> and also the rich Fisherman
> is that king's son, son of the man
> who has himself served with the grail.
> Now do not let the thought prevail
> that from the grail he takes food like
> a salmon, lamprey, or a pike,
> because from it the king obtains
> one mass wafer, and it sustains
> his life, borne in the grail they bring;
> the grail is such a holy thing.
> He is so very spiritual
> that he's required no food at all
> except the host the grail contained…."[30]

We see in those words the closest reference to the "Holy Grail." We see, also, the clearest answer to our abiding questions. If the King is so very spiritual, then what must be said of his relatives? Are they, too, of the spirit rather than of the flesh? That certainly would be in accord with the views of Cathar Christians.

Welsh Tales

The Welsh tales of *The Mabinogion* are filled with Holy Grail images. "*The Mabinogion* itself is something of a mystery, both as to origin and as to content."[31] *The Mabinogion* "lay so dormant that it was not translated into English until 1849…."[32] The use of the title "Mabinogion" is an unfortunate error[33] which has become entrenched, illustrating, once more, that error can become truth merely by repetition. The tales come to us from the *Red Book of Hergest*, circa 1400 A.D.,[34] the *White Book of Rhydderch*, circa 1325 A.D.,[35] and a document known as *Peniarth 6*, circa 1225 A.D.[36] Although scholars have assured us that Britain is the origin of Grail quest stories, you should note that these Welsh tales come to us in manuscripts that are not as old as the earliest continental Grail quest manuscripts. Gantz suggests that the tales of *The Mabinogion* may "derive from French reworkings of Celtic originals," and that this may "account for the veneer of French manners in the Welsh Romances."[37] For our purposes, need we reach conclusions as to who wrote what first?

Before you get yourself "hyped up" in expectation of beautiful stories about King Arthur's court as portrayed by Hollywood, be warned that "Mochdrev" in Welsh means "Pig Town," and "Culhwch" means "Pig Run."[38] Are we reading satire and parody?

Grail concepts as well as Grail images abound in these stories. We read about "shape-changing,"[39] the magic cauldron of Bran into which slain warriors are thrown to be born-again fit to fight but unable to speak,[40] a giant and his wife emerging from a lake,[41] a house or chamber of iron,[42] Bran walking across the Irish Sea,[43] and headhunting.[44] We discover a Grail-image of "a golden bowl fastened to four chains, the bowl set over a marble slab and the chains extending upwards so that he could see no end to them."[45] **Figure 410.** Maxen's dream is a wonderful story on which to practice your Grail-skills.[46] A manform god who walks on the sea? Warriors fit to fight but unable to speak? Like our knights who failed to ask the proper questions when the Holy Grail passed before them? Like all Christian sheep who silently accept whatever they are told by their Christian shepherds?

Blood-magic is encountered in its most primitive form: "The blood will not be effective unless you get it while it is still warm, and no vessel anywhere will keep liquid warm save the bottles of Gwydolwyn the Dwarf…."[47] Yes, there are dwarfs,

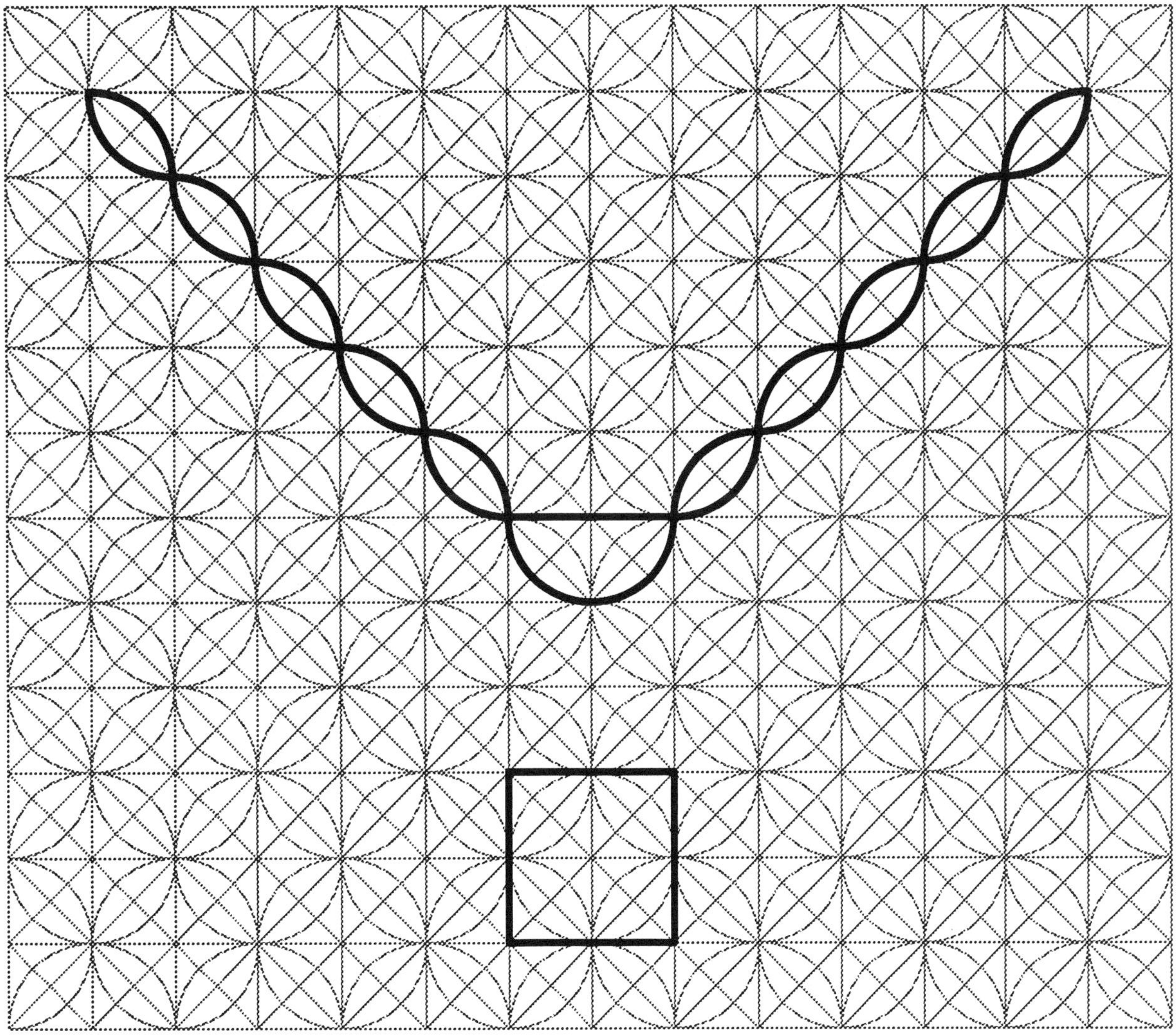

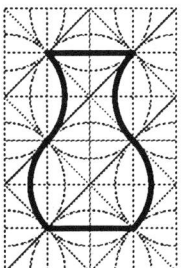

Figure 410

as well as giants, in these stories! We see Gwydolwyn's bottle, or a "wine bottle"[48] in **Figure 411**. Ritual cannibalism of the worst sort is mentioned: "Gwynn killed Nwython and cut out his heart, and forced Kyledyr to eat his father's heart...."[49] Is this a parody of the doctrine of "Real

Figure 411

Presence," which holds that the Holy Magic of the Mass converts the Host into the actual body of God?[50]

The dream-quest of Madawg, son of Maredudd, finds the hero going off to dreamland while lying on a yellow ox-skin on a platform on a floor strewn with holly-stems.[51] King Arthur is found "sitting in the middle of a chamber on a pile of green rushes with a cloth of yellow-red brocade under him and a red-brocade-covered cushion under his elbow."[52] Familiar images!

Grail banqueting images in these stories include cushions, bowls, towels, linen, tables, horns, cups, candles, and cauldrons.[53] Sir Kei (Kay) returns to the banqueting hall "with a pitcher of mead and a gold cup, and his hands full of skewers with

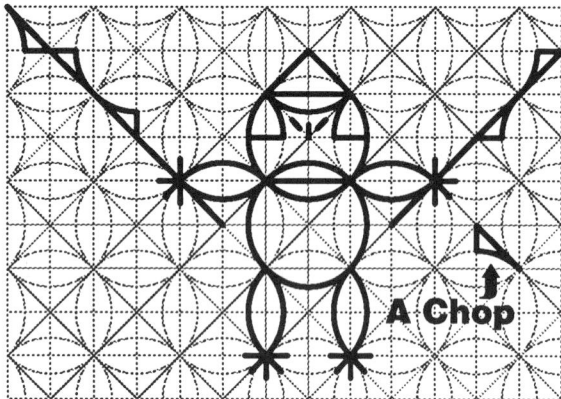

Figure 412

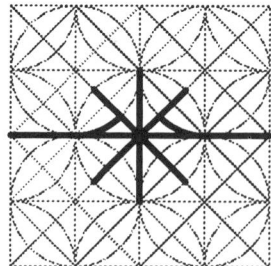

Figure 413

chops on them...."[54] We see Sir Kei with his hands full of skewers with chops on them in **Figure 412**. We have not seen a Grail "chop" before now. You can find the pitcher and cup for yourself. At least one more tale from *The Mabinogion* contains an image of chops roasting on a spit on a fire.[55] **Figure 413**. Once a writer learns the system, he can create new images not previously used by Grail authors.

You will recall that Grail storysmiths often give us a clue that they are not writing about real-world trees, rivers, plains, fortresses, and oceans. We are told, for instance, that "the trees were all the same height."[56] Not likely, even in a modern, man-planted and man-managed forest, but certainly not in a natural, God-planted forest! Is our unknown author trying to tell us, if we will but listen, that we are walking in a Grail forest?

Remember the giant herdsman, the magic spring, the thunderstorm started by pouring water from the spring onto the magic rock, etc., from the *Story of Yvain*? In the *Story of Owein*, from *The Mabinogion*, we are introduced to "a great black man, no smaller than two men of this world. He has one foot, and one eye in the middle of his forehead, and he carries an iron spear which you can be certain would be burden for any two men. Though ugly, he is not an unpleasant man. He is keeper of the forest, and you will see a thousand wild animals grazing about him. Ask him where to go from the clearing; he will be cross with you, but nevertheless he will show you how to find what you seek."[57] Gantz correctly points out in a footnote that the Irish god Lug and the Germanic god Odin also appeared in one-eyed and one-legged forms.[58] A forest in the sky? With wild animals (constellations) grazing about him? Does he stand at the North Pole, and give directions to those who travel

by land or sea? In the Story of Stories, does he show us the Way?

Owein asked the giant "what power he held over the animals" and the giant replied, "'Little man, I will show you.'"[59] The giant "took his cudgel and struck a stag a great blow so that it roared; with that wild animals came until they were like stars in the sky, so that there was scarcely room for me to stand among the serpents and vipers and lions and animals of all sorts. He looked at them and ordered them to graze, and they bowed their heads and worshipped him as obedient men do their lord. Then he said, 'Well, little man, you see the power I hold over these animals.'"[60] Experts in cosmology tell us that the one-legged manform of ancient legends is the keeper of the rotational axis of the world.[61] We see the one-legged and one-eyed man-

Figure 414

Illustration 23-1. The Celtic god Cernunnos as the cosmic master of the animals. From the Gundestrup Cauldron, second century B.C., Denmark. Courtesy of the Werner Forman Archive, London.

form and the world axis in **Figure 414**. Note the reference to stars in the sky! Are we being told that the herdsman is lord of the constellations of the sky; that the constellations of stars rotate around him (i.e., worship him) because they know he will punish them with his cudgel if they do not; and that his cudgel is the *sole* source of his power over the animals? The Roman Catholic Church prevailed over the Cathar Christian Church because of *might* rather than *right*. Humans are animals. The Church tells us that Jesus is our Shepherd. Might there be some relationship between the shepherd of the constellations of the sky and the Church's Holy Shepherd?

The Owein Story from *The Mobinogion* next tells the tale of the tree, the bowl, the stone, the thunderstorm caused by sympathetic magic, the shower of birds in the tree, and the knight who guards the spring. As in *Yvain*, the hero is humiliated rather than slaughtered by the knight of the spring.[62] We Celts are amused by stories in which the hero lands on his duff in a mudpuddle! That gods as well as men find themselves baptized in the cosmic mudpuddle of Celtic parody and satire is a consequence of their having been "demoted" by "backsliding" Celts to anthropomorphic beings instead of being permitted to continue their original aniconic[63] existence? The Hebrew YHWH avoids cream pies in His face by remaining so spiritual that His name is not even pronounced.[64] Should other religions have taken clues from the Jews?

The consequence of creating a "new" name for an "old" god whose myths appear on the Holy Grail can be that Your Man and the other fellow can be compared with each other by anyone who understands the art of Grail storysmithing. In **Illustration 23-1**, we see the god Cernunnos surrounded by animals. He holds a torc and a snake, familiar Aryan sexual symbols. Cernunnos = Thor = Lug = Jesus Christ? Cavendish tells us that we Celts started visualizing our gods as anthropomorphic beings "as a result of cultural interference from the Mediterranean world. Here perhaps the story told of Brennus, the Celtic leader defeated at Delphi in 279 BC, laughing in scorn when he heard that the

Figure 415

Figure 416

Greeks believed in gods in human form lends support."[65]

We previously alluded to the fact that archaeologists have unearthed evidence indicating that our Stone Age ancestors "tripped" using the juice of the opium poppy. Notice the poppies under the wolf and the stag in Illustration 23-1,[66] and compare them with **Figure 415**. Is any resemblance between those shapes illustrated on the Gundestrup cauldron, from Denmark, and the shape of the opium poppy on the Holy Grail purely coincidental? Naughty Celts!

Do the tales of *The Mabinogion* cast subtle barbs into the hide of the Church? "Take this ring and put it on your finger, and keep the stone in your hand and close your fist over it, for as long as you conceal it will conceal you."[67] The story-line is that the ring will conceal its wearer from the view of his potential enemies. What is the allegorical level, if any? Is Christ the stone? Conceal the origins of the Christ story and the Christ story will conceal you? Conceal what about you? That you are a shepherd herding sheep by use of Grail-born myths? For the sake of the sheep? Or for the sake of the shepherd?

You will recall the iron pincers which could not be removed from the grave of the knight. In one of the tales of *The Mabinogion* we are told of a knight's iron tunic which "will not come off, it is part of him...."[68] Is this another clue that we are traveling in the realm of Grail fantasy rather than in the world of reality?

Peredur (the Welsh Perceval) forgot to ask who was served from the Grail because of these instructions from his teacher: "Forget your mother's words, for I will be your teacher, and I will make you a knight. From now on follow this advice: though

you see what is strange, do not ask about it unless someone is courteous enough to tell you...."[69] Eschew the scientific method of inquiry? Ask the Church no questions and the Church will tell you no lies? Believe what the clergy tell you to believe in order to become a Christian?

A maiden puts a stone into Peredur's hand, then vanishes, after telling him: "When you seek me, look towards India."[70] We have progressed westerly in this book from India to the British Isles. Are we going to make a circle? The Chakra? Ezekiel's Wheel? Will we return from whence we came? Not until we reach Ireland!

In the *Story of Peredur*, we are told that "[w]hen a white sheep bleated a black sheep would cross the river and turn white, and when a black sheep bleated a white sheep would cross the river and turn black."[71] Will the yin-yang wheel soon start spinning? Will we return to the place from whence we have come? Not until we reach Ireland!

Peredur is berated for not asking the Grail questions: "Had you asked, the king would have been made well and the kingdom made peaceful, but now there will be battles and killing, knights lost and women widowed and children orphaned, all because of you."[72] Why? Because Roman Catholic knights presumably would not attack and kill Cathar Christian knights in warfare over religious beliefs if they were aware of the origins of their Catholic faith in line-forms visible on the Holy Grail? Peredur does not carry this blame by himself. Human strife and conflict stirred up by the Church has continued because *none* of us has asked questions; because *all* of us have accepted our instructions from our teachers and have believed what we should have questioned. We *all* bear the shame of Peredur! We *all* bear the blame for what mankind has done to itself in the Holy Name of God!

In the *Tale of Gereint and Enid* we are introduced to an interesting Grail-image: "a small green pitcher... with a cup over the mouth of the pitcher...."[73] In **Figure 416**, we see the pitcher, right-side up, and the cup, upside down and over the mouth of the pitcher. Gantz's translation of these stories is not "literal,"[74] but it is accurate enough to allow us to understand and to draw a Grail-image conceived by an unknown author over 600 years ago!

Gereint is told that if he travels a certain road he "will not return alive. Below there is a hedge of mist, and enchanted games within, and no man who has gone there has ever come back."[75] Gereint and Enid eat a meal with the earl who instituted the games. "The earl noticed... [Gereint] lost in thought and supposed that Gereint had stopped [eating] for fear of having to go to the game; and he was sorry he had ever instituted these games, if only so as not to lose a man as excellent as this."[76] Actually, Gereint was worried that he would not be allowed to go to the games.[77] We are told that if Gereint had asked the earl "to call off the game he would have done so gladly."[78] The earl tells Gereint, "If you are fearful of going to the game you will not have to go, and for your sake no one will ever have to go again."

Gereint tells the earl that he *does* want to go to the games.[79] Gereint enters the mist, fights and bests the knight of the mist, gaining the privilege of sitting in the knight's chair.[80] The defeated knight of the mist grants Gereint his wishes, which are: "'... that these games cease, and that the hedge of mist and the magic and enchantment disappear.'"[81] The knight of the mist tells Gereint, "'Blow on that horn, for as soon as you sound it the mist will vanish. Until a knight who had overthrown me sounded the horn, the mist could not vanish.'"[82] We are told that "...Gereint... came and blew on the horn, and as soon as he did so the mist disappeared."[83]

Gantz tells us that "The meaning of the hedge of mist episode remains a mystery."[84] We have studied about sacred kings-for-a-year who died to assure that the fruitful seasons would return. Is Gereint the last of the sacrificial kings to die? Is he Jesus Christ? After Him, no more? What is the magic and enchantment which is to disappear? Human sacrifice to keep the wheel of the seasons turning? Magic made with human flesh and blood? Or do we have here an allegory within an allegory? Is Roman Catholic Christianity blowing its horn to dispel the mist of paganism, or is Cathar Christianity blowing its horn to dispel the mist of Roman Catholicism? Might the magic and enchantment dispelled be that of the Roman Catholic Mass? Such a conclusion would be consistent with Cathar Christian beliefs!

We must leave the rest of the Welsh tales to those of you who are interested in what the *great* Britains (the Welsh) thought about life and death.

Notes
CHAPTER TWENTY-THREE. French and Welsh Grail Stories

1. Cline, *Yvain* xi. The Grail scholar John Matthews indicates that *circa* 1136, Geoffrey of Monmouth almost certainly drew upon earlier sources for his *Historia Regum Britanniae*, dealing with Arthur the King. Matthews, *Reader* 50. Matthews indicates that a version of the Arthur tale by Bleheris, a Welshman, predates Chretien's *Perceval*. Matthews, *Reader* 182. Your author expresses no opinion about who first conceived of the Grail, or who first wrote about it.

2. Cline, *Yvain* 8-9. Is it without significance that the Hindu Avatar Krishna is black and carries a club? Parrinder 81; Cavendish 24. In Joseph Campbell's edition of Heinrich Zimmer's *The King & The Corpse*, we are told (at footnote 1 on page 183) that our cosmic herdsman is none other than Merlin the Magician of Round Table fame! If Merlin was the magician to King Arthur, and Merlin was a cosmic allegory, then what might we conclude about Arthur the King? That the Christian Church was not alone in teaching cosmic allegory as historic reality? If Zimmer and Campbell are correct, is Merlin somehow related to the monster Humbaba, who was slain by the Sumerian-Babylonian hero Gilgamish? Langdon 246-269.

3. Cline, *Yvain* 11.

4. Cline, *Yvain* 12.

5. Cline, *Yvain* 13.

6. Cline, *Yvain* 13.

7. 1 Frazer 1,2; 2 Frazer 364.

8. Cline, *Yvain* 16.

9. Cline, *Yvain* 20-21.

10. Tribbe 221,246.

11. Cline, *Yvain* 13,23.

12. Cline, *Yvain* 14.

13. Cline, *Yvain* 19.

14. Cline, *Yvain* 65-66.

15. Cline, *Yvain* 71.

16. Cline, *Yvain* 115-116.

17. Cline, *Yvain* 114-115.

18. Cline, *Yvain* 111-112,121

19. Cline, *Yvain* 121-123.

20. Cline, *Perceval* 87-89.

21. Cline, *Perceval* 89-91.

22. Cline, *Perceval* 93.

23. Cline, *Perceval* 128.

24. Cline, *Perceval* 99.

25. Cline, *Perceval* 126-127.

26. Cline, *Perceval* 137-153.

27. Cline, *Perceval* 161-167,177.

28. Cline, *Perceval* 206.

29. Cline, *Perceval* 213.

30. Cline, *Perceval* 173.

31. Gantz, *Mabinogion* 9.

32. Gantz, *Mabinogion* 31.

33. Gantz, *Mabinogion* 31.

34. Gantz, *Mabinogion* 29.

35. Gantz, *Mabinogion* 10,29.

36. Gantz, *Mabinogion* 21.

37. Gantz, *Mabinogion* 25.

38. Gantz, *Mabinogion* 20.

39. Gantz, *Mabinogion* 47,50,104,105,115.

40. Gantz, *Mabinogion* 71,79.

41. Gantz, *Mabinogion* 72.

42. Gantz, *Mabinogion* 72.

43. Gantz, *Mabinogion* 75.

44. Gantz, *Mabinogion* 79.

45. Gantz, *Mabinogion* 89.

46. Gantz, *Mabinogion* 119-121.

47. Gantz, *Mabinogion* 157.

48. Gantz, *Mabinogion* 228.

49. Gantz, *Mabinogion* 168.

50. Matthews 54-55.

51. Gantz, *Mabinogion* 179.

52. Gantz, *Mabinogion* 193.

53. Gantz, *Mabinogion* 194-195,202-203.

54. Gantz, *Mabinogion* 194.

55. Gantz, *Mabinogion* 212.

56. Gantz, *Mabinogion* 194.

57. Gantz, *Mabinogion* 196.

58. Gantz, *Mabinogion* 196.

59. Gantz, *Mabinogion* 197.

60. Gantz, *Mabinogion* 197.

61. Talbott 42-43,47-59; Spanuth 91-101.

62. Gantz, *Mabinogion* 198-199.

63. Cavendish 171.

64. Runes 233.

65. Cavendish 171.

66. Cavendish 171. Does the Old Testament tell us that Adam and Eve were expelled from the Garden of Eden because they ate the opium poppy? This question is far less absurd than it first seems! In the Hebrew version of the story found in the Bible, Yaweh created Adam. Genesis 2.7,19. In the earlier Babylonian (Accadian) version, Ea created Adapa. Langdon 175. Langdon posits the existence of an even earlier Sumerian version of the story from the existence of Sumerian illustrations of a man, a woman, a tree, and a snake, Langdon 177-179, from the existence of a Sumerian version of the story of the fall of man, Langdon 181, and from references to a plant, identified as the opium poppy, that the Sumerians called the "plant of life." Langdon 187. Langdon shows us Sumerian art illustrating a deity offering an opium poppy to a worshiper. Langdon 186. Thus, we have an open question whether there might be some relationship between the opium poppy (the Sumerian "plant of life") and the biblical "tree of life," Genesis 3.24, which may, or may not, be the same tree as the "tree of knowledge of good and evil." Genesis 2.17. Note, in passing, that by eating the forbidden fruit, "man is become as one of us." Genesis 3.22. "Us" is plural! Is that plural reference a remnant of an earlier, polytheistic version of the tale? We cannot answer these questions if we limit ourselves to the Bible. However, if we read the equally-ancient Hindu *Rigveda*, we are told about another plant whose extract was drunk by the gods and their priests. Its name was "Soma," called "Haoma" in the Iranian version of the tale. Keith 46. When its shoots were pressed, a ruddy brown liquid was extracted, which flowed clear when passed through a strainer. Keith 46. The extract, when drunk, stimulated speech; had an exhilarating power. Keith 46. Soma was grown in the mountains by hill tribes. Keith 47-48,90. It was drunk from a cup; the drinking vessel of the gods. Keith 57. The great deeds of Indra resulted from his drinking of Soma. Keith 46. However, the plant extract had negative effects. Indra became seriously afflicted from drinking it, and had to be cured through a sacred rite. Keith 88, 93. What do you think? I think that, in passing, we should note that Indra had a "great belly" to contain the vast quantities of soma he drank! Keith 32. Indra also had beautiful lips. Keith 32. Does Indra sound like anyone you met among the pages of this book? Answering the main question: We apparently are forced to conclude that our ancestors may have tripped as well as traveled!

67.   Gantz, *Mabinogion* 201.

68.   Gantz, *Mabinogion* 223.

69.   Gantz, *Mabinogion* 225.

70.   Gantz, *Mabinogion* 243.

71.   Gantz, *Mabinogion* 243.

72.   Gantz, *Mabinogion* 248-249.

73.   Gantz, *Mabinogion* 282-283.

74.   Gantz, *Mabinogion* 34.

75.   Gantz, *Mabinogion* 295.

76.   Gantz, *Mabinogion* 295.

77.   Gantz, *Mabinogion* 295.

78.   Gantz, *Mabinogion* 295.

79.   Gantz, *Mabinogion* 296.

80.   Gantz, *Mabinogion* 296-297.

81.   Gantz, *Mabinogion* 297.

82.   Gantz, *Mabinogion* 297.

83.   Gantz, *Mabinogion* 297.

84.   Gantz, *Mabinogion* 258-259.

Chapter Twenty-Four

Irish Stories Vedantic Beside the Atlantic

The spangled and painted American tourist-lady was visibly upset. Through chilly fog and rain she and her man had come to the cozy pub on the west coast of Ireland to hear "real" Irish music sung and played. My American-style, mountain-climber's, foul-weather jacket distinguished me from the locals. Her questions were addressed to me. She had been assured that this was the best place to come "to get a taste of the local color," a euphemism of American tourists which means, essentially, to cast a cold eye on the local human animals in their natural habitat as you quickly pass by, much as one observes a white rat in its cage during a walk-through tour of a laboratory. When would the musicians start playing *real* Irish music? When would they cease the clatter of spoons, the banging on that Arab drum, and the incessant squawking of that bellows-pumped instrument which looks as if it might be the offspring of a saxophone and a bagpipe? What sort of music are the musicians playing? Is this a local version of Greek, Israeli, or East Indian folk music? When would they play "Danny Boy"?

Smiles. First, for her. Then, for me. Anticipation. A circle of smiling faces awaiting my answer, which was: "Lady, would you like to hear the Story of Indra of the Vedas?" More smiles, and a few comments whispered in the Irish language, but no open laughter. The Irish *are* polite, even to impolite American tourists.

Bad-temper flashed across her face.
"Come, Fred, let's go, let's leave this place."
Fred, at last warm with a beer in his hand.
His coat soaked by the rains of Ireland.
Away from the peat-blaze,
Back into the rain,
Before your author could explain,
Indra, the Dagda, the ancient of daze,
Lady, his music, his songs, they plays.
The Irish — western warriors Vedantic,
Nestled beside the howling Atlantic,
Play his music, or theirs.
Who cares whose it is.
She left without knowing,
Still ignorant, gee whiz.

The Chakra. The Yin-yang Wheel. Ezekiel's Wheel. The cosmic wheel. Things equal to the same thing are equal to each other. Culturally, we have come full circle, although geographically we have progressed ever-westerly. In our chapter on India, we quoted Fairservis as follows: "The story has been repeated for millennia, sung in temples, chanted in halls, told by word and actions of how a warrior people came out of the vastness of inner Asia through the passes of the northwest to fall upon the fortified cities of India and to conquer; riding horse-drawn chariots, driving herds of cattle, sheep, and goats, worshipping cosmic deities like Indra of the thunder and Agni of the fire, sacrificing, quarreling, gambling, drinking, singing, dancing — the Rig Veda account of the Aryan tribes is one of the oldest epics in the world. It is part of an oral tradition which lies at the heart of Hinduism. The Aryans were a pastoral people moving along routes already ages old, a people already affected by the sedentary world with which they were in contact even before arriving in India. They were organized into a rough class system headed by warrior chiefs whose rank was retained partially by accumulated wealth counted by herds and partially by prowess in battle. They spoke an Indo-European language and both by speech and cosmology were one with that group of pastoral nomads who inhabited the heart of the Eurasian continent in the early second millennium B.C. and whose later migrations so profoundly affected the ancient world."[1]

Change "India" to "Ireland" and "Rig Veda" to the "Book of Invasions" and you have described the invasion of Ireland by the people the historians call the Goidelic Celts, the Gaels, or simply the Irish.

We use the word "Aryan" in the sense of a language family of Sanskrit-speakers, not in terms of Nazi fantasies about a racial purity that never existed. An Irishman, for instance, is a person who can pronounce the words *Cumann Luthchleas Gael*.[2] His skin may be milk-white and freckled, his hair red and curly, and his eyes green. Or his skin may be ivory, his hair blond and straight, and his eyes blue. Or his skin may be as brown as an East

Indian's, his hair jet black and kinky, and his eyes dark brown. Physical appearance does not matter. What counts is his love for horses, dogs, dark beer, team sports, and songs with verses that the clergy do not know. We could kick Adolph Hitler's bigoted butt for the permanent damage he did to the ancient and honorable word, "Aryan." Aryan superiority? Right! Try to beat us at football![3] Aryan racial purity? You really must be careful whose myths you swallow!

The "conduct of Irish and Welsh court poets was described by an eminent orientalist as 'almost a chapter in the history of India under another name.'"[4] In India, Wales, and Ireland the telling of tales serves as a benediction over the listeners and the place of recital.[5] Why? Could it be that the telling of a tale which came to the storyteller as a revelation from the Holy Grail was regarded as a way to become "at one with the Creator"? The Mass — the supposed eating of God's flesh and drinking of His blood — is another ritual by which the faithful believe that they unite their bodies with the Creator.

Can the words which flow from the mouth of the storyteller as he creates a story from line-forms visible on the Holy Grail be likened to the "words of power" spoken by the Creator God to start the Chakra spinning? The retired American school teacher was hunchbacked and arthritic. She had suffered sitting there on the rock as the Irish storyteller performed by a small turf fire. "How profound, what he said," she remarked, when he finished his tale — translated, this time, into English, for the benefit of the tourists. "What did he say and what did he mean?", I asked her. She was stunned. "I really do not know," was her response, followed by the request she perhaps should not have made: "Tell me what he meant. His words moved me so deeply." My response shattered her euphoria: "He spoke a concert of words which have no point at all, except to please you, which they did. You have heard of Irish blarney. Now you have heard blarney at its best." A wry grin appeared on her ancient lips. "Blarney is like a Sunday sermon designed to leave the congregation warm and mellow?", she responded. "Yes," I replied. "Ah, well," she said, in a mock Irish accent, "'Tis better for the liver than Irish whisky." She had heard words of power. You cannot understand unless you have experienced the feeling. Grail stories may be mere fantasy; sheer nonsense. The *feeling* created by words of power is *real*. Our shepherds know this. Thus do they herd the sheep.

Nearly everyone realizes that the ancient Irish tales are a mixture of history, cosmology, and good-humored fantasy. You perhaps will decide that they contain elements written around line-forms visible on the Holy Grail. Separating these components and labeling them is beyond the ken of most of us, and far beyond the reach of this book. Much of the story action occurs around Brug na Boinne,[6] the tumulus of Newgrange, located on the River Boyne.[7] Those of you who have read the science chapters realize that Newgrange is a 5000-year-old structure which functions as a solar calculator and calendar. Fomorian towers dot the landscape of these tales.[8] "The Men of Ireland" are tired of Fomorian raiders, and resolve to run them out of Ireland once and for all.[9] We encounter Grail images such as a stone, a spear, a sword, a golden ring, a magic cauldron, and a man "whose mouth was out of his breast."[10]

We are told a tale about the "Dagda," that is, "the good hand," not in the sense of "well-behaved" but in the sense of "all-skilled."[11] We are told that he was one of the gods of the Irish.[12] Here is the story: "Porridge was then made for him by the Fomorians, and this was done to mock him, for great was his love for porridge. They filled for him the king's cauldron, five fists deep, in which went four-score gallons of new milk and the like quantity of meal and fat. Goats and sheep and swine were put into it, and they were all boiled together with the porridge.[13] They were spilt for him into a hole in the ground, and Indech told him that he would be put to death unless he consumed it all; he should eat his fill so that he might not reproach the Fomorians with inhospitality. Then the Dagda took his ladle, and it was big enough for a man and woman to lie on the middle of it. These then were the bits that were in it, halves of salted swine and a quarter of lard. 'Good food, this,' said the Dagda.... At the end of the meal he put his curved finger over the bottom of the hole.... Sleep came upon him then after eating his porridge. Bigger than a house-cauldron was his belly, and the Fomorians laughed at it.[14] Unseemly was his apparel. A cape to the hollow of his two elbows. A dun tunic around him, as far as the swelling of his rump. It was, moreover, long-breasted, with a hole in the peak...."[15] Other translators tell us the Dagda wore: "...a hood over his head, a cape reaching to his elbows, a tunic reaching only to his buttocks...."[16] No mention is made of a kilt, pants, or other clothing to cover his lower body! We see the Dagda in **Figure 417**, which illustrates the hood over his head, the cape reaching

Figure 417

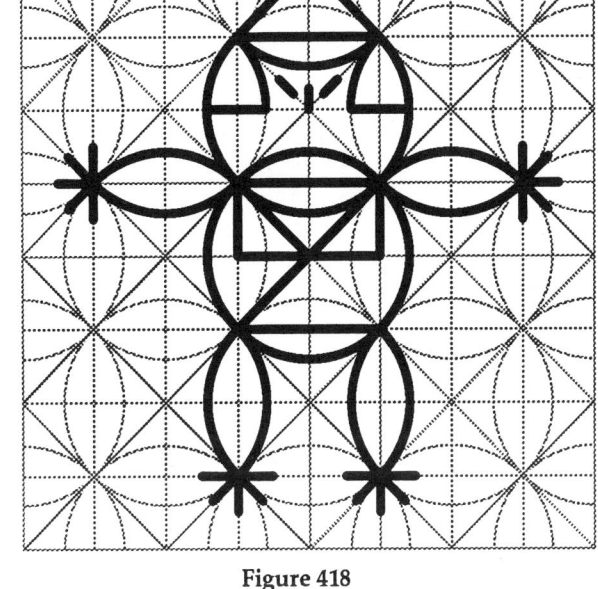

Figure 418

to his elbows, and the tunic down to his buttocks. In **Figure 418**, we have removed the cape to illustrate the two flaps at the neck hole of the tunic. These flaps are hanging open, revealing a portion of his chest, as King Arthur's mailcoat was open in an earlier story. Was he otherwise naked? How could this manform be an Irish god? Because the Irish had not yet stopped ridiculing the concept of Mediterranean people that gods appear in anthropomorphic forms?[17] Because the Christianized scribes who recorded these stories enjoyed humor which was poked at pagan gods? Because the tales were intended to elicit ripples of laughter from the children assembled around the storyteller's campfire under the stars? Was the Dagda one of their cartoon characters?

In another of these stories, we find Lug, one of the two brothers of the Dagda, raising the battle fervor of the men of Ireland, who are fighting the Fomorians. "Singing a chant he went round the host on one foot and with only one eye open."[18] Is he playing the role of the guardian of the world's rotational axis? Lug then confronted Balor, the Fomorian leader, who had a single evil eye which never was opened except on the battlefield, an event which required four of his men to lift the huge eyelid. The Fomorians opened the eyelid of their battle-giant Balor, and guess what Lug did? Right! "Lug cast a sling-stone which carried the eye through his head...."[19] Then what did Lug do? Right again! He "cut off Balor's head...."[20] An Irish parody on

the Biblical story of David and Goliath? Perhaps. Could it be that the Irish story of Lug and Balor and the Hebrew story of David and Goliath have a common origin in ancient cosmology?

The Dagda, the Ogma, and Lug formed an ancient Irish trinity of gods.[21] What did they need? Right, again! They needed an ancient Irish trinity of goddesses — the Morrigan, the Badb, and Macha — "three sinister and destructive female beings who prophesied carnage and haunted battlefields."[22] An Irish female-libber recently quipped that the gods had all the fun on the cosmic battlefields, after which the goddesses picked up the carnage! What do the guys and gals do in these stories? Nothing but eat, drink, and chop off heads, if the translator was a Victorian-minded prude who could not cope with the straightforward honesty of the ancient Irish towards matters sexual. If the translator was a bit more liberal, we find references to men and women "having intercourse."[23] Many an Irish lad has learned just enough of the language of his ancestors to be able to read what these stories *really* say! Modern translations tell it all — including the hilarious tale of the nine-month-long "one-night-stand" between the Dagda and the river goddess Boann.[24] The Victorians evidently thought that homicide was "decent" but sex was "dirty." The ancient Irish poets who wrote these stories apparently believed that humor made life worth living, that sex was natural, and that homicide was obscene. You decide for yourself which view is correct.

On the subject of mixed facts and fantasy, consider this: We are told that the Romans captured parts of Europe by avoiding battles with armies of Celts; by attacking isolated Celtic homesteads one at a time. But this strategy did not always lead to quick and easy victory. One Roman wrote: "A whole troupe ... was not able to withstand a single Gaul if he called his wife to his assistance, who is usually very strong and with blue eyes...."[25] We are told that in Celtic society "the position of women seems to have been high," and that "there were women rulers in the ancient Celtic world."[26] A Roman described one of those Celtic women rulers as follows: "She was huge of frame, terrifying of aspect, and with a harsh voice. A great mass of bright red hair fell to her knees: she wore a great twisted golden torc, and a tunic of many colours, over which was a thick mantle, fastened by a brooch. Now she grasped a spear, to strike fear into all who watched her."[27] Nowadays, she wears a housedress and grasps the kitchen broom. Her terrifying aspect is unchanged. She still rules. Romans who have not given up the idea of invading Ireland, keep these facts in mind: You never succeeded before.[28] Kathleen still is waiting for you, broom in hand, at the kitchen door! While she keeps our hearth, we might sack Rome, as we did in 390 B.C.![29] Irish pub talk! Pub talk like this is founded in truth, but is it "innocent"? Or does it postpone the day when the troubles of the world can be solved?

Stories Vedantic. Beside the Atlantic.[30] Have you been able to digest the idea? Remember the Welsh story from *The Mabinogion* of the white and black sheep crossing the river and changing colors with each other? Like the Hindu Asuras and Devas, these sheep "are in essence consubstantial: 'the Darkness *in actu* is Light, the Light *in potentia* Darkness.'"[31] The crossing of the "river" is an allegory for the transition from Earth to Heaven; white sheep become black and black sheep become white on the other side of the "river" as result of the Hindu inversion principle under which things in Heaven are supposed to be the opposite of things on Earth, i.e., left becomes right, black becomes white, etc.[32]

"The Vedic goddess Danu is mother of Vrtra, the chief adversary of Indra, the king of the gods, but she is also the consort of the sovereign gods of Mitravaruna. Her ambivalent role is paralleled by that of Danann in Irish tradition. Danann is the mother of the gods of Ireland and she gives her

Figure 419

name to the wizard Tautha. On the other hand, 'the Three Gods of Danann' are usually her three sons...."[33] The three gods of Ireland have different names in different stories. We learned the names Dagda, Ogma, and Lug.[34]

Eminent orientalists have identified the Indian goddess Sri Laksmi, who represents sovereignty, with the Irish heroine Queen Medb. The former is the consort of Indra. As Apala, she brings him the intoxicating beverage "soma."[35] The brothers Rees tell us: "Medb's name is cognate with the Welsh *meddw*, 'drunk', and related to the English word *mead*. She is 'the intoxicating one'."[36] The ancients apparently understood that power was more intoxicating than booze! Sovereignty was represented as a loathsome hag with a deranged mind. She became beautiful in the eyes of the king after his marriage to her.[37] We have here the Indo-European version of the sacred marriage of the goddess Inanna (whose role was played by the high priestess) to the Sumerian kings; the new year's sacred marriage ceremony to bring forth a fruitful land![38] "Sovereignty is a bride, the server of a powerful drink, and the drink itself."[39] We Irish performed the ceremony correctly! During inauguration ceremonies, the Irish kings-to-be dived into man-sized cauldrons of beer to "marry Medb." Modern keg-parties on the beach are sober occasions, in comparison!

The brothers Rees draw a careful parallel between the famous Irish stories about St. Moling's leaping about to escape from the specters, and about Suibne Geilt, who grew feathers like a bird and hopped about from tree-top to tree-top, and an Indian story about the god Vishnu, in his dwarfish form, striding about to claim the lands on which mankind might live.[40] We see Mad Sweeny in his bird-form in **Figure 419**, standing on a tree branch. In **Figure 420**, we see the god Vishnu, the sacrifice, in his dwarf-form, lying on the *vedi*, the altar of the Earth, to claim as much of the Earth as possible for mankind.[41] If you are failing to find humor in all of this, go drink a couple of beers, then start reading again.

Why does the "turning point" of Noon play such an important role in Grail quest stories? You have noticed that it does, but we have failed to understand the reason. "Midday and midnight, like sunrise and sunset, were moments when the veil between this world and the unseen world was very thin."[42] The same may be said of *Samain*, the Irish New Year, which we still celebrate as Halloween.[43] Burn her at the stake at Noon because we want to make sure that her spirit will get from "here" to "there" rather than stay around "here" to haunt us! Stupid? Sure! Cathars of the twelfth century would have agreed with you. Their Grail quest stories parody such thinking! Eight hundred years later, are we free from all silly superstitions?

In the *Bhagavad-Gita*, Krishna says of himself: "I am the radiant sun.... I am the moon.... I am Meru among mountain peaks.... I am the ocean among the waters.... I am the Wind...."[44] Amergin of the Irish myths continues the ancient Aryan chant:

> "I am Wind on the Sea,
> I am Ocean-wave,
> I am Roar of Sea,
> etc."[45]

The award for brevity goes to the Hebrews:
> "I AM THAT I AM,"
or, simply,
> "I AM."[46]

Our religious leaders tell us we must fight to preserve our religions; that we must convert the nonbelievers and never must accept any aspect of their religions. For the sake of the sheep? Or for the sake of the shepherds?

We have bandied about the concept of "reality" but never have sought to define it. In ancient Indo-European cultures, "reality is acquired solely through repetition or participation; everything which lacks an exemplary model [in a tribal myth] is 'meaningless', i.e., it lacks reality."[47] The Nicene Creed is reality?

Figure 420

The brothers Rees compare the Irish legends about the five provinces of Ireland with the Indian "Five Kindreds" of the *Rig Veda* and conclude that the "seas" which are crossed and the "lands" which are settled in the Indian and Irish tales "have no place in terrestrial geography."[48] They have no doubts "as to the cosmological significance of the four [provinces] and the central fifth [province] in Ireland."[49] "Although the four great provinces and the centre constitute the state, the ordered cosmos, they do not comprise all that is."[50] There also is the "otherworld" of Celtic legends. Board games such as chess, branfad, fidcheall and gwyddbwyll, often found in Grail quest stories, represent the opposition between the cosmos and the "otherworld."[51] We find the four cosmic divisions of "Earth" and the fifth division, "Heaven,"[52] expressed on the shield of the Irish hero CuCulainn as five interlocking wheels.[53] **Figure 421**.

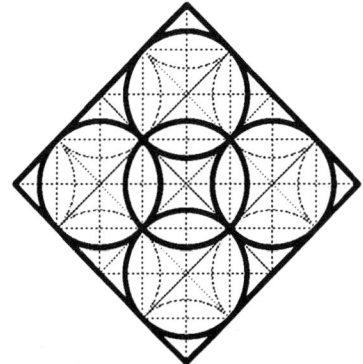

Figure 421

The brothers Rees tell us: "The *Rig Veda* also speaks of the eight supreme Hindu gods known as Adityas as crossing the waters in an amphibious chariot 'with seats where eight may sit.' These may be compared with the [Irish tales of] the eight Sons of Mil."[54] A chariot for the crossing of the "sea" of Heaven? Ezekiel's wheels? The Wain?

The brothers Rees draw a comparison between the Irish CuRoi mac Dairi, who sets the fortress in which he spends the night revolving as swiftly as a millstone so that the entrance cannot be found after sunset,[55] and the Indian god Pusan, who aids in the revolution of day and night and shares other characteristics with CuRoi.[56] They quote an eminent orientalist, who identified the giant herdsman of our Grail tales as Varuna, Prajapati, Atman — the highest of the Indian gods in their sacrificial aspects as the source from which all things come forth.[57]

The Irish banqueting halls and hostels of these tales sometimes are divided into twelves.[58] "Around Conchobar's couch in Bricriu's Hall were the couches of the twelve heroes of Ulster, an arrangement which is paralleled by the beds of the Twelve Peers of France set around the magnificent central bed of Charlemagne. It also brings to mind King Arthur and his twelve knights, Odin seated in a circle with his twelve god-councillors, Hrolf and his twelve berserks, Odysseus and his twelve companions, as well as the Biblical twelves."[59] The Irish are said to have had twelve "free or noble races."[60] Are the

Figure 422

twelve tribes of Ireland mythology whereas the twelve tribes of Israel are history? "The account of the construction of Bricriu's Hall certainly embodies a calendrical symbolism. It took *seven* of the Ulster champions to carry every single lath, and *thirty* of the chief artificers of Ireland were employed in constructing and arranging the building. The hall contained couches of the *twelve* heroes and it was built in the course of *one* year."[61] Remember the Tabernacle and the Tent of the Presence, and Solomon's Temple, from the Old Testament?

The cosmic stone is found in Irish legends as the Stone of Fal at Tara.[62] It also is found as the Stone of Divisions at Uisnech, where it is the navel of Ireland.[63] Note that the navel of our man-form lies at

Figure 423

Figure 424

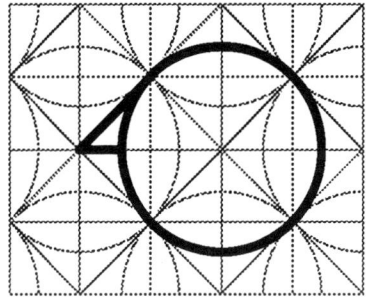

Figure 425   Figure 426   Figure 427

the center of the Holy Grail. **Figure 422**. In the *Rig Veda*, the Five Kindreds and the Eight Adityas kindle a fire on an altar immediately after landing from the sea. In the Irish stories, the landing occurs at *Beltine*, when ship-festivals and fire-lightings are celebrated, and Mide's fire, the archetypal *Beltine* fire, is kindled on the sacred hearth.[64] "Agni, the Vedic sacrificial fire, is the navel of the earth...."[65] We *have* come full circle.

We have insufficient space and time to finish this analysis. We simply must quit, bold-line some Irish stories on the Holy Grail, and move on.

In one Irish saga about Conn of the Hundred Battles, we find a girl seated on a crystal chair wearing a golden crown. By her is a silver vat, a vessel of gold, and a golden cup.[66] In another saga, Cormac enters a beautiful palace and finds a shining spring surrounded by hazel trees. Salmon in the spring eat hazel nuts as they fall from the trees.[67] Who was first to find these fish-forms on the Holy Grail? The Irish? Or the Christians?

The Irish story, *The Fate of the Children of Tuirenn*, is a do-it-yourself kit for an experienced reader like you. Lug demands as compensation: Three apples, the skin of a pig, a spear, two steeds, a chariot, seven pigs, a puppy dog, and a cooking spit.[68] See how easy this stuff becomes as we progress! You saw all those Grail images without any bolded lines!

In *Wooing of Etain*, Mider took Etain "beneath his right shoulder; and he carried her off through the smoke-hole of the house. And the hosts rose up around the king, for they felt that they had been disgraced, and they saw two swans circling round

Tara, and the way that they took was the way to the elf-mound of Femen."[69] We have seen doves on the Holy Grail. **Figure 423**. We see our first Grail-swan in **Figure 424**.

In *The Destruction of Da Derga's Hostel*, we are introduced, one by one, to the cast of characters before the battle begins. "Then, as Conaire was going to Da Derga's Hostel, a man with black, cropt hair, and with one hand and one eye and one foot, overtook them. Rough cropt hair was upon him. Though a sackful of wild apples were flung on his crown, not an apple would fall to the ground, but each of them would stick to a hair. Though his snout were flung on a branch they would remain together. Long and thick as an outer yoke was each of his two shins. Each of his buttocks was the size of a cheese on a withe. A forked pole of iron, black-pointed, was in his hand. A swine, black-bristled, singed, was on his back, squealing continually, and a woman big-mouthed, huge, dark, ugly, hideous, was behind him. Though her snout were flung on a branch, the branch would support it. Her lower lip would reach her knee."[70] In another translation, his hair is "short" instead of "cropped," and was "bristling"; and his snout "would stick" to the branch.[71]

In **Figure 425**, we see our Grail-man with one eye, one hand, and one foot. His hair is "cropt" or "short" on both sides of his head and "bristling" on top of his head. In **Figure 426**, we see Grail-apples stuck to his bristling hairs. In **Figure 427**, we see his head, alone, side-view, showing his nose or snout, which is sharp enough to stick to, or hang over, a

Figure 428

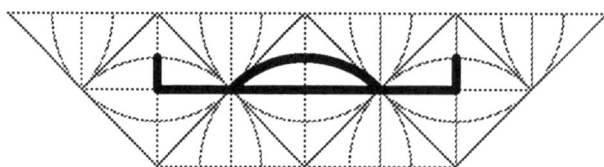

Figure 430

Figure 431

Figure 432

branch. In **Figure 428**, we see that his shin is yoke-shaped, and we see the forked iron pole in his hand. In **Figure 429**, we have bolded his buttocks, and in **Figure 430**, we have turned them upside down, like a cheese on a withe. His swine is seen in **Figure 431**. His big-mouthed woman (She really is!) is seen in **Figure 432**. Her snout is like his. In **Figure 433**, we

see that lines of her lower lip reach her knee. Three cheers for our translators: Cross, Slover, and Gantz! Well done!

The hero of *The Destruction of Da Derga's Hostel* is King Conaire, son[72] of the beautiful Etain, who flew away through the skylight in the form of a swan in *The Wooing of Etain*.[73] Etain is being held

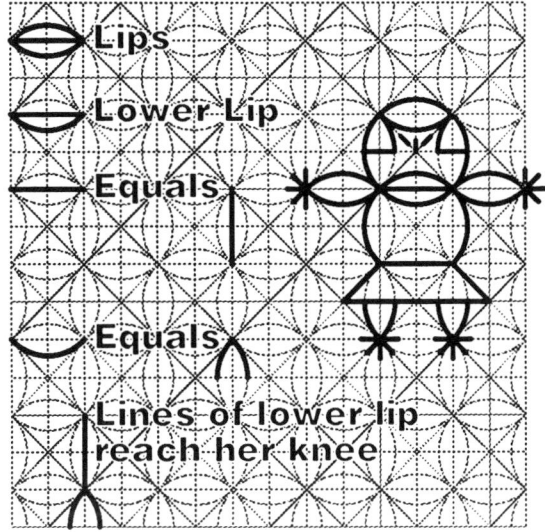

Figure 433

Figure 434

prisoner in a wickerwork house without any door but with a skylight. **Figures 434** and **435.** Is this structure, like the Tabernacle and the Tent of the Presence, a representation of the Earth with a sky-light toward Heaven? She is to marry a king.[74] A bird comes to her through the skylight, sheds its birdskin, has sexual intercourse with her, and tells her that "thou wilt be pregnant by me, and bear a son, and that son must not kill birds."[75] The Holy Spirit came unto Our Lady who was betrothed to Joseph and caused her to bear a Son who was not to kill men? We need more evidence! We get it, too! Our Grail-man, the churl, says to King Conaire, upon his arrival at Da Derga's ("Two Reds") Hostel, "'Welcome to thee, O master Conaire! Long hath thy coming hither been known.'"[76] The churl calls King Conaire "'O fair little master Conaire,'" and tells Conaire, "'[T]hou are the best king that has come into the world!'"[77] The name "Conaire" can be translated, "King of the Road." King of the Way? Enough evidence? The churl has a black boar on his back, which he has brought for Conaire "to con-sume."[78] The boar was a pre-Christian cult object of the ancient Celts.[79] The King of the Way is "to consume" the former pagan cult object of the Celts? Christianity is to consume paganism? Our transla-tors summarize the remainder of the tale thus: "[T]he story goes on to tell how the youthful king met his tragic and untimely death."[80] Are we reading another parody or satire of the Christ story?

We are reading a story with a plot that is very different from the Grail quest stories. Also, it has an entirely different cast of characters from King Arthur and his Knights of the Round Table. "The oldest

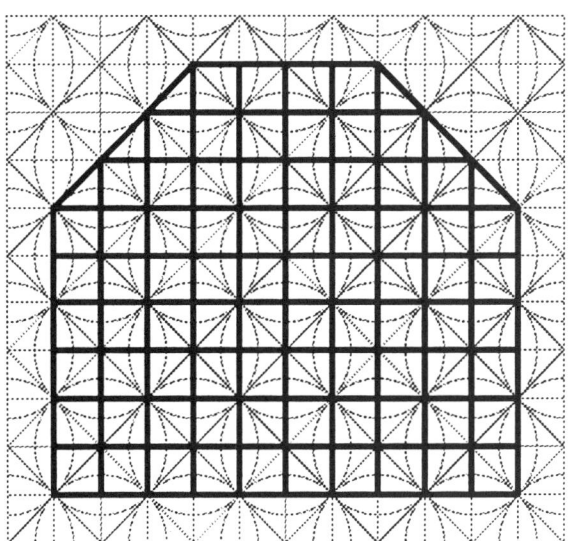

Figure 435

manuscript was copied about the year 1100, but the saga existed in written form as early as the eighth or ninth century. According to the annals, Conaire was high-king of Ireland about the beginning of the Christian era."[81] Does this mean that *The Destruc-tion of Da Derga's Hostel* may be older than any of the Welsh or continental Grail quest stories; that conti-nental authors may not have been the first to parody the Christ story by constructing parallel tales on the Holy Grail? When was the idea of Grail-parody born? At the very beginning of Christianity, among "Eagles" who realized the origin of the Christ story?

Figure 436

Figure 437

Were they emulating a practice of ancient story-smiths who had parodied the Grail-born stories of other gods and goddesses for millennia? For whose amusement? Did only the "Eagles" of the tribe understand the parody? Or did everyone in the tribe — including "Lions," "Oxen," and "Men," understand?

Suppose yourself a time-traveler, whisked forward 100 years to a primitive society of nuclear or environmental holocaust survivors who live in caves. They worship a handcarved wooden statue which looks much like Walt Disney's Donald Duck. You smile and say to their leader, "I used to collect Donald Duck comic books when I was a kid. Donald Duck stories sure are funny!" Their leader groans, then snarls, then puts the sharpened point of a wooden spear deep into your bellybutton. He frowns at you, then speaks: "Donald Duck is our god! He was born, sacrificed for a Sunday dinner, and rose again. He helps us to sustain ourselves by returning to that pond by the cave entrance no matter how many times we catch him and eat him. You have laughed at him. You must die." He runs you through with his spear. One person's religion is another person's entertainment? Could this happen? Did it happen?

The casual reader will not know enough about Irish culture for us to do a very deep analysis of *The Destruction of Da Derga's Hostel*. The story is a goldmine for those who can both read *and* understand the writings of James Joyce and Brian O'Nolan. Go slowly. Use your acquired Grail-skills. Read it in the original Irish Gaelic, if you can. Have a few chuckles. Your parish priest may make you do

penance, but he will not run you through with a wooden spear!

How many "marauders" do you count?[82] Watch out! Our storyteller is full of Irish mischief. Having told you that there are *seven* sons of Ailill and Medb of Connacht, each of whom commands a certain number of marauders, he lists the names of *eight* sons. Is this a translator's error? Or is it a storyteller's trick to see if his listeners were alert and could do sums in hundreds in their heads? Meaning what? I am not sure, but rocks in Aubrey holes make an excellent Stone Age calculator, if you want to read up on such things.[83] We must not scare away our "arts only" readers! Notice, also, that "three reds" go to "the house of red...,"[84] which is the Hostel of "Da Derga," i.e., "Two Reds."[85] This is no more confusing than The Holy Trinity, which is Three but only One! What are "the reds"? The sun? Mars? Something else? Too deep! Let's play Grail-games!

We next are introduced to Ingcel. "A man ungentle, huge, fearful, uncouth was Ingcel. A single eye in his head, as broad as an oxhide, as black as a chafer, with three pupils therein."[86] We see him in **Figure 436**, which illustrates his single eye, with three pupils, in the middle of his forehead. Is this another reference to The Holy Trinity — The Three in One? Ungentle? Huge? Fearful? Uncouth? In **Figure 437**, we see him again, to illustrate the plainly-visible fact that his single eye is, indeed, as broad as an oxhide! A single "black" eye. Like Balor the Fomorian giant? Clergymen of the Christian Church are uncouth and evil? "All 'round the fire sat the priests in a bunch; 'round a big roarin' fire drinkin' tumblers of punch"?

Figure 438

The two opposing bands from Ireland and Britain form a truce under which they agree not to fight each other; rather, to combine their forces and pillage each other's countries alternatively.[87] The Romanized Catholic church of Britain and the Monastic Catholicism of Ireland combine forces to extract the wealth of all peoples in the British Isles? The British "marauders" help their new brothers, the Irish "reavers," kill the parents and brothers of the British "marauders."[88] Christians should stand with their Brothers in the Faith against their parents and blood brothers?[89] The "reaver" with the gift of hearing hears, and the "reaver" with the gift of seeing sees, and the "reaver" with the gift of understanding understands, as they observe the approach of King Conaire's procession.[90] The Christian parallels should be clear enough! They report back to the main body of "reavers," who set sail for shore.

What follows is the best of Irish satire. Imagine yourself twelve years of age, barefooted, wrapped in your blanket, sitting beside a peat-fire on the hearth of your family's croft made of dry-stacked rocks with a thatched roof and a dirt floor. Darkness has fallen and is everywhere around you in the room outside the reach of the firelight. The storyteller's voice rises and falls; he (or she) waves his (or her) arms wildly as he (or she) jumps to his (her) feet, casting moving shadows from the fire onto the lime-whitened walls of the dwelling. The Christ story has been told for less than seven hundred years. Irish storytellers have been telling stories by the firelight for millennia beyond reckoning. You have the scene in mind? Here comes the story: "Just at the time when the boats reached land, then was Mac Cecht striking fire in Da Derga's Hostel. At the sound of the spark the thrice fifty boats were hurled out, so that they were on the shoulders of the sea.... Liken thou that, O Fer Rogain. 'I know not,' answered Fer Rogain, 'unless it be Luchdonn the satirist in Emain Macha who makes this hand-smiting when his food is taken from him... or Mac Cecht's striking a spark, when he kindles a fire before the king of Erin where he sleeps. Every spark and every shower which his fire would let fall on the floor would broil a hundred calves and two half-pigs'.... Their fleet was steered to land. The noise that the thrice fifty vessels made in running ashore shook Da Derga's Hostel so that no spear nor shield remained on its rack therein, but the weapons uttered a cry and fell on the floor of the house.... 'Liken that... what is this noise?' 'I know nothing like unless it be the earth that has broken, or the Leviathan that surrounds the globe and strikes with its tail to overturn the world, or the ships of the sons of Donn Desa that have reached shore.'"[91] You still are that twelve-year-old child. Have you laughed, or snickered, or smiled? What do you suppose was the purpose of this story? To entertain?

In the prow of the lead ship was Ingcel, the one-eyed, to whom we already have been introduced. His single eye is as wide as an *oxhide*. He is "wrathful," a word the ancient Irish applied to appearance of *raptors*, and is "*lion* hard." He is a *man*. All four! Once more! Take him seriously, if you can: "Each of his knees was big as a stripper's cauldron; each of his two fists was the size of a reaping basket; his buttocks as big as a cheese on a withe; each of his shins as long as an outer yoke."[92] He looks like the "churl" to whom we first were introduced at the beginning of this story, but with two legs. We are told that certain of the warriors present wore a "short cloak to their buttocks. Speckled-green drawers they wore...."[93] Is this proof that if the storytellers had wanted the Dagda to wear something from his buttocks down they would have said so expressly?

The story has a heroine, of sorts. "[T]hey saw a lone woman coming to the door of the hostel .... A greyish, wooly mantle she wore. Her lower hair reached as far as her knees. Her lips were on one side of her head...."[94] A real babydoll! Gantz apparently was shocked by the words which Cross & Slover translate as "lower hair." Gantz renders the passage thus: "Her beard reached to her knees."[95] Perhaps the Holy Grail will let us know which translation is correct, without my having to shock you with a literal translation! In **Figure 438**, we see that her "beard" does *not* extend down to her knees.

Figure 439

Figure 440

In **Figure 439**, we see that her "lower hair" *does* extend down to her knees. A picture is worth a thousand words? The "lady," like the Dagda, wore no pants!

Has the parody on the Christ story ended? Has the story become nothing but a ribald romp? The story action is leading up to the "destruction" of the hostel. King Conaire's rule on Earth is being praised. Fer Rogain says: "May God not bring that man [King Conaire] there tonight! 'Tis sad to destroy him.... Sad is the shortness of his life!"[96] The destruction of the hostel occurs at Halloween. "[T]hat it was on the eve of Samain (Allsaints) the destruction of the Hostel was wrought...."[97] Conaire was killed at the Irish year end, as Christ was crucified at the ancient Semitic Babylonian year end. No, the parody has not ended.

We cannot give the entire story its due. We must move on. As the story builds towards the destruction of the hostel, we are introduced, one by one, to the leaders of the combatants. Grail images abound. We read about the raging *torc caille* ("boar of the woods") bonfire of King Conaire, and men seen through the wheels of the warriors' chariots.[98] One champion holds a shield with "five golden circles upon it" and a "five-barbed javelin in his hand."[99] The comedy continues: "An ox with a bacon-pig, this is the ration of each of them, and that ration which they put into their mouths is visible till it comes down past their navels. Bodies of bone without a joint in them all those three have."[100] Take **Figure 440**, and **Figure 441**. Superimpose Figures 440 and 441 on each other and you have a man-form with an ox-face visible in and among the "bones" of

his body. Notice that the arms and legs of Grail-people lack elbow and knee joints, just as the storysmith tells us! Do the same "swallowing trick" with the pig-form in **Figure 442**, and you have the entire image reconstructed on the Holy Grail.

More praise for King Conaire: "He is the most splendid and noble and beautiful and mighty king that has come to the whole world. He is the mildest and gentlest and most perfect king that has come to it, that is, Conaire son of Eterscel."[101]

The battle began. The attackers repeatedly tried to burn the hostel. All of the water in the hostel was used up by the defenders to quench the flames. King Conaire was thirsty, and requested a drink of water. There being no water in the hostel, and the King wanting a drink, Mac Cecht took the King's cup and burst forth from the hostel through the waves of attackers, searching for water for the King. The battle raged on. The King's thirst increased. In

Figure 441

Figure 442

the meantime, Mac Cecht went from river to river throughout Ireland, trying to find enough water to fill the King's cup. He finally found water, filled the cup, and returned to the hostel, only to find that the attackers already had confronted the King and had struck off his head.[102] "Mac Cecht then spilt the cup of water into Conaire's gullet and neck. Then said Conaire's head, after the water had been put into its neck and gullet:

'A good man Mac Cecht!'"[103]

The Story of Stories says that Christ on the Cross of Calvary wanted water but got, instead, a sponge soaked with vinegar. If Mac Cecht had been around, Christ would have gotten the water He wanted? Meaning? The Irish do what the Church asks of them, no matter the costs to themselves? Perhaps the time has come for another Irishman to do what is required for all of humanity — whether the Church likes it or not?

Notes
CHAPTER TWENTY-FOUR
Irish Stories Vedantic Beside the Atlantic

1. Fairservis 345; see also, Nora Chadwick 111; Powell 58,77; Sharkey 5-6.

2. Irish Gaelic for the "Gaelic Athletic Association," sponsor of Irish sports.

3. The reference is to Gaelic football, which is played without the body armor employed in the entirely different American game with the same name.

4. Rees 17.

5. Rees 18-19.

6. Cross 1.

7. McMann 23.

8. Cross 5,6,14.

9. Cross 8.

10. Cross 28-31. The man "whose mouth was out of his breast" sounds like someone we have met?

11. Cross 38-39; Powell 146.

12. Nora Chadwick 173; Rees 53; Powell 146.

13. The recipe for the Dagda's "porridge" is similar to the recipe for haggis!

14. Like a bowl full of jelly?

15. Cross 39.

16. Rees 36.

17. Cavendish 171.

18. Rees 37.

19. Rees 37.   See also, Cross 44.

20. Rees 37.

21. Rees 35.

22. Rees 36.   See also Powell 146.

23. Rees 35.

24. Sharkey 9.

25. Nora Chadwick 50.

26. Nora Chadwick 115.

27. Nora Chadwick 50.

28. Nora Chadwick 83.

29. Nora Chadwick 39.

30. Nora Chadwick 16.

31. Rees 41.

32. Rees 145.

33. Rees 53.

34. Rees 53.

35. Rees 75.

36. Rees 75.

37. Rees 74.

38. Rees 74.

39. Rees 76.

40. Rees 76-80.

41. Rees 79.

42. Rees 92.

43. Rees 91; Powell 146-147.

44. Rees 99.

45. Rees 98. See also Hoagland 3; Cross 21.

46. Exodus 3.14.

47. Rees 106.

48. Rees 107.

49. Rees 148.

50. Rees 154.

51. Rees 154-155.

52. Talbott 122-123.

53. Rees 189.

54. Rees 107.

55. Rees 137-138.

56. Rees 138-139.

57. Rees 139.

58. Rees 149.

59. Rees 150.

60. Rees 151.

61. Rees 152.

62. Rees 146-147.

63. Rees 159.

64. Rees 157-158.

65. Rees 159.

66. Nora Chadwick 177.

67. Nora Chadwick 178.

68. Cross 61.

69. Cross 92.

70. Cross 102-103. In Lady Charlotte Guest's translation of *The Mabinogion*, we are told of a man who would let one of his lips drop below his waist while he wore his other lip as a cap on his head. Guest 227,332. She also wrote of a black-faced woman whose stomach rose from her breast-bone higher than her chin. Guest 115. Our Grail humanforms certainly got around in the world!

71. Gantz, *EIMAS* 71.

72. In other tales, Conaire is Etain's grandson. Cross 93.

73. Cross 92-93.

74. Cross 96.

75. Cross 96.

76. Cross 103.

77. Cross 103. See also, Gantz, *EIMAS* 71-72.

78. Cross 103.

79. Piggott 35.

80. Cross 93.

81. Cross 93.

82. Cross 103-104; Gantz, *EIMAS* 72-73.

83. J.E. Wood 69-78.

84. Cross 101.

85. Cross 100.

86. Cross 104. See also, Gantz *EIMAS* 73.

87. Cross 104.

88. Cross 104.

89. Matthew 10.34-38.

90. Cross 105.

91. Cross 106.

92. Cross 107.

93. Cross 107.

94. Cross 107.

95. Gantz, *EIMAS* 76.

96. Cross 109.

97. Cross 110.

98. Cross 110.

99. Cross 111.

100. Cross 116. Lady Charlotte Guest's translation of *The Mabinogion* refers to a character with a thin or spare (that is, fleshless) body and huge, bony legs. Guest 115.

101. Cross 117-118.

102. Cross 123-125.

103. Cross 125.

Chapter Twenty-Five

An Introduction to Grail Science

We have studied many stories which evidently contain references to line forms visible on the Holy Grail. We have discussed reasons why a storysmith might have wanted to incorporate images visible on the Holy Grail into his work product. Perhaps he thought he was receiving a prophetic "revelation" from his god(s) through the medium of communication known as "symbolism." Perhaps he incorporated Grail images into his story as proof of his membership in the nameless group of scholars who have served the power structures of Church and State by creating the myths which have governed the conduct of the masses. Perhaps he was a critic of those systems of thinking. We have learned that the Holy Grail somehow is related to the following concepts: Earth — the planet, and its sky above; the heavenly bodies — the sun, moon, planets, and stars; time — the hours, days, weeks, months, seasons, years, and longer cycles; spatial relationships — between objects and their component structures; electricity; and light.

Now we must try to answer this question: Who gave us the Holy Grail and what did it mean to them? There may be as many answers to that question as there are readers of this book because of a logic trap from which we will not be able to escape. Your personal answer to the question of who gave us the Holy Grail will depend upon an interaction between your suppositions about who the People of the Holy Grail were and what they knew. This process of "squirrel-cage reasoning" best can be illustrated by a brief discussion of one aspect of Grail science which we have come to appreciate — the passage of white light into quartz crystals, which produces the rainbow-spectrum "interference pattern."

Ezekiel sought to describe for his readers a phenomenon like a wheel within a wheel,[1] positioned on the ground and in the sky,[2] which was also like a rainbow but was not a rainbow.[3] His religion held that phenomena visible on Earth and in the sky were not gods; rather, they were the work products of the Tetragrammaton, the one and only God.[4] Ezekiel tried to relate the unnamed phenomenon he sought to describe to something which was like ice but was not ice.[5] We have come to appreciate the fascination of the ancients with a substance which is like ice but is not ice, that is, quartz crystal, which they evidently knew will throw the rainbow spectrum in an internal "interference pattern" when it is struck by primary and secondary rays of light. We see in Illustration 4-2 that the interference pattern *does* have the appearance of a wheel within a wheel. We may speculate that Ezekiel meant to say that just as a rainbow was not God in the ice-like sky, so the rainbow-spectrum interference pattern was not God in an ice-like rock crystal; rather, that these phenomena were wondrous creations of God, proving that their Creator was even more wondrous.

An ancient Einstein was not required to pick up a piece of quartz, hold it in correct angular position to the sun, and produce the interference pattern.[6] If we suppose that the ancients were Earth-bound dolts, we nonetheless must suppose them to have been capable of such "scientific" observations. But some of you might prefer them to have been space invaders or Earth-bound Einsteins who had learned something of the science of space invaders. We have learned that Ezekiel's Vision also contains references to electricity in the form of lightning and amber.[7] A quick reference to the modern scientific writings at the end of this sentence will teach you that quartz is piezoelectric; that it vibrates when stressed by an electrical current, providing us with high-quality timepieces known as quartz-crystal clocks and watches.[8] Was Ezekiel aware of the piezoelectric effect of quartz crystals? We found some evidence that the ancients knew about the light-splitting property of quartz.[9] We found *no* evidence that the ancients knew that quartz crystal plus electricity equals high-quality timekeeper. But if we ignore that lack of evidence, and suppose, in a flight of fantasy, that Ezekiel *must* have known about the relationship between quartz, electricity, and time because he wrote about all three in his vision, then it is not a very high flight to fantasy number two: that he must have been a space invader or have talked with one. The latter sort of reasoning is, of course, entirely specious, but you get the point: What we suppose the people of the Holy Grail knew depends on who we suppose they were; who we suppose they were depends on what we suppose they knew. We will not extract ourselves from this logic trap in this book, but we shall try.

We do not know the following about the person who gave us the Holy Grail: name; sex; race; tribe; place of origin; color of hair, eyes, or skin; dates of birth and death; and religious or scientific affiliations, if any. We suggest this: the person was a "scientist" in the modern sense of the word, who accurately observed, remembered, collated, and correlated observations about nature, and then postulated in geometric form a relationship between certain natural phenomena; hence, about the Creator of those phenomena. This science was revelatory, in line with the "listen to God but do not inquire of God" thinking of the day. We act similarly in one aspect of our science, called "empirical science," i.e., principles we learn from observing God's handiwork.

We also speculate that the Holy Grail may have been a "committee effort," rather than the work of a single person, which was formulated over a considerable period of time commencing during the Stone Ages but fixed in final form by no later than the time it appeared on our Babylonian school tablet during the second millennium B.C. We saw the points of a Grail-style concave-sided tetragon touching the rim of a pre-Sumerian bowl and another concave-sided tetragon touching the rim of a Grail-born "fantasy bowl" described in the story of the table from the Pseudepigraphal *Letter of Aristeas*. We have learned that the Holy Grail has been kept through the years by a secret society of scholars, who have authored the myths which have governed the conduct of the masses of humanity for thousands of years.

We have been assured that there *is* an ancient sacred science and philosophy; that they can be unlocked with the proper key or unearthed with the proper tool. "There is a sacred science, and for thousands of years countless inquisitive people have sought in vain to penetrate its 'secrets.' It is as if they attempted to dig a hole in the sea with an ax. The tool must be of the same nature as the objective to be worked upon."[10] We have dissected many ancient stories using the Holy Grail as our scalpel. Is the Holy Grail the key by which ancient science and holy philosophy will be unlocked? "The key to

most of the great philosophic conceptions of the ancient world has been lost."[11] Lost but now found? "Obviously, a special training is needed to practice the Symbolic Method...."[12] "This secret is not hidden from anyone, anymore than the esoteric teaching of Ancient Egypt was; one need only have developed the faculties needed to understand it."[13] We have tried to develop those faculties through the specialized training offered in this book. "We stand before a strongbox containing the greatest wealth concerning the history of humanity; we have not been able to open it, because we have insisted on using the rationalist key, rather than that which the makers of this jewelcase used — the symbol and the symbolic."[14]

R.A. Schwaller de Lubicz was writing about the *meaning* underlying the excellent *transliterations* and *translations* which Egyptologists have prepared of ancient Egyptian texts. Although skillfully translated, those texts still defy understanding. We already have used the Holy Grail as key to a sampling of those stories.

R.A. Schwaller de Lubicz wrote of the Christian Gospels: "The purpose of these parables and enigmatical phrases is not to hide anything from 'he who has eyes to see and ears to hear,' according to the evangelical formula. The purpose is to select those who developed the necessary understanding and who are for this reason worthy of those 'secrets' (that is to say, they will not misuse them for selfish motives). There was never any intent to conceal, from those thus prepared, any of the wisdom transmitted by texts, traditions, or monuments. The enigma does not lie in the thing itself but is the result of our understanding, our faculties, and our intelligence, which are not attuned to the mentality according to which the idea was expressed, and it is just this that our present education prevents us from admitting."[15]

A short string of reasoning may lead us to something tangible. We have been told that there was an ancient science and that there was an ancient philosophy. We have good reasons to speculate that they were somehow related to the Holy Grail — which is a series of lines that can be scratched into a rock, into the sand, sewn into a cloth, or printed on this page. Recall the many stories we have studied. All have something in common. All deal with spatial relationships, as, for instance, the fitting together of parts of a "table." Most make reference to emanations from the center and progressions inward toward the center. Recall, for instance, Ezekiel's cherubim on the square defined as unity, which expands outward from and contracts inward towards the center point. Ozark Mountain wisdom insists that if something looks like a frog, feels like a frog, smells like a frog, tastes like a frog, croaks like a frog, and hops like a frog, there is a substantial chance that it *is* a frog. The so-called "ignorant" hillbilly thus wisely uses *probabilities* to circumscribe his "reality," much as do modern students of quantum physics! Have we not proven to our reasonable satisfactions that Ezekiel was "into" (i.e., was an adept of) what we, today, would call Oriental Philosophy — the attempt to approach, and, if possible, to become one with, the mystical unity which Christianity and Judaism call "God"?

Is R. A. Schwaller de Lubicz not saying, in the last quotation above, that we have been taught to accept the Gospels on what we would call the Oxen level — true stories about historic persons — rather than on the Eagle level — allegories about God's principles of Creation?

We often have asked questions rather than making statements throughout the pages of this book, but the time has come for some straight talk. Modern students of comparative religion have at least an inkling of what the Bible's "higher knowledge" consists of: the *same* ancient science and science-related philosophy of cosmology and cosmogony which we have encountered in every culture we have studied. At root, it is Pythagorean — a science of numbers. It is mathematical and geometrical. But it *quickly* can mire up in utter nonsense, just as the very highest of religion or science always can be dissolved into the very lowest forms of magic.

You were promised that we would not wallow in Kabbalistic numerology. That promise has been, and will be, kept. You were *not* promised that we would not delve into the mathematics of ancient science and engineering — that sort of practical number theory which causes the sixth-century Cathedral of Hagia Sophia (now a mosque) still to stand in Constantinople despite earthquakes which long ago would have dissolved many modern buildings into piles of rubble.[16] You were not promised that we would avoid the geometry and number theory which was used to erect the great twelfth-century Christian cathedrals of Europe.[17] We shall speculate that the ancients believed they got those principles from God Himself. In a *very* real sense they did, much as a modern student of quantum physics observes nature at work, distills from those workings the apparent operative principles, and works with those principles although he is unable

to penetrate or comprehend them through reasoned analysis. We are about to embark on a fascinating study which those of you who are *not* mathematically-minded can comprehend just as readily as those of you who are students of higher mathematics. We shall assume that the ancients were *not* space invaders or students of space invaders; that their methodologies were brilliant, albeit basic and simplistic. This is not to say that *all* ancients thought this way. Quite to the contrary, we probably are dealing with the works of elite scholars whose activities supported the thrones of dominion, i.e., church and state.

The Pentateuch correctly expresses an overview of the ancient science, but botches the mathematical details. The Bible tells us that God gave the Hebrews, as it were, a complete set of blueprints for the Temple.[18] In a *very* real sense, He did. We shall learn that a building constructed of stones according to the proportions and geometric forms expressed on the Holy Grail will withstand earthquakes and howling winds for thousands of years. Why? Because such a building was constructed from unit structures observed in nature; from line forms of the structural components of rock crystals, plants, and the human body[19] as expressed geometrically on the Holy Grail. If a unit structure works when God incorporates it into *His* creation, why should it not work just as well when humans employ it in *their* creation? The ancient sages would call this "revelation." We would call it "empirical science." Things equal to the same thing are equal to each other.

The practical problem with using the Temple stories of the Bible as "blueprints" for the construction of a *real* Temple is that evidently the Hebrew sage who wrote those stories was a religionist rather than a structural engineer. For instance, he or she insisted, according to then-outdated Semitic mathematics, that the diameter of the round bronze "sea" was ten *and* its circumference was thirty.[20] Any student of high-school mathematics will tell you, if you have forgotten, that π is 3.1416, an uneven number, as result of which either the diameter of the "sea" has to "come out uneven" or the circumference of the "sea" has to "come out uneven." One cannot be ten and the other thirty, except in the mind of a religionist who was concerned in his or her writings with matters other than the rules of mathematics. Note that the Hebrews employed an outsider to construct the Temple and its furnishings.[21] Here is one safe bet: He did not use the Bible to do it! Many a true believer has tried to use the Bible as a set of building specifications and has failed.[22] There are too many missing structural elements.

If the Hebrew sage who wrote the Biblical Tabernacle story was not attempting to preserve a set of specifications for erection of a *real* tent, what, then, was his purpose? Was he using overlaid round "tents" as allegories for the various calendrical systems which his city-cousins, the Semitic Babylonians, then were learning to coordinate with each other, i.e., was he referring to the Holy Grail in its role as timekeeper?

We have been discussing myths. Now let us look at another reality: The erection of Christian cathedrals. Modern architects and engineers recently have subjected the foundations, frames, and fabrics of European cathedrals to architectural and engineering analysis, which has caused these buildings to "cough up" their secrets; to reveal the number theory expressed in the geometry which holds them together. That geometry or number theory is Platonic, Pythagorean, Hermetic, Pharaonic, Semitic, and Indo-European. It is probably the ancient mathematical science to which the Bible refers allegorically.

Classicists might approach this analysis from another direction; hence, they might fail whereas we shall succeed. The Christian church never was able to find and to burn all of the books discussing this ancient mathematical science.[23] Students of the Classics read *some* of them today. We will approach the analysis by performing an "autopsy" on the great Christian cathedrals, rather than by following the Classical approach, for two reasons: First, the cathedrals are fantastic but real. Mathematics from God, as revealed to the ancients by the Holy Grail, holds these awe-inspiring buildings together. Second, Classical-style writings are philosophical as well as scientific. Classicists discuss the same practical principles which hold up the cathedrals, but substantial portions of their writings shade over into philosophy and finally dissolve into silly "number magic." The lines between science, philosophy born of science, and magic are distinct in the Classics only if you are a student of ancient science and can winnow it out from the other two. The uninitiated are apt to be led astray or confounded utterly. Also, those of you who are trained in modern science and mathematics probably would throw a Classical analysis into the trash can after reading only a few introductory sentences because Classical-style writings are heavily larded with philosophy, then frosted with magic, albeit the

undressed cake underneath is blended, molded, and baked in accordance with empirically-revealed laws of nature.

Some of the Greek classical "mathematicians" suffered from the same problem. They allowed their "science" to become a "religion." Even the followers of Pythagoras fell into this trap.[24] As example: A Greek Classicist might decline to trisect an angle unless he could do it using Euclidian methods because, in effect, he had permitted himself to "worship" Euclidian methods. All angles can be trisected, although *no one*, even until this day, ever has done so strictly by Euclidian methods.[25] Hence, such a person would deny himself the opportunity to trisect every angle because he would rather be bound by, or adhere to, his principles, than to solve the problem at hand. Practically-minded Greeks abandoned Euclidian methods and devised the "conchoid of Nichomedes," which violated Euclidian methodology, to solve the trisection problem.[26] The practical men who erected the great European cathedrals probably would have tossed their heads back and emitted loud guffaws of laughter about self-imposed mental imprisonment caused by dogmatic adherence to mathematical principles — as do the practical mathematicians and engineers of today. The principle-worshiping Classicist fails where the ancient or modern engineer succeeds because the Classicist puts one of his "tools" on a pedestal and worships it as if it were a god, whereas ancient and modern engineers would lay aside any tool not fit for the particular task at hand and either would find or would fashion one which would produce the required result. For these reasons, we shall approach ancient mathematics and science through an "autopsy" of the European cathedrals rather than through the writings of the Classicists.

You are entitled to be confused about the relationship between twelfth-century Christian cathedrals and a Babylonian schoolboy's tablet from the second millennium B.C. This is the same problem about the writing of this book which we have discussed before. We are analyzing a spider's web. We must start somewhere and end somewhere. You will not see the entire picture until you are through. There is no perfect starting point and no perfect ending point, although the chronology of the book may be more apparent to you now than it was when we started. Please accept this for now: We have achieved some degree of success by assuming that the persons who wrote the stories we are analyzing were not Sophistic liars; instead, that they were speaking truth as they perceived it. Take as example the Hebrew sage who authored the Biblical stories about the Temple. He or she was correct in his or her overview of ancient science, albeit he or she was not the equal of Semitic mathematicians of his or her day. Let us assume that *all* of our ancient authors spoke truly: that the Holy Grail *was* brought down to Earth from Heaven.[27] One meaning of the expression "brought down to Earth from Heaven" is that the lines of the Holy Grail can be used to diagram the structures of crystals, plants, and man; that adherence to those diagrams will cause man-made structures to stand. Another meaning may be that Sumerian astronomers, or other persons before them, may have realized that the Earth rotates on its axis once daily while it also rotates once yearly around the sun. Here is the *second*, and certainly the most important, meaning of Ezekiel's "wheel within a wheel." We will speculate that the Holy Grail illustrates, precisely, the solstitial and equinoctial positions of the Earth as it travels along the Ecliptic. We will suggest a very simple methodology by which the ancients might have discovered this. We will learn that history records the fact that at least two ancients held this theory before Galileo. Right now, however, we are going to explore a practical side of Holy Grail studies — the erection of magnificent Houses of God.

Notes
CHAPTER TWENTY-FIVE. An Introduction to Grail Science

1. Ezekiel 1.16.

2. Ezekiel 1.15, 19-21.

3. Ezekiel 1.28.

4. Wisdom of Solomon 13.1-9.

5. Ezekiel 1.22 (Oxford).

6. E.A. Wood 91, 98.

7. Ezekiel 1.4, 13-14, 27.

8. Jespersen 40.

9. Krupp 133-134, 317.

10. Schwaller de Lubicz E&S 3.

11. Schwaller de Lubicz S&S 19.

12. Schwaller de Lubicz S&S 12.

13. Schwaller de Lubicz S&S 25.

14. Schwaller de Lubicz S&S 26.

15. Schwaller de Lubicz TTIM 16-17.

16. *National Geographic*, Dec. 1983, 724-727.

17. Gimpel 82.

18. 1 Kings 6-7; 2 Chron. 3-4. "[T]hou didst tell me to build a temple on thy sacred mountain and an altar in the city which is thy dwelling-place, *a copy of the sacred tabernacle prepared by thee from the beginning.*" (Emphasis added.) Wisdom of Solomon 9.8 (Oxford). The Bible tells us that David gave Solomon plans and specifications for the Temple, its furniture, and its furnishings that had been "drafted by the LORD'S own hand." 1 Chron. 28.11-19 (Oxford). "Make me a sanctuary, and I will dwell among them. *Make it* [the Tabernacle] *exactly according to the design I show you*, the design for the Tabernacle and for all its furniture. This is how you must make it...." (Matter in brackets added.) Exodus 25.8-9 (Oxford). These specifications, first for the holy tent and, later, for the holy building, therefore were believed to have come from God, who "rode on a cherub... [and] flew through the air," 2 Samuel 22.11 (Oxford), and who "sits throned on the vaulted roof of

the earth." Isaiah 40.22 (Oxford). Have we seen God? We surely have seen what the seers saw!

19. Ghyka xi, 13-19, 66, 84-85, 87-91, 98.

20. 1 Kings 7.23; 2 Chron. 4.2.

21. 1 Kings 7.13-14, 40, 45; 2 Chron. 2.13-14; 2 Chron. 4.11, 16.

22. Rosenau 38-43, 65-69, 91-99, 133-140, 161-166.

23. Gimpel 82-86.

24. Ghyka 111-117.

25. Weltner 3384.

26. 1 Heath 225, 238-240.

27. Eschenbach *Parzival* 244.

Chapter Twenty-Six

The Holy Grail as Plan and Elevation for Houses of God

Scholars tell us that the tradition of temple design founded on Cosmic Man still exists in India, and that the architectural plan for the great Gothic cathedrals was Christ on the Cross.[1] This is not to say that the foundation plan of all early Christian churches was cruciform. Some of the earliest Christian churches were copies of the Roman basilica, and were rectangular in plan, with flat wooden ceilings.[2]

We are told that the pendentive was the great Byzantine contribution to structural form; that pendentives enabled the large domed structures of Europe to be built; and that pendentives solved the problem of how to construct a circular form upon a square one.[3]

In **Figure 443**, we see a *plan* view of a dome sitting on four pendentives. In **Figure 444**, we see a *plan* view of a dome sitting on four pendentives which, in turn, are sitting on the four corners of a square. Compare these *plan* Figures with the *isometric* view of a dome in Illustration 7-3.[4] Yes, friends, a "pendentive" is a cusp of a dome-shaped concave-sided tetragon! We have seen our old friend, the concave-sided tetragon, playing many roles in fiction. In Illustrations 7-3 and 22-1, we see him playing one role in the world of reality — supporting a dome.[5] Could it possibly be that our Babylonian scribal student was learning to calculate the areas of pendentives for the erection of domes?

Scholars are unsure where, exactly, the dome supported by pendentives originated, but its use in Christian churches now is accepted as being from Eastern influence rather than from Imperial Rome.

Christianity had taken root in Iran and Armenia earlier than in Rome. Domed churches were erected in the East from the second century A.D., onwards. After Christianity became the official religion of the Roman Empire, churches were built in Rome and the West, but these generally had flat, timber roofs in basilican style, whereas contemporary churches in the eastern part of the Byzantine domains were domed with vaults of brick or stone erected on a square plan.[6]

We got here by the mythological route. Turn back to Figure 444. We see the cosmic circle of Heaven supported by the cosmic square of Earth.[7] Recall how often we have found Persian *cosmology* and *cosmogony* making its way to Rome; thence marching westward across the face of Europe to the British Isles. Now, we have found Eastern-style domed churches spreading westward to the Vatican; thence spreading westward, across the face of Europe, to St. Paul's in London!

If Byzantine stone or brick domes came from Eastern wooden structures, as suggested by some scholars, that might eliminate any chance that our Babylonian student was working with pendentives of stone or brick when he was solving a problem concerning the area of a concave-sided tetragon.[8] However, Joan Oates showed her readers a picture of the earliest known "pitched-brick" vault, at Tell al Rimah, erected on pendentives *circa* 2100 B.C.[9] We have progressed steadily by assuming that the storysmiths have spoken the truth as they per-

Figure 443   **Figure 444**

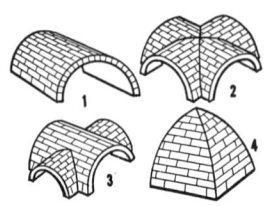

vaults 1a: *1* barrel, *2* cross, *3* Welsh, *4* cloister

Illustration 26-1. The four classical vaults. By permission. From *Webster's Third New International Dictionary* © 1986, at page 2536, by Merriam-Webster, Inc., publisher of the Merriam-Webster ® dictionaries.

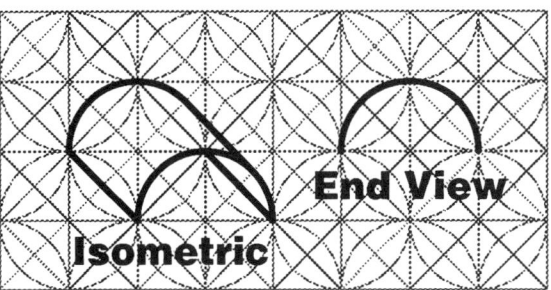

Figure 445

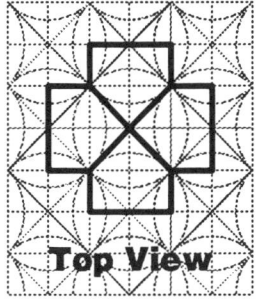

Figure 446

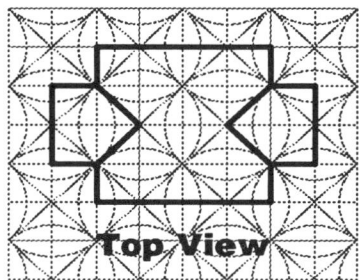

Figure 447

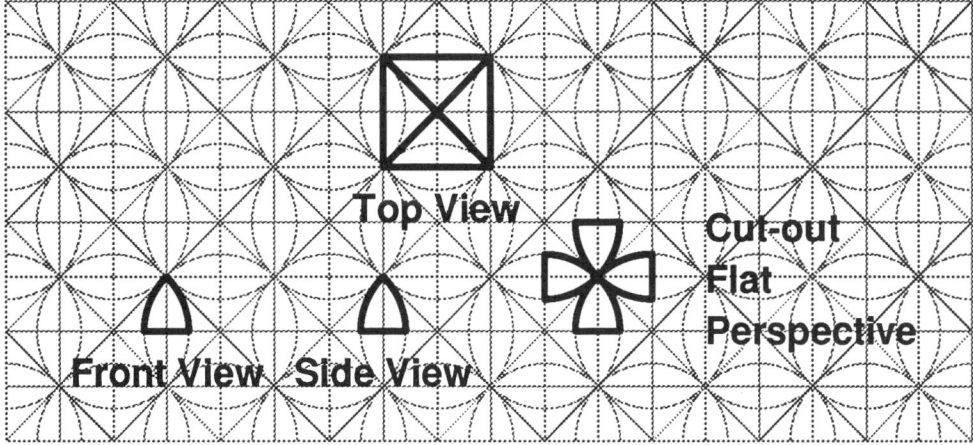

Figure 448

ceived it. Perhaps we should adopt the same approach regarding what the archaeologists dig up?

We Irish have rock domes above ground at Slea Head, and elsewhere, and underground domes at Newgrange, and elsewhere. Similar tholoi are found in Mycenae.[10] We already have found such structures among the pre-Sumerians of Mesopotamia.

Do vaults as well as domes appear on the Holy Grail? **Illustration 26-1** shows *all four* of the "classical vaults."[11] **Figures 445 through 448** show *each* of these vaults on the Holy Grail.

So this structural engineering, based on forms which can be found on the Holy Grail, was passed down from generation to generation until it was used to construct the wondrous Cathedrals of Europe? Yes, by a rather circuitous route. The Christian church had destroyed all of the books of ancient Babylonian, Egyptian, and Greek science that it could find.[12] It never found them all, of course, and more were located after the fervor for book-burning cooled somewhat. But so thorough a job of destruction had been done that, during a now-famous eleventh-century dialogue between two

European scholars, neither was able to figure out how to work a simple proposition of geometry![13] The Christian church found itself unable to build its cathedrals using even the most elementary principles of geometry. The Church had sought to arrest scientific development,[14] apparently having decided that the level of science was high enough to support a Christian society. Having almost succeeded, the Church was in need of science to build its cathedrals! Where was this science to be found? The answer was obvious: outside the zone of destruction under control of the Church; that is, in the parts of Spain under Moorish influence.

Enter the Arabs! "Since... medieval scholars did not re-invent geometry and... Greek documents had almost entirely disappeared from Western Europe, where then did men like Villard de Honnecourt discover their science? Some of it must have been handed down to them directly from Roman geometers or they must have learnt it from studying the works of Vitruvius, the Roman architect from the time of Augustus whose manuscripts were frequently recopied during the early Middle

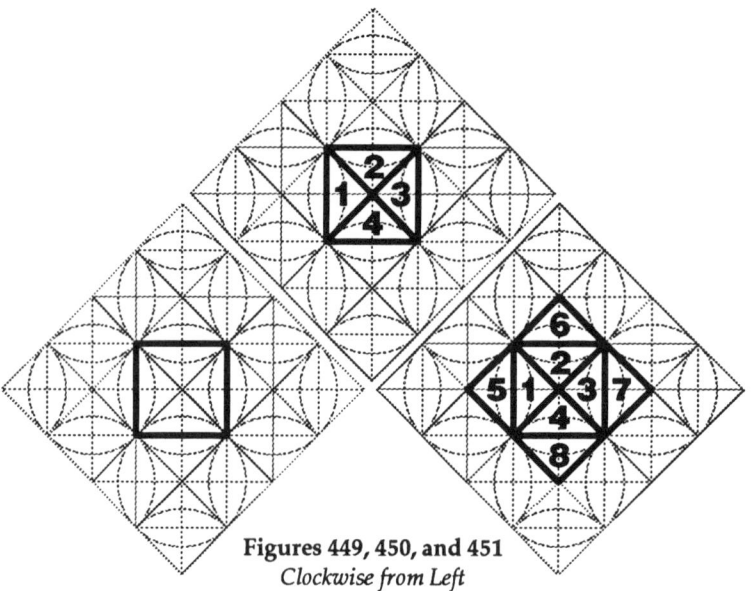

Figures 449, 450, and 451
Clockwise from Left

Ages. In fact, during the ninth and tenth centuries, Muslim scholars had translated into Arabic a considerable number of scientific works from classical antiquity, namely the writings of Aristotle, Plato, Euclid and Ptolemy. The Arabs produced a magnificent synthesis of the knowledge of classical antiquity *and of India*; they assimilated the arithmetic, developed chemistry and algebra and more or less invented trigonometry. This vast culture was taught indiscriminately to Muslims, Christians and Jews *in Arab universities in Spain throughout the eleventh and twelfth centuries.*"[15] And Grail tales were taught to Christians right along with Grail geometry?

"[B]y the middle of the twelfth century, Greek and Arab science was available to Western European scholars. The remarkable Arab contribution to our culture is often underestimated, and yet it was this that made the full flowering of the Middle Ages possible. Without it the Renaissance could barely have developed and the twentieth century might still be technically and scientifically in the nineteenth century."[16]

And of just what did these wonderful secrets of the master operative stone masons consist? Some were amazingly simple; others more complex; none is beyond your understanding. One basic but highly useful geometric proposition was called "doubling the square."[17] In **Figure 449**, we have bolded a square. Do you know how to double it in area? You treat each one of the four numbered triangles in **Figure 450** as a tab, and fold it over, producing the square in **Figure 451**, which has eight such triangles instead of just four; ergo, it is twice as large in area as the square in Figure 449. Simple? You bet! A knowledge of calculus is not necessary for you to come along with us!

How was "doubling the square" useful in the building of cathedrals? Assume that you have laid down on the ground, as part of a foundation *plan*, a square with sides of 10. A square with sides of 10

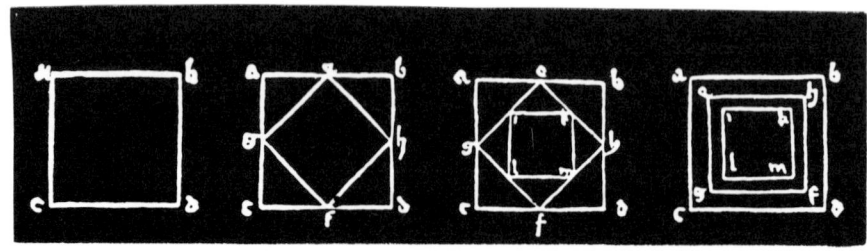

Illustration 26-2. Doubling the square to take an elevation from a plan. Courtesy of Michael Russell (Publishing) Ltd., Wilton, Salisbury, England.

The Holy Grail as Plan and Elevation

Illustration 26-3. Doubling the square, a geometry problem on the other side of the same ancient Babylonian tablet from which came Illustration 2-1. Courtesy of the Trustees of the British Museum, London.

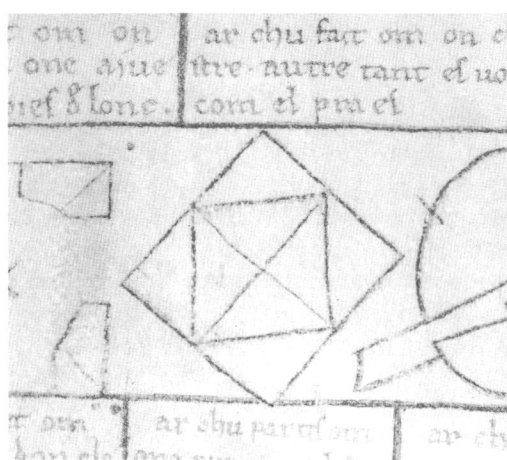

Illustration 26-4. Doubling the square, from the sketchbook of a master mason. Courtesy of Michael Russell (Publishing) Ltd., Wilton, Salisbury, England.

contains 100 square feet. Try doubling that square in *area* so it will contain 200 square feet. Uneven numbers quickly get into your way. Good engineering consists of finding the easy way to a correct solution. In this instance, geometry is a better "tool" than arithmetic.

The geometrical theorem for "doubling the square" also provided a way in which a master stone mason could "take an elevation from a plan," which was one of the secrets which all members of the guild of masons were supposed to keep from outsiders. "'No workman, no master, no journeyman will tell anyone who is not of the craft and who has never been a mason how to take an elevation from a plan.'"[18] Look at **Illustration 26-2**, from a master mason's sketchbook,[19] illustrating the *plan* drawing technique we just have learned. By doubling the square, then rotating the resulting squares into parallel alignment with each other, the master was able to produce what we would call "cut sections" of the vertical church spire — much as you might cut a carrot sideways, rather than lengthwise, into a pile of round slices, then stack the slices on top of each other to "reconstruct" the carrot.

Was Holy Grail geometry actually used by operative stone masons? Turn back to Illustration 7-1,[20] which shows a mason's mark "proved" on the Holy Grail. Turn to **Illustration 26-3**,[21] which shows another panel of the Babylonian tablet from which came our copy of the Holy Grail. Find the Holy Grail in Illustration 2-1. Now, find in Illustration 26-3 the proof of the geometrical technique for "doubling the square." Compare that proof with the same proof which you find on the excerpt from a page of the master mason's sketchbook shown in **Illustration 26-4**.[22] Answer the question for yourself.

Why have we not learned any of this in our history classes? Because the views of the Classicists have prevailed due to the most deadly defensive device used by "scholars" when someone proves them wrong: absolute silence. Many, if not most, teachers of the Classics want us to believe that the Greeks were the world's very first mathematicians, albeit that *real* scholars, such as Sir Thomas Heath, were quick to point out that the Greeks *themselves* admitted that their mathematics had precedents in Egypt and Babylonia.[23] Heath expressly mentions the probability that the Greek mathematician Pythagoras studied in Egypt.[24] Translations of Egyptian and Babylonian texts completed during the twentieth century should suffice to convince even the most skeptical scholar or the most ethnocentric Classicist. For instance: "A second oddity of the history of mathematics was brought to light when the Babylonian clay tablet Plimpton 322 (museum number, Columbia University, New York) was translated by Neugebauer and Sachs in 1945. The translation established beyond any doubt that the Pythagorean theorem was well known to Babylonian mathematicians more than a thousand years before Pythagoras was born."[25] Until 1945, we were justified in referring to the 3-4-5 triangle proposition applicable to right triangles as the "Pythagorean theorem." What do we call it forty-five years after the foregoing translation by Neugebauer and Sachs? We still call it the "Pythagorean theorem." What will we call it one-hundred years from now? The same. Why? Classicists control the textbook publication industry, and most of them have given the findings of Neugebauer and Sachs the shunning of "scholarly silence." They will give this book the same treatment! Why? Because they have allowed their "science" to become their "religion." The Greeks were the first mathematicians! Period! Case closed! No further evidence will be admitted — most particularly if it tends to prove anything to the contrary! Classicists still are apt to insist that Plato and Socrates gave us the proposition concerning the doubling of the square — but *real* scholars know better![26]

How did Egyptian architects, engineers, and construction superintendents work with what we call the "right triangle theorem," which has been attributed incorrectly to Pythagoras; the proposition that the square of the hypotenuse equals the sum of the squares of the other two sides, which we express, customarily, by the algebraic formula $c^2 = a^2 + b^2$? They called it the "Sacred Triangle."[27] They knew from their mathematics and geometry that a triangle whose two sides are 3 and 4 will have a hypotenuse of 5. They knew from their arithmetic that $3 + 4 + 5 = 12$. They divided a rope into 12 equal segments, using knots, or other markers, then staked 4 segments down to the ground, leaving 3 segments free on one end of the rope and 5 segments free on the other end of the rope. They swung the two loose segments of 3 and 5 units upwards, in circular motions until the two ends touched![28] Simple! Also brilliant! Ancient Egyptian surveyors were called *harpedonapti*, that is, those who measure with a cord.[29] Modern building construction surveying still involves use of an engineer's "chain," string lines, and chalked lines "snapped down" with strings. *If* use of ropes and strings for surveying denotes or connotes primitivism, then we are as backwards now as they were thousands of years ago!

We should expect such practical engineering from a people who could level the base of a pyramid without surveying instruments. How did they do that? Using their ability to reason. They built a dike around the building site, flooded it with water, then, as the sun evaporated the water, they marked out the high points of the dirt and rock and shaved them off. Repeating the process several times produced a site which was absolutely level; just as level as moderns would get it with laser-beam surveying instruments![30]

We sampled, rather than surveyed or summarized, the mythology of Egypt and Babylonia, in an effort to avoid losing, as readers, Eagles who are scientifically-minded. We must do no more than sample the mathematics and engineering of the Egyptians and Babylonians in order to keep our liberal-arts-minded Eagles from abandoning ship. Babylonian mathematics included algebraic quadratic equations, and they utilized arithmetical progressions and tables of numerical and linear values to analyze problems of astronomy that we would approach using the "tools" of spherical geometry, spherical trigonometry, and analytical geometry.[31] Their systems of notation and calculation were entirely different from ours.[32]

We must lay a foundation for a somewhat detailed study of the Christian Cathedral at Chartres, in France, without violating our precept that we will not wallow in "number magic." The construction of Chartres reached substantial completion during the 1230's.[33] The clergy at Chartres were Christian Gnostics.[34] They dedicated Chartres to the Bodily Assumption of the Virgin Mary,[35] a doctrine which was generally accepted by Roman Catholics for many centuries before it became official dogma during the 1950's.[36] This doctrine holds that Our Lady stands by God "almost as a divinity in her own right."[37]

Chartres was dedicated to Our Lady in her role of "Queen of Heaven."[38] For a few moments, let us look at the concept of the "Queen of Heaven." "There is one point concerning religion to which the reader's attention should especially be drawn, and this is the growth of the Marian cult which took place during the Middle Ages and which was to have a considerable effect on the building of cathedrals. St. Bernard, who was really a central figure in the history of medieval Christianity, contributed enormously to the growth of the cult of the Virgin, which was celebrated at the time in liturgical hymns:

O Salutary Virgin - Star of the Sea,
Thou who bore the Sun of Justice;
Creator of light, ever Virgin,
Receive our praise.
Queen of Heaven through whom the sick are cured,
The faithful receive grace,
The afflicted joy, and the world celestial light..."[39]

Read those words twice more. The planet we call "Venus," in its role as the "Morning Star," precedes (or, allegorically, "gives birth to") the rising sun.[40] The Sumerians called the planet Venus "Inanna," which literally means "Queen of Heaven,"[41] and said of her:

I say, "Hail!" to the Holy One who appears in the heavens!
I say, "Hail!" to the Holy Priestess of Heaven!
I say, "Hail!" to Inanna, The Great Lady of Heaven!
Holy Torch! You fill the sky with light!
You brighten the day at dawn![42]

My Lady, the Amazement of the Land, the Lone Star,
The Brave One who appears first in the heavens. [43]

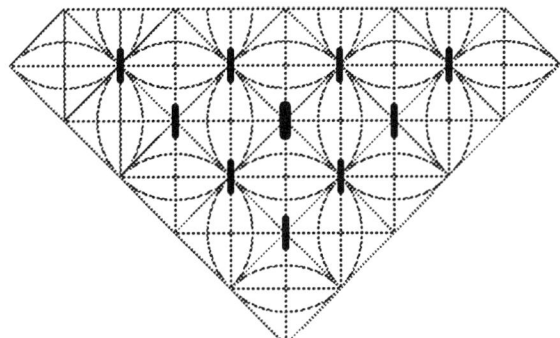

Figure 452

Inanna, seated on the royal throne, shines like daylight.
The king, like the sun, shines radiantly by her side. [44]

Recall that Isis was the Egyptian Queen of Heaven, and that she was called the "Throne of Osiris."[45] The Blessed Virgin, Our Lady, later was called the "Throne of the Almighty."[46] Recall that the Hebrew Prophet Jeremiah spoke against worship of the "Queen of Heaven."[47] You may have looked at the *Sepher Ha-Razim*[48] to learn the Hebrew recipe for cakes made for sacrifice to Inanna, Ishtar, Isis, etc., the Queen of Heaven of *all* ancient Middle Eastern peoples, including the Hebrews. Jeremiah surely was speaking out not only against the worship of the *foreign* Queens of Heaven, such as Inanna, but against the worship of the ancient Hebrew Queen of Heaven, as well.

We have learned that St. Bernard contributed to the growth of the Catholic cult which finally crowned Our Lady as Queen of Heaven.[49] By contributing to the growth of the Marian Cult, St. Bernard thereby contributed to the building of many Christian churches. Was he proud of the building of richly-decorated Cluniac churches? Well, not exactly! He wrote: "O vanity of vanities, but more folly than vanity! Every part of the church shines but the poor man is hungry! The church walls are clothed in gold, while the children of the church remain naked.... Tell me then, poor monks - if indeed you are poor - what is gold doing in the holy place? To speak plainly, greed is the root of all evil, greed, the slave of idols... for the sight of these sumptuous and amazing vanities encourages man to give rather than to pray. So riches attract riches, money attracts money. Why, I do not know, but the greater the abundance of riches, the more willingly men give. The eye is dazzled by gifts of golden roofs to house relics and purse-strings are unloosed. Beautiful statues of saints are thought more venerable if they are richly painted. The faithful come to kiss them and are encouraged to give. They are more concerned with the beauty of the statues than with the virtue of the saints.... A man at prayer seems even to have forgotten the purpose of his prayer.... The poor are allowed to groan in hunger and the money they need is spent on useless luxury."[50] St. Bernard evidently wanted to reorient the Church toward the ancient sky-goddess, but he apparently had no intention to mulct the poor for the construction of churches!

Although we will not wallow in ancient number magic, we must take a peek at it in order to understand why the numbers 7 and 9, which "belonged" to Our Lady,[51] were incorporated into the fabric of Chartres Cathedral. We shall be brief.

In India, it is said that the triangle is the mother of form.[52] Kramer taught us that the triangle in Illustration 10-9 is one of the world's oldest written symbols, representing a female *pudendum*, and meaning "woman."[53] We discussed its possible derivation from the Holy Grail. Figure 183. A triangle composed of ten numerals one is illustrated in **Figure 452**. This triangle, called the *Mystical Tetractys*, was one of the principal secret symbols by which followers of Pythagoras could identify themselves to each other.[54] The Pythagoreans took an oath never to reveal the meaning of this triangle.[55] We know, however, that the Pythagoreans (*circa* 500 B.C.) believed that in the *Tetractys* "are found the source and root of eternal Nature."[56] Notice that the bolded numeral one in the center of the triangle is surrounded by nine unbolded numerals one. We are supposed to see a relationship between a pregnant woman, who holds a fetus in her womb, and this triangle, which holds The Big Number One in its "womb," that is, surrounds the bolded 1 with the nine numerals one. The triangle of nine thus is "pregnant" with the Big Number

One, like Our Lady was pregnant with Christ. "[A]s Dante wrote: 'The Blessed Virgin is nine, for she is the root of the Trinity.'"[57] The number seven was the "Virgin Number."[58] Take away the *four* numerals one on the top row of the *Tetractys*, and then take away the *three* numerals one on the next row, and you have left a trinity of numerals one, i.e., you have *the* Christian Trinity. The numerals you took away, *four* and *three*, equal *seven*, the Virgin number. We must expect to find the numbers seven and nine in profusion when we begin a structural analysis of Chartres! If you fail to understand the point of this stuff, consider the words of St. Augustine: "'[I]gnorance of number prevents us from understanding things that are set down in the scripture in a figurative and mystical way.'"[59]

Three of the five "Platonic Solids" of ancient three-dimensional geometry are composed of (i.e., "born from") triangles.[60] The "Platonic Solids," the "Archimedian Solids," and other three-dimensional geometric forms recognized by the neo-Pythagoreans, define the shapes of structural components of crystals,[61] and also are found to have been used as structural elements of the Gothic Christian Cathedrals, including Chartres, as they were in the ancient temples of the Greeks and Egyptians.[62]

"It is not generally suspected how much... Plato... influenced European... Thought and Art, especially Architecture. In the same way that Plato conceived the 'Great Ordering One'... as arranging the Cosmos harmoniously according to the preexisting, eternal paradigma, archetypes or ideas, so the Platonic — or rather, neo-Platonic — view of Art conceived the Artist as planning his work of Art according to a preexisting system of proportions, as a 'symphonic' composition, ruled by a 'dynamic symmetry' corresponding in space to musical eurhythmy in time. This technique of correlated proportions was in fact transposed from the Pythagorean conception of musical harmony...."[63] "It is also quite recently that, in the field of biology too, it was found that certain morphological intuitions of the Pythagorean and Platonist schools, and their interpretation by the Neo-Platonist thinkers and artists of the Renaissance, are confirmed by modern research. The Pythagorean creed that 'Everything is arranged according to Number' (taken up by Plato) is justified not only in Art (it was a Gothic Master Builder who in 1398 said, '*Ars Sine Scientia Nihil*') but also in the realm of Nature. The use of Geometry in the study and classification of crystals is obvious, but it is only lately that its role

in the study of Life and Living Growth has begun to be recognized."[64] "Curiously enough, the patterns, themes of symmetry, spirals, discovered in living forms and living growth, show those same themes of proportion which in Art seem to have been used by Greek and Gothic architects, and, paramount amongst them, the ratio or proportion called by Leonardo's friend Luca Pacioli 'the Divine Proportion,' by Kepler 'one of the two Jewels of Geometry,' and commonly known as 'The Golden Section,' appears to be the principal 'invariant' (to use an expression popular in modern Mathematical Physics), as remarkable by its algebraical and geometrical properties as by this role in Biology and in Aesthetics. There are then such things as 'The Mathematics of Life' and 'the Mathematics of Art,' and the two coincide."[65]

Ghyka tells us that for the Greeks "Architecture was not only 'Frozen Music' (Schelling) but living Music. The notions of periodicity and proportion, and their interplay, can be used for succession in time as well as for spatial associations.... If Architecture is petrified or frozen Music, so is Music 'Drawing in Time.'"[66] Carrying the same concepts into religion, "Plato (*Timaeus*) mentions the concordance between the rhythm of the harmoniously balanced soul and the rhythm of the Universe...."[67]

The "Golden Section," to which we just referred, is represented by the Greek letter Phi.[68] We shall leave its algebraical and geometrical derivation to those of you who are interested in mathematics, so as not to scare away our liberal-arts-only readers.[69] "The Golden Section also plays a dominating part in the proportions of the human body, a fact which was probably recognized by the Greek sculptors, who liked to put into evidence a parallelism between the proportions of the ideal temple and of the human body (cf. Vitruvius), or even to trace a harmonious correspondence... between the terms Universe-Temple-Man. The correlation Universe-Man as macrocosmos-microcosmos was studied later on by the Kabbala as well as by the Christian mystics of the Middle Ages, and by later dabblers in white and black magic."[70] As we have said before, it is remarkable how mathematics quickly can be dissolved by the human mind into the very lowest levels of religion, that is, magic!

The mathematical proportion represented by the Greek letter Phi "is intimately associated with the regular pentagon and with the regular star-pentagon or pentagram, so much so that the construction of the pentagon... discovered by the Pythagoreans and given by Euclid is directly based

The Holy Grail as Plan and Elevation

on the Golden Section and on... [a certain] formula.... And because of this connection between the Golden Series or Phi series, the Fibonacci Series, and homothetic growth, and between the Golden Section and the pentagon, we shall not be surprised to see the preponderance of pentagonal symmetry in living organisms, especially in botany and amongst marine animals (starfishes, jellyfishes, sea-urchins)."[71]

As we have said before, the ancients were careful observers, recorders, collators, and correlators of the lines, forms, and proportions of God's creations, both animal and mineral, and were competent mathematicians and geometers.

In the number magic built into Chartres, the number 5 is the number of Christ, the "Son of Man," because it is the sum of the number 4, representing the world and material things, including the flesh and blood of Christ, and the number 1, representing the mystical unity of God the Father.[72] The number 5 also is the number of mankind (and of the "Son of Man") because human bodies have five appendages — one head, two arms, and two legs, and the human body fits into the 5-pointed star and pentagram.[73] Silly nonsense? Some moderns would think so! But if you were a Pythagorean true believer, convinced that in the Tetractys "are found the source and root of eternal Nature,"[74] you would not have believed this numerology foolish at all. Let any one of you who is entirely free from silly beliefs about science and religion be the first to throw an unkind remark at the ancient Pythagoreans!

Let us bring these concepts into architecture. Persian architects made use of the 3-4-5 triangle to establish the profile of their domes.[75] We see Ghyka's drawing of this application in **Illustration 26-5**.[76] "The cuboctahedron plays also an important part in architecture, especially in Byzantine (and Moslem) architecture, and wherever we meet the problem of setting a dome on a cubical supporting frame."[77] This is the solution to the problem of erecting a dome on a square "chosen by the architect of Santa-Sophia...."[78] Ghyka's isometric drawings showing the relationship between the cuboctahedron and Byzantine cupolas were shown in Illustration 4-1.[79] Ghyka informs us that "Vitruvius, in a sentence comparing the 'commodation' of a well planned-out temple with that of the human body, had already noticed that the navel is the centre of symmetry of the latter."[80] Perceval's name meant "pierced through the middle" to the Grail quest author Wolfram von Eschenbach. King Arthur was a dweller at the antipodes. The bellybutton of our Grail

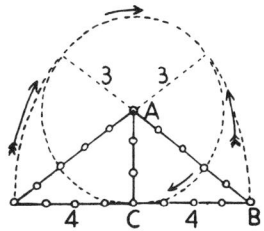

Illustration 26-5. Use of the 3-4-5 triangle to establish the profile of a dome. Courtesy of Dover Publications, Inc., New York.

manform is the exact center of a Grail dome. The evidence is mounting rapidly that we are on the right track.

Other numbers also had their "magic," which was transmitted through the years by the Hebrew Kabbala, medieval magic, Rosicrucian esoterism, and operative and speculative Masonic lodges.[81] As promised, we shall restrict our discussion of the "magic" of numbers to the following two topics: Why churchmen wanted certain numbers incorporated into the foundations, structural members, and fabrics of the Christian Cathedrals, and how operative stone masons pleased their clients by incorporating Christian "number magic" into the cathedrals while, at the same time, following sound principles of design and construction which would cause the cathedrals to stand against the ravages of time. The answer is simple yet brilliant: There was no conflict between the "number magic" desires of the clients (the churchmen) and the engineering requirements of the builders! The same "number magic" which would please the churchmen would cause the cathedrals to stand! Proving what? That magic rather than engineering causes the cathedrals to stand? Of course not! Proving that there was a firm layer of sense under the massive layers of nonsense; that numerical proportions and relationships observed by the ancients in the handiwork of God (crystals, plants, animals, and human beings) would hold up some of the largest buildings ever erected by mankind!

The number five stood for Man, the Microcosmos, and the number ten stood for the World, the Macrocosmos, "with sometimes the Temple as link, as 'proportional mean' between the two."[82] Recall that Pythagorean laws governing the proportions of buildings were derived from musical intervals or "ratios between the lengths of the strings of the tetrachord...."[83] Has the symbolism of the Christian cathedral begun to be apparent to you? Think of a Gothic cathedral. High vaults and domes, as those imagined in Heaven. Stained-glass windows throwing the rainbow spectrum into the building when they are struck by sunlight. Music being played on instruments and sung by choirs. All of this supported on the Church's one foundation, the cosmic manform, Jesus Christ, Our Lord, on the Cross of Calvary![84] The Christian cathedral, like the Hebrew Temple, is God's House on Earth — built according to His very own specifications as revealed to man in His handiworks on Earth! The Hebrew religionist who wrote the Temple story may not have been a very good mathematician or structural engineer, but there was *much* truth in what he or she wrote!

The pentagram and its relationship to the Golden Section and to other geometrical forms, including the circle, was used by the Pythagoreans as "the secret sign of brotherhood" and was "the most important mathematical secret of the Fraternity."[85] The esoteric concept of correspondence between the number ten, representing the Earth, and the number five, representing Man, appeared in the Hermetic "Emerald Table."[86] Ezekiel's Vision referred to a mystic "emerald," which we found on the Holy Grail. Our Grail quest stories were filled with references to the mystic "emerald." We are beginning to understand why!

It is clear that the ancients *thought* that in their number theory they had "found the source and root of eternal Nature."[87] The pentagram was used "as frame of the secret planning diagrams of the architects and Master Masons, handed over from father to son...."[88] "In England the oldest masonic documents... mention King Athelstan (925-940) as having established the first Guilds of Masons in the British Islands."[89] Remember King Athelstan? Remember the gifts on the occasion of his daughter's marriage, which included a piece of the Cross of Calvary enclosed in a crystal? Here is tangible evidence that persons privy to the engineering secrets of the operative stone masons also were privy to the inner secrets of the Christian Faith! The pentagram traveled from the Pythagorean Brotherhood to the operative stone masons; thence, through various channels, including occultist and Rosicrucian circles, "to modern Free-Masonry, where the 'Flaming Star' is none other than our Pentagram, with the letter G in its middle, Latin transcription of the Hebrew Yod, itself the number

Ten or Decad."[90] Most modern speculative Freemasons evidently believe that their passwords, symbols, rites, etc., are derived from Judaism and Christianity. Is another explanation possible? Could it be that Judaism, Christianity, and speculative Freemasonry are not-so-distant "cousins" of the same doctrinal "ancestor"; that they are inheritors of the same underlying traditions?

The number six, signifying the "harmony" and "perfect symmetry" which the ancients had found in the structures of crystals, was represented geometrically by the Jewish Shield of David, the six-pointed star.[91]

Ghyka gives us the point of departure for serious study of the cathedrals: "We shall not be surprised to see... that, according to the converging results of recent researches about Canons of Proportions and plans used by Gothic Master Builders, the fundamental Gothic Diagram, the Key-Diagram transmitted from Master to Master (the third degree of initiation in the craft) was based on the pentagram and decagon, placed within the circle of orientation of the church or cathedral."[92] "Vitruvius describes very clearly the way in which the *line* North-South was placed into the circle of orientation by marking the direction of minimum shadow-length of a vertical pole erected at the center of the circle (true noon and true South); the tracing of a perpendicular direction, in fact of any right-angle, was obtained, as we have seen... by using a continuous rope divided by knots into 3+4+5=12 equal parts."[93]

We call the five regular polyhedra of ancient solid geometry the "Platonic Solids" because Plato wrote about them in *Timaeus*.[94] However, we must not allow the Classicists to convince us that Plato fathered the concept of these geometrical forms. Sir Thomas Heath, a *real* scholar, tells us that at least one dodecahedron of Etruscan origin has been dated to about 1000 B.C., and no less than twenty-six dodecahedrons of Celtic origin have been discovered.[95] The five "Platonic Solids" were found in an archaeological dig at Maes Howe, in Scotland, indicating that the Neolithic inhabitants of the British Isles were skilled mathematicians some 1000 years before Plato![96]

The ingredients are swirling together in our mixing bowl! When we have added a few more ingredients, it will be time to bake the doughnuts!

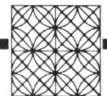

The Holy Grail as Plan and Elevation

Notes
CHAPTER TWENTY-SIX
The Holy Grail as Plan and Elevation for Houses of God

1. Lawlor 92. See also, Schwaller de Lubicz EM 158.

2. Yarwood 81.

3. Yarwood 81.

4. Yarwood 87.

5. Yarwood 87; Ghyka 55.

6. Yarwood 85-86.

7. Yarwood 84; Lawlor 16.

8. Yarwood 85-86; Oates 185.

9. Oates 48.

10. Yarwood 5.

11. *Webster's Third New International Dictionary* 2536.

12. Dreyer 206; Ronan 8.

13. Gimpel 82.

14. The Church now opposes genetic research. Scientists cannot be trusted? Can Church leaders be trusted?

15. Gimpel 82. (Emphasis added.)

16. Gimpel 84.

17. Gimpel 88.

18. Gimpel 85.

19. Gimpel 85.

20. Ghyka Plate XLIV.

21. Saggs Plates 23, 24.

22. Gimpel 74.

23. 1 Heath 5, 24-25, 78-79, 120-121, 137-139, 141, 174, 177, 202, 356.

24. 1 Heath 4-5, 67, 86, 128.

25. Gillings 1. See also Neugebauer 35-36.

26. Gimpel 85-86.

27. Schwaller de Lubicz EM 96.

28. Schwaller de Lubicz EM 95-96; Ghyka 22.

29. Schwaller de Lubicz EM 94; 1 Heath 121-122.

30. *Smithsonian*, April, 1986, p. 90.

31. Oates 184-186; Neugebauer 40, 44, 102-138, 150, 161, 185.

32. Gillings 4-10; Neugebauer 15-23; Oates 184-186.

33. James 1.

34. James 89.

35. James 67.

36. James 67, 107; Graham 360-361. The doctrine of the assumption to Heaven of the Mother of the God "is in no sense peculiar to Christian mythology." Graham 360. Graham lists several mothers of pagan gods who reputedly ascended to Heaven. Graham 360.

37. James 67.

38. Gimpel 25; James 53, 67, 106-108.

39. Gimpel 25. An inscription to the goddess Cybele refers to her as "[t]he virgin in her heavenly place," and as a "constellation seen in the heavens." Vermaseren 138. An inscription to Attis, Cybele's male associate, refers to him as "the shepherd of the white constellation." Vermaseren 182. The same historian notes that at many locations where Cybele formerly was worshiped, shrines to the Virgin Mary have been established. Vermaseren 182. The Semitic "Queen of Heaven," known as Inanna, Ishtar, or Anat, was said to be a harlot; the mistress of the gods. Langdon 30-36. The East Indian goddess Usas (Dawn), of *Rigveda* fame, wore dancing clothes and displayed her bosom when she went forth before the sun to remove the black mantle of night. Keith 32, 76. Usas was said to be the mistress of the sun; also, the mother of the sun. Keith 32. The role of the Planet Venus as the Morning Star, proceeding across Heaven before the sun, was cleaned up considerably when the Ro-

man Catholic Church crowned Our Lady as "Queen of Heaven." How can Usas have been both the mistress of the sun and the mother of the sun? Cathar Christians criticized the Roman Catholic doctrine of the Bodily Assumption of Our Lady to Heaven because, in their view, Our Lady thereby was required to play the conflicting roles of consort to God (Jehovah) and mother of God (Jesus Christ). This theological dispute remained unresolved until the Church of Rome resorted to fire and sword. Cathars who survived kept their opinions to themselves. So do I.

40. Schaaf 148.

41. Wolkstein xvi.

42. Wolkstein 93.

43. Wolkstein 105.

44. Wolkstein 109.

45. 2 Budge *Osiris* 272, 274, 287.

46. James 84.

47. Jeremiah 7.18; 44.17-19, 25.

48. At pp. 33-34.

49. Gimpel 25.

50. Gimpel 12.

51. James 84,101; Ghyka 21, 113.

52. Lawlor 12.

53. Kramer 302, 304.

54. Schwaller de Lubicz EM 80-81, 86.

55. Schwaller de Lubicz EM 81, 109; 1 Heath 75.

56. Ghyka 116.

57. James 84.

58. Ghyka 21, 113.

59. James 85.

60. Ghyka 40.

61. Ghyka 85.

62. Ghyka 50-68.

63. Ghyka ix.

64. Ghyka xi.

65. Ghyka xi-xii.

66. Ghyka 5-6.

67. Ghyka 5.

68. Ghyka 7.

69. Ghyka 7-19.

70. Ghyka 16.

71. Ghyka 17-18.

72. James 101. See also Lawlor 103.

73. Lawlor 58.

74. Ghyka 116.

75. Ghyka 22.

76. Ghyka 23.

77. Ghyka 54.

78. Ghyka 54.

79. Ghyka 55.

80. Ghyka 66. Christian churchmen later elevated the center to the heart. Lawlor 93.

81. Ghyka 113.

82. Ghyka 112.

83. Ghyka 112.

84. James 83.

85. Ghyka 113.

86. Ghyka 115.

87. Ghyka 116.

88. Ghyka 117.

89. Ghyka 117-118.

90. Ghyka 119.

91. Ghyka 117.

92. Ghyka 119.

93. Ghyka 142.

94. Lawlor 96.

95. 1 Heath 160.

96. Lawlor 96-97.

Chapter Twenty-Seven

Chartres Cathedral — God's Engineering Replicated

John James tells us that the tools of the master masons who were the architects, engineers, and builders of Chartres "were the compass, straight-edge and ruler, angles, proportional dividers, and string...."[1] The master masons used geometry to issue instructions to their workers.[2] They incorporated Christian sacred geometry[3] into the structure to reflect the belief of the clergy, their clients, that every detail and element of the structure thereby would reflect the Essence of God.[4] Thus, for reasons of religious expression as well as engineering necessity, "Geometry totally pervaded the building."[5] Geometry allowed the master mason to produce and to check wooden templets which workers used to determine the size and shape of each stone.[6] The master masons who worked at Chartres used different measurements of length, one of which has been traced through Crete to Egypt, "and may have originated on the Persian plateau some five thousand years ago."[7] Another standard length used in building Chartres was "known from India to Ireland."[8] The flow of technology, as well as mythology, seems to have been from East to West.

James concludes that the cathedral builders "had the audacity to believe that they were constructing a slice of eternity itself, and the simplicity to trust that God's Essence would be made manifest in something they built from the materials found on earth. They achieved this by setting into the design as many of the appropriate numbers and symbols as possible, so that the different levels of meaning tumble over one another, layer upon layer, until the mind reels under the weight."[9]

We would violate our precept of brevity were we to spend much time repeating the details of the fascinating discoveries of John James and his assistants. You should read James' book about Chartres from cover to cover — whether or not you are interested in architecture. This is the *real* world of Holy Grail studies!

Another conclusion by James will serve our present purposes: "There was no room in the 1200's for the visual adjustments we find in Classical architecture, like thicker columns against the corner with a narrower bay next to it, or tapering shafts

and the swelling called entasis partway up that were all invented to aid the eye. The mediaeval cathedral was not built to be seen from man's viewpoint, but from the pure and universal view of God himself. Perspective and other optical refinements were irrelevant to people who believed they were building a slice of Paradise."[10] The builders apparently were seeking to apply God's mathematical and geometrical rules of form and proportion as observed in crystals, plants, and animals in order to replicate here on Earth His house in the sky. We soon shall see that this replication required the incorporation of design features which neither appeal to aesthetics nor serve any useful engineering purpose. God built crystals that way. Man would build God's house on Earth the same way.

Chartres is "cruciform in shape, in memory of Our Lord's Passion."[11] The towers are four-sided, that is, two squared, "which in nearly all cultures represents the world of matter."[12] Pilgrims enter the church from the west, between two square towers, representing the mundane, and progress across the nave, representing the ark, toward the altar in the east.[13] "At the apse, the essential design consists of three large circular chapels. Three is the number of the spirit, again an almost universally accepted idea, and the circle, being the perfect figure without beginning or end, is God himself. The pilgrim thus moves from the duality of existence [between the square towers] towards the Trinity and the Spirit."[14] **Illustration 27-1.**[15] In moving

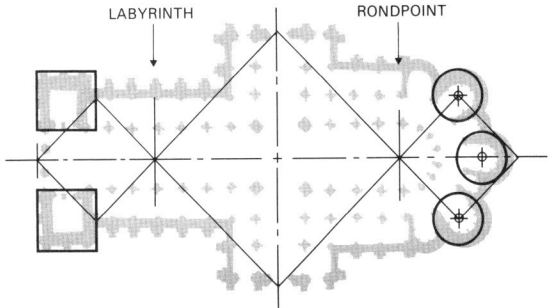

Illustration 27-1. Holy geometry in use to establish forms and proportions for the plan of Chartres Cathedral. Courtesy of Routledge & Kegan Paul, London.

towards the nave and the altar, the pilgrim crosses the labyrinth, a pattern of lines on the cathedral floor.[16] We must pay most particular attention to the labyrinth.

James tells us this about the labyrinth: "Its design is canonic, in that there are many examples in mediaeval churches, and that nearly all of those that date from this time follow exactly the same pattern. There are eleven rings, containing a path that leads by a circuitous but singular route to the middle. It is not a maze, but a way leading to the six-petalled rose at the centre. The arrangement is always the same: you enter on the left and proceed directly to the fifth circle, then the sixth, followed by all the inner rings and so on, to the centre. It must have had an important religious significance, otherwise why install it? Why make them so large? And why always use the same design? As with the masters, the documents are silent."[17]

Remember your numerology? You proceed in the labyrinth to the fifth circle. Meaning that you start a journey toward the Center burdened by your human faults? Then you go to the sixth circle. Meaning that you perfect yourself as a human? Then you journey toward the six-petalled rose at the Center. Meaning what? Back to James: "At one time there was a brass plaque in the centre. The three figures engraved on it, weird as they seem for a Christian church, tell us much about the meaning of the pattern. Two of the figures were the pagan mythological heroes Theseus and the Minotaur, and the third was Ariadne who supplied the string her lover used to find his way home. Theseus voluntarily searches for and finally destroys the devil, be it his original sin or his own inner passions, but having done so would have been lost in the darkness but for the guidance given him by his Virgin Lady. A nice Christian parable, and notice that even in the original myth Theseus, though betrothed to Ariadne, does not marry her, but leaves her behind so she remains a maid. For these reasons it is believed that the labyrinth portrays man's path to God, not after death, but now, while here on earth."[18]

Some of our Stone Age ancestors evidently initiated their adolescents into adulthood by requiring them to go deep into a natural cave, through the darkness, until they reached a lighted grotto where a cult figure had been painted on the cave's wall.[19] When the adolescents made their way back out, they apparently were considered to be adults.[20] The idea might have been to cause the initiate to face and to conquer his childish fears. The experi-

ence is valid today, as anyone who ever has sat alone in a natural cave without light or noise for a few hours will tell you! The symbolism seems apparent: the child returned to the womb of the Earth Mother (i.e., entered the cave) and symbolically "died." The adult then was symbolically "born" from the womb of the Earth Mother. Childhood was over. The initiates were adults. Born again! We are told in a version of the Christ story that Christ was born in a cave rather than in a manger in a stable.[21] We are told that Christ died on the Cross that we might be born again. The mystery religions, like the speculative Freemasons today, conducted ceremonies in dark grottoes during which persons symbolically "died" and were "born again."[22] Is the Christian Church really so different from the oriental faiths from which it was born? Is the current message different from the message of our tribal past? Start out as a human being, with all human faults and frailties, then perfect yourself as a human being, then give yourself up to, and become one with, God, in order to be born again in the image of God? In modern humanistic terms: Give yourself up to the pursuit of excellence in order to become your "personal best." If this is the goal of all religions, why do people kill each other in disputes about liturgical and theological details of their respective faiths? Does it really matter whether the "cave" into which we crawl for our rebirth displays a Christian Cross, the Star of David, an Islamic Moon, or any of the other symbols over which human beings have fought and for which they have died through the years? Why are such religious wars fought? For the sake of the sheep? Or for the sake of the shepherds?

But we have not ended our discussion of the labyrinth of Chartres, and of the other Christian cathedrals. "The labyrinths seem to have had two roles, being not only to exemplify the Way, but also to honour the builders. We can see this in some of the names given to them, for they were not only called 'Jerusalem' but also 'Daedali' after the first architect from mythology, Daedalus. Perhaps we know him better as the first man to fly, but he was also supposed to have invented the builder's tools and to have constructed the labyrinth in Crete, the one with the Minotaur. It is a nice touch that the symbol of man's path to God should also record the names of the men who were able to create the cathedral as the Heavenly Jerusalem on earth, through which the pilgrim could come close to him."[23] Hang onto your framing squares and dividers! In **Figure 453**, we see Daedalus wearing

Figure 453

his flying equipment, that is, two wings and tailfeathers. He is surrounded by tools of the ancient builders: dividers, proportional dividers, and a framing square. He also is surrounded by the geometrical forms he uses to construct buildings: circles, squares, triangles, domes, vaults, arches, etc. An architect from Heaven equipped with tools and building techniques from Heaven! Does this stuff have no end?

Back to other realities — the geometry which holds Chartres together, and the "need" to incorporate Christian number magic into the structure. In Illustration 27-1,[24] we see a *plan* of the structure with the two square towers to the left and the three round chapels to the right. Remember the geometry proposition of "doubling the square"? You see it in use in Illustration 27-1 to establish certain proportions of the structure.[25]

The numbers of Christ and of Our Lady were used to set foundation proportions throughout the structure.[26] The hexagon and pentagon similarly were used in *plan* and *elevations*.[27] "All three of the numbers needed for calculating the cycle of Easter are included in the plan."[28] If the master was responsible for all these things, what sort of man was he? What was his training in religious matters?[29]

The master mason evidently knew about "gematria," an occult pursuit of religious intellectuals of many faiths, which is a system of notation by which numbers are written using letters of the alphabet to which they correspond — as if we used "A" to mean "1," "B" to mean "2," etc.[30] Several of the distances in the foundation *plan* of Chartres correspond to words and phrases in Latin and Greek honoring the Virgin and Child.[31] The master mason knew his religious number magic![32]

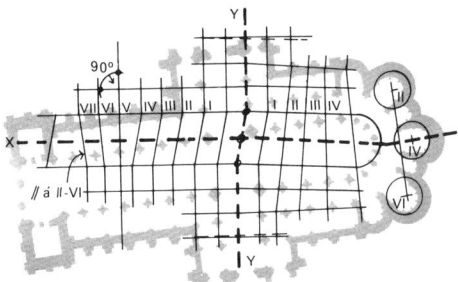

Illustration 27-2. Intentional misalignments of the axes at Chartres Cathedral to emulate dislocation in crystals. Courtesy of Routledge & Kegan Paul, London.

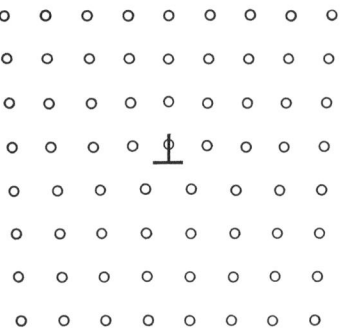

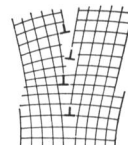

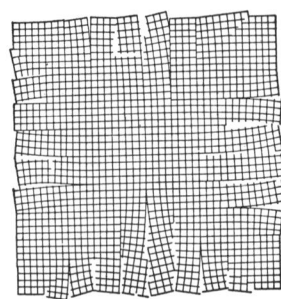

Illustration 27-3. Diagrams of natural dislocation in crystals. Courtesy of Dover Publications, Inc., New York.

He apparently also knew crystallography. James concludes that the master who laid down the foundations "deliberately bent the axes. There was no need to do this…. It could not have been a mistake…. There are some twists in the other axes, too, forming a coherent and orderly system of sways and bends that belie the possibility of randomness, and therefore of error."[33] James tells us that bending of the long axes, nearly always to the south, was a common practice in the construction of Gothic churches.[34] "Architecturally, bending the axis is an attempt to avoid symmetry, for it adds the same sort of imbalance that we find in natural things."[35] James indicates that in India the architect was instructed to bend the temple axis to the south, to create a deliberate discrepancy between the ideal and the actual.[36] Why? Let us venture a guess. **Illustration 27-2**[37] shows an exaggeration of the misalignment of the axes at Chartres. **Illustration 27-3**[38] shows three diagrams of a phenomenon in crystals known as "dislocation."[39] If man was to follow God's design of crystals in the construction of God's house on Earth, was it philosophically necessary, although not structurally necessary, that the "dislocation" of quartz crystals be designed into the structure? The Hebrew religionists who wrote the story of the Temple of Solomon believed that God had "specified" that a spiral staircase be included in His house.[40] Some crystals, including quartz, "rotate the plane of polarized light"[41] in the form of a spiral staircase, as shown in **Illustration 27-4**.[42]

Again, what sort of man was the master mason? Why does this matter so much? Because James and his assistants did a *marvelous* bit of detective work regarding the bending of the axes at Chartres. They discovered that the next master mason on the job straightened the axes that the first master mason deliberately had bent! Proving what? Proving this: "If the clergy had authorized the bent

axis for its sacred significance, surely they would have told the second master to keep it that way. The fact that it was straightened shows otherwise."[43] Suggesting what? "This suggests some fascinating possibilities about the masters' traditions. They must have flowed through the ages independently of their patrons, and have evolved as concepts and theories within a culture of their own. *Maybe there is something in the beliefs held by Masonic lodges after all.*"[44]

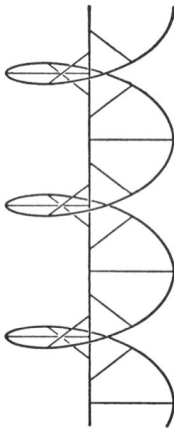

Illustration 27-4. Diagram of the rotation of the plane of polarized light by some optically active crystals, including quartz. Courtesy of Dover Publications, Inc., New York.

Notes
CHAPTER TWENTY-SEVEN
Chartres Cathedral — God's Engineering Replicated

1. James 33.

2. James 33.

3. See, generally, Lawlor.

4. James 33.

5. James 33.

6. James 33-34.

7. James 37.

8. James 41.

9. James 85.

10. James 147.

11. James 83.

12. James 87.

13. James 86-87.

14. James 88-89.

15. James 93.

16. James 86.

17. James 86-87.

18. James 87.

19. Hadingham SOTIA 181-183.

20. These inferences were drawn by scholars from physical evidence left behind by the adults and adolescents whose footprints were found on the cave's floor. The physical evidence indicates that the ceremonies were neither large nor frequent. Does this indicate that the tribe or band was small? Hadingham SOTIA 181-183.

21. *The Protevangelion* XII.14; XIV.3-4, 12; Godwin 95.

22. Godwin 34-36.

23. James 130. A Germanic myth tells us where we might find England's Weylund Smith, a/k/a Scandinavia's Volund the Smith, a limping smith of the genre of the Greek god Hephaistos, who helped Daedalus fashion his wings. Weylund, alias Volund, is to be found hovering, "...'neath very heaven," so high up that no one could haul him down or shoot him down. Hollander 159,166.

24. James 93.

25. James 93.

26. James 101.

27. James 99-100, 110, 116.

28. James 111.

29. James 111.

30. James 106-110.

31. James 107-108.

32. James 164-165.

33. James 103.

34. James 104.

35. James 104.

36. James 104.

37. James 103.

38. E.A. Wood 65,66.

39. E.A. Wood 65,66.

40. 1 Kings 6.8.

41. E.A. Wood 136.

42. E.A. Wood 137.

43. James 104.

44. James 105. (Emphasis added.)

Chapter Twenty-Eight

The Holy Grail in Ancient Astronomy — Paths to Success or Failure

Our final quest is toward an understanding of the relationship between the Holy Grail and ancient astronomy. We are confronted with the proverbial farmer's advice to the out-of-state motorist lost in a maze of rural roads: "You can't get there from here." Yes or no, depending on the route we take. There are several routes available to us. One route dead-ends short of our goal. Another would lead us in circles. Still another is so difficult to traverse that many of us might be forced to abandon the quest. We have been following the Way of the Holy Grail. We have assumed, with some degree of success, that ancient storysmiths *honestly* sought to encode in allegory the truth about their universe as they understood it. Should we abandon our precepts so late in this book?

Classicists would suggest that we should approach ancient astronomy through a comprehensive understanding of Greek astronomy. This would be one of the most certain routes toward failure, for the reasons that follow.

The earliest Greek astronomers recorded by the scholars J.L.E. Dreyer and Sir Thomas Heath lived during the sixth century B.C. They, and others of their kind who followed them, were philosophers rather than mathematicians,[1] and their conclusions about the sun, moon, planets, and stars are so childishly silly[2] that a detailed study of their beliefs likely would cause some of us to become ensnared in this fallacy: The beliefs of these Greek philosopher-astronomers are absurd. (This is true.) Hence, the beliefs of the Egyptians, Babylonians, Sumerians, and other ancient people who preceded these Greek philosopher-astronomers must have been even more absurd. (This is false.) Hence, an exploration of the astronomy of earlier people would be a waste of time. (This would be a big mistake!) Some of these early Greek philosopher-astronomers were aware of a few solar, lunar, and astral realities, but they got much of this knowledge from the Egyptians and Babylonians.[3]

Dreyer and Heath describe the works of other Greek astronomers, dating from as early as the fourth century B.C., who were skilled mathematicians.[4] Their geometric proofs of what they believed was going on in the sky are among the most rigorous the world ever has known. Some of these proofs predict with modest accuracy various periodicities.[5] Several of these men studied in Egypt.[6] We would encounter only two problems in studying this phase of ancient astronomy, but both are formidable: First, we would lose everyone but hard-core theoretical mathematicians. Second, to what avail our efforts? After all, everyone knows that these Greek mathematician-astronomers were wrong about what rotates around what. So why study their theories in this book?

Dreyer and Heath describe the works of a third group of Greek astronomers, dating from as early as the sixth century B.C. Some of them taught an atomic theory of the universe similar in many respects to the atomic theory which began to emerge from hiding during the seventeenth century A.D.[7] Others said that the moon derives its light from the sun,[8] and that solar eclipses are caused by the moon's passing in front of the sun.[9] The Greek astronomer Hipparchus noted the precession of the equinoxes.[10] Some, including followers of Pythagoras, said that the Earth is round, not flat,[11] is inhabited all over by human beings,[12] and that it is in motion, like the other planets.[13] Others said that the Earth inclines on its axis.[14] Still others of the Pythagorean school believed the Earth rotates once daily on its axis, thereby giving us night and day.[15] "Herakleides and Exphantus the Pythagorean let the earth move '...in a turning manner, like a wheel... from west to east round its own centre.'"[16] "Herakleides let Venus [and Mercury] move round the sun instead of round the earth...."[17] "Herakleides, like Kalippas, was aware of the variable velocity of the sun in the course of the year,"[18] as were his Babylonian contemporaries.[19] Space limitations deny us the opportunity to list the names of all these ancient Greek astronomers who saw bits and pieces of reality as we do, but it is obvious that Herakleides deserves special mention!

Vitruvius described Herakleides' theory of the rotation of Mercury and Venus thus: "'Mercury and Venus make their... motions... about the rays of the sun, forming by their courses a wreath or crown about the sun itself as centre.'"[20] Is this the origin of the Crown of Thorns which became the Crown of Gold? Are we beginning to understand New Testament allegory?

And then there was Aristarchus of Samos, who flourished around 281 B.C., about whom Archimedes (287-212 B.C.) wrote: "'[H]e supposes... that the fixed stars and the sun are immovable, but that the earth is carried round the sun in a circle which is in the middle of the course....'"[21] Plutarch wrote that "'Kleanthes held that Aristarchus of Samos ought to be accused of impiety... as the man... supposed... that the heavens stand still and the earth moves in an oblique circle at the same time as it turns round its axis.'"[22] Copernicus gave credit to Aristarchus for the discovery of heliocentricity.[23] Why, then, do we give this credit to Copernicus and Galileo? Did Ezekiel learn about heliocentricity from his Babylonian captors? Is Ezekiel's wheel within a wheel the Wain (the circumpolar stars) within the Ecliptic (the circle of the Zodiac)? Recall that our Babylonian clay tablet was written between 1800 B.C. and 1600 B.C., and may have come[24] from Nippur, the city through which flows the River Chebar, where Ezekiel saw his First Vision in 593 B.C.[25] Was heliocentricity known to the Babylonians for over a thousand years before it first was "revealed" to Ezekiel?

Note that Aristarchus incurred religious condemnation – as did Copernicus and Galileo many years later![26] History books written for popular consumption usually tell us that Copernicus and Galileo were the first persons to discover that the Earth rotates around itself and around the sun,[27] and that Kepler was the first man to discover the variable velocity of the sun [Earth!] during the course of the year.[28] Why should authors and publishers want us to believe those factual and historical misrepresentations? The fathers of the Christian church, as you will recall, demanded that Christian true believers accept as whole truth the theory of Plato and Aristotle that the Earth lies at the center of the universe and that the sun makes an annual circuit around it.[29] If we knew that heliocentricity was known to mankind hundreds of years before Copernicus and Galileo, then we might wonder why mankind "forgot" the sun-centered universe until Copernicus and Galileo "rediscovered" it? That question, then, might lead us to the burning of ancient books and the execution of ancient scholars by early Christian fanatics opposed

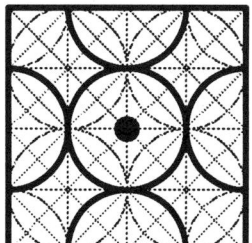

Figure 454

to "pagan" science? Those discoveries, in turn, might lead us to a belief that Christianity has not always been a force for the good, which might lead us sometimes to question, rather than always to believe, our religious leaders? Those discoveries might diminish the absolute authority of our church leaders over us? Are the textbook publishers afraid to print the truth, lest their books be banned, if not burned, by howling or scowling Christian fundamentalists who will not tolerate the publication of any truth contrary to their truths? Better to tell a little white lie about the "discoveries" of Copernicus and Galileo than to open up a can of worms by mentioning Aristarchus? The corporate goal of the publishers, after all, is to sell textbooks!

Aristarchus is credited with having invented an improved sundial which had a concave, hemispherical surface with a shadow-casting pointer or gnomon erected vertically in the middle. The vertical gnomon on this sundial threw shadows so the direction and height of the sun could be read off by means of lines marked on the hemisphere.[30] Remember our pre-Sumerian bowl with lines marked on its hemisphere? Did the Sumerians use bowl-shaped sundials thousands of years before Aristarchus? The Holy Grail can be visualized in top view as such a device! **Figure 454.** The inner circle of the Holy Grail can represent a top view of a hemispherical sundial. The four outer half-circles can represent half-hemispheres. Sundials with half and whole hemispheres were popular among Greek dial-makers.[31] Scientific instruments had been used in astronomy before the time of Aristarchus. Eudoxus had used a *dioptra*, a sextant-like device, and an *arachne* ("spider's web"), a device by which the position of the sun in the sky could be related to the time of day.[32]

A careful study of the ancient astronomers who were at least partially correct about what is going on in the daytime and nighttime skies would lead us nowhere, however, because modern experts know very little about the Egyptian, Babylonian,

and Sumerian astronomy from which the Greek astronomers got their first glimpses of reality.[33] We have the tattered remains of only a few Egyptian papyrus rolls and only a few shards of Babylonian clay tablets which contain materials relating to their mathematics and astronomy.[34] We are lucky to have these. Had they not been buried in tombs or in rubbish heaps at the beginning of the Christian era, they, too, doubtless would have been intentionally destroyed, along with the thousands of scientific writings which fell prey to the Christian and Moslem bookburners.

The largest library in the ancient world was in Alexandria, Egypt. It may have contained upwards of half a million separate works.[35] "At all events, it was the largest collection of written material in the ancient world, and if it had remained unscathed by time it would have been a treasure house of the accumulated wisdom not only of Egypt and the entire Greek civilization, but even of those who lived beyond the boundaries of the Mediterranean basin."[36] What happened to this library? Some of its contents were destroyed or damaged when the Roman Emperor Julius Caesar laid siege to Alexandria.[37] "[B]ut the tragic wholesale destruction of the Library did not come until late in the fourth century AD. Then the despoilers were not the Romans but the Christians.... On the advice of the fanatical Theophilos, bishop of Alexandria, who detested all pagan learning with pathological vehemence, the emperor Theodosios ordered the Library to be burned. Although some books were secretly carried to safety, by 416 AD the destruction was to a great extent complete. And what little remained was finally demolished two centuries later by the Muslims under the Caliph Omar, who used as his reason that either the material still there was already in the Koran - in which case it was superfluous - or it was not and must, therefore, be heretical!"[38]

There were other ancient libraries, of course, but most of their writings did not survive wars and mobs of raging religious fundamentalists.[39] The scholars who wrote the books received similar treatment.[40] "Theon of Alexandria... was probably the last scientific man who could make use of the celebrated library, as it was destroyed in his lifetime by the savage Christian mob.... His renowned daughter Hypatia, who was justly considered a personification of the highest Greek culture and thought, was... barbarously murdered some years later...."[41] "[S]he was murdered by Christian fanatics in A.D. 415."[42] The commentaries of Hypatia are the sole source of our knowledge of the works of some ancient Egyptian and Greek scholars of science and mathematics.[43] Did God *really* call upon religious fundamentalists to burn science books and to slaughter science scholars in His Holy Name?

Heath gives us a brief glance into the analysis of Archimedes, and, perhaps, of *all* Greek geometers. "There is... a certain mystery veiling the way in which he arrived at his results. For it is clear that they were not *discovered* by the steps which lead up to them in the finished treatises.... '[N]early all the ancients so hid from posterity their method of Analysis (though it is clear that they had one)....'"[44] Archimedes drops one clue: "'[C]ertain things,' he says, 'first became clear to me by a mechanical method, although they had to be demonstrated by geometry afterwards because their investigation by the said method did not furnish an actual demonstration.'"[45] Shall we wonder whether some Greek geometers were less theoretical than some professors of classical literature would have us to believe? Shall we speculate that some Greek geometers had a practical side to their personalities akin to that of the Babylonian mathematicians that the Greeks admit they studied?

In summation: We have just enough bits and pieces of the mathematical astronomy texts of the ancient Egyptians, Babylonians, and Sumerians to know they were careful observers and methodical recorders of the apparent movements of the sun, moon, stars, and planets, but not enough to know very much about what they knew or how they went about discovering it. We dead-end at a river which has not been bridged by the experts. We must take another route.

We have an abundance of cosmological, as distinguished from astronomical, literature from these ancient people, much of which made its way into the Old Testament.[46] A cosmic mountain. A cosmic sea. A vault of Heaven dividing the waters of Heaven from the waters of Earth. Familiar concepts.[47] Round and round the Holy Grail we could go, finding little of substance relating to mathematical astronomy. We have spent almost an entire book finding storybook drawings on the Holy Grail. We should leave the remainder for another book.

We shall collect one tidbit of cosmology for brief analysis, then return to the real world: "In early (Sumerian) texts there are twin mountains between which the sun passes."[48] We see the sun setting between twin mountain peaks in **Figure 455**. In **Figure 456**, we see the sun, in the horns of the "bull of heaven," rising between two mountain

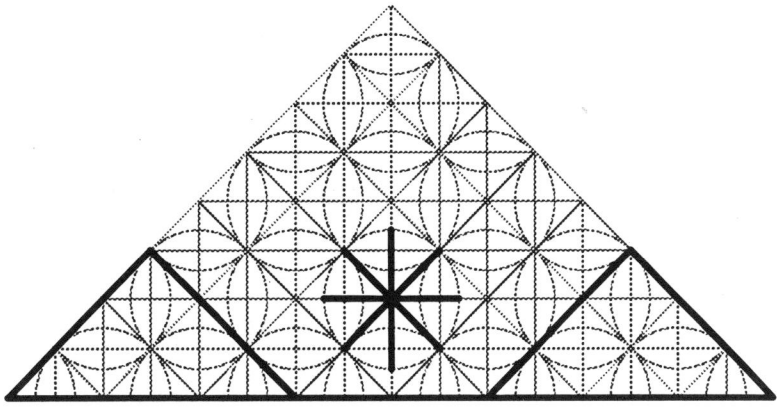

Figure 455

Figure 456

peaks. The Egyptians held sacred the twin mountain peaks, between which they said the sun rises and sets. Dora Jane Hamblin writes as follows in the April, 1986, issue of *Smithsonian*, "Two other astonishing alignments were revealed as the study went on, both involving the Egyptian hieroglyph *akhet*, which means "places where the sun rises and sets." The *akhet* is rendered as a sun between two mountains. Viewed from the Sphinx at the time of the summer solstice when the sun is at its greatest distance north of the celestial equator, it sets directly between the pyramids of Khufu and Khafre, thus writing across the horizon an *akhet* 'on the scale of acres,' as Lehner says."[49] She continues, quoting Lehner: "'We know from the study of archaeoastronomy it is not so difficult to orient a structure to the equinox or to the solstice. But in the case of the Sphinx, the solar temple and the second pyramid, the surveyors had to project this line when the

ground to be occupied by that complex presumably existed at the height of the Sphinx's head. They managed not to deviate from their survey reference lines as they quarried 70 feet down – quite an accomplishment.'"[50] She concludes: "It is Lehner's conviction that he and his team can figure out the builders' ingenious way of aligning the pyramids and the temples...."[51] Would the Holy Grail help to explain how the Egyptians executed their surveys for this *akhet* of acres?

Another route we could travel toward an understanding of ancient astronomy might be through the medieval cosmology of the Christian church.[52] These writings were founded on a "narrow-minded literal interpretation of every syllable in the Scriptures... and anything which could not be reconciled therewith was rejected with horror and scorn."[53] "At first there was no enmity to science exhibited by the followers of the Apostles."[54] "But this kind of

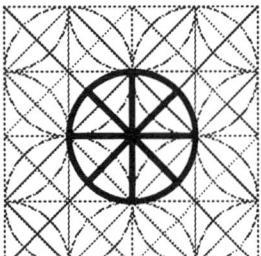

Figure 457

teaching was not to the taste of those who would have nothing to do with anything that came from the pre-Christian world, and to whom even 'the virtues of the heathen were but splendid vices.'"[55] "In no branch of knowledge was the desire to sweep away all the results of Greek learning as conspicuous as with regard to the figure of the earth and the motion of the planets."[56] The Church insisted that "heaven is not a sphere, but a tent or a vault."[57] Scripture said the Earth has four corners; hence, Christian cosmologists concluded that the Earth must be square.[58] Scripture said the sun stood still in the sky,[59] and its shadow moved backward on the sun-dial,[60] so Christian cosmologists believed that the sun, not the Earth, is in motion.[61]

There were more moderate thinkers among the clergy, of course, and St. Augustine was one of them, but "[w]ith regard to the heavens, Augustine was, like his predecessors, bound hand and foot by the unfortunate water above the firmament."[62] Augustine did not "treat Greek science with ignorant contempt; he appears to have had a wish to yield to it whenever Scripture did not pull him in the other way, and in times of bigotry and ignorance this is deserving of credit."[63]

There were rebels within the Church, of course, and, as you might expect, at least one of them was an Irishman. His name was Fergil. He lived in the eighth century, and is better known as Virgilius of Salzburg.[64] He taught that the Earth was a sphere and that people lived on the other side.[65] The Holy Father ordered him excommunicated.[66] Why? Because if people lived on the other side of the Earth, how could they have been descended from Adam or redeemed by the death of Christ?[67]

Islam outgrew its hostility towards science and mathematics earlier than Christianity.[68] "[T]here is no record of any Arabian having been persecuted [during the Middle Ages] for asserting that the earth is a sphere capable of being inhabited all over."[69] Hebrews of the Middle Ages also had no trouble accepting the reality of a round Earth. The *Zohar* refers to a certain Rabbi Hamnuna the Elder,

Illustration 28-1. Carved stones in Loughcrew "Passage Grave," Ireland. Courtesy of Thames & Hudson Ltd., London.

who taught that "'the earth turns like a sphere in a circle round itself, and that some people are above and others below.'"[70]

We would get nowhere by exploring Medieval Christian church cosmology. We must choose another route. But what shall it be? Grail-related symbols? Let us test the waters and see where this might lead us.

In her fabulous catalog of Greek and Roman sundials, Sharon L. Gibbs illustrates a decorated stone from the front step of a house.[71] She says this is not a planar sundial, but is an example of sectioned circles which were used to pave the streets of many Greek and Roman cities.[72] She concludes that these carvings have the characteristics of the wind diagrams described by Vitruvius, but have nothing in common with accurately constructed planar sundials.[73] Their exact form appears on the Holy Grail. **Figure 457.** They have eight spokes like the symbol for the ancient Sumerian goddess of love and of the Planet Venus![74] Eight-spoked "wheel carvings" are found in the Megalithic "passage-grave" at Loughcrew in Ireland! **Illustration 28-1.**[75] Coincidences?

In **Illustration 28-2,**[76] we see side and top views of the stacked stone inner structure of the megalithic construct at Newgrange, Ireland, which dates from before 3000 B.C., and which is cruciform in design![77] When the sun reaches the midwinter solstice, "At dawn on the shortest day of the year, for about a quarter of an hour, the sun's rays shine through a slit beneath the roof-box to illuminate the whole passage and the rear wall of the chamber."[78] "[A]t sunrise on the shortest day of the year, direct sunlight can enter Newgrange, not through the

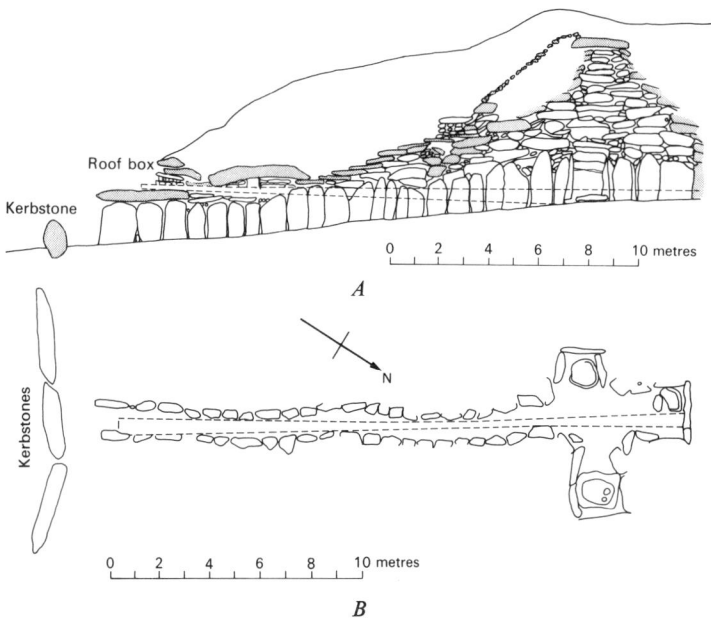

Roof box

Kerbstone

0 2 4 6 8 10 metres

A

N

Kerbstones

0 2 4 6 8 10 metres

B

Illustration 28-2. Plan and elevation of the underground stone structure of the megalithic construct of Newgrange, Ireland. Courtesy of Oxford University Press, Oxford, England, and reprinted by permission from *Nature*, Vol. 249 (1974), J. Patrick, "Midwinter sunrise at Newgrange," copyright © Macmillan Magazines Limited.

doorway, but through the specially contrived narrow slit which lies under the roof-box at the outer end of the passage roof."[79] Basins (for offerings to the sun?) are in each of the three niches at the top of the cross.[80] The front exterior wall of Newgrange, which faces the rising sun at the midwinter solstice, was faced "with shining white quartz from the river."[81] Quartz? Ezekiel's Vision? Grail stories? The rainbow-hued interference pattern in the form of a Celtic Cross? Does it matter that this is white quartz instead of clear quartz? Suppose we were to learn that white quartz was considered to be the sun's dried semen, fallen to Earth?

"At Newgrange the focus was certainly on the rebirth of the sun at the winter solstice."[82] "New Grange can no longer be considered as a simple chambered tomb; it was also an astronomical clock for establishing the time of midwinter."[83]

McMann tells us that "During the Neolithic, or Late Stone Age (from 5000 to 2000 B.C. in Europe), the realistic and often light-hearted representations of hunters and animals disappear. The art becomes abstract. Spirals and geometric designs appear on stones and rock surfaces, sometimes executed with great care and finesse, at other times hastily scratched - like a doodle."[84] Could it be that these carvings are more than mere "doodles"; that they are early geometrical representations of what their inscribers thought was going on in the sky? Radio-

carbon dating has revealed that these Megalithic tombs of Ireland are older than the pyramids of Egypt, and that similar Megalithic tombs in mainland Europe are another thousand years older![85] Could our Stone Age ancestors possibly have observed *and recorded* the periodicities of the sun, moon, stars, and planets? Stonehenge, on the Salisbury Plain of England, immediately comes to mind, but it is of later date, construction having commenced there at about 2800 B.C. to 2300 B.C.[68] Could Stonehenge be the culmination of the efforts of ancient astronomers? Shall we close our eyes to these possibilities? Or shall we take a peek at the written record of discoveries?

What does McMann believe might be the explanation of these "doodles" or symbols? The concepts are familiar to us. Spirals on rocks might be symbols of a labyrinth, representing the growth outward from, and the return to, the womb of the Neolithic "earth mother goddess."[87] The cycle of the seasons, including the "regeneration of the sun" which commences after the midwinter solstice, is another, related possibility.[88] The path from, and back to, the sacred center point, which we encountered in the modern Hindu faith, is another.[89] Other speculations about these symbols or "doodles" include ancient knowledge of magnetic forces.[90] The ancients apparently *did* observe the interactions of lodestones and iron,[91] so speculations about magnetism may not be as absurd as they appear, and may prove to be not at all helpful to those persons who are bent on proving that Earth was invaded by ancient space travelers.[92]

Having twice been inside Newgrange, and being a lawyer who rows a boat and paddles a canoe for recreation, I am of the opinion that some of the "doodles" look like fingerprints, and others look like whirlpools created in water by oars or paddles. Moreover, I wonder whether the ancients were celebrating the rebirth of the sun at the solstice, or were celebrating the fertilization of the earth mother by the sky father.

What surely is proven, in any event, is that the limits of speculation are a product of the knowledge of the speculator multiplied by his unrestrained imagination! Let us proceed to more tangible speculations which are confined by data we have gathered during our quest.

"Cup and ring" carvings are found on rocks throughout the British Isles. The "cups" are surrounded by "rings," inside of which are carved eight, eleven or sixteen small circles.[93] Do the "cups" represent the sun? Do the "rings" represent the "dome of Heaven"? Do the small circles outside the "cups" but inside the "rings" represent either constellations within the band of the Zodiac or the seasonal positions of the Earth as it moves along the Ecliptic? Each "cup" could be filled with water, giving the viewer a safe way to observe the sun indirectly, and thereby putting the sun's reflection on the "cup" of water in the middle of the "cup and ring" carving – exactly where it belongs! What is the significance of the number eleven? "Servius, about A.D. 400, said that for a long time… [the Zodiac] consisted of but eleven constellations, Scorpio and its claws being a double sign…."[94] Talbott says that a ring of eleven dots around a central cup represented to the Babylonians "the circle of the gods…."[95] Grains of sand? Nothing more! But we already have a cupful!

What might have been the meaning of the eight-spoked "Inanna symbol" to the ancients? The British archaeologist Aubrey Burl suggests that a circle cut into eight segments of forty-five degrees each *might* have symbolized an eight-fold division of the solar year. He says: "Alexander Thom suggested that prehistoric people divided the year into sixteen equal periods. This brilliant deduction may be a slight over-refinement of a simpler calendar. If, instead, one took every other one of Thom's 'months,' the eight declinations correspond very closely to those of iron age feast days three thousand years later. Later still, Christianity adopted and adapted these when the Church was struggling to overcome heathen customs…. It is interesting to see how many alignments in the early stone circles correspond to the times of the Celtic festivals of Beltane, Lughnasa, Samain and Imbolc."[96] The eight-fold division of the year, Celtic-style, runs like this, starting in May: "Beltane, Midsummer Solstice, Lughnasa, Autumn Equinox, Samain, Midwinter Solstice, Imbolc, Vernal Equinox."[97]

North of Stonehenge lie the great earthen ditches and standing stone circles of Avebury, which are connected by a double row of standing stones, known as the "West Kennet Avenue," to Overton Hill, where several concentric circles of post holes and stones, called "The Sanctuary," have been excavated. Windmill Hill, Silbury Hill, and the White Horse of Uffington lie in the same general vicinity, which was a Stone Age ceremonial center of no mean proportions.[98] Phase I of "The Sanctuary" was a circular structure erected on nine posts, eight of which stood forty-five degrees apart in a circle. The ninth post stood at the center of the circle.[99] Was an "Inanna symbol" incorporated into the Sanctuary, much as Christian symbols were incorporated into Chartres Cathedral thousands of years later? Phase II saw the structure enlarged in diameter, and constructed on an inner circle of eight posts and an outer circle of twelve posts.[100] Have the builders changed from the Indian Zodiac of eight symbols to the latter-day Babylonian and Egyptian Zodiac of twelve symbols? Later construction increased the diameter of the structure, utilizing a circle of sixteen posts.[101] The sixteen-fold division of the year according to Thom? The time-frame seems to have been 2500 B.C. to 2000 B.C.[102] We must be careful not to read too much into the numbers of posts utilized to support a circular building, which apparently was used in ceremonies somehow related to the cycle of the sun and the seasons.

The great stone circle at Avebury was a favorite site for stonesmashing among the good Christian folk of the vicinity. Generations of English, commencing as early as the thirteenth century, put their Christian faith into practice by undermining and overturning the "pagan" standing stones of Avebury, heating them with fires, then pouring cold water over them to break them into pieces small enough to be smashed further by sledge-hammers for eventual burial.[103] Stonesmashing, as well as book-burning, has been a characteristic of Christian fundamentalism. The fault of the sheep? Or of the shepherds?

Notes
CHAPTER TWENTY-EIGHT
The Holy Grail in Ancient Astronomy — Paths to Success or Failure

1. Heath, *Aristarchus* 1.

2. Dreyer 6-17; Heath, *Aristarchus* 7-11, 24-45, 5 9-61, 66, 86-88.

3. Dreyer 12-13; Heath, *Aristarchus* 12-13; 16-18.

4. Dreyer 87-88, 149-170, 191-206; Heath, *Aristarchus* 190-216.

5. Dreyer 91, 200-201; Heath, *Aristarchus* 208; Neugebauer 153.

6. Dreyer 88, 100, 103; Heath, *Aristarchus* 13, 192.

7. Dreyer 26-27, 30; Heath, *Aristarchus* 126-127.

8. Dreyer 21; Heath, *Aristarchus* 77-78, 91.

9. Dreyer 25; Heath, *Aristarchus* 92.

10. Dreyer 48, 161, 164, 202-203; Heath, *Aristarchus* 101, 172.

11. Dreyer 17, 20, 37-38, 53; Heath, *Aristarchus* 21, 48, 51.

12. Dreyer 37, 39.

13. Heath, *Aristarchus* 94-95, 97-101.

14. Dreyer 31.

15. Dreyer 50-51, 123; Heath, *Aristarchus* 49; Fanning 17.

16. Dreyer 125-126. See also Heath, *Aristarchus* 254, 282-283.

17. Dreyer 126. See also Heath, *Aristarchus* 255.

18. Dreyer 126.

19. Neugebauer 6.

20. Heath *Aristarchus* 255.

21. Dreyer 137. See also Heath, *Aristarchus* 302; 2 Heath *GM* 2, 3.

22. Dreyer 138. See also Heath, *Aristarchus* 304; 2 Heath *GM* 2. In a Germanic myth, the moon is referred to as "Wheel" and the sun as "Fair Wheel." Hollander 113. However, the Earth's spinning like a wheel as it wheels around the Ecliptic seems to your author to be the more probable meaning of Ezekiel's wheel within a wheel.

23. Heath, *Aristarchus* 301.

24. See note 9 of Chapter 2 of this book.

25. Oxford Bible 886.

26. Fanning 20-24.

27. Dreyer 305, 308, 328, 416-417.

28. Dreyer 392-393.

29. Dreyer 55-56, 59, 122-123, 125, 147, 416-417; Heath, *Aristarchus* 141-143; Washburn 7; Fanning 17, 22.

30. Heath, *Aristarchus* 300, 312; 2 Heath *GM* 1.

31. Gibbs 66-73, 325, 387.

32. Heath, *Aristarchus* 192-193.

33. Neugebauer 29-30, 99, 105-106.

34. Neugebauer 29-30, 99, 105-106.

35. Ronan 7.

36. Ronan 7-8.

37. Ronan 8.

38. Ronan 8; Hapgood 190.

39. Ronan 8; Hapgood 190-191.

40. Dreyer 206.

41. Dreyer 206.

42. 2 Heath *GM* 453.

43. 2 Heath *GM* 453, 519, 528-529.

44. 2 Heath *GM* 21.

45. 2 Heath *GM* 21. Mathematicians interested in a succinct statement about the rediscovery of "The Method" of Archimedes, and its proof, should read van de Waerden 212-214.

46. Dreyer 2-3; Heath, *Aristarchus* 19-20.

47. Dreyer 1-8.

48. Dreyer 2.

49. Hamblin 92-93.

50. Hamblin 93.

51. Hamblin 93.

52. Dreyer 207-239.

53. Dreyer 207.

54. Dreyer 208.

55. Dreyer 209.

56. Dreyer 208.

57. Dreyer 211.

58. Isaiah 11.12; Dreyer 226.

59. Joshua 10.12-13.

60. Isaiah 38.8; Cousins 13.

61. Dreyer 235.

62. Dreyer 213.

63. Dreyer 213-214.

64. Dreyer 224.

65. Dreyer 224-225.

66. Dreyer 224.

67. Dreyer 225.

68. Dreyer 249.

69. Dreyer 249.

70. Dreyer 272.

71. Gibbs 128, Plate 1.

72. Gibbs 84.

73. Gibbs 84.

74. Wolkstein 67.

75. McMann, Fig. 43. These "passage-graves" may not be graves at all but sun shrines or chronometers. Brennan 7-126.

76. J.E. Wood 80, Fig. 5.1. See also McMann 24, Fig. 14.

77. Service & Bradbery 144, 221.

78. McMann 25.

79. McMann 25. See also Service & Bradbery 41.

80. McMann 24, Fig. 14. See also McMann 26. "The three recesses, or niches, at the west, north and east of the chamber, remind one of the cruciform plan of Christian churches." McMann 26. Is this just another coincidence?

81. McMann 23. See also Service & Bradbery 221.

82. Service & Bradbery 221.

83. J.E. Wood 81.

84. McMann 11.

85. McMann 12; Walsh 55; Service & Bradbery 15.

86. McMann 11; Newham 10; Atkinson 4.

87. McMann 151.

88. McMann 150.

89. McMann 149.

90. McMann 149.

91. 28 Great Books 3.

92. McMann 144.

93. McMann, Fig. 93. The Pythagoreans put the cosmic "central fire," or "hearth of the universe," or "watch-tower of Zeus," at the cosmic center, "round which the earth and all the other heavenly bodies moved in circular orbits." Dreyer 41. Plato put "Hestia," the earth, at the cosmic center, "the hearth of the universe." Dreyer 55. Are both systems references to what they saw on the Holy Grail? We saw the cosmic "hearth" replicated as an ancient Hebrew altar. We encountered the crystal "watch-tower" during our analysis of the Grail tales.

94. Allen 1.

95. Talbott 80, 231, 235.

96. Burl 34-35.

97. Burl 34. See also Service & Bradbery 42.

98. Vatcher 10-30.

99. Vatcher 31-32.

100. Vatcher 31-32.

101. Vatcher 31-32.

102. Vatcher 30-33.

103. Vatcher 42-43.

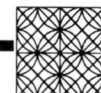

Chapter Twenty-Nine

The Holy Grail as Clock, Calendar, and Navigational Instrument

Previous chapters surely have left you with the impression that the Holy Grail somehow is related to ancient concepts of *space* and *time*. Was being at the proper *place* at the proper *time* important to our ancestors? Was the Holy Grail used by the ancients to orient themselves in *space* and *time* in the real world they observed with their eyes, and in the greater Cosmos of which they supposed they were a part?

We started our studies with Lion, Ox, Man, and Eagle, from Ezekiel's Vision. We found them on the Holy Grail. We found them in the roles of Matthew, Mark, Luke, and John. We mentioned their roles as the Guardians of Heaven, the Cosmic Archers, or the Four Royal Stars of Persia.

By observing the comings and goings of constellations of stars which lie along the band of the Zodiac — the Ecliptic of mathematical astronomy — we can determine the month of the year. Put simply: The Zodiac is a calendar in the sky. We are not overly concerned with precession of the equinoxes, caused by the wobbling of the Earth's axis, which causes the polestar to change, and the band of the Zodiac to slip loose from our calendar, because precession of the equinoxes occurs slowly over thousands of years, and its effect is not significant within our lifetimes.

Richard Hinckley Allen tells us this about the star *Antares*: "It was one of the four Royal Stars of Persia, 3000 B.C...."[1] Recall that Newgrange, in Ireland, a solar timeclock which establishes the advent of the shortest day of the year, has been dated to this period. Allen says that in Egyptian astronomy, *Antares* "represented the goddess Selkit, Selk-t, or Serk-t, heralding the sunrise through her temples at the autumnal equinox about 3700-3500 B.C., and was the symbol of Isis in the pyramid ceremonials."[2] *Antares* currently lies within the constellation Scorpio, the scorpion,[3] but Allen quotes authority for the proposition that "in the zodiac which the patriarch Abraham knew it was an Eagle...."[4]

Allen says of the star *Regulus*, which lies in the constellation of Leo, the Lion, that its name is the diminutive of Rex, "from the belief that it ruled the affairs of the heavens, — a belief current, till three centuries ago, from at least 3000 years before our era."[5] *Regulus* "was the leader of the Four Royal Stars of the ancient Persian monarchy, the Four Guardians of Heaven. Dupuis, referring to this Persian character, said the four stars marked the cardinal points, assigning *Hastorang*, as he termed it, to the North; *Venant* to the South; *Tascheter* to the East; and *Satevis* to the West; but did not identify these titles with the individual stars. Flammarion does so, however, with *Fomalhaut*, *Regulus*, and *Aldebaran* for the first three respectively, so that we may consider *Satevis* as *Antares*. This same scheme appeared in India, although the authorities are not agreed as to these assignments and identifications; but, as the right ascensions are about six hours apart, they everywhere probably were used to mark the early equinoctial and solstitial colures, four great circles in the sky, or generally the four quarters of the heavens. At the time that these probably were first thought of, *Regulus* lay very near to the summer solstice, and so indicated the solstitial colure."[6]

The star *Aldebaran* or *Al Dabaran*, Allen says, "was one of the four Royal Stars, or Guardians of the Sky, of Persia, 5000 years ago, when it marked the vernal equinox."[7] It lies in the constellation Taurus, the bull, which "was one of the earliest and most noted constellations, perhaps the first established, because it marked the vernal equinox from about 4000 to 1700 B.C., in the golden age of archaic astronomy; in all ancient zodiacs preserved to us it began the year."[8] *Aldebaran* was related to the Egyptian bull-god Osiris, the Apis Bull, the husband of Isis, "whose worship as god of the Nile may have preceded even the building of the pyramids,"[9] and also is related to "Moses' allusion to... Joseph in the 33rd chapter of *Deuteronomy*, — that 'his horns are the horns of the wild ox.'"[10] The constellation Taurus also was directly related to the Cult of Mithras and to Babylonian worship of Marduk.[11] We have seen the bull-god on the Holy Grail. Three stars down. One to go!

The last of the four Guardians is the star *Fomalhaut*, from the Arabic for "the fish's mouth," because it now lies in the constellation of the Southern Fish.[12] Ptolemy and the *Alfonsine Tables* of 1521 clearly located it in Aquarius, the waterbearer, the Man of our four Guardians.[13] "Flammarion says it was *Hastorang* in Persia 3000 B.C., when near the winter solstice, and a Royal Star, one of the four Guardians of Heaven, sentinels watching over other stars; while about 500 B.C. it was the object of sunrise worship in the temple of Demeter at Eleusis...."[14]

Lion, Ox, Man, and Eagle. The four Guardians. The four Cosmic Archers. Each near the Ecliptic or the Zodiac.[15] They serve as markers of the course traversed by the "wandering stars," which the Greeks called the "planets."[16] Lion, Ox, Man, and Eagle appeared in Ezekiel's Vision. Why did the Christian church think it necessary to carry these symbols forward as Matthew, Mark, Luke, and John? Because the concepts were so ancient and venerable that they could not be obliterated from the minds of the common folk; hence, had to be tolerated and Christianized? Or were they essential features of the ancient astrophysics which gave rise to the Christ story?

What do we see in **Figure 458**? Is this a representation of the polestar surrounded by the four guardian stars, with each guardian being surrounded by a equinoctial or solstitial colure, a great circle in the sky?

The ancient Sumerians, Babylonians, Egyptians, Greeks, and Hebrews believed stars to be gods.[17] Stories about their "gods" thus are apt to be stories about the stars.[18] The latter-day Hebrews made a significant advance in theology when they abandoned the old opinion that stars were gods and adopted the view that "the circle of the starry signs" (the Zodiac) and the "great lights in heaven" (the sun and moon) are the handiwork of YHWH, the Christian Jehovah.[19] You should decide for yourself which direction the Christian church moved in theology when it pictured Christ sitting on a throne surrounded by a circle, wearing a Grail cross on his chest, with a Grail interference pattern as his halo, and surrounded by four circles covered with eyes, on which circles appear, respectively, the images Lion, Ox, Man, and Eagle.[20] You will recall that Lloyd Graham suggested that "there is not an incident in the whole Christ story that is not written in the stars...."[21]

Could it be that stories about ancient gods, that is, about the stars, were composed to aid the memory of the storyteller about astral periodicities, or apparent motions of the sun, moon, and planets? Is

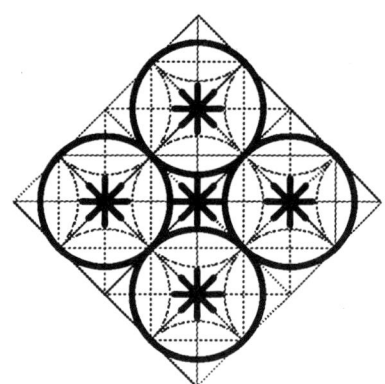

Figure 458

this how the ancients remembered the long cycles of events in the sky before written symbols first were utilized for that purpose? If so, can we regard these stories as scientific databases? Modern memory experts still memorize long strings of hard-to-remember numbers by encoding the numbers in easily-remembered stories. This ancient skill can be learned by almost anyone from paperback memory-improvement books available in most book stores. Recall that Eusebius, one of the founding fathers of the Christian church, wrote that the Gospels are allegorical,[22] and that Saint Augustine declared that "[i]gnorance of number prevents us from understanding things that are set down in the scripture in a figurative and mystical way."[23] Graham quotes from Thomas Jefferson, as follows: "'The day will come,' said he, 'when the mystical generation of Jesus by the supreme being as his father in the womb of a virgin will be classed with the fable of the generation of Minerva in the brain of Jupiter.'"[24]

Precisely how might the Holy Grail have been used by ancient astronomers to represent solar, lunar, or astral periodicities? And how might those representations have been used in navigation or travel?

In Medieval times, there were two distinct categories of world maps. There were academic maps,[25] which expressed the view of the world which the Church insisted that people believe. Religious beliefs are nice, of course, but if you are a deep-water seaman, you have the very practical problem of getting by ship from where you are to where you are going. Academic maps were not very good for that purpose.[26] So there was another type of maps, now called "portolan maps," which were prepared by navigators for navigators.[27] No one wanted to be tried by Church Inquisition for heresy but, on the other hand, the cargo needed to get where it was going. Sailors long had known that the Earth is

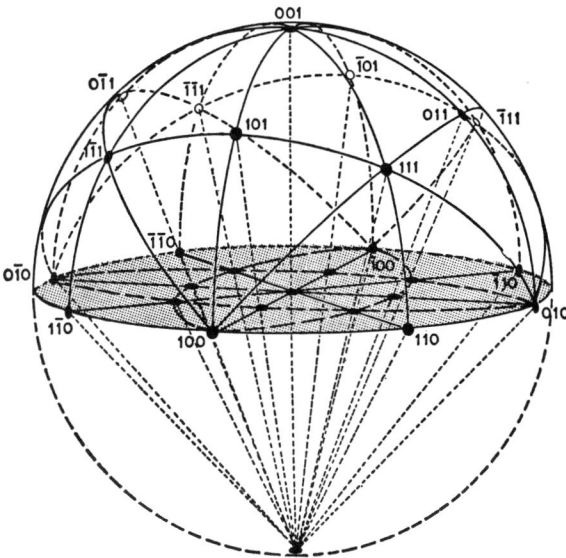

Illustration 29-1. Stereographic projection of a crystal. Courtesy of Dover Publications, Inc., New York.

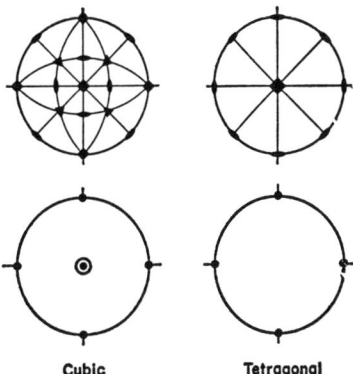

Cubic   **Tetragonal**

Illustration 29-2. Stereographic projections of cubic and tetragonal system crystals. Courtesy of Dover Publications, Inc., New York.

round.[28] They learned about the shape of the Earth in a most simple and direct way: As you sail south, along the African coast, you begin to see stars you cannot see further north, and the northern circumpolar stars are seen in the south dipping below the horizon.[29] Ergo: the Earth is round. No big deal. Every deep-water sailor knew this. It had been known for untold generations.

If you treat the Earth as a sphere, and Heaven above as a dome, then how do you measure distances on the sphere of the Earth or dome of Heaven? Modern high-school students would use spherical trigonometry, but the authorities tell us that the ancients did not know spherical trigonometry.[30] A very interesting book entitled *Maps of the Ancient Sea Kings*, by Charles H. Hapgood, which analyzes the accuracy of the portolan maps, and speculates as to who might have drawn them,[31] repeatedly states that the map-makers *must* have used plane trigonometry,[32] or spherical trigonometry,[33] or that they must have treated the round surface of the Earth as a series of flat plates.[34]

Practically every educated person now living is aware that a flat map can be made illustrating our round Earth. Not many people realize, however, how many different types of "projections" can be used for that purpose, and the accuracies and distortions inherent in each. This book is no place for such analysis. Suffice it to say that the experts tell us that the ancient Greeks were quite aware of "stereographic projections,"[35] a system used not

only by modern map-makers[36] but by modern students of crystallography![37] The advantage of a stereographic projection is that "great circles," that is, the courses a ship would sail on the ocean, become straight lines on the flat map.[38] See **Illustration 29-1**,[39] a stereographic projection of a crystal. See also **Illustration 29-2**,[40] stereographic projections of crystals. Crystals? Fact and fantasy interwoven with each other in Grail stories?

Portolan maps are covered by what we call "Inanna symbols," or what Gibbs called "wind diagrams."[41] Hapgood refers to these symbols as "wind systems."[42] The ancient map-maker drew his "compass rose," that is, our "Inanna symbol," at various points, treating the sphere as if it were a flat surface.[43] Several portolan maps thereafter could be put together, forming a "world map" which favorably compares with our modern maps,[44] and which has about as much resemblance to a medieval Church-theory academic map as a modern Indianapolis racecar has to a T-Model Ford! Another very disturbing fact about these portolan maps is that our Church-approved world history books tell us that Columbus was the first explorer to cross the ocean to the "New World." Pre-Columbian portolan maps illustrate, quite accurately, the coasts of Central and South America![45]

Treating Heaven as if it were a dome, a stereographic projection of the "dome of Heaven" can be done the same way. Ergo, we have an ancient system of map-making for navigation on the seas of Heaven and Earth!

This discussion of portolan maps and stereographic projections not only helps us to appreciate how ancient astronomers solved map-making

Illustration 29-3. The Home of the Buffalo People, a Navajo sandpainting. Courtesy of Dover Publications, Inc., New York.

problems we attack using spherical trigonometry, but leads us to our next discussion of ancient astronomy relating to the planet Venus. The Sumerian goddess Inanna was said to be the daughter of the Moon, and was represented in the sky by the planet we call Venus.[46] The planet Venus has connections with a far distant place and time, and what we find there may help us to understand Stonehenge, which we visit in the next chapter.

Few scholars of the arts or sciences would dare to do what you and I are about to do next. They would be afraid of being laughed out of their profession. The ideas are far too radical. Peer pressure often causes scholars to oppose radical breakthroughs or innovations in their respective fields of expertise, leaving to amateurs or outsiders the task of initiating major departures from the consensus of the experts.[47]

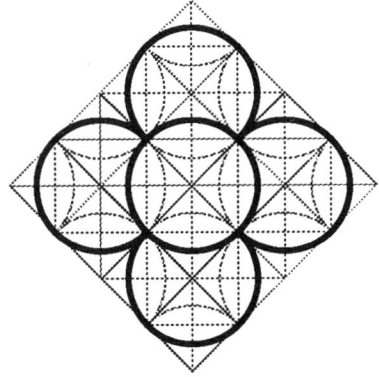

Figure 459

You and I are not experts in these fields. We are amateurs, wandering like babes in the woods, staring wide-eyed at what we encounter. We have been foundering in foolish fables since this book began, so this latest incursion into fields into which we have not been invited should pose for us no problems with which we cannot cope.

Flash forward in time from Sumeria and Britain of 3000 B.C. to the Navajo country of the western United States in the year 1977. **Illustration 29-3**[48] shows a black-and-white line drawing of a Navajo sand painting, complete with labels for many of its principal symbols. This drawing would be rendered by the Navajo sandpainter in a variety of brightly-colored sands. It is called "The Home of the Buffalo People."[49] In the center is "Big Water," a Navajo cosmic concept, situated exactly in the position on the Holy Grail where we found the cosmic "sea" in the Story of Solomon's Temple. Big Water is surrounded by four mountains,[50] over which are superimposed four dragonflies. The dragonflies are symbols of pure water.[51] We see "Big Water" surrounded by the four sacred mountains in **Figure 459**. We see a "dragonfly" in **Figure 460**. The entire Navajo sandpainting is sectioned into four parts by four sprigs of herbs. Sixteen tipis, four in each quadrant, are illustrated. Each buffalo is separated from his nearest neighbor by a clockwise-spinning swastika (They knew the correct direction!) and is connected with the *Cosmic Center* of the drawing, that is, Big Water, by a trail to Pure Water! Is each trail to Pure Water the Navajo equivalent of the Christian "Way" to the "Saviour"? Out of each Christian true believer's "belly shall flow rivers of living water"?[52] As in **Figure 461**? The trails to pure water lead to Big Water along S-shaped curves, which impart to the entire drawing the same clockwise-spinning motion as illustrated by the swastikas. Shall we continue?

Figure 460

"The Navajo likes nothing better than a trip, and he himself always has hopes of finding the lost mountain...."[53] The Navajo tell tales of "Whirling Mountain."[54] The Navajo "ritualistically lights the prayersticks with a crystal held to the sun...."[55] Many of the stories told by the Navajo, such as the one about Holy Boy, who arose into the sky,[56] can be rationalized as borrowings from Christianity, but we safely can assume that no Christian missionary, priest, or minister ever taught the Navajo the Grail-based cosmology we discovered in the drawing of "The Home of the Buffalo People"!

How could the Navajo have come into the possession of a Grail-based cosmology? Perhaps they developed it independently of everyone else in the world. Perhaps they know about it like everyone else in the world once did because it dates

Figure 461

back to the period during which the thinking people of all races travelled widely, visited with each other, and shared beliefs about the world in which they lived.

Books about Phoenicians or Carthaginians who sailed to the New World before Columbus belong far less to the "lunatic fringe" of human studies than most scholars would have us to believe. Most still are written by amateurs and are scorned by the "experts" for reasons we already have discussed. Many do not deserve the ridicule so often heaped upon them. Take, for instance, *Gods of the Cataclysm*, by Hugh Fox, who offers us a few bits of circumstantial evidence which tend to indicate that the Indians of Mexico may have gotten the idea of sacrificing human beings to the sun from sailors seeking tin who came to the New World from Mediterranean countries.[57] Absurd? If so, who furnished the data to the navigators who drew the pre-Columbian portolan maps of the coasts of Cuba and Central America? Why do pre-Columbian Central and South American pottery mugs portray the heads and faces of every racial and ethnic group in the world — European, Asiatic, African, etc.?[58] Why do Grail-related symbols appear on pre-Columbian pottery?[59] The cross is a universal symbol, used everywhere by ancient people who never heard the Christ story,[60] so a pre-Columbian pottery figure of a man on a cross might be regarded as no proof of pre-Christian world-wide circulation of the cosmic story of the man on the cross?[61] Why were the Indians of Central and South America not surprised by the coming of bearded Europeans?[62] Because their legends told of the earlier comings of bearded white men, who would return again some day![63]

Another cosmologist whose book, *The Saturn Myth*, is deserving of reading is David N. Talbott. His *conclusions* are not attractive to your author because they adopt the theories of Velikovsky, an author with whom many people disagree.[64] Regardless of the validity of Talbott's *conclusions*, his *research* into ancient cosmology and cosmogony is exquisite. It almost seems, at times, that he is aware of the Holy Grail, although he must not be. If he were, he surely would not struggle so hard to present in words that which can be seen immediately if the reader casts a quick glance at bolded lines on the Holy Grail.

Reading Talbott is an *excellent* way to summarize points of international cosmology and cosmogony we have learned from observing the Holy Grail in use by ancient storysmiths. For instance:

"Santa Claus, descending yearly from his polar home to distribute gifts around the world, is a muffled echo of the Universal Monarch, the primordial Osiris, Yama, or Kronos spreading miraculous good fortune.... The home of the great father is the cosmic center — the 'heart,' 'midst,' or 'navel' of heaven. As the earth rotates on its axis the northern stars wheel around a fixed point.... All of the ancient world looked upon the polar center as the 'middle place,' 'resting place,' or 'steadfast region' occupied by the Universal Monarch."[65] Most adherents of Judaism presumably will deny that the man on the throne at the Cosmic Center of the Holy Grail is YHWH. Similarly, most Christians will deny that the man at the Cosmic Center of the Holy Grail is Jesus Christ on the Cross of Calvary. So be it.

Talbott again: "That the Egyptians conceived the unified 'land' or celestial 'bread' as the *body* of the creator is crucial to the symbolism; in eating the cake, or in drinking the sanctified beer, the initiates symbolically enjoyed the abundance of the primeval age, or, what is the same thing, they consumed the body of the creator."[66] The concept of Christian Mass clearly predates Christianity!

Talbott summarizes quickly cosmology which you and I have learned slowly: The cosmic sea, river, rock, mountain, man, woman, throne, sun, moon, womb, egg, seed, garden, city, holy land, wheel, chariot, boat, way, crossroads, crown, shield, spear, staff, sword, cup, vase, table, eye, serpent, bull, eagle, etc., are *not* to be found here on Earth. Rather, they are emanations from the Creator — who is located at the rotational center of the sky.[67] For instance: "Ancient cosmology locates the primordial 'place,' not 'down here,' but at the celestial pole, the center and summit."[68] We have found *all* of the foregoing, and more, on the Holy Grail. Hence, may we conclude that the Holy Grail is the wellspring from which the constellations and asterisms, and the stories told of them, were drawn? Is this why our Grail author Wolfram von Eschenbach wrote: "The heathen Flegetanis could tell us how all the stars set and rise again and how long each one revolves before it reaches its starting point once more. To the circling course of the stars man's affairs and destiny are linked. Flegetanis the heathen saw with his own eyes in the constellations things he was shy to talk about, hidden mysteries. He said there was a thing called the Grail whose name he had read clearly in the constellations. 'A host of angels left it on the earth and then flew away up over the stars.'"?[69]

Figure 462

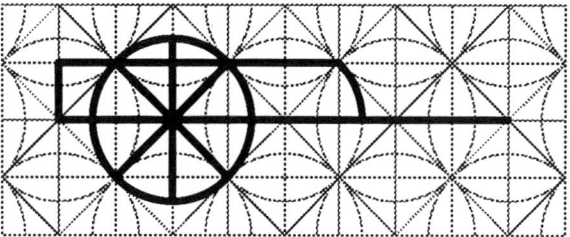

Figure 463

In regard to stars revolving in a circling course, measuring the passage of time, the Egyptians and Babylonians used the "star decans," and the "lunar mansions," as well as the Wheel of Zodiac, to measure time, thereby converting the nighttime sky into both a calendar and a clock![70] Science encoded in allegory? "In my Father's house are many mansions: if it *were* not so, I would have told you."[71] Does the Christ story refer to the *lunar* mansions? If so, then it *is* allegorically true that His house (Heaven) has many mansions!

Talbott labors long regarding the cosmology of the horn-shaped boat and the wheeled vehicle which carry the cosmic sun, not across the real-world sky but around in a circle in the cosmic sea.[72] **Figure 462** shows the sun's boat sailing around the cosmic "sea" in the middle of the Holy Grail. The top of the boat's mast is connected with the Cosmic Center. **Figure 463** shows the sun's two-wheeled chariot in similar position. It, too, rotates around the Cosmic Center. We can understand Talbott's frustration when he writes: "But if the analysis set forth here is correct, *the twin peaks of the Mount, being synonymous with the ship of heaven, must have revolved daily around the sun-god's enclosure — in flagrant contradiction of natural geography!*"[73] True! The cosmology of the ancients described *the central sun symbol on the Holy Grail*! Along the same vein, Talbott writes concerning the twin-peaked cosmic mountain: "The twin peaks are anything but a fixture of the local landscape. Though the most common position of the mountain image is upright, some illustrations depict it in an *inverted* position... again contradicting geography. Moreover, the distinction between the upright and inverted positions of the revolving twin peaks is crucial to the symbolism of the archaic 'day' and 'night,' as I shall show."[74] Well done! It is remarkable what Talbott learned, considering that he *apparently* is unaware of the Holy Grail as the source of all this cosmology!

The horned ship and the horned altar are identical in ancient cosmology. "'The horned altar' and 'the horns of the altar' were, of course, common phrases among the ancient Hebrews."[75] Correct, again! We saw a real Hebrew altar, complete with "horns," and such an altar on the Holy Grail.

Talbott writes: "Mesopotamian reliefs show the sun-god standing upon a cleft peak virtually identical to the Egyptian 'mountain' symbol...."[76] Recall the article in *Smithsonian* about the giant *akhet* symbol formed by the sun setting between the pyramids of Khufu and Khafre as viewed from the Sphinx? How important was the Holy Grail to the Egyptians? Important enough to justify in their minds the expenditure of hundreds of thousands of man hours of labor to build the pyramids of Khufu and Khafre in the form of an enormous *akhet* symbol! Talbott says there is a "curious feature" of the Babylonian twin-peaked mountain: One mountain is the mountain of night or of sunset, and the mountain of the morning or sunrise, and also the mountain of the Center.[77] Correct, again! That would be a "tough act" for a real-world mountain, but our twin-peaked Grail Mountain, **Figure 464**, has no difficulty playing all three roles! Talbott continues:

Figure 464

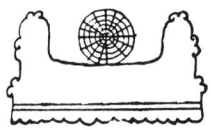

Illustration 29-4. The twin peaks of Assyro-Babylonian and Mexican Native American cosmology. Courtesy of Doubleday & Company, Inc., New York.

"And what is most interesting about the Egyptian symbol of the cleft peak is that it finds strikingly similar parallels in other lands. The Mesopotamian sun-god rests upon a twin-peaked world mountain of identical form... and the same dual mount occurs also in Mexico — here too revealing the sun-god between the two peaks."[78] We see Talbott's sketches of the Babylonian and Mexican twin-peaked mountain framing the sun, the equivalent of the Egyptian *akhet*, in **Illustration 29-4.**[79]

We leave any further consideration of Talbott's writings to you, after this quote from the Egyptian Pyramid texts:

"I know the secret of Hieraconopolis.

"It is the *two hands of horns* and what is in them."[80]

What is in the upraised hands of Egyptian gods and goddesses is the *cosmic* sun.[81] Is this cosmic sun the polestar of the real world, at rest as the circumpolar stars apparently revolve around it? Is it, instead, the real sun of the real world, "at rest" while the Earth and the other planets revolve around it? Or is it *both*, depending upon the use to which the Holy Grail is being put by the ancient astronomer at any given moment?

Did Native Americans in Mexico have the same cosmic mountain in their religion as the Egyptians and the Babylonians? By coincidence? By separate development? By bearded white men who brought Grail cosmology, including human sacrifice, to the new world before Columbus? Or could it possibly be true that this common cosmology is so old that Native Americans brought it with them across the former land bridge connecting Russia with Alaska? In **Figure 465**, we see a Grail human form lying on his back on the cosmic altar, awaiting sacrifice to the sun. Our Grail sun symbol is seen on the belly of

this sacrificial victim at the Cosmic Center. Abraham did not sacrifice his first-born son, Isaac, as his ancestors before him had sacrificed theirs. He sacrificed a lamb instead. We see the lamb which Abraham sacrificed in lieu of Isaac in **Figure 466**. The Hebrews learned from a priest to sacrifice their first-born sons. They later learned from a priest-humanist not to sacrifice their first-born sons. The Phoenicians and Carthaginians continued infant sacrifice long after the Hebrews gave it up in favor of animal sacrifice.[82] They, too, gave it up when their neighbors got tired of their raiding parties to capture children as sacrificial victims.[83] But the Aztecs did not give up the practice of capturing and sacrificing human victims to the sun until the Catholic priests arrived.[84] What shall we say of this?

Figure 465

Figure 466

That religious humanism ultimately will prevail over inhumane practices which masquerade as religion?

"The Mesoamericans, like the Egyptians, became pyramid and temple builders and at great ceremonial centres erected clusters of grand and imposing structures."[85] "Among the cycles depicted in the great Calendar Stone [of the Aztecs] are lunar cycles and the cycle of the Venus year, which, as in Babylonia, had important ritualistic significance."[86] "Part of the Dresden *Codex* includes a calendar for the planet Venus covering a period of 384 years which shows that the Maya (like the Babylonians) knew that five synodic revolutions of the planet (2920 days) equalled *eight solar years*. Also like the Babylonian Venus Tablets, the Maya Venus observations are loaded with astrological omens referring to danger periods."[87] "The Venus count was very important too in tying in with other cycles.... They had no leap year, and to reconcile the various cycles of time and correct errors they looked for significant intervals when the various cycles coincided and could then be manipulated in grand large-number reconciliation schemes. One of the most beautiful of these Maya schemes was the interval of 37,960 days. This they discovered was the lowest common multiple of the 365-day solar year, the 260-day sacred year, *and* the 584-day (average) period of Venus's synodical revolution. The Maya Venus reckoning shows an error of only 0.08 days in the span of 481 years.... This is a remarkable achievement.... The precise detail of how the Maya made their astronomical observations and with what instrumentation, if any, is not known. Nevertheless, it seems probable that they

used their Megalithic architecture to provide alignments in much the same way as the Stone-Age astronomer-priests used the sarsens of Stonehenge."[88]

The Dresden *Codex* is a Mayan book which escaped the wrath of the book-burning and stone-smashing Roman Catholic priests.[89] It includes eclipse tables which indicate that through long periods of observation "the Maya priesthood discovered that eclipses fell into well-defined patterns; and in doing this they discovered the eclipse-important swing of the lunar nodes (in 18.61 years) without actually knowing precisely what it was they had discovered. It is the Maya eclipse reckoning using simplistic whole-number counts which provides insights into an exciting methodology that might also have been used at an earlier period by the Stone-Age astronomer-priests of North-West Europe."[90] "But how *did* the astronomer-priests of the Maya and the other pre-Columbian American races make their observations to provide high accuracies in time-keeping cycles as demonstrated? The short answer is that at present their *modi operandi* are not clear. Nevertheless, there are indications that some buildings were purpose-oriented.... The best known of these is El Caracol (circular) Tower (the Snail). It has four outer doors facing the cardinal points of the compass and owes its name to its inner spiral staircase."[91] The Temple of Solomon had a spiral staircase! So did the crystal tower in our Grail stories and the Watch Tower of Zeus. Did the ancient solar-lunar-astral priesthood extend itself worldwide? Was the Christian church confronted by its ancient enemy almost everywhere it went?

At least we got the answer for which we went fishing. The cycles of Venus of *eight solar years* help to reconcile various other periodic cycles in the sky and thereby to correct errors in the calculation of the year. Suppose we were to find the eight-pointed Inanna symbol at Stonehenge? Would this indicate that they, too, might have used the Venus cycle to reconcile the various periodicities and to correct errors?

Did the Holy Grail really make it to the Americas? When four Mexican Native-Americans "fly" as "ceremonial birds" by tying ropes to their legs and spinning to the ground from a tall pole, a fifth man rotates on a platform at the top of the pole.[92] Does the man on the platform represent our cosmic Grailperson spinning around the polestar or around the sun?

Near Teotihuacan, the largest of Mexico's ancient ceremonial centers, are found cross and circle

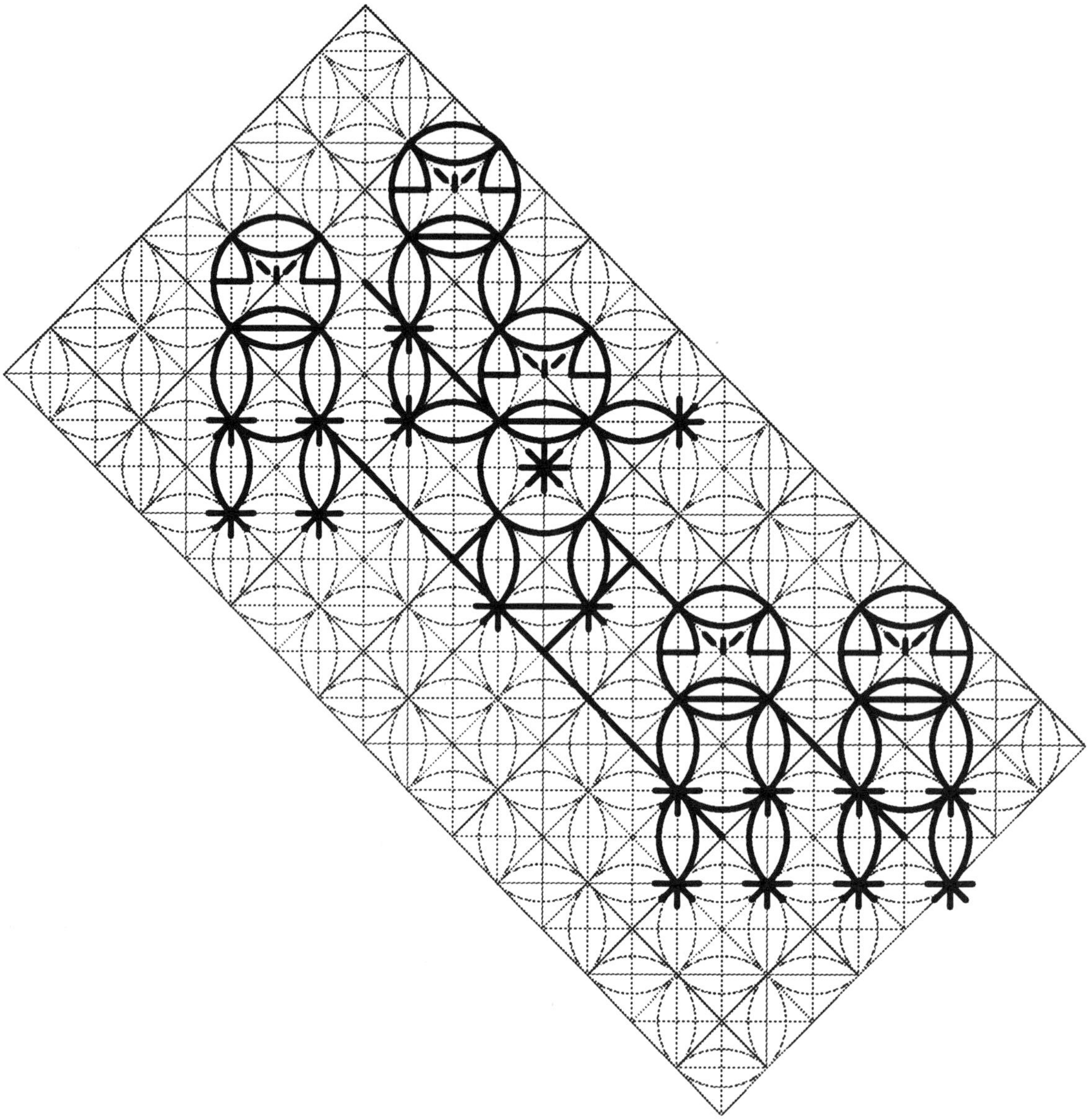

Figure 467

markings.[93] These diagrams suggest to the experts that "the true cardinal directions were important to the builders...."[94] The presence of a pair of almost identical cross and circle markers within three miles of the Tropic indicates to the experts that Native Americans may have been able to locate the Tropic![95]

The experts recently have begun to discover that the elaborate mosaics of the ancient step-pyramids of the Maya contain hidden numerical messages in stone, including the Venus count.[96] Recall the number-counts we found in the stone foundation, frame, and fabric of Chartres Cathedral!

Modern Mayan cosmology has become entangled with the Christian dogmas of the Spanish invaders. Christ has become the sun god and Our Lady the goddess of the moon.[97] However, one does not have to look very hard to find Grail-related cosmology which no Catholic priest would have taught to his Native American flock. For instance, we are told that an elderly Native American told our informant that, "The deity having the day's duties carries the sun in his chest, setting out at dawn on a litter supported by four lesser divinities."[98] As in **Figure 467**? The Barasana Indians of Colombia told another informant that when the sun reaches its zenith, that is, when the sun is straight overhead, thereby causing an upright staff to lose its shadow, the sun's rays penetrate directly into the earth (soil) and the Earth (planet) thereby is seasonally renewed.[99] As in our Grail quest stories

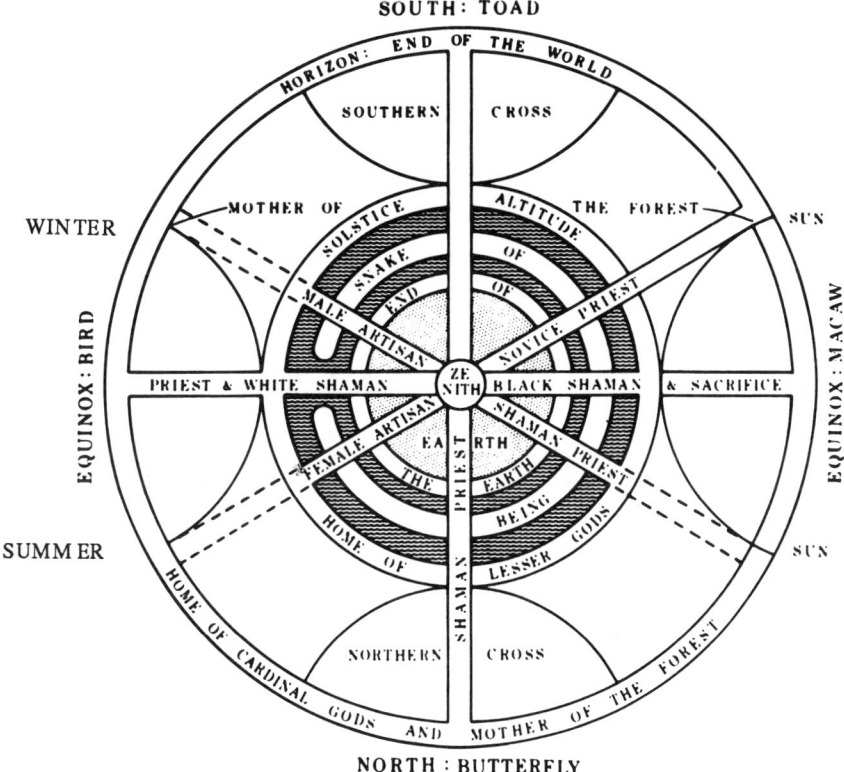

Illustration 29-5. Corrected diagram of the cosmos of the Warao Native Americans of Venezuela. Courtesy of Dr. Johannes Wilbert, Director, Latin American Center, University of California, Los Angeles.

about the manform which plunges into the fountain at noon? Another informant tells us that the Desana Indians of Colombia determine the arrival and departure of the seasons by the stars; that Orion's belt is one of their seasonal indicators; and that they tell a tale about the Master of the Animals, a supernatural gamekeeper,[100] whose role in the Cosmos parallels that of the Grail giant who herded the constellations of stars in a tale from the Welsh *Mabinogion* and from the writings of Chretien de Troyes!

You remain unconvinced? Look, then, at **Illustration 29-5**,[101] which is a diagram of the Cosmos as conceived by the Warao Indians of the Orinoco River delta of Venezuela. The Warao say that the concentric circles in that drawing represent the flat disc of the Earth surrounded by the great snake, which is the source of all life, and the dwelling places of the lesser and greater gods![102] The world surrounded by a great snake! Familiar cosmology to those of us who have read the preceding chapters of this book! Note that the cosmic Earth, the cosmic snake, and the heavenly spheres of the lower and

higher gods are centered by a version of our Inanna symbol! A Roman Catholic priest taught the Warao this cosmology? Not likely!

You remain skeptical? Then consider the construction and cosmic function of the temple of the Kogi Indians of Colombia as told by Dr. E.C. Krupp of the Griffith Observatory: "With a rope, knotted to preserve key lengths, the shaman traces out a circle around a stake driven into the center point. The rope and its knots are used to determine the placement of other features of the temple. The height equals the diameter at the base, about 25 feet.... Once a circle establishes the temple's outer wall, large posts are placed on it at the intercardinal directions. These four wall posts form a square, but the wall is built of smaller posts set along the circle. Pairs of larger posts mark the north and south points on the ring, and entrances are placed at cardinal east and cardinal west.... On the temple floor are four fireplaces also positioned as the corners of a square at the intercardinal points. When the June solstice arrives, the sun travels north of the zenith, and at about 9 A.M. shines through a hole in

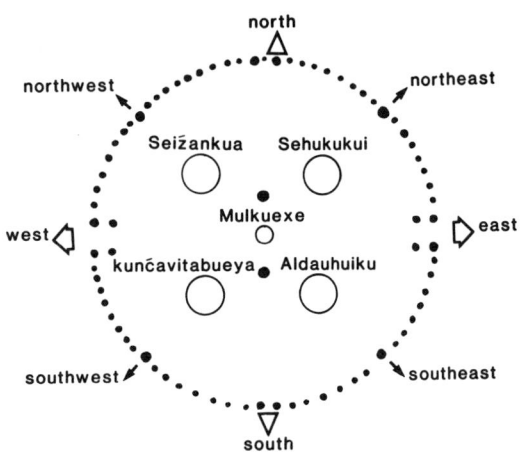

north
northwest
northeast
Seiẑankua   Sehukukui
Mulkuexe
west   east
kunčavitabueya   Aldauhuiku
southwest
southeast
south

Illustration 29-6. Diagram of the four fireplaces of the cosmos-temple of the Kogi Native Americans of Colombia. Courtesy of Dr. E.C. Krupp, Director, Griffith Observatory, Los Angeles, and of Harper & Row, Publishers, New York.

the very top of the temple... and the first light strikes the southwest fireplace. As the day continues, the beam traces out a line to the east and stops in the southeast fireplace. At that time, about 3 o'clock in the afternoon, the sunlight can no longer enter the roof hole, and the spot of light fades."[103] Recall that 3:00 o'clock P.M., the Nones, is the traditional hour at which Christ Jesus died! Continuing with Dr. Krupp's narrative: "If we were to leave the roof hole uncovered and watch each day, we would see this line of sunlight gradually edge north until, on the December solstice, the first beam fell on the northwest fireplace and ended its display on the northeast fireplace. Now the sun is south of the zenith, as far as it will travel, and each day following, the threads of daily sunlight will weave the fabric on the floor back to the south. Weaving is exactly the metaphor used by the Kogi to describe this hierophany that takes place in their temples. The four fireplaces are the four corners of a loom to which the sun adds a thread. Through the year, as the sun moves north, south, and north again, it is said to spiral about the world spindle. It weaves the thread of life into an orderly fabric of existence, and the cyclical changes of the sun's daily path are transformed into a cloth of light on the temple floor. Just as the daytime sun weaves a white thread, from west to east, its nighttime alter ego, traveling in the underworld from west to east, weaves a black thread through the year's fabric between each pair of white threads."[104] Dr. Krupp's diagram of these activities is seen in **Illustration 29-6.**[105] "When a Kogi shaman builds a temple, he actually makes a model of his

universe"; he is "imitating the cosmos."[106] Do you suppose that the master masons who built Chartres Cathedral would have understood the goal of the Kogi shaman? Did some Catholic priest teach this Grail-born cosmology to the Kogi? Or could it be that these Indians brought this cosmology with them on their trek across the former land bridge from Asia to the Americas? Need I bold lines for you on the Holy Grail?

But you remain unconvinced? We lack time and space to continue this process, so your author will skip much of what we could consider and will conclude with this: In his excellent analysis of the "sun temples" of Native Americans, Dr. E.C. Krupp discusses shamans who employ quartz crystals and hallucinogenic drugs in their cosmic magic "to communicate with the unseen world."[107] Modern investigators discovered in one such "house of the sun" that "with a natural quartz crystal... they could send rainbows all around the shelter by letting sunlight fall upon it."[108] The common feature of these shrines of Native American tribes is that a person who positions himself correctly in the rock cleft, crevice, or other viewing position will see the sun move across or touch a "sun symbol" or other marker on a rock wall at sunrise or sunset on the day of the solstice and/or equinox, "reminiscent of the play of winter solstice sunlight in the inner chamber at Newgrange."[109] "Although the Chumash do not refer to the 'death' of the sun, they say that the sun, the year, and the cosmos are reborn with the sunrise at the winter solstice. At Window Cave, winter solstice sunset is the key moment. Here, then, the... [shaman] experienced the prelude to renewal of the world's order. The eight-spoke disk may represent the new sun fathered by the old, or it may just be an emblem of the shelter's solar connotations. Either

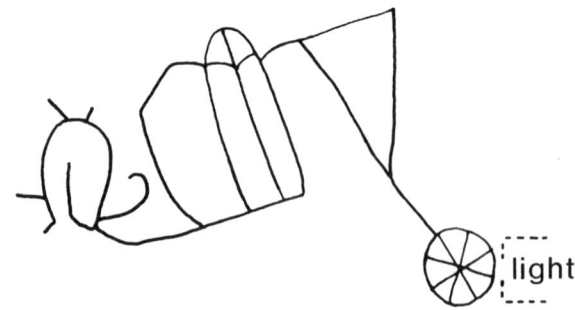

light

Illustration 29-7. Sun symbol and stylized genitalia from Window Cave, a "sun temple" of the Chumash Native Americans of California. Courtesy of Dr. E.C. Krupp, Director, Griffith Observatory, Los Angeles, and of Harper & Row, Publishers, New York.

way, it and the vulva petroglyph restate the familiar metaphors: fertility and sun. Both imply renewal — the end of the one cycle and the start of another."[110] Dr. Krupp's drawing of this sun diagram at Window Cave is seen in **Illustration 29-7**.[111]

Let us open our King James Bibles to Exodus 33.20-23. In order to use one of these Native American "sun temples," the shaman positions himself at the predetermined spot. Exodus 33.21 tells us: "[T]hou shalt stand upon a rock." The sun's rays penetrate between a cleft in the rocks or through a man-made hole. Exodus 33.22 says: "'[W]hile my glory passeth by... I will put thee in a clift of the rock." The Oxford Bible uses the word "crevice" instead of "clift." At the appointed time, sunrise or sunset, equinox or solstice, the Native American shaman or sun priest then sees the light of the sun strike the marker on a rock wall of the cave or cleft. Exodus 33.23 reads: "[A]nd thou shall see my back parts: but my face shall not be seen." The ancients knew the consequences of looking the sun in its "face."

Shall we conclude that the people of the world shared one belief once upon a time long ago? If so, we certainly have changed. Was that change for the sake of the sheep or for the sake of the shepherds? Christianity taught us to eat God rather than eating each other, and to sacrifice our children as Christian soldiers rather than on bloodstained altars. Christianity taught us that the world and its creatures are ours for the taking, rejecting the ancient concept that we should maintain, rather than destroy, the ecosystems of which we are a part. Christianity also taught us that we should believe, rather than question, all aspects of Christian religion, shifting our rational intellect into neutral when we hear the call of the church bells. We sheep profited from Christianity. So did our shepherds! The Cosmos lost. Shall we continue to sacrifice the Earth's ecosystems to the gods of "progress" until we have destroyed ourselves?

Notes
CHAPTER TWENTY-NINE
The Holy Grail as Clock, Calendar, and Navigational Instrument

1. Allen 366.

2. Allen 366.

3. Allen 360.

4. Allen 362.

5. Allen 255.

6. Allen 256.

7. Allen 385.

8. Allen 378.

9. Allen 381.

10. Allen 381; Deuteronomy 33.17. The King James Bible says that "his horns *are like* the horns of unicorns…," a seeming oxymoron.

11. Allen 382.

12. Allen 344-345.

13. Allen 345.

14. Allen 346.

15. Rey 50, 52, 56, 130, 139.

16. Rey 130-136.

17. Allen 26.

18. Allen ix.

19. Wisdom of Solomon 13. 1-9.

20. Beckwith 71.

21. Graham 354.

22. Eusebius 89-93.

23. James 85. A thorough understanding of how the Mayas of Guatemala *still* memorize complex, numerical, astronomical data, which forms the basis for their accurate calendrical system, by encoding that data in easily remembered myths, may be obtained by reading Dennis Tedlock's translation of *Popol Vuh*, Simon & Schuster, Inc., New York, 1985. See, especially, Tedlock 32, 37-46, 58. Grail questers will feel at home in the pages of *Popol Vuh*, one of a handful of sixteenth-century, Mayan cosmogony codexes that escaped the bonfires of ardent, Christian missionaries. Tedlock 27. We are told how "Heart of Sky," an anthropomorphic, one-legged, trinitarian god, created humankind and the world of light. Tedlock 73, 343. We are told that the Mayan icon for the Planet Venus is a severed head. Tedlock 236. The story action proceeds from the beginning of creation "as if the writers were starting at the bottom of something vertical and working their way up." Tedlock 241. Through Tedlock's excellent translation, the Native American authors of *Popol Vuh* tell us that their council book was "a place to see 'The Light That Came from Across the Sea.'" Tedlock 71. Tedlock comments that the Mayan words he translates as "a place to see" refer to "an instrument (or place) for the seeing of something," and that the something to be seen "could variously mean 'figure,' 'drawing,' and even 'picture.'" Tedlock 242-243. He says that one of those Mayan words would refer today "to crystals used for gazing by diviners and to eyeglasses, binoculars, and telescopes." Tedlock 243. He refers to another Mayan codex which indicates that "Heart of Sky" or "Heart of Heaven" is a "bead of precious stone." Tedlock 254. The Mayan gods-heroes of *Popol Vuh* engage in form-changing; and they spend days in ritual combats, and nights in a variety of perilous "houses" and "citadels," including the citadel of the bearded place! Tedlock 43-45, 55-56, 137-150. Does any of this sound familiar to you Grail questers? The Mayan gods are sustained by "the ultimate fruits of the earth and sky, which were themselves described as the 'blue-green plate' and 'blue-green bowl.'" Tedlock 58. Do you remember the story of the Holy Grail sewn with golden threads on emerald-green silk? Is the Mayan creation myth played out on the Holy Grail?

24. Graham 304.

25. Hapgood 9.

26. Hapgood 9.

27. Hapgood 4.

28. Dreyer 6, 39, 172.

29. Dreyer 118, 172; Heath, *Aristarchus* 236.

30. Hapgood 17, 27.

31. Hapgood 115.

32. Hapgood 23, 27, 30, 36, 46, 98, 102, 110.

33. Hapgood 43, 103, 104, 140.

34. Hapgood 43.

35. Neugebauer 161, 185, 218-220; 2 Heath *GM* 292-293.

36. Hapgood 212.

37. E.A. Wood 44-53.

38. Hapgood 212.

39. E.A. Wood Fig. 4-6.

40. E.A. Wood Fig. 4-11.

41. Gibbs 84.

42. Hapgood 4, 14, 106, 108.

43. Hapgood 4 ,43, 211-212, 217, 219-220, 224.

44. Hapgood 25.

45. Hapgood 48-62.

46. Wolkstein xvi.

47. Hapgood 2-3.

48. Reichard Plate XXIII.

49. Reichard Plate XXIII.

50. Reichard 70.

51. Reichard 69.

52. John 7.38.

53. Reichard 17.

54. Reichard 26, 61.

55. Reichard x.

56. Reichard 73.

57. Fox 8,115-116, 130-136, 149-158.

58. Fox 45.

59. Fox 79, 89.

60. Washburn 5-6. The Toltec Fejervary Screenfold illustrates symbols now familiar to us. Xiuhtecutli, the fire god or year god, stands at the center of the cross. Two humanforms stand facing each other on each of the four arms of the cross. Cavendish 245. The mystic center surrounded by the cosmic eight? Like Christ Pantocrator, identified by His monograms IX and XC and by the interference pattern halo around His head, surrounded by eight angels, centering the cupola of *Cappella Palatina*, Palermo, *circa* 1143? Beckwith 260.

61. Fox 3.

62. Fox 33.

63. Fox 15.

64. Talbott 3-5, 328-332; P.L. Brown 194-209.

65. Talbott 42. Is the Tooth Fairy of Germanic mythology and American culture to be found on the Holy Grail? Regarding the origin of the Tooth Fairy, see Hollander 55.

66. Talbott 98.

67. Talbott 8-12, 23-32, 37, 42-293.

68. Talbott 92.

69. Eschenbach, *Parzival* 244.

70. Allen 7-10; Neugebauer 58, 81-82, 84, 87-88, 94.

71. John 14.2.

72. Talbott 268-282.

73. Talbott 281.

74. Talbott 282.

75. Talbott 315.

76. Talbott 186.

77. Talbott 186.

78. Talbott 240.

79. Talbott 240.

80. Talbott 290.

81. Talbott 286-290; Lamy 64.

82. Fox 131, 148-158.

83. Fox 153-154.

84. Fox 115-116, 152.

85. P.L. Brown 213.

86. P.L. Brown 214.

87. P.L. Brown 219. (Emphasis added.)

88. P.L. Brown 220-221.

89. P.L. Brown 216.

90. P.L. Brown 221.

91. P.L. Brown 221.

92. Krupp 209-211. This "dance" plays out the numerical relationship between the ancient sacred count of 260 days and the 365 day year. Krupp 210.

93. Krupp 280. See also Krupp 277-285.

94. Hadingham *EMATC* 183.

95. Hadingham *EMATC* 183-185.

96. Hadingham *EMATC* 193.

97. Hadingham *EMATC* 194.

98. Hadingham *EMATC* 198.

99. Krupp 318.

100. Krupp 319.

101. Krupp 321. The version of this drawing of the Warao Cosmos which appears in Dr. Krupp's work indicates Winter and Summer at positions reversed from those in Illustration 29-5. Dr. Krupp's drawing was based upon a drawing published by Dumbarton Oaks, based upon a drawing by Dr. Johannes Wilbert, Director, Latin American Center, the University of California, Los Angeles. By letter to me of January 4, 1988, Dr. Wilbert asked me to make the Winter and Summer corrections as in Illustration 29-5 to "set the record straight."

102. Krupp 321.

103. Krupp 239-240.

104. Krupp 241. See also Hadingham *EMATC* 168-169.

105. Krupp 240.

106. Krupp 238-239.

107. Krupp 317. See also Krupp 129, 131, 133, 138, 140-141, 318, 322.

108. Krupp 133.

109. Krupp 131. See also Krupp 129-137, 152-156; Hadingham *EMATC* 152-156. Some of these "sun shrines" are not arranged precisely enough to pinpoint the actual day of the solstice to closer than a week. Krupp 131. Hadingham *EMATC* 154. Others, such as Loughcrew, Newgrange, Knowth, and Dowth, in Ireland, are much more precise in fixing the solar events. Brennan 7-126.

110. Krupp 135-136.

111. Krupp 136.

 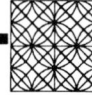

Chapter Thirty

The Wheel in the Middle of the Wheel

We discussed in the last chapter a round tower located in Mesoamerica, complete with spiral staircase, which may have been used by Native Americans as an astronomical observatory.[1] We suggested that there may have been contacts between those Americans and seafarers from the Mediterranean who came to the New World.[2] Were similar towers, used for astronomy, built around the Mediterranean Sea? Megalith-builders constructed huge, round towers of large stones as early as 1500 B.C. along the coasts of Sardinia and, afterwards, elsewhere around the coasts of the Mediterranean Sea — including Corsica, the Balearics, and mainland Europe.[3] Their towers are linked to the sea and the sky. "[A] knowledge of navigation and the tides would in itself provide one reason for studying the movement of the stars, the sun and especially the moon."[4] These megalith-builders gave us a sub-stantial clue about their seafaring origins by excavating chambers and erecting stone structures in the form of overturned boats.[5]

Were these Mediterranean Sea megalith-builders aware of the Holy Grail? At Li Muri, Arzachena, Sardinia, are four circular stone structures which intersect with each other to form a somewhat lopsided concave-sided tetragon. We are told this about those four intersecting stone structures: "The position of the circles seems strongly linked to the sky, for ritual invocation and perhaps for celestial observations aligning the small standing stones with markers on the rugged horizon."[6] The "mother earth goddess" is associated with even earlier megalithic temple construction in Malta,[7] where her legs and short skirt compare exactly with her legs and short skirt as illustrated in Figure 432.[8]

Just how far back into pre-history might Grail-born astronomical concepts go? In **Illustration 30-1**,[9] we see the "mother earth goddess" holding a horn incised with thirteen marks. Thirteen is the round number of days in half a lunar month and the round number of lunar months in a solar year. The horn and the circle it encloses are shaped like an irradiation crescent (a light phenomenon) on the moon.[10] The "mother earth goddess" in Illustration 30-1 has been dated to 30,000 B.C.[11]

What fueled the fertile imaginations of the ancients to transform patterns of stars and their motions into fantastic stories of gods, goddesses, and animals romping around Heaven? Archaeologists have uncovered evidence that Stone Age people cultivated opium poppies![12] Our distant ancestors apparently tripped as well as travelled!

Did those stories about the movements of the constellations serve any purpose other than to entertain? Modern memory experts remember long strings of numbers by encoding them in graphic images that are woven into stories which easily can be remembered.[13] When the numerical data is needed, the stories are remembered and decoded, yielding the raw-number strings.[14] Upon the (perhaps erroneous) assumption that Stone Age people could not write, did they memorize long strings of

Illustration 30-1. The "great goddess" of Laussel, *circa* 30,000 B.C., holding a buffalo horn (?) inscribed with 13 marks – possibly representing either the round-number count of lunar months in a solar year or the number of days from new crescent moon to full moon. Courtesy of Robert Hale Limited, London, and of Peter Lancaster Brown.

astronomical periodicities by using the technique utilized by modern memory experts? Are some ancient legends and myths the astronomical databases of our distant ancestors?

Megalithic solar and lunar astronomy was founded on a system of observing and recording the points along the horizon where the sun and moon "pop" up and "sink" down.[15] "The sun's annual pattern is the easiest to follow."[16] "It soon appears to an observer that the longer the sun's passage, from its rising to its setting, the warmer the season. Thus by noting, at any one place on the earth's surface, the point on the horizon where the sun rises each day, a pattern of the year is readily detected."[17] To utilize the horizon system, it is *not* necessary that the observer understand what actually is going on in the sky.[18] The horizon system works the same way whether the observer assumes that the Earth is standing still and the sun is moving along the Ecliptic, or whether he assumes that the sun is standing still and the Earth is rotating yearly around the Ecliptic, or whether he makes no assumptions *at all* about what is in motion! The horizon system is *pure science*, that is, a method of working with something that the observer does not necessarily understand.

Stone Age people often are portrayed as ape-like creatures captivated by magic — the very lowest form of humanity practicing the very lowest form of religion. In the next few pages of this book, we shall come to appreciate the fact that they had achieved scientific breakthroughs using the best techniques of "modern" empirical science. Apparently, they learned to collect, store, and use astronomical data[19] before they developed theories to explain its causes and significance, and a system of cosmological myths as a repository for long-term storage of their theories.

A writer should be sensitive to racial undertones in anything written these days. Your author has not suggested that Northern European Stone Age people were scientists whereas persons from more Southern regions were magicians. You will find a plethora of books to that effect, but this is not one of them. In point of fact — assuming that anyone is interested in the facts — human skeletons found in association with astronomy-linked megalithic structures from Africa to the Northernmost reaches of Europe include a grand assortment of skull and body types — indicating that Stone Age builder-astronomers varied widely from short, squat people with round skulls and heavy eyebrows to tall, lanky people with long, narrow skulls.[20] The

dark-complexioned, seafaring Fomorian giants we met in Irish legends apparently were builders of coastal megalithic towers who "brought their skills from Africa, by way of what we now call Spain."[21] We apparently are dealing with a *culture* which spanned many racial or ethnic stocks. Dark-skinned Eagles reading this book have no cause to duck their chins in a gesture of self-imposed inferiority, and light-skinned Eagles have no cause to raise their noses in a gesture of self-bestowed superiority. To avoid leaving our friends from the Pacific Islands out of this commentary, please turn to **Illustration 30-2**,[22] where we see Holy Grail symbols Hawaiian-style! All that said, may we now move on?

Before we digressed, we were discussing the fact that solar observations along the horizon are easier than lunar observations along the horizon. Why? The Earth spins on its axis approximately once daily.[23] It rotates around the sun, along the Ecliptic, approximately once yearly.[24] All the while, the axis of the Earth tilts,[25] and it also "precesses" over a period of approximately 26,000 years.[26] "Precession" resembles the wobbling of the axis of a toy top as the top winds down after a spin.[27] Precession causes the polestar to change over the period of approximately 26,000 years.[28] Excluding consideration of precession, and excluding certain other motions, such as the nodding called "nutation,"[29] the axis of the Earth, generally speaking, always points at the polestar, while the Earth makes its once-a-year trip around the Ecliptic.[30] This combination of motions causes the sun to be higher in the sky in certain seasons and lower in the sky in other seasons, and to "pop" up out of and "sink" into the horizon at different points along the horizon as the seasons progress — whereas the fact is that, in a "two-wheel system," the sun really "stays put" and the angle at which the sun's rays strike the Earth varies with the seasonal position of the Earth along the Ecliptic.[31]

Illustration 30-2. Holy Grail symbols Hawaiian-style! Courtesy of Doubleday & Company, Inc., New York.

The Wheel in the Middle of the Wheel

Precession also causes the equinoxes to slip from Zodiac constellation to Zodiac constellation along the Ecliptic over the period of approximately 26,000 years.[32] The first day of spring romantically is called "The First Point of Aries," because that was its location in the time of Classical Greece, but the first day of spring now falls in Pisces because of precession.[33]

The Earth's course along the Ecliptic really is neither Aristarchus's circle[34] nor Kepler's ellipse.[35] Every 100,000 years, the Earth's orbit changes from almost circular to nearly elliptical.[36] The reason is that the Earth revolves around the center of all the mass in the solar system instead of around the sun. The sun contains 98 percent of that mass. Most of the remainder is in Jupiter. The effect of the mass not contained in the sun is to move the focus of the Earth's orbit slightly off center in respect to the sun. This causes periodic changes in the shape of the Earth's orbit.[37]

At night, "the movements of the earth affect the apparent positions of the stars in many different ways. Rotation gives us rising and setting; revolution around the sun changes the constellations visible during each season; precession and nutation alter the position of stars on the celestial sphere and thus change not only the stars associated with the different seasons, but also those which can be seen from different parts of the earth."[38]

Ezekiel wrote of a wheel (the circumpolar stars?) within a wheel (the Ecliptic?) but modern astronomers know that there is a third "wheel" — our sun and its planets moving in a circle around our galaxy, the Milky Way.[39] Now you understand what *really* is happening up there? If you do not, it does not matter for our purposes because, as we said earlier, solar observations along the horizon work the same way whether or not you know — or even care — what is rotating around what!

If you understand the motions of the sun, you might want to try your hand at understanding the even more complicated motions of the moon. By way of a gross oversimplification, add to what you learned about the sun the following: "Twice in each lunar month, the moon's orbit cuts across the plane of the ecliptic. These crossing points are important in lunar astronomy — they are called the nodes. After every three lunar cycles of 18.61 years, i.e., every 55.83 years, the pattern of the nodes is completed and recommences."[40] The synchronized rotations of the Earth and its moon explain why we always see the same side of the moon; the positions of each in relation to each other and to the sun

determine how much of the moon's surface we see lighted.[41] If you understand the motions of the moon, that is great! If you do not, that is equally great, for our purposes! Our Stone Age ancestors did not need to understand the reasons why the moon hops around on the horizon in order for them to study and record its motions over extended periods of time. Did they understand the 18.61-year cycle? Probably not in terms of modern decimal points. In terms of extended periods of years, which we erroneously refer to as the "Metonic" and "Saros" cycles, the answer appears to be a resounding "Yes." We soon will discuss in detail the 56 "Aubrey Holes" at Stonehenge, which can be used for eclipse prediction! The European megalith-builders, like the latter-day Mayas of Mesoamerica, evidently could predict eclipses of the moon.[42] Eclipses and nodal crossings of the Ecliptic are directly related to each other.[43]

How could Stone Age people, whom our artists often portray as ape-like beings with barely enough brain power to kill animals for food, possibly have achieved more in the field of astronomy than the Babylonians of 1500 years later[44] and our ancestors of the early Middle Ages? Could it be that these artists are not correct about an important aspect of Stone Age people? "[A]fter several hundred thousand years of very rapid growth the expansion of the [human] brain slowed down, and in the last one hundred thousand years it has not changed size at all."[45] "The [human] brain reached its present size about one hundred thousand years ago, and its growth ceased."[46] You have been encouraged not to assume that short, squat, round-headed Stone Age people with protruding eyebrows were inferior, mentally, to tall, lanky, long-headed Stone Age people. Shall we take this inferiority-superiority question one step further? Shall we consider the possibility that *we* may have no more brain power than Stone Age people of the year 3000 B.C.?[47] If we assume that the brain power of people of the Stone Ages and people of the Middle Ages was equal, then was the difference between astronomical achievements of the two groups the result of the presence or absence of totalitarian religious precepts which could be questioned only by risking your life to the "tender mercies" of a priest-appointed holy executioner, or a priest-incited mob of true believers?

We finally reach a consideration of Stonehenge. Legends say its stones were erected by Merlin the Magician of Round Table fame,[48] or by the Druids.[49] Caesar tells us about the Druids that " 'the cardinal

doctrine which they seek to teach is that souls do not die, but after death pass from one to another… beside this, they have many discussions as touching the stars and their movement, the size of the universe and of the earth….' "[50] Stonehenge *may* be the temple of the Hyperboreans described by Diodorus: "'This island… is situated in the north, and is inhabited by the Hyperboreans, who are called by that name because their home is beyond the point whence the north wind (Boreas) blows…. And there is also on the island both a magnificent sacred precinct of Apollo and a notable temple (Stonehenge?) which is adorned with many votive offerings and is spherical in shape. Furthermore, a city (Avebury Stone Circle?) is there which is sacred to the god, and the majority of its inhabitants are players on the cithara; and these continually play on this instrument in the temple and sing hymns of praise to the god…. They say also that the moon, as viewed from this island, appears to be but a little distance from the earth and to have upon it prominences, like those of the earth, which are visible to the eye. The account is also given that the god visits the island every nineteen years, the period in which the return of the stars to the same place in the heavens is accomplished; and for this reason the nineteen-year period is called by the Greeks the 'year of Meton.'"[51] Hawkins tells us: "The fifth century B.C. Greek astronomer Meton noted that 235 lunar months equal 19 solar years, so that after one 'metonic cycle' of 19 years the full moon occurs again on the same calendar date."[52] Stone Age people apparently were aware of the cycle we call "Metonic" for many years before Meton.[53]

Mythmakers, historians, and archaeologists said Stonehenge was a temple.[54] The only debates were as to which people built it for which god(s) or goddess(es). Then there came to the Salisbury Plain of England an astronomer affiliated with the Smithsonian Astrophysical Observatory, one Gerald S. Hawkins,[55] who said in a magazine article published in 1963,[56] and in a book entitled *Stonehenge Decoded*, published in 1965, that Stonehenge was an astronomical observatory; a Stone Age computer.[57] His working hypothesis was simple but elegant: "If I can see any alignment, general relationship or use for the various parts of Stonehenge then these facts were also known to the builders."[58] Hawkins' conclusions were equally short but sweet: "There can be no doubt that Stonehenge was an observatory; the impartial mathematics of probability and the celestial sphere are on my side."[59] "From Bernoulli's theorem, the probability that these ten positions are marked by chance alignment in the two structures seems less than one in a million."[60] Our "single grains of sand soon equal a sandbox" approach to Grail studies is just another way of expressing the laws of probability!

Some archaeologists are men and women of the arts. All astrophysicists are mathematicians. Some archaeologists ultimately, and courageously, accepted Hawkins' mathematical explanations.[61] Others rallied around the written record and counterattacked. Mathematical astronomy which they could not or would not understand,[62] they nonetheless bombarded with words! What will the scholars say of your author's writings? Either that they are the rubbish of a rank amateur or, worse, they will say nothing at all, employing the deadly device of the learned — scholarly silence!

In the estimation of some of the ladies and gentlemen of the arts, Hawkins did a dastardly deed, although he only did what scientists and mathematicians do best. He fed astronomical alignments into one of the gigantic digital computers of that era, pushed the switch, and out came an answer which (for the sake of our arts-only readers) your author will express as follows: Prince Charming, that is, an IBM 7090 computer, gave Sleeping Beauty, that is, Stonehenge, a kiss on the cheek and she awakened from a sleep of millennia. Soon, the IBM Prince Charming and Lady Stonehenge were clasping hands and whispering into each others' ears the innermost secrets of their manufacturers. Not exactly, but you get the point: It took one to know one. We dare not get ourselves involved in the mathematical technicalities of how this was done, lest we lose our friends of the arts who, by their refusal to consider the details of mathematical astronomy, close their ears to the enchanting music of the heavenly spheres which this magnificent lady can play on the cosmic cithara!

When was Stonehenge built? Hawkins says between 1900 B.C. and 1600 B.C.[63] Newham says between 2350 B.C. and 1350 B.C.[64] The official guidebook for Stonehenge says it was occupied between 2800 B.C. and 1100 B.C.[65] It depends, in part, upon what an author means by "built" or "occupied," and whether his dating was put into print before, or after, the bristlecone pinetree recalibration of the carbon 14 dating system.[66] Generally speaking, the more recent the publication the older the datings.[67] Any of these windows is accurate enough for our purposes. All fall within the period that Lion, Ox, Man, and Eagle, in their

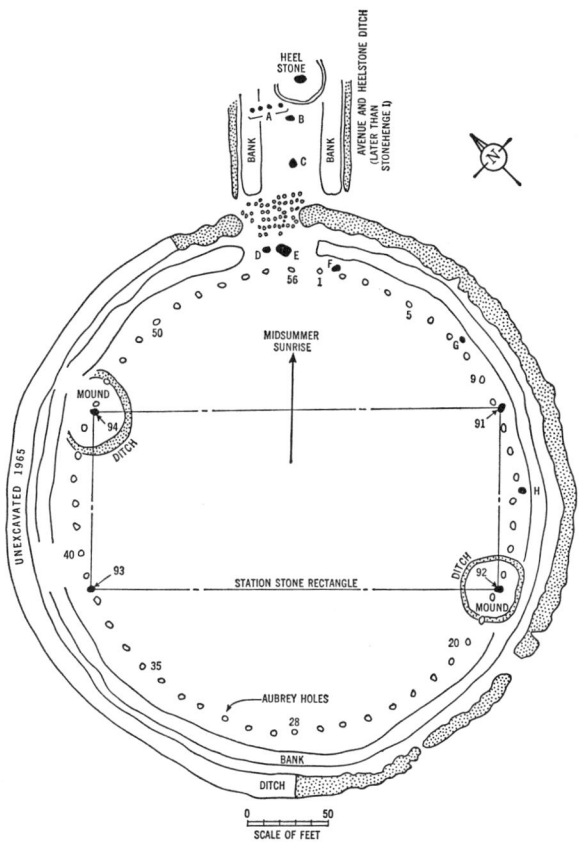

Illustration 30-3. A plan of Stonehenge I, illustrating the "Station Stone Rectangle." Courtesy of Doubleday & Company, Inc., New York.

roles of the Guardians of Heaven, were firmly stuck in the minds of thinking people.

The wonder of Stonehenge to most of its visitors is *how* its builders transported such large stones so far. If, like most moderns, you reject the notion that Merlin "zapped" them there with his magic, then the obvious answer is: either over land or over water. Both routes were possible, considering the presumed population available for the task.[68] Given our theory that the megalith-builders were seafarers, we probably should opt for the Bristol Channel and connecting river route for the bluestones from the only place they can be found — the Prescelly Mountains of Wales.[69] If we choose the water route for the bluestones, consistency would dictate that we choose for the sarsen stones the river route from Malborough Downs.[70]

The better question, for our purposes, is not *how* they transported the stones but *why* they wanted to erect them so far from their places of origin! Why carry construction materials so far to the building site? Why not move the building site closer to the source of the materials? Ask those

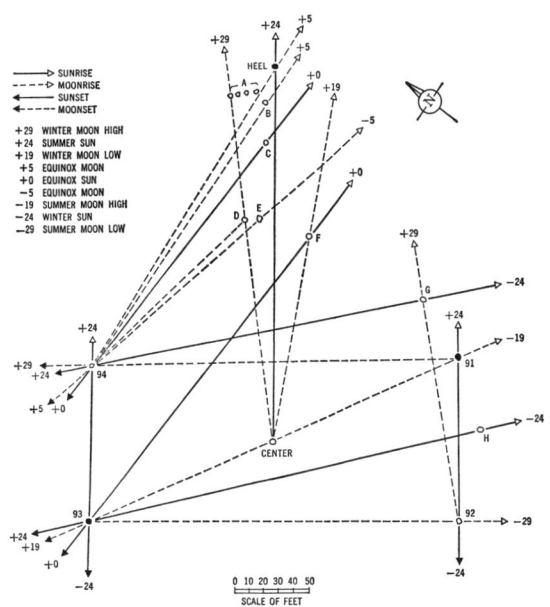

Illustration 30-4. Astronomically-significant alignments for Stonehenge I. Courtesy of Doubleday & Company, Inc., New York.

questions to a member of the official staff at Stonehenge and listen to the official polite and truthful, but evasive, answer: "No one knows the reason." True enough, but there *are* excellent theories! Here is the theory which is important for *this* book: The first-stage builders of Stonehenge did not employ circles or horseshoes of large standing stones in the observatory they built.[71] Hence, they could have put their observatory almost anywhere. Why did they construct it where they did? Why did the second-stage and third-stage builders not erect their new, different, and more imposing structures somewhere else, nearer to the large stones they utilized? Was it important that Stonehenge remain where it first was constructed?

Stonehenge I, as shown in **Illustration 30-3**,[72] was a circular ditch, the contents of which were pitched up to form a circular bank inside the ditch, which surrounded two mounds and the 56 "Aubrey Holes." Notice in Illustration 30-3 the "birdshot" patterns of moon-locator postholes[73] at the opening of the ditch and bank through which appears the midsummer sunrise. Notice in Illustration 30-3 the rectangle which Hawkins calls the "Station Stone Rectangle."[74] This rectangle is our First Wonder of Stonehenge. It appears again, minus ditch, bank, mounds, "Aubrey Holes," and moon markers, in **Illustration 30-4**,[75] in which its sun and moon

alignments are plotted. A legend appears at the top left corner of Illustration 30-4, indicating the sun and moon alignments of the rectangle. This is the significance of that rectangle: "Stonehenge is at the latitude where at their extreme positions along the horizon the sun and the moon rise at a right angle on the horizon. From the standpoint of astronomical measurement Stonehenge could not have been built further north than Oxford or further south than Bournemouth. Within this narrow belt of latitudes the four station stones make a rectangle. Outside this zone the rectangle would be noticeably distorted. Perhaps these latitudes were deliberately chosen, and perhaps these people were aware that the angles of the quadrangle formed by the station stones would change as one moved north or south.... [T]he builders may have been aware of some of the fundamental facts which served later as the basis of accurate navigation and led to a knowledge of the curvature of the earth."[76]

Where does this lead us? To the conclusion that the real wonder of Stonehenge is not how its builders could have transported and erected such large stones but is, instead, whether, and, if so, how, the *original* builders of Stonehenge I knew exactly where to put their observatory on the face of the English countryside to produce near-90-degree angular relationships between seasonal risings and settings of the sun and moon? Hawkins' modern surveying indicated that the actual angles vary from 91 degrees to 94 degrees. How many of us could find on the face of the Earth, using modern plane or geodetic surveying, or by use of a modern sextant, the location of Stonehenge within that degree of accuracy? Is the Holy Grail the answer? Were the builders of Stonehenge I seafaring builder-navigator-astronomers whose map-making techniques later were incorporated into the portolan maps we have studied? Had they *already* circumnavigated the World, or substantial parts of it, by land and sea, using the stars as their roadmaps? Are some of our questions answered by Hawkins' findings that Stonehenge I apparently is as good a calculator as Stonehenge II and III?[77]

Are Hawkins *and* the historian-archaeologists *both* correct? Perhaps Stonehenge I was a calculator, and Stonehenge II and III were calculators which also were used as temples? Does this mean that science preceded religion on the Salisbury Plain? Does this mean that later arrivals from Continental Europe may have created a religion around the science of the original settlers? Was Stonehenge converted from a simple but effective

calculator into an impressive ceremonial precinct of a later-evolved religion? Did the old science remain in the minds of the people as tenets of the new religion — much as the separation of the waters of Heaven and Earth still is stated as religious precept in the Book of Genesis? Did the new science not need such an expensive and unportable calculator as Stonehenge — much as in our own times when $2,000 mechanical calculators which weighed over 100 pounds and covered an entire desktop have been replaced by $4.98 pocket models the size of a credit card? Speculation leads to speculation! Suppose we were to find at Stonehenge our Inanna symbol, the ancient Sumerian symbol for star, god, or Heaven? Might that help us to find answers to some of our questions?

By no means was Hawkins the very first person to suggest that Stonehenge might have connections with a system of ancient astronomy,[78] but he certainly deserves credit for waking modern astronomers up to the possibilities of what they might find in that old pile of rocks on the Salisbury Plain! Of course, all astronomers do not agree with everything that Hawkins wrote. Also, it should come as no surprise that many astronomers have started where he stopped and have gone further.

In his book *Sun, Moon and Standing Stones*, John Edwin Wood takes exception to Hawkins' theory about the use of the 56 Aubrey Holes as eclipse predictors.[79] Wood points out that the erroneously-named "Metonic Cycle"[80] is *not* an accurate eclipse-predictor[81] but that the erroneously-named "Saros Cycle,"[82] which was known to Babylonian and Chaldean astronomers, *is* an accurate eclipse-predictor.[83] Wood then explains how the 56 Aubrey Holes could have been used, accurately, to predict *every* eclipse, whereas the method proposed by Hawkins would have predicted only *some* lunar eclipses.[84] Readers are invited to read these materials for themselves, remembering, always, that the ancients did not *necessarily* understand what was rotating around what. Instead, they only may have understood the time cycles on which these events occurred, based upon their accurately-recorded observations of the apparent motions of the sun, and the apparent antics of the moon, along the morning and evening horizons. "[I]f the Stonehenge astronomer-priests did succeed in predicting eclipses, they preceded the rest of mankind in doing so by nearly two millenniums."[85]

It was difficult for your author to accept the possibility that the ancients had translated their horizon observations into a theory of what was

Illustration 30-5. Diagram of the limiting directions of sunrise and sunset at the latitude of Stonehenge. Courtesy of Oxford University Press, Oxford, England.

Illustration 30-6. Sunrise at Stonehenge. Courtesy of The Photo Source, New York.

rotating around what until the full import of the following sentence struck me between the eyes: "In Hoyle's suggested use of the Aubrey Holes, the circle of holes represents the ecliptic."[86] Ouch! There *is* some chance they may have understood both "wheels."

Remember Hawkins' Station Stone Rectangle, which he found incorporated by the original builders into Stonehenge I?[87] There is another way to express those alignments to the rising and setting sun during the cycle of the seasons. This other method is shown in **Illustration 30-5**.[88] Is it a coincidence that we again are looking at our Inanna symbol? Is it coincidental that the rays of the sun passing between the standing stones of Stonehenge are seen in the form of our Inanna symbol? See **Illustration 30-6**.[89] What was the original meaning of our Inanna symbol? At Stonehenge, it records the fact that the sun can rise only within the indicated arc to the east, and can set only within the indicated arc to the west, during the entire cycle of the seasons! As with Hawkins' Station Stone Rectangle, "If the observer went further south the two sunrise lines would be closer to the east, and if he went further north, they would open out and be closer to north and south."[90] *If* there is a relationship between our Inanna symbol and the seasonal rising and setting points of the sun along the horizon, might our Inanna symbol have originated at a place on the face of the Earth where the lines of the "X" are positioned in relationship to each other as at Stonehenge?

You will recall that the Sumerian goddess Inanna, who was "Queen of Heaven" thousands of years before Our Lady assumed that throne, was represented in the sky by the Planet Venus, the third brightest object in the sky after the sun and the moon, and was said to have been the daughter of the moon.[91] Inanna, Queen of Heaven, was a cosmic figure, as was the Hebrew Adam,[92] because we are told that she was:

"'As tall as heaven,
As wide as earth.'"[93]

Suppose our Inanna symbol *also* describes the seasonal swings of the moon's risings and settings along the eastern and western horizons at Stonehenge. What, then, would you say? See **Illustration 30-7**.[94] Notice how each of the major and minor standstill lines limiting the directions of the rising and setting moon during the cycle of the year, straddles the lines limiting the directions for the rising and setting of the sun during the same cycle!

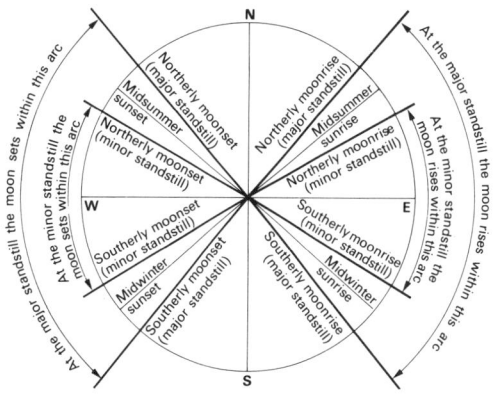

Illustration 30-7. Diagram of the limiting directions of moonrise and moonset at the latitude of Stonehenge. Courtesy of Oxford University Press, Oxford, England.

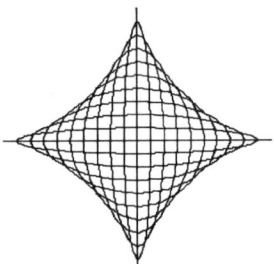

Illustration 30-8. The concave-sided tetragon as an envelope of ellipses. Courtesy of Dover Publications, Inc., New York.

The Inanna symbol, either by coincidence or by intent, is a precise scientific drawing, which records the limits of the seasonal swings of the sun and the moon along the horizon during the cycle of a year! Good science is a powerful ingredient for magic and mythmaking! Is this why Inanna's symbol appears in Loughcrew Passage Grave in Ireland? We have been digging hard for many pages. Have we struck the "mother lode?" Or have we done no more than mire up in the filth of ages? Of what *practical* value would be our Inanna Symbol to the builders of Stonehenge? John Edwin Wood gives us an answer we have heard before: it would "give all the sightlines needed for an eight-month calendar."[95] Did the Stonehenge astronomers also use the eight year Venus count in the manner of the Maya? Your author does not know.

Consider the findings of the archaeo-astronomers that some of the "stone circles" of the British Isles are not *circles* at all; rather, that they are ellipses,[96] or "Type A" or "Type B" flattened circles,[97] or "Type I" or "Type II" egg-shapes.[98] Is this the source of the cosmic eggs we encountered in mythology? All of these egg-like figures can be set down on the ground without knowledge of formal geometry[99] and with surprising ease, using nothing but wooden pegs hammered into the ground and lengths of rope.[100] "In summary, the skill and knowledge needed to draw the various shapes is not very great. It pales beside the engineering ability demanded of the builders of the megalithic tombs or Silbury Hill."[101]

Why did they draw these "eggs" on the ground? Were they seeking to avoid the irrationality of π in the formula for the circumference of a circle, that is, to make π come out even?[102] Is this what the author of the story of the Temple of Solomon was attempting? Was he trying to produce a circular "sea" with an even-numbered diameter *and* an even-numbered circumference?[103] Could the megalith-build-

ers have had another objective in mind? Could they have been seeking to describe the flight path of the Earth and the other planets around the sun? Before Kepler arrived at his theory that planets travel in elliptical orbits around the sun, he gave consideration to a theory that the flight path of planets around the sun was an egg-shaped oval, "broader at the aphelion and more pointed at the perihelion."[104] Could Stone Age astronomers have arrived at this conclusion thousands of years before Kepler? These questions bring us to what is perhaps the most fascinating geometrical form set forth on the Holy Grail — our old friend, the concave-sided tetragon. What was his role in the *real* world of Grail-based astronomy?

The real-world name of our old friend, the concave-sided tetragon, is "hypocycloid" or, more specifically, "asteroid."[105] A hypocycloid is a curve generated by a mark on the circumference of a circle which rolls on the inside of the circumference of a fixed circle. There is a cusp at every point where the mark touches the fixed circle. A four-cusped hypocycloid is known as an asteroid.[106] The mathematically-inclined will appreciate the relationships that necessarily exist between a fixed circle and its inscribed asteroid.[107] All others, we can be assured, could not possibly care less.

The big question, however, is not the correct name for our old friend, the concave-sided tetragon, but what he is capable of doing when put where we found him on our Babylonian schoolboy's tablet. An asteroid (a four-cusped hypocycloid) can serve

Figure 468

Figure 469

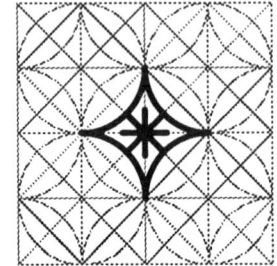

Figure 470

the function of an "envelope of ellipses." See **Illustration 30-8.**[108] Let us recall the various elements of the "sandwich of suppositions" that we already have put together. Suppose that the four circles surrounding the central circle on the Holy Grail represent the four solstitial colures, four great circles in the sky, each centered by one of the four Guardian Stars, which are located on or near the Ecliptic. **Figure 468.** Suppose that the central circle on the Holy Grail is centered by the ancient pre-Sumerian symbol for "star," "god," or "Heaven," and is surrounded by four ancient pre-Sumerian symbols for our planet, Earth, thereby indicating the four positions of the Earth along the Ecliptic at the Solstices and Equinoxes. **Figure 469.** Notice, next, that a concave-sided tetragon (a four-cusped hypocycloid or an asteroid) surrounds the central star symbol. **Figure 470.** Most recently, we have learned that a four-cusped hypocycloid or asteroid can perform the function of an envelope of ellipses. According to one of Kepler's theorems, the planets travel around the sun at variable velocities along flight-paths resembling ellipses.[109]

Does this mean that the Holy Grail could have been used by the ancients as a line-drawing of our solar system?

Did the ancients *actually* use the Holy Grail as a depiction of our solar system, as well as a depiction of Earth's rotation around the polestar? Suppose that an archaeologist has unearthed a flint chip from a pit containing a human burial. He determines from the skeletal remains that the deceased was a woman. What was the function of the flint chip buried with her? The archaeologist quickly determines that the chip is too small to be an axehead, and is not shaped properly to be a spearhead or arrowhead. Having been buried with a woman, it probably was a tool associated with work that her relatives thought she might be required to perform where she was going after her death. Women of her era dressed animal hides brought home by their hunter-husbands. The archaeologist determines the flint chip is sized and sharpened correctly for use as a hide-scraper. Ergo, the archaeologist gives the chip a number and writes opposite that number on the next page of his record book: "Hide-scraper found at [exact location horizontally and vertically on the dig-site]."

You get the point. The archaeologist does not *know* that the flint chip is anything other than a flint chip! He *speculates* that it was used as a hide-scraper because of *where it was found* and *what could be done with it.* Hawkins used this method to "decode"

Stonehenge. We have adopted the same method for our speculations. A concave-sided tetragon, alias four-cusped hypocycloid, alias asteroid, can be used as an envelope of ellipses, and we found one surrounding the ancient pre-Sumerian sun symbol signifying "star," "god," or "Heaven." According to Kepler's principles of astronomy, the planets travel around the sun in ellipses. If the archaeologist may write "hide-scraper" in his notebook, and Hawkins may write "Stone Age computer" in his, why are we less entitled to write "line drawing of solar system" in ours? Because we are rank amateurs, who are not entitled to have opinions about such matters? I cannot help but remind myself of a question that a well-respected scientist asked about an amateur who was dabbling in the scientist's field of expertise: "What can Thomas Edison possibly know about electricity?"

Yes, we cannot prove it. Why do we lack evidence? Because the Christian church burned the ancient astronomy books and slaughtered the ancient astronomers? Why did the Church seek to erase all knowledge of ancient astronomy? Because a person who discovers the fundamental precepts of ancient astronomy discovers also the very origins of the Christ story? Because the Church has something to hide, and this is the closet in which it is hidden? Because we are supposed to obey the dictates of our religious leaders rather than asking questions like these? Did the Holy Creator give us minds with which to think and then expect us not to use them? Did He *really* ordain a few human beings to tell everyone else what they must believe if they wish to avoid their deaths at the hands of the holy executioner, the holy army, or the holy mob?

Those of you who have been reading the notes after each chapter of this book know something that other readers have missed. Read note 43 of Chapter 20, where we quote from the writings of Meister Eckhart, a Roman Catholic priest, *circa* 1260-1239, about his religious beliefs centered on "heaven's revolution." Have some members of the clergy known all along not only the truth of heliocentricity, but the reason why the Church sought to obliterate heliocentricity from the minds of true believers? Note that although Meister Eckhart wrote about Heaven's being in motion, much as we speak of the sun's coming up in the morning, his theology revolved around the concept of the Cosmic Center. Can he have known, and believed in, that heretical cosmology, and not known its origins in the equally heretical mathematical astronomy of heliocentricity? Can he have failed to understand why, in the minds of true believers, the Church had stopped the Earth from spinning?

How and when did the priests get the power of life and death over the common herd of humanity? The *how* is easy to answer. They got the power by creating the illusion in the minds of the common folk that they knew how to placate, if not to please, the Holy Creator, and thereby how to keep the cycle of the seasons and of nature working so as to produce abundant drinking water and foodstuffs and a climate which was survivable if not always pleasant. They kept their jobs by creating and perpetuating further illusions in the minds of true believers, and by wholesale genocide committed on non-believers. When this job specialization began is difficult to say. Archaeologists speculate that a priesthood had arisen by the time the Stone Age megalith-builders erected their enormous structures on Crete at about 3500 B.C.[110] Human skeletal remains found in association with these presumed-to-be "temples" are wanting in evidence of strong muscle-to-bone connectors, indicating that they could not have been the skeletal remains of workmen who had the physical strength to erect structures using large stones; indicating, to the contrary, that *some* people labored while *others* enjoyed the fruits of that labor and worked with their minds, if at all.[111]

Why do present-day religious leaders still wield the power of life and death over so many thousands of people? President Marcos was preparing to attack Mrs. Aquino's rebels with tanks when thousands of Filipinos lay down in the streets, thereby blocking all routes by which his tanks could reach her soldiers. Those brave Filipinos, not Mrs. Aquino, toppled the Marcos government. Terence MacSwiney, Mohandas Gandhi, and Martin Luther King, Jr., were correct, you know! At times, the common folk must stand up (or lie down) peacefully for the sake of human rights!

Why did ancient priests seek power over the common folk? To live a comfortable life without labor? Because they had the ability to see "revelations" on the Holy Grail which they interpreted as messages from the gods? Because they interpreted natural phenomena as proof that the gods favored them over the rest of humankind? In short, were they callous power-grabbers, who were perfectly aware of what they were doing, or had they managed to fool themselves as well as the common folk?

We have tangible proof that priests of religions may have fooled themselves as well as their true believers. "In the early morning, when the sun is still low and casts… [a person's] long shadow on the dewy grass… [that person *alone* can] perceive a remarkable aureole of light, uncoloured, lying near and above the shadow of… [his or her] head…."[112] The phenomenon is called the "Heiligenschein."[113] "When Benvenuto Cellini, the famous Italian artist of the sixteenth century, noticed it, he thought that the shimmer of light was a sign of his own genius!"[114] A person might interpret another natural light-phenomenon as evidence of his special favor. "If we happen to be on the top of a hill when the sun is low we can sometimes see our own shadow outlined against a layer of mist, in which case the head of the shadow will be surrounded by a glory having the same vivid colours as those shown by coronae around the sun and moon. On one occasion a fivefold glory of this kind was observed. Note, however, that although everyone sees his own shadow and also the shadows of those around him if they are near enough to him and if the mist is far enough away, the glory can be seen by each one around his own head only."[115] The phenomenon is called "The Spectre of the Brocken" because it often occurs on a high peak by that name in Germany.[116] Can you imagine a Bud Abbot and Lou Costello comedy act about the Spectre of the Brocken? Bud insists that he is the "chosen one" and Lou is not, while Lou insists that he, not Bud, wears the Halo of Glory! Amusing when done as comedy. Not so amusing when done by power-mongers who already are impressed with their own greatness!

Minnert states the problem succinctly: "Whenever we are unable to find the cause of any natural phenomenon, it is our own ignorance which is to blame!"[117] Put another way, one person's science is another's religion. Evidently, things have been that way for a long time! The only distinction, it would seem, is that the *truly great* among us find in such phenomena no special favor for themselves. "'I looked at the fine centrifugal spokes around the shape of my head in the sunlit water…. Diverge, fine spokes of light from the shape of my head, or anyone's head, in the sunlit water!' WALT WHITMAN, 'Crossing Brooklyn Ferry' (*Leaves of Grass*)."[118]

"In a few very rare cases most remarkable mirages have been seen by quite reliable observers, who describe them as landscapes with towns and towers and parapets, rising above the horizon, transforming, crumbling, fairy-like scenes, producing a deep sense of happiness and an endless longing…."[119] Castles in the air, or Heavenly Jerusalem, may have been less a figment of the

unaided imagination of mythmakers than we might have supposed! Rainbows, dewbows, haloes, light pillars, coronae, aureoles, glory rings, etc., as well as the color spectrum thrown by light-weight oil floating on water, are natural phenomena which no longer impress most of us with the feeling that we have been visited, spoken to, or specially favored by the Creator.[120]

"On July 14, 1865, the alpinist Whymper and his companions were the first to reach the top of the Matterhorn.... Toward the evening Whymper saw an awe-inspiring circle of light with three crosses in the sky...."[121] Three crosses in the sky? *If* humanity is victimized by our religious leaders, is this the fault of the shepherds? Or the fault of the sheep?

Shall we conclude with the thought that the priests took labor from the people but gave nothing in return? That would be unwarranted. Some priest somewhere apparently looked at the line-forms on the Holy Grail and had the revelation that the gods expected human beings to sacrifice each other to keep the sun on its appointed course. This was an enormous step backward. The Bible tells us that YHWH had told the Israelites to attack the Moabites,[122] but when the Moabites' leader sacrificed his first-born son on the walls of the Moabite city, the Israelites immediately ceased battle and headed home![123] Considering the fact that the Israelites were about as far from being cowards as anyone you could find, might we be led to the conclusion that the Israelites were more afraid of this form of Moabite magic than they were afraid of the wrath of YHWH? Abraham was a "good" Israelite in the sense that he was prepared to sacrifice his first-born son, Isaac, according to the ancient custom, but the Bible tells us that YHWH provided a lamb as surrogate.[124] Did some priest-reformer consult with the line-forms on the Holy Grail and receive a revelation that dumb animals should be substituted for human infants? Whatever the source or reason, the abolition of infant sacrifice certainly was a step in the right direction. Most people did not stop infant sacrifice as early as did the Israelites, and it still was being practiced quite generally at the time of the Christ story. However, after God so loved the world that He gave His only begotten Son in sacrifice to all of humanity, to save us from ourselves, and from each other, and from all else, tribesmen probably were not as willing to give up their children as sacrifices for the supposed well-being of the tribe. It would appear that Christian priests found a convincing justification for ending infant sacrifice!

Did priests do anything else for us? Our ancestors, quite generally, were of the opinion that, in the words of Pliny, human flesh was "most wholesome meat."[125] Even the "civilized" Romans, whose laws had abolished such practices, continued, in the words of Pliny, to "lay for the marrow-bones, and the very braine also of young infants, and... to find some good meat and medicine therein."[126] But how could such pagan practices be as effective to renew youth and to maintain health as the weekly consumption of the *actual* flesh and blood of the Son of God? The Christian priests put an end to cannibalism! The Roman civil authorities and army merely had driven the practice underground. The list could go on. The priests took our labor. If they did not give us civilization, they gave us the next-best thing to it. They continue to preach fables, but they *do* still earn their keep. If they were to get completely honest with us for the first time in almost two thousand years, the Age of Aquarius might become the Golden Age of humanity!

Shall humankind wait for our religious shepherds to become completely honest with us about religion? Instead, shall we sheep jump from pen to pen, in search of the perfect shepherd? Or shall we vault *all* of the fences erected by our shepherds to divide us into separate flocks, and run as one mixed herd toward freedom on the holy mountains? Shall we there shed our wool, sprout wings, and soar like eagles?

What should religion be during the next millennium? A system of mind control or thought control? If so, then should Christian fundamentalists draw up a "plan of attack,"[127] and organize "Holy Ghost swat teams on every campus,"[128] giving their Christian soldiers or thought police standing orders to seek out non-Christians in their schools and colleges while insisting that "non-Christians are not allowed to seek out anyone?"[129] If so, should Islamic, Hebrew, and Hindu fundamentalists do the same thing? And what should happen when the groups meet, face to face? Should they start a "rumble" for Christ, Allah, YHWH, and Siva, as their ancestors and cousins often have done in Belfast, Beirut, Bombay and elsewhere? Holy-war mentality mandates that one religion shall prevail over *all* other religions either by friendly persuasion or force of arms!

Or shall we listen, instead, to Mother Theresa, who believes that God and compassion are one and the same, and to the Dalai Lama, who insists that the essence of all religions is love, compassion, and tolerance?[130]

Notes
CHAPTER THIRTY
The Wheel in the Middle of the Wheel

1. P.L. Brown 221.

2. Fox 15.

3. Service & Bradbery 14, 18-19, 113-142.

4. Service & Bradbery 19.

5. Service & Bradbery 129-130, 132-134.

6. Service & Bradbery 108. These stone circles may have been constructed as early as 2500 B.C. Service & Bradbery 108.

7. Service & Bradbery 93, 100-101.

8. Service & Bradbery 100. The Tarxien statue has been dated to a period before 2500 B.C. Service & Bradbery 100.

9. P.L. Brown Fig. 28.

10. Minnaert 104-105.

11. P.L. Brown Fig. 28. Joseph Campbell suggested for the "Venus of Laussel" a period of 20,000 to 18,000 B.C. 1 Campbell HAOWM 47,66. He also suggested a possible connection between our cosmic master of the animals and the "dancing shaman" at the center of the animal illustrations in the "sanctuary" of the Cave of Les Trois Freres. 1 Campbell HAOWM 73-79. Does a connection exist between Cundrie La Sorciere, of Grail tale fame, and the painting in the Cave of Les Trois Freres that popularly is known as "the sorcerer"? Please note that Cundrie of the Grail tales and the "sorcerer" of Les Trois Freres are composites of many animals' parts! Just how far back does our Grail-related solar-lunar-astral symbolism go? In Christianity, Jesus Christ assumed the role of the cosmic herdsman. Does totemism, as well as shamanism, exist to this day in Christianity? The Ainu of Hokkaido believe that a bear dies willingly and gratefully during painful sacrificial rites because the bear's spirit thereby is released from the bear's flesh to return to the spirit world. The Ainu honor and remember the sacrificed bear by consuming its flesh during a sacramental meal hosted by the bear's pelt. Our Celtic ancestors engaged in bear-related religious practices in Bern ("Bear City"), Switzerland, as late as 200 A.D., and the English banned "sport" with bears by act of Parliament in 1835. The same Parliament banned human sacrifice in India. The Classical Greeks sacrificed little girls known as "bears," and the Bible (2 Kings 2.23-25) says that some children who were not sufficiently respectful of the Prophet Elijah, of heavenly whirlwind and cosmic chariot fame, were mauled by bears. 2 Campbell HAOWM 152-155. Us-uns versus them-uns? Our ways are sacred; theirs are blasphemy? How much progress have we made during the last 20,000 years? Some, apparently. During Mass or Communion, bread it is and bread it remains! Osiris-Jesus saved us from anthropophagy!

12. Service & Bradbery 93.

13. Lorayne & Lucas 83-93. The authors are aware that memory systems were used by the ancients. Lorayne & Lucas 1.

14. Lorayne & Lucas 83-93.

15. Service & Bradbery 24-25.

16. Service & Bradbery 24.

17. Service & Bradbery 24.

18. Service & Bradbery 24.

19. J.E. Wood 99.

20. Service & Bradbery 21-22, 234.

21. Hawkins 28-29.

22. Talbott 232. The pattern of lines of the Holy Grail is the predominant feature of many of the sand drawings of Vanuatu. "Sand Drawings of Vanuatu," by Phillip Nissen, *Mathematics in a Multicultural Society* (1988), pages 34-39, published by The Mathematical Association, 259 London Road, Leicester LE2 3BE, England. A. B. Deacon, an anthropologist, was told by the natives of South Malekula, Vanuatu, formerly the New Hebrides Islands, stories about their culture-heroes, the *Ambat*.

The islanders said the *Ambat* were white men with narrow noses who were not cannibals. Deacon also mentions stories told on other islands about Tangaroa, who reputedly had sandy hair, and whose home was in the sky. Deacon alludes to the Maori tradition of a people of white complexion who lived on the sea and worked only at night. The islanders of Vanuatu with whom Deacon conversed apparently were of the opinion that our now-familiar pattern of lines was brought to their shores by white-skinned seafarers. "Geometrical Drawings From Malekula And Other Islands Of The New Hebrides," by A. Bernard Deacon, *The Journal of the Royal Anthropological Institute* (1934), Vol. 64, pages 129-176. Grail-related research has only begun!

23. Fanning 53; H. Brown 1-3; J.E. Wood 57.

24. Fanning 53; H. Brown 4-5; J.E. Wood 57.

25. H. Brown 5; J.E. Wood 58.

26. Fanning 59-62.

27. H. Brown 5.

28. Fanning 60.

29. Fanning 59.

30. Fanning 59-62; H. Brown 4; J.E. Wood 58-59.

31. J.E. Wood 58-63.

32. Fanning 61.

33. Schaaf 234-235; Fanning 61.

34. Dreyer 137-138.

35. Fanning 88-89; Dreyer 390.

36. Washburn 120.

37. Washburn 120.

38. Fanning 62-63.

39. Fanning 153; Jastrow 5; Schaaf 241-243.

40. Service & Bradbery 25.

41. Fanning 67.

42. P.L. Brown 111, 124, 127.

43. Hawkins 183; J.E. Wood 13; P.L. Brown 110-111.

44. P.L. Brown 11.

45. Jastrow 123.

46. Jastrow 127. See also J.E. Wood 14-15.

47. Jastrow 123,127.

48. Hawkins 6.

49. Hawkins 14.

50. Hawkins 15.

51. Hawkins 129-130. See also Hawkins 174.

52. Hawkins 130, footnote.

53. Hawkins 188; J.E. Wood 74-78; P.L. Brown 112-127.

54. Hawkins 1-27.

55. Hawkins, Forward.

56. Hawkins 169.

57. Hawkins vii.

58. Hawkins vii.

59. Hawkins vii. Your author has no intention of allowing himself to become embroiled in a dispute with learned mathematicians about whether or not Hawkins correctly used probability theory to reach these conclusions. Your author's "sandbox theory" of probability, or the hillbilly "frog theory" of probability, is sufficient for our purposes. A cupful of sand is not a children's sandbox. On the other hand, several buckets' full of sand, placed into a wooden box that has been surrounded by a wooden bench and topped by a brightly-colored awning, and into which have been placed a plastic shovel, rake, bucket, and assorted sand molds is, in all probability, a children's sandbox. Moreover, something that looks like a frog, smells like a frog, croaks like a frog, hops like a frog, catches insects like a frog, swims like a frog, and produces eggs that become tadpoles that become frogs is, in all probability, a frog! Whether expressed in rigorous mathematics or in folksy parable, the probability that your author has found the Holy Grail and, with it, the origins of Christianity, is sufficient to convert a single one dollar bill into megabucks in a few minutes of play at any licensed casino! I challenge mathematicians to dispute the verity of my last sentence while avoiding quibbles over the most rigorous mathematical theorem to be employed for their calcula-

tions! Most people would accept such a high degree of probability as near-certainty were it not for the impact of such acceptance upon their most cherished religious beliefs!

60. Hawkins 172. See also Hawkins 135-136. Sir Fred Hoyle puts it thusly: "No documentary evidence about the distant past could be so strong. Documents are frequently wrong, sometimes because of inadvertent errors, sometimes by design. For Stonehenge, on the other hand, it is implausible to argue that a people ignorant of astronomy chose positions for the stones that happened by chance to display great astronomical subtlety." Hoyle 94.

61. J.E. Wood 17-18.

62. J.E. Wood 14.

63. Hawkins 39.

64. Newham 10.

65. Pitkin Guide 4.

66. McMann 12; P.L. Brown 169-173.

67. J.E. Wood 2, 4-7; P.L. Brown 169-173.

68. Hawkins 64-74.

69. Hawkins 64.

70. Hawkins 43.

71. Hawkins 40.

72. Hawkins 41.

73. Hawkins 41. See also J.E. Wood 101.

74. Hawkins 41.

75. Hawkins 134.

76. Hawkins 190.

77. Hawkins 134-136.

78. Hawkins 21-22, 169; P.L. Brown 7, 53-79.

79. J.E. Wood. 13. See also P.L. Brown 112.

80. P.L. Brown 38.

81. J.E. Wood 74.

82. P.L. Brown 109-110.

83. J.E. Wood 74.

84. J.E. Wood 74-78. See also P.L. Brown 118-123, 125-127.

85. P.L. Brown 109.

86. J.E. Wood 75. See also P.L. Brown 119. Hoyle 105, 121.

87. Hawkins 41.

88. J.E. Wood 9, Fig. 1.2.

89. The Heavens 12.

90. J.E. Wood 9.

91. Wolkstein xvi.

92. Graves & Patai 61.

93. Wolkstein 56.

94. J.E. Wood 10, Fig. 1.3.

95. J.E. Wood 11.

96. J.E. Wood 40.

97. J.E. Wood 41, 42.

98. J.E. Wood 44, 46.

99. J.E. Wood 42.

100. J.E. Wood 43, 48.

101. J.E. Wood 48.

102. J.E. Wood 49-50.

103. 1 Kings 7.23; 2 Chron. 4.2.

104. Dreyer 389. Where did Kepler get the idea that the Earth's path around the sun might be egg-shaped? His mother apparently was learned in ancient science, for which the Church burned her as a witch! See note 18 of Chapter Ten. You will recall that the Church considered the mathematical science of the ancients to be Christian heresy!

105. Heafford 104.

106. Heafford 104. Is this two-circle geometric method for the generation of a concave-sided tetragon, alias "hypocycloid," alias "asteroid," another possible meaning of Ezekiel's wheel within a wheel? Not if the familiar King James translation of Ezekiel 1.16, used in the title of this chapter, is correct! The King James translation of Ezekiel 1.16 says that one wheel is "in the middle of" the other wheel, whereas this method for generating a concave-sided tetragon requires one wheel to

roll inside the rim of the other wheel. The Oxford translation of Ezekiel 1.16 ("inside" rather than "in the middle of") is faithful to the Hebrew word "betoch," which means "inside," "within," or "in the midst of." Relying upon Oxford's correct translation of "betoch," we find ourselves presently unable to exclude the possibility that Ezekiel was referring to this two-wheeled geometric method for the generation of concave-sided tetragons! Is Ezekiel saying that the rotation of the Earth around the Ecliptic (one wheel) as the Earth rotates around itself (the other wheel) can be described on the ground and in the sky by a concave-sided tetragon? If so, Kepler would have agreed!

107. Lawrence 173.

108. Lawrence 38.

109. Dreyer 390.

110. Service & Bradbery 97.

111. Service & Bradbery 97.

112. Minnaert 230.

113. Minnaert 230-234.

114. Minnaert 231.

115. Minnaert 224.

116. Schaaf 43.

117. Minnaert 35.

118. Minnaert 333.

119. Minnaert 52.

120. Minnaert 38, 170, 184, 190, 201, 203, 208, 214, 224; Schaaf 19, 22, 26, 30, 32, 38, 43.

121. Minnaert 202-203.

122. 2 Kings 3.15-26.

123. 2 Kings 3.27.

124. Genesis 22.2-13.

125. Hawkins 17.

126. Hawkins 17.

127. Utne Reader 86.

128. Utne Reader 87.

129. Utne Reader 86.

130. Utne Reader 92-93.

List of Illustrations

and the fruitful earth. Courtesy of the Werner Forman Archive, London.

Bibliography

Ali, Allama Abdullah Yusuf. *The Meaning Of The Illustrious Quran.* Kitab Bhavan, New Delhi, 1978.

Allegro, John. *The Mystery Of The Dead Sea Scrolls Revealed.* Gramercy Publishing Company, New York, 1981.

Allen, Richard Hinckley. *Star Names: Their Lore And Meaning.* Dover Publications, Inc., New York, 1963. [Quotations reproduced by permission of Dover Publications, Inc.]

Angus, S. *The Mystery-Religions: A Study In The Religious Background Of Early Christianity.* Dover Publications, Inc., New York, 1975. [Quotations reproduced by permission of Dover Publications, Inc.]

Aristeas, The Letter Of. See *The Forgotten Books Of Eden.*

Atkinson, R.J.C. *The Prehistoric Temples Of Stonehenge & Avebury.* Pitkin Pictorials Ltd., London, 1980.

Aveling, J.C.H. *The Jesuits.* Dorset Press, New York, 1981.

Baer, Randall N. and Vicki. *Windows Of Light: Using Quartz Crystals As Tools For Self-Transformation.* Harper & Row, Publishers, San Francisco, 1984.

Baigent, Michael; Richard Leigh; and Henry Lincoln. *Holy Blood, Holy Grail.* Dell Publishing Co., Inc., New York, 1983.

Barnstone, Willis (Editor). *The Other Bible.* Harper & Row, Publishers, San Francisco, 1984.

Beckwith, John. *Early Christian And Byzantine Art.* Penguin Books, Ltd., Harmondsworth, Middlesex, England, 1970, 1979.

Beltz, Walter. *God And The Gods: Myths Of The Bible.* Penguin Books, Harmondsworth, Middlesex, England, 1983.

Bible, Interpreter's, The. Abingdon-Cokesbury Press, Nashville, 1952.

Bible, King James Version.

Bible, The New English, With The Apocrypha, Oxford Study Edition. Oxford University Press, Inc., New York, 1976. [Quotations from The New English Bible. Copyright © the Delegates of the Oxford University Press and the Syndics of the Cambridge University Press, 1961, 1970. Reprinted by permission.]

Booth, John Nicholls. *Introducing Unitarian Universalism.* Unitarian Universalist Distribution, Boston, Massachusetts.

Branston, Brian. *The Lost Gods Of England.* Oxford University Press, New York, 1974. [Quotations reproduced by permission of Oxford University Press.]

Brennan, Martin. *The Stars And The Stones.* Thames and Hudson, New York, 1983.

Brooke, Rosalind and Christopher. *Popular Religion In The Middle Ages: Western Europe 1000-1300.* Thames and Hudson Ltd., New York, 1984. [Quotations reproduced by permission of Thames and Hudson, Ltd.]

Brown, Hanbury. *Man And The Stars.* Oxford University Press, Oxford, 1978. [Quotations reproduced by permission of Oxford University Press.]

Brown, Peter Lancaster. *Megaliths and Masterminds.* Robert Hale Limited, London, 1979. [Quotations reproduced by permission of Robert Hale Limited and Peter Lancaster Brown.]

Bryant, Nigel. (Translator.) *The High Book Of The Grail: A Translation Of The Thirteenth Century Romance of Perlesvaus.* Rowman and Littlefield, Totowa, New Jersey, 1978. [Quotations reproduced by permission of Boydell & Brewer Ltd., Woodbridge, Suffolk, England.]

Budge, E.A. Wallis, Sir. *Amulets And Superstitions.* Dover Publications, Inc., New York, 1978. [Quotations reproduced by permission of Dover Publications, Inc.]

Budge, E.A. Wallis, Sir. *Egyptian Magic.* Dover Publications, Inc., New York, 1971. [Quotations reproduced by permission of Dover Publications, Inc.]

Budge, E.A. Wallis, Sir. *Osiris & The Egyptian Resurrection.* Dover Publications, Inc., New York, 1973. [Quotations reproduced by permission of Dover Publications.]

Burl, Aubrey. *Prehistoric Astronomy And Ritual.* Shire Publications Ltd., Aylesbury, England, 1983. [Quotations reproduced by permission of Shire Publications Ltd.]

Burman, Edward. *The Templars: Knights Of God.* The Aquarian Press, Wellingborough, Northamptonshire, 1986.

Campbell, F.W. Groves. *Apollonius Of Tyana: A Study Of His Life And Times.* Argonaut, Inc., Publishers, Chicago, Illinois, 1968.

Campbell, Joseph. *Historical Atlas Of World Mythology,* Harper & Row, Publishers, New York, 1988.

Campbell, Joseph. *The Hero With A Thousand Faces.* Princeton University Press, Princeton, 1973.

Cavendish, Richard. *An Illustrated Encyclopedia Of Mythology.* Orbis Publishing Limited, London, 1980. [Quotations reproduced by permission of Macdonald & Co (Publishers) Ltd., London.]

Cerny, Jaroslav. *Ancient Egyptian Religion.* Greenwood Press, Publishers, Westport, Connecticut, 1979. [Quotations reproduced by permission of Century Hutchinson Publishing Group Limited, London.]

Chadwick, Henry. *The Early Church.* Dorset Press, New York, 1986.

Chadwick, Nora. *The Celts.* Pelican Books, New York, 1982. [Copyright © the Estate of Nora Chadwick, 1970. Quotations reproduced by permission of Penguin Books Ltd., London.]

Charlesworth, James H. (Editor.) *The Old Testament Pseudepigrapha,* Doubleday & Company, Inc., Garden City, 1985.

Childe, V. Gordon. *New Light On The Most Ancient East: The Oriental Prelude To European Prehistory.* W.W. Norton & Company, Inc., New York, 1953.

Chretien de Troyes. *Perceval, Or The Story Of The Grail.* Translated by Cline, Ruth Harwood. The University of Georgia Press, Athens, Georgia, 1985. [Quotations reproduced by permission of The University of Georgia Press and Ruth Harwood Cline.]

Chretien de Troyes. *Yvain, Or The Knight With The Lion.* Translated by Cline, Ruth Harwood. The University of Georgia Press, Athens, Georgia, 1984. [Quotations reproduced by permission of the University of Georgia Press and Ruth Harwood Cline.]

Cirker, Blanche. *The Book of Kells: Selected Plates In Full Color.* Dover Publications, Inc., New York, 1982.

Cirlot, J.E. *A Dictionary Of Symbols.* Second Edition. Philosophical Library, Inc., New York, 1983.

Cook, Theodore Andrea. *The Curves Of Life.* Dover Publications, Inc., New York, 1979.

Cousins, Frank W. *Sundials: A Simplified Approach By Means Of The Equatorial Dial.* John Baker, London, 1969.

Coxeter, H.S.M. *Regular Polytopes.* Dover Publications, Inc., New York, 1973.

Cross, Tom Peete, and Clark Harris Slover. *Ancient Irish Tales.* Henry Holt and Company, Inc., New York, 1936. [Quotations reproduced by permission of Henry Holt and Company, Inc.]

Crossley-Holland, Kevin. (Translator.) *The Norse Myths.* Andre Deutsch Limited, London, 1980.

Cumont, Franz. *The Mysteries Of Mithra.* Dover Publications, Inc., New York, 1956. [Quotations reproduced by permission of Dover Publications, Inc.]

Cumont, Franz. *The Oriental Religions In Roman Paganism*. Dover Publications, New York, 1956. [Quotations reproduced by permission of Dover Publications, Inc.]

Darrah, John. *The Real Camelot: Paganism And The Arthurian Romances*. Thames and Hudson, Inc., New York, 1981.

Davidson, H.R. Ellis. *Gods And Myths Of The Viking Age*. Bell Publishing Company, New York, 1981. [Copyright © MCMLXIV by H.R. Ellis Davidson. Quotations reproduced by permission of Penguin Books Ltd., London.]

Dobin, Joel C., Rabbi. *The Astrological Secrets Of The Hebrew Sages: To Rule Both Day And Night*. Inner Traditions International, Ltd., New York, 1983. [Quotations reproduced by permission of Inner Traditions International, Ltd., Rochester, Vermont.]

Dreyer, J.L.E. *A History Of Astronomy From Thales To Kepler*. Dover Publications, Inc., New York, 1953. [Quotations reproduced by permission of Dover Publications, Inc.]

Dupont-Sommer, A. *The Essene Writings From Qumran*. Basil Blackwell, Oxford, 1961.

Earle, Alice Morse. *Sun Dials And Roses Of Yesterday*. The Macmillan Company, London, 1902.

Egyptian Book Of The Dead, The. The University of Chicago Press, Chicago, 1960.

Erbstosser, Martin. *Heretics In The Middle Ages*. Edition Leipzig, German Democratic Republic, 1984.

Erman, Adolf. *Life In Ancient Egypt*. Dover Publications, Inc., New York, 1971.

Eschenbach, Wolfram von. *Parzival*. Translated by Mustard, Helen M., and Charles E. Passage. Alfred A. Knopf, Inc., and Random House, Inc., New York, 1961. [Quotations reproduced by permission of Alfred A. Knopf, Inc., and Random House, Inc.]

Eschenbach, Wolfram von. *Willehalm*. Translated by Gibbs, Marion E., and Sidney M. Johnson. Penguin Books, Harmondsworth, Middlesex, England, 1984. [Copyright © Marion E. Gibbs and Sidney M. Johnson, 1984. Quotations

reproduced by permission of Penguin Books Ltd., London.]

Eusebius. *The History Of The Church*. Translated by Williamson, G.A. Penguin Books Ltd., Harmondsworth, Middlesex, England, 1983. [Copyright © G.A. Williamson, 1965. Quotations reproduced by permission of Penguin Books Ltd., London.]

Evans, H. Meurig. (Editor.) *Y Geiriadur Cymraeg Cyfoes* (The Dictionary of Modern Welsh), Hughes, Llandybie, 1981.

Evans, Sebastian. (Translator.) *The High History Of The Holy Grail*. The Attic Press, Inc., Greenwood, South Carolina, 1969.

Fairservis, Walter A., Jr. *The Roots Of Ancient India*. The Macmillan Company, New York, 1971. [Quotations reprinted with permission of Macmillan Publishing Company. Copyright © 1971 by Walter A. Fairservis, Jr.]

Fanning, A.E. *Planets, Stars And Galaxies: Descriptive Astronomy For Beginners*. Dover Publications, Inc., New York, 1966. [Quotations reproduced by permission of Dover Publications, Inc.]

Farbridge, Maurice H. (Edited by Harry M. Orlinsky.) *Studies In Biblical And Semitic Symbolism*. KTAV Publishing House, Inc., New York, 1970.

Forgotten Books Of Eden, The. Bell Publishing Company, New York, 1981.

Fox, Hugh. *Gods Of The Cataclysm: A Revolutionary Investigation Of The Cultures Of The World Before And After The Great Flood*. Dorset Press, New York, 1981.

Fox, Matthew. (Translator.) *Breakthrough: Meister Eckhart's Creation Spirituality in New Translation*. Doubleday, New York, 1980.

Fox, Matthew. (Editor.) (Herein referenced "1 Fox.") *Illuminations of Hildegard of Bingen*. Bear & Company, Inc., Santa Fe, 1985.

Fox, Matthew. (Editor.) (Herein referenced "2 Fox.") *Hildegard of Bingen's Book of Divine Works*. Bear & Company, Inc., Santa Fe, 1987.

Frankfort, Henri; H.A. Frankfort; John A. Wilson; Thorkild Jacobsen; and William A. Irwin. *The Intellectual Adventure Of Ancient Man.* The University of Chicago Press, Chicago, 1977. [Quotations reproduced by permission of The University of Chicago Press.]

Frazer, James G. *The Golden Bough: The Roots Of Religion And Folklore.* Avenel Books, New York, 1981.

Gantz, Jeffrey. (Translator.) *Early Irish Myths And Sagas.* Dorset Press, New York, 1985. [Copyright © Jeffrey Gantz, 1981. Quotations reproduced by permission of Penguin Books Ltd.]

Gantz, Jeffrey. (Translator.) *The Mabinogion.* Dorset Press, New York, 1985. [Copyright © Jeffrey Gantz, 1976. Quotations reproduced by permission of Penguin Books Ltd.]

Ghyka, Matila. *The Geometry Of Art And Life.* Dover Publications, Inc., New York, 1977. [Quotations reproduced by permission of Dover Publications, Inc.]

Gibbs, Sharon L. *Greek And Roman Sundials.* Yale University Press, New Haven, 1976.

Gillings, Richard J. *Mathematics In The Time Of The Pharaohs.* Dover Publications, Inc., New York, 1982. [Quotations reproduced by permission of Dover Publications, Inc.]

Gimbutas, Marija. *The Language Of The Goddess.* Harper & Row, Publishers, San Francisco, 1989.

Gimpel, Jean. *The Cathedral Builders.* Grove Press, Inc., New York, 1983. [Quotations reproduced by permission of Michael Russell (Publishing) Ltd., Wilton, Salisbury, England.]

Ginsburg, Christian D. *The Essenes: Their History And Doctrines; and The Kabbalah: Its Doctrines, Development And Literature.* Routledge & Kegan Paul Ltd., London, 1956.

Ginzberg, Louis. *The Legends Of The Jews.* The Jewish Publication Society of America, Philadelphia, 1913.

Godwin, Joscelyn. *Mystery Religions In The Ancient World.* Harper & Row, Publishers, Inc., San Francisco, 1981. [Copyright © 1981 Thames and Hudson Ltd., London. Quotations reproduced by permission of Harper & Row, Publishers, Inc.]

Graham, Lloyd M. *Deceptions And Myths Of The Bible.* Bell Publishing Company, New York, 1979. [Quotations reproduced by permission of Lyle Stuart, Inc., Secaucus, New Jersey.]

Graves, Robert, and Raphael Patai. *Hebrew Myths: The Book Of Genesis.* Greenwich House, New York, 1983.

Great Books Of The Western World. Vol.35. Encyclopaedia Britannica, Inc., Chicago, 1952. [Quotations reprinted by permission from Encyclopaedia Britannica, Inc.]

Gregg, Robert C., and Dennis E. Groh. *Early Arianism – A View Of Salvation.* Fortress Press, Philadelphia, 1981.

Guest, Charlotte, Lady. (Translator.) *The Mabinogion.* John Jones Cardiff Ltd., Cardiff, 1977.

Hadingham, Evan. *Early Man And The Cosmos.* William Heinemann Ltd., London, 1983. [Quotations reproduced by permission from William Heinemann Ltd.]

Hadingham, Evan. *Secrets Of The Ice Age: The World Of The Cave Artists.* Walker and Company, New York, 1979.

Hall, A. Rupert. *From Galileo To Newton.* Dover Publications, Inc., New York, 1981. [Quotations reproduced by permission of Dover Publications, Inc.]

Hapgood, Charles H. *Maps Of The Ancient Sea Kings: Evidence Of Advanced Civilization In The Ice Age.* E. P. Dutton, New York, 1979.

Harrelson, Walter. *From Fertility Cult To Worship.* Scholars Press, Missoula, Montana, 1969.

Hawkins, Gerald S., and John B. White. *Stonehenge Decoded.* Doubleday & Company, Inc., Garden City, 1965. [Quotations reproduced by permission of Doubleday & Company, Inc.]

Heafford, Philip. *Fun With Mathematics*. Bell Publishing Company, New York, 1983.

Heath, Thomas, Sir. *A History Of Greek Mathematics*. Dover Publications, Inc., New York, 1981. [Quotations reproduced by permission of Dover Publications, Inc.]

Heath, Thomas, Sir. *Aristarchus Of Samos*. Dover Publications, Inc., New York, 1981. [Quotations reproduced by permission of Dover Publications, Inc.]

Heidel, Alexander. *The Gilgamesh Epic And Old Testament Parallels*. The University of Chicago Press, Chicago, 1963. [Quotations reproduced by permission of The University of Chicago Press.]

Hermas, Book Of The Shepherd Of. See *Lost Books Of The Bible, The*.

Hoagland, Kathleen. *1000 Years Of Irish Poetry: The Gaelic And Anglo-Irish Poets From Pagan Times To The Present*. The Devin-Adair Company, Old Greenwich, Connecticut, 1981.

Hollander, Lee M. (Translator). *The Poetic Edda*, Second Edition, Revised. University of Texas Press, Austin, 1987.

Hoyle, Fred, Sir. *On Stonehenge*. W. H. Freeman and Company, San Francisco, 1977. [Copyright © 1977 by W. H. Freeman and Company. Quotations reproduced by permission of W. H. Freeman and Company.]

Hozeski, Bruce. *Hildegard of Bingen's Scivias*. Bear & Company, Inc., Santa Fe, 1986.

Hughes, David. *The Star Of Bethlehem Mystery*. J.M. Dent & Sons Ltd., London, 1979.

Iamblichus. (Translated by Taylor, Thomas.) *The Life Of Pythagoras*. Inner Traditions International, Ltd., Rochester, Vermont, 1986.

Infancy. See *Lost Books Of The Bible, The*.

Ireland, The Encyclopaedia of. Allen Figgis, Dublin, 1968.

James, John. *Chartres: The Masons Who Built A Legend*. Routledge & Kegan Paul, London, 1985. [Quotations reproduced by permission of Routledge & Kegan Paul.]

Jastrow, Robert. *Until The Sun Dies*. Warner Books, New York, 1980. [Quotations reproduced by permission of Robert Jastrow.]

Jespersen, James, and Jane Fitz-Randolph. *From Sundials To Atomic Clocks: Understanding Time And Frequency*. Dover Publications, Inc., New York, 1977. [Quotations reproduced by permission of Dover Publications, Inc.]

Jones-Wake. See *Lost Books of the Bible, The*.

Jung, C.J. *Mandala Symbolism*. Princeton University Press, Princeton, 1973. [Quotations reproduced by permission of Princeton University Press.]

Kahane, Henry and Renee. *The Krater And The Grail: Hermetic Sources Of The Parzival*. The University of Illinois Press, Urbana, 1965.

Keith, A. Berriedale. Volume VI, Indian. *The Mythology Of All Races*. Cooper Square Publishers, Inc., New York, 1964.

Kramer, Samuel Noah. *The Sumerians: Their History, Culture, and Character*. The University of Chicago Press, Chicago, 1963. [Quotations reproduced by permission of The University of Chicago Press.]

Krupp, E.C. *Echoes Of The Ancient Skies: The Astronomy Of Lost Civilizations*. Harper & Row, Publishers, New York, 1983. [Copyright © 1983 by Edwin C. Krupp. Quotations reprinted by permission of Harper & Row, Publishers, Inc.]

Kunz, George Frederick. *The Curious Lore Of Precious Stones*. Dover Publications, Inc., New York, 1971. [Excerpted materials utilized by permission of Dover Publications, Inc.]

Lambert, W.G. *Babylonian Wisdom Literature*. Clarendon Press, Oxford, 1960. [Quotations reproduced by permission of Oxford University Press.]

Lamy, Lucie. *Egyptian Mysteries: New Light On Ancient Spiritual Knowledge*. The Crossroad Publishing Company, New York, 1981. [Excerpted materials utilized by permission of Thames and Hudson Ltd., London.]

Landels, J.G. *Engineering In The Ancient World.* University of California Press, Berkeley & Los Angeles, 1981.

Langdon, S. *Babylonian Menologies And The Semitic Calendars.* Oxford University Press, Oxford, 1935.

Langdon, S. *The Babylonian Epic Of Creation.* Clarendon Press, Oxford, 1923.

Langdon, Stephen Herbert. Volume V, Semitic. *The Mythology Of All Races.* Cooper Square Publishers, New York, 1964.

Larson, Martin A. *The Essene-Christian Faith: A Study In The Sources Of Western Religion.* Philosophical Library, New York, 1980.

Lavelle, Des. *Skellig: Island Outpost Of Europe.* The O'Brien Press, Dublin, 1981.

Lawlor, Robert. *Sacred Geometry.* The Crossroad Publishing Company, New York, 1982.

Lawrence, J. Dennis. *A Catalog of Special Plane Curves.* Dover Publications, Inc., New York, 1972. [Excerpted materials utilized by permission of Dover Publications, Inc.]

Leyden Papyrus: An Egyptian Magical Book, The. Edited by Griffith, F. Ll., and Herbert Thompson. Dover Publications, Inc., New York, 1974. [Quotations reproduced by permission of Dover Publications, Inc.]

Litany of Re, The. Random House, Inc., New York, 1964.

Lloyd, Seton. *The Archaeology Of Mesopotamia: From The Old Stone Age To The Persian Conquest.* Thames and Hudson Ltd., London, 1984.

Loewe, Michael, and Carmen Blacker. *Divination And Oracles.* George Allen & Unwin, London, 1981.

Lorayne, Harry, and Jerry Lucas. *The Memory Book.* Ballantine Books, New York, 1986.

Lost Books Of The Bible, The. Bell Publishing Company, New York, 1979.

Lubicz. See Schwaller de Lubicz, R.A.

Malone, Dumas; Robert Llewellyn; and Charles Granquist. *Thomas Jefferson's Monticello.* Thomasson-Grant, Inc., Charlottesville, Virginia, 1983. [Quotations reproduced by permission of Thomasson-Grant, Inc.]

Malory, Thomas, Sir. *Le Morte d'Arthur.* (Translated by Baines, Keith.) Bramhall House, New York, 1962.

Malory, Thomas, Sir. *Le Morte d'Arthur.* (Translated by Strachey, Edward, Sir.) Macmillan and Co., Ltd., London, 1898.

Martin, Malachi. *Rich Church, Poor Church.* G.P. Putnam's Sons, New York, 1984.

Mather, Kirtley F. *Science In Search Of God.* Henry Holt and Company, New York, 1928.

Matthews, John. (Editor.) *An Arthurian Reader.* The Aquarian Press, Wellingborough, Northamptonshire, 1988.

Matthews, John. *The Grail: Quest For The Eternal.* The Crossroad Publishing Company, New York, 1981. [Copyright © 1981 Thames and Hudson Ltd., London. Quotations reproduced by permission of Thames and Hudson Ltd., London.]

McMann, Jean. *Riddles Of The Stone Age: Rock Carvings Of Ancient Europe.* Thames and Hudson Ltd., London, 1980. [Copyright © 1980 Thames and Hudson Ltd., London. Quotations reproduced by permission of Thames and Hudson Ltd., London.]

Mercier, Jacques. *Ethiopian Magic Scrolls.* George Braziller, Inc., New York, 1979.

Meyer, Marvin W. (Editor) *The Ancient Mysteries: A Sourcebook.* Harper & Row, New York, 1987.

Minnaert, M. *The Nature Of Light & Color In The Open Air.* Dover Publications, Inc., New York, 1954. [Quotations reproduced by permission of Dover Publications, Inc.]

Moortgat, Anton. *Die Entstehung Der Sumerischen Hochkultur.* J.C. Hinrichs Verlag, Leipzig, 1945.

Morison, Samuel Eliot. *The European Discovery Of America: The Northern Voyages A.D. 500-1600.* Oxford University Press, New York, 1971.

Nag Hammadi Library, The. Harper & Row, Publishers, San Francisco, 1981.

Neugebauer, O. *The Exact Sciences In Antiquity.* Second Edition. Dover Publications, Inc., New York, 1969. [Quotations reproduced by permission of Dover Publications, Inc.]

Newham, C.A. *The Astronomical Significance Of Stonehenge.* Moon Publications, Shirenewton, Gwent, Wales, 1972.

Oates, Joan. *Babylon.* Thames and Hudson Ltd., London, 1979. [Copyright © 1979 Thames and Hudson Ltd., London. Quotations reproduced by permission of Thames and Hudson Ltd., London.]

O'Shea, Tim. *The Skelligs.*

Owen, Gale R. *Rites And Religions Of The Anglo-Saxons.* Dorset Press, New York, 1985. [Quotations reproduced by permission of David & Charles Publishers, Newton Abbot, Devon, England.]

Parker, Derek and Julia. *The Compleat Astrologer.* Greenwich House, New York, 1982.

Parrinder, Geoffrey. *Avatar And Incarnation, A Comparison Of Indian And Christian Beliefs.* Oxford University Press, New York, 1982.

Partner, Peter. *The Murdered Magicians.* The Aquarian Press, Rochester, Vermont, 1987.

Piggott, Stuart. *The Druids.* Thames and Hudson, Inc., New York, 1985.

Platt & Brett. See *Forgotten Books Of Eden, The.*

Powell, T.G.E. *The Celts.* Thames and Hudson Ltd., New York, 1980.

Protevangelion, The. See *Lost Books Of The Bible, The.*

Rees, Alwyn and Brinley. *Celtic Heritage: Ancient Tradition In Ireland And Wales.* Thames and Hudson Ltd., London, 1961. [Copyright © Alwyn and Brinley Rees 1961. Quotations reproduced by permission of Thames and Hudson Ltd., London.]

Reichard, Gladys A. *Navajo Medicine Man Sandpaintings.* Dover Publications, Inc., New York, 1977. [Quotations and other materials reproduced by permission of Dover Publications, Inc.]

Rey, H.A. *The Stars: A New Way To See Them.* Houghton Mifflin Company, Boston, 1976.

Robbins, Rossell Hope. *The Encyclopedia Of Witchcraft & Demonology.* Bonanza Books, New York, 1981. [Quotations reproduced by permission of The Crown Publishing Group, New York.]

Robertson, J.M. *Pagan Christs.* Dorset Press, New York, 1987.

Ronan, Colin. *Lost Discoveries.* Bonanza Books, New York, 1981. [Quotations reproduced by permission of Roxby Press, London.]

Rosenau, Helen. *Vision Of The Temple: The Image Of The Temple Of Jerusalem In Judaism And Christianity.* Oresko Books Ltd., London, 1979.

Rudolph, Kurt. *Gnosis.* Harper & Row, Publishers, San Francisco, 1987.

Runes, Dagobert D. *Dictionary Of Judaism.* Philosophical Library, Inc., New York, 1959.

Saggs, H.W.F. *Everyday Life In Babylonia & Assyria.* G.P. Putnam's Sons, New York, 1965.

Saggs, H.W.F. *The Greatness That Was Babylon.* Hawthorn Books, Inc., Publishers, New York, 1962.

Sahi, Jyoti. *The Child And The Serpent: Reflections On Popular Indian Symbols.* Routledge & Kegan Paul Ltd., London, 1980. [Quotations reproduced by permission of Routledge & Kegan Paul Ltd., London.]

Sandars, N.K. *The Sea Peoples: Warriors Of The Ancient Mediterranean 1250-1150, B.C.* Revised Edition. Thames and Hudson, London, 1985.

Schaaf, Fred. *Wonders Of The Sky: Observing Rainbows, Comets, Eclipses, The Stars, And Other Phenomena.* Dover Publications, Inc., New York, 1983. [Quotations reproduced by permission of Dover Publications, Inc.]

Schwaller de Lubicz, R.A. *Esoterism & Symbol*. Inner Traditions International Ltd., New York, 1985. [Quotations reproduced by permission of Inner Traditions International Ltd., Rochester, Vermont.]

Schwaller de Lubicz, R.A. *Symbol And The Symbolic: Ancient Egypt, Science, And The Evolution Of Consciousness*. Inner Traditions International, New York, 1978. [Quotations reproduced by permission of Inner Traditions International Ltd., Rochester, Vermont.]

Schwaller de Lubicz, R.A. *The Egyptian Miracle: An Introduction To The Wisdom Of The Temple* . Inner Traditions International, Ltd., New York, 1985. [Quotations reproduced by permission of Inner Traditions International Ltd., Rochester, Vermont.]

Schwaller de Lubicz. R.A. *The Temple In Man: Sacred Architecture And The Perfect Man*. Inner Traditions International, New York, 1977. [Quotations reproduced by permission of Inner Traditions International Ltd., Rochester, Vermont.]

Sepher Ha-Razim: The Book Of The Mysteries. (Translated by Morgan, Michael A.) Scholars Press, Chico, California, 1983.

Service, Alastair, and Jean Bradbery. *Megaliths and Their Mysteries*. Macmillan Publishing Co., Inc., New York, 1979. [Quotations reprinted with permission of Macmillan Publishing Company. Copyright © 1979 by Alastair Service.]

Sharkey, John. *Celtic Mysteries: The Ancient Religion*. The Crossroad Publishing Company, New York, 1975.

Smith, Morton. *Jesus The Magician*. Harper & Row, Publishers, San Francisco, 1981. [Copyright © 1978 by Morton Smith. Quotations reproduced by permission of Harper & Row, Publishers.]

Spanuth, Jurgen. *Atlantis Of The North*. Sidgwick & Jackson, London, 1979.

Splendors Of The Past: Lost Cities Of The Ancient World. The National Geographic Society, 1981.

Stafford, Thomas Albert. *Christian Symbolism In The Evangelical Churches*. Abingdon-Cokesbury Press, New York, 1942.

Staniforth, Maxwell. (Translator.) *Early Christian Writings*. Penguin Books Ltd., Harmondsworth, Middlesex, England, 1984. [Copyright © Maxwell Staniforth, 1968. Quotations reproduced by permission of Penguin Books Ltd.]

Talbott, David N. *The Saturn Myth*. Doubleday & Company, Inc., Garden City, 1980. [Quotations reproduced by permission of Doubleday & Company, Inc.]

Tedlock, Dennis. (Translator.) *Popol Vuh*. Simon & Schuster, Inc., New York, 1985.

The Heavens. World Book, Inc., Chicago, 1986.

Tribbe, Frank C. *Portrait Of Jesus? The Illustrated Story Of The Shroud Of Turin*. Stein And Day, Publishers, New York, 1983.

van der Waerden, B.L. *Science Awakening I*. The Scholar's Bookshelf, Princeton, 1988.

Van Treeck, Carl, and Aloysius Croft. *Symbols In The Church*. The Bruce Publishing Co., Milwaukee, 1936.

Vatcher, Faith de M. and Lance. *The Avebury Monuments*. Her Majesty's Stationery Office, London, 1980.

Vermaseren, Maarten J. *Cybele And Attis*. Thames and Hudson, Ltd., London, 1977.

Walker, Benjamin. *Gnosticism*. The Aquarian Press, Wellingborough, Northamptonshire, England, 1983.

Walsh, Jill Paton. *The Island Sunrise*. The Seabury Press, New York, 1976.

Washburn, Mark. *In The Light Of The Sun: From Sunspots To Solar Energy*. Harcourt Brace Jovanovich, New York, 1981. [Quotations reproduced by permission of Harcourt Brace Jovanovich, Inc.]

Waugh, Albert E. *Sundials: Their Theory And Construction*. Dover Publications, Inc., New York, 1973.

Webber, F.R. *Church Symbolism.* J.H. Jansen, Publisher, Cleveland, 1927.

Webster's Third New International Dictionary Unabridged, G. & C. Merriam Company, Springfield, Massachusetts, 1966.

Weingreen, J. *Introduction To The Critical Study Of The Text Of The Hebrew Bible.* Clarendon Press, Oxford, 1982. [Quotations reproduced by permission of Oxford University Press.]

Wheeler, David R. *Journey To The Other Side.* Ace Books, New York, 1977.

Wilmshurst, W.L. *The Meaning Of Masonry.* Bell Publishing Company, New York, 1980.

Wolkstein, Diane, and Samuel Noah Kramer. *Inanna: Queen Of Heaven And Earth: Her Stories And Hymns From Sumer.* Harper & Row, Publishers, New York, 1983. [Copyright © 1983 by Diane Wolkstein and Samuel Noah Kramer. Quotations reproduced by permission of Harper & Row, Publishers, Inc.]

Wood, Elizabeth A. *Crystals And Light: An Introduction To Optical Crystallography.* Second Revised Edition. Dover Publications, Inc., New York, 1977. [Excerpted materials utilized by permission of Dover Publications, Inc.]

Wood, John Edwin. *Sun, Moon And Standing Stones.* Oxford University Press, Oxford, 1980. [Quotations reproduced and excerpted materials utilized by permission of Oxford University Press.]

World Book Encyclopedia, The. World Book, Inc., Chicago, 1983.

Yarwood, Doreen. *The Architecture Of Europe.* Chancellor Press, London, 1974. [Excerpted materials utilized by permission of Bounty Books, London, and Doreen Yarwood.]

Zimmer, Heinrich. (Campbell, Joseph, Editor.) *The King & The Corpse: Tales Of the Soul's Conquest Of Evil.* Princeton University Press, 1973.

Periodicals :

Deacon, A. Bernard. "Geometrical Drawings From Malekula And Other Islands Of The New Hebrides." *The Journal of the Royal Anthropological Institute,* 1934, Vol. 64, pages 129-176.

Hamblin, Dora Jane. "A Unique Approach To Unraveling The Secrets Of The Great Pyramids." *Smithsonian,* April, 1986, pp. 78-93. [Quotations reproduced by permission of Smithsonian Magazine.]

Muller, Kal. "Tanna Awaits The Coming Of John Frum." *National Geographic,* Vol. 145, No. 5, May, 1974, pp. 706-715.

Nissen, Phillip. "Sand Drawings of Vanuatu." *Mathematics in a Multicultural Society,* 1988, pages 34-39, The Mathematical Association, Leicester, England.

Utne Reader, No. 43, Jan./Feb. 1991.

Weltner, Charles Longstreet. "The Heavens Of Babylon – Ezekiel's Vision And The Trisection Problem." *Congressional Record,* Vol. 125, No. 89, June 29, 1979, pages E3384-E3387.

Index

A

Achmardi, Holy Grail on an, 205-206.
Adonis, 145-146.
Africa, 120-123.
Aldebaran. *See* Guardian stars.
Amber. *See* Electricity.
Anat. *See* Queen of Heaven, the, a/k/a Inanna, Is(h)tar, Anat, Cybele, Usas, Venus, Isis, Mary.
Anglo-Saxons. *See* Germanic cosmology.
Antares. *See* Guardian stars.
Apocrypha, 35.
Arabs, mathematics and science from, 293-296.
Archers, the cosmic. *See* Tetramorphs.
Architecture, Holy Grail used in, 286-290, 292-300, 303-306.
Aristeas, Letter of. *See* Letter of Aristeas.
Ark of the Covenant, 55-68.
Aryans, 98-107.
Assyrians. *See* Sumerians, etc.
Astral mythology and theology, 69-70, 81, 104, 110, 130-131, 138, 158-159, 161-162, 163-164, 186, 236-237, 240, 318.
Astronomy, Holy Grail used in, 200-201, 308-314, 317-329, 333-343.
Athelstan, Masonic King of England, 184, 300.
Attis, 146-147.

B

Babylonians. *See* Sumerians, etc.
Baptist, St. John the. *See* Saint John Christians.
Blasphemy *vel non*, 81.
Boaz, the column of. *See* Jachin, column of.
Bread, the cosmic. *See* Sacrifice, the cosmic.
Bridegroom, the cosmic, 129.
Brocken, Spectre of the. *See* Rainbow.
Buddhism, 2, 98-107, 110-118.

C

Calendar, Holy Grail used as, 317-329.
Canon of the Bible. *See* Fathers of the Church.
Cargo cults, 8-9.
Cathars. *See* Docetic (Gnostic) Christianity.

Center, the cosmic, 106, 113, 115-118, 169, 195, 206, 209, 316, 322-329, 330, 344.
Chalice, image of, seen on Holy Grail, 238-239, 247.
Chashmal. *See* Electricity.
Cherub, or Cherubim, 25, 26-27, 58-59, 63-64.
Christ. *See* Christianity.
Christianity, 1-2, 29-33, 35-36, 37-38, 81, 98-107, 110-118, 125-129, 133-141, 145-154, 157-165, 169-186, 191-194, 196-208, 212-250, 258-267, 279-283, 286-290, 292-300, 303-306, 308-314, 317-329, 333-343.
Classify yourself, 1.
Clock, Holy Grail used as, 317-329.
Cloth, Holy Grail on a, 205-206, 210.
Colures, 95.
Corona. *See* Rainbow.
Correspondence theory, 26, 80, 110.
Cosmogony. *See* Cosmology.
Cosmology, 35-38, 95-97, 98-107, 110-118, 169-186, 286-290, 292-300, 303-306, 308-314, 317-329, 330, 333-343.
Crucifixion, 33.
Cybele. *See* Queen of Heaven, the, a/k/a Inanna, Is(h)tar, Anat, Cybele, Usas, Venus, Isis, Mary.

D

Daniel, vision of, 159.
Daystar, the Planet Venus. *See* Queen of Heaven, the, a/k/a Inanna, Is(h)tar, Anat, Cybele, Usas, Venus, Isis, Mary.
Dionysus, 135, 147-148.
Docetic (Gnostic) Christianity, 164-165, 168, 191-194, 212-216, 237, 239-240, 243, 251.
Drugs, used in religious worship, 134-135, 147, 154, 163, 266, 269, 333.

E

Eagle. *See* Tetramorphs.
Egyptian religion, 32, 125-131, 150-154.
El. *See* YHWH, Yahweh, or Jehovah.
Electricity, 12, 22, 132.
Elements, the, 36, 102, 140.

Enlil, 29, 88.
Ethiopia. *See* Africa.
Evangelists. *See* Guardian stars; Tetramorphs.
Ezekiel, visions of, 4-5, 11-22, 25-32, 100.

F

Fathers of the Church, 35-36, 38, 112-113.
Fire, the cosmic, 117, 277, 322-329.
Firmament, the "vault" of Heaven, 15, 20, 310, 312.
Fisher, 53.
Fleur-de-lis, 41.
Flood, the cosmic, 103. *See also* Utnapishtim, story of.
Fomalhaut. *See* Guardian stars.
Freemasonry. *See* Masons.
French Grail quest tales, 258-267.

G

Galileo, 2, 84, 93, 129.
Gate, the cosmic, 37-38, 95, 140.
Germanic cosmology, 169-186.
Gilgamesh. *See* Utnapishtim, story of.
Glories. *See* Rainbow.
God of Moses, 85-86, 93, 329.
Grail. *See* Holy Grail.
Greek gods, 133-141, 145-154.
Guardian stars, 17, 81, 95, 317-318. *See also* Tetramorphs.

H

Haloes, light. *See* Rainbow.
Harrapans. *See* India; Pakistan.
Hermas, Shepherd of. *See* Parable of the tower.
Hildegard of Bingen, Saint, visions on the Holy Grail, 257.
Hinduism, 2, 98-107, 110-118.
Holy Grail, 2, 3, 4-5, 31-32, 191-194, 196-208, 212-250, 258-267, 286-290, 292-300, 303-306, 308-314, 317-329, 333-343.
House of the Forest of Lebanon, 72-75.
Hypothesis, proofs, etc., 1-3, 13, 41-42, 79, 208-209, 345-346.

I

Inanna. *See* Queen of Heaven, the, a/k/a Inanna, Is(h)tar, Anat, Cybele, Usas, Venus, Isis, Mary.
India, 98-107, 110-118.
Indus, River. *See* India; Pakistan.
Interference pattern, 18, 27, 39, 164, 286.
Is(h)tar. *See* Queen of Heaven, the, a/k/a Inanna, Is(h)tar, Anat, Cybele, Usas, Venus, Isis, Mary.
Isis. *See* Queen of Heaven, the, a/k/a Inanna, Is(h)tar, Anat, Cybele, Usas, Venus, Isis, Mary.
Islam, 89, 95, 104, 120-121, 124, 165, 173, 205, 304, 312.
Islam is not affected by Holy Grail mystique, 173.

J

Jachin, column of, 75, 77.
Jefferson, Thomas, 5, 318.
Jehovah. *See* YHWH, Yahweh, or Jehovah.
Jesus. *See* Christianity.
John, the Evangelist. *See* Tetramorphs.
Judaism, 2, 11-22, 25-32, 42-43, 52, 55-68, 71-78, 125-126, 130-131, 154, 318.

K

Katapetasma, 193-195.
KISS, 79.
Koran, the Holy, 97, 173, 245, 310.
Koran, the Holy, does not contain Holy Grail images, 173.

L

Lamps, the cosmic, 63.
Letter of Aristeas, 41-53, 125-126.
Light, the cosmic, 38.
Lion. *See* Tetramorphs.
Loaves and fishes, the cosmic, 60, 161-162.
Luke, the Evangelist. *See* Tetramorphs.

M

Magi, 11-12, 140.
Magic, versus science and religion. *See* Science, versus religion and magic.
Magicians, Holy, Jesus and Moses as, 11-12, 35, 166.

Man. *See* Tetramorphs.

Mandaeans. *See* Saint John Christians.

Manichaeism, 140, 191-192.

Mark, Secret Gospel of, 189.

Mark, the Evangelist. *See* Tetramorphs.

Mary, Our Lady, Mother of Jesus. *See* Queen of Heaven, the, a/k/a Inanna, Is(h)tar, Anat, Cybele, Usas, Venus, Isis, Mary.

Masons, 41-42, 184, 192, 286-290, 292-300, 303-306.

Masses, the religion of, 81, 107, 141, 183-184.

Matthew, the Evangelist. *See* Tetramorphs.

Mayan Codex. *See Popol Vuh*, Mayan Codex, Holy Grail in.

Memory systems, 318, 333-334.

Menorah, 31, 60-63, 154.

Mithraism, 2, 96, 133-141.

Moses, 85-86, 329.

Mountain, the cosmic, 52-53, 100, 116-118, 310-311, 322-329.

Mystery religions, 2, 96-97, 133-141, 145-154, 157-165.

Mythmakers. *See* Storysmiths.

N

Nasoraeans. *See* Saint John Christians.

Navajo sandpainting, Holy Grail used in, 321-322.

Navigational instrument, Holy Grail used as, 317-329.

Noah Story. *See* Utnapishtim, story of.

Numerology, 15, 51-52, 297-300, 305, 318.

O

Orpheus, 148-150.

Osiris. *See* Egyptian religion.

Our Lady, Mary, Mother of Jesus. *See* Queen of Heaven, the, a/k/a Inanna, Is(h)tar, Anat, Cybele, Usas, Venus, Isis, Mary.

Ox. *See* Tetramorphs.

P

Pakistan, 98-107.

Pantocrator, 100, 331.

Parable of the tower, 35-38.

Persians. *See* Sumerians, etc.

Peter, vision of, 53.

Phi, the "golden section," in nature and architecture, 298-300.

Pi, 8, 63, 75-77, 288, 340.

Pictographs, Sumerian, 85-86, 340-341.

Pillars, the cosmic, 70, 101, 171, 185-186, 322-329.

Plans for Tabernacle and Temple from God, 55-56, 67, 290-291.

Popol Vuh, Mayan Codex, Holy Grail used in, 330.

Portolan maps, 318-320.

Principles and procedures, 4-5.

Pseudepigrapha, 35, 41.

Q

Quartz crystal, 36, 39, 286-287, 306, 316, 319, 328-329.

Queen of Heaven, the, a/k/a Inanna, Is(h)tar, Anat, Cybele, Usas, Venus, Isis, Mary, 69, 85, 106, 132, 146-147, 150-154, 158-159, 167, 190, 260, 296-297, 301, 301-302, 339-340.

R

Rainbow, 18, 27, 104-105, 139, 342-343.

Regulus. *See* Guardian stars.

Religion, versus science and magic. *See* Science, versus religion and magic.

Revelation, Book of, 143.

Rock, the cosmic, 37-38, 95, 137, 276, 322-329.

Roman gods, 133-141, 145-154.

Royal Stars of Persia. *See* Guardian stars.

S

Sacrifice, the cosmic, 114-115, 126, 145, 147, 151, 163-164, 166, 173, 226-227, 236-237, 240-241, 247, 303-304, 322.

Saint John Christians, 95, 194, 239-240.

Sandpainting, Navajo, Holy Grail in, 321-322.

Scarab, 32.

Science, versus religion and magic, 2-3, 7-9, 11-12, 35-38, 103-104, 134-135, 140-141, 164, 197, 200-201, 286-290, 292-300, 303-306, 308-314, 317-329, 333-343.

Sea, the cosmic, 36, 75-77, 86, 96, 130, 288-289, 322-329.

Seven, the sacred, 15, 117-118.

Shepherd of Hermas. *See* Parable of the tower.

Shroud of Turin, 254-255.

Solomon's Temple, 71-78, 117, 290-291.

Sophists, 41, 45, 49-51.

Source, common of all symbolism, 110.

Spectre of the Brocken. *See* Rainbow.

Star of David, 31, 72, 300.
Stone, Holy Grail on a, 202-205.
Stone masons. *See* Masons.
Storysmiths, 11-12, 25-26, 41-53, 91-92, 148.
Structural engineering, 286-290, 292-300, 303-306.
Sumerians, etc., 79-92, 95-97.
Swastika, as ancient solar symbol, 83, 106.

T

Tabernacle, 55-68, 290-291.
Table, story of the. *See* Letter of Aristeas.
Tachyon, the, 9.
Tammuz, 112, 145, 181, 191.
Templar, Knights. *See* Docetic (Gnostic) Christianity.
Temple, Solomon's. *See* Solomon's Temple.
Tent of the Presence, 55-68.
Tetramorphs, 1, 3, 11-22, 25, 35, 65, 91, 95, 102, 117, 152, 260, 281, 317-318.
Teutons. *See* Germanic cosmology.
Tower. *See* Parable of the tower.
Tree, the cosmic, 105, 171, 173, 185-186, 187, 190, 322-329.
Trinities, various, 118, 157.
Turin, the Shroud of. *See* Shroud of Turin.

U

Utnapishtim, story of, 86-91.
Usas. *See* Queen of Heaven, the, a/k/a Inanna, Is(h)tar, Anat, Cybele, Usas, Venus, Isis, Mary.

V

Vanuatu, Holy Grail found in, 344-345.
Vault. *See* Firmament, the "vault" of Heaven.
Venus. *See* Queen of Heaven, the, a/k/a Inanna, Is(h)tar, Anat, Cybele, Usas, Venus, Isis, Mary.
Vesica piscis, 30-31, 106.
Vision. *See* Daniel, vision of; Ezekiel, visions of; Hildegard of Bingen, Saint, visions on the Holy Grail; Peter, vision of.

W

Water, the cosmic, 36, 322-329.
Way, the cosmic, 36, 38, 140.
Welsh Grail quest stories, 262-267.
Witches, 11, 93, 346.

Y

Yahweh. *See* YHWH, Yahweh, or Jehovah.
YHWH, Yahweh, or Jehovah, 12-13, 26-27, 73, 75-76, 100, 142, 167, 290-291, 343.

Z

Zoroastrians, 96-97.

Epilogue

Peace efforts failed. War commenced tonight between the United States and Iraq. The outcome is certain. Thinking that they are dying for Church and State, i.e., for God and Country, "sheep" will die to protect the power and wealth of their "shepherds." This book did not get to press in time to avert the beginning, but it may be published in time to help bring war to a quick end, assuming, of course, that the news media does not suppress it, people read it, and it achieves the goal of helping the "sheep" to understand how their "shepherds" herd them. If this book fails to convey that message, then at least I tried. If this book conveys its message, success will come despite the efforts of Christian fundamentalists in the publishing, typesetting, and printing businesses to prevent or delay its publication. The pen has not been mightier than the sword. With book in one hand and sword in the other, religions have conquered people's minds for the benefit of Church and State. The question now is whether the computerized wordprocessor is mightier than the computerized missile. If so, humankind may cease being the servants of Church and State. Instead, the world's religious and civil leaders may become the servants of humankind.